August 2014   Ottawa

La Mulți Ani!

Cu drag!

Pusa și Robi

THE
HISTORICAL ATLAS
OF
WEAPONRY

A CARTOGRAPHICA BOOK

This edition published in 2011 by
CHARTWELL BOOKS, INC.
a division of BOOK SALES, INC.
276 Fifth Avenue Suite 206
New York, New York 10001
USA

ISBN 13: 978-0-7858-2595-1
ISBN 10: 0-7858-2595-9

QUMHAWP

This book is produced by
Cartographica Press
6 Blundell Street
London N7 9BH

Publisher: Sarah Bloxham
Editor: Valeria Kogan
Assistant Editor: Jo Morley
Production: Rohana Yusof
Design: Andrew Easton at Ummagumma Creative

Cartography:
Red Lion Mapping

Printed in Singapore by
Star Standard Industries Pte Ltd.

THE
HISTORICAL ATLAS
OF
WEAPONRY

BRENDA RALPH LEWIS AND RUPERT MATTHEWS

CHARTWELL
BOOKS, INC.

CONTENTS

MAP LIST

INTRODUCTION

THE HISTORY OF WEAPONRY AND WAR HAS BEEN MARKED BY MANY SIGNIFICANT MILESTONES. THE FIRST WAS DISTANCE WARFARE, THE ABILITY TO STRIKE FROM AFAR WHILE REMAINING SAFE FROM THE DANGER OF CLOSE-QUARTER COMBAT.

Dagger with decorated handle and scabbard. Throughout history weapons makers have used decorations to finish off finely crafted implements of war.

The weapons that would be used for distance warfare — stone knives or wooden spears, for example — were already to hand for use by early humans for hunting animals for food. However, it was not long before the hunters realized that flinging a spear was much more logical than risking death or injury in close combat with fierce, enormous prey such as a mammoth. Bows and arrows, which were already in use in the Stone Age, were similarly effective, allowing for even greater distance between predator and prey. Applied to combat, these primitive forms of distance warfare led, in time, to the use of firearms and artillery after the discovery of gunpowder some time before the 14th century. Distance warfare has seen the development in more recent times of the intercontinental ballistic missile (ICBM), a constant threat during the Cold War (1945–1991). The distances involved were more immense than ever before and the nuclear bomb, first dropped on Japan in 1945, was the ultimate threat.

It is likely that early warfare involved limited groups of fighters, but one of the consequences of the city living that typified civilization in around 4000BC was the gathering of more concentrated populations. This, in turn, allowed for larger, more organized armies, which provided another milestone in the development of war and weaponry. On the battlefield, armies could now exploit strategies that required large numbers of men drilled to perform in concert to outflank enemies or provide a tightly packed human wall in the face of attack. The phalanx employed by the city-states of ancient Greece and the wedge-shaped or square formations used by the Romans were examples of this harmonizing of forces. These disciplined arrangements have characterized regular armies ever since.

The appearance of the horse-drawn chariot on the battlefield, after the Sumerians of Mesopotamia became the first to introduce it in around 3000BC, undoubtedly stepped up the pace of warfare and injected an added element of danger to the fighting with the hit-and-run shock tactics used by the archers or spearmen who made up the chariot crew. At the same time, this milestone highlighted the formal participation of horses in warfare, an activity which continued long after the war chariot was replaced by cavalry. Although actions such as the cavalry charge ceased at the end of the 19th century, horses were still widely used, mainly for transportation, in both the World Wars of the 20th century.

Conical helmet like those worn by medieval knights during and after the Battle of Hastings in 1066.

Arguably the most fundamental change in weaponry before the advent of the atomic bomb in 1945 was the introduction of guns and gunpowder into European warfare after around 1325. This not only altered the conduct of war but also did away with several conventions of the time. Now, the description "artillery" no longer applied to ranks of longbowmen firing their arrows in unison on medieval battlefields. Instead, it described batteries of field guns, which in time increased in size, range, and destructive power to thunder massive bombardments at the big battles of World War One and World War Two.

Both World Wars of the 20th century saw an escalation of weaponry deployment that far outpaced anything that had previously gone before. The machine gun, which could mow down rows of troops during World War One, was countered by the armored tank, which first appeared in 1916. Air warfare brought a new, though not yet decisive, dimension to World War One but more than proved its deadly nature in World War Two. The first significant change in naval warfare occurred in the 16th century, when war at sea as a floating version of war on land was superseded by naval gunnery — another instance of distance warfare. A further change took place in World War Two, when the big-gun battleships were replaced at sea by aircraft carriers. Their airplanes could strike over distances so immense that these ships were out of sight of their targets.

In the 21st century the latest innovation has been robot weapons, such as the unmanned drone programmed to hit targets on its own, or machines that can carry out forward reconnaissance, launch artillery, conduct patrols, or defuse mines and bombs. This is not just the ultimate in distance warfare, conducted by operators sitting in front of their computers thousands of miles from the scene of battle. It is also a completely new kind of military action — one without fear or emotion, something never before known in the long, dramatic history of warfare and its weaponry.

WEAPONS IN PREHISTORY

EARLY PROTO-HUMANS ENCOUNTERED A PROBLEM WHEN THEY FIRST APPEARED ON EARTH SOME 20 MILLION YEARS AGO: OTHER CREATURES WERE LARGER, STRONGER, AND FIERCER THAN THEM. IN ORDER TO OVERCOME THIS DISADVANTAGE AND SURVIVE, HUMANS HAD TO ARM THEMSELVES.

Of the many differences between humans and animals, the most important is that animals are well equipped with natural weapons, while humans appear to have none. Elephants have their tusks and scorpions their sting. Crocodiles have sharp teeth and tails that can kill with one powerful flick. Some snakes, such as cobras, have sacks of poison which they can use to kill. Others, such as pythons, have powerful muscles that choke or crush other creatures to death.

By comparison, humans possess very little in the way of natural armor. Human skin is soft and easily pierced by sharp implements. Many animals are much faster, heavier, and physically stronger. Nature, it seems, has neglected us. However, it can be argued that the human brain is superior, with its powers of reasoning and the ingenuity to develop better, deadlier skills than animal brains. By this means, early humans were able to increase their limited bodily powers, and it is from this simple fact of prehistoric life that the whole story of arms and armor has sprung.

In prehistory, the need for us to arm and protect ourselves was vital. Without weapons for attack and defense, we might never have survived in a world full of creatures so much more powerful than us. In addition, for many thousands of years we needed weapons to help us hunt animals, birds and fish for food. This was so even after around 7000BC, when we ceased to be totally reliant on hunting or fishing and learned to cultivate the land, grow crops, and become farmers.

The first weapons were objects found lying around on the ground or in caves, in rivers and on mountain sides: pieces of flint, large stones, the branches or roots of trees, or the bones of dead animals. Anything that could strike and injure was probably used for precisely those purposes. Fire was one weapon humans encountered very early on. In fact, it was a discovery that could hardly have been

The first offensive weapons were chipped and sharpened pieces of flint, which were also used for hunting prey and cutting animal hides.

avoided; fire was found everywhere. For example, a bolt of lightning striking a clump of trees or bushes during a thunderstorm would set them ablaze and the flow of red-hot lava rolling down the side of a volcano could set alight the vegetation in its path.

Although humans, like all living creatures, were naturally afraid of fire, they soon learned its many valuable uses. When it came to using fire as weaponry, it was very effective for hunting. By deliberately setting ablaze a stretch of brushwood or vegetation, hunters could frighten animals into stampeding, and that made them easier to see and easier to kill.

Another early and important discovery came in the Paleolithic (Old Stone) Age, which began some 2.5 million years ago: the discovery that flint could be used as a cutting tool. This was the first great technological advance made by humans. Flint could cut or chip other pieces of flint into small, sharp pointed "flakes" and larger pieces of flint could be sharpened into hand axes. Lengths of hard wood were scraped into sharp spears and larger pieces of wood shaped into clubs with long, easy-to-grip handles and thick, round heads. Another technological step forward came in the Mesolithic (Middle Stone) Age that ended around 6,000 years ago, when stones were used to grind sharp edges on weapons instead of being laboriously chipped away at by hand.

It appears that in the Mesolithic era new, sharper, and much more deadly weapons were already being put to use in Europe. Evidence of this was discovered around the turn of the 20th century by paleontologists working in the Ofnet Cave in Bavaria, southern Germany, where in around 5500BC an entire community was butchered — men, women, and children. There were two pits in the cave containing 38 skulls, mainly those of children under the age of 15. They were all covered in red ochre a form of burial regularly practiced in Mesolithic times. Two-thirds of the adults found were women, but there were also several men, who had obviously fought hard to fend off their attackers. Some of the men's heads had been battered up to seven times, by blows presumably from clubs, that had left large holes in their skulls. There were also cut marks on some of the skulls, suggesting that they had been scalped. It seems likely that this violent attack had taken place during the absence of most of the men of the community, who perhaps were away hunting for food. Alternatively, it may be that the skulls represented booty from a head-hunting expedition.

The Ofnet Cave is by no means a lone example of a mass assault that may have wiped out most members of a prehistoric community. At another Mesolithic site in Germany, at Talheim in the south-west, the mass grave of 34 men, women, and children was found in a pit. It is believed that the slaughter occurred in around 5000BC, and it appears to have been even more brutal than the massacre at the Ofnet Cave. Most of the victims suffered axe and adze blows, but three of them were shot in the back by arrows. This time there were no formal burials: all 34 dead were thrown into the pit without ceremony. It has been suggested that the Talheim massacre was the final fatal act in a dispute between two communities over land and possibly livestock.

Massacres, it seems, were fairly frequent in prehistoric Europe, and evidence of death in suspicious circumstances has been found at Mesolithic sites in Portugal, Spain, France, Switzerland, Sweden, Romania, and Greece. One set of remains found at Dyrholmen in Jutland, Denmark, points toward cannibalism: the bones of at least nine people were found among them. However, murder and mayhem were nothing new in the prehistoric world and went on even further back in time than the Mesolithic Age. Serious armed combat designed to exterminate rivals seems to have developed after humans acquired the kind of weapons that made it most damaging. In around 12,000BC, the simple clubs and spears of earlier prehistory were augmented by bows and arrows, slings and maces.

All of these were examples of distance weapons which allowed attackers to avoid dangerous close-quarter combat and assault their enemies with some impunity. The reach of the bow and arrow and the sling was much greater than that of the mace, but the mace presented its own danger to anyone who came within range. Made from a spiked ball attached by a rope to a long stick, the mace could be flicked at an opponent while the attacker stood at a distance that combined the length of the stick and the length of the rope. The mace was the first example of a true weapon of war, as it had no role to play other than in warfare: the specific purpose of the mace was to kill opponents. The first maces were made of wood, but the danger they presented was amplified by pieces of flint or obsidian (volcanic glass) embedded in the ball. The discovery of metals also served to increase the damage a mace could inflict on an opponent: pieces of copper, and later bronze, had even more destructive properties than flint or obsidian. The need for protection against the damage a mace embedded with bronze could inflict, in turn led to the development of leather armor for protection.

Having evolved effective weaponry, warfare proceeded with ever-increasing violence. In 11000BC, there were clear cases of murder being committed in Paleolithic Italy, where people died after being struck by flint arrows. The points were still in their skeletons when they were found by modern palaeontologists. At the Grotta dei Fanciulli, one of an extensive network of caves at Balzi Rossi, near Ventimiglia in Liguria, a child was found with a flint point lodged in its spine and at the San Teodoro cave in Sicily, a woman was discovered with a flint embedded in her pelvis.

The presence of bows and arrows in prehistory has been supported by several pieces of evidence found in the rock art of south-eastern Spain. Mesolithic or, as some experts believe, Neolithic archers are depicted in threatening poses on the cave walls of Cueva del Roure confronting four men. At Les Dogues, 11 men oppose a group of nine, presumably rivals, with bows armed and ready for firing. Even larger groups appear on the walls of Molino de las Fuentes where 15 archers are ranged against a force of 20. Most cave art discovered in Europe depicts animals that were hunted by prehistoric humans, and these kinds of cave drawings have been widely interpreted as representing their hopes for good luck when hunting. However, there are three examples from Spain that can be seen as evidence of a high degree of aggression in prehistoric society and perhaps symbolically depict all-out battles.

Finds made by paleontologists from many other places in Europe have confirmed that warfare of the most violent kind was virtually endemic on the continent in prehistory. Skeletons found in France, Denmark, and the Ukraine have provided plenty of evidence of foul play in early times. The finds made in caves or pits were largely fortuitous, but after about 7000BC, when the first purpose-built cemeteries were used for burying the dead, it becomes commonplace to find victims whose deaths were caused by violence. As well as by axes and bows and arrows, a large number of these deaths seem to have been caused by clubs, especially injuries to the head, which probably offered the best chance of killing or disabling an enemy.

A study carried out at the University of Copenhagen almost 30 years ago by the paleopathologist Pia Bennicke revealed that among serious skull fractures in Danish records of prehistory, more were inflicted in the Mesolithic Age than in any other prehistoric period. A similar proportion of head injuries has been found among skulls from Mesolithic California and among the Yanomamo, a tribe that lives today as their prehistoric ancestors did in the Amazon regions of central Brazil and Venezuela. The Yanomamo are essentially hunter-gatherers, following the same basic lifestyle as the first humans. They are thought to be among the last tribes on Earth that have survived to encounter the modern world.

The continuance of the prehistoric way of life in the Amazon, the more remote areas of Africa and some Pacific Islands has been largely due to geography and the bounty of nature which has provided everything a tribe needs to survive — food, shelter, clothing, tools — in an environment well away from outside interference. This isolation has also perpetuated the kind of tribal warfare that was probably fought in prehistoric times, including raids on neighboring tribes, the kidnapping of women and slaves, and the preservation of ancient fighting methods and weapons. However, there has been a price to pay for remaining apart from the modernization that has transformed other parts of the world. Historically, this was demonstrated most tellingly by the Native Americans of the United States, who experienced no Renaissance, no Industrial Revolution, no urbanization, and no advancement in weaponry or warfare.

Above: Sharpened flint was a development of the flint shown on page 11. The triangular shape was intended as the head of a spear for hunting or fighting at a distance.

Opposite page: Prehistoric flint sharpened by another flint. The idea was to strike off chips of stone while shaping the flint into a sharp weapon for cutting or use in war. It may look rough and primitive, but it was hugely effective.

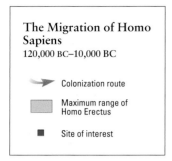

The Migration of Homo
Sapiens
120,000 BC–10,000 BC

Colonization route

Maximum range of
Homo Erectus

Site of interest

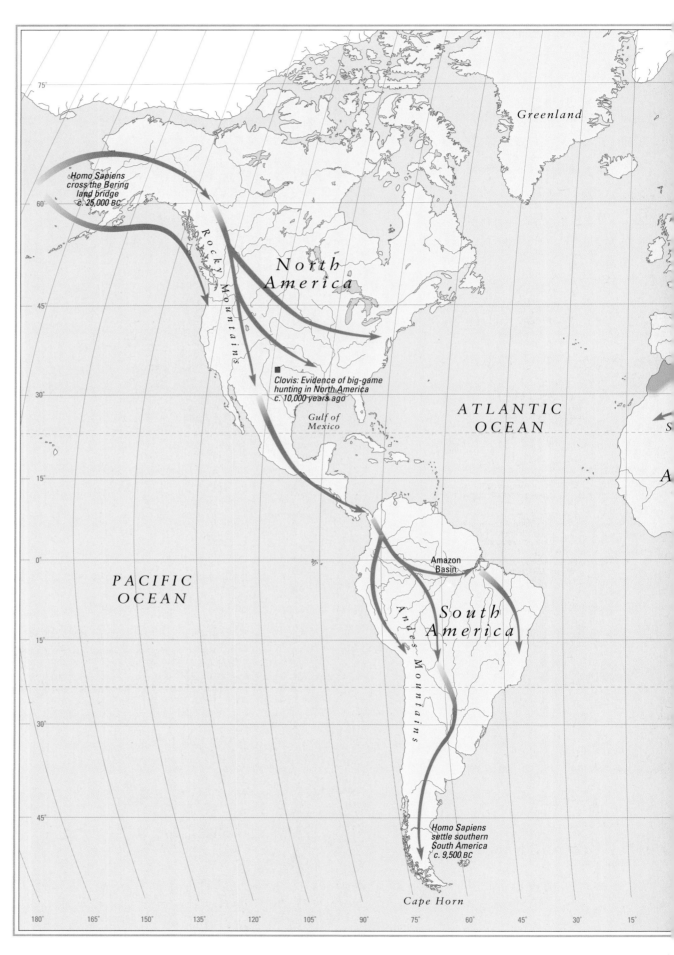

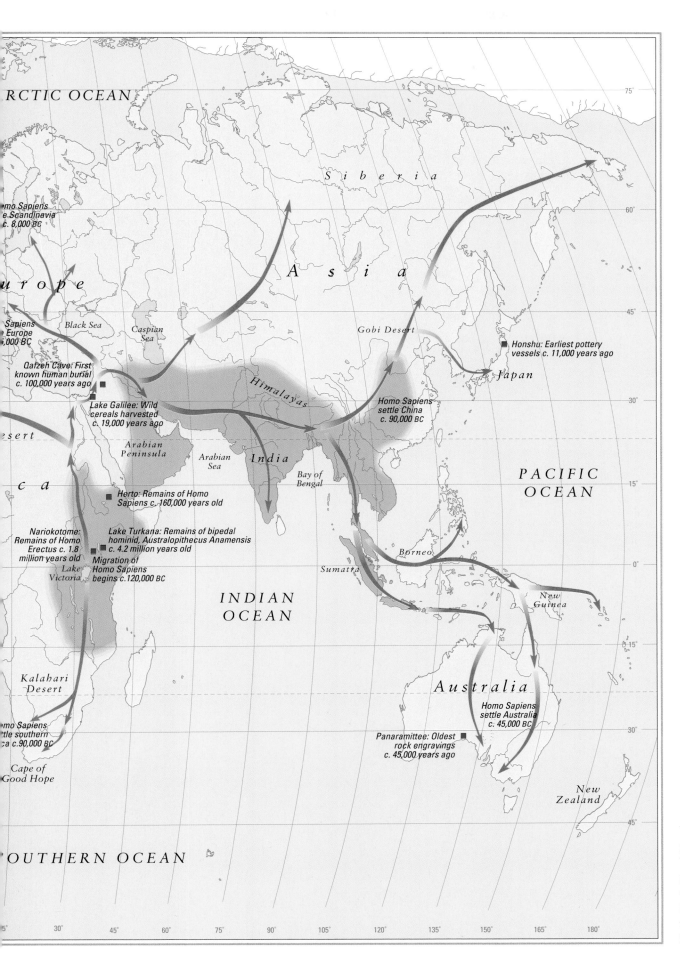

RCTIC OCEAN

Siberia

Asia

mo Sapiens
e Scandinavia
c. 8,000 BC

urope

Sapiens
Europe
,000 BC

Black Sea

Caspian Sea

Gobi Desert

■ Honshu: Earliest pottery
vessels c. 11,000 years ago

Qafzeh Cave: First
known human burial
c. 100,000 years ago ■

Himalayas

Japan

Lake Galilee: Wild
cereals harvested
c. 19,000 years ago ■

esert

Arabian Peninsula

Arabian Sea

India

Homo Sapiens
settle China
c. 90,000 BC

Bay of Bengal

PACIFIC OCEAN

Herto: Remains of Homo
Sapiens c. 160,000 years old ■

c a

Nariokotome:
Remains of Homo
Erectus c. 1.8
million years old

Lake Turkana: Remains of bipedal
hominid, Australopithecus Anamensis
c. 4.2 million years old ■

Borneo

Migration of
Homo Sapiens
begins c.120,000 BC

Lake Victoria

Sumatra

INDIAN OCEAN

New Guinea

Australia

Homo Sapiens
settle Australia
c. 45,000 BC

Kalahari Desert

Panaramittee: Oldest
rock engravings
c. 45,000 years ago ■

mo Sapiens
tle southern
ca c.90,000 BC

Cape of
Good Hope

New Zealand

OUTHERN OCEAN

The prehistoric world was
peopled by extensive migrations.
These probably began with
population moves out of Africa,
where humans are thought to
have first developed. Eventually,
they spread all over the world,
including migrations overseas.

Opposite page: The Americas were peopled by migrations across a land bridge (now covered by the Bering Strait), which may once have led from eastern Asia into what is now known as Alaska.

Instead, they lived with nature, although this way of life did nothing to prepare them for the arrival of Europeans on their continent after Christopher Columbus' first voyage in 1492.

The contest that followed was bound to be unequal. Native American weaponry had changed very little from ancient times, when warfare meant battling it out hand to hand with clubs, axes, bows and arrows, or spears. Before the first European settlers arrived, the Native Americans knew nothing of firearms or the methods of warfare of Europe, where gunpowder and its destructive uses had been discovered centuries earlier. By the 1860s some Native Americans had been introduced to modern rifles such as Springfields and Winchesters and had soon learned how to use them. The Cheyenne, armed with their new rifles, confronted the forces of General George Armstrong Custer at the battle of Little Big Horn in 1876, where they inflicted what has been widely judged as the greatest disaster ever suffered of the U.S. Army.

Their victory at Little Big Horn did not mean that the Native Americans had abandoned their traditional methods of making war — with knives, tomahawks, long lances, clubs, and of course bows and arrows. Native American warriors were extremely adept at using bows and arrows on horseback. Their arrowheads were made of flint, bone, or metal, and an experienced warrior could fire 20 arrows in the same time that it took a European to load and fire a musket. Even more chillingly, the lances used by the Native Americans in their struggle to keep European settlers away from their ancestral lands were decorated not only with feathers, but also with the scalps of their defeated enemies. The Native Americans were well protected from the bullets or arrows of their rivals by oblong shields, commonly made from tanned buffalo skins. These shields were virtually impenetrable, and the only hope a rifleman had of piercing one of these shields was to hit it square on: any other angle of shot made the weapon bounce off it. Yet despite the skill of the native warriors, the European settlers ultimately prevailed and the Native American traditional way of life came to an end.

Far back in history though, in Mesopotamia and the Near East, the techniques of war that were still being used in the 19th century by the Native Americans had given way to much larger conflicts involving whole armies. This came about some 6,000 years ago, at the dawn of the Neolithic Age when people began to settle down to live in one place, cultivating land in the more fertile areas such as the River Nile in Egypt or the Indus Valley in north-western India. The more extensive these civilizations grew, the more important it was for people to claim sufficient cultivable land and stretches of river needed to water it. The larger the population became, the easier it was to raise large armies when contesting the possession of land: the first large, organized armies of the sort that have fought wars ever since.

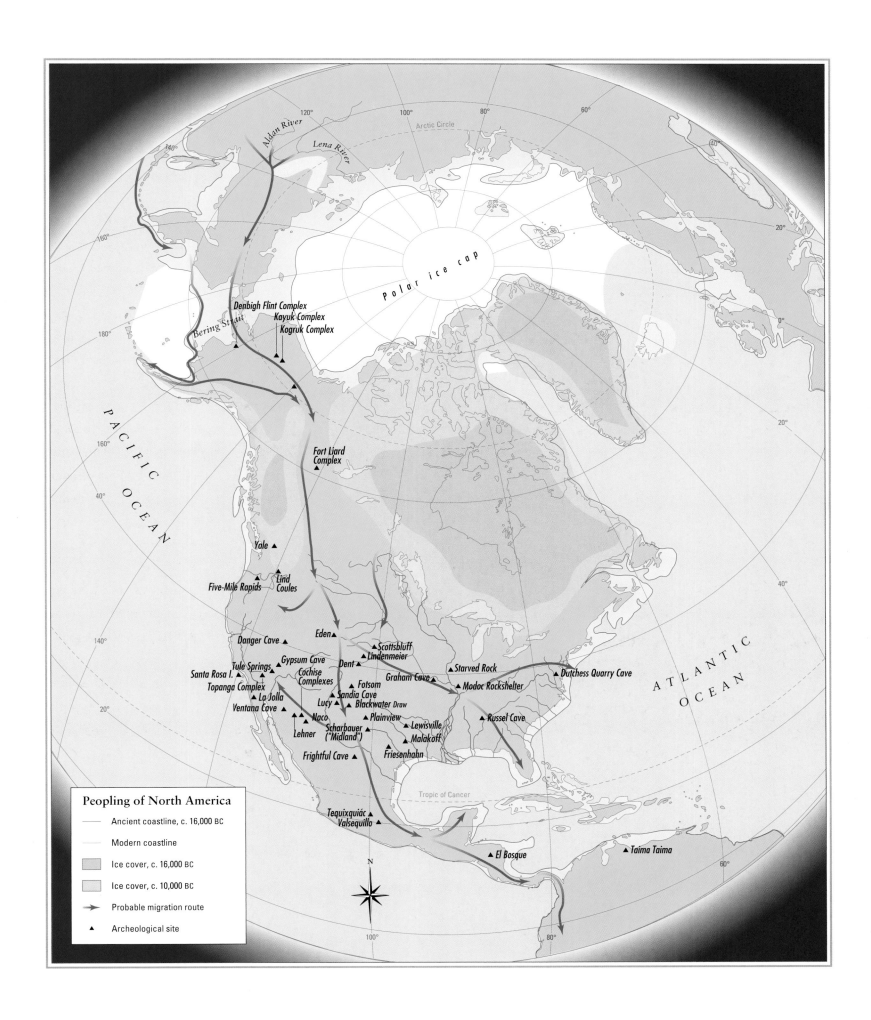

Peopling of North America

— Ancient coastline, c. 16,000 BC

— Modern coastline

■ Ice cover, c. 16,000 BC

■ Ice cover, c. 10,000 BC

→ Probable migration route

▲ Archeological site

USING METALS FOR WAR – THE METALS OF ANTIQUITY

UNTIL THE 13TH CENTURY AD ONLY SEVEN METALS — THE METALS OF ANTIQUITY — WERE KNOWN. THE FIRST OF THEM, GOLD, WAS DISCOVERED AROUND 6000BC. TWO OTHERS, COPPER AND IRON, REVOLUTIONIZED WEAPONRY AND TURNED WAR INTO A SCIENCE.

Gold was the first metal found among the seven known as the Metals of Antiquity. The others were copper, silver, lead, tin, iron, and the liquid metal mercury. The first practical metal for use in producing weaponry discovered was copper, which was found in around 4200BC. It was soon realized though, that copper was relatively soft. It broke when small pieces were hammered and ground down. Something stronger than copper was required, but a long wait lay ahead to find it. The principle of smelting metals was already known as far back as 6000BC, but it took a long time before bronze was discovered. Smelting copper with tin to make the alloy bronze did not appear until long after the discovery of tin around 3000BC. Smelting copper with tin was taking place in Sumeria in around 2500 BC, when an axe head was made containing 11 percent tin and 89 percent copper.

Metal weapons did not immediately replace those made of stone. For one thing, stone was much more readily available, it was simply lying around virtually everywhere, and unlike metals it did not have to be extracted from ores. Besides this, stone weapons were also very effective, as were those made of animal bone, and so they were not quickly discarded and the transition to metal weapons was a gradual process. Despite this, metal did prove to be a much more versatile material. By smelting metal it was easier to shape and sharpen and it could be crafted into many different types of weapon: swords with deadly blades, lightweight knives, and sharp, arrow-shaped spear tips and lances. Metal also provided

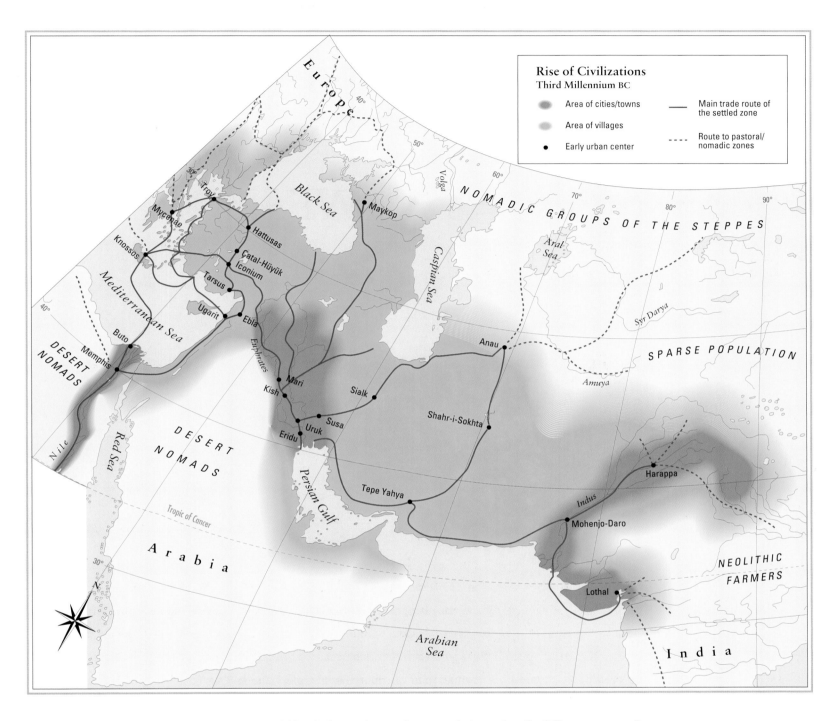

effective protection in battle because it could be fashioned into sheets and shaped to fit different parts of the body. With all these uses, metal eventually came to outclass stone. However, metal replacing metal would continue to be a part of the process of weapons development in its earliest stages.

Bronze replaced copper for the obvious reason that it was much stronger, having been smelted from copper and tin, and in time iron came to replace bronze. Naturally occurring iron was first discovered in about 1500BC, but it was known long before that, for it was occasionally found in meteorites that had landed on Earth. Iron meteorites were composed of metallic iron-nickel, and stony-iron meteorites comprised material that was both metallic and rocky. Whatever its composition, meteoric iron was quite rare and there was never enough of it to make weapons on any practical scale, but naturally occurring iron went on to revolutionize weapon making because iron objects could be made much more cheaply.

The earliest civilizations developed in Mesopotamia around the rivers Tigris and Euphrates. The first of them was Sumer, the "Land of the Lords of Brightness", which was established in what is now southern Iraq.

THE FIRST METAL WEAPONS

THE USE OF METALS — FIRST COPPER AND ITS ALLOY BRONZE, THEN IRON AND ITS VARIOUS ALLOYS — GREATLY INTENSIFIED THE CONDUCT OF WAR, INTRODUCING MORE EFFICIENT METHODS OF KILLING AND WOUNDING OPPONENTS. IN RESPONSE TO THIS METAL ARMOR ALSO DEVELOPED.

Metal first appeared in warfare not as individual weapons but as adjuncts to or elaborations of existing ones. Weapons used for smashing objects, or opponents, received extra destructive power from the addition of metal to their surfaces. Spears acquired sharp metal points and battle axes were given cutting edges. All these first appeared in Mesopotamia and the surrounding areas in the Bronze and Iron Ages. However, this first use of metals as small additions indicated that it took time to develop metallurgy to the point where it could provide suitable arms for warfare. The task was to develop ways of working hard, malleable metals into the right consistency and shape for effective weapons to be produced. Several stages had to be mastered. First, the metal ores had to be sized before they could be used. Next they had to be combined with other substances under a controlled temperature and gas atmosphere before being cast into the desired shape. And finally, the metal had to be worked to attain the desired properties. This process took a long time to perfect, and did not occur until some time before 2000BC, during the Bronze Age.

The first new weapon to emerge in the age of metals was the comparatively modest dagger. It was soon followed by the sword, which relied on advances in metallurgy for the power of its long, thin blade. At the same time, protective armor improved markedly, even though leather remained the most common material used. Leather armor was often reinforced with metal and the helmet, breastplate and greaves for the shins were made entirely of bronze, and later iron.

Sumeria, the earliest civilization to develop around the rivers Tigris and Euphrates in Mesopotamia, was also the first civilization whose army appears in historical records. Figurines dating from about 4000BC have been found by archeologists; they show Sumerian soldiers wearing copper helmets and

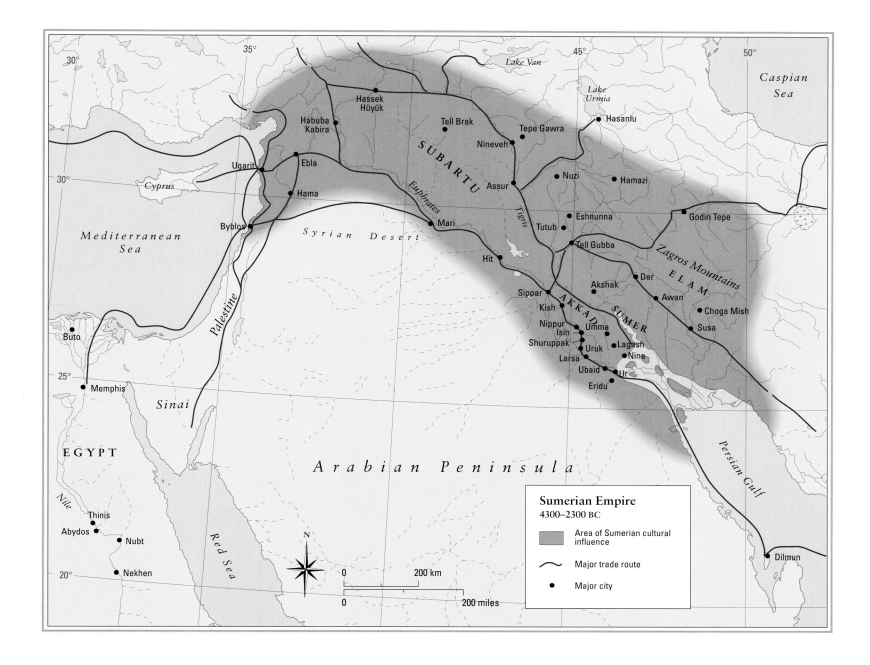

carrying short spears. The Sumerian army, which consisted almost entirely of infantry, also used simple bows, slings, battle axes, and daggers. They wore leather kilts and protective cloaks made of felt or thick, hard-to-penetrate leather and other animal skins. Chariots, a Sumerian invention, also featured in the army's equipment. These were not the swift, nimble fighting machines later used by the Hittites, ancient Egyptians and the ancient Greeks, but lumbering affairs with four solid wheels pulled by onagers (wild asses)– not very fast animals. Chariots, the first mobile weapons to be manufactured for use in war, would one day revolutionize warfare, but the Sumerians primarily used them as transportation for a pair of crewmen who would have carried battle axes and lances.

War has always been the spur to weapons development, and the prevalence of war in Sumeria and the rest of ancient Mesopotamia certainly served this purpose and made the Sumerians the most sophisticated fighters of their time. In addition to their prime innovation, the war chariot, the Sumerians also introduced the composite bow, a much more sophisticated weapon than the original bow and arrow,

By 2,340BC the Sumerian Empire extended from southern Iraq and the Persian Gulf to the eastern Mediterranean Sea. This empire was a secular rather than religion-based state and was particularly dominant and influential between 2500BC and 2000BC.

made from a single piece of wood and used in the Stone Age. Eventually, the composite bow became the weapon of choice in many parts of Asia and was used by mounted horsemen as well as infantry. The secret of the composite bow and its greatly increased power lay in the materials which were laminated together to lend their particular properties to the finished article. Composite bows had wooden cores, ideally made from hard maple. The core was laminated with several types of horn taken from water buffalo, antelope such as oryx or ibex, and goat or sheep. The lamination process employed glues derived from animal hides or fish bladders.

The composite bow and the much greater power it brought to the battlefield added to the ferocity of the many wars fought in Sumeria over some 2,000 years. Initially, Sumeria was not a single country under the control of one ruler, but a mass of small states that were forever quarrelling over the same bones of contention: control of the rivers Tigris and Euphrates and a monopoly of the opportunities the rivers offered for transportation and irrigation. There were also innumerable boundary disputes and feuds over supplies of timber, stone, and metals.

Inevitably, some of these quarrels led to fighting. In 2525BC, war broke out between two cities, Lagash and Umma, which lay 18 miles (29 km) apart on the River Euphrates near the Persian Gulf. The fertile agricultural region of Guendena had been disputed by the two cities for generations and when Umma violated a boundary treaty, Lagash went to war. Lagash was triumphant. In honor of its victory, the city's king, Eannatum, raised a stele which contained a near complete pictorial record of his army, its weaponry and an image of Eannatum in his chariot: the first depiction of the wheel in military use.

Opposite page: The Hittite (Hatti), Hurrian (Mittani) Assyrian, and Babylonian kingdoms were among the most ancient civilizations in what is now the Middle East. The aggressive, militaristic Assyrians, though appearing the smallest on this map, would later expand to dominate the rest.

Below: Mosaic from the Royal cemetery at Ur (c. 2500BC) showing the army of Lagash going to war and the defeat of Umma. The heavy four-wheeled Sumerian chariots depicted sharply contrasted with the swift, nimble chariots that later evolved.

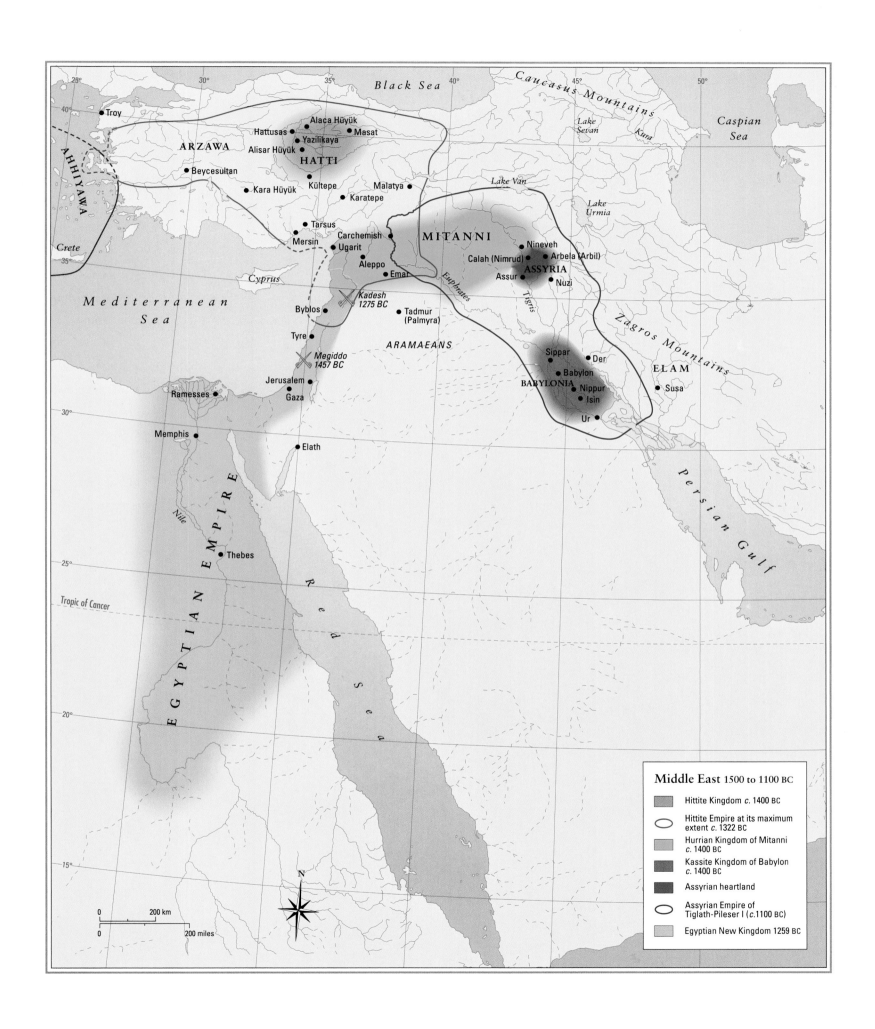

Black Sea

Caucasus Mountains

Caspian Sea

Troy

AHHIYAWA

Crete

ARZAWA

Alaca Hüyük
Hattusas •
Alisar Hüyük •
Yazilikaya •
Masat •
HATTI

Beycesultan •

Kara Hüyük • Kültepe •
Karatepe •
Malatya •

Lake Sevan

Kura

Lake Van

Tarsus •
Mersin •
Carchemish •
Ugarit •
Aleppo •
Emar •
MITANNI

Nineveh •
Calah (Nimrud) •
Arbela (Arbil) •
ASSYRIA
Assur •
Nuzi •

Lake Urmia

Mediterranean Sea

Cyprus

Byblos •
Kadesh 1275 BC
Tadmur (Palmyra) •

Euphrates

Tigris

Zagros Mountains

Tyre •
Megiddo 1457 BC

ARAMAEANS

Sippar •
Der •
Babylon •
BABYLONIA
Nippur •
Isin •
Ur •

ELAM

Susa •

Jerusalem •
Gaza •

Ramesses •

Memphis •

Elath •

EGYPTIAN EMPIRE

Nile

Red Sea

Persian Gulf

Thebes •

Tropic of Cancer

N

0   200 km
0   200 miles

Middle East 1500 to 1100 BC

Hittite Kingdom *c.* 1400 BC

Hittite Empire at its maximum extent *c.* 1322 BC

Hurrian Kingdom of Mitanni *c.* 1400 BC

Kassite Kingdom of Babylon *c.* 1400 BC

Assyrian heartland

Assyrian Empire of Tiglath-Pileser I (*c.*1100 BC)

Egyptian New Kingdom 1259 BC

The king also appeared on the stele wielding a sickle-shaped sword, another Sumerian invention, dating from 2500BC. This type of sword later became a regular infantry weapon in ancient Egyptian and biblical armies. The ancient Egyptians, whose sickle-shaped sword was called the *khopesh*, used it for slashing at their enemies. It was horrifically effective: it could cut halfway through a man's neck at a stroke, the curved *kopis* used by the ancient Greeks could do much the same. Elsewhere on Eannatum's stele, the spear-bearers of Lagash are shown marching in a phalanx. They wear helmets, probably made from copper and lined with leather, or a cap on their heads. They also appear to be wearing armored cloaks made of leather, with metal disks sewn on them. The raised centers or spines on the disks were intended to protect soldiers from the copper socket-axe and other weapons used during the Lagash-Umma war. It would appear, though, that the cloaks were awkward to wear in battle and generally unsatisfactory, as overlapping plate armor was soon introduced.

Below: The Battle of Kadesh, fought between the armies of Ancient Egypt and the Hittite Empire probably saw the most extensive chariot battle that ever took place. Some historians reckon that up to 6,000 chariots took part.

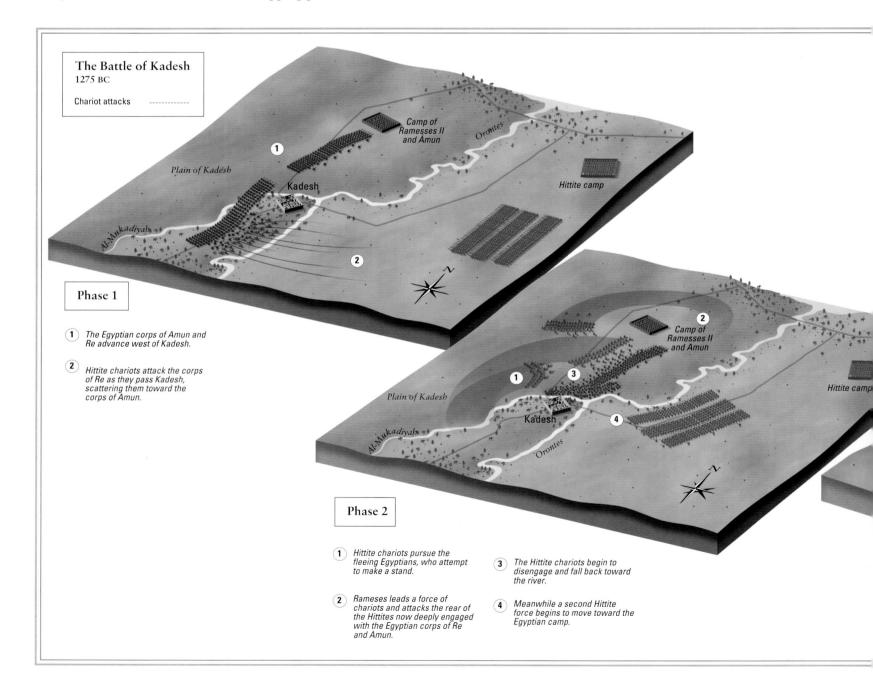

The Battle of Kadesh
1275 BC

Chariot attacks ------------

Camp of Ramesses II and Amun

Orontes

Plain of Kadesh

Kadesh

Hittite camp

Al-Mukadiyah

N

Phase 1

① The Egyptian corps of Amun and Re advance west of Kadesh.

② Hittite chariots attack the corps of Re as they pass Kadesh, scattering them toward the corps of Amun.

Camp of Ramesses II and Amun

Plain of Kadesh

Kadesh

Al-Mukadiyah

Orontes

Hittite camp

N

Phase 2

① Hittite chariots pursue the fleeing Egyptians, who attempt to make a stand.

② Rameses leads a force of chariots and attacks the rear of the Hittites now deeply engaged with the Egyptian corps of Re and Amun.

③ The Hittite chariots begin to disengage and fall back toward the river.

④ Meanwhile a second Hittite force begins to move toward the Egyptian camp.

The history of arms and armor has, of course, always been a dynamic of offensive weapons producing better defenses, and better defenses producing even more deadly offensive weapons. The inevitable response to Sumerian body armor was the invention of a mightier socket-axe, which replaced copper with stronger, harder bronze. But this was not the only advance of the new socket-axe: the blade was made thinner and ended in a point which was capable of piercing bronze plate armor, making the new socket-axe one of the most devastating weapons used by armies in the ancient world. Just how effective these weapons could be was amply illustrated by the axe heads found in the 1930s in a tomb at Til Barsip, a town on the Euphrates, by the French archeologist François Thureau-Dangin. The axe heads that were found came in a variety of blade shapes, but all of them were capable of opening up a suit of armor and killing the man inside.

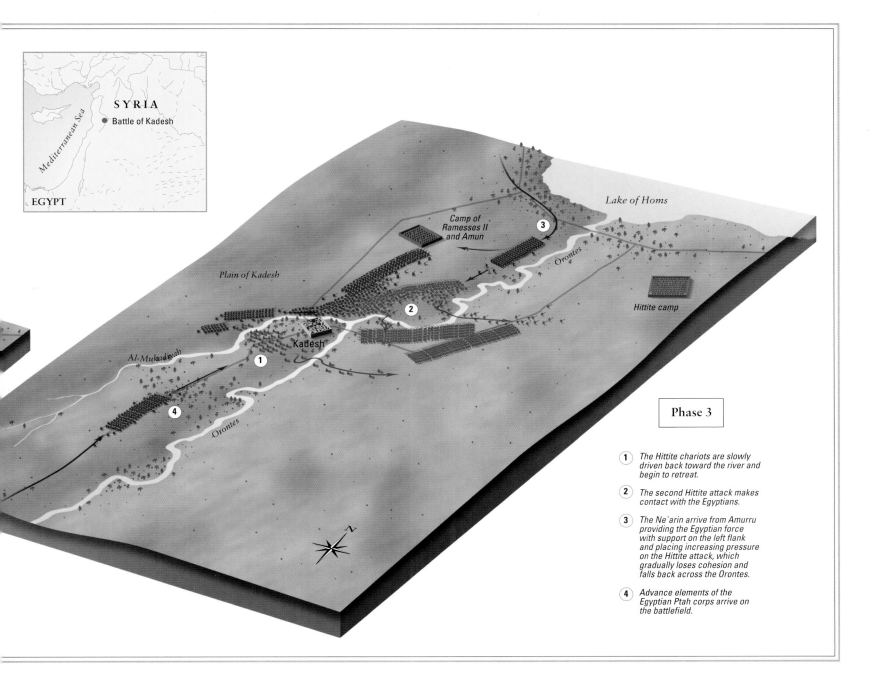

Phase 3

1   The Hittite chariots are slowly driven back toward the river and begin to retreat.

2   The second Hittite attack makes contact with the Egyptians.

3   The Ne`arin arrive from Amurru providing the Egyptian force with support on the left flank and placing increasing pressure on the Hittite attack, which gradually loses cohesion and falls back across the Orontes.

4   Advance elements of the Egyptian Ptah corps arrive on the battlefield.

DECORATING WEAPONS

WEAPONRY ACHIEVED PRESTIGE AMONG ITS PRACTITIONERS AND EVEN BECAME A SYMBOL OF STRENGTH AND POWER. DECORATING WEAPONS WITH PATTERNS AND SYMBOLS WAS A WAY OF EXPRESSING STATUS, AND A GREAT DEAL OF ARTISTRY AND CRAFTSMANSHIP WAS LAVISHED UPON THEM.

For the Sumerians, as for many fighters throughout history, weapons were not just practical tools for making war; in many ways they were works of art as well. In almost the whole story of arms and armor, the makers of weapons have used decorations to finish off finely crafted swords, shields, helmets, and other implements of war. In part, this was done in order to show pride in workmanship or to reflect the owner's prestige and wealth. In ancient times, arms, armor, and the whole panoply of war represented strength and power. These qualities were highly valued in an age when success in battle was regarded as heroic and conquest was seen as a sign of greatness. Adornments also served as a form of what later became heraldry: designs and motifs were personal statements by kings and commanders that could be recognized in the heat of battle and spur on soldiers to greater effort.

The Sumerians realized the psychological value of decorating weapons very early on. The practice dated at least from the Bronze Age, which began in Mesopotamia and the Near East around 3300BC. Daggers found in the Sumerian city of Ur had handles with criss-cross stud and fish designs on them. Similarly, the light, two-wheeled chariots used by the ancient Egyptians were beautifully decorated with plates of gold, intricately engraved with elegant flower motifs. Sword hilts were also often adorned with gold thread or gold sheeting.

Even the Vikings of Scandinavia, arguably the most ferocious and dangerous of the raiders who rampaged over Europe after the fall of

Intricately carved wooden handled hunting knife.

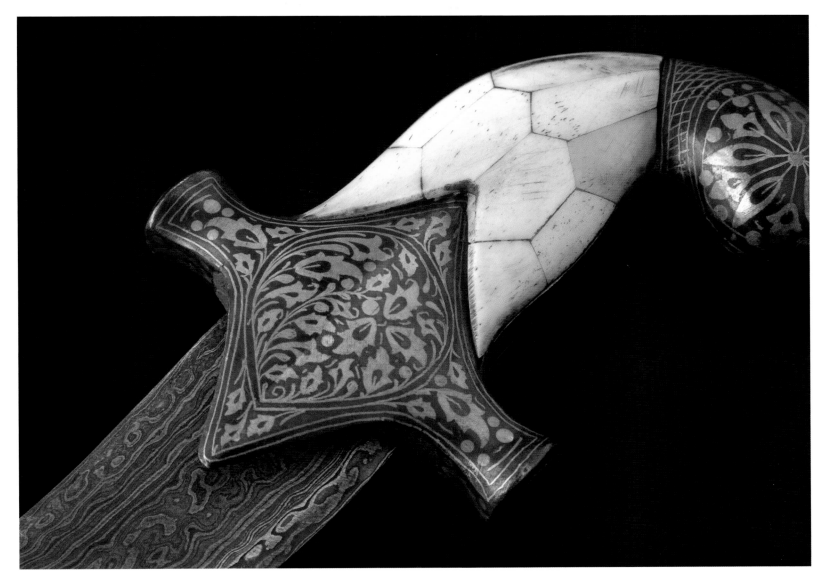

Intricately decorated handle and blade of an ancient dagger. Decorating weapons was a tradition in many early civilizations and indicated the pride in weaponry that characterized warlike societies. The blade was probably made from obsidian (volcanic glass).

the Roman Empire in about AD476, displayed a penchant for intricate decoration and applied real artistry to some of their weapons. For example, the throwing spears they carried into battle were terror weapons, designed to reduce an enemy to a state of helpless fear before the Vikings weighed in with their swords or axes at close quarters. Yet the spearheads were adorned with intricate patterns that used an alloy of silver and other metals mixed with sulfur. The alloy was rubbed into an engraved pattern and then fired in a furnace. The pattern remained black where the alloy was rubbed into the pattern, but the rest of it could be polished to a bright, colorful finish. It was the Vikings who used military imagery to depict the belief in Norse mythology: that the sun was pulled each day from east to west by a horse. This was the message on the Trundholm Sun Chariot, which features a 10 in (25 cm) bronze disk representing the sun. It is gilded on one side to depict the daytime sun, with a bronze horse in front of it standing on a rod. The ungilded reverse side of the disk represents the night, when the chariot is pulled from west to east to await the next dawn. The Sun Chariot was discovered in Denmark in 1902 in Trundholm Moor, on the north-western coast of Zeeland island.

Artistry and pride in craftsmanship were by no means the only reasons for decorating weapons; another was that they had to be well and carefully made in order to do their job properly. A spear, for example, would be of little use if its metal tip were not finely turned and well pointed, and arrows were useless if they could not fly straight to their target. Swords had to have properly sharpened edges and, like shields, had to be well balanced when held in the hand. Shields also had to be tough and thick enough to ensure, as far as possible, that an opponent's weapons could not pierce them and armor needed to be carefully molded to the shape of the body so that the wearer could move easily.

The one-time Hollywood image of a knight, encased in armor and apparently unable to move or walk, being winched up into the saddle was total nonsense: knights had to be nimble in battle; otherwise they would be unable to fight and were unlikely to survive. It was a test of the armorer's craft as well as of the knight's athleticism that he should be able to leap into the saddle without using a stirrup while wearing a full suit of armor. Knights were also required to roll over on the ground while similarly armored and jump to their feet in one movement.

Among the many ways of decorating arms and armor, heating the metal, a method already used in ancient times, was the most versatile. Heating metal not only made it change color — from yellow to purple to deep blue — but also ensured that the color change was retained. Deep blue, acquired from a process known as "blueing", was the most popular color for armor, swords, and other edged weapons and, after the discovery of gunpowder in Europe in the 14th century, for the barrels of guns. In the 18th and 19th centuries firearms' barrels were commonly colored a rich brown. The effect was not purely cosmetic: patination, the process of applying a film of brown or green color to metal, also protected the surface from rust, as did painting metal surfaces, a method already in use in ancient times.

Gilding, by applying gold or silver to the surface, was used to beautify weapons and armor in European, Islamic, and Asian armies by using an adhesive to apply a very thin sheet of gold or silver to a surface, or by using powdered metal suspended in gold paint or lacquer. "Fire" gilding was a particularly long-lasting method, and involved combining powdered gold with mercury: when a metal surface was covered with this mixture it was heated to get rid of the mercury and to bond the gold to the metal.

Other ways of decorating arms and armor included enameling, embossing, engraving, etching, fretting (cutting decorative patterns into a surface), carving, and chiseling. Ancient Greek armor, for instance, was frequently engraved and embossed. The Greeks had a tradition of decorating their armor that went back as far as the Bronze Age, and most of the decoration was devoted to the cuirass, which was frequently embossed to mimic the wearer's chest and back. Greek helmets too were often embossed or engraved, usually with geometric designs or with emblems, symbols, and other figurative decoration. The Greek *aspis*, or shield, could be elaborately painted with geometric designs, portraits of animals, and even scenes from Greek myths. Lower-leg armor was usually left unadorned; in fact, the Romans' horses were more decorated than were their legionaries, and wore armor that was embossed.

The Romans, who lacked the artistic instincts of the Greeks, had a plain, practical view of war and its weapons. The decorations on a legionary's shield, for instance, normally signified little more than the unit to which he belonged and for the rest, his bronze or iron armor was plain. But even the Romans turned decorative when it came to adorning armor for ceremonial purposes, and in these cases Roman decoration was rather more graphic than the Greek. A signifier or standard bearer would wear the hide of a lion, bear, or wolf over his armor, with the animal's head over his helmet to make him more ferocious.

Opposite Page: By the time the battle of Crécy was fought in 1346, during the Hundred Years' War, knights were wearing complete suits of plate armor. The horses the knights rode were also covered against close-quarter fighting.

DISTANCE WARFARE

DISTANCE WARFARE WAS A FIGHTING TECHNIQUE PECULIAR TO HUMANS, ORIGINALLY DEVELOPED IN ORDER TO CONFRONT LARGER, STRONGER ANIMALS HUNTED AS PREY. LATER, THROWING SPEARS, SHOOTING ARROWS, OR FLINGING STONES FROM SLINGS ALSO OFFERED GREATER SAFETY IN BATTLE.

Opposite page: The smaller English army triumphed at the Battle of Crécy on August 26 1346, due to superior weaponry and the success of their longbowmen against the French armored knights.
Below: The story of David slaying Goliath is one of the oldest examples of distance warfare.

U sing weapons at long range for hunting is something that animals, apart from poison-spitting snakes, cannot do. But from the earliest days of weaponry the armed human could throw a spear or axe over a distance, shoot stone-tipped arrows even farther with a bow, and with a sling or catapult send a missile speeding through the air at a great rate — all the while keeping a safe distance from the target. This ability to use weapons for distance warfare made humans formidable and dangerous hunters, and before long it was employed in war.

One of the classic tales of long-range warfare is the Biblical exploit of the boy David, who felled the Philistine giant Goliath with a single stone flung from a sling. The ancient Israelites, led by King Saul, confronted the Philistines at Socoh, in Judea, but there was no actual battle. Instead, Socoh would be decided by single combat between a champion from each side. The Philistines' champion was the giant Goliath, who according to the Biblical Book of Samuel was the equivalent of 9 ft 9 in (2.97 m), another reckoning puts his height at a more reasonable 6 ft 6 in (1.98 m). Twice a day Goliath paraded in front of the Israelites, in full armor and attended by his personal shield-bearer demanding that a challenger come out and fight.

"He had a helmet of brass upon his head, and he was armed with a coat of mail; and the weight of the coat was five

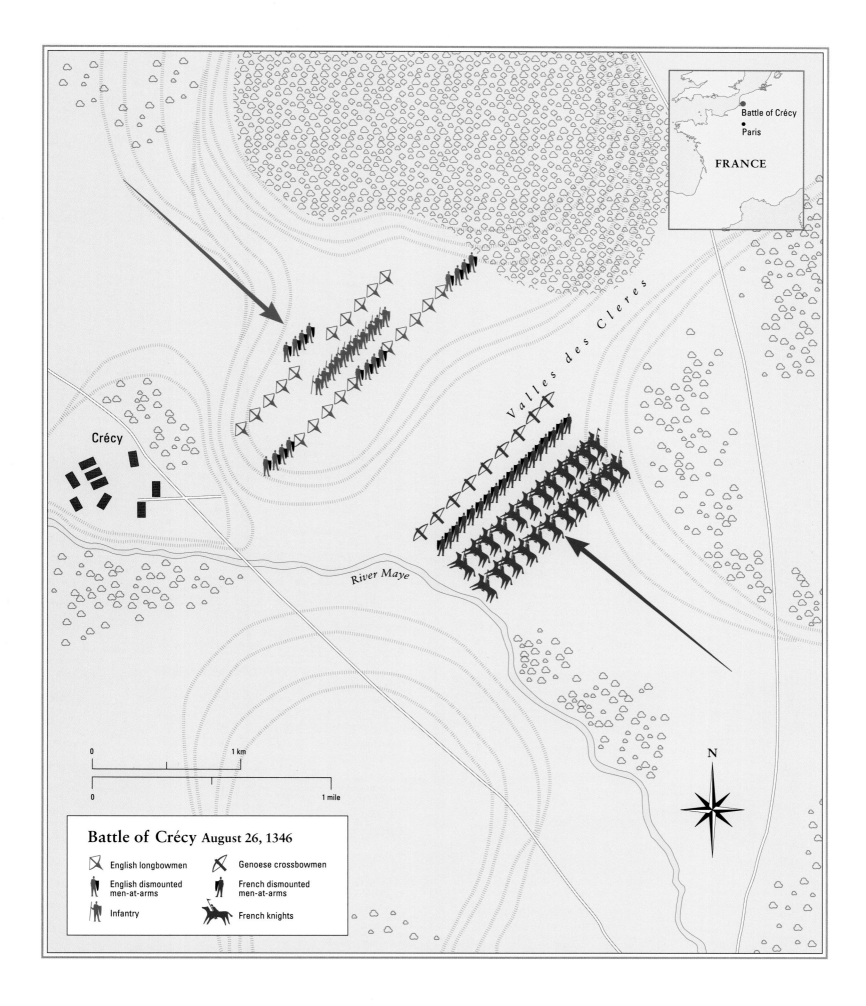

FRANCE

Battle of Crécy
• Paris

Valles des Cleres

Crécy

River Maye

N

0   1 km

0   1 mile

Battle of Crécy August 26, 1346

⊠ English longbowmen	⊠ Genoese crossbowmen	
English dismounted men-at-arms	French dismounted men-at-arms	
Infantry	French knights	

thousand shekels of brass [125 lb (57 kg)]. And he had greaves of brass upon his legs, and a target of brass between his shoulders. And the staff of his spear was like a weaver's beam; and his spear's head weighed six hundred shekels [15 lb (6.8 kg)] of iron."

Unsurprisingly, there was no volunteer willing to take on Goliath, despite the reward offered by King Saul. Then the least likely candidate, almost laughably inappropriate, offered to take up the challenge — the youth David. King Saul offered to lend David his own armor, helmet, and sword, but he was too small for any of it. David then chose to do battle with Goliath armed only with a sling and five round stones which he took from a nearby stream. With the sling, David threw one of his stones at Goliath, from a distance and managed to hit him squarely on the forehead. Goliath collapsed, unconscious, and with that David ran over to him, took his sword and cut off his head. The Philistines, shocked and dismayed at this unexpected outcome, fled in disarray.

The sling David used to fell Goliath was already an ancient weapon in Biblical times. It was used by New Stone Age peoples in the Mediterranean but may date back as far as the Old Stone Age, when it could have been contemporary with the simple bow and arrow and the atlatl, the spear-thrower later used by the Aztecs of Mexico (see picture on the next page). Two finely braided slings were discovered in the tomb of the pharaoh Tutankhamun who died in around 1325BC. It seems likely that in Tutankhamun's time these slings were used for hunting game, but their transition to use as weapons of war was easy. The sling extended the length of the human arm as it was swung around by its two cords: when one of the cords was released, the stone or other projectile flew off at a tangent and was capable of hitting a target many times farther away than could be reached had it been thrown by hand.

Using the sling became a specialization in many armies. One famous instance of the damage this simple weapon could do was related by the ancient Greek author Xenophon. He described how at the battle of Cunaxa in 401BC the "Ten Thousand" Greeks were forced to retreat under a hail of large stones flung by slingers in the army of King Artaxerxes II of Persia. The Greeks learned their lesson and subsequently recruited slingers into their own forces. Then they went one better than Artaxerxes: their slingers, specialists from the island of Rhodes, used sling-bullets made of lead and could throw them twice as far as their Persian counterparts.

Another simple but immensely effective long-range weapon that began as an aid to hunting or herding but ended up in battle, was the *bolas*. In South America *gauchos* still use the *bolas* to capture cattle and game by entangling their legs and bringing them down. The *bolas* was used in pre-Hispanic times to do the same to opponents in battle and several examples have been unearthed by archeologists in Patagonia in the far south of South America. The force of the *bolas* depends on the number of weights used. A *bolas* with one weight is called a *perdida*; one with two, a vestrucera or nanducera; and one with three, a boleadora. Using them involves swinging them around and around to achieve momentum, then releasing them in the direction of the target — a technique requiring fine judgment of distance.

The crossbow, another weapon with a long and dangerous reach, originated in China so long ago as to feature in Sun Tzu's influential *The Art of War*, which was written some time before 300BC. There is a record of a crossbow being used in an ambush at the battle of Ma-Ling in 341BC, and several remnants of crossbows were found when the Terracotta Army was discovered in 1974 in the tomb of the 3rd-century BC Chinese emperor Qin Shi Huang. The crossbow consisted of a bow mounted on a tiller or stock with a drawn bowstring held by a mechanism. To fire the weapon, a rod was pushed up through a hole to force out the bowstring and release the projectile, known as a bolt or quarrel. Armies in North Africa, Asia, and Europe commonly used the crossbow in war and there were many variants: these included a Chinese repeating crossbow with a pull lever and automatic magazine, a pistol-fired crossbow, and the arbalest, a giant steel crossbow invented in Europe that could fire two bolts per minute and guarantee to be accurate at up to 1640 ft (500 m).

Before the age of rifles and guns, the ultimate in distance warfare, the most renowned long-range warriors were archers who staged mass assaults and won some of the most dramatic victories in the history of warfare. In 53BC, for example, Roman legionaries were overwhelmed at Carrhae in Persia by mounted Parthian archers who slaughtered 20,000 of them with arrows shot from strong, flexible, and composite bows made from layers of horn. In the 6th century AD, Byzantine archers were trained to fire very rapidly, showering their opponents with arrows and killing hundreds at a time. The medieval longbow created similar havoc during the Hundred Years' War between England and France at the battles of Crécy in 1346, Poitiers in 1356 and Agincourt in 1415. Reputedly, the French became so infuriated at the prowess of the English longbowmen that any of them they managed to capture had the drawstring fingers of their hands severed. Archers who escaped this unenviable fate were said to waggle their drawstring fingers at the French to show they were still in action.

Aztec warrior's Atlatl or spear thrower, Mexico. As early as the Stone Age the spear was one of the most commonly used personal weapons developed for hunting animals for food.

Opposite page: The Battle of Liegnitz (Poland) in 1241 comprised two engagements between armies drawn from several European states and the Mongol invaders from Asia. The Europeans' aim was to halt the Mongol invasion of their continent.

The medieval longbow has been called the machine gun of the Middle Ages owing to the rate at which experienced longbowmen were able to fire it: the firing rate was reckoned to average six arrows per minute. This was considerably greater than the firing rate obtained from crossbows and much faster than the early hand-held gun. The arquebus and boys were employed to deliver replacement arrows to the longbowmen should they run out. Marksmanship was not necessarily involved, for the intention was to loose a cloud of arrows into the air, causing them to fall in a thick concentration that was difficult for opponents to avoid. To make matters even worse for the longbowmen's opponent, the plate armor that replaced chain mail in the 14th century as protection against firearms was no defense against longbow arrows, which could easily pierce it.

Although its earliest example, found in Somerset in southwestern England, dates from 2665BC, the heyday of the longbow came between AD1250 and 1450. The longbow was not a composite, but a self-bow, made from a single piece of yew or ash. The traditional method of making a longbow was long and laborious; the yew had to dry out for up to two years before being shaped over the next three. However, a well made longbow could last a long time in use, particularly if the traditional coating of wax, resin, and fine tallow was applied to it.

Unusually, archers had to be "fitted" for their longbows, as the weapons were supposed to be as tall as their users. Longbows had to be tailor-made for the archer who used them so that they were tall enough for archers to draw the string — which was made of hemp, flax, or silk — to a suitable point on his face or body. From there, the longbowman was required to line up his target which meant that his line of sight had to be very precise — eyes and hands had to work together in order to score a hit. Ideas about the range of medieval longbows have also varied. A range of 540 ft (165 m) has been mooted, so has the idea that a longbowman was able to strike an enemy at 748 ft (228 m). Archers mounted on horses needed smaller bows that could be moved from one side of the horse to the other quickly. These tended to be composite bows made up of layers of horn, wood, and sinew rather than simple wooden bows. At the Battle of Liegnitz in 1241 Mongol horse archers skirmishing ahead of the main army, shot thousands of arrows at the heavy European cavalry of Duke Henry II of Silesia. At the same time as peppering the Europeans with arrows, the Mongol light cavalry fell back through smoke, luring the Europeans forward. This disrupted the European formation and reduced their numbers so that they fell easy victim to a charge by Mongol heavy cavalry armed with lances and swords. The horse archers then returned to complete the rout.

A replica of a longbow was found on the Tudor carrack (warship) *Mary Rose* which sank on July 17, 1545, during the Battle of the Solent while fighting against a French invasion fleet. Among the 20,000 artefacts discovered on board was a crossbow that was able to fire a 2 oz (57 g), arrow over a distance of 1079 ft (329 m), and a 3 ¼ oz (94 g) arrow over 814 ft (248 m). At the time the *Mary Rose* was constructed, between 1509 and 1511, warfare at sea was still generally regarded as a floating version of war on land; although unusually, the English warships carried guns that could fire broadsides from gunports. Traditionally, though, fighting between opponents was carried out at close quarters, usually on the decks of ships that had been grappled to keep them close and then boarded. This form of "grapple and board" sea battle was dramatically superseded later in the 16th century when the English ships bombarded vessels of the Spanish Armada in 1588 with cannons fired from a distance.

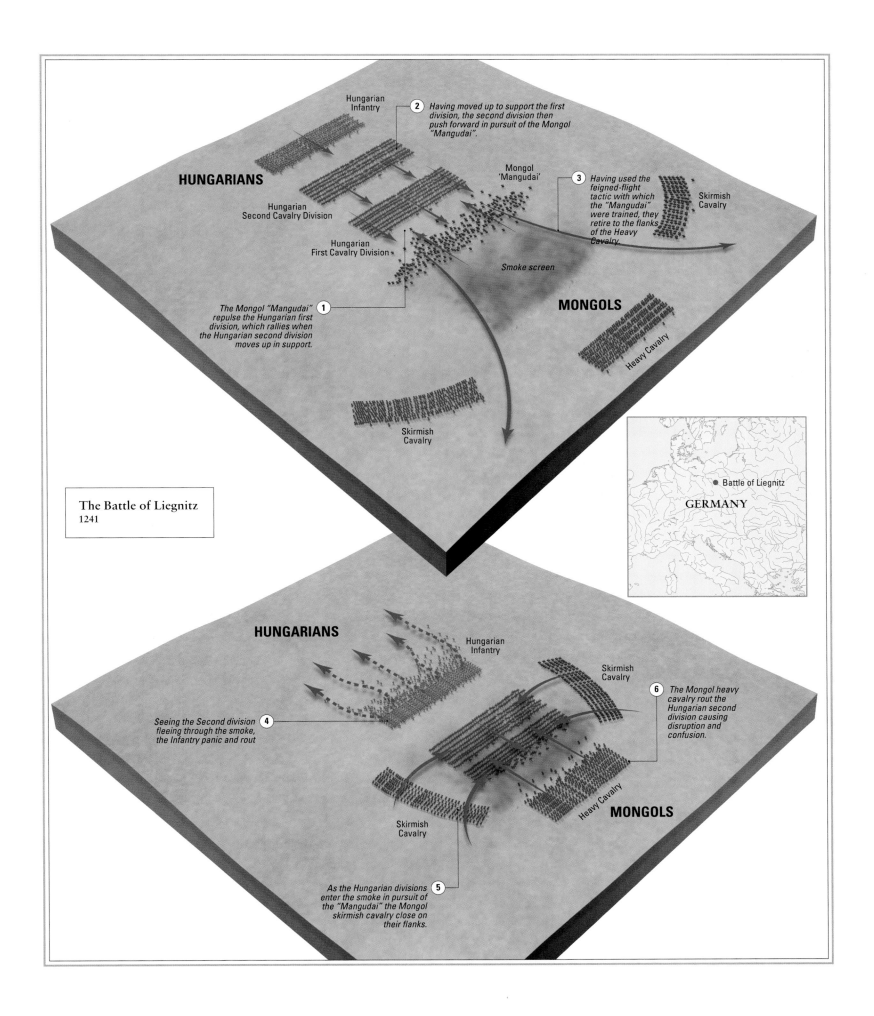

Hungarian
Infantry

2 Having moved up to support the first division, the second division then push forward in pursuit of the Mongol "Mangudai".

HUNGARIANS

Hungarian
Second Cavalry Division

Mongol
'Mangudai'

3 Having used the feigned-flight tactic with which the "Mangudai" were trained, they retire to the flanks of the Heavy Cavalry.

Skirmish
Cavalry

Hungarian
First Cavalry Division

Smoke screen

1 The Mongol "Mangudai" repulse the Hungarian first division, which rallies when the Hungarian second division moves up in support.

MONGOLS

Heavy Cavalry

Skirmish
Cavalry

The Battle of Liegnitz
1241

● Battle of Liegnitz

GERMANY

HUNGARIANS

Hungarian
Infantry

Skirmish
Cavalry

6 The Mongol heavy cavalry rout the Hungarian second division causing disruption and confusion.

4 Seeing the Second division fleeing through the smoke, the Infantry panic and rout

Heavy Cavalry

MONGOLS

Skirmish
Cavalry

5 As the Hungarian divisions enter the smoke in pursuit of the "Mangudai" the Mongol skirmish cavalry close on their flanks.

THE CHARIOT: TERROR WEAPON OF ANCIENT WARFARE

THE INTRODUCTION OF THE CHARIOT INTO WARFARE, WITH ITS MOBILITY AND POWER, BROUGHT A NEW KIND OF TERROR TO THE BATTLEFIELD. CHARIOTS, AND THE HIT-AND-RUN TACTICS THEY EXPLOITED, SOON BECAME A REGULAR FEATURE IN BATTLE.

Chariots were the first mobile weapons to be manufactured specifically for use in war. They originated in Sumeria around 3000BC, and some 500 years later they made their first pictorial appearance on the standard of Ur, a city in southern Mesopotamia near the Persian Gulf. Sumerian chariots were hefty affairs, not made for speed and usually pulled by onagers (wild asses) as part of a military baggage train rather than fighting duties. Later on, in about 2000BC, the Sumerians developed a lighter version of the chariot with two wheels instead of four, although thewheels were still solid and the chariot was pulled by four asses.

It fell to other peoples to transform the chariot into something better suited to the demands of war. The military use of chariots, which required speed, easy handling, and the use of fleet-footed horses rather than slow, if sturdy, onagers or oxen, developed only after spoked wheels replaced solid ones. Examples of chariots with spoked wheels were discovered by archeologists in the Andronovo burial sites in what are now Russia and Kazakhstan. From there, chariots and chariot warfare soon spread to India and Persia and appeared in Mesopotamia in the 18th century BC, when the Hittites of Canaan began to use two-wheeled chariots drawn by horses. A contemporary document, the Old Hittite Anitta Text, records the use of 40 teams of horses in the siege of Salatiwara, a Bronze Age city in Anatolia (Turkey) that was besieged by the forces of Anitta, the king of Kussara. The Hittites were assiduous in training their horses to peak condition, with rules and exercises that probably followed a special Hittite training text.

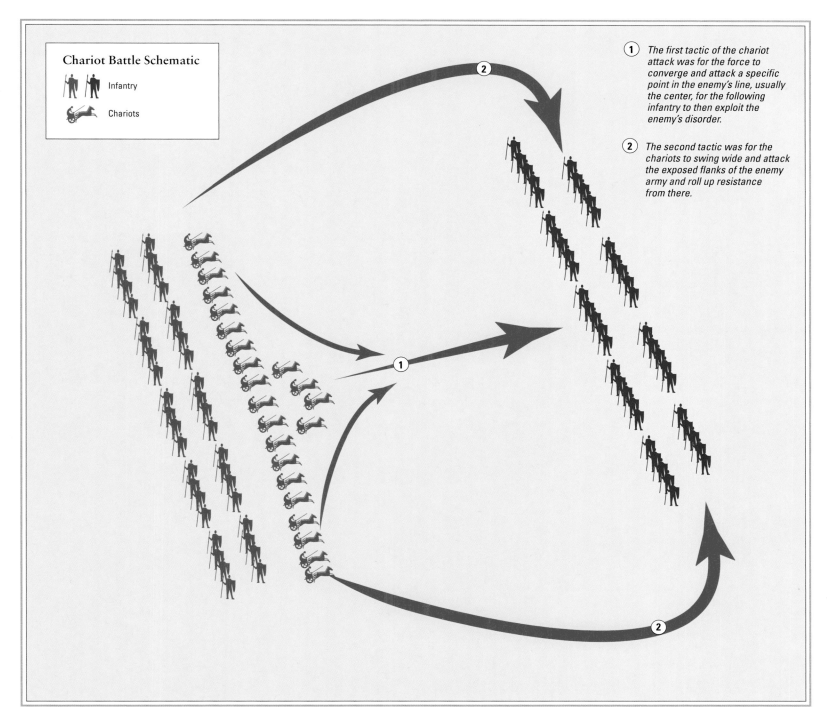

Chariot Battle Schematic

Infantry

Chariots

 The first tactic of the chariot attack was for the force to converge and attack a specific point in the enemy's line, usually the center, for the following infantry to then exploit the enemy's disorder.

② The second tactic was for the chariots to swing wide and attack the exposed flanks of the enemy army and roll up resistance from there.

The Hittites soon became renowned, and much-feared, charioteers. They developed chariots with lighter wheels of four spokes rather than eight, and by placing the wheels along the middle of the chariot they provided better support for the driver and crew so the chariot could hold three warriors. The Hittites became the terror of Mesopotamia, which they occupied after 1900BC, and went on to vanquish Syria as well. In the first known account of a battle in detail — the battle of Kadesh in 1275BC — an anonymous Egyptian scribe recorded how the Hittites and Egyptians clashed at Kadesh, the Hittite stronghold in Syria. There the Egyptian pharaoh Rameses II found himself ambushed by a mass of Hittite chariots that scattered the Egyptian army, chasing it back to their camp and surrounding it. Eventually, Rameses managed to extricate his army and peace was concluded between him and the Hittite king Muwatallish.

The chariot was the first fast-moving weapon used in warfare. Armies relied on the chariots' speed to throw enemies into disarray. The second wave of chariot assaults, on the opponents' flanks, helped the attacking infantry to pick them off.

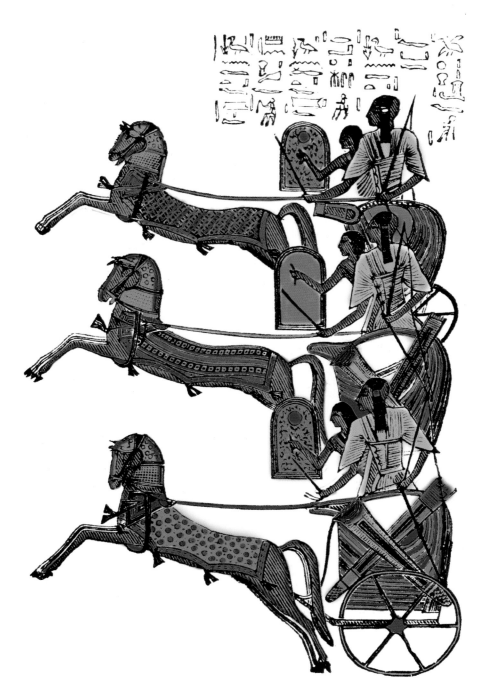

Above and opposite page: The Pharaoh Rameses II (circa 1303 BC - 1213BC), son of Seti I and considered one of the most powerful pharaohs of ancient Egypt, is shown storming a fortress by chariot flanked by his three sons.

But Kadesh had been a painful lesson in the power of the chariot as a weapon of war, one that the ancient Egyptians never forgot.

The Egyptians developed their own chariots in the 15th century BC; and like the Hittite models they were extremely graceful, yet sturdy enough to withstand the strain of being driven at high speed over rough ground. Egyptian chariots, which carried two men, a driver, and an archer or spearman, were smaller than the Hittites' and their wheels were placed at the back, not along the center. Egyptian chariot horses were sometimes employed as weapons in themselves: their charioteers made them rear up just as they reached the enemy lines and batter away at enemy soldiers with their hooves.

Chariots are frequently mentioned in the Old Testament, and were depicted by the prophets not only as instruments of war but also as symbols of glory and power. They acquired so much prestige, in fact, that the second Book of Kings recounted the death of the prophet Elijah in supernatural terms: a chariot of fire appeared, pulled by four horses, and Elijah was carried directly to heaven in a whirlwind. Another religious record, the Rigveda, one of the four Hindu sacred texts, tells how several deities, such as Usha, goddess of the dawn, and Agni, the messenger of the gods, rode in chariots. It was also in India that the military uses of the chariot were exploited. Scythed wheels were introduced by Ajatashatru, king of the Magadha Empire in northern India, in around 475BC. Razor-sharp, sickle-shaped blades were attached to the end of the axles, extending some 36 in (91 cm) on both sides of the chariot.

By this time, however, the age of the chariot as a principal weapon of war was nearing its close in the Near East. Its swansong occurred at the Battle of Gaugamela in 331BC, when Alexander the Great's Agrarians, his javelin-throwers, demolished the chariots launched against them by King Darius III of Persia. The Agrarians had rehearsed a special stratagem. The first Agrarian line withdrew, to open up a gap. The chariot horses entered, only to run into the lances of the rear ranks. Thus trapped, the chariots, their drivers, crews and horses could be dealt with at leisure. This was the first time the otherwise dreaded Persian chariots had been rendered useless, and the ingenious but simple means by which it was done severely dented their fearsome reputation. After that, the cavalry took their place as the force responsible for front-line shock action.

Chariots continued to feature in European warfare, notably in Britain, where Julius Caesar encountered them during the first of his two excursions into what the Romans termed the "Sacred Isle" in 55BC. The Britons' expertise was such that even though Caesar described them as "barbarians", he was greatly impressed. As he wrote in the fourth book of his *Gallic Wars*:

Rameses II leading the storm of a fortress in an Egyptian chariot.

"Their mode of fighting with their chariots is this: firstly, they drive about in all directions and throw their weapons and generally break the ranks of the enemy with the very dread of their horses and the noise of their wheels; and when they have worked themselves in between the troops of horse, leap from their chariots and engage on foot. The charioteers in the meantime withdraw some little distance from the battle, and so place themselves with the chariots that, if their masters are overpowered by the number of the enemy, they may have a ready retreat to their own troops. Thus they display in battle the speed of horse, [together with] the firmness of infantry; and by daily practice and exercise attain to such expertness that they are accustomed, even on a declining and steep place, to check their horses at full speed, and manage and turn them in an instant and run along the pole, and stand on the yoke, and thence betake themselves with the greatest celerity to their chariots again."

The Britons made plenty of trouble for the Romans, first by crowding the landing beaches with their chariots in an attempt to prevent them from coming ashore. The attempt failed, but later they attacked a Roman foraging party at work in a field of barley. From the thick forests of alder and oak, the Britons watched the Romans as they laid aside their arms and jerkins, and began to reap the field. they were thoroughly occupied, the Britons rushed out of the trees yelling fearsome war cries, brandishing spears, and driving their chariots at speed. At Caesar's camp, the sentries were alerted by clouds of dust rising into the sky from the direction that the foraging party had marched. Immediately, Caesar and a handful of troops stormed out of the camp and raced along the path that led to the field, buckling on their armor as they ran. When they arrived, they saw the foraging party cramped together, surrounded by chariots and about to be overwhelmed by the Britons, who were throwing spears and other weapons at them from all sides. Several Romans had been killed, but fortunately the Britons got the idea that Caesar had come to deal with them in force. They immediately broke off their attack, leapt into their chariots, and fled back to the safety of their forests.

Caesar paid a second visit to the Sacred Isle in 54BC, but the result was no more satisfactory than before. Ultimately, the elusive Britons, who specialized in sneak attacks and ambushes and never came out to fight a proper battle, combined with the appalling British weather — torrents of rain fell for days on end — to make Caesar and his troops withdraw from Britain. Caesar never returned, but some 90 years later, Emperor Claudius sent an invasion force that conquered the island and added it to the Roman Empire, as the province of Britannia, for the next four centuries.

Unlike their previous responses to weaponry that had taxed them in battle, the Romans never added the chariot to their equipment. Instead, in a thorough overhaul of their army that took place in the 3rd century AD, they opted for cavalry units, an advancement that would lead to cavalry becoming the successors to chariots. Nevertheless, the Romans found a role for them: chariot-racing, which was so dangerous and so frequently fatal that the charioteers were usually dispensible slaves. Chariot-racing became the most popular mass entertainment at the Circus Maximus in Rome, where the spectators might number a quarter of a million, with the same number again viewing the proceedings from the surrounding hills.

Opposite page: Human habitation in the Middle East as it existed in around 900BC. Significantly, populations are shown as settling mainly on coasts, that is, close to water, or in the case of Ancient Egypt, along the River Nile.

Roman arena in Arles, which would have hosted entertainments including chariot races, a hugely popular form of entertainment during the Roman times.

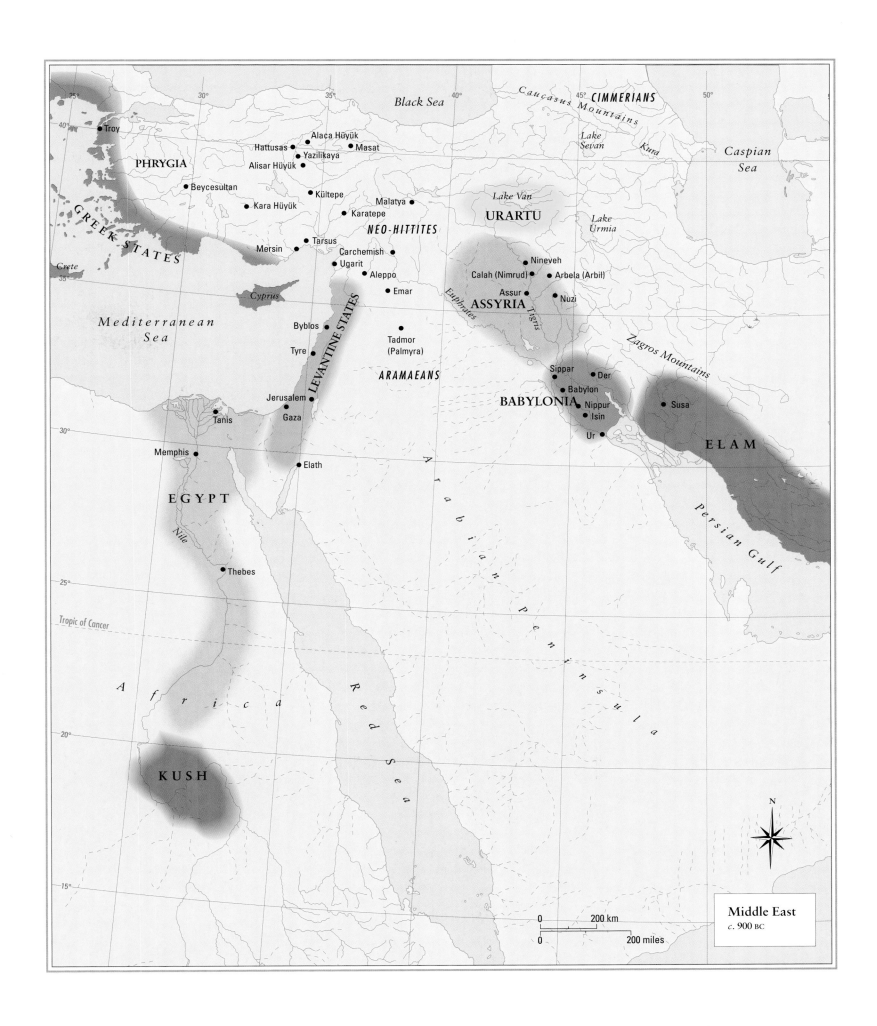

Black Sea

CIMMERIANS

Caucasus Mountains

Caspian Sea

Troy

PHRYGIA

Alaca Hüyük

Hattusas

Masat

Yazilikaya

Alisar Hüyük

Lake Sevan

Kura

Beycesultan

Kültepe

Lake Van

Malatya

URARTU

Lake Urmia

GREEK STATES

Kara Hüyük

Karatepe

NEO-HITTITES

Crete

Mersin

Tarsus

Carchemish

Nineveh

Ugarit

Calah (Nimrud)

Arbela (Arbil)

Cyprus

Aleppo

Assur

ASSYRIA

Nuzi

Euphrates

Tigris

Emar

Mediterranean Sea

Byblos

LEVANTINE STATES

Tadmor (Palmyra)

Zagros Mountains

Tyre

ARAMAEANS

Sippar

Der

Babylon

Jerusalem

BABYLONIA

Nippur

Susa

Gaza

Isin

Tanis

Ur

ELAM

Memphis

Elath

EGYPT

Arabian Peninsula

Persian Gulf

Nile

Africa

Red Sea

Thebes

Tropic of Cancer

KUSH

N

Middle East
c. 900 BC

0   200 km

0   200 miles

ASSYRIA: THE WORLD'S FIRST MILITARY STATE

"THE ASSYRIANS CAME DOWN LIKE A WOLF ON THE FOLD", WROTE 19TH CENTURY ENGLISH POET LORD BYRON. HE NEEDED NO POETIC LICENSE, THE RUTHLESS, WARLIKE ASSYRIANS CONQUERED AN EMPIRE AND TERRORIZED MESOPOTAMIA FOR THREE CENTURIES.

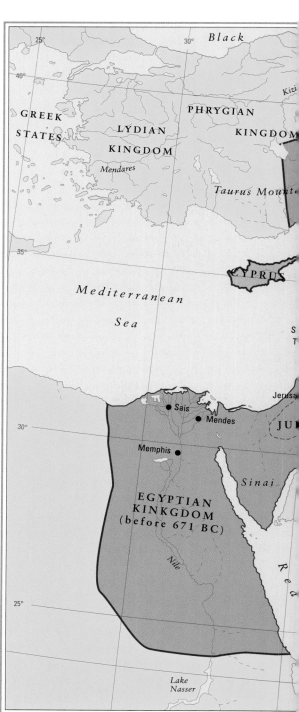

The Assyrians created the world's first military state. To support it, their empire was constantly geared for war. Assyrian soldiers and their commanders were its most important citizens, and most money and effort went on perfecting the army. This was not just a matter of military acquisition and the creation of power: the Assyrians believed that conquest was a divine mission bestowed on them by their gods and that it was their duty to spread the worship of those gods over the territories they conquered. To this end, maximum effort was concentrated on building up their army to the highest peak of efficiency with the best equipment and training. Little wonder that the Assyrians became the most successful military power in Mesopotamia, with an empire that ultimately stretched from Persia in the east into Anatolia (Turkey) in the north, along the shores of the eastern Mediterranean and from there into Egypt. Throughout this vast area, the Assyrians inspired great terror with the gigantic size of their armies — a field force numbering up to 50,000 men could be mustered at any time — the mass onslaughts of their chariots, and the large cavalry squadrons which they were the first to create.

However, it took the Assyrians almost a millennium of effort to reach this paramount stage in their history. By comparison, their beginnings were very modest. They began in about 3000BC in north-eastern Mesopotamia, where the upper reaches of the River Tigris run across a flat, otherwise featureless plain. With its lack of natural barriers, this was difficult country to protect against incursions by nearby peoples,

Although the Assyrians overran their extensive empire by systematic aggression, they were following a defensive policy: their original territory was virtually indefensible against attack and so they resolved to conquer rather than be conquered and proved to be harsh rulers over their conquered territories.

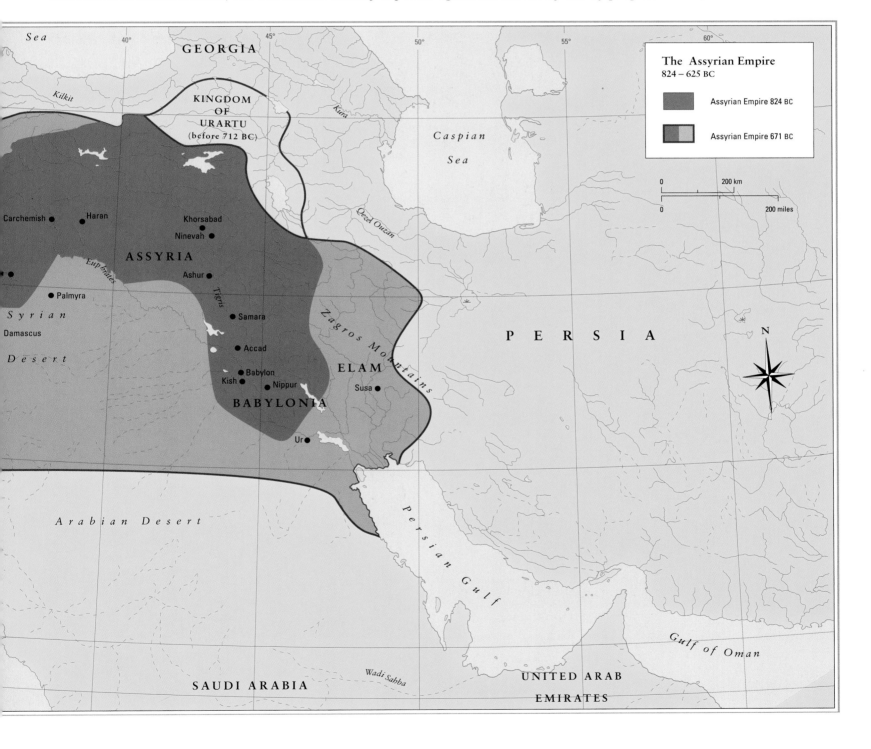

Ancient Assyrian fresco depicting a soldier. The Assyrian militia were equipped with iron spears, iron-tipped arrows, and iron armor.

and the Hittites in the north-west and the Babylonians to the south-east lost no opportunity to threaten the Assyrians. The great effort needed to survive in a hostile environment bred a strain of defiant resistance in the Assyrians that evolved into a warlike mentality that made theirs the most successful, and aggressive, army in Mesopotamia.

One king in particular was responsible for this transformation from vulnerable neighbor to mighty military power. Before Tiglath-Pileser III came to the throne in around 745BC, the state had relied on a militia that fought campaigns as and when required but afterward returned to their civilian occupations. Tiglath-Pileser believed that the defense of Assyria and the acquisition of new territories was not just an occasional activity. What was required was a standing army, well trained and drilled, adept at strategy and tactics, and equipped with the best weapons available.

As early as 1000BC, the Assyrians had recognized the superiority of iron weapons over those made of bronze; and even in its militia days, their army had been equipped not only with iron spears or iron-tipped arrows but also with iron armor. Modern tests have shown that this armor was capable of resisting shot from the muskets used in Napoleon's army. Assyrian chariots were often made of heavy-paneled, iron-covered wood, which was painted in brilliant colors and sometimes studded with jewels or pieces of ivory. Drawn by two horses, Assyrian chariots carried a two-man crew, the driver and an archer. A spare horse was later tethered to the rear of the chariot and a third man was added to protect the other two.

Through constant training and practice, Assyrian archers became superlative bowmen, greatly feared by their opponents for their ability to fire arrows over a distance of up to 820 ft (250 m). An archer's quiver contained some 50 arrows; and apart from its role in chariotry, the Assyrian bow served as the principal weapon of the infantry. A single captain of infantry could have up to 100 bowmen and their shield-bearers under his command, often operating in groups. Their deadly accuracy quickly became legendary. One important use of the Assyrian bowmen was to create confusion and dismay among the enemy by blasting them with a storm of arrows as a prelude to a charge by chariots and cavalry. The chariots were the main strike force of the Assyrian army. Their purpose was to build up speed as a prelude to colliding head on with the enemy infantry. It was certainly brute force, but brute force used in far greater numbers than was normal and closely co-ordinated with the spearmen, archers, and cavalry. Although numerous by contemporary standards, the cavalry was the smallest element in the immense Assyrian army. Curiously, the Assyrians did not work out the multiple roles a horseman might play in combat. Their horses were ridden bareback by two men, who between them performed the same functions as the driver and crew of a chariot: the man in front controlled the horse while his companion used the lance or the bow. The bulk of an Assyrian army consisted of spearmen, who were trained to maneuver with a nimbleness that belied their large number and who were superior to the infantry of other armies of the time. Once the spearmen began to advance en masse in a battle, they tended to become an irresistible force and a sign that an Assyrian victory was imminent.

An important part of military planning was the diet on which Assyrian soldiers were fed. The stringent drilling and training, the long route marches, and the demanding Mesopotamian climate made it imperative that Assyrian soldiers were properly nourished in order to keep up their physical strength and well-being. It was reckoned, therefore, that their diet needed to contain at least 3,450 calories per day, including around 2 ½ oz (71 g), of protein and 2 ¼ gallons (8.5 litres) of water. Also essential, once the Assyrian Empire grew in size, were proper communications; and for this the Assyrians constructed a road system, the first of its kind, that enabled their armies to reach troublespots fast. The roads also eased the movement of military supplies, which were carried by donkeys or, for the first time, camels. Mountains were no barrier: the Assyrian engineers simply

Height: 0·95 m. 119402.

Siege of a city.
Tiglathpileser III; provenance unknown.

cut through them. Regular way-stations were provided for messengers to rest en route, and here too their horses were changed. Like the empire-spanning roads later built across Europe by the Romans, the Assyrian system also benefited commercial traffic, allowing the easier distribution of goods throughout the empire.

A wall carving of the siege of a city, during the reign of Tiglath-Pileser III, king of Assyria, c. 730BC.

The Assyrians also concentrated their military expertise on siege warfare, a very necessary skill in view of the large number of heavily fortified towns and cities in the turbulent Middle East of their time. The art of fortification had already been thoroughly developed by 1000BC or earlier, and numerous cities were protected by massive walls that were all but impregnable to the many armies of the region. The

Assyrians, however, used sophisticated methods to circumvent the technological limitations of their weaponry in reducing the defenses of well-fortified cities. This often included the use of fire, a terrifying prospect for soldiers trapped high above the ground on scaling ladders or inside wooden towers.

The wooden towers were part of the equipment the Assyrians included in their siege trains, and they came protected from flaming arrows with ready-wetted leather hides. A supply of water was carried in case the leather dried out and caught fire in the baking Middle Eastern sun before the tower's task was accomplished. Archers were posted in the small tower at the top and showered defenders brave or unwary enough to attempt to prevent the siege machine being brought up close to the city wall. Once the tower was in place, soldiers wielding long, sharp spears would remove pieces of the wall, which was usually made of mud rather than stone and was therefore relatively easy to chip away. As and when stone walls became more common, the Assyrians simply devised larger, stronger spears capable of destroying the harder material. Heavy battering rams with ends armored by iron were also included in the Assyrians' siege equipment.

Another strategy in siege warfare was the most insidious: "mining", which involved removing bricks or, later, stones at the base of a city's walls, propping up the walls with sticks and packing the spaces made with flammable materials. The "miners" would then set fire to the material, hastily withdraw, and then wait until the flames burned through the supporting sticks and collapsed the wall. The advantage of "mining" was that it could be carried out in a protected position out of sight of the defenders while all the attention was being directed at the battle going on at the top.

Once a city fell to the Assyrians, the fate of its inhabitants was appalling. It was normal for the Assyrians to kill every man, woman, and child inside a vanquished city. Either that or they deported whole populations as captives and slaves. King Tiglath-Pileser III, for example, removed 65,000 people from what is now Iran to the River Diyala on the border between Assyria and Babylonia. Two years later, he displaced another 330,000 from Hamath in Syria to the Zagros Mountains in what is now in southwestern Iran. The Assyrians were adept at the psychology of terror, of which slaughter and deportation were essential ingredients. Records engraved on plaques, which were ordered by individual kings, leave no doubt that fearful vengeance would follow any resistance to the mighty Assyrian army and its all-powerful, all-avenging royal commander. An inscription describing a victory over the King of Elam won by King Sennacherib, the son of Sargon II and his successor in 704BC, could hardly have been more gruesomely specific.

"At the command of the god Ashur, the great Lord, I rushed upon the enemy like the approach of a hurricane ... I put them to rout and turned them back. I transfixed the troops of the enemy with javelins and arrows. Humban-undasha, the commander in chief of the King of Elam, together with his nobles ... I cut their throats like sheep ... My prancing steeds ... plunged into their welling blood as into a river: the wheels of my battle chariot were bespattered with blood and filth. I filled the plain with corpses of their warriors like herbage ..."

Just over 90 years later, in 612BC, this same fate overcame Nineveh, an "exceeding great city", according to the Biblical Book of Jonah, and the capital of Assyria. With that, the Assyrian Empire came to an end after three centuries of dominance. It was the victim of the Babylonian and Medean Empires, which had risen to power and taken its place.

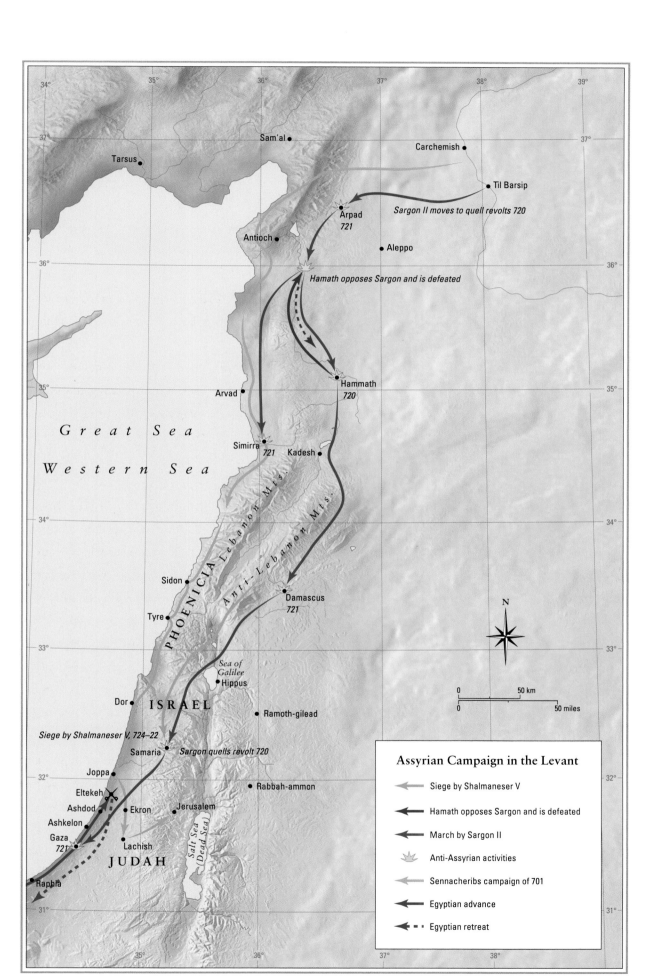

34°   35°   36°   37°   38°   39°

37°   37°

• Sam'al   Carchemish •

Tarsus •

                                                    • Til Barsip

                                                Sargon II moves to quell revolts 720

                            ☀ Arpad
                               721

                    Antioch •   • Aleppo

36°   36°

                        ☀ Hamath opposes Sargon and is defeated

                                        ☀ Hammath
                                           720
                    Arvad •

35°   35°

G r e a t   S e a

W e s t e r n   S e a

                    Simirra ☀
                            721   Kadesh •

34°   34°

                              Lebanon Mts.

                              Anti-Lebanon Mts.

                    Sidon •

                                        Damascus ☀
                    PHOENICIA   721

                    Tyre •

33°   33°

                        Sea of
                        Galilee
                        • Hippus   N

                                                        ⭐ (compass rose)

        Dor • ISRAEL

                        • Ramoth-gilead   0   50 km
                                                          0   50 miles

Siege by Shalmaneser V, 724–22

32°   Samaria Sargon quells revolt 720   32°

        Joppa •

    Eltekeh ✗   • Rabbah-ammon
  Ashdod • • Ekron   Jerusalem •
  Ashkelon •
    Gaza •
        721   Lachish •   *Salt Sea*
              JUDAH   *(Dead Sea)*

  Raphia •

31°   31°

Assyrian Campaign in the Levant

→ Siege by Shalmaneser V

→ Hamath opposes Sargon and is defeated

→ March by Sargon II

☀ Anti-Assyrian activities

→ Sennacheribs campaign of 701

→ Egyptian advance

⇢ Egyptian retreat

35°   36°   37°   38°

After the mid-8th century BC, the Assyrians swept through the entire length of the Levant, overrunning Phoenicia and Ancient Israel as far as Gaza in the extreme south. At the time, Assyria was the greatest military power in the world.

The hoplites of ancient Greece

THE HOPLITES OF ANCIENT GREECE WERE SPEARMEN WHO FOUGHT IN TIGHTLY ORDERED PHALANXES. ALTHOUGH THEY BELONGED TO A MILITIA RATHER THAN A STANDING ARMY, THEY DEFEATED THEIR MOST FORMIDABLE ENEMY, THE PERSIANS, AND TWICE SAVED GREECE FROM INVASION AND OCCUPATION.

The hoplite first appeared in battle in the 7th century BC; and in the early, classical period of hoplite warfare, most battles were somewhat stylized. They took the form of brief, armed clashes in which opposing phalanxes approached each other until their front lines, the protostates, were close enough to stab out with their spears, a form of fighting known as *doratismos*. At the same time, as one theory on Greek military strategy puts it, the hoplite front line was gently pushed by the ranks behind: this procedure, known as *othismos*, imposed pressure on the enemy, and was designed to overbalance and panic them. Meanwhile, light infantrymen, the *psiloi*, would throw stones and javelins at the enemy from behind their lines. If the *doratismos* and the *othismos* failed to produce withdrawal or surrender, the opposing hoplites would draw the *xiphos*, their straight-bladed, double-edged sword, about two feet (61 cm) in length, and attempt to settle matters at close quarters.

Opposite page: The geography of Greece, with its terrain of mountains and valleys, prearranged both its politics and history. A series of separate, mutually hostile city-states developed, resulting in regular warfare, although the states would unite against a common enemy such as Persia.

These clashes usually continued for an hour before one or other of the phalanxes broke and fled. The hoplite who broke and ran from an enemy, particularly if he abandoned his *aspis* (shield), earned disgrace not only for himself but also for his family and friends. Unfortunately, the ancient Greek shield was very likely to be discarded in flight, as it was unusually large and heavy: it was made of wood and covered in bronze and it measured some 36 in (91.5 cm) in diameter and weighed up to 33 Ib (15 kg). The purpose of the *aspis* was to defend the hoplite but also to carry him from the field should he be killed or wounded. The aspis did provide safety in numbers, as the hoplites were in phalanx formation.

Mycenaean Greece

- ■ Mycenaean capital
- ● Major city
- · Mycenaean site

Tiryns Citadel

— Old citadel, 1400 BC

1. Main gateway
2. Inner gateway to palace
3. Greater propælum
4. Lesser propælum
5. Court to chief Megaron
6. Chief Megaron
7. Court to lesser Megaron
8. Lesser Megaron

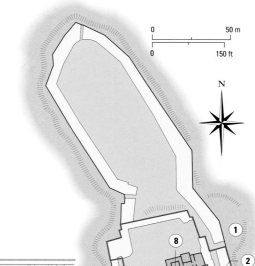

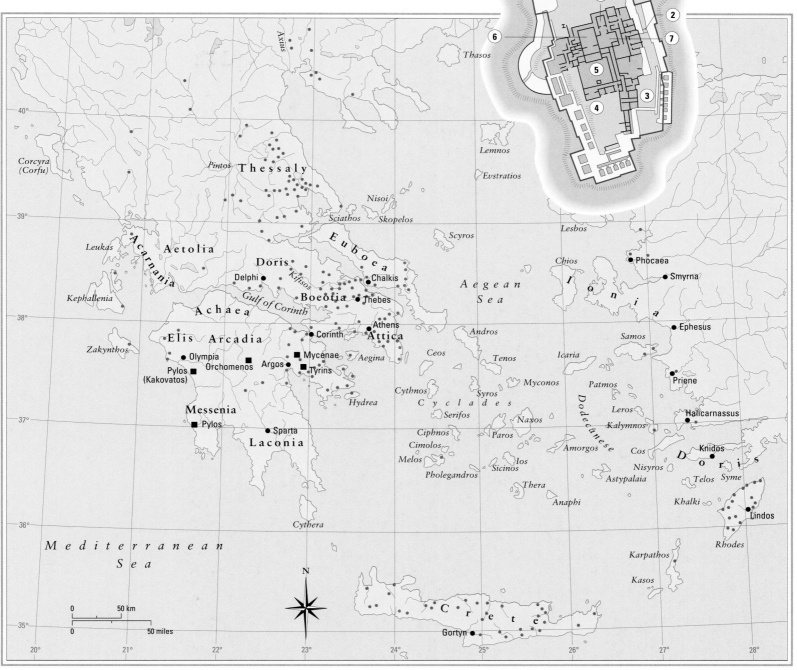

Of course hoplite warfare had limitations. There was not enough wealth or population in most Greek cities to support a large or standing army, and the only alternative was the militia, formed by citizen soldiers. Every man of military age was liable for war service, and the most famous ancient Greeks did their time as hoplites. Among them were the philosopher Socrates, whose bravery in battle was recounted by Plato in his *Dialogues*, and the playwright Aeschylus, who fought at the battle of Marathon in 490 BC and against the Persians at Salamis in 480BC, the first recorded naval battle in history.

The hoplites were required to supply their own panhopla, or panoply, that is their weapons and their bronze armor. This included a helmet, greaves, a cuirass, a spear, and a sword and shield, all expensive items which normally only middle-class Greeks could afford. For this reason, the hoplites were drawn from the class of *zeugitai*, a term which meant "plowman" but more likely described middle-class farmers. There were three other classes, all with military duties to perform: the *thetes* provided rowers for the Athenian navy; the *hippeis*, or knights, formed the cavalry and furnished their own horses for the purpose; and, most favored of all, the wealthy *pentacosiomedimnoi*. When young, they fought as cavalry and when older, they paid to equip *triremes* for the navy.

Individual wealth also affected the quality of the armor worn by the hoplites. The better-off could choose linothorax, an armor comprising stitched or laminated linen reinforced with animal skins or bronze scales. A financial step up was a bronze breastplate or a bronze helmet with plates protecting the cheeks and greaves. There were several types of helmet, such as the Corinthian, its lighter version the Chalcidian, or the plain and simple Pilos helmet favored by the ascetic Spartan hoplites.

Opposite page: Engraving showing Hoplite soldiers guarding a gateway.

This fearsome formation of hoplite forces dates from the time when King Philip of Macedonia ruled Greece. The hoplites' *sarissas* (spears), would appear terrifying to the enemy before commencing battle.

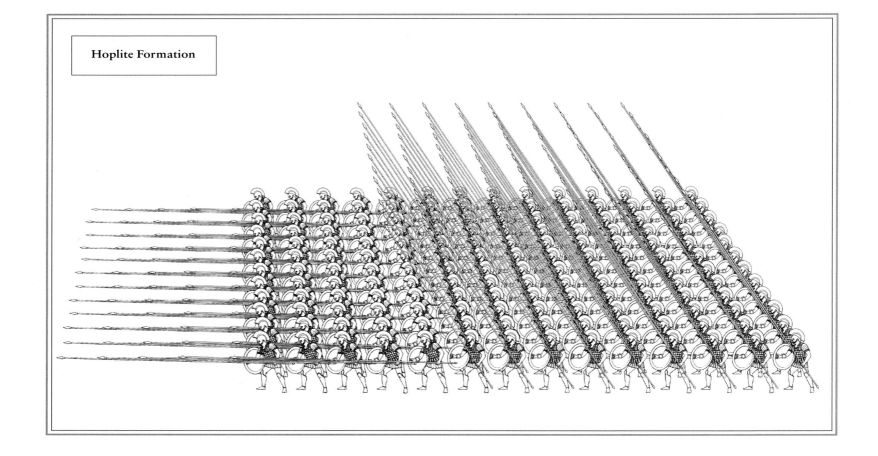

Hoplite Formation

SPARTA: THE MILITARY STATE OF ANCIENT GREECE

SPARTA WAS A CITY-STATE TOTALLY FOCUSED ON WAR. NOTHING INTERFERED WITH ITS STRINGENT MARTIAL ETHOS — INFANTS DEEMED UNSUITABLE TO SERVE THE STATE WERE KILLED AT BIRTH.

GREECE
Battle of Thermopolae

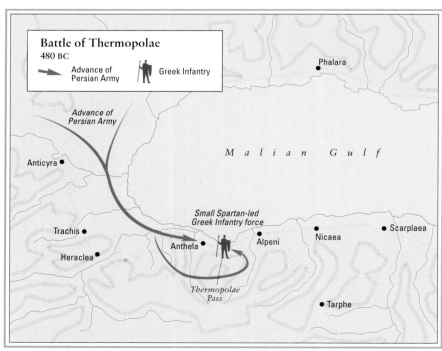

Battle of Thermopolae
480 BC

→ Advance of Persian Army   Greek Infantry

Phalara

Advance of Persian Army

Anticyra

M a l i a n   G u l f

Small Spartan-led Greek Infantry force

Trachis
Anthela
Alpeni
Nicaea
• Scarplaea
Heraclea

Thermopolae Pass

• Tarphe

The Spartans were the Assyrians of ancient Greece. Unlike in other Greek city-states, especially luxury-loving, commercially minded Athens, the sole ethos of Sparta was war. Spartans were born to be soldiers, and at the age of seven began their training for a life of warfare. The boys were taken away from home and female influence, and sent to an *agoge*, a military camp, where they were taught to endure hardship and were deliberately deprived of sufficient food and clothing. At the age of 12, they were classed as *meirakion* (youths) and the punitive nature of their training was increased.

They became subject to even more severe discipline: they were allowed to dress only in a thin tunic and went unshod in both summer and winter. At 20, they became eligible for military service. Service would last for 40 years, if they survived, and sometimes longer.

By the time they became full-fledged soldiers, Spartans had been taught to fear defeat and the disgrace it brought more than they feared death. Every effort had been made to eradicate any sign of individualism from their mind, and every Spartan soldier knew that if a Spartan were suspected of cowardice — by returning from battle without his shield, for instance — the penalty could be execution. Plutarch, the Greek historian of the 1st century AD, wrote in his *Life of Lycurgus* that Spartans were "the only men in the world with whom war brought a respite in the training for war". Tyrtaeus,

Statue of King Leonidas in warrior dress, Sparta, Greece.

Left: In 480BC, an alliance of Greek city-states resisted a Persian invasion of Greece. The Persians were blocked at the pass of Thermopolae. The Persian fleet was defeated at Artemisium. The final victory, scored by the Athenians, was won at Marathon.

Overleaf, page 54 The Peloponnesian War of 431-404BC between Athens and the Peloponnesian League led by Sparta was a struggle for power that wrecked Athens while promoting Sparta to the leadership of Greece.

the Spartan poet, whose works were required study in the training camps, wrote in his *War Songs*: "It is beautiful when a brave man of the front ranks falls and dies, battling for his homeland... Young men fight shield to shield and never succumb to panic or miserable flight, but steel the heart in your chests with magnificence and courage. Forget your own life when you grapple with the enemy."

Only the fittest could survive the physical and mental strain involved in such a regime, and the Spartans themselves saw to it that the unfit did not survive: there was no place for newborn infants judged to be too weak or disabled to fight for Sparta. They were "exposed", that is, left out in the open on mountainsides to die. Or, as another, even harsher tradition had it, a weak or sickly infant was taken to Mount Taygetos after being declared unfit by a committee of elderly men and was thrown over the edge as unsuitable for war and, therefore, unsuitable for Sparta.

Peloponnesian War
431–404 BC

◼ Athens and members of the Delian League, c. 431 BC

◼ Athens' allies

➡ Athenian campaign

✗ Athenian victory

◼ Sparta and Spartan allies, c. 431 BC

➡ Spartan campaign

✗ Spartan victory

✳ Revolt against Athens

◼ Persian Empire

◼ Neutral states

This stringent regime was established in Sparta in or around the 8th century BC, when Lycurgus, possibly a mythical figure, is said to have established the city as a military state. It was in a famous war that the Spartans made their first appearance in ancient literature: they featured in the *Iliad*, the account of the last year of the Trojan war, believed to be the work of the legendary epic poet Homer. In the 12th century BC, Sparta, together with other Greek city-states, sent a contingent to fight against Troy in what was then the "heroic" age of warfare.

Despite its dazzling name, war in the heroic age involved simple tactics, such as charging the enemy head on and killing every opponent in range. At the time, it was a tradition that use of the bow and arrow was "unmanly", and most of the fighting was done by infantry using short spears and swords. The style of warfare was, it seems, that of a "free-for-all" involving a great deal of killing, even to the extent that when an army was routed, it was pursued and butchered to the last man. After Lycurgus' reforms, Sparta began to expand its territory until, by the 6th century BC, it had grown from a small village on the banks

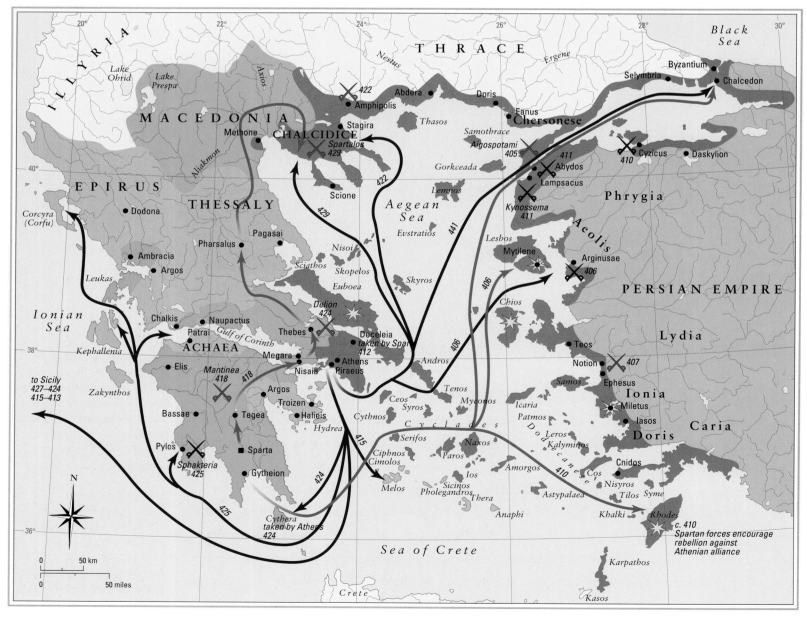

of the River Eurotas in Laconia into the most important of the Greek city-states. When the Persians under Xerxes invaded Greece in 480BC, Sparta led the Greek forces in repelling the invaders.

However, the Spartans were not suited to the role now required of them: protector of the Greek city-states from foreign intrusions. They were unwilling to campaign far from Sparta, and tended to withdraw into isolation from Greek affairs. Their narrow mindset put military matters above all else, and their belief, freely expressed, that "one Spartan is worth several men of any other state", alienated their allies, who soon became disgruntled by their unwillingness to reform their ways.

Numerous wars ensued, with the city-states of Argos, Athens, Corinth, and Thebes. Despite some success, notably the defeat of Athens in 425BC, the Spartans were reduced to the status of a third-class power after 371 BC, when they were crushed at the battle of Leuctra by the Thebans, losing more than 2,000 *spartiartes* of their elite warrior class. The *spartiartes* were men who enjoyed full citizenship in Sparta, and it could not afford the loss of so many in one battle. Sparta's military prestige was shattered; and after 197BC, the Spartans lost their independence when their city came under Roman rule.

At the Battle of Leuctra in 371BC, Theban forces outflanked their Spartan enemies, attacking them from both front and rear. The defeat of the Spartans weakened the influence gained by Sparta after its victory in the Peloponnesian War of 431-404BC.

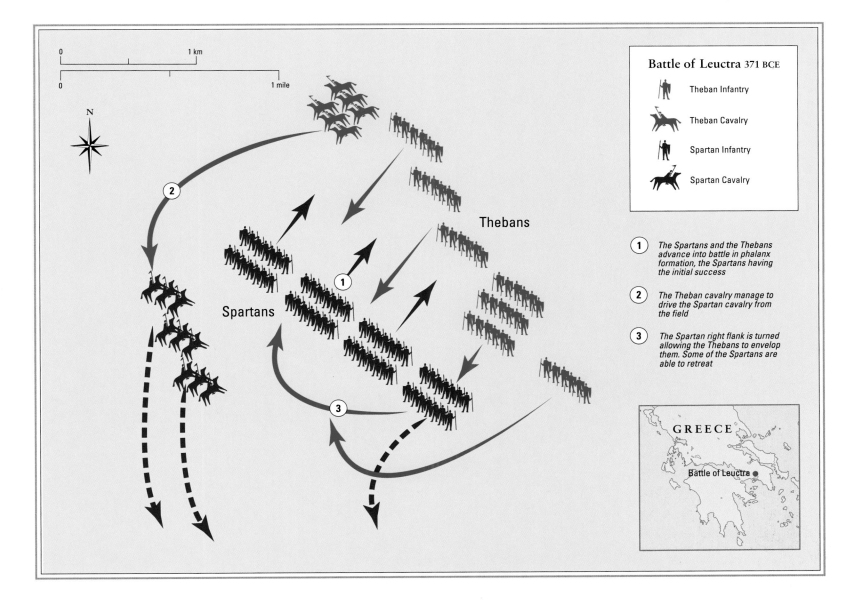

Battle of Leuctra 371 BCE

Theban Infantry

Theban Cavalry

Spartan Infantry

Spartan Cavalry

Thebans

Spartans

1. The Spartans and the Thebans advance into battle in phalanx formation, the Spartans having the initial success

2. The Theban cavalry manage to drive the Spartan cavalry from the field

3. The Spartan right flank is turned allowing the Thebans to envelop them. Some of the Spartans are able to retreat

GREECE

Battle of Leuctra

THE RISE OF MACEDONIA

MACEDONIA, IN NORTH-EASTERN GREECE, WAS A WEAK, UNSTABLE STATE EXPLOITED BY ITS NEIGHBORS UNTIL KING PHILIP II AND HIS SON ALEXANDER THE GREAT TURNED ITS ARMED FORCES INTO THE MOST POWERFUL AND IRRESISTIBLE FORCE IN THE ANCIENT WORLD.

Opposite page: After the mid-4th century BC, King Philip II of Macedonia and his renowned son, Alexander the Great, greatly expanded their kingdom to reach the Black Sea in the east and assume power in at least half of Ancient Greece.

Below: The core of the Macedonian infantry was the Macedonian phalanx, armed with the long *sarissa*, or spear.

I n the 4th century BC, King Philip II of Macedonia and his son Alexander III, Alexander the Great, took the Greeks out of their parochial style of warfare and turned them into world-class conquerors. Macedonia, in the north-eastern corner of the Greek peninsula, had long been the prey of its neighbors: the Illyrians, Triballians, and Thracians. The royal family's hold on power was so tenuous that the only way to keep its enemies at bay was to lodge Philip with them as a hostage. Philip endured this fate twice, the second time in 368BC, when at the age of 14 he was sent to Thebes, then the most prominent city-state in Greece. In Thebes, Philip learned a great deal about politics, diplomacy, and warfare from Epaminondas, the Theban general who had broken the power of Sparta at the battle of Leuctra. In 364BC, Philip returned home determined to transform Macedonia into a strong military and imperial power and become dominant in the intensely competitive world of ancient Greece.

Among Philip's first moves after he became king of Macedonia in 359BC was to make army service a full-time profession. Intermittent experience of soldiering, the cardinal weakness of the militia system, could not offer regular drilling and weapons practice or achieve the

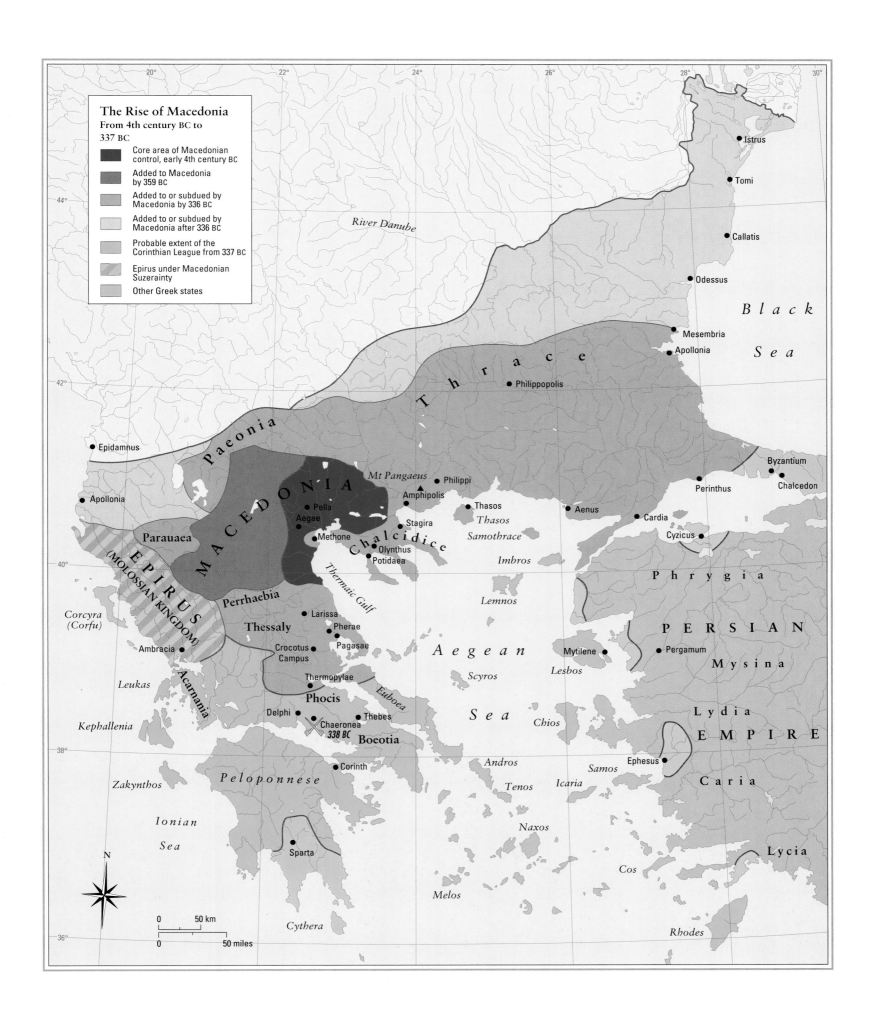

The Rise of Macedonia
From 4th century BC to
337 BC

- Core area of Macedonian control, early 4th century BC
- Added to Macedonia by 359 BC
- Added to or subdued by Macedonia by 336 BC
- Added to or subdued by Macedonia after 336 BC
- Probable extent of the Corinthian League from 337 BC
- Epirus under Macedonian Suzerainty
- Other Greek states

Istrus

Tomi

Callatis

River Danube

Odessus

Black

Sea

Mesembria

Apollonia

Thrace

Philippopolis

Paeonia

Epidamnus

Byzantium

Chalcedon

Apollonia

Mt Pangaeus   Philippi

Perinthus

MACEDONIA   Amphipolis

Pella

Aegae   Stagira   *Thasos*   Aenus

Cardia

Cyzicus

Parauaea   Methone   *Chalcidice*   *Thasos*

EPIRUS   Olynthus   *Samothrace*

(MOLOSSIAN   Potidaea   *Imbros*   *Phrygia*

KINGDOM)   *Thermaic Gulf*

Perrhaebia   *Lemnos*

Corcyra   *PERSIAN*

(Corfu)   Larissa   Pergamum

Pherae   *Aegean*   Mytilene

Thessaly   *Scyros*   *Lesbos*   *Mysina*

Ambracia   Crocotus   Pagasae

Campus   *Sea*   *Chios*   *Lydia*

Leukas   Thermopylae   *EMPIRE*

Acarnania   Phocis   *Euboea*

Kephallenia   Delphi   Thebes   Ephesus

Chaeronea   *Andros*   *Caria*

338 BC   Boeotia   *Samos*

Corinth   *Tenos*   *Icaria*

Zakynthos   *Peloponnese*

Ionian

Sea   *Naxos*   *Lycia*

N   Sparta   *Cos*

Melos

Cythera   *Rhodes*

0   50 km

0   50 miles

cohesion that enabled an army to perform in the co-ordinated way he had in mind. Philip's idea was that the various elements of the Macedonian army — the cavalry, the *psiloi*, the missile-throwing troops, and the phalanx — should work in unison to disconcert the enemy and continually present him with different challenges on the battlefield.

His innovations were of particular importance in handling the phalanx. Philip armed the Macedonian phalanx with the *sarissa*, a spear up to 21 ft (6.4m) long; it was almost 40 percent longer than the traditional hoplite *doru*. Its increased length meant that the *sarissa* had to be used with both hands, which made the large, heavy *aspis* (shield) obsolete. In its place, the hoplites wore a small pelte strapped to their left forearm. The *sarissa* also disposed of the wall of shields which the front line of a phalanx had previously presented to an attacker. But this loss was more than made good by the extreme length of the new spears, which prevented an opponent from coming too close. Up to five ranks of hoplites in Philip's new phalanx were able to project their spearheads straight at an advancing enemy at a time. It was a form of distance warfare that was all the more dreaded because when struck downwards, the spearhead of a *sarissa* was extremely difficult, if not impossible, to remove. The hoplites of the Macedonian phalanx were known as *pezhetairoi*, or foot companions. They were subject to regular and extensive drilling, which kept them at a peak of efficiency barely known in other armies.

The *hetairoi,* the "companion" cavalry of the Macedonian army, achieved similarly high standards and eventually became known as the best of its kind in the ancient world. Raised from the landed nobility, its members were equipped with the *xyston*, a spear nearly 10 ft (3 m) long, and fought in eight 200-man squadrons called *ile*. In battle, it was formed into wedges, which gave it great maneuverability and added power to the shock cavalry charge. Later, when fighting under Alexander the Great, the Macedonian cavalry was responsible for applying the decisive assault in battles. Philip's new army also contained light cavalry, known as *prodromoi*, whose task was to guard the wings in battle and carry out reconnaissance missions. The task of the *hypaspistai*, the elite mobile infantry, was to protect the right flank of the Macedonian phalanx. Like the *hetairoi*, its members came from the privileged Macedonian class, and later it formed a bodyguard, 3,000 strong, for Alexander the Great.

King Philip lost little time in fielding his army. Among his first conquests, in 357–356BC, were Amphipolis in central Macedonia, which controlled the goldmines of Mount Pangaeion, and the town of Crenides in eastern Macedonia, which brought him more goldmines. Philip, who changed the name Crenides to Philippi, was able to use the enormous wealth he acquired in order to pay thousands of mercenaries and reinforce his army. They included crack bowmen from Crete, heavy cavalry from Thessaly, spearmen from Pontus and *peltast*, light infantry, from Phrygia.

The Macedonian army, re-formed by King Philip, made relatively short work of subduing the city-states of Greece, thus making him master of the peninsula and ready to embark on war against Persia, the principal enemy of the Greeks. But in 336BC, Philip's forces were about to invade the Persian empire when he was assassinated, and the task was taken up by Alexander. In the next 13 years, before his own premature death aged 32 in 323BC, Alexander used the magnificent military instrument his father had left him to create one of the great empires of ancient times. It stretched from Macedonia through Turkey, Babylonia, and Persia into India, which was the eastern limit of the known world. It was said that Alexander wept when he realized that there was no more world for him to conquer.

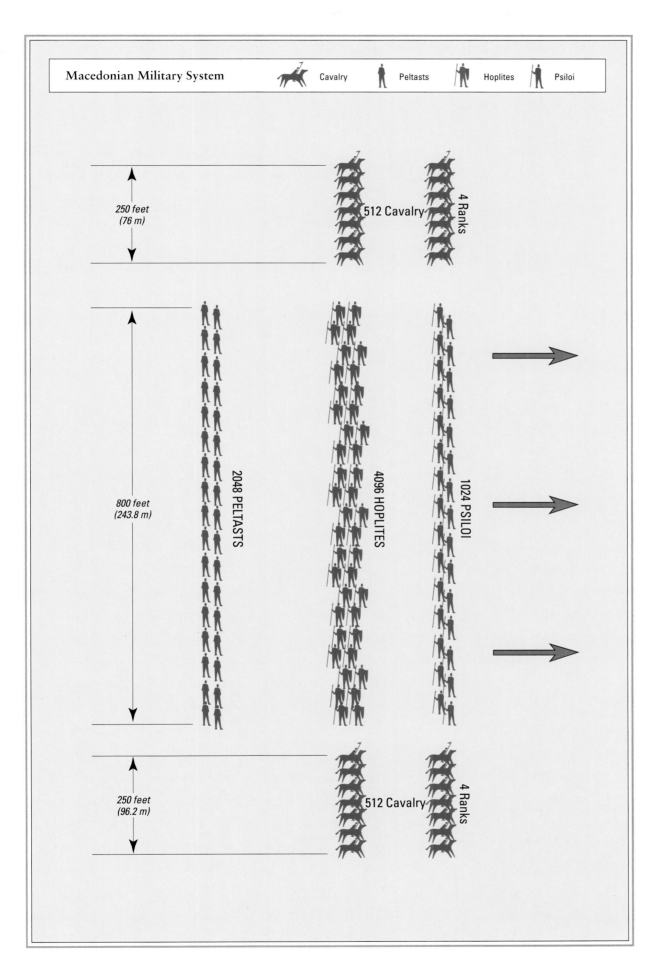

Macedonian Military System — Cavalry | Peltasts | Hoplites | Psiloi

250 feet
(76 m)

512 Cavalry — 4 Ranks

800 feet
(243.8 m)

2048 PELTASTS

4096 HOPLITES

1024 PSILOI

250 feet
(96.2 m)

512 Cavalry — 4 Ranks

After conquering Ancient Greece, Philip of Macedonia expanded the power of the Greek army by arranging ranks of *psiloi* (light infantry) backed by hoplites (spearmen) flanked on either side by cavalry. Behind the hoplites stood ranks of *peltasts* (skirmishers).

SIEGE MACHINES: PART 1

IN ORDER TO TAKE A TOWN OR CITY, AN ARMY WOULD FIRST HAVE TO GET INSIDE. RULERS UNDERSTOOD THAT GOOD DEFENSES MAY DETER, OR AT LEAST DELAY, ATTACKING ARMIES, SO THE TREND OF BUILDING CITY WALLS WAS BORN. THESE DEFENSES GAVE RISE TO A NEW TYPE OF WEAPON—THE SIEGE MACHINE.

Opposite page: The siege of Jerusalem in AD70, during the first Roman-Jewish War, was a disaster for the Jews. The city was destroyed as well as its Temple, an event that has been mourned by Jews every year since.

Below: Engraving of a medieval army laying siege to a fortified town in the 14th century.

Because building protective walls was a very early form of defense, besieging towns, cities, or castles became a very early form of warfare. Around 11,000 years ago, the walls of Jericho were some 10 ft (3 m) thick and possibly half a mile (0.8 km) long. As the biblical Book of Chronicles records, Uzziah, King of Judah in the 8th century BC, "made in Jerusalem engines ... to be on the towers and upon the bulwarks, to shoot arrows and great stones withal". In 424BC, during the Peloponnesian War, a huge blowpipe was employed to throw fire at the wooden palisades of Delium, a city near the Gulf of Corinth. Once the palisades had burned down, the Spartans were able to capture the town.

At this time, the Greeks were also using siege towers and catapults. One catapult was the *katapelte*, which hurled arrows, javelins, and a stone weighing eight pounds (3.6 kg) in one devastating load. Both the *katapelte* and the *petrobolos*, which threw heavy rocks, used the torsion method of propulsion. This involved twisting a length of sinew, human hair, cords, or fibers until they reached their tightest and then letting them unravel very quickly: the force generated by this process gave impetus to the missiles, which hurtled to their target at high speed. With larger machines, such as the springal, which used a spring to throw stones, arrows, or a firebrand or pieces of burning wood, planks were drawn back by a thick rope attached to a winch. When released, the top end of the plank sprang forward and dealt the missile a hefty thwack.

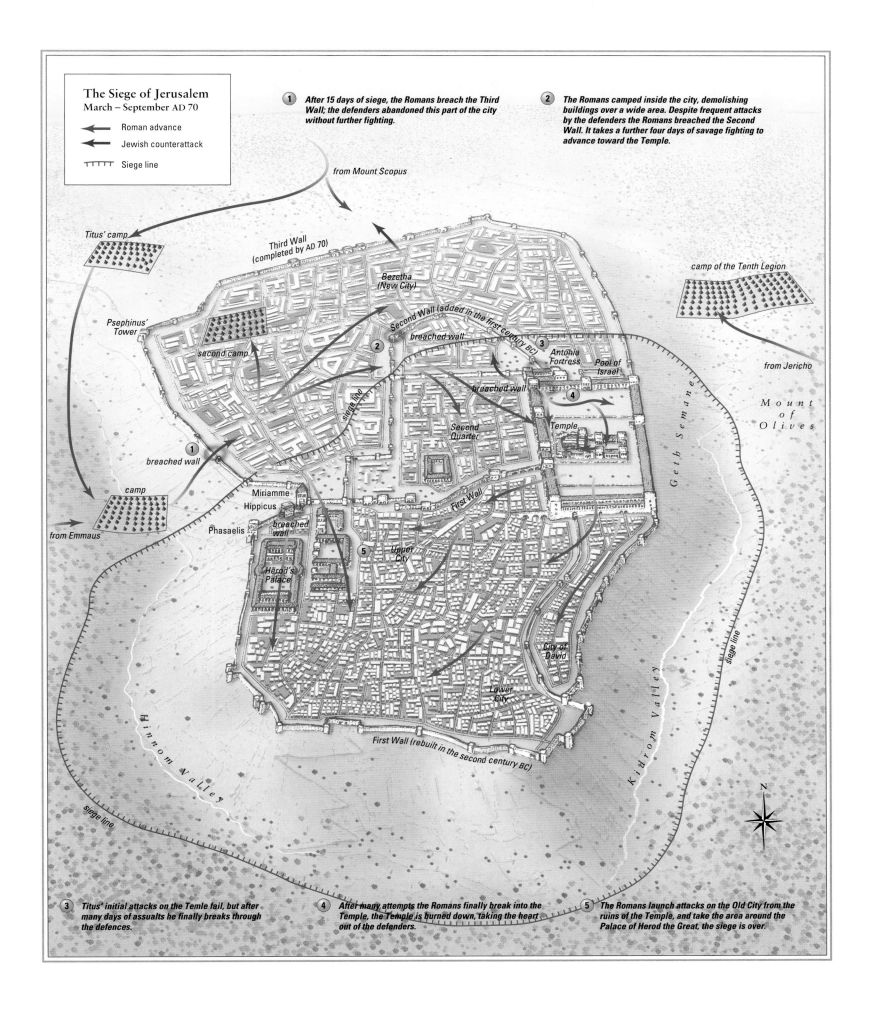

The Siege of Jerusalem
March – September AD 70

← Roman advance

← Jewish counterattack

⊤⊤⊤⊤⊤ Siege line

① After 15 days of siege, the Romans breach the Third Wall; the defenders abandoned this part of the city without further fighting.

② The Romans camped inside the city, demolishing buildings over a wide area. Despite frequent attacks by the defenders the Romans breached the Second Wall. It takes a further four days of savage fighting to advance toward the Temple.

from Mount Scopus

Titus' camp

Third Wall
(completed by AD 70)

Bezetha
(New City)

camp of the Tenth Legion

Psephinus'
Tower

Second Wall (added in the first century BC)

breached wall

from Jericho

second camp

siege line

② Antonia
Fortress

③ Pool of
Israel

Mount
of
Olives

breached wall

④

Temple

Gethsemane

breached wall

① Second
Quarter

Miriamme

Hippicus

First Wall

camp

breached
wall

⑤ Upper
City

from Emmaus

Phasaelis

Herod's
Palace

City of
David

Kidron Valley

Hinnom Valley

Lower
City

First Wall (rebuilt in the second century BC)

siege line

N

siege line

③ Titus' initial attacks on the Temle fail, but after many days of assaults he finally breaks through the defences.

④ After many attempts the Romans finally break into the Temple, the Temple is burned down, taking the heart out of the defenders.

⑤ The Romans launch attacks on the Old City from the ruins of the Temple, and take the area around the Palace of Herod the Great, the siege is over.

THE ROMANS AT WAR

THE ROMAN EMPIRE, WHICH STRETCHED ACROSS EUROPE, WAS CONQUERED BY AN ARMY WHOSE FIGHTING METHODS, EXPERTISE, AND MORALE WERE LEGENDARY IN THE ANCIENT WORLD. ITS SOLDIERS ALSO PRESERVED THE *PAX ROMANA* (THE ROMAN PEACE) THAT EXISTED WITHIN ITS BORDERS.

T he Roman army was the most successful fighting force of the ancient world and the first great military power in Europe, losing the odd battle but never a war. The secret of Rome's military success was strict discipline, a strong sense of honor, iron nerve, and clever tactics. One tactic was the t*estudo* (tortoise), in which the legionaries formed themselves into an armored column by locking their shields above their heads and around the sides. This sheltered them from missiles flung by opponents, and enabled them to use their swords to stab out at opponents in relative safety.

The *gladius* was one of the two basic weapons carried by Roman legionaries. The other weapon was the throwing spear (*pilum*). Roman legionaries also carried the *scutum*, a rectangular shield made of wood and leather, which gave them protection from the neck to the knees. This was augmented by a metal breastplate made from strips of metal that would cover legionaries from the neck to the waist. Roman legionaries also wore metal helmets that covered the entire head, and had a flange at the back to guard the base of the skull.

Despite their undoubted military superiority, the Romans were not too proud to learn from some of their more innovative opponents. They adopted the javelin from the Samnite tribes, siege artillery, spear-throwing, and body armor from the Greeks. Often, the Romans had to learn their military lessons the hard way, by sustaining heavy defeats. At Trebbia in 218BC, and at Cannae two years later (during the second Punic War with Carthage), the Carthaginian cavalry charged the Roman foot-soldiers from the rear and scattered them in a panic. The Romans won the war but took note of this tactic and later turned the tables on the Carthaginians. At the battles of Ilipa in 206BC and Zama in 202BC, specially formed and trained squadrons of Roman cavalry charged the Carthaginians from behind and annihilated them.

Opposite page: In the makeup of the Roman Army as it existed in around 200BC, the spear- and sword-carrying infantry was the most important component. By contrast, the cavalry, which later came to dominate Roman battle tactics, was relatively minor.

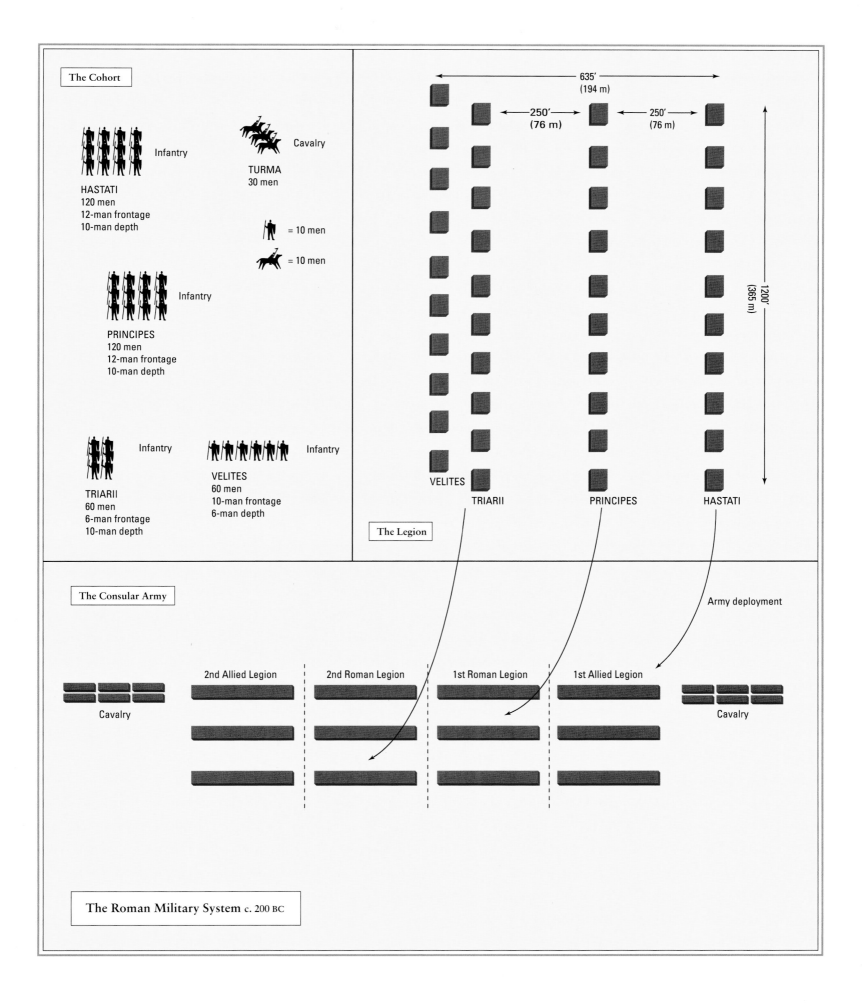

The Cohort

HASTATI
120 men
12-man frontage
10-man depth

Infantry

TURMA
30 men

Cavalry

= 10 men

= 10 men

PRINCIPES
120 men
12-man frontage
10-man depth

Infantry

TRIARII
60 men
6-man frontage
10-man depth

Infantry

VELITES
60 men
10-man frontage
6-man depth

Infantry

The Legion

635'
(194 m)

250'
(76 m)

250'
(76 m)

1200'
(365 m)

VELITES

TRIARII

PRINCIPES

HASTATI

The Consular Army

Cavalry

2nd Allied Legion

2nd Roman Legion

1st Roman Legion

1st Allied Legion

Cavalry

Army deployment

The Roman Military System c. 200 BC

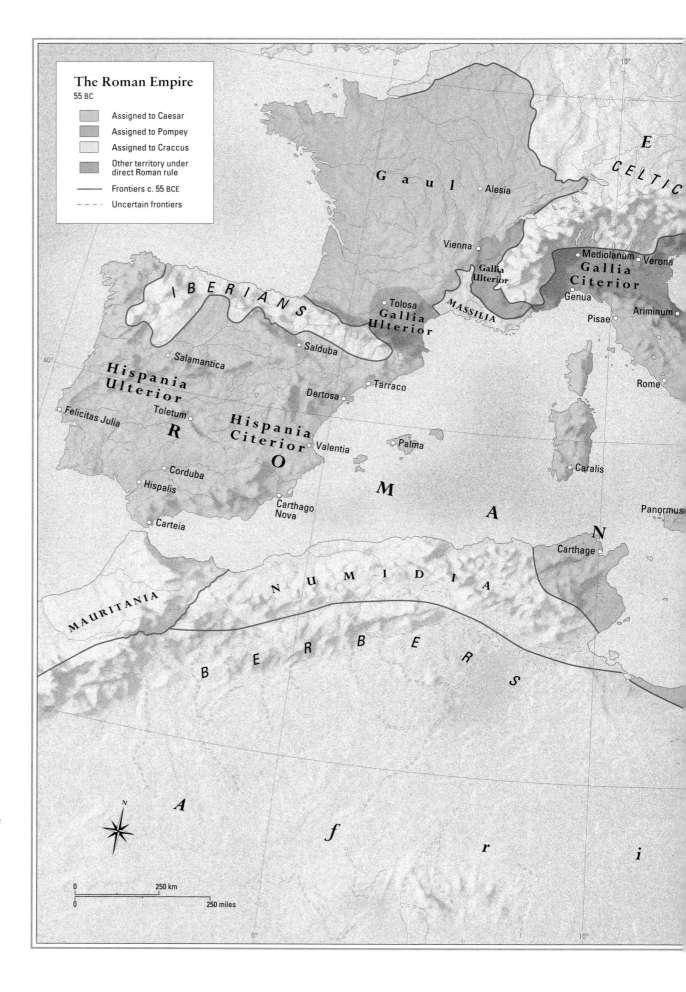

The Roman Empire
55 BC

Assigned to Caesar
Assigned to Pompey
Assigned to Craccus
Other territory under
direct Roman rule
——— Frontiers c. 55 BCE
- - - Uncertain frontiers

The Roman Empire remains the
largest land empire Europe has
ever known. This map shows
Roman imperial possessions in
55BC, which excludes several
later acquisitions, for example
Britain (subsequently Britannia),
which was not conquered until
after AD43..

The fighters who made the most profound difference to Roman military methods were some of the auxiliaries who were recruited into the Roman army. Auxiliaries came from within the Roman Empire — from Spain, Britain, and France — but also from outside — from Germany, Arabia, and Russia. They were tempted into the Roman ranks by the chance to become Roman citizens after 25 years' service. It also helped recruitment that they were able to bring their own weapons and fighting methods with them.

For example, the Spanish, Russian, British, French, and German auxiliaries had long been accustomed to fighting on horseback. Because cavalrymen had to reach much farther than a foot-soldier in order to get at the enemy, their swords and spears had to be longer. The longer sword, called the *spatha* by Spanish cavalrymen, was probably twice as long as the original Roman *gladius*. Likewise, cavalry lances were lengthier and heavier than the Roman javelin, which was designed mainly for throwing.

Eventually, the weapons and tactics used by these auxiliary soldiers from around the Roman Empire completely transformed the Roman army. In the 3rd century AD, a thorough overhaul of Roman arms and fighting methods took place. The *gladius* and the javelin were replaced by the long, barbarian-style sword and the cavalry lance. After that, the cavalry became of prime importance, replacing the legion of infantrymen as the "star" of the battlefield.

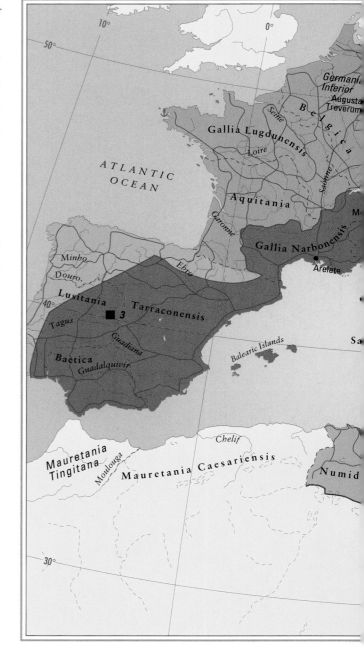

The Roman soldier had other duties besides fighting wars. By far the most important was preserving the *Pax Romana*, the Roman Peace, inside the the empire by forming a permanent armed guard on its frontiers. It was a giant task, for the Roman Empire stretched from the border with Scotland in the north-west to Arabia in the south-east, from Spain in the west to Mesopotamia in the east, and into Egypt and the Middle East. Roman territory offered security and living standards that were inconceivable beyond its frontiers. Inevitably, the empire was constantly under the threat of attack, especially from the lands beyond the Rhine and the Danube, from where intruders made, or sought to make, incursions into Roman territory.

The role of military policemen for the empire was a lonely one, carried out far from Rome or any other civilized place. The scale of the problem of barbarian attack was illustrated in AD9 by the fate of three legions commanded

Opposite page: The Romans had acquired more territory by AD14. However, the Emperor Augustus had already decided to restrict further growth after an entire Roman legion was ambushed and slaughtered in Germany five years earlier.

by Quintilius Varus comprising 16,000 men. They were making their way through wooded hill country when suddenly they were attacked by the Cherusci, a German tribe that was after revenge for a massacre recently masterminded by Varus. The Cherusci killed every legionary. Varus survived, but realizing what would happen if he were captured, he took the decision to kill himself in the Roman fashion, by falling on his sword.

The fate of Quintilius Varus and his three legions was echoed by Roman soldiers throughout the years they served on the dangerous frontiers of the Roman Empire. For the most part the legionaries had the skills needed to survive in such a challenging environment and it was the Roman army that built roads, which were the network of the empire, and also towns, bridges, aqueducts, and mighty defenses such as Hadrian's Wall in the north of Britain. The soldiers of the mighty Roman Empire were tool-makers, smiths, carpenters, and stonemasons — not only jacks of all trades but also masters of them all.

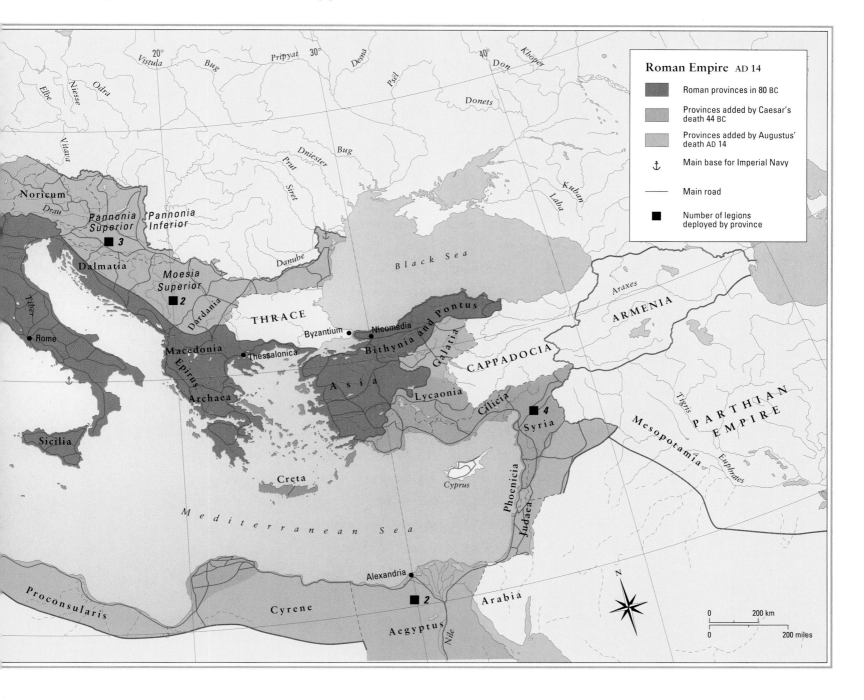

SIEGE MACHINES: PART 2

THE ROMANS REGULARLY EMPLOYED THE USE OF SIEGE MACHINES IN ATTACKS, AND DEVELOPED SYSTEMS THAT INVOLVED THE USE OF HEAVY ARTILLERY FIRE TO DISTRACT DEFENDERS FROM THE SOLDIERS BUILDING RAMPS UP THEIR WALLS, OR SIMPLY TO BREAK THROUGH DEFENSES.

By the 1st century AD, siege machines were a standard part of a legion's equipment. Each legion possessed up to 10 catapults and 60 "*ballistae*". The ballista was larger than the catapult, and a really big *ballista* could hurl a 50 lb (23 kg) stone over a distance of around 400 yd (365 m). Although missiles fired by these monster machines could destroy or badly damage anything they struck, they were difficult to move and could normally be used from only one position during a siege or battle. More mobile was the smaller "scorpion" which could be operated by only two soldiers. The scorpion was a very large bow with wooden arms drawn back by winches for firing a very large arrow.

The Romans used their siege machines named, collectively, *tormentae*, to pound the walls of a city, town or castle they wanted to capture with javelins, arrows, hardwood beams, or rocks. This "artillery fire" was meant to make it easier for legionaries to break through defenses or give covering fire for those engaged in building ramps, as a prelude to scaling the walls. The technology for the *tormentae* — usually onagers as well as *ballistae* and scorpions — had been imported from Greece, which had been absorbed into the Roman Empire after 146BC. Compared to their new masters, the Greeks possessed vastly superior talents for science, mathematics, architecture, and other skills, and it was the Romans who served as "publicity agents" for these Greek ideas and innovations. These Greek ideas eventually spread all over the vast Roman Empire.

The *ballista* was one of the most destructive of the Romans' siege machines. It was a heavy duty missile weapon made of wood with iron plates around the frames. The ballista could lob large rocks at

Siege Machines

ramparts and walls with chilling accuracy. For good measure, it let out a sinister whirring when fired and the sound alone, it seems, created deep fear inside towns and cities besieged by the Romans.

Julius Caesar took the *ballista* with him for his excursions into Britain in 55BC and 54BC and it seems that the Britons were frightened by the very sight of these strange contraptions being unloaded onto the beach. In 52BC, the machines saw action when Caesar's forces besieged Alesia in Gaul and hoisted the *ballistae* to the top of siege towers to batter away at the defenders from a height.

Another siege machine used by the Romans was the battering ram. In their simplest form, battering rams were large logs or tree trunks that pounded away at walls until they cracked or otherwise disintegrated. Other rams were more sophisticated with the battering end reinforced by iron. An iron ram was used at the battle of Jotapata, a fortified Jewish village in Gallilee where the Romans erected towers 50 ft (15 m) high. Jewish historian Josephus described the ram as "similar to a ship's mast... It is drawn back by a huge number of men who then push it forward with all their might so that it hits the walls with its iron head. There is no tower strong enough nor any wall thick enough to withstand [it]".

A Roman siege in progress with three scaling ladders in use. On the siege tower, the battering ram is at work and there are three separate attacks on the walls. "Mining" operations (foreground) are shown going on underground.

THE SWORD

THE SWORD WAS USED IN WAR FOR ALMOST 5,200 YEARS, AND SURVIVED AS A PRACTICAL WEAPON FOR NEARLY 600 YEARS AFTER THE INTRODUCTION OF GUNS. IN SOME CULTURES, IT GAINED AN ALMOST MAGICAL REPUTATION AND ACQUIRED ADMIRING NAMES.

The sword was the longest-lasting of all the weapons of war. It was used in battle from the Bronze Age, which began in and around Mesopotamia in about 3300BC, until the 19th century AD. The sword developed from the dagger, which had itself evolved from prehistoric tools and weapons. The earliest daggers were made of flint, ivory, or bone. But the discovery of metals opened up new possibilities offered by swords, which at first had resembled elongated daggers. Swords made of copper, the second of the Metals of Antiquity, and dating from around 2300BC, have been found by archeologists at Harappa on the Indus River; others, dating from around 1700BC, have been found at Fatehgarh in north-western India.

Copper was a relatively soft metal. Much stronger was bronze, the alloy of copper and tin. It is likely that the first "true" swords were made of bronze, but there was a disadvantage: the longer a bronze blade became, the more likely it was to lose tensile strength and bend. This was why swords longer than about 24 in (60 cm) had to wait until the development of even stronger alloys such as steel and advances in the heat processes used to manufacture them. This meant that longer swords became possible, at the earliest, after 1500BC. At that time iron, the major ingredient of steel, was discovered; experiments with alloying iron with carbon or other ingredients such as manganese or chromium produced swords with long blades whose strength made them fearsome weapons. There was good reason why the various words for sword in European languages came from the word root "swer", meaning to wound or cut. Swords were complete killing weapon: their sharp edges cut and sliced and their pointed ends could be used for stabbing and thrusting.

The use of swords extended virtually around the world — to wherever there were armies or wars. Some acquired legendary reputations, such as the swords that were made in Toledo, Spain which earned

THE SWORD ✳ 71

a name for their perfection from the superlative quality of the steel from which they were made, and their exceptional hardness.

The history of the Toledo sword goes back more than 2,000 years, to the 5th century BC when early Toledan swords called *falcata* were being forged by Spanish blacksmiths and soon became renowned for their excellence. Two centuries later, Hannibal, the renowned Carthaginian general who fought the Romans in the second Punic War of 218-201 BC equipped his army with Toledan swords and subsequently won such resounding victories that the Romans adopted these same weapons for their own forces.

In the 12th century, the Moorish conquerors of Spain encountered the famed Spanish hero Rodrigo de Vivar, El Cid, who used a Toledo sword in his many victories against them. Before long, the Moors adapted this same sword for their own two-edged scimitars. In the 16th century, the Spanish conquistadors took their Toledan swords with them during their conquests in Mexico, Peru, and the rest of what later became Latin America. The fame of Toledo swords went around the world. So much so that the *daimyos*, the great lords of feudal Japan, are said to have visited Spain for the precise purpose of having their own weapons forged by Spanish swordsmiths.

What no outsider managed to do, though, was to learn the secret that made the swords of Toledo such excellent weapons. It was not until the 20th century that this became known. Hard steel with a very high content of soft steel and carbon had to be forged at a very high temperature of at least 1,545˚F (840˚C) for a precise amount of time.

Before the late 18th century, the accuracy of clocks could be uncertain, so the Toledo swordsmiths could not afford to use them to keep accurate time as required. Instead, they used to recite psalms and prayers, taking care to maintain a constant rhythm for as long as the sword was inside the furnace. Unless the timing was precise, the steel could melt if left in the furnace too long, whereas insufficient time would prevent it from reaching melting point. After the forging process, the swordsmith would cool the steel with water or oil. The idea was to give the sword a clear, clean welded seam.

In other countries, many attempts were made to produce Toledo-standard swords, but without success. For example, swords made in Damascus, Syria, were forged from steel that was too hard and inflexible: the trouble was the unsuitable iron and carbon content and the fact that Damascus swords were not refined: instead, they retained a certain amount of impure minerals.

In Spain, however, the manufacture of swords continued to flourish and between the 15th and the 17th centuries, maintained its reputation for producing the best swords in Europe. A swordmakers' guild was in charge of preserving the quality of Toledo weaponry, which also included the manufacture of daggers.

However, when production went into decline in the late 17th and 18th centuries, the Spanish King Carlos III stepped in to set up the Royal Arms factory in 1761. Under this royal umbrella, the swordsmiths' guilds of Toledo were brought together.

From then on, the importance of swordmaking revived and increased, so much so that its premises were constantly expanding until they became virtually a city within the city of Toledo. Also notable for their excellence were the two swords

Japanese hand made *daito-katana* sword traditionally used by the samarai.

used by the Japanese samurai who dominated Japan for 700 years from the 12th century. These famous and prestigious weapons were the 24 in (60 cm) long *daito-katana*, which were light, sharp, and easy to use, and the *shoto-wakizashi*, which could be half the size. The samurai believed that a sword with a name personalized the weapon and represented the "soul" of the warrior ethos.

Japanese swords named *jokoto* started out as straight-bladed, but after AD987 they were made curved for attacking an opponent more quickly by drawing it from its scabbard in one instead of two movements. It was said that a samurai could draw his sword and strike with it so fast that his opponent was always taken by surprise. Apart from bronze, two types of metal were used in making Japanese swords: hard steel and soft steel, which were folded over many times so as to make a curved shape. This treatment made the sword strong enough to survive a strike against stone.

Like the Japanese, the Chinese have a long history of swordmaking. In their case, it goes back to prehistoric times when, it appears, they made swords out of stone. The more practical bronze sword appeared in China in the middle of the 3rd century BC; and in due course, swords were forged from iron and steel. Chinese iron swords were not cast in a mold; they were wrought by forging or rolling. Swords with blades measuring more than 35 in (90 cm) were common, and some discovered by archeologists were even longer. There were two types of Chinese sword, which were produced in both bronze and steel. *Jian* swords were double-edged, and *dao* were single-edged. Like the Japanese, the Chinese gave their swords names: for instance, *changdao* (long knife), *dadao* (big knife), *liuye dao* (willow-leaf saber), or *yanmao dao* (goose-quill saber).

Chinese sword-makers experimented with the metals of the weapons they made. For example, they cast high-tin edges onto low-tin cores or gave the bronze blades diamond-shaped patterns. As things turned out, high-tin bronze, which contained more than 17 percent tin, was not a feasible idea: it produced blades that were too hard and tended to break under stress. The Chinese used bronze swords along with iron swords for several centuries. It was only in the 3rd century BC that iron finally prevailed.

The Romans were too practical to give their swords semi-poetical names, but the prestige of their standard-issue short sword, the 24 in (60 cm) long *gladius*, was great, if only for the warriors who used it and for what they achieved with it. Unlike their less strictly organized enemies, who tended to storm into battle in a wild, undisciplined weapon-wielding mob yelling fearsome war cries, the Romans did not deliberately expose themselves to attack when using their swords. Instead, they wielded the *gladius* from the "cover" provided by the *testudos* they formed in battle or from behind their large, oblong shields. This tactic enabled soldiers to stab out at their enemies when they came too close, a technique that usually dispatched most of them.

As with so much else in Roman culture, the Romans copied sword design from the ancient Greek *phasganon* or *xiphos*, but they soon adapted both for their own purposes. Greek swords were wide at the hilt and featured leaf-shaped blades, but the Romans preferred using the straight blade, which was more effective for the stabbing, thrusting techniques they employed. In the absence of the blast furnace, not yet invented, the *gladius* was made in a bloomery furnace by smelting iron from its oxides and producing pieces of slag, or "blooms", which could then be forged into the necessary blade shape.

The *gladius* was used until the 2nd century AD, when it was replaced by the *spatha*, the long cavalry sword the Romans introduced after a complete overhaul of their methods of warfare. The *spatha* was a straight-bladed sword, measuring some 35 in (90 cm). It had a long, sharp point, suitable for doing mortal damage when thrust downward from the saddle at an opponent. The *spatha*, which was also used by gladiators who provided popular entertainment in the Roman arena, became the weapon of heavy infantry. The *spatha* enjoyed a long history of its own, lasting well into the Middle Ages. It was used by German barbarian tribes and the Scandinavian Vikings.

The Vikings also used swords made of quenched, hardened, and tempered steel, a process introduced in about the 10th century. Blades of this type, said to be manufactured by a Nordic smith named Ulfberht, were used by Viking raiders to attack the Franks of north-eastern France. They were so damaging that the Holy Roman Emperor Charles II, who was also the Frankish king, attempted to stop suppliers from exporting them to the raiders.

In Asia, sword design and manufacture were developing fast. Damascus steel was being made in India using special smelting and reworking techniques. In neighboring Sri Lanka, the steel being produced in a wind furnace — a unique method of its time — gave sword blades a particularly hard cutting edge and enabled them to be decorated with beautiful patterns. The late Middle Ages and early Renaissance period in Europe saw innovations in sword design: longer blades and grips, making it possible to use the weapon with two hands. Swords were made too that were strong and sharp enough to pierce body armor. The French *estoc* longsword was an innovative instrument. It had a point but no cutting edges. Its blade was more than 4 ft (1.2 m) long and its sole purpose was to work its way through mail or plate armor and kill the man inside.

However, the weapon that finally ended the era of full body armor and with it the age of the medieval knight on horseback, was not an ingenious device for "unlocking" the plates that protected him but the introduction of gunpowder and with that, the advent of hand-held firearms.

Very soon, it became obvious that a musket bullet could pierce even so hard a metal as high-tempered steel. With that, armorers began to make their armor thicker, but the trouble was that a bullet-proof suit of full armor was so heavy that the man inside it could barely move.

No wonder, then, that full armor was soon discarded. It was discarded so rapidly that by around 1600, armor as worn by infantry and cavalry consisted of helmets and the cuirass — breast-and-back plates fastened together. In actual fact, the 17th century cuirassier wore rather more than this: his protection comprised three-quarter armor, a cut-down version of full armor without the leg and feet pieces. Instead, a cuirassier's legs and feet were covered by knee-high leather boots. It was a sign of the times, though, that they were frequently armed with a pair of wheel-lock pistols in addition to their customary swords.

The knight in armor had been a close-quarter fighter, clashing in person with his opponent on the battlefield, thereby earning a reputation for courage and honor. Using firearms did not have the same cachet or require the same skills and qualities. So, something else was discarded when knights and their swords were replaced by musketeers waging war from a distance: the age-old concept of war as a valiant and noble undertaking.

THE WEAPONS OF THE VIKINGS

AT THE END OF THE 8TH CENTURY AND FOR SOME 300 YEARS AFTERWARDS, THE MOST FRIGHTENING SIGHT TO BE SEEN ON THE WATERS OF EUROPE WAS AN APPROACHING VIKING LONGSHIP. IT SIGNIFIED VIOLENCE, BLOODSHED AND TERROR ...

Opposite page: The Vikings were superb sailors, crossing seas out of sight of land and navigating rivers in shallow draft ships. They also circumnavigated Europe by sailing north to south along the rivers of western Russia.

Below: Viking vessels became a familiar sight around European coasts in the 9th century AD. The broad-bodied trading vessels were not to be feared but the sight of slim-shaped warships meant attack was imminent.

The first Viking raid in Europe took place on January 8, 793 and prompted the Anglo-Saxon scholar Alcuin to remark: "There is the beginning of woe and calamity". It was all too appropriate. That day, the long, slim Viking warships with their serpent or dragon prows appeared on the horizon and headed for Lindisfarne Island, 2 miles (3.2 km) off the north-eastern coast of England. Anchoring offshore, the Vikings leaped into the water, yelling bloodcurdling war cries and brandishing wicked-looking spears, axes, and swords. Scrambling up the beach, they ran toward the nearby monastery, battered down the door, and burst inside, cutting down any monk who tried to stop them. They grabbed all the gold, silver, jeweled ornaments, crosses, and sacred emblems that they could lay their hands on. They tore them off the walls, pulled them from the altars, and ransacked chests and cupboards, flinging the contents all over the floor in an attempt to find more treasure. Before leaving, the Vikings butchered or drowned most of the monks who had survived the initial assault and carried off the rest as slaves.

This scene was repeated many more times in Britain and across Europe, from France to Russia, in the ensuing centuries. Eventually the Vikings settled down to live and work in England, France, and other areas they raided, but until then they were scourges terrifying whole populations. The Viking longships carried the sinister signs of their purpose, easily visible by petrified observers onshore: there was a line of round wooden shields along its sides, indicating many more weapons on board. These shields were covered in leather and reinforced with metal, and featured a bar in

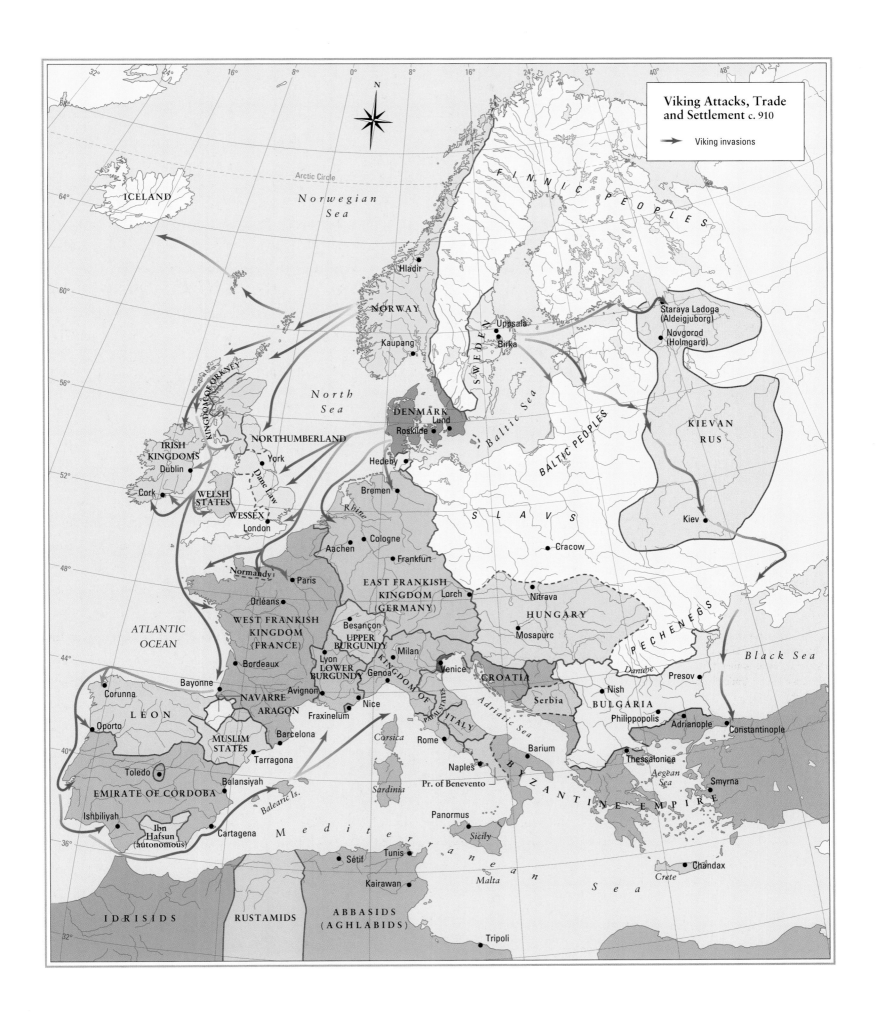

Viking Attacks, Trade
and Settlement c. 910

→ Viking invasions

Arctic Circle

ICELAND

Norwegian
Sea

FINNIC PEOPLES

Hladir

NORWAY

Staraya Ladoga
(Aldeigjuborg)

Novgorod
(Holmgard)

Uppsala

Kaupang

Birka

North
Sea

SWEDEN

Baltic Sea

KIEVAN
RUS

BALTIC PEOPLES

KINGDOM OF ORKNEY

DENMARK
Lund
Roskilde

NORTHUMBERLAND

IRISH
KINGDOMS
Dublin

York

Hedeby

SLAVS

Dane Law

Bremen

Kiev

Cork

WELSH
STATES

Rhine

WESSEX
London

Cologne

Aachen

Frankfurt

ATLANTIC
OCEAN

Normandy

Paris

EAST FRANKISH
KINGDOM
(GERMANY)

Lorch

Cracow

Orléans

Nitrava

HUNGARY

WEST FRANKISH
KINGDOM
(FRANCE)

Besançon
UPPER
BURGUNDY

Mosapurc

PECHENEGS

Lyon
LOWER
BURGUNDY

Bordeaux

Milan

Black Sea

Corunna

Bayonne

Avignon

Genoa
Venice

CROATIA

Danube

Presov

NAVARRE
ARAGON

Nice

Serbia

Nish

BULGARIA

Adriatic Sea

LÉON

Fraxinelum

Oporto

Barcelona

MUSLIM
STATES

Rome

KINGDOM OF ITALY

Corsica

Philippopolis

Adrianople

Constantinople

Tarragona

Toledo

Balansiyah

Sardinia

Naples

BYZANTINE EMPIRE

Thessalonica

Aegean
Sea

Smyrna

EMIRATE OF CÓRDOBA

Balearic Is.

Pr. of Benevento

Ishbiliyah

Ibn
Hafsun
(autonomous)

Cartagena

Panormus

Mediterranean

Sicily

Chandax

Crete

Sétif

Tunis

Malta

Sea

IDRISIDS

RUSTAMIDS

ABBASIDS
(AGHLABIDS)

Kairawan

Tripoli

Opposite page: After much fighting, King Alfred of Wessex and the Viking leader Guthrum made a treaty in AD884 ceding the 'Danelaw' to the Vikings, so giving them half of England. Danish law prevailed within the Danelaw and lasted for 70 years.

the center for the Viking warrior to grasp. For attack, the Vikings used axes, swords, leaf-bladed spears, and longbows which shot barbed arrows. The axe was the characteristic Viking weapon, and came in several types. The *skeggox* had a "bearded" blade projecting downward: it was probably used originally by carpenters for woodwork; but like so many other practical or hunting tools, it was eventually recruited into warfare. There were also the *handox* (hand axe), the *breidox* (broad axe), the *scramasax* (big knife), and axes with wedge-shaped and T-shaped blades. The "Danish axe", which was wielded with both hands, had a blade some 35 in (90 cm) long and could decapitate a horse at one stroke. Danish axes appeared in the Bayeux Tapestry, the 230 ft (70 m) long embroidery depicting scenes from the Battle of Hastings in 1066 between the Norman invaders and the English defenders. The English nobility, including descendants of Viking settlers, are shown attacking the Norman cavalry two-handed with the mighty axe.

The weapon the Vikings valued most highly was the sword. The immense strength of Viking swords was due to the fact that their long, double-edged tapering blades were carbonized. This was achieved by placing iron ore in a charcoal furnace and heating it to a very high temperature. After cooling, the metal was removed from the furnace, reheated, and then hammered out on an anvil. This process converted the iron into steel.

On the subject of swords, the Vikings became very romantic, and it was a common belief among them that swords had supernatural powers. Many poems were written in praise of these weapons and the Vikings gave them all sorts of lyrical names. "Fire of Battle", "Lightning Flash of Blood", and "Snake of Wounds" were some of them. Viking swordsmiths lavished much loving skill and care upon their work: they could take up to a month to complete a sword to their satisfaction and finish decorating it with snake shapes, scrolls, and jewels.

The short Viking sword was called the sax. It was single-edged, carried a blade measuring between 12–24 in (30–60 cm) and had hilts made of horn, bone, or wood. Saxes of different lengths were indicated by their names, such as the *langsax* (long sax). The sax differed from the more carefully crafted Viking sword in that the blades were heavier and thicker. Most probably, they were the work of local smiths rather than specialists, and they were carried in a scabbard suspended crosswise from the belt.

As with their swords, the Vikings used more than one size of bow. Short Viking bows measured about 35 in (90

Below: Viking battleaxe with an iron blade. Axes might not pierce the skin but when swung with sufficient force they could cause bruising and internal injuries.

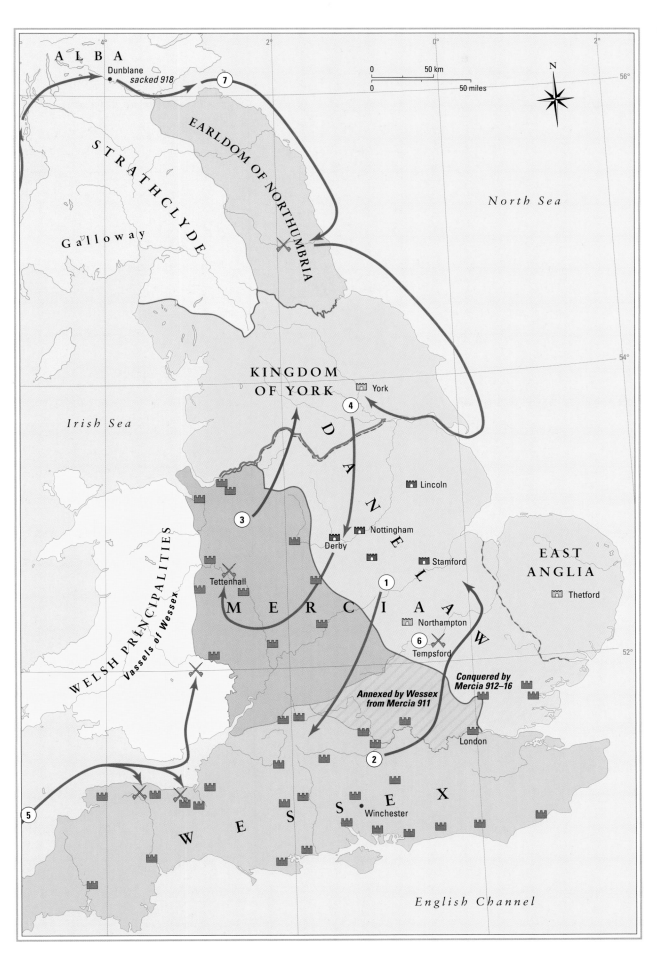

Viking Rule in England
902–919

	English Kingdoms or under English control c. 902
	Extent of Danelaw c. 902
🏰	The Five Boroughs of Danelaw
🏰	Other major fortified towns
🏰	English fortified towns (*burh*) established by 916
—	Wessex border after the annexation of Mercia c. 919
→	Major Scandinavian movements
→	Major English movements
✕	Major battle site

① 903: Danes attack English Mercia and Wessex.

② 903: English reprisal attack defeated.

③ 909: English army ravages Kingdom of York.

④ 910: Danes launch reprisal raid, they are badly defeated at Tettenhall.

⑤ 914: Viking raids launch from Brittany, defeated by English.

⑥ 917: Danish King of East Anglia killed in battle of Tempsford after which Danish resistence crumbles. The English conquest of Danelaw completed under the leadership of Wessex.

⑦ 918: Norse chieftan based in Dublin took control of the English-ruled Earldom of Northumbria and then seized control of the Kingdom of York.

In 911, the Viking Rollo was granted the fiefdom of Normandy by the Frankish king Charles in exchange for his feudal homage. Normandy had been conquered by Rollo previously, so acquired its name from Rollo's Viking or 'Northman' origins.

cm) in length, and the largest could be twice as long. Either of these bows, made of ash or yew, could shoot over a distance of 27 in (70 cm); and the arrows, which could be up to 27 in (70 cm) long, were capable of piercing a mail shirt, but only at short range. The Vikings themselves most commonly wore the mail shirt, or *byrnie*, as armor. This was made of iron rings, each of which was linked to four others. The average *byrnie* consisted of more than 30,000 links. Half the arm was protected and it covered the body down to the mid-thigh or knee. A mail shirt could protect against a slash with an axe or sword. But

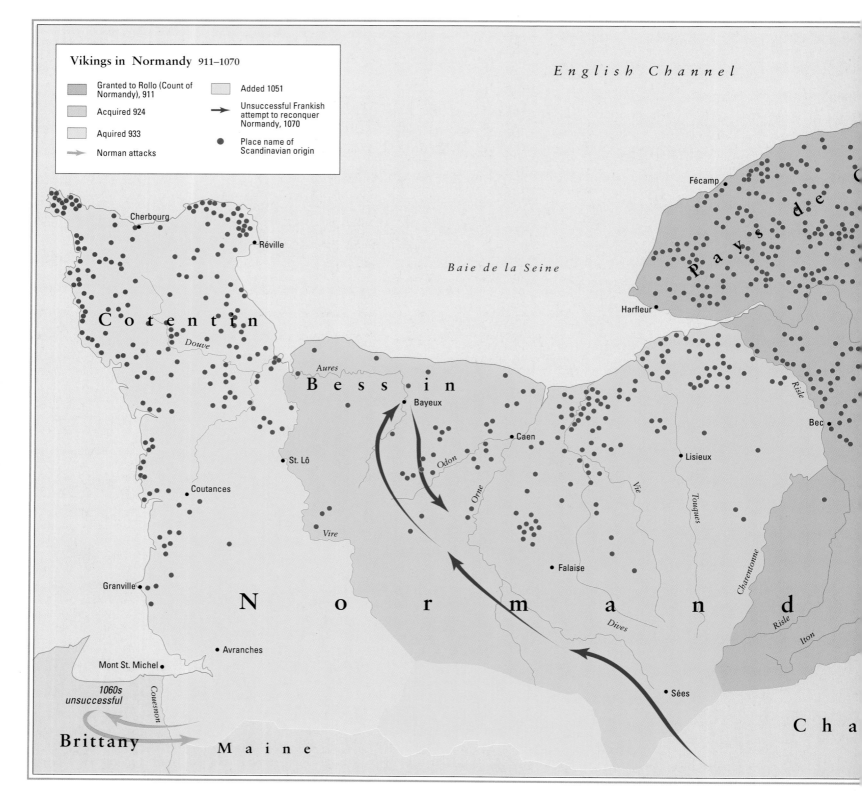

Vikings in Normandy 911–1070

- Granted to Rollo (Count of Normandy), 911
- Acquired 924
- Aquired 933
- → Norman attacks
- Added 1051
- → Unsuccessful Frankish attempt to reconquer Normandy, 1070
- ● Place name of Scandinavian origin

English Channel

Baie de la Seine

Fécamp

Cherbourg

Réville

Harfleur

Pays de C

Cotentin

Douve

Aures

Bessin

Bayeux

St. Lô

Odon

Caen

Lisieux

Bec

Coutances

Vire

Orne

Vie

Touques

Granville

Falaise

Charentonne

N   o   r   m   a   n   d

Dives

Risle

Iton

Avranches

Mont St. Michel

Sées

1060s
unsuccessful

Couesnon

Brittany   Maine

Cha

the axe could still do damage: an axe blade swung with sufficient force could cause bruising; and even though it might not pierce the skin, there could be internal injuries. A strike with a spear that was used with both hands was a more serious matter, for it could easily penetrate a standard mail shirt. However, most of the enemy spearmen whom the Vikings encountered did not bother with armor. They struck instead at the unprotected parts of the body: the throat or the face.

Although the Vikings could fight on horseback, particularly when they went raiding, they also fought as foot-soldiers in set-piece battles. Their weapons then were mainly infantry weapons, and their favorite means of defense was typical of the foot-soldier: a wall of shields placed edge to edge. The typical Viking shield measured up to 35 in (90 cm) across, and so a shield wall could be of considerable length and make a formidable defense. Each shield overlapped with the next shield on both sides. This formed a barrier that was usually strong enough to prevent opponents from rushing it and penetrating it. For the individual fights and melées that followed, the shield wall was loosened, to enable the combatants to wield their axes and swords. Attacks could also be launched from behind the shield wall. The *Heimskirngla*, a compilation from various Norwegian sagas dating from the 13th century, described an assault by a shield wall formation that took place some 200 years earlier: "They who stood foremost struck blows, they who were next thrust with spears, and all who came up behind shot with spears or arrows or cast stones or hand axes or javelins".

Since the Vikings were a warrior people, and warfare was a regular activity, strict laws were laid down about the arms or folk weapons that every adult male needed to prosses. Each Viking had to have a shield, sword or axe, and a quiverful of arrows; and each year an official made a careful check to see that these rules were observed.

Replica of a viking axe used by foot solidiers

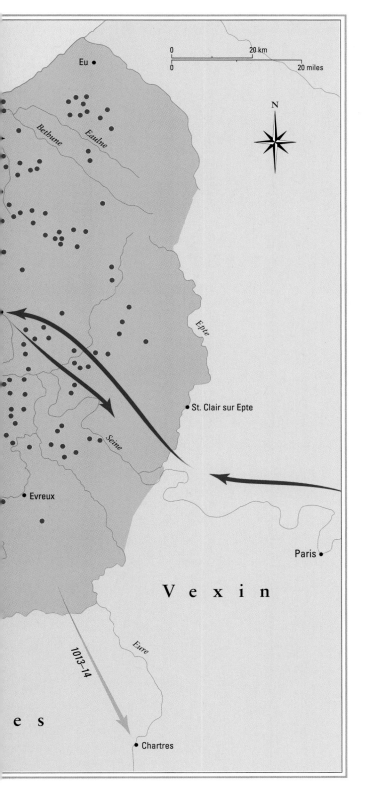

THE CAVALRY

CAVALRY HAS FEATURED IN WAR THROUGHOUT MOST OF HUMAN HISTORY. FIGHTING ON HORSEBACK DEVELOPED FROM CHARIOT WARFARE, AND ALONG WITH THE USE OF CAVALRY GREATLY INCREASED THE FIGHTING VALUE OF THE SMALLEST FORCE.

Opposite page: Battle of the Kalka River, 1223. The Mongol cavalry stormed across the river and sliced up the ranks of Cumans and forces from Kiev and other principalities of Rus to score a stunning victory.

Below: Medieval knights on horseback in full armor.

T he cavalry was the most mobile of all the elements of warfare until the introduction of motorized columns into 20th-century armies. Cavalry was able to outflank an enemy, make surprise appearances on the battlefield, deal opponents sudden shock attacks and, where necessary, escape from a battle at speed.

Fighting on horseback required special weapons that not only served the convenience of the warrior-horseman but also made the most of the agility that cavalry warfare afforded. One of these weapons was noted in the first report of cavalry used in war, which appeared in Assyrian records of the 9th century BC. Describing the tactics of Persian tribes, the records reported an army that included mounted archers. Later on, crossbows, javelins, and lances also became cavalry weapons.

The Assyrians faced problems in raising sufficiently large numbers of cavalry and finding horses large and strong enough to carry heavily armored riders into battle. Reliefs dating from around 865BC depict men on horseback

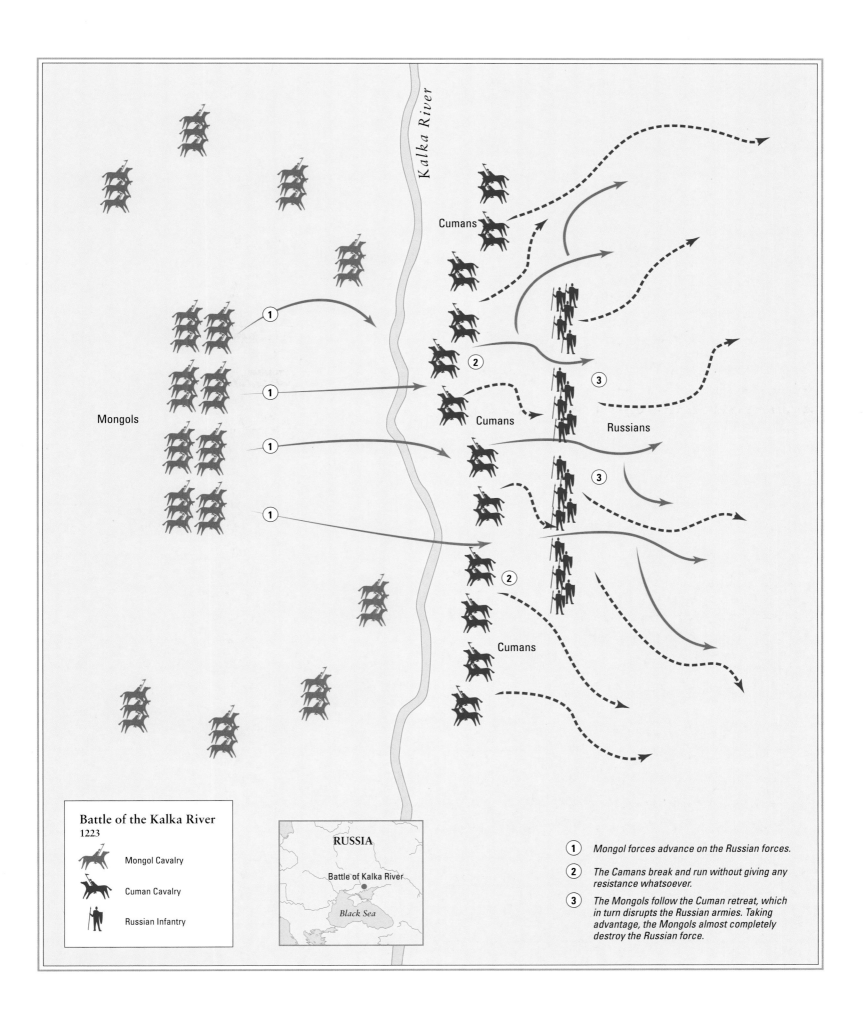

Kalka River

Cumans

Mongols

Cumans

Russians

Cumans

Battle of the Kalka River
1223

 Mongol Cavalry

Cuman Cavalry

Russian Infantry

RUSSIA

Battle of Kalka River

Black Sea

(1) Mongol forces advance on the Russian forces.

(2) The Camans break and run without giving any resistance whatsoever.

(3) The Mongols follow the Cuman retreat, which in turn disrupts the Russian armies. Taking advantage, the Mongols almost completely destroy the Russian force.

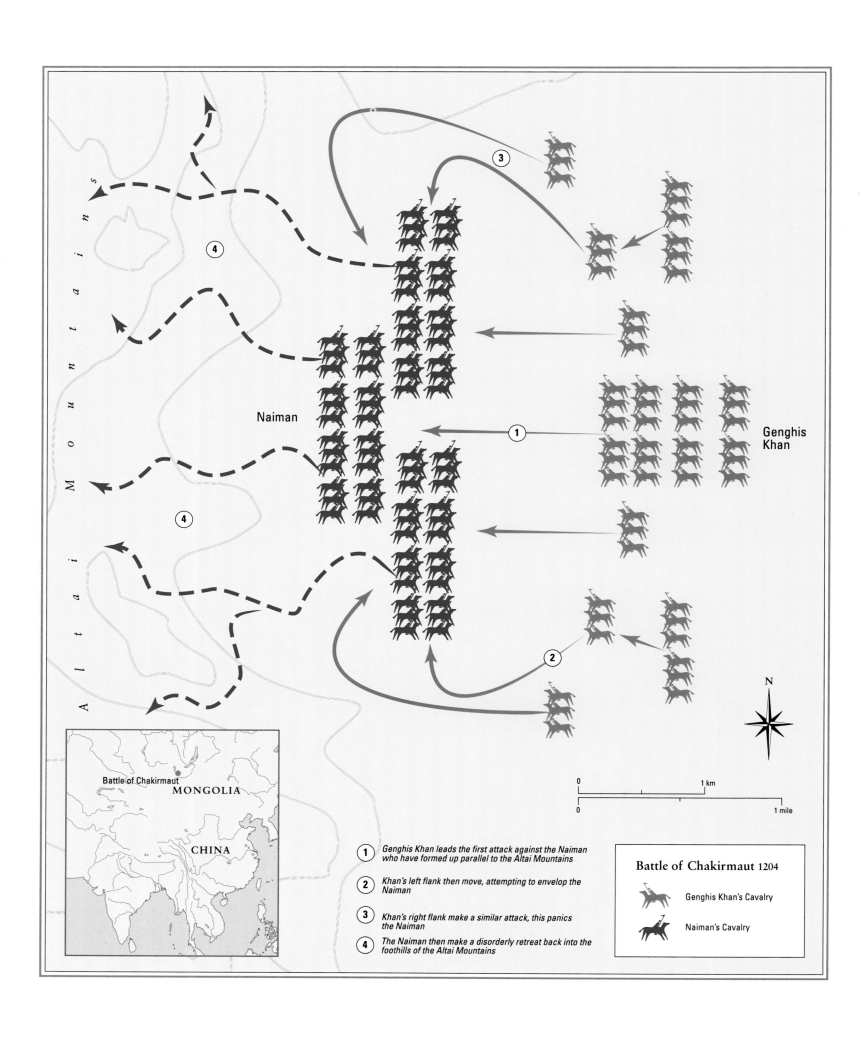

Naiman

Genghis
Khan

N

Battle of Chakirmaut
MONGOLIA

CHINA

0   1 km

0   1 mile

1 Genghis Khan leads the first attack against the Naiman
   who have formed up parallel to the Altai Mountains

2 Khan's left flank then move, attempting to envelop the
   Naiman

3 Khan's right flank make a similar attack, this panics
   the Naiman

4 The Naiman then make a disorderly retreat back into the
   foothills of the Altai Mountains

Battle of Chakirmaut 1204

Genghis Khan's Cavalry

Naiman's Cavalry

without any of the equipment that could make riding steady and leave them free to handle weaponry: there were no saddles or saddle cloths, spurs or stirrups; all effort had to be devoted to controlling the horse. At first, the Assyrians dealt with this problem by having their cavalry operate in pairs. A second horseman controlled the reins for the mounted archer riding alongside, leaving the archer free to fire his arrows at the enemy. Later, archers and other riders using swords and shields were able to control their own horses after they were equipped with crude saddles in the form of saddle cloths. These were sometimes intricately decorated and were held in place by straps fastened around the horse's belly.

The quest for suitable horses for cavalry purposes was resolved, probably in the late 5th century BC, by mounts described by the Greek historian Herodotus as "of unusual size". They were bred on the Nisaean Plain, part of the Zagros Mountains in western Iran. The cavalry could now be equipped with mounts able to carry riders wearing increasing amounts of armor and heavy equipment, but these horses remained relatively rare for some time. Bucephalus, the famous horse owned by Alexander the Great, was said to be one of them. It was Alexander's father, King Philip II, who developed the heavy cavalry, the *hetairoi*, which was made possible by more robust war horses in the 4th century BC. And it was Alexander who employed them in a combined arms system that enabled him to conquer Persia, and, later, the north-west of India (see pages 56–59).

The Macedonian army also included light cavalry called *prodromoi*, which was used for reconnaissance and screening, two functions that were still being performed by cavalry in European armies until aircraft took over the task during World War One more than 2,000 years later. The Macedonians' mounted forces were completed by the *ippiko* (horse-riders). They were medium cavalry and performed reconnaissance duties, but they were also used for skirmishing.

Apparently, even in the army of Alexander the Great, a force famous, and feared, for its innovative strategies and unexpected tactics, the Macedonian cavalry was still riding its horses bareback or sitting on a piece of cloth or animal hide. The Moors of Morocco, in North Africa, are thought to have been the first to use saddles as such, in the form of padding between the rider and the horse's back. But discoveries made in a Scythian tomb in Siberia dating from the 5th century BC include a cover for a cushioned saddle made from leather, felt, and hair.

At around the same time, a companion innovation, the stirrup, first appeared, possibly in India; but several other peoples, including the Scythians and Mongols, have been credited with its introduction. The stirrup is counted among the most significant technological advances in warfare before the advent of gunpowder. It increased the power of the cavalry by enabling archers to stand up in the saddle to use the bow. A cavalry tactic employed by the Sassanid Persians in the 6th and 7th centuries AD was the "shower shoot", which involved a line of cavalry and its horses, both heavily armored, loosing arrows at an enemy from a fixed position while shortening the draw length in order to fire as rapidly as possible. The heavy cavalry, thundering down on the enemy at full speed, lances thrust out in front, could smash into opponents, unhorsing them with such force that they were hurled backward to the ground.

The ancient Greeks and Romans, with their infantry-based forces, made little use of cavalry, at least initially. Before the military reforms pioneered by Philip of Macedonia, the Greek phalanx served the city-states well enough and certainly saved mainland Greece from the Persians. In Republican Rome, the cavalry, known as the *equites*, was used as support for the infantry, the legions that made up around four-

Opposite page: Battle of Chakirmaut, Mongolia. The Mongol leader Ghengis Khan used his cavalry to defeat a force of Naimans despite being vastly outnumbered by them. Ghengis' victory at Chakirmaut completed his conquest of Mongolia

fifths of the army. But after 27BC, with the advent of the Roman Empire, cavalry became more and more important in the business of defending its far-flung possessions. With that, the *equites*, an elite drawn from the landed aristocracy, was augmented by recruits from the Italian *socii*, or allies, and by barbarian auxiliaries from Gaul (France), Spain, Germany, and Numidia in North Africa, where the recruits were particularly skilled skirmishers. The Romans were well aware of the fighting qualities of the foreign cavalry, having fought against them on many occasions. Admitting some of them to the ranks of the army certainly improved the scope of operation of the Roman forces, but it could not nullify the danger the foreign tribes presented to the security of the empire. The foreign contribution to the Roman cavalry bought the Roman Empire perhaps another two centuries of survival. But the barbarian depredations continued nonetheless; eventually, in the 5th century AD, the Roman army, once the greatest army in the then-known world, was too weak to hold the frontier against the massive incursions from outside. Barbarians flooded across the borders, running wild through Germany, France, and Spain while Anglo-Saxon invaders assailed Britain, which had been abandoned so that its garrison could help to defend the city of Rome. The barbarians pillaged, plundered, killed, and destroyed as they went. Finally, unable to withstand their relentless onslaught, Rome and the empire fell.

Among those barbarians, the Goths, who were especially skilled and dangerous on horseback, probably did the most to bring about the end of the Roman Empire in Europe. The military power of the Goths was a grim fact of life that the Roman emperor Valens learned to his cost when he attacked a Gothic camp at Adrianople in western Turkey in 378AD. The result was a humiliating disaster for the Romans. The Gothic cavalry crashed through the mass of legionaries, laying about them with their swords and massacring them by the score. This was the first time heavy cavalry had scored such a stunning victory over infantry, and it marked the start of a long period when the fighter on horseback became predominant in warfare.

The Goths made great use of the stirrup, which enabled their horsemen to balance themselves in the saddle and withstand the shock of impact when they struck opponents with their lances. Just as brilliant on horseback and equally terrifying in battle were the Huns, a nomadic barbarian tribe that probably originated in China and invaded south-eastern Europe in about 370AD. In battle, a Hun horseman could turn and maneuver his mount at high speed while firing showers of arrows from the saddle with deadly accuracy. The Huns also used long iron swords and were clever at entangling an enemy by lassoing him or throwing a net over him. By these means, the Huns sent many opponents crashing helplessly to the ground, where they were quickly finished off with a lance- or sword-thrust.

The Huns and the Goths demonstrated valuable lessons in cavalry warfare, that were taken up and copied in the Byzantine (eastern Roman) Empire, centered around Constantinople (modern Istanbul). From about 520 AD, a brilliant young Byzantine general, Belisarius, began to train his heavily armed and armored cavalry to become nimble, all-purpose fighters. They carried four weapons: the bow and arrow, which the Byzantines learned to fire rapidly in the Hun fashion by loosing an arrow from the bowstring at a point opposite their right ear; the lance; small feathered darts with which the Byzantines could pepper their enemies at close quarters; and the heavy broadsword.

Belisarius trained the Byzantine cavalry to become proficient at using all this equipment, and where necessary, in quick succession and with great skill. At the same time, they had to control their horses

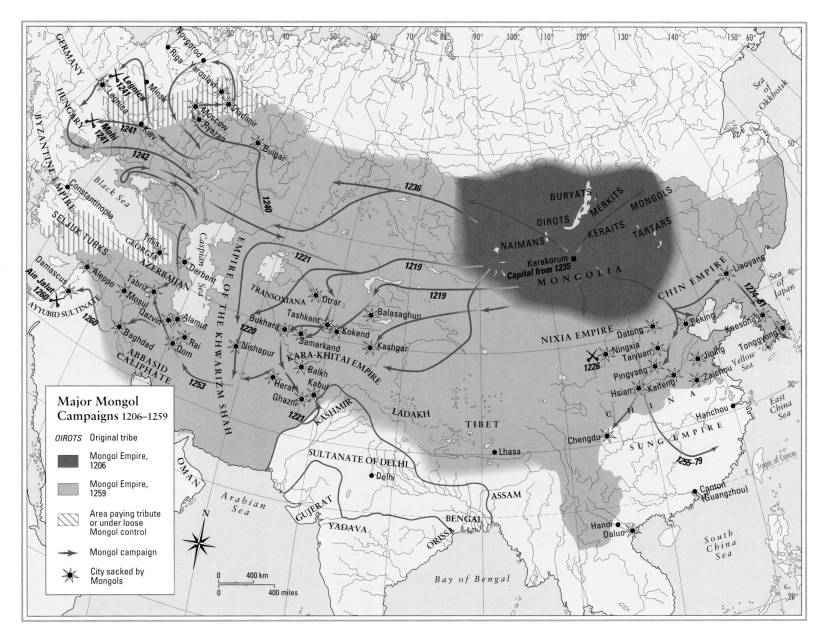

Major Mongol Campaigns 1206–1259

OIROTS Original tribe

Mongol Empire, 1206

Mongol Empire, 1259

Area paying tribute or under loose Mongol control

→ Mongol campaign

✳ City sacked by Mongols

0   400 km
0   400 miles

The Mongol Empire extended right across Eurasia, from the River Danube to the Sea of Japan, covering almost a quarter of the world's land, and ruling a total population of more than 100 million people.

in all the sudden twists and turns of battle. The Byzantines used stirrups, as the Goths had done, and Belisarius taught them how to control and turn a horse by pressing their knees into its sides. All this sounds very much like a military juggling act, and in many ways it was.

Nevertheless, large numbers of Byzantines learned how to fight in this complex fashion, and did so brilliantly. Part of the training exercises for Byzantine soldiers included having to "attack" a stuffed dummy, later called a quintain, hit it with three arrows as they galloped toward it, and then finish by sticking a lance or a set of darts into it. With fighting men of high quality and expert training, and by the cunning use of battle tactics, Byzantine armies were able to conquer the barbarian Vandals in Africa, thrash the Goths in Italy, and hold back barbarian tribes attempting to cross the River Danube. As a result, the Byzantine Empire never fell to the barbarians as the western Roman Empire had done. The Byzantine empire could not, of course, remain completely immune to attack, but the eastern empire did manage to outlive its western equivalent for nearly 1,000 years, until Constantinople fell to the Muslim Ottoman Turks in 1453.

MEDIEVAL KNIGHTS

THE KNIGHT ON HORSEBACK WAS THE HERO OF MEDIEVAL TIMES. HE REPRESENTED ALL THE GREAT VIRTUES THAT WERE VALUED THEN AND IN MANY WAYS PERSIST TODAY: COURAGE, CHIVALRY, PHYSICAL STRENGTH, RELIGIOUS DEVOTION, LOYALTY AND, WHEN IT BECAME NECESSARY, SELF-SACRIFICE.

The knight on horseback made his first appearance in England at the Battle of Hastings in 1066. On October 14 of that year, the face of warfare as it had been known in England changed for ever. Duke William of Normandy, who was intent on claiming the crown of England allegedly promised him by a previous king, Edward the Confessor, brought with him up to 4,000 Norman infantry, consisting of bowmen with 5 ft (1.5 m) bows, crossbowmen, pikemen, and swordsmen, all of them clad in mail shirts. William's forces also included some 3,000 heavily armored, mounted knights, whose mail protected them from the tops of their heads to their knees. They fought with swords, lances, and maces (metal-headed spiked clubs). Added protection came from the knights' kite-shaped shields, which extended from neck to toe, and also from their conical helmets, which had bars projecting over their noses.

Their English opponents, the descendants of Anglo-Saxon and Viking invaders, put up the traditional shield wall to resist the Normans, but confronted by a new and unfamiliar form of warfare, their efforts were futile. Late in the afternoon, Duke William ordered his bowmen to unleash a hail of arrows against the defenders; and in the confusion that followed, the knights thundered in and started hacking about them with their weapons. The defensive shield wall held for a while but finally disintegrated.

The knights' action at Hastings was the first "performance" in England by warriors who became, and still remain, the most admired, most romanticized fighters in the history of warfare. Thirty years after Hastings until the early 14th century, the knight on horseback journeyed to the Holy Land to fight the Muslims in the Crusades. The knight was greatly admired for his physical strength and agility. As well as being renowned warriors, knights were also the most famous sportsmen of their time.

Opposite page: At the Battle of Evesham in 1265, the rebel baron Simon de Montfort was defeated by the forces of King Henry III. Henry's troops, led by his son Edward I, prevented de Montfort from driving through the royal front and attacked the baronial army on both flanks.

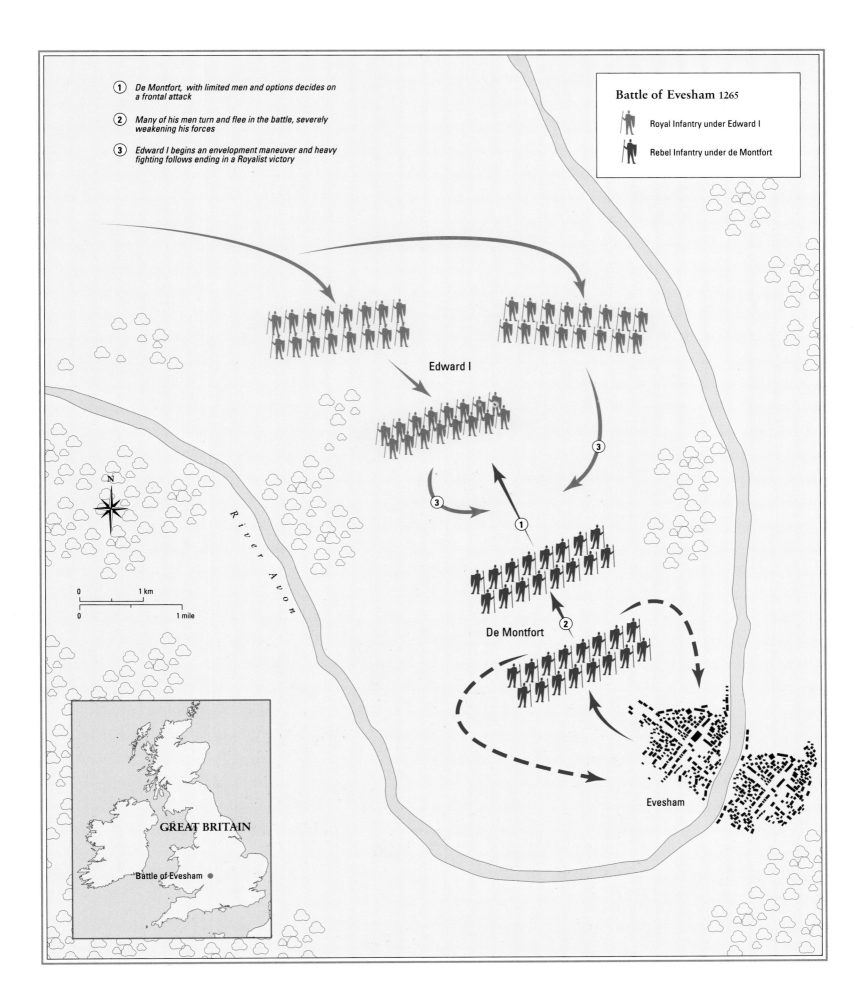

① De Montfort, with limited men and options decides on a frontal attack

② Many of his men turn and flee in the battle, severely weakening his forces

③ Edward I begins an envelopment maneuver and heavy fighting follows ending in a Royalist victory

Battle of Evesham 1265

Royal Infantry under Edward I

Rebel Infantry under de Montfort

Edward I

De Montfort

River Avon

N

0   1 km

0   1 mile

Evesham

GREAT BRITAIN

Battle of Evesham ●

Opposite page:: The Battle of Navarette (Najera) was fought in 1367 between English and French armies, each supporting rival Castilian princes. The English prevailed, mainly due to heavy fire from their longbowmen, which caused the enemy cavalry to flee the battlefield.

The most thrilling sport in their day was the tournament, where fully armored knights galloped toward each other on beautifully caparisoned horses, their lances at the ready. The tournament was essentially a rehearsal for war; and it was just as dangerous and, sometimes, just as fatal as fighting on the battlefield. It was not a pursuit for weaklings. The armored knight had to carry heavy, cumbersome equipment. There was his 9ft (2.75 m) lance, a 4ft (1.2 m) shield, and a double-edged sword 42 in (1.1 m) long. All of it needed to be handled while wearing a full suit of armor weighing up to 55 lb (25 kg).

After Hastings, the knight's mail armor gradually covered more and more of the body. The hauberk (mail shirt), for instance, acquired longer sleeves. In about 1350, armorers began to provide plates of steel for the knees, elbows, and shins. Gradually, they became more adept at making plate armour supple, so that it would move as the body moved. Before long, knights were riding into battle completely covered in plate armor from their visored basinets (helmets) to the gauntlets on their hands and the shoes on their feet. Even so, knights were not entirely safe from attack. Swordmakers introduced narrow, rigid blades that could be worked between the joins of plate armor, and longbows could shoot arrows at speeds that enabled them to penetrate it. This is what happened at the Battle of Crécy in 1346, during the Hundred Years' War, when English archers killed some 1,500 French knights. But by then, gunpowder, which was going to bring the age of the armored knight to an end, was already in existence.

The mounted knight in armor, seen here taking part in a tournament, the rehearsals for real battle, was the most admired fighter of medieval warfare. He encapsulated all the military virtues of heroism, self-sacrifice, military skill and chivalry..

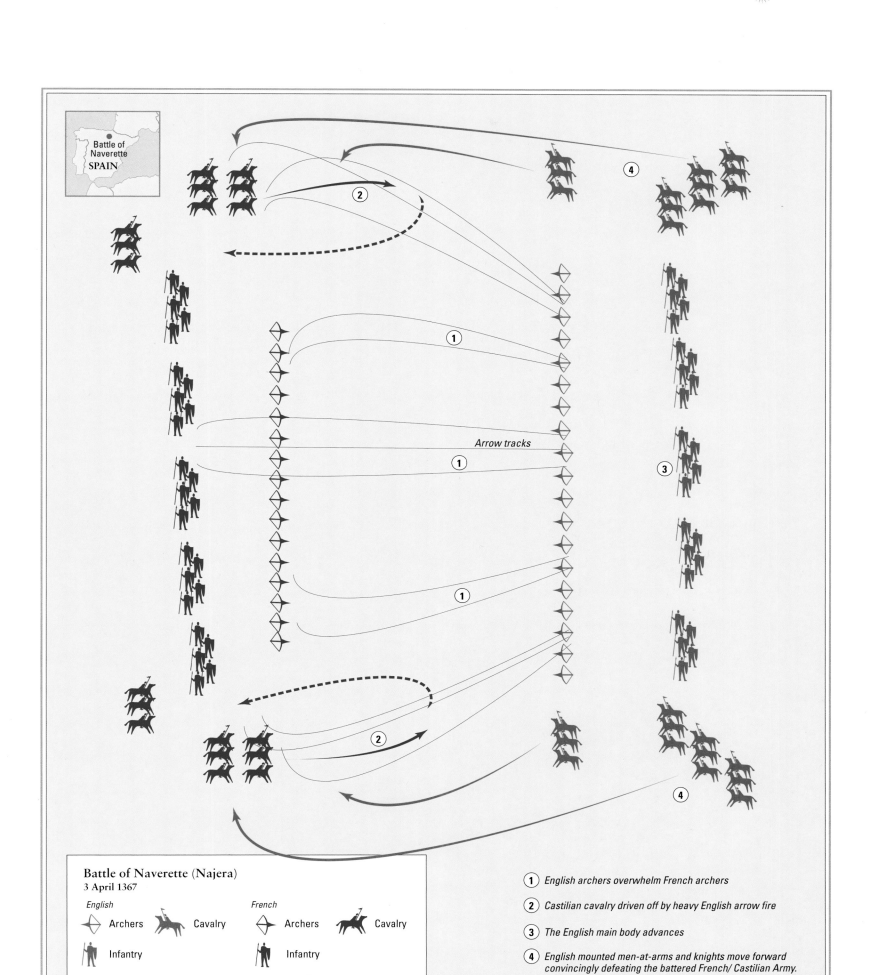

Battle of Naverette (Najera)
3 April 1367

English
Archers   Cavalry

Infantry

French
Archers   Cavalry

Infantry

1 English archers overwhelm French archers

2 Castilian cavalry driven off by heavy English arrow fire

3 The English main body advances

4 English mounted men-at-arms and knights move forward convincingly defeating the battered French/ Castilian Army.

Arrow tracks

Battle of
Naverette
SPAIN

SIEGE MACHINES: PART 3

THE SIEGE WAS ONE OF THE MOST ANCIENT FORMS OF WARFARE AND SIEGE MACHINES WERE THE MECHANISMS THAT MADE IT TERRIFYING. YET WITHIN A FEW YEARS IN THE 14TH CENTURY, THEY WERE SUPERSEDED BY A NEW, EVEN MORE DESTRUCTIVE INVENTION.

Opposite page: Chateau Gaillard, on the River Seine, was a fortress built for Richard the Lionheart in 1197–1199. Richard was Duke of Normandy as well as King of England and the Chateau was meant to protect his Duchy from French attacks.

A thousand years after the Romans, siege warfare had not changed a great deal. Medieval armies besieging a castle still used catapults, flame-throwers, ballistae, and battering rams. They employed equipment used even before actual siege machines were devised, such as scaling ladders and siege towers. And just as the Romans had once protected themselves with the testudo of overlapping shields, medieval armies engaged in a siege used "cats" or "penthouses" as shields against missiles thrown down at them from the walls above.

One of the siege engines used in medieval warfare was the trebuchet, which had been developed from the Roman *onager*. Its name came from the old French verb "*trebucher*", meaning to overthrow. Like the *onager*, the trebuchet administered a mighty "kick" to fire a missile at its target. A windlass was operated in order to twist ropes or springs, which forced a spoke down. When the ropes or springs were suddenly released, the spoke "kicked" at a crosspiece on the wooden frame and missiles contained in a large cup attached to the trebuchet were propelled forward. The firing method used with the trebuchet was known as the "counterweight" system.

The trebuchet was normally used to hurl large stones, just like its near-relative the torsion-operated mangonel, a much older siege machine once used by the Romans. The mangonel was not as accurate as the trebuchet but it could hurl projectiles much faster and at a much lower trajectory. Its purpose on the battlefield was to bombard concentrations of troops, kill as many of them as possible, and throw the rest into confusion. During a siege, the mangonel was used to destroy castle or town walls, enabling a besieging army to get inside and slay the defenders. But the crew operating a mangonel or a trebuchet did not always confine themselves to throwing stones.

Chateau Gaillard, Normandy

This drawing shows the castle as it
would have looked around 1204. It
was an exceptionally strong fortress
and proved extremely difficult to
capture.

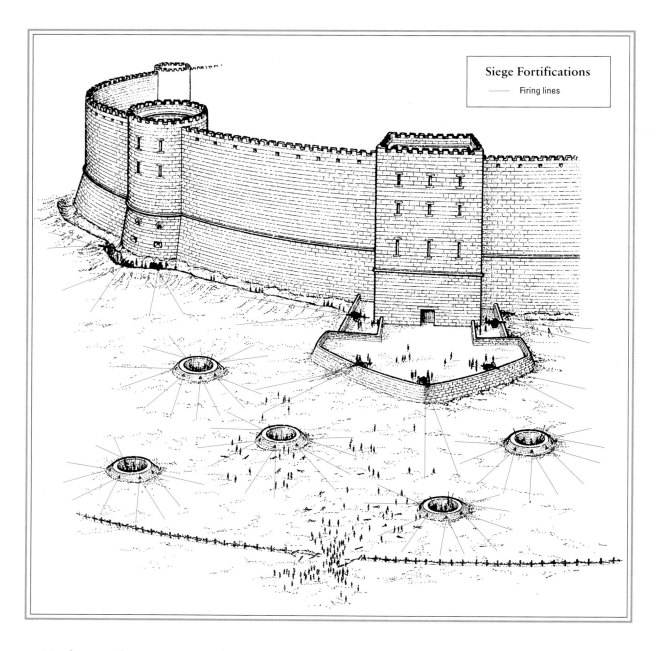

Siege Fortifications
——— Firing lines

Much more fearsome projectiles were available, including flaming pots, burning pitch, blazing oil, and Greek Fire. The ingredients of Greek Fire, often used by the Byzantines to drive invaders from the walls of their capital Constantinople, were apparently kept secret, by allowing those who prepared it to know only one component of the mixture. The contents of Greek Fire remain a mystery even today, but saltpeter, quicklime, or distilled petroleum have been suggested as possible components of Greek Fire. Whatever it contained, Greek Fire had only to be wetted in order for it to blaze up uncontrollably. No amount of water, it appeared, could put it out, which is suggestive of the explosive reaction between water and quicklime.

Greek Fire, invented in around 672AD, was the true terror weapon of medieval times. However, another, more sinister payload better deserved that reputation. The cause and cure of disease was poorly understood in medieval times, but its ability to spread, and spread quickly, was well known. This was why human and animal corpses, sometimes partly decomposed, were loaded into the buckets of siege machines together with excrement and catapulted — over the walls of castles or cities — to infect the

High, thick walls, crenellated battlements with built-in towers were the essentials of medieval fortifications. The towers were provided with slit "windows" shaped to protect the bowmen who shot their arrows through the openings.

people inside. The chances of disease spreading by this means were high in view of the depredations already caused by hunger and bad hygiene.

The most terrifying of all infections was bubonic plague, and there were instances of the bodies of dead victims being used as a weapon. In 1346, during a war in the Crimea of southern Russia, both combatants, the Tartars and the Genoese, delivered this deadly payload to each other during the hostilities. Nor was this form of biological warfare confined to the Middle Ages. In 1710, during a war between Russia and Sweden, plague-infected corpses were thrown over the walls of Revel (Tallin, now the capital of Estonia) for the purpose of infecting the Swedish garrison.

Mangonels, trebuchets, and other siege machines were not quickly replaced by guns, which first appeared on European battlefields during the first quarter of the 14th century. Early cannons were very unreliable, and often posed a greater danger to the attacker than the attacked. It took the best part of a century for guns and gunpowder to become sufficiently destructive that they could batter down castles and reduce the walls of fortified towns to rubble. In 1415, during the latter stages of the Hundred Years' War between England and France, Harfleur, in northern France, was one of the first towns to receive this treatment. With that, the age of monster siege machines and their deadly payloads came to an end.

Generally, siege machines like this one would have thrown their missiles from a distance, lobbing it over the wall to fall directly among the defenders on the other side.

GUNS AND GUNPOWDER

THE INTRODUCTION OF GUNPOWDER AS A MISSILE PROPELLANT WAS AMONG THE GREAT MILESTONES IN WARFARE. FIRST USED IN EUROPE IN AROUND 1325, GUNS EVENTUALLY SWEPT AWAY SEVERAL ESTABLISHED FEATURES OF WAR, INCLUDING THE MOUNTED KNIGHT AND THE TRADITIONAL SIEGE.

T he basic ingredients of gunpowder — saltpeter (potassium nitrate), charcoal, and sulfur — were well known in ancient times, but the precise mixture that made them explode was not discovered for some time. The finding of the formula has been ascribed to Taoist monks in China in the 9th century AD and to the authors of two books which included recipes for gunpowder: the Islamic scholar Hassan al-Rammah, who wrote a treatise on military technology in around 1240, and Huo Lung Ching, the author of *Huolongjing* [*Fire Dragon Manual*] in the 14th century. However, in 1904 an artillery officer, Lieutenant-Colonel H.W.L. Hime, found that a treatise written some time between 1249 and 1260 by the English philosopher Roger Bacon contained an anagram which, when decoded, turned out to be a cipher for the preparation of gunpowder. Bacon had every reason to conceal his recipe by ciphering it because in his time, scientific investigation was condemned by the Church as works of the devil, and perpetrators were liable to execution. Nevertheless, Bacon included a stark description of the explosive effect created: "We can with saltpetre and other substances compose artificially a fire that can be launched over long distances ... By only using a very small quantity of this material, much light can be created, accompanied by a horrible fracas. It is possible with it to destroy a town or an army."

Whatever the Church thought of it, a weapon of this potential soon came to the attention of kings and governments. In 1346, gunpowder was being manufactured in England and in 1461, a "powder house" was installed in the Tower of London, then a royal palace. Gunpowder was also manufactured and stored at the royal palaces in Edinburgh, Scotland, and Portchester on the south coast of England. Elsewhere, in Europe and the East gunpowder was already being used in war, for instance at the Siege of Belgaum

Opposite page: The siege of Constantinople by the Muslim Turks in 1453 brought about the end of the Byzantine Empire. The struggle took place on both land and sea and Turkish gunpower was used to smash through the city walls.

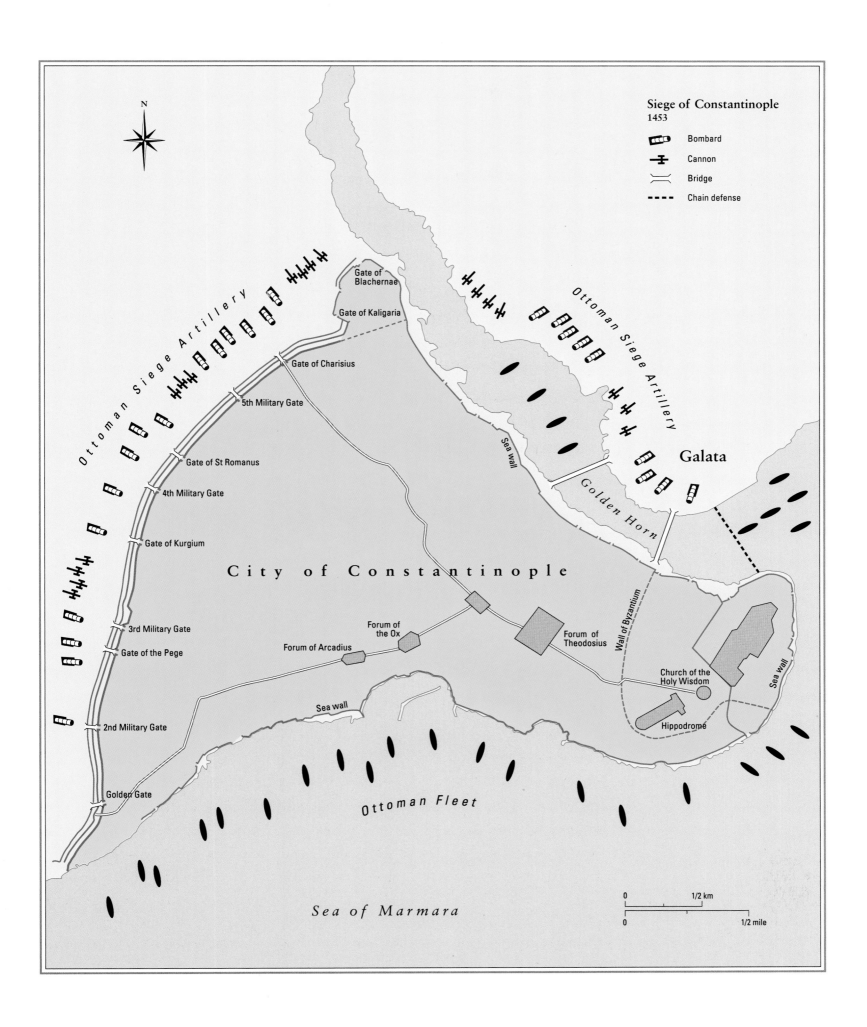

N

Siege of Constantinople
1453

◗▬ Bombard

╪ Cannon

⟩⟨ Bridge

- - - Chain defense

Ottoman Siege Artillery

Gate of
Blachernae

Gate of Kaligaria

Gate of Charisius

5th Military Gate

Gate of St Romanus

4th Military Gate

Gate of Kurgium

3rd Military Gate

Gate of the Pege

2nd Military Gate

Golden Gate

City of Constantinople

Ottoman Siege Artillery

Galata

Golden Horn

Sea Wall

Wall of Byzantium

Forum of
the Ox

Forum of Arcadius

Forum of
Theodosius

Church of the
Holy Wisdom

Sea wall

Sea wall

Hippodrome

Sea wall

Ottoman Fleet

Sea of Marmara

0   1/2 km

0   1/2 mile

in western India in 1473 and at the siege of Constantinople in 1453, where gunpowder was used by the Turks to break the city walls.

Early guns were cast from a non-ferrous alloy such as brass, the alloy of zinc and copper, which was widely used to make church bells. The name given to the first guns, *vasi*, suggests that they were made in Italy, where the metal-working industry was the most advanced in 14th-century Europe. However, gun-making skills soon spread to Germany and France and from there to England. At first, production faced the same difficulty: guns made of non-ferrous alloys were very expensive. Many gun-makers turned instead to a cheaper alternative, wrought iron. Wrought-iron guns, known as bombards, did not entirely supersede those made of non-ferrous alloys.

In the pre-gun era, arrows served as the principal projectile in war; and when guns made their appearance, arrows were simply transferred to them. The first illustration of a *vaso*, which appears in a document dated 1327, shows a vase-shaped "gun" with a large arrow sticking out of it. Gun arrows went by many names such as as darts, quarrels, or *carreaux* (tiles). They had short shafts made of oak, with iron points and metal "wings" instead of the feathers fitted to the arrows used by bowmen. Besides being expensive to make, gun-arrows were of very light caliber. They were soon replaced by lead balls. These projectiles were suitable for firing from guns as long as the guns remained of small caliber — on average, around 5 in (12.7 cm). But although effective against soldiers, small-caliber guns were as yet unable to match the destructive capabilities of the mechanical siege machines.

Nevertheless, it was clear that a gun was far quicker than a *ballista* or trebuchet to set up and fire. It followed that guns must be bigger if they were to become more powerful. The projectiles they fired needed to be more effective too. The arrows and lead shot had to go. In 1364, the Italians, who were still well ahead of other Europeans in gun-making, introduced a weightier alternative — stone.

Stone was cheap and readily available in suitably large chunks owing to the prevalence of church-building in the 14th century. There was a problem, however. When fired at a well-built target, gun stones, as the new projectiles came to be called, tended to disintegrate, leaving the target scratched but otherwise unharmed. But by the 15th century, the technique of casting iron was sufficiently developed for iron roundshot to replace stone. The casting of iron began in Italy in 1364 and afterward spread throughout Europe. At the Battle of Formigny in 1450 culverins guns were used to devastating effect by the French forces to bombard the English, their culverinswere able to fire from beyond the range of the longbows of the English, therefore bringing the French to resounding victory.

By 1512, the English were also producing iron projectiles. The young King Henry VIII, who had come to the throne of England three years earlier, sought to make up for the relative backwardness of English gunners, who always appeared to come late to new developments. Henry enthusiastically promoted the production and organization of artillery, and ordered "patterns", or models, of guns to be made as examples to gun-founders. They were probably illiterate: written instructions and even drawings would have been of no use to them as guidelines. Instead, they were told to copy the models and simply increase their size. Although stone remained in use in England until 1578, iron eventually replaced it. Iron projectiles were fired from guns throughout the smoothbore era, until well into the 19th century.

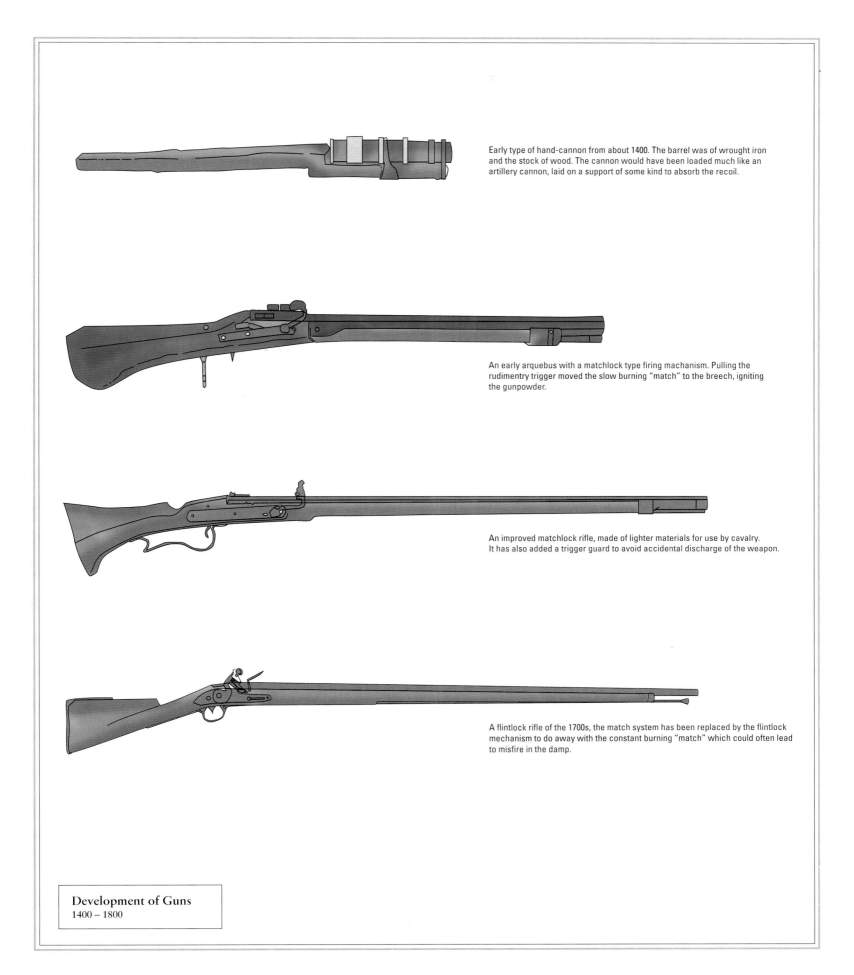

Early type of hand-cannon from about 1400. The barrel was of wrought iron and the stock of wood. The cannon would have been loaded much like an artillery cannon, laid on a support of some kind to absorb the recoil.

An early arquebus with a matchlock type firing machanism. Pulling the rudimentry trigger moved the slow burning "match" to the breech, igniting the gunpowder.

An improved matchlock rifle, made of lighter materials for use by cavalry. It has also added a trigger guard to avoid accidental discharge of the weapon.

A flintlock rifle of the 1700s, the match system has been replaced by the flintlock mechanism to do away with the constant burning "match" which could often lead to misfire in the damp.

Development of Guns
1400 – 1800

Opposite page: The Battle of Formigny, fought between English and French forces in 1450, resulted in a resounding victory for the French. A crucial factor in this victory was French use of culverins firing beyond the range of the English longbows.

By the 16th century, the caliber of guns had greatly increased. Some were reportedly enlarged to calibres of 35¼ in (91 cm). One celebrated bombard, Mons Meg, constructed in Scotland in the mid-16th century, was 15 ft (4.6 m) long, weighed 15,365 lb (6,970 kg), and had a caliber of 20 in (50.8 cm). The average caliber was a good deal less than either of these but it was still an increase in size. The basilisk, for example, had a caliber of 8¾ in (22.2 cm) and the caliber of the culverin measured up to 8½ in (21.6 cm). Guns such as these were powerful enough to batter down castles and reduce the walls of fortified towns to ruins. This sort of destruction, which could be rapid, brought an end to conventional siege warfare. And with it, the mighty castle and the fortified city lost whatever remained of their invulnerability.

This was particularly true after 1460, when incendiary material was added to projectiles, making it easier to burn down castles or town gates, many of which were still made of wood. At sea, gunners used iron shot to develop their own version of assault by fire. After King Stefan Bathory of Poland reputedly gave the first demonstration in 1579, they began to use "hot shot" against wooden ships or onshore buildings. This involved heating a cast-iron shot until it glowed red and loading it into the ship's guns together with a thick wad of turf, to make sure that it did not ignite the propellant. The gun was fired and the hot shot, landing on an enemy's deck, could easily start a fire and engulf his ship in flames. As an alternative to the fireship, which was commonly used in sea battles to set an enemy vessel ablaze, the hot shot was much more accurate and, therefore, much more deadly.

Although it was not until the late 16th century that stand-off warfare at sea began to replace the grappling and boarding technique of fighting naval battles, there were some very effective predecessors to the actions of King Stefan Bathory and the English galleons which kept ships of the Spanish Armada at bay nine years later, in 1588. Guns were being used on board ship a great deal earlier to convince attackers with assault in mind that it was unwise to approach a galleon or other sailing ship too closely. In the mid-15th century, merchantmen or, indeed, any vessel with valuable cargo on board could be in danger from prowling pirates or from enemies in time of war. This was why it became common practice for sailing ships, which by the end of the 15th century dominated the sea lanes, to be equipped with the verso, a mounted swivel gun.

The bombard and the verso were relatively small, powerful, guns that were taken on board large sailing vessels and used to fight off attacks by galleys. The verso, a versatile lightweight swivel gun, was not a long-range weapon. Nevertheless, it was used to kill enemies attempting to get on board and bring down an attacker's rigging. The bombard, on the other hand, could create significant damage on galleys which were subject to several limitations when it came to firing guns. The galley was much smaller than a sailing ship and was "driven" by banks of oars, whereas their larger adversaries could rely on the wind to take them through the water. The galley could not mount heavy guns to fire broadsides since this would interfere with the rowers. The only place available was in the bow, but the bow was used for ramming and without the ability to ram, there was no chance of attackers getting on board a target ship. The bombard was a breech-loader and the first heavy gun to be used at sea. It was usually mounted on a bed of timber and, lacking any means of recoil, had to be tied down with ropes to secure it while firing. Later on, cast iron barrels permitted more powerful charges to be fired, recoil ability was provided, and bombards were fitted with guiding bars and wheels.

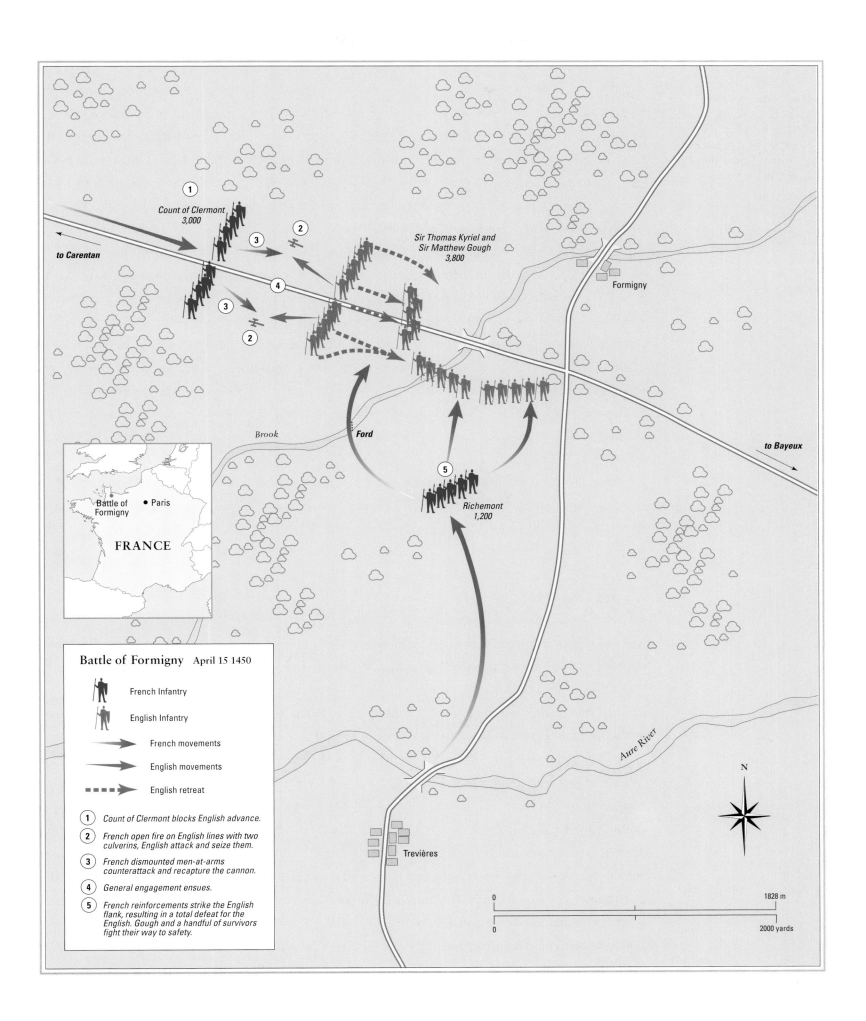

to Carentan

Count of Clermont
3,000

Sir Thomas Kyriel and
Sir Matthew Gough
3,800

Formigny

Brook

Ford

to Bayeux

Richemont
1,200

Battle of
Formigny

Paris

FRANCE

Aure River

N

Trevières

Battle of Formigny April 15 1450

French Infantry

English Infantry

French movements

English movements

English retreat

1. Count of Clermont blocks English advance.

2. French open fire on English lines with two culverins, English attack and seize them.

3. French dismounted men-at-arms counterattack and recapture the cannon.

4. General engagement ensues.

5. French reinforcements strike the English flank, resulting in a total defeat for the English. Gough and a handful of survivors fight their way to safety.

0   1828 m

0   2000 yards

HAND-HELD FIREARMS

HAND-HELD FIREARMS QUICKLY FOLLOWED THE INTRODUCTION OF ARTILLERY GUNS AND BOMBARDS AND, LIKE THEM, SOON BEGAN TO TRANSFORM THE CONDUCT OF WAR AND CONDITIONS ON THE BATTLEFIELD. EVENTUALLY, THEY REPLACED WEAPONRY OF WAR THAT HAD BEEN USED FOR CENTURIES.

The Chinese first described incendiary devices in a manuscript dated 1040AD. Some two centuries later, a sculpture was discovered in Sichuan, western China, depicting a soldier wielding a gun. This, it is believed, placed the first known use of firearms in China in the 12th century AD, an idea backed up by a 13th century firearm found in Manchuria in the north-east of the country.

From China, it appears that knowledge of gunpowder and guns moved westward into the Muslim lands of the Middle East, including Persia, on to North Africa and from there into Moorish Spain and the rest of Europe.

The first example of guns in action in the Muslim world occurred when the Egyptian Mamelukes, a slave warrior caste, employed them against the invading Mongols at Ain Jalut in the valley of Jezreel, Palestine, on September 3, 1260. In this first known battle to feature explosives, the Mamelukes fired their hand cannons, or *midfa* in Arabic, to frighten the Mongols' horses and disrupt their cavalry. The tactic appears to have been successful, for the Mamelukes prevailed

Sixty-five years passed after Ain Jalut before hand-held firearms made their debut on a European battlefield, in around 1325. These early examples of small arms were miniature versions of artillery cannons attached to a long stick and were sometimes called hand bombards, they were not particularly efficient and had to be leaned against a wall in order to fire them. Alternatively, they became two-man weapons, with one soldier holding the cannons and another igniting the charge. The introduction of the slow-burning match in around 1400 made firing the hand bombard easier but also more dangerous. The bombard was loaded with gunpowder, the match was lit and allowed to smolder over the touch-hole.

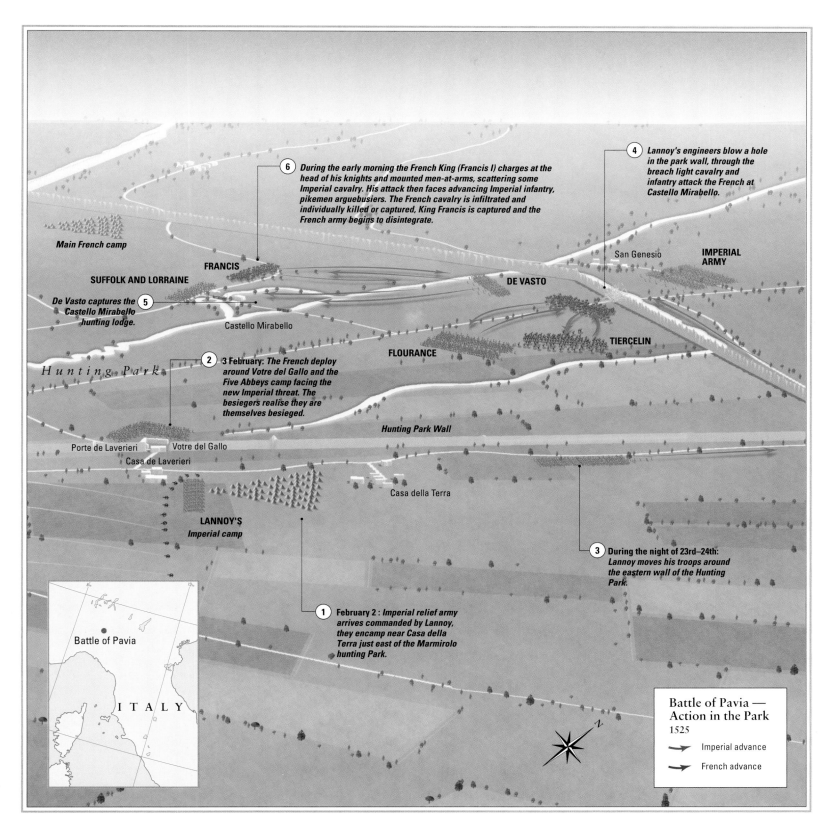

6 During the early morning the French King (Francis I) charges at the head of his knights and mounted men-at-arms, scattering some Imperial cavalry. His attack then faces advancing Imperial infantry, pikemen arguebusiers. The French cavalry is infiltrated and individually killed or captured, King Francis is captured and the French army begins to disintegrate.

4 Lannoy's engineers blow a hole in the park wall, through the breach light cavalry and infantry attack the French at Castello Mirabello.

Main French camp

FRANCIS

SUFFOLK AND LORRAINE

San Genesio

IMPERIAL ARMY

DE VASTO

5 De Vasto captures the Castello Mirabello hunting lodge.

Castello Mirabello

TIERCELIN

Hunting Park

FLOURANCE

2 3 February: The French deploy around Votre del Gallo and the Five Abbeys camp facing the new Imperial threat. The besiegers realise they are themselves besieged.

Hunting Park Wall

Porte de Laverieri

Votre del Gallo

Casa de Laverieri

Casa della Terra

LANNOY'S
Imperial camp

3 During the night of 23rd–24th: Lannoy moves his troops around the eastern wall of the Hunting Park.

Battle of Pavia

ITALY

1 February 2 : Imperial relief army arrives commanded by Lannoy, they encamp near Casa della Terra just east of the Marmirolo hunting Park.

Battle of Pavia — Action in the Park
1525

→ Imperial advance

→ French advance

Meanwhile, the gunner took cover so that when the powder exploded and the gun fired, he had a chance of escaping injury. The successor to the hand bombard was the arquebus, a firearm whose name derived from the Dutch *haakbus*, meaning "hook gun" which was possibly a reference to its slightly bent butt. The arquebus, which first appeared in Europe in the 15th century and remained in use until the 17th, was much easier to handle than the hand bombard. It was a light, smoothbore muzzle-loading

Battle of Pavia, 1525. The Spanish Army confronted the French Army of Francis I. The French cavalry were driven back, its infantry overwhelmed and Francis was captured. Pavia ended French influence in Italy.

matchlock firearm which prefigured the rifle and other long-barrelled hand guns and featured a trigger much like that of a crossbow. The arquebus was, however, so slow to load that arquebusiers could often manage little more than one volley in 15 minutes.

A dramatic success for the arquebus came at the Battle of Pavia in 1525. An Imperial army led by Charles de Lannoy launched a surprise dawn attack on the army of King Francis I of France which was laying siege to the city of Pavia. The attack began as a conventional asssault using cavalry, artillery, pikemen, and arquebusiers in combination. However, the broken nature of the ground and confusion caused by the poor light soon caused the battle to break up into a number of separate engagements. At about 8am a large body of Imperial arquebusiers pinned a group of French cavalry against dense woodlands and mowed them down with concentrated fire. One of the French horsemen to have his mount shot dead under him and to be captured was Francis himself. With their king lost, the French army broke up and fled. The arquebusier officer responsible, Alonsa Pita da Veiga, was raised to the nobility and granted extensive estates by the Emperor Charles V.

Apart from being slow to load, the low velocity of the hand-held arquebus meant that it was unable to pierce plate armor at anything but close range. This problem was so common that armorers would test the protection afforded by armor by firing an arquebus or pistol at it at various ranges. The dent in the armor where a bullet had failed to penetrate was marked by an engraved circle to prove the success of the test. However, by the early 17th century, the damage an arquebus could do at close range and the power of the English longbow to shoot arrows at speeds that could pierce right through armor even from a distance finally did away with the use of plate armor among the infantry.

Despite drawbacks, though, the arquebus was used in many places across the world. The Divine Engine Division, one of three military elites formed by the Ming Dynasty, which ruled China between 1368 and 1644, was the only one armed with guns. In the late 14th century, the Division's cavalry and arquebusiers combined to drive the Mongols out of China and in 1387, a triple line of arquebusiers fighting rebels overcame a force of elephants: two lines of arquebusiers reloaded their guns while the other shot at the rebels and each took its place in turn in the firing line. It was the nearest they could get to continuous fire. In addition to the arquebus, the Division used fire lances, which comprised spears equipped with tubes filled with black gunpowder, and fire arrows, which were the first rockets used in war. The arrows were fitted into a bamboo stand that was used as a launch pad to fire salvoes, as many as 1,000 of them at a time.

In Europe, the arquebus was first used in large quantities in the 15th century by the army of King Matthias Corvinus of Hungary in which one third of his men were arquebusiers. The Spanish and Portuguese conquistadores who conquered South and Central America in the 16th century terrified their native opponents with their use of this fearsomely noisy weapon.

Later on in the 16th century, during the reign of the Safavid Shah Esma'il II in Persia, the arquebus was added to a range of weapons, all of which were in use in battle when Vincenzo di Alessandri, a Venetian envoy, reported in 1572 that the Persians "used for arms, swords, lances, arquebuses which all the soldiers carry and use ...The barrels of the arquebuses are generally six spans long (4½ ft (1.3 m)) and carry a ball little less than 3 oz (85 g) in weight. They use them with such facility that it does not hinder them (from) drawing their bows nor handling their swords, keeping the latter hung at their saddle bows

Opposite page: These infantry formations date from the Renaissance (c.1450-1600) and involve the early use of the "shot-and -pike" technique. In both formations, the pikemen greatly outnumber the musketeer, since the latter needed some time to prepare their weapons for firing.

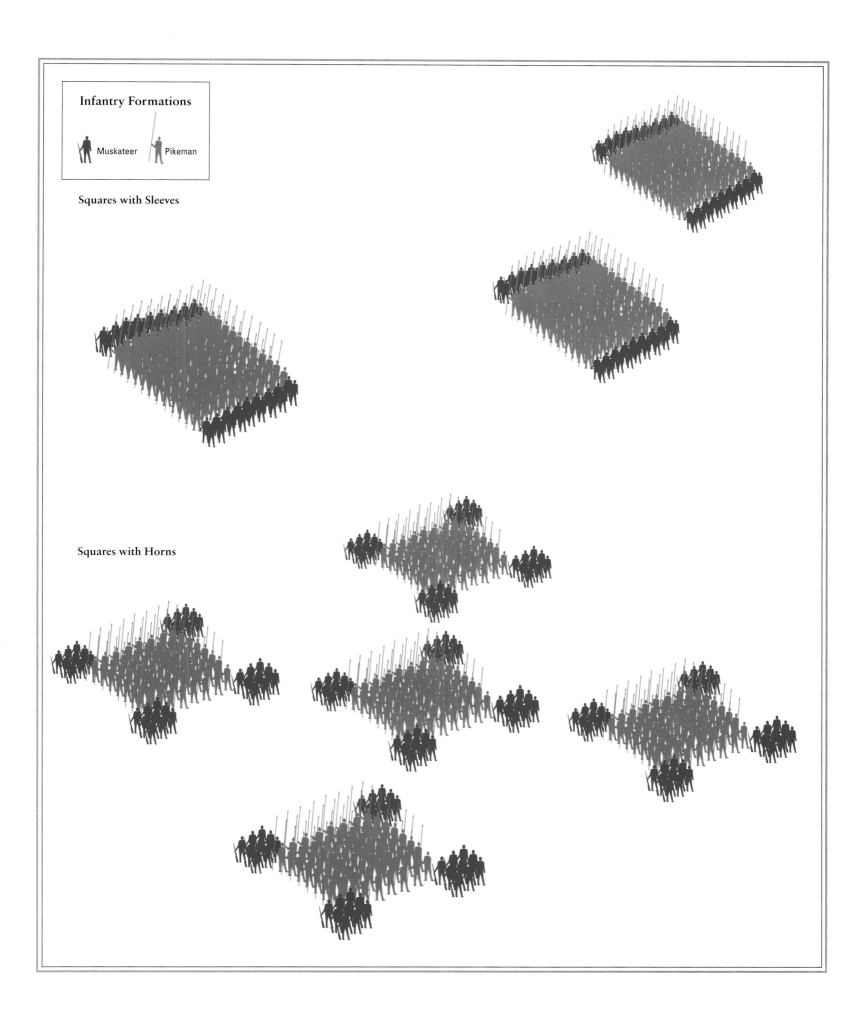

Infantry Formations

Muskateer   Pikeman

Squares with Sleeves

Squares with Horns

till occasion requires them. The arquebus is then put away behind the back so that one weapon does not impede the use of the other."

It is possible, though, that instead of an arquebus, di Alessandri was describing a musket, which had a significantly longer barrel, measuring up to some 5ft (1.5 m). In Europe, the musket had been around for several decades by 1572, and for even longer in Asia, where it was in use in China in the 14th century. The Janissaries, the renowned infantry that comprised the first standing army of the Ottoman Turkish Empire, were equipped with muskets in the mid-15th century and the weapons were being used in India in the early 16th century, around the time they were also introduced in Spain.

In 1543, traders from Portugal reached Japan. They brought with them a number of matchlock muskets that soon revolutionized the persistent warfare that was virtually a way of life for the samurai warrior caste, their immensely powerful leaders, the *daimyos* (landowner rulers), and the *shoguns* (warlords). Although the Japanese appeared to be technologically backward compared to Europeans, they learned fast and possessed a great deal of ingenuity. For example, they invented a device that enabled the matchlocks to fire in rainy weather: this was an important advance considering the perennially wet climate that prevails in Japan and interfered with the musket's ignition system.

By the 1560s, the Japanese had a thriving arms industry and an organized infrastructure, with officials appointed to oversee and monitor the manufacture of guns. Copies of the muskets, called Tanegashima by the Japanese after the island near Kyushu where the Portuguese had first landed, were being produced in quantity. The Tanegashima differed from European designs by the absence of a shoulder-stock. Instead, the butt was placed against the cheek while the hands applied pressure — the left hand forwards, the right hand rearwards — to steady the gun for firing. The Tanegashima was still in use in the second half of the 19th century, when Japan was forced to modernize in line with the modern world, a process that included the formation of a modern army and navy.

The powerful 16th century *daimyo*, Oda Nobunaga, took the Japanese acquisition of firearms a step further when he devised a system of separating the functions of loading and firing muskets in battle: he assigned three guns to each musketeer, who fired at the enemy while his loaders primed the other two firearms. There was, therefore, never a time when a musketeer did not have a ready-to-fire weapon to hand. In 1575, Nobunaga confirmed the effectiveness of his system at the battle of Nagashino castle where his musketeers defeated the cavalry of the rebel samurai Takeda Katsuyori. In 1600, when a Japanese army invaded Korea their ranks included some 20,000 musketeers.

In Europe, the smoothbore musket started out as a weapon that aimed to pierce body armor, a function the arquebus had singularly failed to perform at more than a few yards' distance. In response, armor became thicker, weighing around 55 lb (25 kg), a rise of more than 40 percent over its average weight a century earlier. Ironically, the musket itself had to be heavier in order to use the sort of shot that could penetrate the thicker armor, and required a forked rest before it could be fired.

Initially, the musketeers themselves wore armor, which slowed their reactions and reduced their agility. Eventually, in the mid-17th century, both weapons and armor were downsized and not long afterwards the musketeers became the first infantry to discard armour altogether. The musket barrel was reduced to 3ft (0.9 m) and the forked rest became redundant. With this, warfare became faster and infantry became more nimble. There was now no place for the armored knight on horseback and with muskets now lighter and easier to carry, the arquebus and the pikemen who had once protected arquebusiers from enemy cavalry also lost their place in the order of battle.

The musket, however, was going to have a very long history. Although it remained a smoothbore weapon for most of its time in action, its firing mechanism went through several evolutions. In the matchlock musket, a lighted match was lowered into the flashpan to prime the gunpowder. This was a distinctly dangerous procedure which was improved with the addition of a serpentine, a small curved lever which held a slow-burning match at one end. One pulled the lever and the smoldering match was lowered into the flashpan where it ignited the powder. The matchlock was replaced in around 1500 by the wheel lock musket, which used a rotating steel wheel to ignite the powder.

The next two mechanisms for firing a musket, the snaplock and the snaphance, employed the shower of sparks method. In the snaplock, the sparks to ignite the musket's propellant were produced by a firing lever equipped with a flint that was designed to strike a piece of hard steel. The snaphance, which appeared in the mid-16th century, used the same means to produce sparks, although the flint involved was secured in a clamp at the end of the lever. The snaphance was equipped with a trigger which, when pulled, sprang forward to hit a curved hardened steel plate — colloquially known as a "frizzen". This produced a shower of white-hot steel shavings which fell into the flashpan.

The last method of firing a smoothbore musket was the flintlock, which made its appearance in around 1630. The flintlock musket also used the shower of sparks method, but in much greater safety as far as the musketeer was concerned. The musket had a hammer with a safety lock that was released when the hammer was moved from half-cock to full-cock. When the trigger was pulled, the flint held by the hammer struck the frizzen and the resultant sparks hit the gunpowder held in the flashpan and the musket fired.

Because of the bullet's smaller size, the smoothbore musket had to be rifled by giving the bore spiral grooves. These enabled the bullet, when fired, to spin towards its target, so increasing its accuracy and its range: with rifling the musket could hit its target at a range of 1,500 ft (457 m), compared to the 900 ft (274 m) of the smoothbore musket. Now known as 'rifled muskets' and equipped with bayonets, they were extensively used in the American Civil War of 1861-1865. But shortly afterwards, in 1868, they were replaced by the breech-loading Springfield rifle — the so-called Trapdoor Springfield — and the musket's more than 300 years of service in warfare came to an end.

Flintlock pistols were so called because the lock uses a flint to strike sparks into the priming pan when the trigger is pulled. A small amount of gunpowder in this pan is ignited, which in turn ignites the main gunpowder charge in the barrel and fires the lead ball. Often the priming charge would burn, but fail to ignite the main charge —which is where we get the expression "a flash in the pan". Powder horns were used with 18th-century muskets, but were rendered obsolete by the development of breech the development of breech loading firearms. loading firearms.

SPANISH SUPREMACY IN THE 16TH CENTURY

DURING THE 16TH CENTURY, SPAIN WAS THE GREATEST MILITARY POWER IN EUROPE. IT NEEDED TO BE, FOR IT WAS ALSO THE COUNTRY MOST FREQUENTLY AT WAR.

Opposite page: Spain's long struggle to control and protect the Mediterranean, or at least its western half, was regarded as important as its campaigns to hold on to territories in northern Europe. The Ottoman empire and its allies proved implacable enemies, capable of raiding the coasts of Spain itself.

Peace was at a premium in Spain; for a large part of the 16th century, its forces were at war — fending off raids by the Barbary pirates on coastal villages and towns, tussling with France in Italy over control of the Kingdom of Naples and Sicily, invading Ireland with a view to obtaining a springboard to attack England, conquering an empire in Central and South America, and fighting rebels in the Spanish Netherlands (the present-day Belgium and the Netherlands).

With such extensive military commitments, Spain was unique in having a standing army, the only one in Europe. This status afforded Spanish soldiers better training and greater discipline than was possible for the foreign civilian militias that other countries called up only for specific wars or battles.

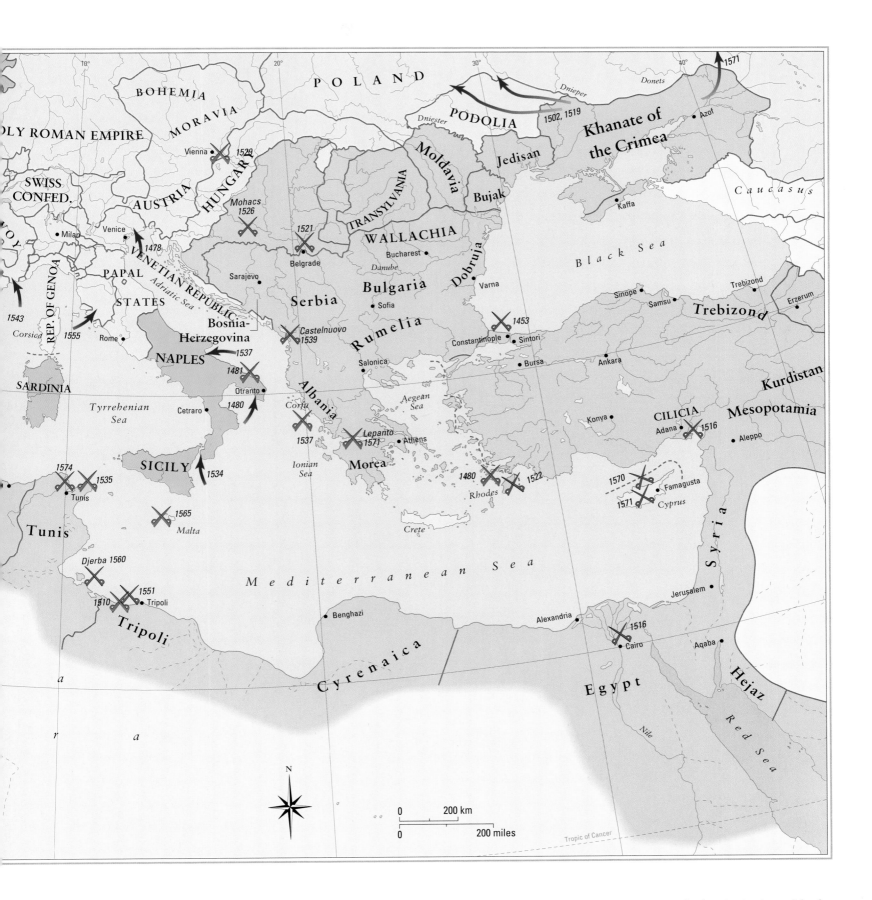

Spanish Christians entered the 16th century fresh from completing the *Reconquista*, the reconquest of Islamic Spain, with the capture in 1492 of Granada, the last state ruled by the Muslim Moors. This final victory was the climax of nearly 800 years of effort: the *Reconquista* had begun very soon after the Moorish conquest of AD711. The Spaniards now emerged from those years with a new self-confidence, a sense of unity, and a deep respect for the fighting valor on the battlefield, and the dedication of their armies.

The hero of the hour was El Gran Capitan, the Great Captain, General Gonzalo Fernandez de Cordoba, who led the Christian forces in virtually every type of action known in warfare: sieges, defenses of cities and castles, skirmishes, ambushes, and even guerrilla warfare in the mountains. De Cordoba was to go on to be one of the architects of the Spanish standing army. The calibers and mechanisms of small arms were standardized, making the supply of ammunition and the business of training much more simple, straightforward and effective, and the infantry he trained was almost invincible on the battlefields of 16th-and early 17th-century Europe. De Cordoba also derived valuable lessons from his experience of campaigning in Italy at the start of the 16th century, when Spain was embroiled with France in a contest over Naples and Sicily. He perceived that they were able to shelter in entrenchments and that a force of arquebusiers could hold extensive lines of defense even against greatly superior forces. Furthermore, he

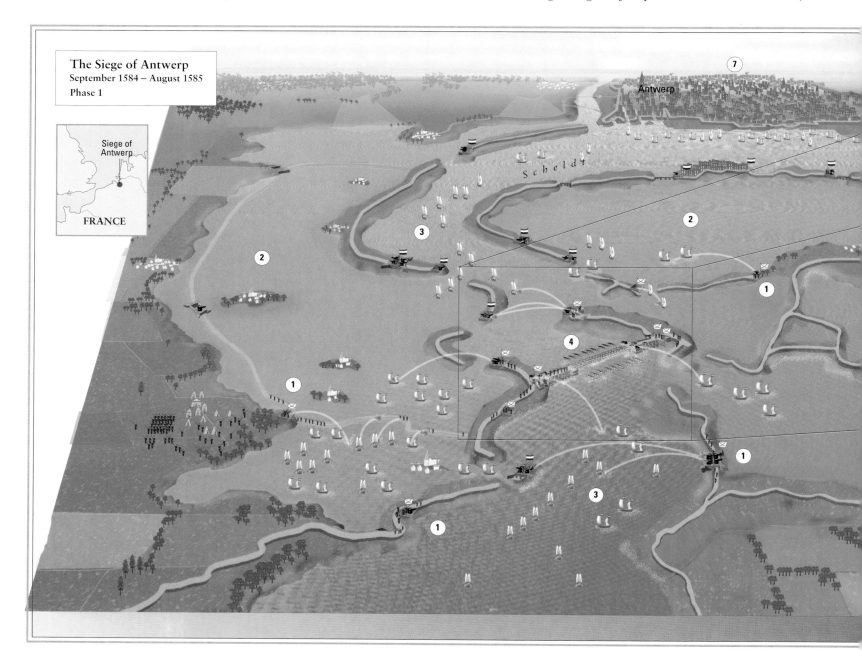

The Siege of Antwerp
September 1584 – August 1585
Phase 1

Siege of Antwerp

FRANCE

realized that with their slow rate of fire and lengthy time to reload, arquebusiers in the open had to be protected from enemy fire. De Cordoba's solution to the exposure of the arquebusiers to enemy fire was to use a line of pikemen to screen the arquebusiers from attack and to use shock action to see off any enemy who came too close. An impressive demonstration of de Cordoba's new tactic took place at the Battle of Cerignola on April 26 1503.

During the fighting, the Spanish artillery met with disaster when its powder supply exploded, rendering its big guns useless. After this, it was left to the Spanish arquebusiers, positioned in a ditch surrounded by a palisade of stakes and supported by pikemen, to let fly with a shower of shot, mowing down dozens of French cavalrymen. The French commander, Louis d'Orléans, Duc de Nemours, was among the dead. Cerignola has been counted as the first time that a battle was won by small-arms fire alone. After this encounter the pike-and-shot tactic featured in battles fought by several European armies until it was eventually replaced by the flintlock musket, with its bayonet, at the end of the 17th century.

The siege of Antwerp (1584–1585) occurred during the Eighty Years' War when the Dutch fought for independence from Spain. However, the Dutch failed to destroy the forts supplying the Spanish army, and were forced to surrender on August 7 1585.

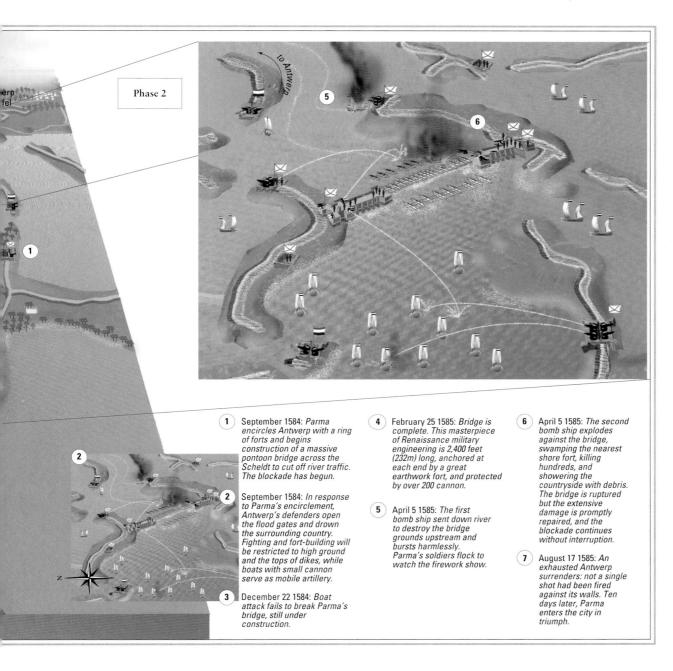

Phase 2

1. September 1584: *Parma encircles Antwerp with a ring of forts and begins construction of a massive pontoon bridge across the Scheldt to cut off river traffic. The blockade has begun.*

2. September 1584: *In response to Parma's encirclement, Antwerp's defenders open the flood gates and drown the surrounding country. Fighting and fort-building will be restricted to high ground and the tops of dikes, while boats with small cannon serve as mobile artillery.*

3. December 22 1584: *Boat attack fails to break Parma's bridge, still under construction.*

4. February 25 1585: *Bridge is complete. This masterpiece of Renaissance military engineering is 2,400 feet (232m) long, anchored at each end by a great earthwork fort, and protected by over 200 cannon.*

5. April 5 1585: *The first bomb ship sent down river to destroy the bridge grounds upstream and bursts harmlessly. Parma's soldiers flock to watch the firework show.*

6. April 5 1585: *The second bomb ship explodes against the bridge, swamping the nearest shore fort, killing hundreds, and showering the countryside with debris. The bridge is ruptured but the extensive damage is promptly repaired, and the blockade continues without interruption.*

7. August 17 1585: *An exhausted Antwerp surrenders: not a single shot had been fired against its walls. Ten days later, Parma enters the city in triumph.*

By the 16th century, it was clear that gunpower did a great deal more than simply introduce new and deadlier weapons to warfare: it had also made obsolete the organization of the battlefield as it had been known for the past three or four centuries. The combat formation of medieval times was still being employed on the battlefield and was proving to be very vulnerable to both hand-held firearms and artillery.

Once again, the Spanish took the lead in solving the problem of organizing a combat formation able to withstand gunpowder weaponry. In 1505, King Ferdinand II of Aragon ordered the creation of 20 *colunellas* (columns) of between 1,000 and 1,250 pikemen, halberdiers, arquebusiers, and swordsmen. The *colunella* was the ancestor of the modern battalion and regiment, and was commanded by a *cabo de colunella* (chief of the column), or colonel, an officer whose rank still features in armies today. The advantage of the *colunella* was that it combined different types of weaponry on-site so that it was able to deal with any type of emergency that might arise during a battle. The *counella* has been compared to the ancient Roman cohort, in which raw recruits, trained troops, and veterans fought side by side or in which cavalry and infantry fought together. By 1535, the *colunella* had grown into the *tercio*, which was finally standardized into three columns containing a total of some 3,000 men. Its name, meaning "one-third", is thought to indicate that the *tercio* contained one-third of the infantry in a typical Spanish army. But by this time, the swordsmen and halberdiers had been phased out and the *tercio* consisted of the original "pike-and-shot" personnel, the pikemen and the arquebusiers.

By the end of the 16th century, the power, range, and most important kinds of artillery were essentially fixed and became the standard model for the next 300 years. The major Spanish artillery fell into three types. The first was the culverin, a long-barrelled gun of 30 calibers (diameter of barrel) which had thick walls and was designed to fire at long range. The cannon was shorter and lighter than the culverin and was made to fire heavy projectiles over a shorter distance. The advantage of the cannon was that it possessed greater mobility than the culverin and it could still destroy its targets with the power of its shot. A third type of major artillery had a short barrel with thin walls and fired projectiles over an even shorter range. One design in this category was the *pedrero*, which was up to 15 calibers in length and, as its name indicated, fired stone projectiles — *pedrero* is Spanish for "stone quarry". The other category of *pedrero* was the very short 10-caliber mortar, which fired its projectiles in a high, curved trajectory.

The siege of Antwerp in the 1580s proved to be a masterclass in the use of the new types of artillery. The Spanish commander, the Duke of Parma, constructed a series of earth and timber forts mounting modern heavy guns and manned by experienced troops that between them blocked all road and river access to or from the city. So well were these forts constructed and positioned that after some desultory efforts, the Dutch gave up all hopes of attacking them and resorted to the use of floating mines to try to break the barrier of boats blocking the Scheldt. That barrier was also covered by Parma's guns and all efforts failed. Antwerp surrendered.

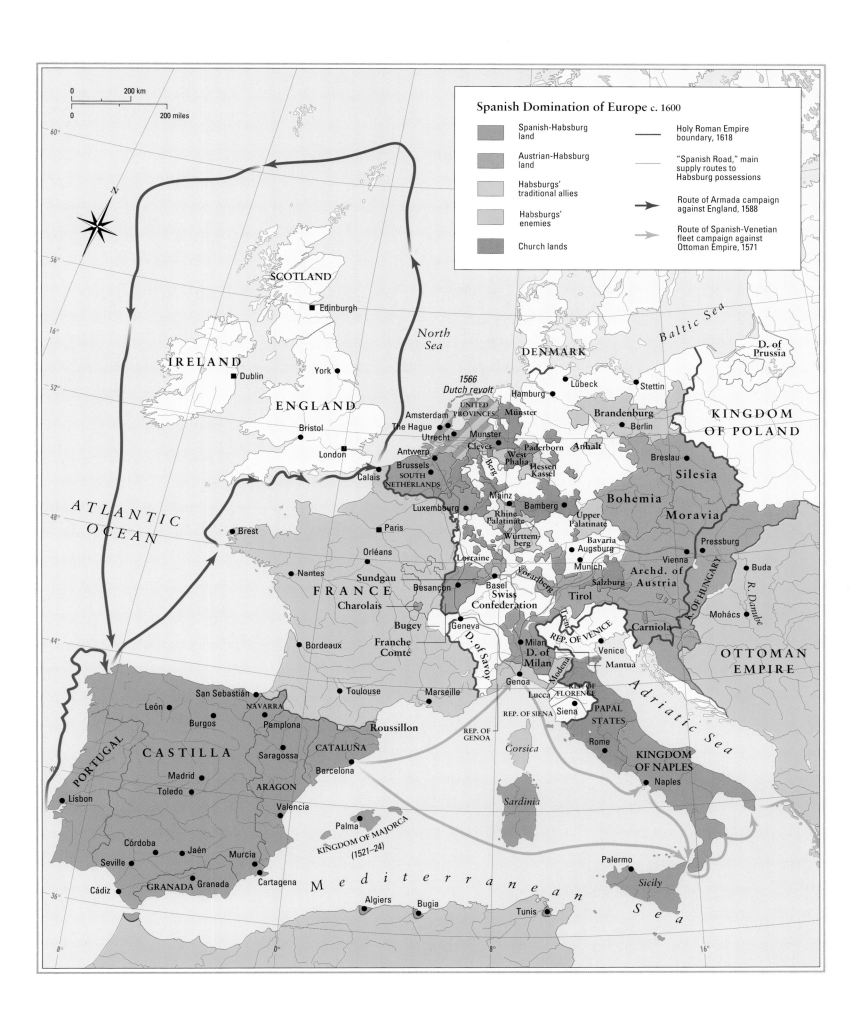

Spanish Domination of Europe c. 1600

- Spanish-Habsburg land
- Austrian-Habsburg land
- Habsburgs' traditional allies
- Habsburgs' enemies
- Church lands

— Holy Roman Empire boundary, 1618

— "Spanish Road," main supply routes to Habsburg possessions

→ Route of Armada campaign against England, 1588

→ Route of Spanish-Venetian fleet campaign against Ottoman Empire, 1571

0   200 km
0   200 miles

N

SCOTLAND
Edinburgh

IRELAND
Dublin

York

North Sea

DENMARK
Hamburg   Lübeck   Stettin

Baltic Sea

D. of Prussia

1566 Dutch revolt

UNITED PROVINCES
Amsterdam   Münster
The Hague
Utrecht   Munster
Antwerp   Cleves   Paderborn   Anhalt
Brussels   West Phalia   Hessen Kassel
SOUTH NETHERLANDS   Berg
Calais   Mainz   Bamberg   Bohemia

Brandenburg   Berlin

KINGDOM OF POLAND

Breslau   Silesia   Moravia

ENGLAND
Bristol
London

ATLANTIC OCEAN

Luxembourg   Rhine Palatinate   Upper Palatinate
Brest   Paris   Württemberg   Bavaria   Augsburg
Orléans   Lorraine   Vorarlberg   Munich   Archd. of Austria   Pressburg   Buda
Nantes   Basel   Salzburg   Tirol   Vienna   R. OF HUNGARY   R. Danube
FRANCE   Sundgau   Besançon   Swiss Confederation   Trent   Mohács
Charolais   Geneva   REP. OF VENICE   Carniola
Bugey   D. of Savoy   Milan   Venice   OTTOMAN EMPIRE
Bordeaux   Franche Comté   D. of Milan   Mantua
Genoa   Modena   Adriatic Sea
San Sebastián   Toulouse   Marseille   REP. OF FLORENCE
León   NAVARRA   Lucca   Corsica   PAPAL STATES
Burgos   Pamplona   Roussillon   REP. OF GENOA   Siena   Rome   KINGDOM OF NAPLES
CASTILLA   Saragossa   CATALUÑA   REP. OF SIENA
Madrid   ARAGON   Barcelona   Sardinia   Naples
Toledo   Valencia
PORTUGAL   Palma   KINGDOM OF MAJORCA (1521–24)
Lisbon   Córdoba   Jaén   Murcia   Palermo
Seville   GRANADA   Granada   Cartagena   Sicily
Cádiz   Algiers   Bugia   Tunis

Mediterranean Sea

THE SPANISH CONQUEST OF THE NEW WORLD

THE SPANISH CONQUEST OF THE NEW WORLD WAS THE FIRST VENTURE IN MODERN TIMES DESIGNED TO CREATE A FAR-FLUNG OVERSEAS EMPIRE. IT ALSO SAW THE FIRST ENCOUNTERS BETWEEN MILITARILY ADVANCED EUROPEANS WITH SOPHISTICATED WEAPONS AND PRIMITIVELY ARMED "NATIVE" FORCES.

Opposite page: Defeat by Hernán Cortés, his conquistadors, and their Mexican allies saw the downfall of the coast-to-coast Aztec Empire after the Aztec capital, Tenochtitlan was besieged, bombarded from specially built ships on Lake Texcoco, and captured in 1521.

Temple of the Warriors at the Mayan religious center at Chichen Itza in the Yucatan peninsula.

The Spanish were the first Europeans to acquire an extensive overseas empire, with territories in Italy, the Netherlands, west and north-west Africa, the Philippine islands, the Caribbean and, most prestigious of all, Central and South America. The "jewels in the crown" of the Spanish Empire were Aztec Mexico (Anahuac) and Inca Peru (Tahuantinsuyu), the "land of the four quarters". Here the Spanish encountered two extraordinary "native" empires that astounded them with their sophisticated civilization and advanced skills in astronomy, architecture and mathematics but had no writing system or wheeled vehicles, and confronted them in battle with primitive weapons not seen in Europe for centuries.

The Aztecs and the Incas had the skills to construct magnificent cities such as Tenochtitlan in the Valley of Mexico or Cuzco in the high Andes of Peru; and in Peru, the Incas built a network of roads that spanned great mountains and deep valleys. Both were aggressive conquerers in their own right, taking large swathes of territory for their own empires. The Aztecs ruled tribes and territory from the Atlantic to the Pacific coasts of Central America and the Inca Empire covered an area of some 1,250,000 miles² (3,237,500 km²) stretching from Ecuador in the north through Peru and Bolivia to central Chile in the south. But neither the Aztecs nor the Incas nor any other local tribe used metal attack weapons, although the Incas made body

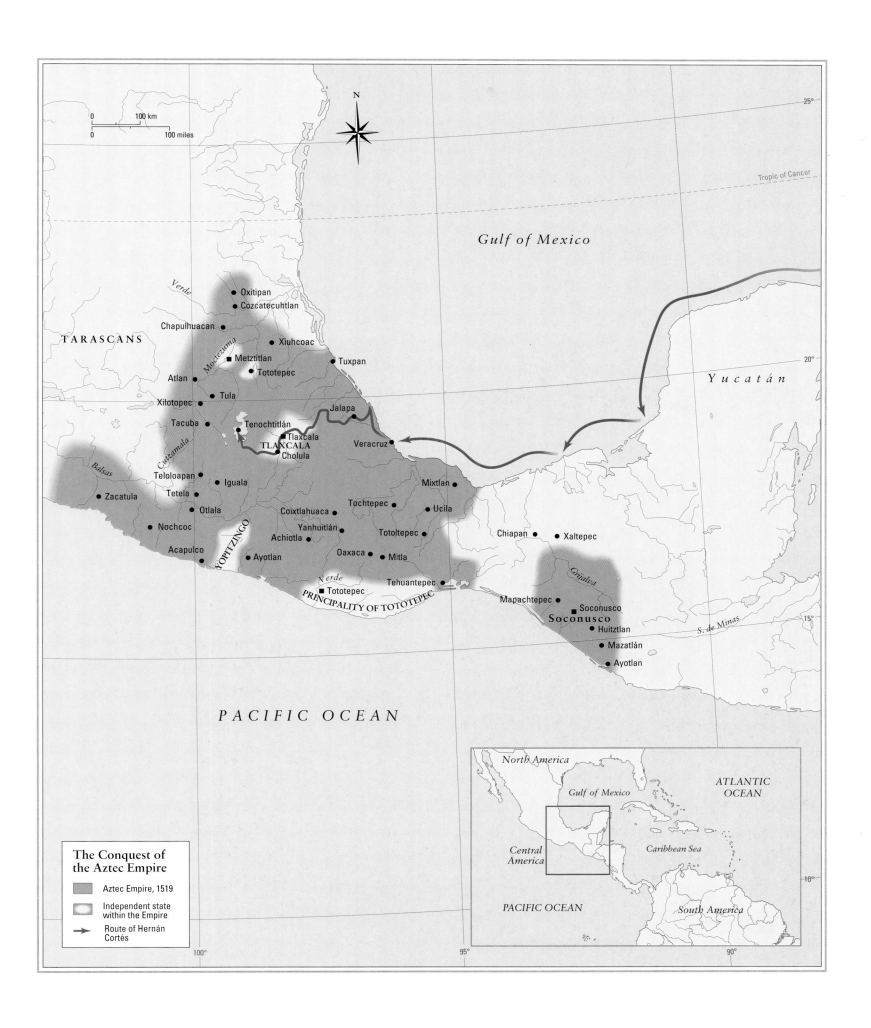

25°

Tropic of Cancer

Gulf of Mexico

Verde

Oxitipan

Cozcatecuhtlan

Chapulhuacan

TARASCANS

Xiuhcoac

Moctezuma

■ Metztitlan

Tuxpan

Tototepec

Y u c a t á n

Atlan

Xilotepec

Tula

20°

Jalapa

Tacuba

Tenochtitlán

Tlaxcala

Cutzamala

TLAXCALA

Veracruz

Cholula

Balsas

Teloloapan

Iguala

Mixtlan

Zacatula

Tetela

Tochtepec

Otlala

Coixtlahuaca

Ucila

Chiapan

Xaltepec

Nochcoc

Yanhuitlán

Tototepec

Achiotla

Grijalva

Acapulco

Ayotlan

Oaxaca

Mitla

YOPITZINGO

Verde

Tehuantepec

Mapachtepec

■ Soconusco

■ Tototepec

Soconusco

PRINCIPALITY OF TOTOTEPEC

Huiztlan

S. de Minas

15°

Mazatlán

Ayotlan

PACIFIC OCEAN

North America

Gulf of Mexico

ATLANTIC OCEAN

Central America

Caribbean Sea

PACIFIC OCEAN

South America

10°

The Conquest of the Aztec Empire

Aztec Empire, 1519

Independent state within the Empire

Route of Hernán Cortés

100°

95°

90°

armor from copper. They knew nothing of cavalry in warfare or of explosives and guns. There was too a difference in the command structure of their armies: their generals were regarded as so indispensable to the prosecution of war that if they were killed or captured, the morale of their forces and their ability to fight on fell apart.

The Spanish, by contrast, were typical Renaissance men: outspoken, individualistic, and enterprising, well able to take over from a fallen commander if need be. These military and psychological differences help to explain how a handful of conquistadores subjugated an estimated 25 million Aztecs and almost 13 million Incas and exploited their territory for their own purposes. These purposes were to find gold, silver, and other riches and to convert the heathen natives to Christianity, especially those, like the Aztecs, who practiced human sacrifice. To achieve these goals, Hernán Cortés and Francisco Pizarro seized and imprisoned, respectively, the Tlatoani (Great Speaker) Motecuhzoma Xocoyotzin in Mexico, better known as Montezuma, and the Sapa Inca Atahualpa in Peru. By this means, the head was severed from the body politic and the Spanish seized authority — and unquestioning obedience to authority was the centerpiece of life in Mexico and Peru.

Pizarro arrived in Peru in 1532 with only 106 foot-soldiers and 62 horsemen. In 1519, Hernan Cortes had come ashore in Mexico with 32 crossbowmen, 13 musketeers, and 463 other soldiers, including cavalrymen, and 109 seamen. Two years later, at the Siege of Tenochtitlan, which sealed the fate of the Aztec capital, Cortès' forces consisted of 86 cavalry, 118 crossbowmen and arquebusiers, 700 foot-soldiers, and some 45,000 "native" allies, who were only too pleased to help the Spanish vanquish their oppressive

Hernán Cortés de Monroy y Pizarro (1485–1547), the Spanish conquistador who led the expedition that caused the fall of the Aztec empire.

Aztec masters. It was the cavalry that made the greatest impact on the Aztec defenders, as the Spanish soldier-chronicler Bernal Diaz del Castillo recounted: "When the people of the city saw that there were no horsemen with us, they turned ... on the Spaniards and drove them from the towers and courts. The Spaniards ... would have suffered great loss had it not pleased God that at that moment, three horsemen should arrive ... the horsemen killed some of [the enemy] and we regained the courts and enclosure."

The Aztecs who first saw the Spanish soldiers' horses in Mexico concluded that horse and rider must all be one animal, and their terror at this strange sight grew in magnitude when the Spanish gave a demonstration of their artillery. A contemporary account describes the scene: "The great lombard gun expelled the shot which thundered as it went off", the Aztecs reported back to Montezuma.

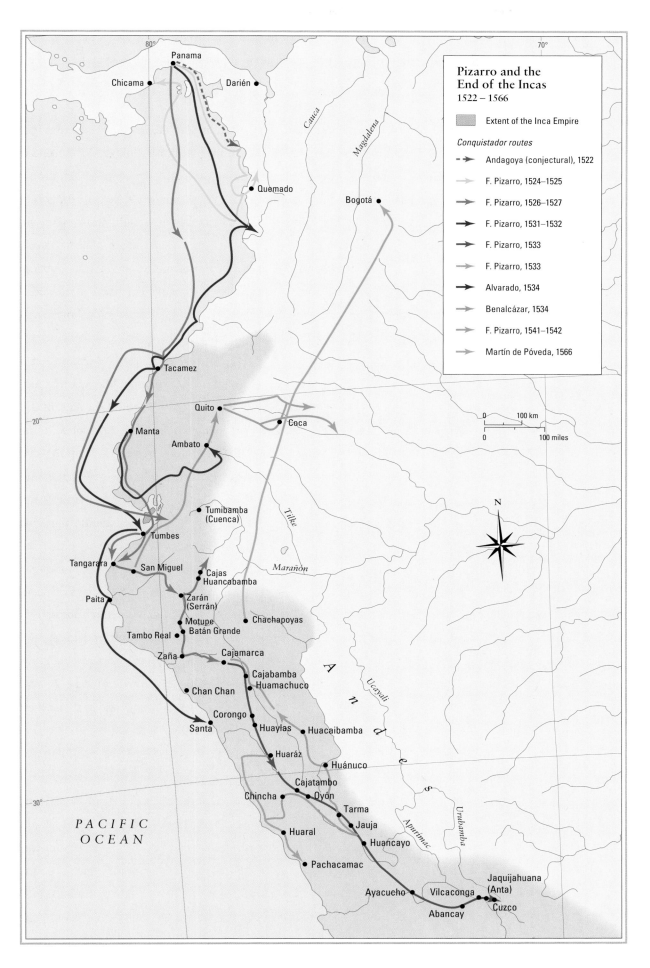

Pizarro and the End of the Incas
1522 – 1566

Extent of the Inca Empire

Conquistador routes

- - → Andagoya (conjectural), 1522

→ F. Pizarro, 1524–1525

→ F. Pizarro, 1526–1527

→ F. Pizarro, 1531–1532

→ F. Pizarro, 1533

→ F. Pizarro, 1533

→ Alvarado, 1534

→ Benalcázar, 1534

→ F. Pizarro, 1541–1542

→ Martín de Póveda, 1566

Left In 1532, Francisco Pizarro and a few hundred Spanish conquistadores climbed the Andes Mountains to reach the Inca Empire of Tahuantinsuyu (Land of the Four Quarters). Subsequently, they succeeded in overrunning Tahuantinsuyu by capturing and manipulating its ruler, Atahualpa.

"Something like a stone came out of it in a shower of fire and sparks ... and the shot, which struck a mountain, knocked it to pieces."

The arquebus and the lighter harquebus, or carbine, used by the Spanish cavalry were just as much a frightening mystery to the Aztecs. But they also encountered another mighty Spanish weapon to which they had no real equivalent: the Toledo steel sword (*falcata*), which possessed a superlative hardness owing to its carbon and soft-steel content, forged at very high temperatures, and its iron interior. These swords were of great antiquity, dating from around the 5th century BC, when they were first produced by Iberian swordsmiths. Three centuries later, during the second Punic War with Rome, the Carthaginian general Hannibal armed his soldiers with Toledo swords and got the better of Roman legions, which afterward adopted the sword themselves.

The weapons the Aztecs and the Incas brought to the battlefield were fearsome and damaging but, unlike the armory of the Spanish, not ultimately decisive. The contest was always unequal; and the armed struggle between two civilizations — one scientifically advanced, the other disciplined and courageous but lagging far behind in social, military and political development — had only one outcome: the Spanish conquest of Central and South America.

Inca armies were usually divided into three sections, each of which specialized in one type of weapon. The first was the slingshot, with which expert Inca warriors were able to hit a moving enemy at a distance of up to 210 ft (64 m). Waves of shot were launched at opponents, showering them with deadly downpours of stones. The *boleadora* or *bolas* (see pages 30-31), used by both the Aztecs and the Incas, was a very effective distance weapon designed to trip up opponents by entangling their legs. After these preliminaries, the main attack would be launched, consisting of close-quarter fighting using spears as well as axes and truncheons in which sharp pieces of copper or stone were embedded. Defensive weaponry consisted of copper or wooden shields, copper, leather and cotton armor for the upper body, and more copper to protect the arms and legs. Inca helmets were made of wood or copper decorated with feathers.

Arguably the most deadly of the Aztec weapons was the *maquahuitl*, a close-quarter weapon which could be used both one- and two-handed. The *maquahuitl* was usually made of oak, and had a blade around 4 in (10 cm) wide and 4 ft (1.22 m) long. Pieces of obsidian (volcanic glass) were embedded in its edges and made it so sharp that it was said to be capable of cutting off a horse's head with one blow. The *huitzauhqui,* a wooden club, also featured inlaid obsidian blades. The Aztec *quauhololli*, a wooden mace with a ball at one end, was used for smashing and crushing; other maces had embedded stone pieces. Like the Incas, the Aztecs used spears, notably the *tepoztopilli.* This was more than 7ft (2.13 m) long and had a 12 in (30.5 cm) wide composite stone blade made up of smaller blades. Aztec spears were often thrown over a distance with the help of a special launcher called an *atlatl* (see image page 33). Bows and arrows — *tlahuitolli* and *yaomime* — were also in the Aztec armory, in addition to slings using specially shaped stones which, it was said, could be shot over more than 650 ft (198 m).

For defense, Aztec warriors carried the *cuauhchimalli,* or wooden shield, or other shields made from maize cane called *otlachimalli.* For body protection, the warriors wore quilted cotton armor called *ichcahuipilli,* up to 4 cm thick and was capable of resisting obsidian weapons and spears. Some of the elite Aztec aristocracy would carry an extra layer in the *ehuatl,* which they wore over their armor.

Opposite page: Spain created the first extensive European empire overseas. Moving out from their initial conquests in Mexico and Peru, the Spaniards extended their power over parts of the present day United States, Canada, Central America, and half the land area of South America

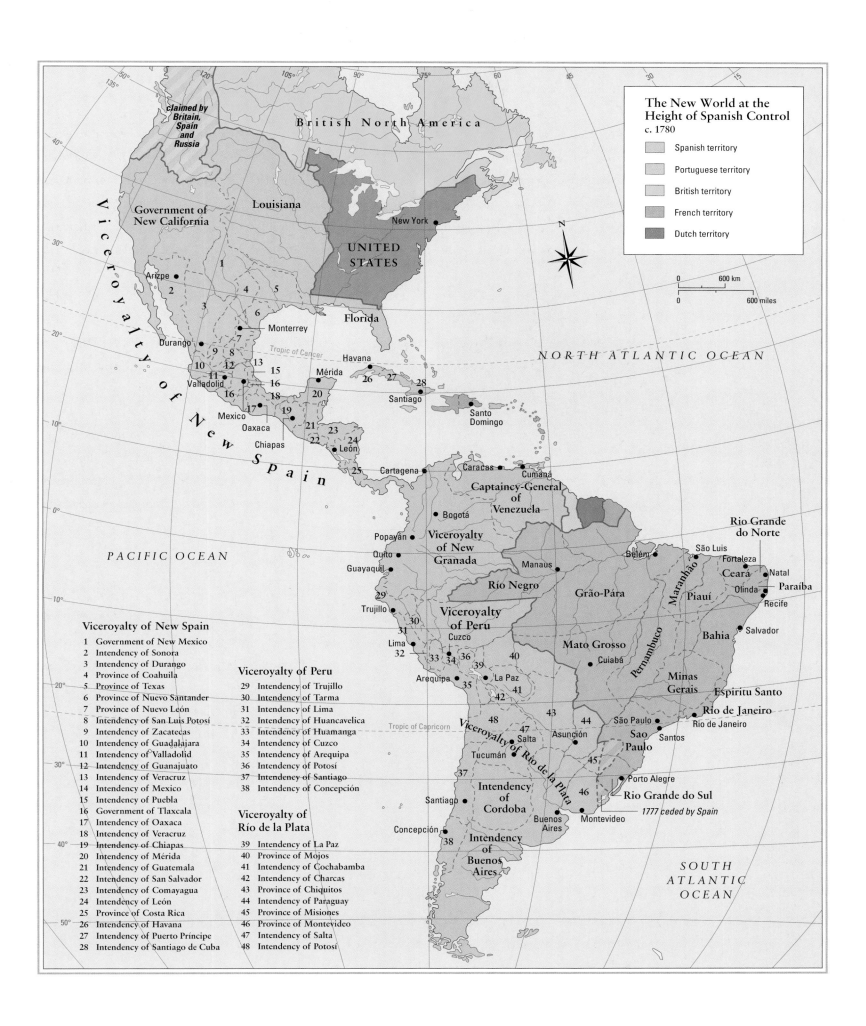

The New World at the
Height of Spanish Control
c. 1780

Spanish territory
Portuguese territory
British territory
French territory
Dutch territory

600 km
600 miles

British North America

claimed by
Britain,
Spain
and
Russia

Government of
New California

Louisiana

New York

UNITED
STATES

Florida

Monterrey

Tropic of Cancer

Havana

NORTH ATLANTIC OCEAN

Arizpe

Durango

Mérida

Santiago

Santo
Domingo

Valladolid

Mexico

Oaxaca

Chiapas

León

Cartagena

Caracas

Cumaná

Captaincy-General
of
Venezuela

Bogotá

Popayán

Viceroyalty
of New
Granada

Rio Grande
do Norte

São Luis

Belém

Fortaleza

Quito

Ceará

Natal

Guayaquil

Manaus

Olinda

Paraíba

Recife

Río Negro

Grão-Pára

Piauí

PACIFIC OCEAN

Trujillo

Maranhão

Pernambuco

Salvador

Lima

Cuzco

Viceroyalty
of Peru

Mato Grosso

Bahia

Arequipa

La Paz

Cuiabá

Minas
Gerais

Espiritu Santo

Rio de Janeiro

Tropic of Capricorn

Asunción

Salta

São Paulo

Rio de Janeiro

Santos

Sao
Paulo

Tucumán

Viceroyalty of Río de la Plata

Santiago

Intendency
of
Cordoba

Concepción

Buenos
Aires

Montevideo

Porto Alegre

Rio Grande do Sul

1777 ceded by Spain

Intendency
of
Buenos
Aires

SOUTH
ATLANTIC
OCEAN

N

Viceroyalty of New Spain

1 Government of New Mexico
2 Intendency of Sonora
3 Intendency of Durango
4 Province of Coahuila
5 Province of Texas
6 Province of Nuevo Santander
7 Province of Nuevo León
8 Intendency of San Luis Potosí
9 Intendency of Zacatecas
10 Intendency of Guadalajara
11 Intendency of Valladolid
12 Intendency of Guanajuato
13 Intendency of Veracruz
14 Intendency of Mexico
15 Intendency of Puebla
16 Government of Tlaxcala
17 Intendency of Oaxaca
18 Intendency of Veracruz
19 Intendency of Chiapas
20 Intendency of Mérida
21 Intendency of Guatemala
22 Intendency of San Salvador
23 Intendency of Comayagua
24 Intendency of León
25 Province of Costa Rica
26 Intendency of Havana
27 Intendency of Puerto Príncipe
28 Intendency of Santiago de Cuba

Viceroyalty of Peru

29 Intendency of Trujillo
30 Intendency of Tarma
31 Intendency of Lima
32 Intendency of Huancavelica
33 Intendency of Huamanga
34 Intendency of Cuzco
35 Intendency of Arequipa
36 Intendency of Potosí
37 Intendency of Santiago
38 Intendency of Concepción

**Viceroyalty of
Río de la Plata**

39 Intendency of La Paz
40 Province of Mojos
41 Intendency of Cochabamba
42 Intendency of Charcas
43 Province of Chiquitos
44 Intendency of Paraguay
45 Province of Misiones
46 Province of Montevideo
47 Intendency of Salta
48 Intendency of Potosí

Viceroyalty of New Spain

ARTILLERY IN THE 16TH CENTURY

IN THE 16TH CENTURY, FIELD ARTILLERY BECAME TOO HEAVY TO BE SUFFICIENTLY MOBILE ON THE BATTLEFIELD. FOR A TIME, THIS LED TO ITS USE DURING SIEGES, OR ON SHIPS IN ACTIONS AT SEA.

During the 16th century, artillery failed to make the same advances as small arms. The problem was the difficulty of combining long-range firepower with mobility. Early guns (see pages 94-99) such as Vasi used gun arrows so were of small caliber and the arrows rhemselves were expensive to make. To get the most out of artillery in land warfare, guns had to measure 20 caliber or more and have thick walls. Thick walls were vital to ensure that the gun barrel could withstand the pressure that built up inside the barrel when a large powder charge detonated. Working with artillery with thinner walls firing lighter charges was feasible, but the disadvantage was reduced accuracy and a more limited range.

Longer range also came with a price: the longer the range, the larger and heavier the artillery. In the 16th century, when heavy artillery was usually made of cast bronze rather than the wrought iron employed in the 15th century, some cannons were made with barrels measuring around 10 ft (3 m) in length, and these could weigh a hefty 20,000 lb (9,072 kg). Moreover, they required very large amounts of gunpowder. A heavy English cannon, for example, needed 23 horses before it could be moved, and even the smaller culverin required nine.

The problem was ameliorated by the introduction of the wheeled gun carriage and the invention of the limber, a two-wheeled, horse-drawn vehicle used to tow a field gun; but neither was adequate to allow artillery to keep pace with an army on the move. Sometimes, the artillery was so slow that it was captured by the enemy. Politics also entered the equation. By around 1500, the French became supreme in artillery; and the Spanish, their long-term foe, counteracted this advantage with improvements in small arms and the tactic of pike-and-shot (see pages 106-111).

Opposite page: The challenge for armies using big cannons was how to make sure they could handle the stresses involved when they were fired. This illustration shows how gun design progressed to meet this challenge, and how firing techniques helped ensure success on the battlefield.

The Development of the Cannon

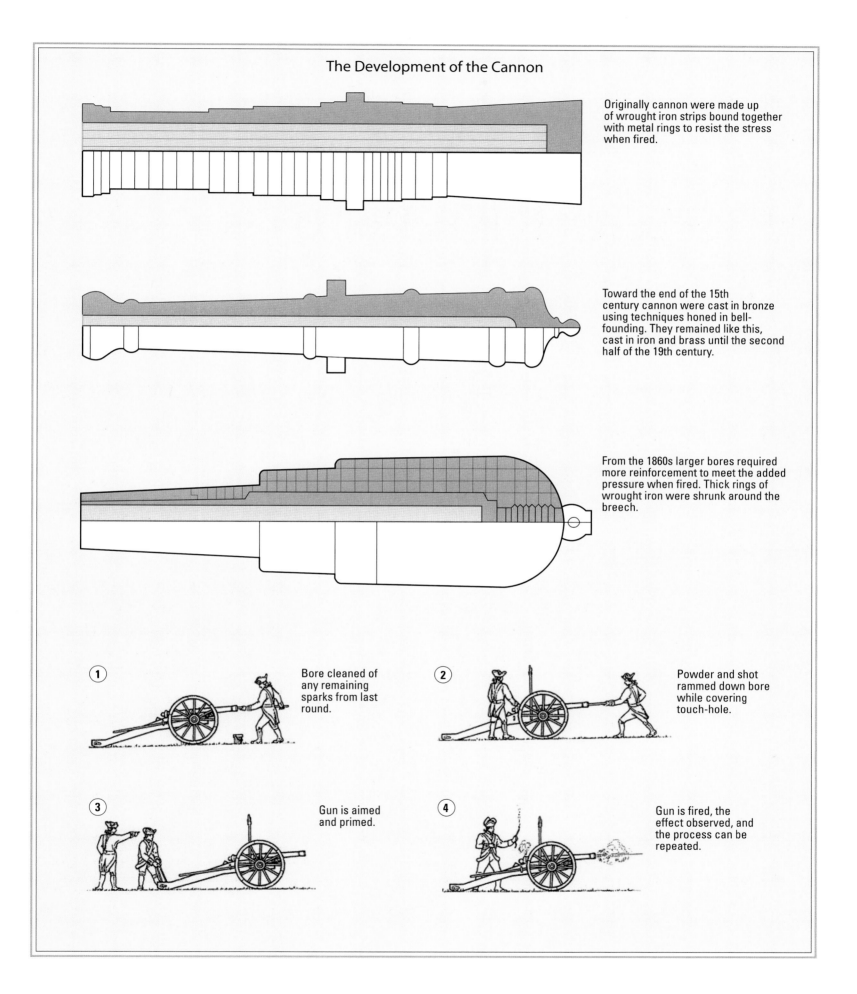

Originally cannon were made up of wrought iron strips bound together with metal rings to resist the stress when fired.

Toward the end of the 15th century cannon were cast in bronze using techniques honed in bell-founding. They remained like this, cast in iron and brass until the second half of the 19th century.

From the 1860s larger bores required more reinforcement to meet the added pressure when fired. Thick rings of wrought iron were shrunk around the breech.

1 Bore cleaned of any remaining sparks from last round.

2 Powder and shot rammed down bore while covering touch-hole.

3 Gun is aimed and primed.

4 Gun is fired, the effect observed, and the process can be repeated.

Consequently, pike-and-shot continued to dominate the battlefield and French artillery lost its supremacy. As the Italian diplomat Niccolo Machiavelli put it in his *The Art of War* (1519-1520), "It is true that the arquebuses and the small artillery do much more harm than the heavy artillery". Although artillery did not entirely leave the 16th-century battlefield, it was more frequently used in in sieges or sea battles where mobility was not so vital. In these more static contexts, the heavy artillery, usually firing from an optimum range of around 180 ft (55 m), was impressive. For example, in 1552 at the

seige of Kazan during the wars between Russia and the Tartar Khanate of Kazan, the Russian artillery was instrumental in breaking through the city walls. The Russians used wooden "battery towers" containing 10 large-caliber cannons and 50 lighter guns, and ultimately Kazan, the Khanate capital, was destroyed. This and similar artillery actions completely changed the profile of the fortress and city wall, creating "star forts" with lower but thicker walls (see pages 122-125).

At sea, artillery could be just as decisive, as proved in two major naval battles in the 16th century, each of which saved the victors from invasion and war. The first was the Battle of Lepanto in 1571, which was fought between an Ottoman Turkish fleet and the Holy League of several European powers, including Spain, the Republic of Venice, and the Papacy. At stake was the Christian future of Europe, which the Turkish Muslims were resolved to destroy. The Turks' chance of achieving their aim was stunted by a decisive advantage for the Holy League: the superiority in guns on board their ships. The number of ships, mainly galleys, brought to the battle by the two sides was roughly equal: 284 for the Holy League and 277 for the Ottoman Turks. But the ships of the Holy League had 1,815 cannons and other guns to the Ottomans' 750.

The League had a further advantage: the expertise of the Venetian gunners, who were regarded as the best in the Mediterranean. The Venetians were expected to hit an oncoming enemy galley at a distance of about 1,500 ft (457 m), considered to be the effective limit of 16th-century naval gunnery. A further drawback for the Ottomans at Lepanto was their bowmen. They were skilled but were no match for the League's arquebusiers and musketeers.

As a result, the Turks lost 230 ships and up to 20,000 soldiers and sailors at Lepanto, compared to the League's losses of 13 galleys and 7,566 dead. Afterward, Lepanto was named "the Last Crusade", for the Ottoman Turks never made another serious attempt to Islamicize Europe. Seventeen years after Lepanto, the danger posed by the Spanish Armada of 1588 was an invasion of England. Gunpowder won the day, as the mighty but lumbering Spanish galleons were foiled by the nimble English ships, which fired the latest artillery pieces at a range beyond the reach of the Armada's guns (see pages 126-129).

Although this object resembles a vase, tub, or similar container, it was actually something a great deal more dangerous and destructive — the first type of gun, introduced early on in the 14th century and called Vasi.

SIEGECRAFT IN THE 16TH CENTURY

ONE OF THE MANY ASPECTS OF WARFARE THAT WAS CHANGED BY THE ADVENT OF GUNPOWDER WAS THE TRADITIONAL SIEGE. DEFENSIVE WALLS BUILT BY THE OLD METHODS WERE NO LONGER IMPREGNABLE.

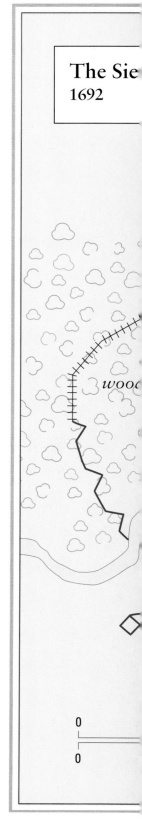

The Sie
1692

wood

0

0

T he 16th century had finally made obsolete and consigned to the past the trebuchet, the onager, the mangonel, and other siege engines that had once smashed their way through castle and city walls, and other defenses. The arrival of artillery outdid them all for the terror and devastation it brought, and because it could do this much more efficiently. The revolution in siegecraft that the artillery signalled was so pronounced that it caused a total rethink of the science of siegecraft and led to the complete redesign of the castles and cities that were vulnerable to attack and likely to come under siege in the new world of gunpowder and explosives.

Towering masonry walls, that were near-impossible to scale, and, were replaced by lower, thicker structures which had two main purposes: firstly, they provided safer emplacements for guns to fire back at a besieging army; secondly, the thicker they were, the more difficult they were for even big guns to breach. In addition, triangular bastions were built outward from the low walls to enable the defenders to survey all possible approaches by enemy forces and, when necessary, to pour down artillery fire on any attacker daring to enter the area.

The history of all warfare has been that of offense countered by defense, and offensive attempts to break down new defenses. As the science of fortification improved, mighty siege guns, including

Opposite page: Namur saw an 11 day siege in May-June of 1692, and was finally captured by the French on June 5. Dutch attempts to relieve Namur were foiled by rains and the flooding of the its tributary River Mehaigne.

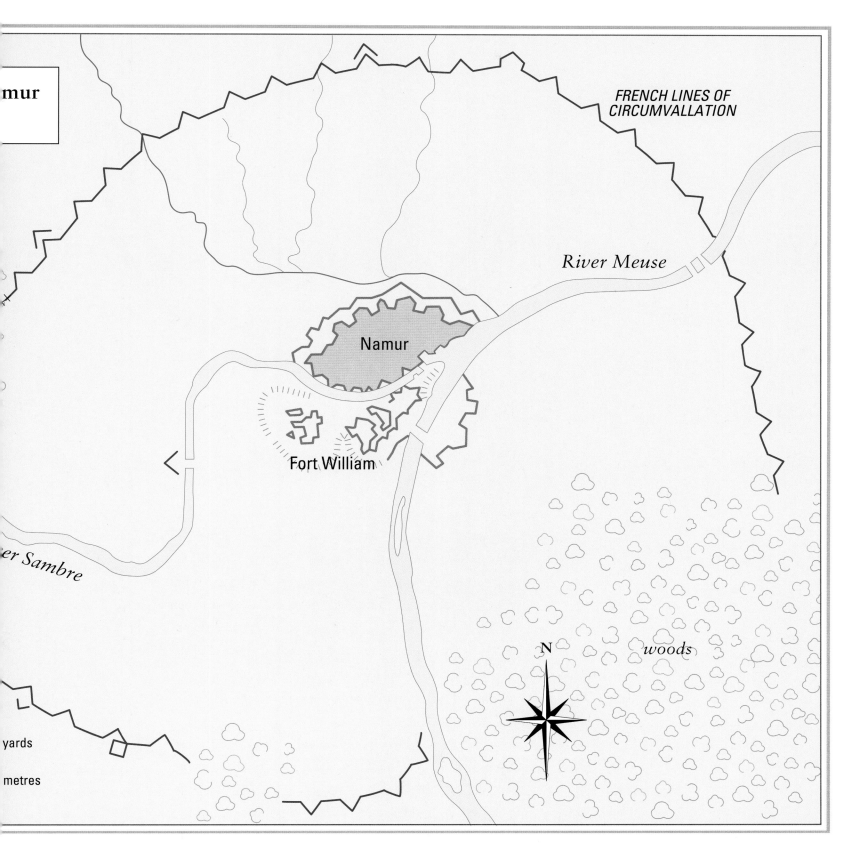

powerful cannons and basilisks directed more prolonged and concentrated fire at castle and city walls.
This situation gave rise to a new form of defense: by widening the ditches around the fortifications
and adding further protection and by building an outer wall where light artillery, arquebusiers, and
musketeers could be placed to prevent siege guns from coming too close.

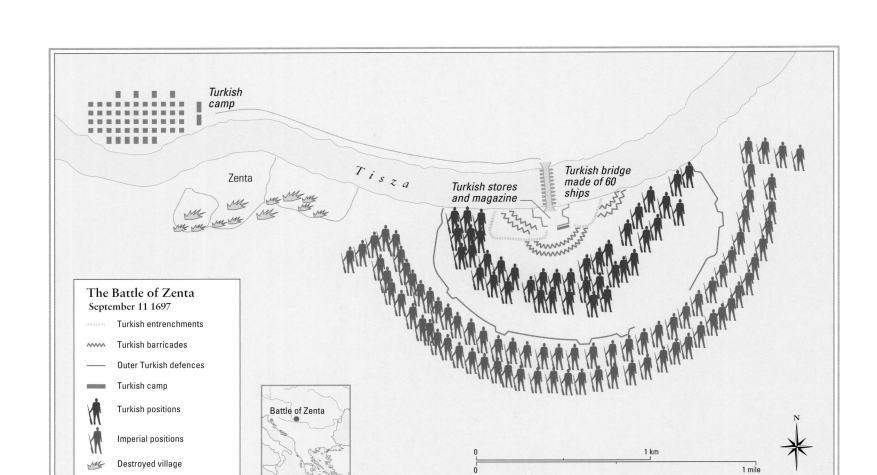

Turkish camp

Zenta

T i s z a

Turkish stores
and magazine

Turkish bridge
made of 60
ships

The Battle of Zenta
September 11 1697

〰〰	Turkish entrenchments
⋀⋀⋀	Turkish barricades
—	Outer Turkish defences
▮	Turkish camp
🯅	Turkish positions
🯅	Imperial positions
⅏	Destroyed village

Battle of Zenta

0   1 km

0   1 mile

N

In 1697, Muslim Turks invaded Hungary and were attacked by forces under Prince Eugene of Savoy at Zenta, near the River Theiss. The attack was so ferocious that the Turks were virtually annihilated. Zenta was the last serious Turkish threat to Hungary.

Even the earth dug out to make the ditch had its uses. It would be laid out in front of the outer wall in a gradually sloping bank known as a glacis. The glacis not only supported the wall but also made it more difficult for attackers to direct fire at the defenders behind it.

The new low walls also complicated an old technique of siege warfare, mining. In medieval times, mining was bele to cause a terrifying collapse of the entire outer structureof a fortification by setting fire to it. This involved tunnelling through the earth surrounding the stones at the bottom of a wall, inserting temporary wooden supports, and then packing the tunnel with flammable material before they were able to set the tunnel alight. But new lower, thicker walls required longer tunnels, which could take a large amount of time to dig. The fact that gunpowder could be used to collapse a wall was no compensation, as it was expensive to buy and dangerous to carry.

The new fortifications won out over gunnery for a time, but this encouraged greater efforts to improve siegecraft. Potential attackers began to consider ways and means of reaching the outer wall without the defensive artillery and firearms teams being aware of them. One solution was to pick a vulnerable spot in the defenses and use infantry and engineers to dig trenches leading to it while under covering fire from long-range culverins. If the besiegers managed to reach an area from which they could direct their artillery fire against the fortifications, they could build up walls of earth in front of the trenches, where they could house their siege guns. For obvious reasons, getting the guns into position was done after nightfall. Supposing that all this was done without the defenders realizing that anything was going on, the attackers would open fire on the fortifications and might be able to take the advantage and push forwards their assault until they overcame the defenders at the outer wall. If the attackers could take the outer wall, then siege guns could be moved in to begin battering away at the main defenses.

That was the theory, but it proved hard to pull off when defenders at the outer wall were alert to the ploy their opponents were likely to attempt. There were also situations in which a 16th-century fortress provided with plenty of food and ammunition could hold out for many months in the event of a siege, if not years, and wear down their attackers, who had to survive in far less salubrious circumstances.

A besieging army that fell victim in this way was the Turkish force laying siege to Szeged, Hungary, in 1697. After fruitless months living in camp and short of food, the Turkish Sultan Mustafa II decided to give up and retreat. He began to march his army over the fortified pontoon bridge across the Tisza at Zenta when the Austrian Prince Eugene launched a surprise attack led by dragoons advancing under cover of artillery. The dragoons overran the Turkish fieldworks and stormed on, followed by infantry and cavalry to massacre the Turks on the south bank of the river. The Turks lost 30,000 out of 80,000 men while Austrians lost only 429 men. By nightfall, Prince Eugene was surprised to find himself in possession of Mustafa's harem.

The dominant influence on siegecraft and fortification at this time was the Frenchman, Sebastien le Prestre, Marquis de Vauban, who tackled both sides of the subject. The prime military engineer of the 17th century, he designed fortifications and also worked out how to break through them.

Vauban was born into the minor French nobility in 1633 but after he was orphaned at age ten, he was fortunate enough to receive an ideal education for his future career from the Carmelite prior of Semur in his native Burgundy; the prior's syllabus majored in science, mathematics, and geometry. At 17, Vauban joined the army and fought with exemplary valor in the civil war of the Fronde. Subsequently, despite his youth — he was still only in his early twenties — Vauban's engineering skills earned him a commission to work on the fortification of Clermont-en-Argonne. His expertise was afterward honed during several other sieges - for example at Maastricht and Trier in 1673 and Ghent and Ypres in 1678. By this time, Vauban had developed his own unique systems of fortification and also the means of attacking and reducing them.

Vauban's siegecraft system used the entrenchments technique, but did so systematically. The entrenchments permitted attackers and their artillery to reach, and breach, a fortress's defensive wall. The first trench was dug parallel to the line of defenses, which were to be assaulted at a distance of some 2,100 ft (640 m) from the fortifications. From this point, Vauban's engineers, or sappers as they were known, dug trenches that approached the fortress, but did so at an angle, with zigzags back and forth to prevent the defenders from pouring down enfilading fire along the trenches as they worked. Gabions, or shelters, were provided to protect the sappers from the defenders' fire. Digging continued until the trench had advanced to a point some 900 ft (274 m) from the defenses, and here new artillery emplacements were created.

That done, siege guns would open up from their new position much closer in an effort to drive the defenders away from the wall and disable their artillery, perhaps starting to create a breach. The idea was to move even closer to the fortifications by means of more entrenchments so that siege guns could be brought up farther and finally pound a decisive breach in the fortifications. A full-scale assault would follow, culminating in the capture of the fortress.

THE DEFEAT OF THE SPANISH ARMADA

THE DEFEAT OF THE SPANISH ARMADA IN 1588 BY A VASTLY OUTNUMBERED ENGLISH FLEET WAS A MOTE IN THE EYE OF SPAIN'S MILITARY SUPREMACY. THE ENGLISH ACHIEVED THIS UNEXPECTED FEAT THROUGH YET ANOTHER INNOVATION OF THE NEW AGE OF GUNPOWDER.

When King Philip II of Spain launched his Armada against England in 1588, the potential for war between the Catholic Spaniards and Protestant English had been rumbling for 30 years. Philip's fleet of 130 vessels not only outnumbered the English ships two to one, but was fully expected to win and achieve the long-threatened invasion and conquest of England and the capture and execution of its "illegitimate" queen, Elizabeth I. This expectation was totally demolished when the English stunned the Armada in the English Channel with a heavy and costly defeat so shaming that on hearing of it, King Philip prayed for death. This unlooked for outcome owed a great deal to characteristically vile weather in the Channel that prevented the Armada from entering harbors in the Spanish Netherlands where an army waited to embark for the invasion of England. Nevertheless, it was just as much the new naval technology that the upstart English employed against the Spanish superpower that sealed their unexpected victory.

Philip's Armada was designed to fight according to the old, outdated concept of grappling and boarding that made naval warfare a floating version of war on land. This was why the Armada carried a one in three ratio of sailors to soldiers whose role it was to board an opponent's ships and fight it out hand to hand on the decks. The Spaniards never got the chance to put this plan into action, for the English had other, revolutionary, ideas. Their 18 small, fast galleons were equipped with 1,800 light, long-range culverins. The Armada's armament comprised 2,400 guns, but 23 percent of them were heavy, short-range weapons designed to smash hulls or dismast enemy ships at

Opposite page: The Armada, the Spanish invasion fleet, encountered disaster in the English Channel where revolutionary English galleons capable of firing deadly broadsides awaited them. Tormented by English gunfire, battered by Channel storms, the Armada was forced to return home in disgrace.

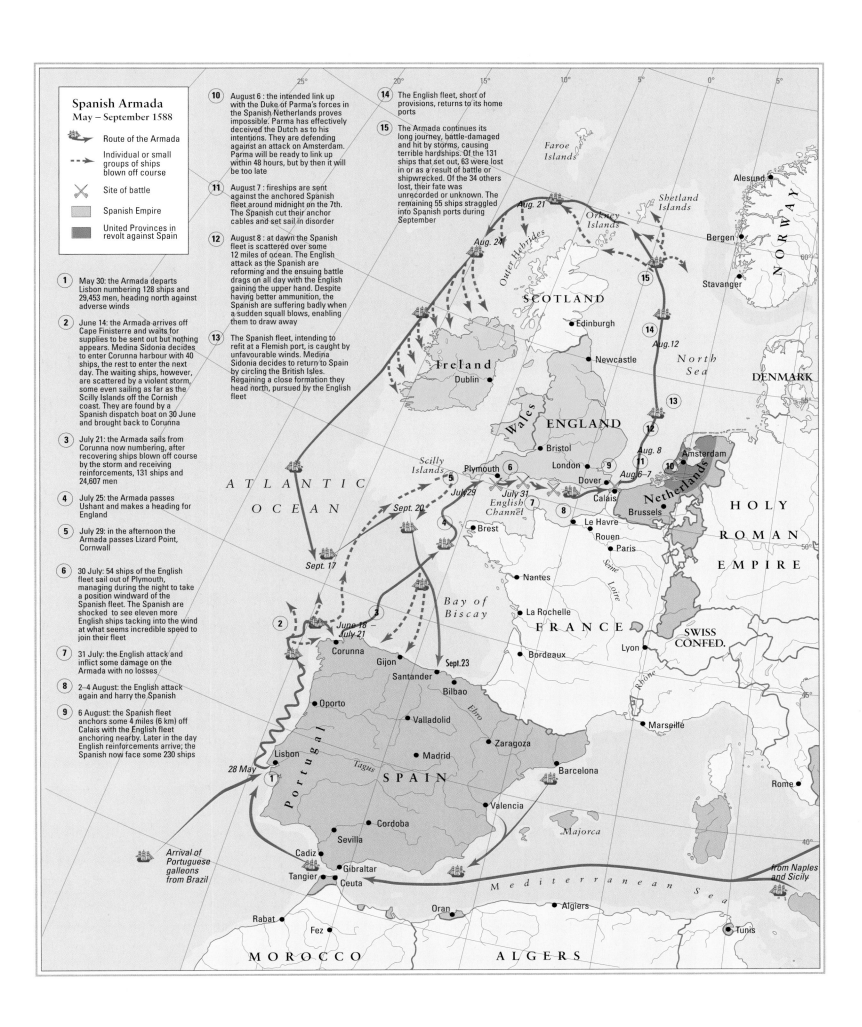

Spanish Armada
May – September 1588

- 🚢 Route of the Armada
- ⇢ Individual or small groups of ships blown off course
- ⚔ Site of battle
- ▢ Spanish Empire
- ▢ United Provinces in revolt against Spain

1 May 30: the Armada departs Lisbon numbering 128 ships and 29,453 men, heading north against adverse winds

2 June 14: the Armada arrives off Cape Finisterre and waits for supplies to be sent out but nothing appears. Medina Sidonia decides to enter Corunna harbour with 40 ships, the rest to enter the next day. The waiting ships, however, are scattered by a violent storm, some even sailing as far as the Scilly Islands off the Cornish coast. They are found by a Spanish dispatch boat on 30 June and brought back to Corunna

3 July 21: the Armada sails from Corunna now numbering, after recovering ships blown off course by the storm and receiving reinforcements, 131 ships and 24,607 men

4 July 25: the Armada passes Ushant and makes a heading for England

5 July 29: in the afternoon the Armada passes Lizard Point, Cornwall

6 30 July: 54 ships of the English fleet sail out of Plymouth, managing during the night to take a position windward of the Spanish fleet. The Spanish are shocked to see eleven more English ships tacking into the wind at what seems incredible speed to join their fleet

7 31 July: the English attack and inflict some damage on the Armada with no losses

8 2–4 August: the English attack again and harry the Spanish

9 6 August: the Spanish fleet anchors some 4 miles (6 km) off Calais with the English fleet anchoring nearby. Later in the day English reinforcements arrive; the Spanish now face some 230 ships

10 August 6 : the intended link up with the Duke of Parma's forces in the Spanish Netherlands proves impossible. Parma has effectively deceived the Dutch as to his intentions. They are defending against an attack on Amsterdam. Parma will be ready to link up within 48 hours, but by then it will be too late

11 August 7 : fireships are sent against the anchored Spanish fleet around midnight on the 7th. The Spanish cut their anchor cables and set sail in disorder

12 August 8 : at dawn the Spanish fleet is scattered over some 12 miles of ocean. The English attack as the Spanish are reforming and the ensuing battle drags on all day with the English gaining the upper hand. Despite having better ammunition, the Spanish are suffering badly when a sudden squall blows, enabling them to draw away

13 The Spanish fleet, intending to refit at a Flemish port, is caught by unfavourable winds. Medina Sidonia decides to return to Spain by circling the British Isles. Regaining a close formation they head north, pursued by the English fleet

14 The English fleet, short of provisions, returns to its home ports

15 The Armada continues its long journey, battle-damaged and hit by storms, causing terrible hardships. Of the 131 ships that set out, 63 were lost in or as a result of battle or shipwrecked. Of the 34 others lost, their fate was unrecorded or unknown. The remaining 55 ships straggled into Spanish ports during September

close quarters. The English took care to keep their galleons beyond the Spaniards' reach while they pounded the Armada with broadsides from their culverins, which were fired through the recently invented "ports" along the sides of their ships.

This strategy was very much in line with the new role artillery played in contemporary naval warfare (see pages 118–121) and depended firstly on an altered perception about seafaring that, ironically, the Spaniards had themselves pioneered in the early 16th century when they created their American empire across the Atlantic Ocean. Until then, sailing out of sight of land was considered unwise if not downright foolish. Instead, most voyages "hugged" the coasts so that landmarks and other aids to navigation could remain in sight at all times. Voyaging to America, however, meant sailing the "open sea" with no land to be seen for weeks on end and the dangers involved included the lack of a method by which longitude could be easily reckoned: this was not available until the invention of the chronometer in the late 18th century.

The English victory over the Spanish Armada in 1588 can be seen as due to the skilful tactics in tracking the Spanish ships (p.128) and using their guns at ranges that prevented the Spaniards from grappling and boarding their vessels (p.129).

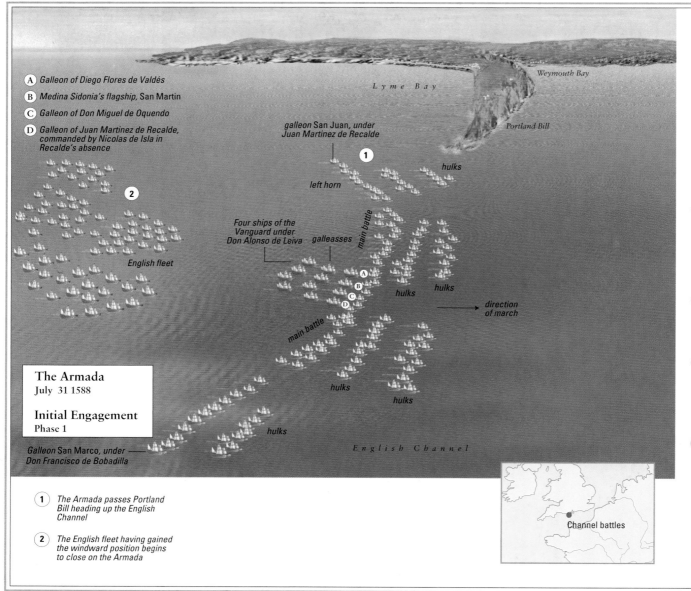

(A) Galleon of Diego Flores de Valdés

(B) Medina Sidonia's flagship, San Martin

(C) Galleon of Don Miguel de Oquendo

(D) Galleon of Juan Martinez de Recalde, commanded by Nicolas de Isla in Recalde's absence

galleon San Juan, under Juan Martinez de Recalde

left horn

hulks

Four ships of the Vanguard under Don Alonso de Leiva

galleasses

main battle

English fleet

hulks

hulks

hulks

main battle

direction of march

hulks

hulks

The Armada
July 31 1588

Initial Engagement
Phase 1

Galleon San Marco, under — Don Francisco de Bobadilla

hulks

English Channel

Weymouth Bay

Lyme Bay

Portland Bill

Channel battles

(1) The Armada passes Portland Bill heading up the English Channel

(2) The English fleet having gained the windward position begins to close on the Armada

(3) Lord Howard of Effingham leads the English fleet into action; his squadron attacks the Armada's vanguard

(4) Drake, Frobisher and Hawkins lead their respective squadrons into attack on the Spanish rearguard

(5) By the end of the afternoon the battle was over; the Spanish commander ordered the fleet to re-form. In attempting to do so there was a collision in the Andalusian squadron

(6) Late afternoon, San Salvador, the flagship of the Vice Admiral and Paymaster General of the Armada suffered a magazine explosion. She was later boarded and captured by the pursuing English and taken to Weymouth

(7) Nuestra Señora del Rosario, flagship of Don Pedro de Valdés, is damaged in a series of collisions and loses her foremast. Unmanageable, she is left behind during the night and surrenders the next morning to Francis Drake. Drake's discovery that English gunfire had inflicted only modest damage on Rosario may have been behind the subsequent English decision to engage at closer range on August 3 and 4

The English Channel was not exactly an ocean in extent, but the "tacking" performed by the English galleons in order to alter their line of assault against the Armada could not be a coast-hugging tactic. At its greatest breadth, the western end of the Channel was 100 miles (160 km) wide, narrowing to the 21 miles (34 km) that separated Dover and Calais at the eastern end, so that the northern French and southern English coasts could disappear below the horizon at the same time. On such occasions, the English Channel was "open sea" for all practical purposes. Secondly, the culverins on board the English galleons were not simply guns translated from land to ships but were given extra power by a new development: an increased rate of fire produced by the harnessing of a gun's recoil with ropes so that after firing, it came to rest in a position inboard where it could be easily reloaded.

The fight against the Spanish Armada was not, therefore, just another naval action, but the start of a completely new strategy, later widely copied by other navies, including the Spanish fleet, which used broadside warfare instead of the warship as floating fortress.

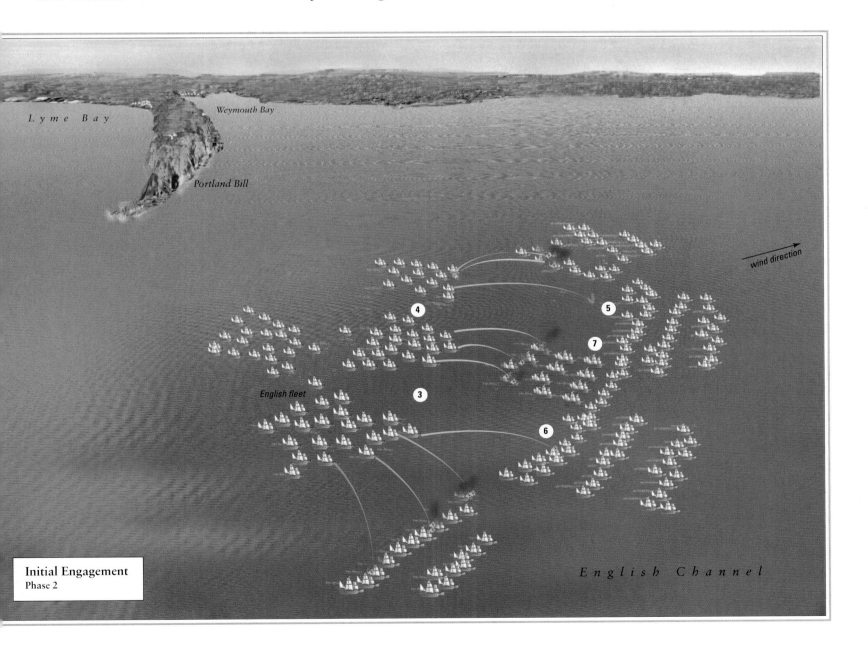

Lyme Bay

Weymouth Bay

Portland Bill

wind direction

English fleet

4

5

7

3

6

Initial Engagement
Phase 2

English Channel

KING GUSTAVUS II ADOLPHUS OF SWEDEN AND MODERN WARFARE

IN THE 17TH CENTURY, SIGNIFICANT CHANGES IN WEAPONS AND THEIR USE IN WARFARE, REMOVED THE LAST TRACES OF ANCIENT AND MEDIEVAL PRACTICE FROM THE BATTLEFIELD AND INTRODUCED THE ERA OF MODERN WARFARE.

King Gustavus II Adolphus of Sweden is considered to be one of the great military commanders and innovators of the 17th century. He died in 1632, aged 37, during the Thirty Years' War while leading the Swedish forces at the Battle of Lützen but his influence lasted until well into the 20th century. Carl von Clausewitz, the Prussian army officer, military historian, and author of *On War*, published in 1832, was one of Gustavus' many admirers. So was Napoleon Bonaparte, who copied the Swedish king's policy of teaching his infantry and gunners to ride. Clausewitz, Napoleon, and, more recently, the American World War Two general George Patton all considered Gustavus Adolphus one of the greatest military leaders of all time.

At the start of the 17th century, the musket and the pike were rivaling each other for supremacy on the battlefield. Battle formations had hardly changed since the days of the Ancient Greek phalanx and the armored cavalry had still not accepted that, though the concerted charge with swords outstretched might be dramatic and glorious, it was irrelevant, in fact suicidal in the age of gunpower. The artillery was dogged by problems over mobility, and the excessive weight of many guns, and was basically unable to keep up with the faster and more agile style of warfare that the use of gunpowder had introduced (see pages 118–121). Yet, by 1700, the pike had virtually disappeared from the battlefield, infantry was fighting in lines rather than phalanx "boxes" and the artillery had become a support for infantry and cavalry.

Opposite page: The Thirty Years' War of 1618–1648, mainly fought on German soil, involved 21 belligerent states and over one million men. The fighting caused such devastation in Europe that it took well over a century for participant nations to recover.

The Thirty Years' War
1630–1639

Imperial campaigns

→ Gallas and Piccolomini 1636

Protestant campaigns

→ Gustav II

→ Banér 1637

✕ Battle

— Border of Holy Roman Empire

Spanish Habsburg territories

Austrian Habsburg territories

King Gustavus was responsible for most of these transformations and made his first priority the problem of the heavyweight musket, which weighed up to 25 lb (11.4 kg). Gustavus reduced it to 10 lb (4.5 kg) and adopted a new cartridge that doubled the musket's rate of fire to one round per minute. Gustavus created a new concept for artillery to provide massed, mobile fire by reducing the weight of guns, standardizing gunpowder, and limiting size to 3 calibers: 24-pounder, 12-pounder, and a light, but stoutly built 3-pounder. These limitations reflected the king's preference for maximum mobility and, in effect, created the first light field artillery used in warfare. The overall result of Gustavus' military reforms was the modern standing army, complete with the organization and system of officers' ranks which persist to this day.

Gustavus also introduced the principle of combined arms, which allowed the cavalry to benefit from the safety of a line of infantry and cannons and not only mount an attack from this shelter but return to it to regroup afterward. Gustavus replaced the thick blocks of pike-and-shot formations with a thinner arrangement of up to six ranks.

In addition, he dispensed with the Spanish Square and the Tercios, which could be up to 50 ranks deep — far too cumbersome for the fast-moving warfare he had in mind. What Gustavus wanted — and in effect

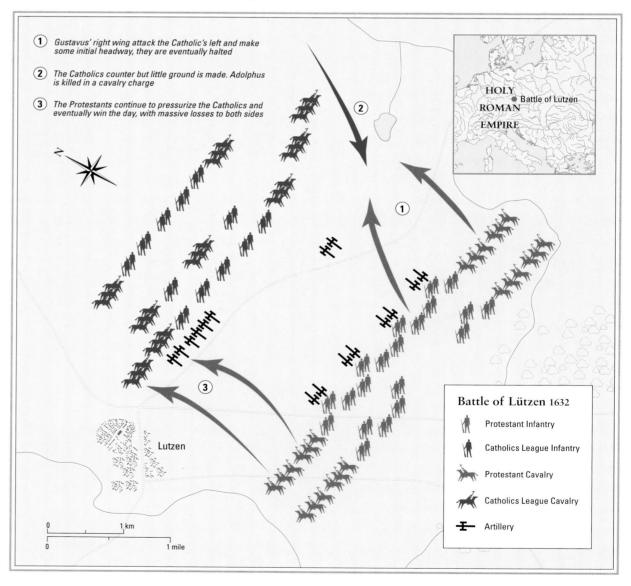

① Gustavus' right wing attack the Catholic's left and make some initial headway, they are eventually halted

② The Catholics counter but little ground is made. Adolphus is killed in a cavalry charge

③ The Protestants continue to pressurize the Catholics and eventually win the day, with massive losses to both sides

HOLY ROMAN EMPIRE
● Battle of Lutzen

Lutzen

0   1 km
0   1 mile

Battle of Lützen 1632

Protestant Infantry

Catholics League Infantry

Protestant Cavalry

Catholics League Cavalry

Artillery

At the Battle of Lützen, the Swedes, facing the Imperial Army of the Holy Roman Empire, drove off their opponents' infantry and cavalry and forced the enemy commander, Wallenstein, to withdraw. But during the fighting, the Swedish king, and commander, Gustavus II Adolphus was killed.

created — was an army whose manpower could be quickly reassigned or take on a new configuration at short notice. This had the virtue of disturbing his opponents and making them wonder what the Swedish king was going to do next. Gustavus was something of a martinet when it came to training his musketeers, who soon became renowned for their accuracy with a weapon that, being a smoothbore, was not always known for its precision. The Swedes were also remarkable for the speed at which they could reload their weapons — they were able to do this three times faster than most musketeers in other armies.

In the 17th century and for some time afterward, elitism was common in all European forces. The organization of most of the forces saw the cavalry the most highly regarded element, the artillery commanded somewhat less in status, though still esteemed, and the infantry as the lowest element, despised by those above it. King Gustavus, however, refused to have anything to do with such snobbery. Gustav saw to it that all sections of his forces were treated as equal and equally valuable and this encouraged a certain esprit de corps that served as a boost to the army's morale. The Swedish soldiers were encouraged to multi-task: for example, artillery could be serviced by the infantry and cavalry and Gustavus' pikemen learned how to fire muskets.

At Breitenfeld, the Imperial troops of the Holy Roman Empire forced the Swedes' Saxon allies from the field, and attacked the now exposed Swedish left flank. The Swedish King Gustavus II Adolphus countered the attack with his cavalry and opened up with his artillery. The Imperial troops fled.

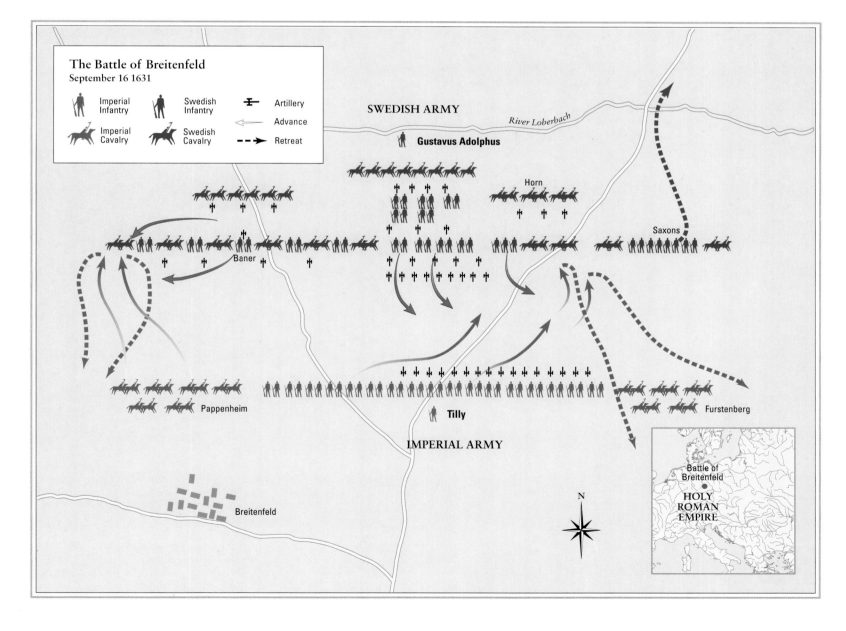

The Battle of Breitenfeld
September 16 1631

Imperial Infantry
Swedish Infantry
Artillery
Imperial Cavalry
Swedish Cavalry
Advance
Retreat

SWEDISH ARMY
River Loberbach
Gustavus Adolphus
Horn
Saxons
Baner
Pappenheim
Tilly
Furstenberg
IMPERIAL ARMY
Breitenfeld
N
Battle of Breitenfeld
HOLY ROMAN EMPIRE

ENGLISH SUPREMACY AT SEA

VICTORY OVER THE SPANISH ARMADA IN 1588 INAUGURATED A PROCESS THAT EVENTUALLY MADE ENGLAND THE WORLD'S GREATEST SEA POWER, A STATUS IT MAINTAINED UNTIL WELL INTO THE 20TH CENTURY.

After the English fleet defeated the Spanish Armada in 1588, the future at sea belonged to gunnery and broadside warfare. The Spanish absorbed the lesson they had so painfully been taught. They reorganized and re-equipped the Spanish fleet with the new technology, armaments, and fighting vessels that were more in line with the revolutionary galleons that had triumphed in 1588. Designed by the Elizabethan "sea dog" John Hawkins, these fast, streamlined ships were much more maneuverable than previous vessels: they had a length-to-breadth ratio of three to one; unwieldy forecastles and sterncastles were reduced in height; and mainmasts were placed further forward on the deck.

Second Anglo-Dutch War 1665-1667. English fleet under Monck and the Dutch under de Ruyter in the English Channel, 1666. After engraving published Amsterdam, 1666.

But, however advanced the English galleons were, during the 16th century the Portuguese and the Dutch in Asia, as well as the Spanish in the Americas, were still ahead of the English in exploiting the opportunities for wealth and empire that were opening up overseas. This picture was different by the 17th century, when England was acquiring colonies and settlements of its own, in Virginia and New England, India, and the Caribbean. In 1651, the English came into conflict with the Dutch after the parliamentary government in England, which had taken power after winning the English Civil War in the 1640s, passed the Navigation Act. This stipulated that imports into England could not be carried by foreign ships. The Act was designed to protect English trade and badly hit at the Dutch freight trade, leading to

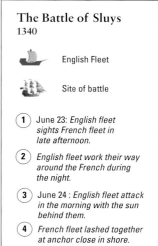

The Battle of Sluys
1340

English Fleet

Site of battle

1) June 23: English fleet sights French fleet in late afternoon.

2) English fleet work their way around the French during the night.

3) June 24 : English fleet attack in the morning with the sun behind them.

4) French fleet lashed together at anchor close in shore.

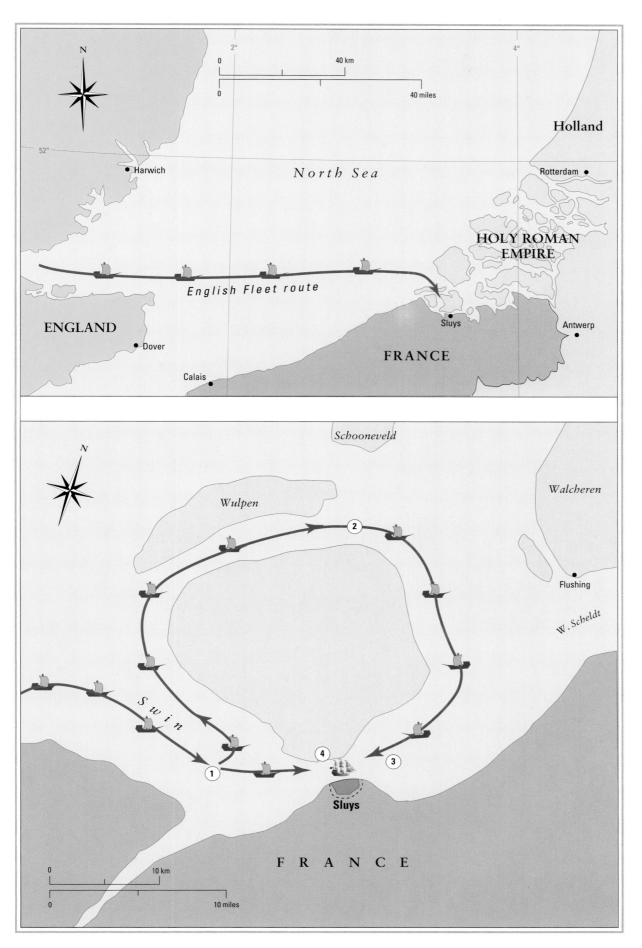

The Anglo-French Battle of Sluys was representative of the "grappling and boarding" method of warfare used at sea. Most of the fighting took place at close quarters. After the fleets grappled and boarded each other, the fighting would have included firing arrows at the enemy as well as hand-to-hand combat.

the first of four Anglo-Dutch wars in 1652. Sensing itself isolated and threatened in Europe, the English Parliament embarked on a major ship-building program, which greatly expanded the size and power of the English Navy. This enabled the fleet, led by General at Sea (Admiral) Robert Blake to triumph against the Dutch in 1654, and it also led him to adopt a new strategy for naval warfare. Blake opted for the line-ahead formation in which all ships sailed in a column, each spaced at equal distances apart. This enabled them to fire broadsides at an enemy at regular intervals as they passed by, although the problems of distance required the provision of clear fighting instructions and detailed orders.

The Anglo-Spanish war that began in 1655 revealed how far Spain had fallen from the heights of its supremacy in the 16th century, and also how far English sea power had come since she had been an underdog facing the mighty Armada. Admiral Blake blockaded the port of Cadiz in southern Spain and destroyed most of the ships of the Spanish treasure fleet berthed there. One Spanish treasure galleon was seized, incurring a loss to Spain of around £2 million. Blake continued the blockade throughout the winter of 1656-1657, the first time a fleet had remained at sea throughout the winter months.

Like the Spanish after the Armada, the Dutch copied English practice and adopted the line-ahead formation for battle warfare at sea. However, the influence of the Dutch admirals Maarten Tromp, his son Cornelis and Michiel de Ruyter, with their fondness for the old grappling-and-boarding system, meant that the Dutch still lagged behind the English in terms of gunnery.

In 1688, it was the turn of the French to challenge the fgrowing supremacy at sea earned by the Royal Navy, as the English fleet had been known since 1660. Using the Royal Navy as his model, the French king, Louis XIV, ordered the construction of a scientifically designed fleet equal in number to the fleets of England and the Dutch Republic combined. Once construction of the French fleet had been completed it temporarily gave France pre-eminence at sea. The largest of the French ships were the *Soleil Royal*, which was 200 feet (61 m) long and designed to carry 112 guns, and the *Royal Louis*, with 118 guns.

The firepower of the French and English vessels was about equal, but King Louis himself crippled the French capabilities by putting the new fleet to work as support for land and amphibious operations and for bombarding coastal targets, instead of using the French fleet as a competitive rival for the British Fleet for action at sea. The War of the Grand Alliance dragged on for nine years, ultimately emasculating Louis' outwardly splendid fleet. Virtually all the French could do to threaten England was to attack English merchant shipping and attempt to seize or destroy their cargo, hoping to damage British trade.

At the beginning of the 18th century, the Royal Navy was the foremost navy in the world. Until 1805, it was numerically outclassed by its opponents on several occasions, but by then supremacy no longer relied on mere numbers. The Royal Navy's tactics and training, its organization, dockyard facilities, logistic support, and standards of hygiene had proved to be of higher quality and superior to those of its rivals. After about 1750, the Royal Navy's levels of design and construction could also be called superior to its rivals as well. During the Napoleonic Wars, which lasted from 1793 to 1815, the Royal Navy attained its peak of power and efficiency. The British fleet succeeded in blockading enemy navies in port and also frustrating Napoleon's plans to invade Britain, and finally smashing his fleet at the battle of Trafalgar in 1805 under the leadership of Admiral, Lord Nelson. By then, Britain's navy exercised a mastery of the seas that no other nation was in a position to contest. The Royal Navy retained this position for the entire 19th century and well into the 20th century.

Opposite page: During the First Anglo-Dutch War, in 1653, at the Battle of Gabbard Shoal each side employed different, mutually exclusive tactics. The English fleet employed "line-of-battle" tactics, whereas the Dutch used the old-fashioned "grappling and boarding" technique. The English tactic proved victorious.

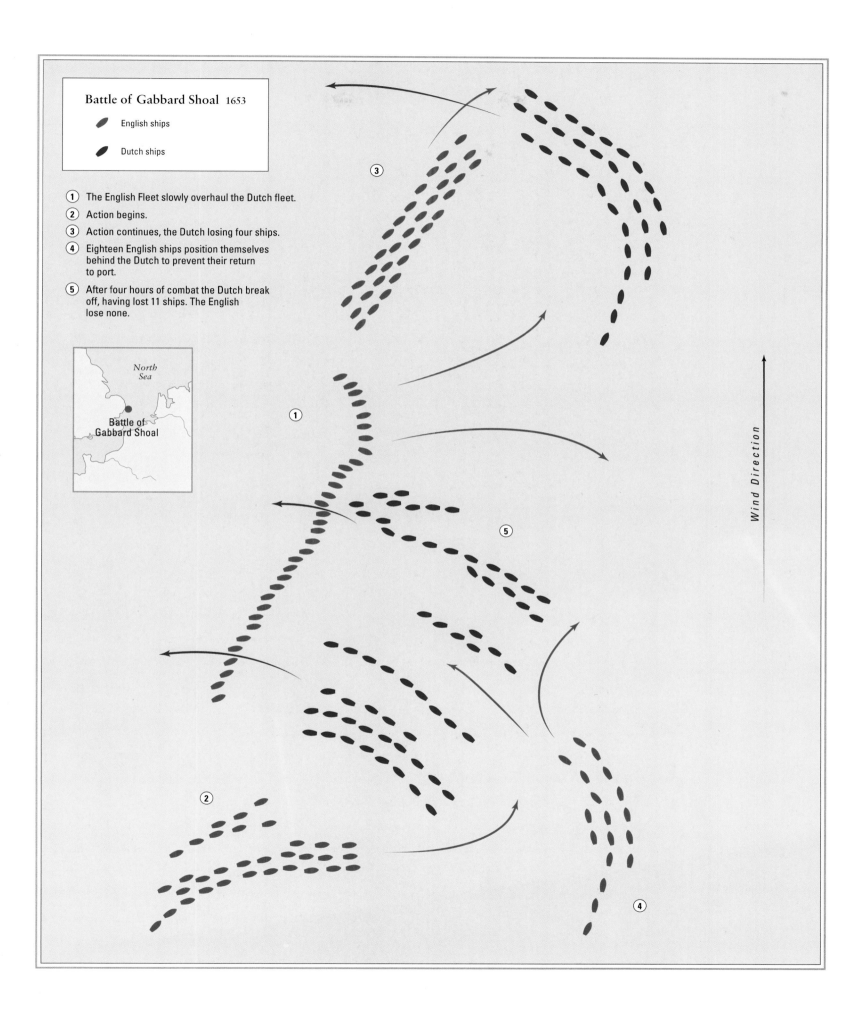

Battle of Gabbard Shoal 1653

- English ships
- Dutch ships

1. The English Fleet slowly overhaul the Dutch fleet.
2. Action begins.
3. Action continues, the Dutch losing four ships.
4. Eighteen English ships position themselves behind the Dutch to prevent their return to port.
5. After four hours of combat the Dutch break off, having lost 11 ships. The English lose none.

North Sea

Battle of Gabbard Shoal

Wind Direction

THE INNOVATIONS OF FREDERICK THE GREAT

KING FREDERICK II OF PRUSSIA, AND HIS FATHER FREDERICK WILLIAM I, WERE THE ARCHITECTS OF PRUSSIAN MILITARY EXCELLENCE IN THE 18TH CENTURY. BETWEEN THEM, THEY FORGED THE PRUSSIAN ARMY INTO A SUPERLATIVELY DISCIPLINED AND DOMINANT FIGHTING FORCE.

When Frederick II, later known as Frederick the Great, succeeded his father Frederick William I to the throne of Prussia in 1740, he inherited a 60,000-strong army that was the fourth largest in Europe. Yet Prussia was a relatively minor state: its population of 2.5 million was 12th in size among the nations of the continent. Frederick William I was obsessed with military matters, so much so that more than 70 percent of Prussia's annual budget of seven million thalers was allocated to the army. The king concentrated on training and drilling until his soldiers became virtual automatons, responding to orders as a single unit, changing direction and shifting from marching column into battle formation and back again. Under this relentless regime, the firepower of Prussian musketeers, using iron ramrods to tamp down the charge in muzzle-loading flintlock muskets, was increased to six times per minute — three times greater than that of most European armies. Frederick William I also reorganized the Prussian cavalry into 55 squadrons of 150 horsemen each and the infantry into 25 regiments.

Frederick the Great's military innovations exceeded his father's; he recruited the entire population of Prussia into the army. Their tasks were strictly divided along social lines with Junkers, the Prussian nobility, making up the officer class whilst the middle class were expected to run the bureaucracy that supported the army and provided quarters for the soldiery. The army's manpower was drawn from the masses of peasants. By the end of Frederick II's reign in 1786 the size of the army had reached 193,000.

When he became king, Frederick II's potential for making war was considerable, but he had to make do with a lesser title, King in Prussia, for his territories were strung out over a wide area. Frederick was determined to reconnect his scattered lands into a great empire. In his way stood Austria, with its connection to the Holy Roman Empire, whose rulers were members of the Austrian Habsburg dynasty. Austria's allies also weighed in, hoping to put down the upstart Prussia, which meant that Frederick was also confronted by France, Russia, Saxony, and Sweden. His allies were Great Britain and the German state of Hanover, whose ruling elector, his uncle George II, was also the king of England.

Despite this apparent imbalance of power, Frederick managed to overcome all his enemies; and by 1772, he ruled over a united state and was, at last, able to claim the title King of Prussia. Frederick had been active throughout this long endeavor. He was a serving officer in the Prussian army at age 18, and later he personally led his armies into battle on several occasions. He was so often involved in the heat of battle that he had six horses shot from under him.

The new army regulations which Frederick issued shortly after the start of his reign were, therefore, drawn from personal experience and observation and from that sense, so valuable in a commander, of where to draw the line between intelligent attack and assault by bravado. Frederick favored speed and offense in war, which meant that light, fast cavalry was preferred and that the smaller but versatile 3-pounder gun was the weapon of choice for the artillery. Frederick considered wars of attrition needlessly wasteful because they could lead to doubtful outcomes in battle. His preference was for overpowering

During his reign between 1740 and 1786, the reforms instituted by Frederick II (the Great) of Prussia gave his relatively tiny kingdom the military dominance that ultimately made it the mighty power which unified the whole of Germany.

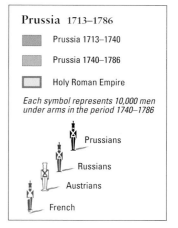

Prussia 1713–1786

■ Prussia 1713–1740

■ Prussia 1740–1786

□ Holy Roman Empire

Each symbol represents 10,000 men under arms in the period 1740–1786

Prussians

Russians

Austrians

French

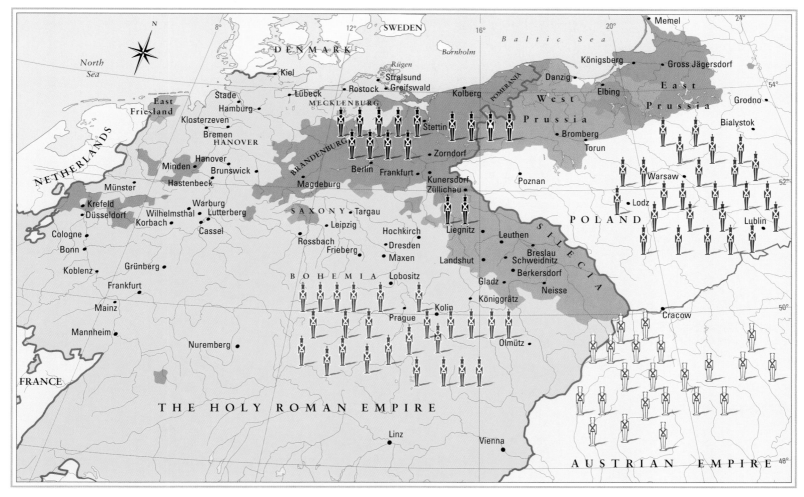

attack and speedy action. He dispensed with the frontal attack and the large numbers of casualties it caused in favor of the oblique approach. In this, the Prussian army set its strongest wing against an opponent's weakest.

This technique of oblique attack was brilliantly carried out against the Austrians at the Battle of Leuthen near Breslau in Prussian Silesia. It took place on December 6 1757, during the Seven Years' War. At Leuthen, the Austrian left flank was broken by heavy bombardment from the Prussian artillery and then thrown back when charged by the Prussian cavalry. The cavalry then went on to foil an attempt by the Austrian cavalry against the Prussian left flank. Caught off balance, the Austrians were unable to rally themselves and ended up making an ignominious escape to nearby Breslau across the River Schwiednitz. Many years later, Napoleon Bonaparte described the Prussian tactics at Leuthen as a "masterpiece of maneuver and resolution"

Frederick the Great was a keen admirer of another "great" king, Gustavus II Adolphus of Sweden (see pages 130–133), whose tactical developments had transformed artillery in the early 17th century. Frederick added his own innovation to the Swedish king's reforms: he introduced horses to the artillery. This provided a solution to the problem that had been so acute in the 16th century: guns that were too heavy and bulky to be moved at a reasonable speed (see pages 118–121). In Frederick's army, all the gunners and ammunition handlers were mounted, to ensure that the Prussian artillery, which was of the lighter variety, did not fall behind the fast-moving Prussian cavalry. In addition, Frederick exploited the high trajectory of the howitzer by concealing the gun so that it could fire from behind trees or hills, where the enemy, not suspecting its presence, could be taken by surprise.

Frederick also made important changes in the tasks of the cavalry, restoring it to its original function of administering shock action on the battlefield and providing reconnaissance off it. The Prussian cavalry went into action in triple formation, later amended to double, and did so at full gallop. But Frederick banned his cavalry from carrying firearms, preferring instead that they should be armed with long sabers. This did not apply to the dragoons, who fought on foot as well as on horseback. Although elsewhere in Europe the intermingling of cavalry with infantry in a battle line was still common, this was not permitted for Prussian horsemen, who were already acting separately in battle, even before the last use of this formation, at Minden in 1759.

Napoleon Bonaparte, who regarded Frederick the Great as the greatest military tactician of all time, was only one of his many admirers. Frederick also drew praise from his deadliest enemy, the Austrian Emperor Josef II, who considered him a knave, yet despite this he wrote in a letter to his mother Maria Theresa: "When the King of Prussia speaks on problems connected with the art of war, which he has studied intensively and on which he has read every conceivable book, then everything is taut, solid and uncommonly instructive. There are no circumlocutions, he gives factual and historical proof of the assertions he makes, for he is well versed in history." He was "a genius," the emperor concluded, "and a man who talks admirably".

The genius, however, had his military weaknesses. One was the reluctance frequently displayed by Frederick the Great to pursue a fleeing enemy after a victory in battle. However, it has been suggested that this was likely due to the rigid military system in which 18th century commanders had to operate and the draconian discipline that was necessary to keep in line the good-for-nothing undesirables who often made up the average European armies of the 18th century. This was a situation greatly exacerbated by the relatively small number of men available for military service and the difficulties that were so often involved in obtaining new recruits.

In this context, it was better to maintain discipline, even if it sometimes mirrored sadism, rather than allow an army to disperse while ostensibly in pursuit that risked the possibility of desertion in the field. There were also too many temptations that might lure soldiers into wrongdoing. After all, it was not unknown for pillaging, raping, or terrorizing the local populace to take place while armies foraged for food and supplies in the vicinity of a battle.

King Frederick, who took so much time and trouble to train, drill, and discipline his armies, was well aware how expensive it was to produce soldiers of the right caliber and how valuable were the skills they acquired in handling their weaponry. No prudent commander was likely to risk losing men who were so important to achieving victory on the battlefield for the sake of a chase that could easily turn out to be no more than an exercise in bloody revenge.

Frederick the Great's victory at Rossbach in 1757 saw the success of his "rapid movement" strategy against the armies of France and the Holy Roman Empire. The Prussians destroyed their enemies while suffering few casualties of their own.

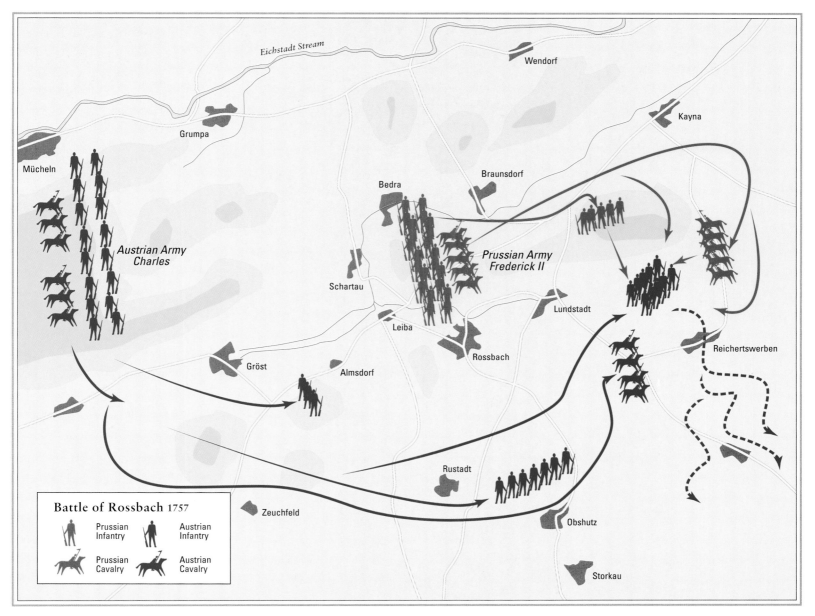

Battle of Rossbach 1757

Prussian Infantry   Austrian Infantry

Prussian Cavalry   Austrian Cavalry

ARTILLERY COMES INTO ITS OWN

SEVERAL PROBLEMS AFFLICTING ARTILLERY WERE FINALLY SOLVED IN THE 18TH CENTURY BY LIEUTENANT-GENERAL JEAN BAPTISTE VAQUETTE DE GRIBEAUVAL, A FRENCH OFFICER. HIS REFORMS WERE SO EFFECTIVE THEY WERE LATER ADOPTED BY THE U.S. ARMY.

Even the military genius of Frederick the Great of Prussia had not entirely solved the cumbersome nature of artillery in battle. Despite the changes Frederick introduced during the Seven Years' War of 1756–1763, there were still too many calibers and the guns themselves remained too weighty to be sufficiently mobile on the battlefield. Then, two years after the end of the Seven Years' War in Europe, an obscure French army officer, Lieutenant-General Jean Baptiste Vaquette de Gribeauval, inaugurated changes that revolutionized artillery and later provided Napoleon Bonaparte with a mighty military arm for his early all-conquering campaigns.

Before de Gribeauval, French artillery had been designed and constructed under a system devised by another French officer, Florent-Jean de Vallière, who reorganized and systematized the army's ordnance along new lines that gave them greater precision. One important innovation was the core drilling of cannon bores that had been made from a single piece of bronze. Another was the use of decorative animal heads, which enabled artillerymen to quickly identify the rating of individual guns: for example, a rooster head motif for a 12-pounder and a lion head motif for a 24-pounder. The French supplied de Vallière guns to the colonists in the American War of Independence, and George Washington was so pleased with their performance at Saratoga in 1777 that he described them as "most valuable". Yet problems remained. De Vallière guns were useful in siege warfare, when mobility was not an issue, but did not perform so well in wars of movement and maneuver that characterized much of 18th century combat. Nor did the de Vallière system include a howitzer, which fired shot with a high trajectory and steep descent.

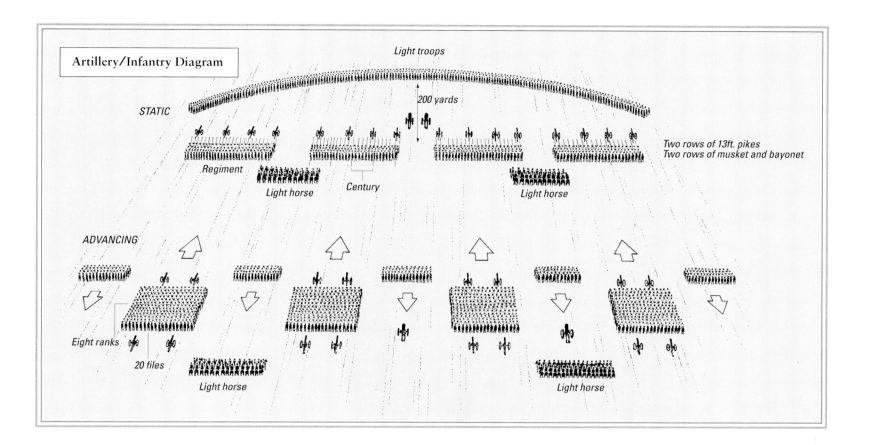

Artillery/Infantry Diagram

Light troops

STATIC

200 yards

Two rows of 13ft. pikes
Two rows of musket and bayonet

Regiment

Light horse Century Light horse

ADVANCING

Eight ranks

20 files

Light horse Light horse

The de Gribeauval system, which was officially announced by an order from Louis XV in 1765, furnished a howitzer of six-inch caliber. The system restricted gun weights to 4-, 8-, and 12-pounders, which subsequently became dominant on battlefields worldwide. All were smoothbores cast in bronze or iron and were comparatively light cannons, designed for use as field artillery. De Gribeauval also provided specialized siege guns which were heavier: his *canon de 24, canon de 16,* and two *canon lourd* (heavy cannon), a *canon lourd de 8,* and a *canon lourd de 12.* To these were added a series of mortars: an 8-inch mortar, a short mortar, the *mortier court de 10,* a long mortar, *the mortier longue de 10,* and the mortier de 12. In addition, de Gribeauval borrowed a 38 cm anti-personnel stone mortar from the de Vallière system. De Gribeauval's artillery was also used after 1780 alongside the de Vallière guns in the American War of Independence by the French expeditionary corps commanded by General Jean-Baptiste, Comte de Rochambeau. They were present at the Siege of Yorktown in 1781.

When de Gribeauval tackled the problem of artillery production, especially for large guns, he found that they were being cast in one piece by melting the iron or bronze and pouring it around a clay cylinder. The clay was removed once the metal had cooled, in this way creating the bore of the gun. The trouble was that this was a crude system that left the core of the gun in faulty condition. That had several unsatisfactory consequences. It stopped cannon balls from achieving a tight fit inside the barrel. The explosive force of the gunpowder was reduced, which affected range and accuracy.

To correct this problem, de Gribeauval radically revised the production system along lines previously advocated by Jean Maritz, a Swiss inventor who became *Commissaire des Fontes* (Commissioner of the King's Foundry) at Strasbourg in eastern France. In 1713 Maritz invented a vertical drilling machine for use on cannons. This was imprecise, so Maritz followed it up in 1734 with a method for drilling

Infantry formation first used by the French Marshak Maurice de Saxe (1679-1750). De Saxe recommended that light artillery should advance with the infantry to provide extra firepower and that skirmishers should front the main advance.

cannons horizontally. His methods meant that a cannon bore had to be drilled from a solid casting. The cannon itself revolved while the drill remained fixed, in much the same manner as a lathe. The result was a perfectly straight bore that tightly fitted the diameter of the cannon ball. The Maritz method also permitted the founding of thinner, lighter barrels, but did not affect the range of the guns. In addition, because the cannonball was a better fit for the gun barrel, the barrel itself could be shortened. This combination of less weight and a more convenient, smaller size made handling and transporting a gun much easier.

De Grieauval facilitated the use of artillery even more by developing interchangeable gun parts. Tackling the longstanding problem of mobility, he changed the role of horses, which had provided traction in tandem, and rearranged them in pairs. Drivers had previously been hired civilians, but they had proved largely unreliable. They were replaced by serving soldiers. Gun carriages were provided with limbers: detachable fronts consisting of two wheels and an axle, a pole and a frame holding one or more ammunition boxes. Tangent scales and elevating screws made aiming a gun easier and more accurate.

De Gribeauval's reforms were so fundamental that a great deal of existing weapons in use by the

French army became redundant almost immediately. However, hostilities were still going on in Britain's American colonies where the colonists were fighting for their independence.

The outdated artillery, including the guns designed by de Vallière, were shipped under cover of secrecy to America where one of de Gribeauval's assistants, Philip Tronson du Coudray, oversaw their delivery. Unfortunately for du Coudray, his involvement in shipping the artillery to America cost him a promotion to General of artillery and ordnance for which he was being considered by the American Congress. A British general, Henry Knox, was chosen instead.

Nevertheless, de Gribeauval had a more direct effect on American military men who were much impressed by his work and adopted his reforms for their own weaponry. De Gribeauval's systems and designs continued to exert an influence on American military practice in both the U..S. Civil War, which took place between 1861 and 1865 and even as long after the Frenchman's lifetime, as in World War One in which the United States was involved in 1917 and 1918.

De Gribeauval's reordering of French artillery lasted for almost 90 years, until his system was replaced by *canons obusier de 12* (shell-firing cannon) introduced in 1853.

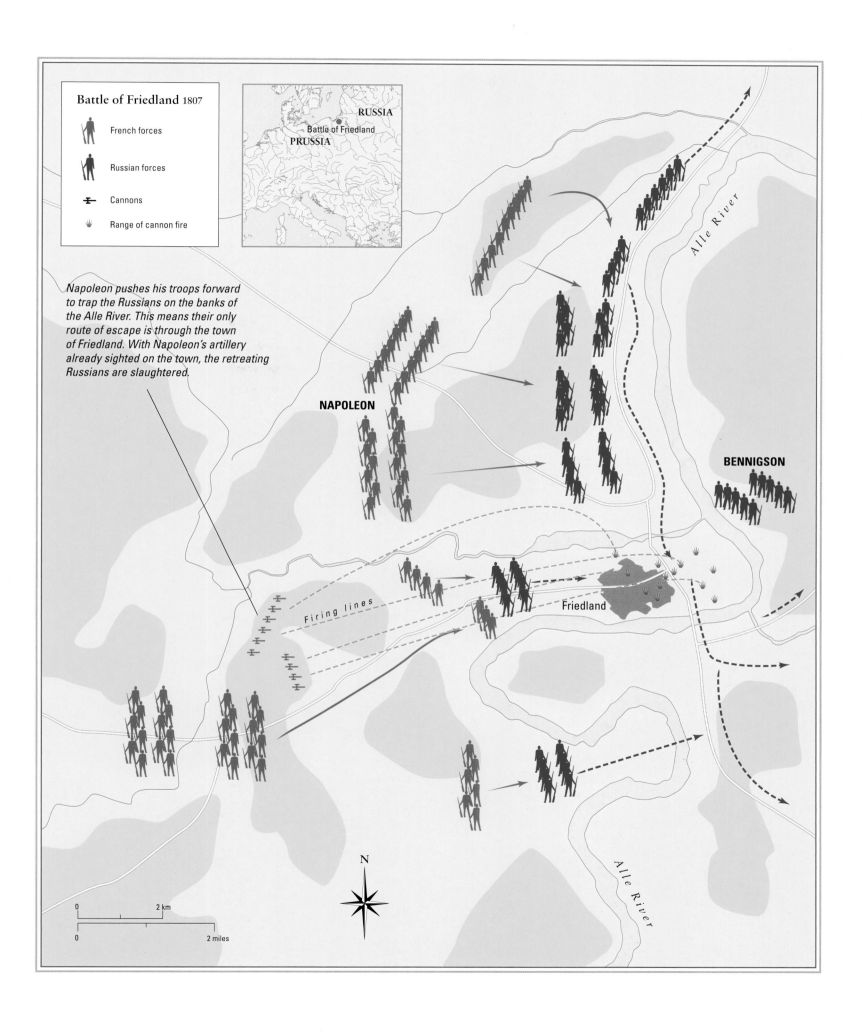

Battle of Friedland 1807

- French forces
- Russian forces
- Cannons
- Range of cannon fire

RUSSIA

Battle of Friedland

PRUSSIA

Napoleon pushes his troops forward to trap the Russians on the banks of the Alle River. This means their only route of escape is through the town of Friedland. With Napoleon's artillery already sighted on the town, the retreating Russians are slaughtered.

NAPOLEON

BENNIGSON

Alle River

Firing lines

Friedland

Alle River

N

0   2 km

0   2 miles

THE BIRTH OF THE RIFLE

18TH CENTURY GUNSMITHS INTRODUCED A REVOLUTION IN WEAPONRY AND WARFARE BY ADDING GROOVES TO SMOOTHBORE GUN BARRELS, CAUSING THE BULLETS TO SPIN. THIS INNOVATION INCREASED THE ACCURACY AND RANGE OF THE RIFLE.

The value of rifling was already known before the hand-held firearm was properly developed. As early as the 15th century, archers realized that if they twisted the tail feathers at the ends of their arrows, the arrows would fly on a truer trajectory and achieve greater accuracy. However, the technological knowledge and expertise required to rifle the barrel of a smoothbore arquebus or musket of the time did not exist until almost four centuries later. Thus the development of the rifle was unable to go ahead for another 300 years or more.

It was not until the early 18th century that an English mathematician named Benjamin Robins recognized that an elongated bullet was able to cut through the air much more easily and smoothly than a round musket ball, which was usually fired at a very low velocity. Furthermore, the musket tended to be inaccurate: the ball did not fit the barrel tightly, so that when the musket was fired, the ball would ricochet along the barrel wall and, on emerging from the muzzle, shoot off in a direction that no one could predict. Additionally, the cloud of smoke caused by the black powder explosive used in muskets was likely to obscure the target so that aiming at an opponent was usually ineffective. In practice, the function of the musket was more likely to be unaimed volley-fire, a hit-or-miss recourse that could kill some opponents but miss many others.

A handful of rifles were produced for civilian hunters in the later 18th century. These proved to be highly accurate, but the black gunpowder then in use meant that the rifling grooves clogged up with residue after only three or four shots. The additional pressures created by pushing a ball up a rifled barrel meant that the barrel had to be stronger, and therefore thicker and heavier. Such rifles were deemed to be too cumbersome and unreliable for use on the battlefield and were not taken up by the military.

The first military rifle to enter service in large numbers was the British Baker Rifle. This weapon was produced by London gunmaker Ezekiel Baker in 1800 and submitted to the British Board of Ordnance. The British army was in the process of forming a special force of light infantry and wanted a weapon more accurate than the standard 'Brown Bess' musket for use in skirmishing. Baker produced a gun that had a shorter barrel than a musket and fired a smaller ball. The result was a rifle that was no heavier than the 'Brown Bess' and so could be carried on campaign. The problems of fouling in the barrel were in part solved by equipping each rifle with a cleaning kit that fitted into a compartment within the stock. Even so, Baker rifles often fouled and so the ramrod was strengthened so that in an emergency men could literally hammer a ball down the barrel.

At first the rifles were used by entire regiments specially trained in using them. The 95th Rifles was equipped in 1800, at the same time adopting a uniform of dull green and black that contrasted with the usual red coats and white braid of the British infantry. The 60th Regiment was converted to rifles soon afterward, and likewise adopted the more camouflaged green uniform to aid thier skirmishing role. The riflemen proved to be highly effective against French skirmishers, who were still using standard muskets, and by 1820 most British infantry regiments had a light company armed with rifles. However, the Baker Rifle, and its various improved versions, remained slow to fire, difficult to handle, and liable to foul in battle.

In 1848 the man who solved the problem of hit-or-miss musket fire mentioned earlier in the chapter was Claude Etienne Minié, the French inventor of the ball and the rifle that were named after him. Minié became interested in a ball devised by two French army captains, had the advantage that it could be loaded rapidly into the muzzle of a rifled musket and rammed down until it had expanded to fill the grooves inside the barrel. This had been achieved by one of the French captains, Henri-Gustave Delvigne, in 1826.

Russian standard infantry cap gun from the time of the Crimean war (1853-1856) which was fought between the Russian Empire on one side and an alliance of France, the Ottoman Empire and Great Britain on the other.

Painting of the confrontation between the Russians and the allies in Ukraine during the Crimean war, 1854-1855. .

After Minié adopted Delvigne's idea as a basis for experiment, he designed a conical soft lead bullet that had four grooves filled with grease on the outside and a cone-shaped hollow in the base. The base also contained a small iron plug, which helped to drive the ball forward, thus reducing the amount the bullet would ricochet along the barrel wall. The Minié ball came separately wrapped in a paper cartridge and was inserted into the barrel while the rifleman poured in the gunpowder. When the rifle was fired, the gas expanded, pushed hard on the base of the ball and made it press against the rifle grooves. As the bullet became subject to pressure from the gunpowder gases, it would swell until the hollow at its base filled up and the lead skirting around its edge gripped the rifling grooves of the barrel. In this way, the bullet was provided with spin, meaning it would fly a truer trajectory and achieve greater accuracy. This was the same spin that the 15th century archers created by twisting the ends of their arrows. Another advance that came with the Minié bullet was that the seal inside the barrel, and the barrel itself, was cleaned in the process of firing.

The Minié bullet was tested at Vincennes, near Paris, in 1849. The result of this test showed that when a rifle was fired at a distance of 45 in (1.14 m), the Minié bullet could slice through two planks of poplar wood, each measuring ⅝ in (1.7 cm) with a 20 in (51 cm) space between them. The key advantage of the Minie system was, however, that the bullet was slightly smaller than the bore of the rifle. This allowed men on the battlefield to load their rifles just as fast as did men armed with smoothbore muskets. The problem of fouling the barrel with residue from black powder remained, but this now affected the accuracy and range of the fired shot not the speed with which weapons could be loaded and fired. So long as the weapon was cleaned at the first possible opportunity after being fired, even this did not prove to be a great problem. On the battlefield, the muzzle-loaded Minie rifle quickly ousted its smoothbore counterpart.

Soon other nations were adapting the essentials of the French system to their own infantry weapons. In 1853 the British produced the Enfield Rifle, which was reckoned to be accurate up to about 700 yd (640 m) and to have a useful range of about 1,200 yd (1,097 m). By the time of the Crimean War of 1854 about half the British infantry were equipped with Enfields, the rest still retaining the brown bess. The Enfield proved to be a popular export model, especially to the USA. More than a million Enfields were in the hands of the various state militias when the American Civil War broke out in 1861. In that year the US government approved its own version of the Minie system in the shape of the Springfield 1861 Rifle. By the end of the Civil War the Springfield 1861 equipped most of the Unionist infantry, while the Confederates still favored the Enfield. The power of the Minié bullet caused huge numbers of casualties — some 714,000 men died on both sides in the Civil War. The use of the Minié bullet also resulted in injuries more severe than was normally expected in the warfare of the time.

Below: Lexington and Concord saw the first battles of the American War of Independence in 1775 and some of the heaviest losses of the entire war due to the role of the rifle. British troops intent on destroying the colonists' military supplies met fierce opposition.

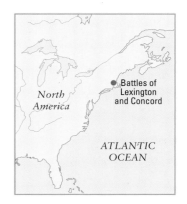

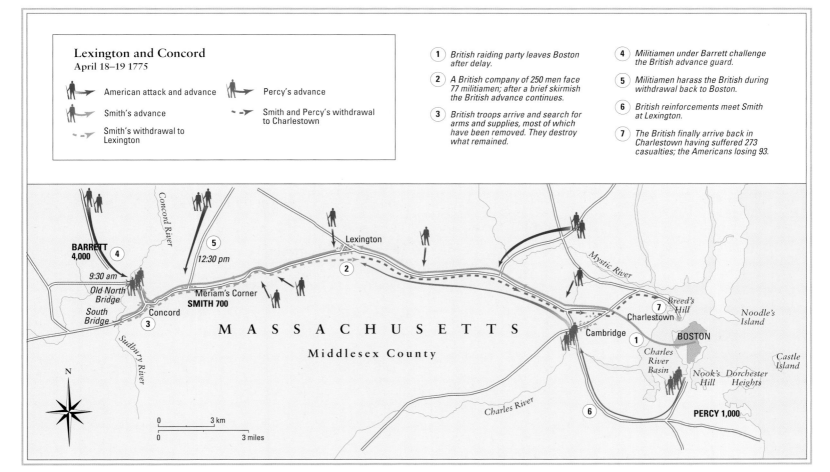

Lexington and Concord
April 18–19 1775

→ American attack and advance

→ Smith's advance

⇢ Smith's withdrawal to Lexington

→ Percy's advance

⇢ Smith and Percy's withdrawal to Charlestown

1. British raiding party leaves Boston after delay.

2. A British company of 250 men face 77 militiamen; after a brief skirmish the British advance continues.

3. British troops arrive and search for arms and supplies, most of which have been removed. They destroy what remained.

4. Militiamen under Barrett challenge the British advance guard.

5. Militiamen harass the British during withdrawal back to Boston.

6. British reinforcements meet Smith at Lexington.

7. The British finally arrive back in Charlestown having suffered 273 casualties; the Americans losing 93.

WEAPONS OF THE AMERICAN REVOLUTION

THE QUICKLY ACQUIRED WEAPONS USED IN THE AMERICAN REVOLUTION AGAINST THE BRITISH ARMY INCLUDED A MIXTURE OF OLD AND UP-TO-DATE WEAPONS: SMOOTHBORE RIFLES AND MUSKETS, CANNONS AND SWORDS, PISTOLS AND AXES.

Opposite page: The 1,900 British troops were outnumbered by the 4,400 colonial forces at the battle of Guilford Courthouse in 1781, yet the British managed to drive their opponents from the field because the forest hampered the effectiveness of the American artillery that included guns that had to be manoeuvred by manned drag ropes. Sensing that they faced disaster, the colonial forces broke off the fighting and retreated.

The colonists' military supplies came, first of all, from the colonial militias in which men from age 16 to 60 were required to own a longarm, such as a flintlock musket, together with a sword, a bayonet, or a belt axe. The muskets were an assortment of hunting and military weapons, some of which had been taken from Loyalists, who supported the British colonial rulers. Others were obtained from European dealers with a surplus to spare. Yet others had been obtained from the British before the disputes that led to the revolution. Among these older weapons were several "Brown Bess" flintlock black-powder muzzle-loaders, a smoothbore with a .75 caliber barrel and a weight of up to 11 lb (5 kg). The "Brown Bess" muskets came in two barrel lengths: the Long Land 46 in (1.2 m) and the Short Land 42 in (1.1 m). Many of the Long Land muskets used in the Revolutionary War were dated 1756. Others, mainly those used by the colonists early on in the war, were even older muskets dating from 1730 or 1742. They belonged to the Long Land series, which was more than 55 years old when they were pressed into the service of the Revolution.

The British forces were equipped with precisely the same muskets when hostilities began, as they had around 5,200 stored in New York and in Quebec in Canada. Later on, like the revolutionaries, the British acquired the more recent Long Land muskets of 1756. The crucial difference between the older Long Land muskets and the 1756 models was that the former used wooden ramrods to tamp down their charge; the latter employed the stronger and more reliable iron ramrods.

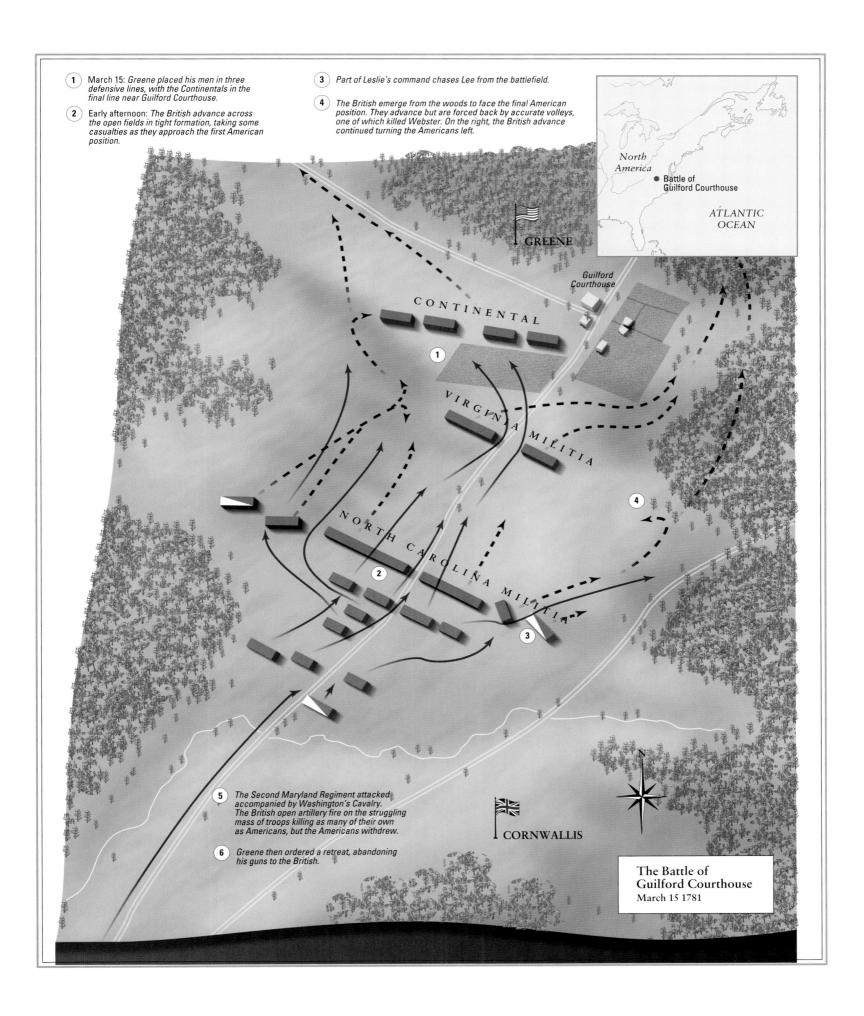

1 March 15: *Greene placed his men in three defensive lines, with the Continentals in the final line near Guilford Courthouse.*

2 Early afternoon: *The British advance across the open fields in tight formation, taking some casualties as they approach the first American position.*

3 *Part of Leslie's command chases Lee from the battlefield.*

4 *The British emerge from the woods to face the final American position. They advance but are forced back by accurate volleys, one of which killed Webster. On the right, the British advance continued turning the Americans left.*

North America

Battle of Guilford Courthouse

ATLANTIC OCEAN

GREENE

Guilford Courthouse

CONTINENTAL

VIRGINIA MILITIA

NORTH CAROLINA MILITIA

5 *The Second Maryland Regiment attacked accompanied by Washington's Cavalry. The British open artillery fire on the struggling mass of troops killing as many of their own as Americans, but the Americans withdrew.*

6 *Greene then ordered a retreat, abandoning his guns to the British.*

CORNWALLIS

N

The Battle of Guilford Courthouse
March 15 1781

Opposite page: On September 30, 1781, at Yorktown, the British commander General Cornwallis withdrew his forces to the inner fortifications. This, however, exposed the British to the combined artillery of the colonists and their French allies. The siege was primarily an exchange of artillery fire, waged at long range with relatively few direct troop confrontations. Estimates place the total number of siege and field artillery pieces at upwards of 375. During the eight-day siege, the Allies fired an average of 1,700 cannon balls and bombs per day. This comes to about 1.2 every minute. Cornwallis had no option but to surrender to the colonists..

During the eight years of the Revolution, gun-makers in England produced over 218,000 Land Service muskets for the theater of war across the Atlantic. The colonists were supplied by the French, who harbored their own resentments against the British after suffering grievous defeats at their hands during the Seven Years' War. After 1757, the French lost control of their highly lucrative trade in India; and two years later, they lost New France, their much-prized colony in Canada.

In 1778, the French exchanged support from the wings for active military participation and entered the war on the American side. They continued to supply the colonists with much-needed materials such as muskets with bayonets. These included the 42 in (1.1 m) Charleyville as well as uniforms, cannons, and cartridge boxes. The French muskets could fire every 15 seconds, a great improvement on previous, poor rates of fire. In battle, the bayonets, which the colonists had formerly lacked, served as important weapons against the British cavalry: by forming a rectangle or square, the colonists, facing outward, could present attacking horsemen with a "hedgehog" of bayonets that prevented them from coming too close.

Even so, among the French cynical self-interest was involved. Some of the cannons they were shipping to America were out of date, for many of them were manufactured under the de Vallière system, which had been superseded by the de Gribeauval system in 1765 (see pages 142–145). The British response was to add to their arsenal another 100,000 Short Land pattern firearms made in Liège in Belgium and in Germany. The colonists too increased their store of muskets by managing to capture 17,000 from the British during the fighting.

Although the rifle, which featured a grooved barrel to spin the bullet and make it more accurate, eventually made the musket obsolete, it was actually less efficient at this stage. It was slower to load than the musket, taking between 30 seconds and a minute. Rifles were therefore secondary firearms in the American Revolution. Another drawback, before the French supplied them with artillery, was a shortfall in the cannons the American colonists could bring to the battlefield. Knowing that infantry without cannon support usually lost, the American militias preferred to avoid confrontation when their better-equipped British opponents arrived on the battlefield with batteries of guns.

At the time of the Revolution, cannons had a range of hundreds of feet. For example, the range of a 3-pounder firing solid shot was around 798 yd (730 m) or, if firing grapeshot, 133 yd (122 m). Grapeshot, so-called because of its resemblance to a bunch of grapes, was an anti-personnel weapon composed of metal slugs, shards of glass, stones, rocks, and iron or lead balls about 1 in (2.5 cm) thick. When packed in a canvas bag and fired from a cannon at high speed, the grapeshot spread out into a shower of small but deadly missiles capable of slaughtering an entire company of men at close range.

The cannons used in the Revolutionary War were smoothbore muzzle-loaders of relatively modest size, usually 3-, 4- or 6- pounder (1.4-, 1.8-, or 2.7- kg) guns. Occasionally larger, 12-pound guns were used on the battlefield, but more often they were confined to fortifications and ships. Some 3-pounders were mounted onto carriages, which had large wheels to facilitate movement over rough ground. Among these cannons were "grasshopper" guns which stood on iron legs. Ammunition for most cannons were solid balls, small shot or, occasionally, shells. These were iron balls filled with black powder and they carried a fuse. Buckshot, musket balls, or grapeshot provided the ammunition.

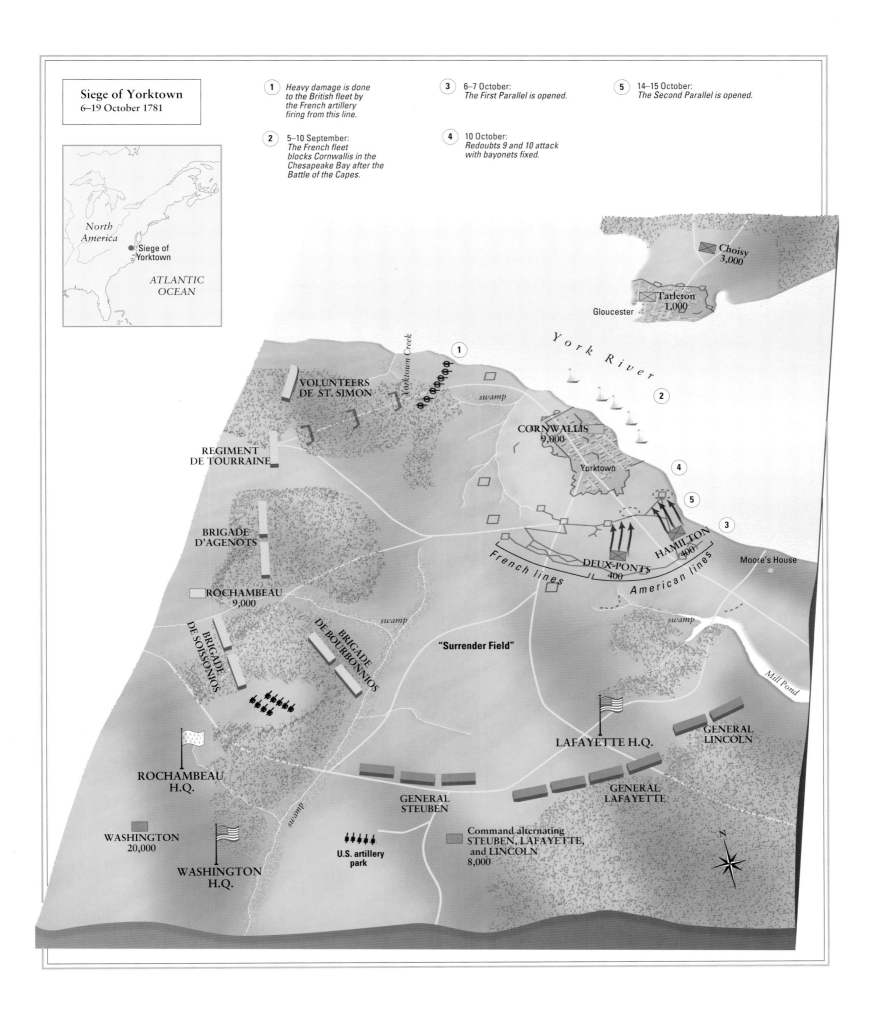

Siege of Yorktown
6–19 October 1781

North America

ATLANTIC OCEAN

● Siege of Yorktown

1 Heavy damage is done to the British fleet by the French artillery firing from this line.

2 5–10 September: The French fleet blocks Cornwallis in the Chesapeake Bay after the Battle of the Capes.

3 6–7 October: The First Parallel is opened.

4 10 October: Redoubts 9 and 10 attack with bayonets fixed.

5 14–15 October: The Second Parallel is opened.

Choisy 3,000

Gloucester

Tarleton 1,000

York River

Yorktown Creek

swamp

VOLUNTEERS DE ST. SIMON

REGIMENT DE TOURRAINE

CORNWALLIS 9,000

Yorktown

BRIGADE D'AGENOTS

ROCHAMBEAU 9,000

DEUX-PONTS 400

HAMILTON 400

French lines

American lines

Moore's House

BRIGADE DE SOISSONIOS

BRIGADE DE BOURBONNIOS

swamp

swamp

Mill Pond

"Surrender Field"

ROCHAMBEAU H.Q.

LAFAYETTE H.Q.

GENERAL LINCOLN

GENERAL STEUBEN

GENERAL LAFAYETTE

WASHINGTON 20,000

U.S. artillery park

Command alternating STEUBEN, LAFAYETTE, and LINCOLN 8,000

WASHINGTON H.Q.

N

WEAPONS IN THE NAPOLEONIC ERA

THE NAPOLEONIC ERA LASTED FROM NAPOLEON'S SEIZURE OF POWER IN 1799 AND ENDED WITH HIS DEFEAT AT WATERLOO IN 1815. BUT HIS MILITARY GENIUS WOULD GO ON TO INFLUENCE THE FACTORS THAT MODERNIZED WEAPONS AND WARFARE, MOVING THE BATTLEFIELD CLOSER TO WHAT WE KNOW TODAY.

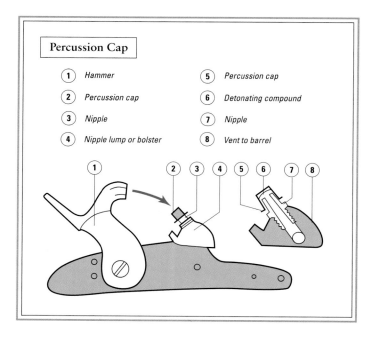

Percussion Cap

①	Hammer	⑤	Percussion cap
②	Percussion cap	⑥	Detonating compound
③	Nipple	⑦	Nipple
④	Nipple lump or bolster	⑧	Vent to barrel

After the introduction of guns and gunpowder in around 1325, 500 years passed before weapons and tactics became properly harmonized. This did not occur until the early 19th century, when Napoleon Bonaparte, a military genius comparable to Alexander the Great (see page 58), was making his appearance on the battlefield. By Napoleon's time, the flintlock musket and the smoothbore cannon had reached their maximum potential and the techniques of employing these weapons with cavalry had been developed.

The Industrial Revolution began in northern England in the middle of the 18th century and by the 19th century, had brought fundamental change to the manufacturing of goods through mass production. The wealth generated by the Industrial Revolution in turn generated new and rapid developments in weapons manufacture. The early 19th century was the era of the great steel and ordnance empires in Germany, the US, Britain, and Sardinia (part of Italy). Of all the elements of weaponry, gunnery was the first to benefit from this huge industrial effort. The percussion cap was developed and introduced in 1830, supplanting the flintlock. This was the crucial invention that enabled muzzle-loading firearms to fire reliably in any weather, therefore leading the way for the invention of the revolver in 1835. The accuracy and range of the muzzle-loading rifle was improved in 1849 by the new Minié bullet (see page 146–149). The now enhanced rifle replaced the smoothbore musket and became the principal weapon of the infantry.

At this time a new weapon also emerged on the battlefield — the rocket, which was developed by the English ordnance expert Sir William Congreve. Congreve's rocket, devised in 1808, was soon taken up by the British army and navy and several foreign countries. The Rocket appeared in the same year as the commencement of the Peninsular War between Britain and France, fought in Spain. It was again used against the French and their allies at the battle of Leipzig in 1813: Leipzig resulted in arguably the most decisive defeat Napoleon ever suffered. The Rocket went on to appear at Waterloo in 1815.

However, the Rocket was not Congreve's only contribution to early 19th century weaponry. In 1815, he invented a new method for the manufacture of gunpowder. This included a new machine for mixing the ingredients of the gunpowder. Congreve first demonstrated his solid-fuel rockets at the royal arsenal in 1805 and seven years later, the rockets, which had a maximum range of ⅘ mile (1.37 km), were used in the Anglo-American war of 1812. They made such an impression that a reference to them — the "rockets' red glare" — was included in the national anthem of the United States.

Opposite page: The percussion cap, introduced in 1830, enabled muzzle-loading firearms to be used in all weathers. Previously, flintlocks habitually misfired in wet conditions. The hammer (1) striking the percussion cap (2) stopped this from happening.

Below: Western armies put rockets to military use: Congreve's rocket was first used in the Napoleonic Wars, Hale rockets were used during the American Civil War and the French produced artillery rockets in the 18th and 19th centuries.

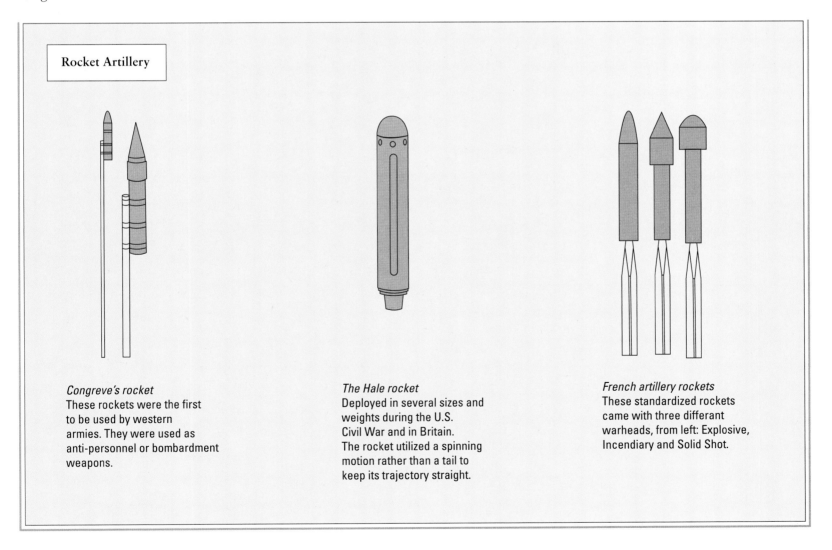

Rocket Artillery

Congreve's rocket
These rockets were the first to be used by western armies. They were used as anti-personnel or bombardment weapons.

The Hale rocket
Deployed in several sizes and weights during the U.S. Civil War and in Britain. The rocket utilized a spinning motion rather than a tail to keep its trajectory straight.

French artillery rockets
These standardized rockets came with three differant warheads, from left: Explosive, Incendiary and Solid Shot.

NAPOLEON'S ARTILLERY

IN USING ARTILLERY, NAPOLEON BUILT ON THE REFORMS OF DE GRIBEAUVAL, EXPLOITING THE EXTRA BATTLEFIELD MOBILITY ACHIEVED WHEN THE LENGTH AND WEIGHT OF GUN BARRELS AND THE WEIGHT OF GUN CARRIAGES WAS REDUCED.

For a long time, the mobility of artillery on the battlefield — or rather, the lack of it — was a thorny problem for military commanders and a big drawback in realizing the full potential of cannons and other big guns. The solution to the problem, which arrived after 1765 with the innovative designs of the de Gribeauval system, accounted for much of the success enjoyed by the French Revolutionary armies as they faced the might of the European monarchies attempting to restore the ousted French monarch to his throne.

Napoleon Bonaparte acquired much of his early experience of warfare in the French Revolutionary Wars, which began in 1792. He was 23 years old and about to be appointed to his first important command, in charge of the revolutionary artillery at Toulon. His military brilliance soon became apparent; and only three years later, he was appointed Commander-in-Chief of the French Revolutionary Army. In 1796, Napoleon commenced the series of military campaigns which, over the next 17 years, enabled him to create an empire in Europe and bestow his name upon an entire era.

Artillery, and especially the mobility it gained under the de Gribeauval system, was the most important factor in Napoleon's style of warfare. He made his own contribution when he provided his gun carriages with axletrees made of iron and gave them large-diameter wheels, which were an advantage on rough ground and helped to maintain the stability of the artillery when in motion. Napoleon's artillery also benefited from greater precision introduced in the manufacture of cannon balls, which became properly rounded and of strictly correct diameter. This had the advantage of reducing the amount of gunpowder needed to fire them. Gunpowder itself underwent a metamorphosis: loose powder, which had always had its dangers, notably premature explosion, was replaced by prefabricated cartridges. With this, the rate of fire intensified. In addition, the arrangement of the horses that drew artillery was changed. It took six horses to draw a 12-pounder (5.4 kg) gun but only four for the lighter 4- and 8-pounder (1.8- and

3.6 kg) guns the 6 in (15.24 cm) howitzers. Under the new arrangement, the horses were harnessed in double rather than single files. There was a commensurate increase in power and strength and, with that, even greater mobility.

Maneuverability was another feature of early 19th-century French artillery, and Napoleon was a master of this military art. One technique, which he frequently employed, was *la grande batterie* (the big battery), which involved massing his artillery in support of his main force on the battlefield. The huge bombardment that resulted virtually annihilated the enemy lines, which made it easier and, of course, less costly for the French infantry to advance. *La grande batterie* was an important component of Napoleon's preferred approach to war, which began with maneuvers to gain the strategic advantage. Then Napoleon continued with a general battle plan whose execution destroyed his opponent's ability to resist. He launched two simultaneous strikes: one at the enemy flank, the other at his front line. Or he would order another double blow comprising a mighty thrust at the center of his opponent's battlefront while attacking his flank. The French divisions assaulting vital objectives were usually given massed artillery support. Once an opponent's main armed force was destroyed, and only then, Napoleon proceeded with the next stage: occupying the enemy's strategic and political centers.

In complete contrast, Napoleon's great rival, Arthur Wellesley, Duke of Wellington, and one of the victors at

Waterloo in 1815, when Napoleon was finally defeated, used his artillery in a much less full-blooded fashion. Wellington's strategy was very sparing. He used his gun batteries only in selected places and in small numbers, strictly reserving them for crucial stages in a battle. Wellington disposed his artillery along the battlefront, where it could support his infantry. Although it lacked the drama and shock-action quality of Napoleon's all-out approach, its relatively minor role in battle was still important to Wellington's successes.

Although they were classed as "heavy artillery", Napoleon's guns were about one-third lighter than Wellington's or, indeed, the artillery of any other European country. For instance, the barrel of a British 12-pounder (5.4 kg) together with its carriage and limber weighed around 6,613 lb (3,000 kg). The gun barrel alone weighed 3,152 lb (1,430 kg). By contrast, the 12-pounder (5.4 kg) built under the de Gribeauval system weighed); 4,367 lb (1,981 kg) with its carriage and limber; the gun barrel weighed 2,173 lb (986 kg). The fact that bronze was used for French gun barrels helped to reduce their weight. Lighter guns

In 1853, France introduced the *canon-obusier de 12*, a 12-pounder (5.4 kg) capable of using either shells, shot, or canisters. The 12-pound cannons had been a favorite weapon of the *Grande Armée* during the Napoleonic Wars; 1806–1812 and 1812–1815. These muzzle-loading smoothbore 12-pounders (5.4 kg) were later known as Napoleon cannons in honor of the French emperor, himself a former artillery officer.

that fired like "heavy artillery" suited Napoleon very well, as his style of warfare was all about mobility and speed. During his campaigns, this gave him a distinct advantage over the many coalition armies he encountered, which almost always outnumbered his own. The French army also had a large choice of shot with its extensive stocks of furnace bombs, grapeshot, canister shot, and mortars. In addition, the capabilities of the French artillery increased greatly during Napoleon's years as an active commander of armies. For example, the army he led into Italy in 1796 possessed 60 guns. But in 1812, at the Battle of Borodino, which was fought during Napoleon's ill-fated invasion of Russia, both sides employed a total of almost 1,200 guns. They fired an average of 15,000 rounds per hour during one day's fighting. The effect of so many guns firing at one time was to cause a high-pressure area. For one Russian messenger, this meant keeping his mouth open as he crossed the battlefield so that he could stabilize the pressure and keep on moving. On the French side, the heaviest standard field gun used at Borodino and elsewhere was the 12-pounder (5.4 kg). The normal bore diameter of these guns was around 9 inches; the equivalent diameter of the 6-pounders (2.7 kg) was around 3½ in (9 cm).

Transporting the 12-pounders (5.4 kg) to and from the battlefield required loading the gun barrel onto a set of supporting cylindrical projections, which held them in place on each side of the gun. By this means, the barrel's center of gravity moved toward the middle of the limber assembly. This arrangement had the advantage of allowing the gun to travel over rough, uneven ground and reduced the chance of overturning. Once on the battlefield, the gun barrel was moved into the forward firing position, ready for action.

The Battle of Austerlitz, December 2 1805. The first engagement of the War of the Third Coalition was one of Napoleon's greatest victories. His 68,000 troops defeated almost 90,000 Russians and Austrians nominally under General M.I. Kutuzov, forcing Austria to make peace with France (Treaty of Pressburg) and keeping Prussia temporarily out of the anti-French alliance.

The organization of Napoleon's artillery differed from the traditional conventions. In the 18th century, there was a pool of artillery units that were alloted to various commanders. Although the Austrians and the Russians employed this system, they still managed to mass artillery into larger units, a method also used by Napoleon. But he began from a different base, for French practice was powerfully influenced by the democratic nature of the French Revolution. The social background of other European armies, notably the Austrian and Russian, was much more despotic in character; the army structure was strictly hierarchical and operated on unthinking obedience to orders. There was more scope for individuals in the French army, which had been rearranged into divisions and corps. This allowed for self-determination among artillery formations, which were under the command of independent-minded young officers much like the young Napoleon in his early years as an artillery officer. They were not afraid to speak their minds to their commanders when proposing innovations of their own devising, something no Austrian or Russian soldier would have dared to attempt. This freedom of ideas was particularly important when it came to co-ordinating artillery fire, and it was noteworthy that Napoleon's armies made gun batteries into particularly powerful offensive weapons.

Battle of Marengo, fought in Italy in 1800. The Austrians had driven Napoleon's forces back for two miles (3.2 km) and mistakenly believed they had won. Napoleon, however, rallied his men, sent for reinforcements and hit back. The Austrian resistance collapsed.

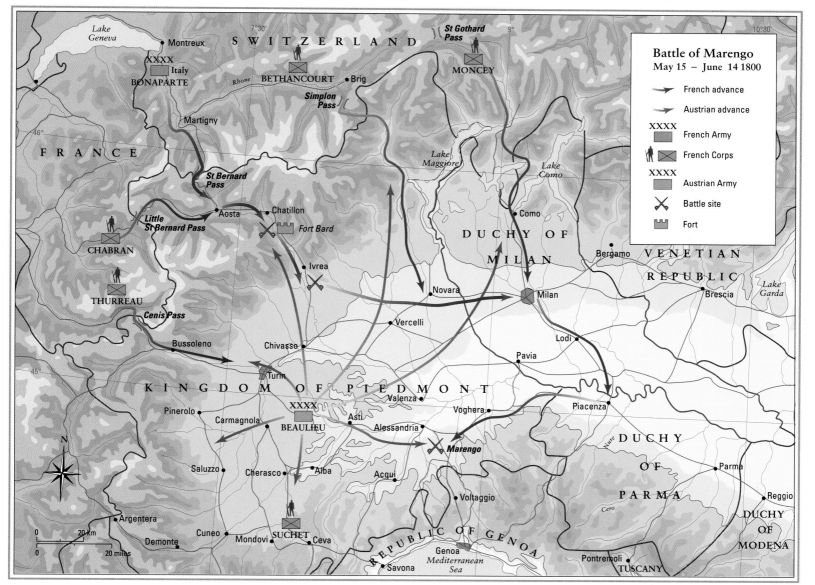

The Battle of Borodino
September 7 1812

French commander

Russian commander

A Army

C Corps

D Division

French Infantry

Russian Infantry

French Cavalry

Russian Cavalry

Prepared defensive position

Artillery

Unit movements:

First position

Later position

Direction of movement

- - -> Retreat

RUSSIA

Battle of Borodino

The last battle of Napoleon's ill-fated Russian campaign was fought at Borodino on September 2 1812. It was also the greatest and most costly one-day battle of Napoleon's invasion, causing 28,000 French casualties and 40,000 Russian.

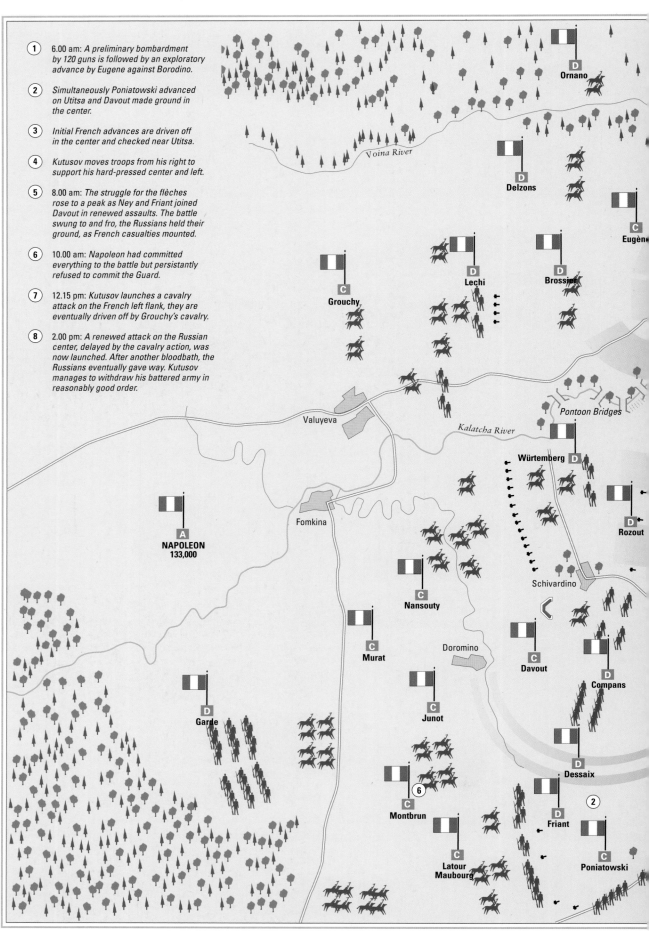

① 6.00 am: A preliminary bombardment by 120 guns is followed by an exploratory advance by Eugene against Borodino.

② Simultaneously Poniatowski advanced on Utitsa and Davout made ground in the center.

③ Initial French advances are driven off in the center and checked near Utitsa.

④ Kutusov moves troops from his right to support his hard-pressed center and left.

⑤ 8.00 am: The struggle for the flèches rose to a peak as Ney and Friant joined Davout in renewed assaults. The battle swung to and fro, the Russians held their ground, as French casualties mounted.

⑥ 10.00 am: Napoleon had committed everything to the battle but persistantly refused to commit the Guard.

⑦ 12.15 pm: Kutusov launches a cavalry attack on the French left flank, they are eventually driven off by Grouchy's cavalry.

⑧ 2.00 pm: A renewed attack on the Russian center, delayed by the cavalry action, was now launched. After another bloodbath, the Russians eventually gave way. Kutusov manages to withdraw his battered army in reasonably good order.

Voina River

Ornano **D**

Delzons **D**

Eugène **C**

Lechi **D**

Brossier **D**

Grouchy **C**

Pontoon Bridges

Kalatcha River

Würtemberg **D**

Valuyeva

Fomkina

Rozout **D**

Schivardino

A NAPOLEON 133,000

Nansouty **C**

Doromino

Davout **C**

Compans **D**

Murat **C**

Junot **C**

Dessaix **D**

Garde **D**

Montbrun **C**

Friant **D**

Poniatowski **C**

Latour Maubourg **C**

Maloe

⑦

C Bagavout

D Platov

C Ostermann

D Korf

D Urarov

Gorki

Borodino

A Barclay de Tolly

Moscowa River

Stonetz River

④

C Doctorov

C Raevski

D Sivers

C Constantine

⑧

Semiovovskaya

Semiovovskya Stream

③

⑤

C Borozdin

A Kutusov
120,800

A Bagration

D Moscow Militia

Old Post Road

C Tutchkov

③

Utitsa

N

0 ———— 1 km

0 ———— 1 mile

Napoleon's Cavalry

NAPOLEON'S CAVALRY, USING THE TRADITIONAL SABER AND LANCE, WERE USED AS A SHOCK FORCE IN BATTLE. NAPOLEON ALSO PROVIDED THEM WITH HORSE ARTILLERY AND USED THEM IN GREAT NUMBERS IN SURPRISE OPERATIONS AGAINST HIS OPPONENTS.

Before going on the attack, Napoleon softened up his opponents with artillery barrages or strong infantry attacks. Normally the French cavalry was superior to the best cavalry of other European nations. When in pursuit, the French moved at lightning speed and so suffered fewer casualties than might otherwise have been the case. Napoleon was also adept at using his cavalry for screening his other forces and for reconnaissance. Cavalry regiments consisted of between 1,200 and 1,800 men. They went into action at a walking pace, but this leisurely approach was deceptive. Once the order to charge was given, they spurred their horses into a gallop. Accompanied by the blaring of trumpets and their own ferocious shouts and yells, they brandished their sabers and bore down on their opponents at speed through the showers of shot and shells directed at them.

Napoleon's cavalry comprised both light and heavy formations. The heavy units, classed as *cuirassiers*, wore helmets and plates of armor, front and back, or were known as *carabiniers à cheval*, mounted men equipped with carbines. Both *cuirassiers* and *carabiniers* were big, brawny men riding huge horses, the biggest among the formations of Napoleon's cavalry. Their horses measured up to 5 ft 3 in (1.6 m) in height, compared to the mounts ridden by the dragoons, which were 5 ft 1 in (1.55 m) or those of the *chasseurs* and *hussars*, which were up to 5 ft (1.52 m). The heavy cavalry was normally used for crashing into lines of enemy infantry; and for this purpose, they carried pistols and heavy sabres that they used for thrusting. The light cavalry, which did not wear armor, carried curved swords for slashing at opponents. They were employed mostly to carry out flanking maneuvers or pursuit. The light cavalry, it seems, had a sense of theater, for they gave themselves dramatic names, such as *Hussars* of Death or Revolutionary *Chasseurs*,

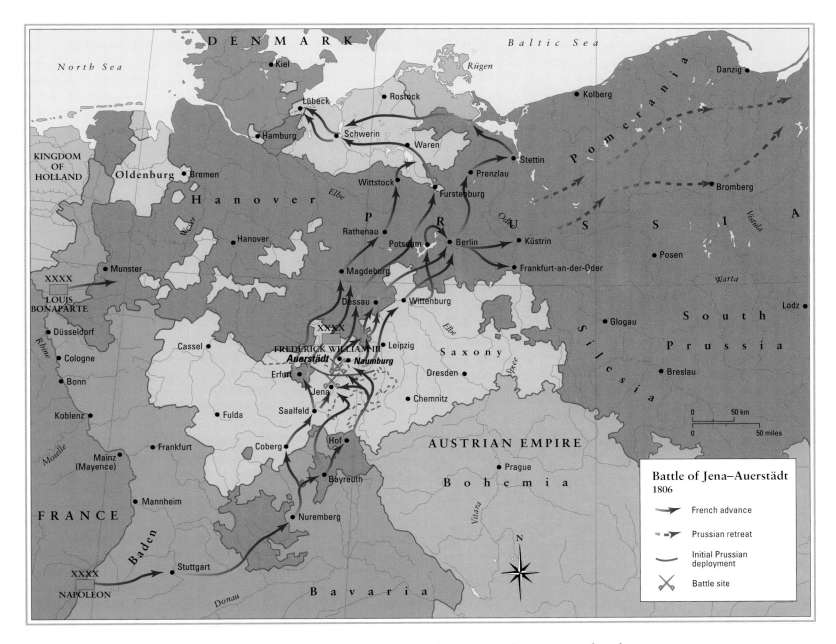

Battle of Jena–Auerstädt
1806

→ French advance

- - → Prussian retreat

⌣ Initial Prussian deployment

✕ Battle site

and were known for their colorful and elaborate uniforms. The dragoons, infantrymen who also fought on horseback, were armed with sabers and carried muskets. These firearms were superior to the carbines carried by the light cavalry, for they had longer barrels and a greater range of fire. However, the dragoons could not store their muskets in the sling used to hold the light cavalry's carbines. Instead, a boot was attached to the saddle and the stock of the musket was placed in it, with a strap attached to the pommel to prevent it from falling out. As the dragoons were about to go into action, they slung their muskets on their backs and drew their sabers.

Albert-Jean-Michel de Rocca was a Swiss-born lieutenant in the Second Regiment of Hussars of Napoleon's army. He served in the Peninsular War in Spain and fought to defeat an attempted British landing at Walcheren, Belgium in 1809. De Rocca wrote accounts of both these campaigns, describing the differences between the *hussars* and other elements of Napoleon's forces.

"The troops that composed our army, especially the cavalry and infantry, differed extremely in manners and habits" de Rocca wrote. "The infantrymen, having only to think of themselves

In 1806, as Napoleon prepared to cut their line of communications, the Prussians moved to intercept. But Napoleon attacked a weak spot in the Prussian defence — a 15-mile (24 km) front north of Jena — and the Prussians were swept from the battlefield.

Napoleon Bonaparte (1796-1821) leading his cavalry in Marengo.

and their muskets, were selfish, great talkers and great sleepers ... They were apt to dispute with their officers and sometimes were even insolent to them ....

"The *hussars* and *chasseurs* were generally accused of being plunderers and prodigal, loving drink ,,, Accustomed ... to sleep with an open eye, to have an ear always awake to the sound of the trumpet, to reconnoitre far in advance during a march, to trace the ambuscades of the enemy ... they could not fail to acquire superior intelligence.... Forever smoking ... the cavalryman, under his large cloak, braved in every country the rigor of the seasons."

Napoleon regarded his cavalry as all-purpose formations. "Cavalry", he said, "is useful before, during and after the battle." He greatly valued its audacity and ensured that it was carefully trained in order to achieve maximum discipline. It took some time for the cavalry to reach its full potential, but when it did, in around 1807, it was mightily impressive on the battlefield and drew much praise from Napoleon's commanders. One of his generals, Antoine-Henri, Baron Jomini, said of them: "When I speak of excellent French cavalry, I refer to its impetuous bravery..." The French cavalry was equally admired by its British opponents. Arthur Wellesley, Duke of Wellington, considered them "irresistible" and General Sir Charles James Napier, who fought in the Peninsular War in Spain from 1808 to 1814, thought of the French cavalry in much the same way. Wellington went so far as to rate it superior to his own cavalry.

The exploits that drew these golden opinions from commanders on both sides in the Napoleonic Wars were typified by two dramatic cavalry charges that took place in 1807, at the Battle of Eylau on February 8 and at Friedland on June 14. At Eylau, where the French were led by the flamboyant Marshal Joachim-Napoléon Murat, the cavalry advanced through the ranks of Russian infantry around Eylau and then split into two sections. One charged into the flank of the Russian cavalry, which was then assaulting a French division led by General Louis-Vincent-Joseph de St. Hilaire. The second charged into the area where a French corps led by General Charles Pierre François Augereau, Duc de Castiglione was having a hard time fending off the Russian infantry. Both Russian units were thrown off balance by the fierce French assault. But not content with that, Murat's cavalry reformed and rode at speed against the Russian center, where it smashed into gunners who had just destroyed the French VII Corps. The French paid heavily for their exploit, losing 1,500 men. Their intervention was later classed as one of the greatest cavalry charges ever on record.

At Friedland, just over four months later, Marshal Emmanuel, Marquis de Grouchy led the French dragoons in a battle that pitted 17,000 French troops against 61,000 Russians. The cavalry was also vastly outnumbered, facing an attack by 60 Russian squadrons. Realizing he had little or no chance of overcoming the Russians, de Grouchy retreated; he hoped to tire out the pursuing

Opposite page: The Battle of Waterloo took place on June 18 1815 near the village of Waterloo in what was then the Netherlands. Napoleon's forces made early advances, but later, during the afternoon, the Prussians commanded by General Blücher joined the battle and French resistance collapsed. In 1815 the Netherlands included the country of present-day Belgium. Belgium broke away from the Netherlands and became independent in 1830 so the Battle of Waterloo was actually fought in present-day Belgium.

enemy. De Grouchy's plan was clearly not working; but as the Russians came nearer, another French general, Etienne-Marie-Antoine Champion de Nansouty suggested a plan to trap them. As the Russians approached, de Nansouty's *cuirassiers* made a sudden, shock appearance and charged the enemy flank. Simultaneously, de Grouchy wheeled around and charged into the Russian cavalry, sending it reeling back in disarray. It regrouped and put up a fight, but the French cavalry charged again and again until the Russians gave up and returned to their own lines.

This was the sort of inspired action that set an example to Napoleon's enemies. They emulated the exploits of the French cavalry; and by the time Napoleon was finally defeated at Waterloo in 1815, they excelled at it. At Waterloo, the British cavalry destroyed the final attack mounted by the French, something that would have been extremely unlikely, if not impossible, earlier on in the illustrious career of Napoleon Bonaparte and his once-magnificent cavalry.

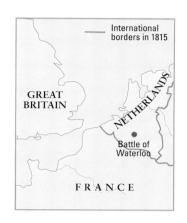

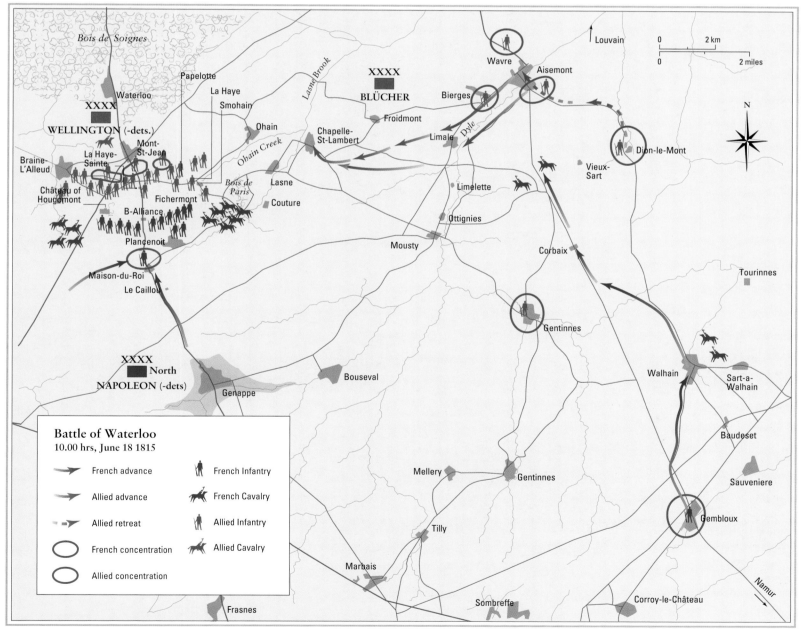

Battle of Waterloo
10.00 hrs, June 18 1815

- → French advance
- → Allied advance
- ⇢ Allied retreat
- ◯ French concentration
- ◯ Allied concentration
- 🏃 French Infantry
- 🐎 French Cavalry
- 🏃 Allied Infantry
- 🐎 Allied Cavalry

THE IMPACT OF THE INDUSTRIAL REVOLUTION

THE INDUSTRIAL REVOLUTION BEGAN IN ENGLAND IN THE MID-18TH CENTURY AND HAD IMMENSE SOCIAL AND ENVIRONMENTAL EFFECTS. IT FUNDAMENTALLY AFFECTED THE PRODUCTION OF WEAPONS, THE CONDUCT OF WAR, AND THE PROVISION OF TRANSPORTATION, COMMUNICATIONS, AND MANPOWER.

Opposite page: The American Civil War was the first conflict in which railroads played an important role in transporting men and supplies. The railroads were about five times faster than mule-drawn wagons and faster still than armies tramping the roads on foot.

When, in 1733, John Kay introduced his flying shuttle to enable looms to weave cloth faster than ever before, it was the start of something momentous. Kay's invention was the first of several machines that transformed the English textile industry and ultimately the way goods of all kinds were produced, distributed, and used. The Industrial Revolution removed manufacturing activity from small workshops and transferred it to factories, eventually replacing individual craftsmanship with mass production. This profound transformation included the manufacture of weapons and, with it, the conduct of war. Using existing trade routes counties such as Britain and the U.S were able to trade goods, including weapons and slaves, all over their empires.

The artillery systems promoted by de Vallière and de Gribeauval (see pages 142-145) and the influence of Napoleon (see pages 158-164) were also revolutionary. But industrialization affected weapons and warfare across the board completely altering arms manufacture as it had been known. The hand-crafting of weapons virtually disappeared from the 19th century onward, as mass production enabled the making of more and more weapons in less and less time. Similarly, industrialization made the repair of weapons faster and easier. All this enabled more men to be equipped for war than ever before. Consequently, the size of armies grew, and with it the extent of battles and the destruction they caused.

Several inventions were the direct products of the Industrial Revolution. They included the percussion cap of 1830, which proofed muzzle-loading firearms against the effects of weather, and the Dreyse breech-

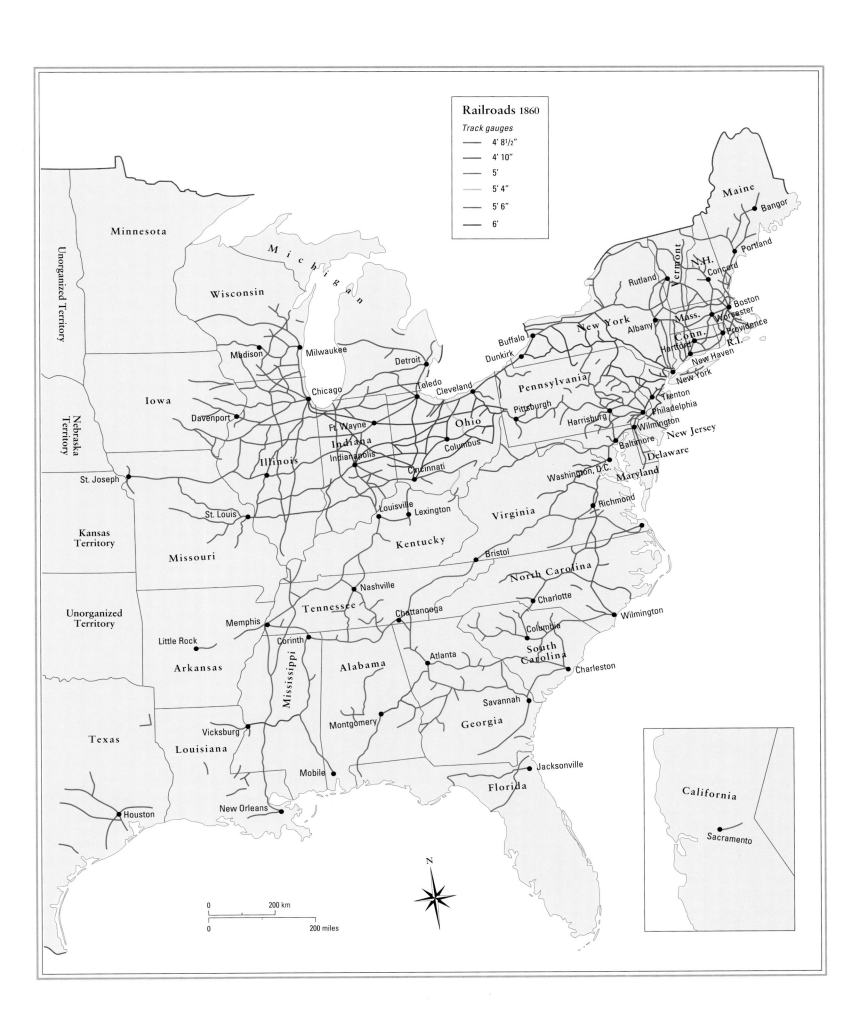

Railroads 1860

Track gauges
— 4′ 8½″
— 4′ 10″
— 5′
— 5′ 4″
— 5′ 6″
— 6′

loading needle rifle of 1841, which incorporated a needle-like firing pin and was later adopted as the main infantry firearm of the Prussian army.

Two further inventions of the time were the Minié soft-lead bullet of 1848, which enabled faster loading for muskets and also increased their range and accuracy, and the machine gun. This soon proved itself to be one of the greatest mass killers ever introduced into warfare (see pages 174-177).

Inevitably, manufacturing firms were set up, concentrating exclusively on the production of arms and armaments, and many of them became very big industrial names. Among them was the Remington Arms company, the U.S. firearms and ammunition manufacturer founded in Lion Gulch, New York in 1816. It supplied a large proportion of the small arms used in the Civil War and in the 20th-century world wars.

In Europe, the Skoda works was founded in 1859 and purchased by Emil Skoda 10 years later. Skoda became the leading arms manufacturer in the empire of Austria-Hungary and was inherited by Czechoslovakia (now separate countries: the Czech Republic and Slovakia) when the empire fell after World War One. Skoda specialized in producing heavy naval guns, mortars, and a range of armaments including several types of mountain gun — artillery designed for mountain warfare — and also the M1909 machine gun. In the first decade of the 20th century, Skoda became the contractor for both the army and the navy of Austria-Hungary, supplying mainly heavy guns and ammunition.

During and after the Industrial Revolution, the German Krupp family company was arguably the most famous name in arms manufacturing — or perhaps the most notorious in view of its involvement with the armed forces of Nazi Germany before and during World War Two. Krupp was established in Essen in 1810 as a steel foundry; but by the 1840s the company was making steel cannons for the armed forces of Tsarist Russia, the Ottoman Turkish Empire, and Prussia. In fact Alfred, son of the founder Friedrich Krupp, who became head of the family firm in 1826 when he was only 14, became known as the "Cannon King'" He invested heavily in the new technology, such as the Bessemer process for mass-producing inexpensive steel from molten pig iron.

Alfred Krupp made his first cast-steel cannon in 1847. Four years later, at the Great Exhibition held in London, he put on display a 6-pounder (2.7 kg) gun made entirely from cast steel and a steel ingot weighing 4,229 lb (1,950 kg). This was more than double the weight of any previous steel cast. Steel castings, a specialized form of casting using different kinds of steel, were used to provide weapons with added strength and resistance to shock. In 1855, at the Paris Exposition, Krupp went even further and displayed a 99,997 lb (45,359 kg) ingot, which caused a sensation among the engineering community and assured the Krupp works at Essen worldwide fame.

Krupp had long been convinced that breech-loading cannons were superior

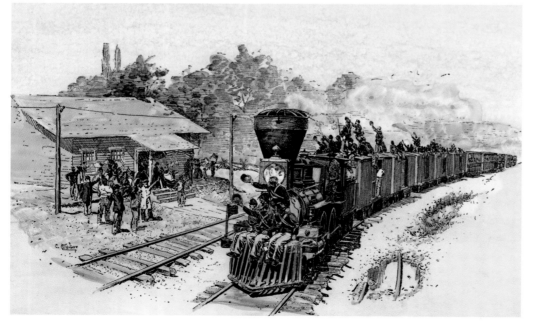

Union troops transported to the front by railroad during the U.S. Civil War, 1861-1865.

to the muzzle-loading kind, and they certainly had important advantages. One was protection for gunners, who could shelter behind the cannons while loading it. In addition, breech-loaders had proved to be more accurate and speedier. But this cut no ice with traditionalist officers, who clung to the tried-and-tested muzzle-loaders, making it virtually impossible for Alfred Krupp to sell his breech-loading steel cannons. He decided instead to make a gift of one to King Friedrich Wilhelm IV of Prussia, who regarded it as an exotic decoration. His brother Wilhelm was more perspicacious. He saw the true import of the Krupp cannons. In 1859, on becoming regent after a stroke incapacitated the king, he purchased 312 steel cannons from a delighted Alfred Krupp and made his company the chief manufacturer of arms for the Prussian army.

Alfred's only son and successor, Friedrich Alfred Krupp, became head of the family firm on his father's death in 1887 and soon followed in his innovative footsteps. In 1890, he introduced nickel steel, an alloy that was hard and strong enough to allow thinner armor to be fitted to battleships. Nickel-steel artillery had similar advantages: cannons were able to use the new and much more powerful explosives invented by the Swedish gunpowder manufacturer Alfred Nobel. In 1892, Krupp became a manufacturer of armor plate and ships' turrets; and in the following year, Friedrich Alfred was asked by Rudolf Diesel, the inventor and mechanical engineer, to construct the new car engine he had designed. Three years later, Krupp expanded again when Friedrich Alfred took over the Kiel ship-building company Germaniawerft and became the main warship-builder in Germany. The first German U-boat was constructed by Krupp in 1906, and 84 were made during World War One. Krupp also produced most of the artillery used by the Imperial German army. Among them was the super-sized howitzer Big Bertha, which had a 12-caliber barrel, weighed 95,998 lb (43,545 kg), was 19¼ ft (5.9 m) long, and had an effective range of 7¾ miles (12.4 km). Big Bertha was one of the most enormous artillery pieces to see action in war.

After 1918, Germany's defeat in the war brought difficult times for Krupp. Under the Treaty of Versailles, the country's peacetime armed forces were strictly limited. Krupp was obliged to renounce arms manufacture, and turned instead to making steel teeth and jaws for injured veterans. There was a market in Prussia for building and furnishing railroad locomotives, but some 70,000 Krupp workers had to be laid off. Versailles was fiercely resented in Germany; and before long, the design and manufacture

The noise of machines, the crush of workers, the heat and smoke that attended the daily tasks performed in 19th century manufacturing were intense and uncomfortable. This was a considerable contrast from the previous method of producing goods at home.

of armaments was being conducted in secret. Krupp, which designed artillery and received an order for 135 Panzer tanks in 1934, was intimately involved in this subterfuge. The secret, long suspected by individual observers, including Winston Churchill, was not fully revealed to the outside world until Adolf Hitler announced in 1935 that Germany had been re-arming behind the scenes and intended to go on doing so.

By the outbreak of World War Two in Europe in 1939, Krupp and its head Alfred Krupp were deeply implicated with Hitler and his Nazi regime, and became a central element of Nazi Germany's wartime arms policy. During the war, Krupp produced artillery and also made tanks, naval guns, armor plate, and the superlative 88-mm anti-aircraft gun, among other munitions. The Krupp Germaniawerft shipyard

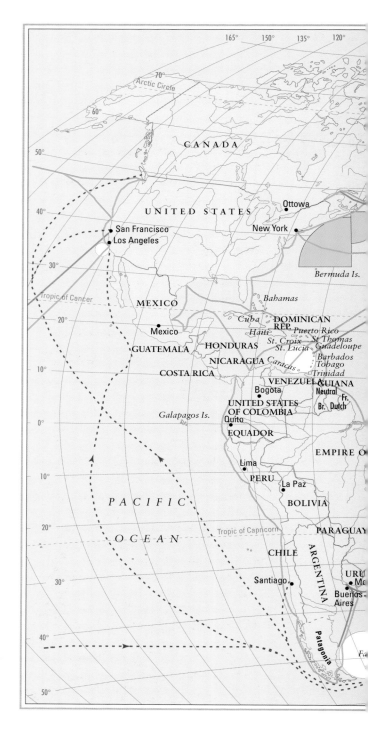

at Kiel launched 134 U-boats up to 1945, as well as the 18,408 ton (16,700 tonne) heavy cruiser *Prinz Eugen*. Krupp took over several industries in Nazi-occupied Europe, including the Skoda Works in Czechoslovakia, and used an estimated 100,000 slave laborers, one-quarter of them Jews taken from concentration camps. Because of the use of slave labur in the Krupp wartime factories, Alfred Krupp was indicted and convicted of war crimes after the war.

As shown by the career of the Krupp family and the advances made by its contemporaries, the keynote of the Industrial Revolution as it affected arms and armament was a very significant advance in the strength, effectiveness, accuracy, range, speed, and power of weapons and warfare.

This was also the case with the career of Alfred Nobel, the Swedish chemist and engineer who concentrated on the safe manufacture and use of explosives that, in his day, could be dangerously volatile. Nobel himself suffered the grievous consequences of this unpredictability when his younger brother Emil was among five people killed by an explosion at the Nobel factory at Heleneborg, Stockholm on September 3 1864. Three years later, Alfred Nobel was conducting experiments with nitroglycerin, which had useful potential in the mining, construction, demolition, and armaments industries. But it had a dangerous drawback: in its pure form, nitroglycerin is a primary contact explosive; it could blow up from the slightest jolt or other physical shock. This meant that it was extremely dangerous to transport or to use, particularly undiluted. However, Nobel discovered that nitroglycerin could be moved and handled more safely if it were mixed with *kieselgurh*, or diatomaceous earth, a soft, crumbly, sedimentary deposit formed from the fossil remains of diatoms (single-celled algae). Nobel named his discovery dynamite, from the Greek word for "strength", and went to England in 1867, where he successfully demonstrated the explosive at a quarry in Redhill, Surrey. Dynamite played an important part in warfare, as did other substances created by Nobel from various combinations based on potassium nitrate, the oxidizing component of gunpowder. Nobel's explosives vastly increased the power of artillery, making possible the

During the 19th century, Britain ruled a worldwide empire on which, it was said, the "sun never set" because it was always daytime somewhere in its far-flung territories. As a result, the oceans were crisscrossed with imperial trade routes.

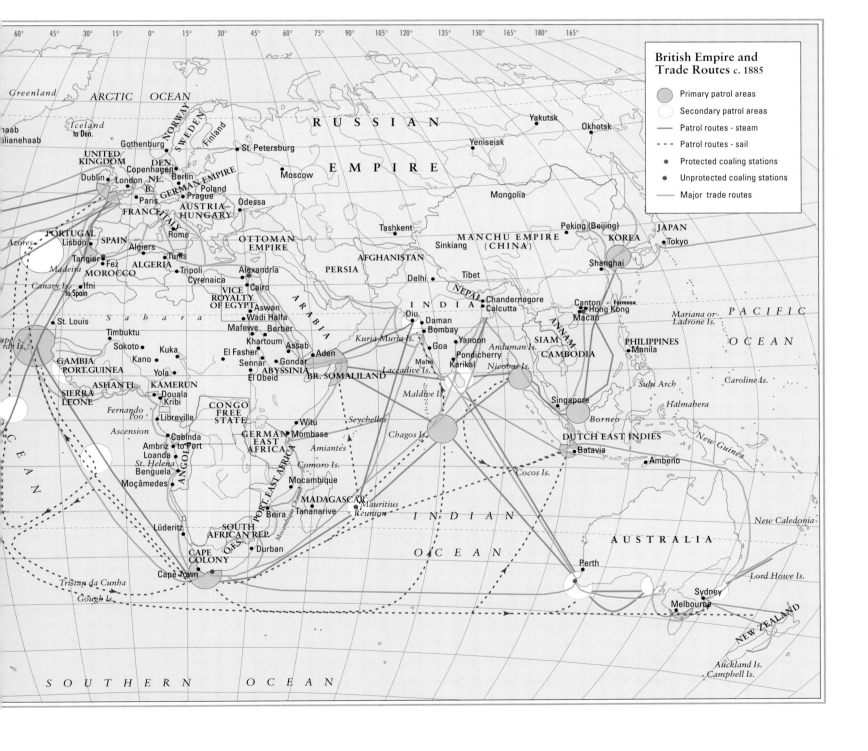

British Empire and Trade Routes c. 1885

- Primary patrol areas
- Secondary patrol areas
- Patrol routes - steam
- Patrol routes - sail
- Protected coaling stations
- Unprotected coaling stations
- Major trade routes

heavy bombardments that characterized the preliminaries battles leading up to the two world wars of the 20th century.

Alfred Nobel had long been a controversial figure. A bogus obituary published in a French newspaper in 1888 was headlined, *"Le marchand de la mort est mort"* (The merchant of death is dead) and said: 'Dr. Alfred Nobel, who became rich by finding ways to kill more people faster than ever before, died yesterday.' Nobel's reply to that was the series of Nobel Prizes for science, chemistry, medicine, literature, and peace that he instituted in 1895, a year before his death from a stroke in San Remo, Italy.

Weaponry in its various forms was not the only influence on war that stemmed from the Industrial Revolution. Although intended as a civilian convenience, the advent of steam-powered railroads in the early 19th century was a vital factor in transforming the way in which war was conducted. Railroads did away with the long, time-consuming route march and could deliver armies to battlefields in a much fresher condition. They also made it possible to rush troops to trouble spots before an emergency might get out of hand.

Like the Industrial Revolution itself, steam-powered trains began in the north of England when the Stockton and Darlington railroad, using locomotives designed by the civil and mechanical engineer George Stephenson, opened for passenger traffic on September 27 1825. Subsequently, railroads were

Top: September 27, 1825 opening of first British Railroad route between Stockton and Darlington.
Bottom: 1829 Locomotive race at Rainhill near Liverpool. George Stephenson's Rocket won.

built all over Britain, Europe, and the Americas. The difference this made to warfare was dramatically demonstrated in the American Civil War, when troops were transported by train over vast distances: exploited by the North, this advantage contributed to its ultimate victory. Similarly, in the Franco-Prussian War of 1870-1871 the use of railroads by the Prussian forces enabled them to advance rapidly. By the start of World War One in Europe in 1914, railroads had become so vital to the mass movement of troops that they were an integral part of military planning.

The new speed that innovations of the Industrial Revolution gave to warfare was also reflected in communications, which underwent radical change in the 19th century. Until then dispatching orders on the battlefield had been a dangerous business for the couriers charged with delivering them. Otherwise, flags or torches were used for signalling, although their usefulness could be limited. The telegraph, invented in 1837, allowed orders to be sent by instant, electrical means. For civilians at home the telegraph, and also the telegram, introduced in 1844, carried information far more rapidly than ever before. Inevitably, news sent by telegraph increased the shock factor inherent in war, which was why the dispatches from the Crimean War of 1853-1856 sent to London by William Howard Russell, reporting for *The Times* newspaper, created such a furore among his readers. Half a century later, news of the Boer War in South Africa, as reported by the young Winston Churchill, had a similarly realistic effect.

New weapons, new outcomes

BY THE START OF THE 20TH CENTURY, ANOTHER, TACTICAL, REVOLUTION HAD FOLLOWED IN THE WAKE OF THE INDUSTRIAL REVOLUTION. NEW WEAPONS, SOME OF THEM OF GREAT INGENUITY, HAD BEEN INTRODUCED AND HAD RADICALLY ALTERED FIREPOWER AND CONDITIONS ON THE BATTLEFIELD.

The totality of effects that stemmed from the new technologies of the Industrial Revolution was to change almost everything that had previously characterized warfare. For a summary of the hindrances and deficiencies of the tactics, equipment and capability of forces in battle in the mid 19th century we can look to the events and confusion of the British forces at the Battle of Balaclava in 1854, during the Crimean War. Due to poor communication between the generals in charge of the British forces, poor visibility of the battle arena, and in the absence of the delayed infantry divisions, it fell to the cavalry to lead a disasterous charge straight at the Russian guns. They were, inevitably, decimated.

While the effects of the Industrial Revolution served to improve conditions on the battlefield, warfare became ever more lethal. Arguably, the most startling alteration to affect the battlefield itself was the introduction of smokeless gunpowder. For over five centuries, ever since the advent of gunpowder in battle, the black powder used by arquebuses, muskets, and cannons of all kinds had shrouded the battlefield in great banks of smoke, obscuring the terrain and hiding opponents from view. The smokeless *Poudre B* (white powder), invented in 1884 by the French chemist Paul Vieille, not only cleared the battlefield but also ended the fouling of guns that black powder involved.

Strictly speaking, *Poudre B* was not an entirely smokeless powder. It produced much less smoke because its composition was mainly gaseous, whereas black powder produced up to 60 percent solid products comprising potassium carbonate, sulfate, and sulfide. Vieille produced *Poudre B* from collodion and guncotton, two types of nitrocellulose, which he softened with ethanol and ether. *Poudre B*, three times more powerful than black powder, was an immediate success and was quickly taken up by the French army. The new gunpowder enabled firearms to attain a higher muzzle velocity, which made for a flatter trajectory. This, in turn, increased the accuracy of long-range fire, enabling it to hit a target at a distance of up to ²/₃ mile (1 km). Much less smokeless powder was required to propel bullets, and so smaller, lighter cartridges could be made. If black powder became wet, it was useless; but *Poudre B* would burn even when soaked.

British soldiers on horseback wearing Khaki uniforms at the relief of Ladysmith, February 27 1900, during the Boer War (1899 –1902). The number of horses killed in the war was at the time unprecedented in modern warfare.

Greater visibility on the battlefield made opponents much easier to see than before and therefore much easier to aim at and kill. This spelled the end of brilliantly colored uniforms. Eventually, the "thin red line" that had once marked out the British infantry became the duller, less visible khaki. Also, camouflage patterns were created that helped soldiers to blend in with the scenery. Movement on the

battlefield had to change too, because better visibility meant that frontal attacks by infantry or cavalry in the face of small arms or artillery fire could be suicidal. So could mounting attacks in formation now that individuals could easily be picked off as they approached. Instead, soldiers under fire either spread out or resorted to rifle pits, foxholes, and, finally, trenches and trench warfare. The new conditions on the battlefield reduced the role of cavalry warfare, confining units to reconnaissance and screening now that shock action such as the frontal assault was so dangerous and likely to be needlessly wasteful.

In any case, the guns that infantry and cavalry now faced were much more deadly than before. Instead of solid shot, they used streamlined shells with explosive charges that were detonated by new, improved fuses. Similarly, the smoothbore cannon was replaced by the rifled gun. Controlled springs solved the problem of cannon recoil. The single-shot muzzle-loader gave way to the repeating magazine rifle. Breech-loading artillery replaced muzzle-loading field guns, a process that was complete by 1900. Field fortifications, once used only in siege warfare, became a regular part of infantry tactics. The Minié ball was replaced by the elongated cone-shaped bullet. In consequence, the range, accuracy, and frequency of fire improved so greatly that it was possible for the first time to pepper an enemy's front line with iron, lead, and steel missiles and send casualty figures soaring.

But the most lethal firearm of all, and the one that would earn itself a name as the most terrifying on the modern battlefield, was the machine gun. This weapon would not reach its full potential until World War One, but its extraordinary killing power was evident from the outset. First in the field, in 1861, was Richard Jordan Gatling, a dentist from North Carolina. He produced a mechanically operated machine gun, the.42 Gatling, which could fire more than 300 rounds per minute. The Gatling gun had six barrels mounted on a revolving frame. In 1882, Gatling designed a larger version, with 10 barrels, which could fire four times as many rounds per minute. The United States Army and other armies around the world were impressed by the Gatling gun; and within a few years, most major armies were equipped with it. But Gatling and another machine-gun designer, Captain William Gardner of Toledo, Ohio, who fought for the North in the American Civil War, were eclipsed in 1885 by Hiram Stevens Maxim and his invention, the world's first automatic portable machine gun.

In the Maxim, spent cartridges were ejected and the next bullet was inserted after firing by the energy of the gun's recoil. By this means, the Maxim could fire continuously until a complete belt of bullets was exhausted. The Maxim's rate of fire was 500 rounds per minute, which gave it the equivalent firepower of 100 rifles. The British Army was pleased with the results of the Maxim's trials and adopted his machine gun in 1889. Their approval was soon justified, when the Maxim gun made its debut in one of Great Britain's colonial wars. This took place in Matabeleland (now a province of Zimbabwe in southeastern Africa) in 1893–1894. In one confrontation, 50 British soldiers using four Maxim machine-guns managed to rout 5,000 Matabele warriors. Other versions included the German *Maschinengewehr* and the Russian *pulemyot maxima*, both of which were based on the Maxim model. Another model, the Browning machine gun, appeared in 1890 and was adopted by the U.S. Navy in 1895. The Hotchkiss, another machine gun, was purchased by the French Army two years later.

At the start of World War One in 1914, machine guns were cumbersome weapons of heavy calliber, weighing between 60 and 132 lb (27 and 290 kg), that is without adding the weight of their mountings, supplies, and carriages. Theoretically they could fire 400–600 small caliber rounds per minute and by

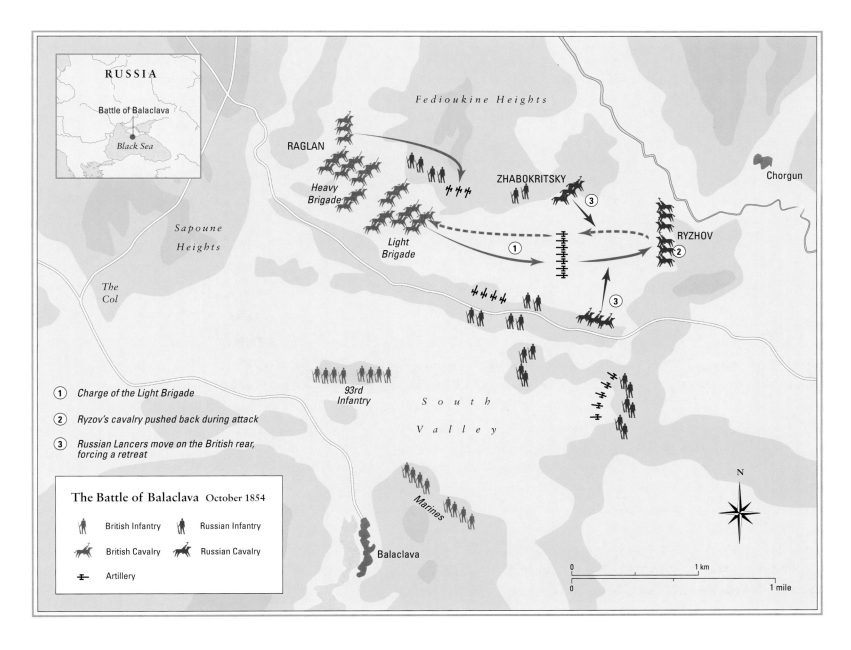

RUSSIA

Battle of Balaclava

Black Sea

Fedioukine Heights

RAGLAN

ZHABOKRITSKY

Chorgun

Heavy Brigade

RYZHOV

Sapoune Heights

Light Brigade

The Col

① Charge of the Light Brigade

② Ryzov's cavalry pushed back during attack

③ Russian Lancers move on the British rear, forcing a retreat

93rd Infantry

South Valley

N

The Battle of Balaclava October 1854

🏃	British Infantry	🏃	Russian Infantry
🐎	British Cavalry	🐎	Russian Cavalry
⚔	Artillery		

Marines

Balaclava

0   1 km

0   1 mile

the end of the war in 1918 this had increased to twice the number of rounds, and the guns were fed with fabric belts or metal strips of ammunition. However, these machine guns also had a tendency to overheat and therefore cease to operate. To overcome these disadvantages machine gun crews, numbering between four and six men, took to firing the machine guns in short bursts. Heat-reducing systems were subsequently developed and used in aircraft. These used either water or air to cool the weapon. Air-cooling the weapon was made possible by air vents built into the weapon itself and was therefore less cumbersome than water-cooling; air-cooling was the preferred method by the end of World War One. Another difficulty of the machine guns was that they frequently jammed. This was common in hot weather or when the weapon was used by an inexperienced crew. To counteract the problem armies adopted a technique that had been used with slow-firing muskets centuries before: guns grouped together so that crews could maintain continuous fire allowing them to maintain a defensive position.

Forward-flying Vickers machine guns used in British and French aircraft were fitted with interrupter gears after 1916 to synchronize them with the movement of the propellers.

Battle of Balaclava, 1854 during the Crimean War. This was the scene of an extraordinary action, the Charge of the Light Brigade, in which British cavalry rode straight at the Russian guns and were, inevitably, decimated as a result.

THE AMERICAN CIVIL WAR

THE AMERICAN CIVIL WAR OF 1861-1865 HAS BEEN CALLED THE "FIRST MODERN WAR" AND THE FIRST "TOTAL WAR". THIS WAS AN ALL-OUT CONFLICT IN WHICH ALL RESOURCES — MILITARY, HUMAN, AND NATURAL — WERE USED TO ENSURE VICTORY AT ANY COST.

T he American Civil war between the Confederate states of the slave-owning South and the anti-slavery Union forces of the North was savage, as only radically conflicting ideologies could make it. For the North, the eventual victor, an important purpose of this mighty struggle was to stop the South from seceding from the United States. But at its heart was a fundamental principle of national life and what today we term human rights. On June 16 1858, Abraham Lincoln set out the problem at the Republican convention in Illinois after it chose him as its candidate for the U.S. Senate.

Opposite page: Map of U.S. employment in weapon manufacturing 1820-1860. In the run up to the American Civil War employment rose sharply, reflecting the increase in weapon production. This is certainly evident from the figures for the east coast Union states.

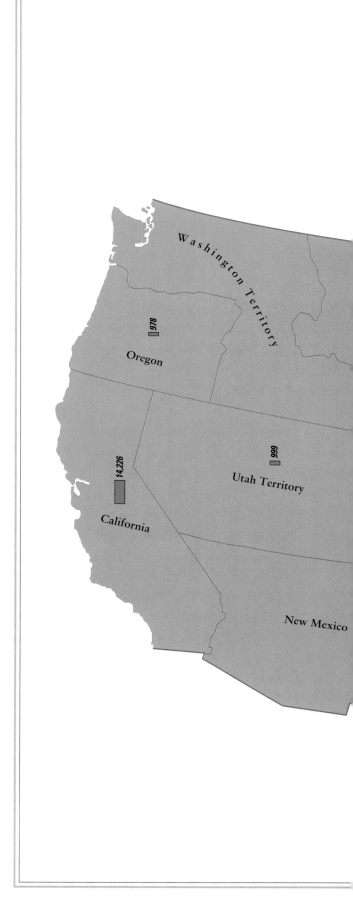

Manufacturing Employees
1820 – 1860

- 1820
- 1840
- 1860
- Union States, 1861
- Confederate States, 1861

100
90
80
70
60
50
40
30
20
10

Employees in thousands

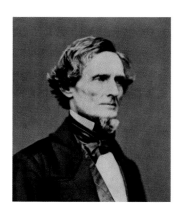

Top: Abraham Lincoln 1809-1865 16th President of the United States.
Below: Jefferson Davis (1808-1889) President of the Confederate States of America.

Opposite page: The opening engagement of the American Civil War took place at Fort Sumter at Charleston Harbor, South Carolina where the Confederates bombarded the fort for 34 hours. The Union forces holding the fort ran out of supplies and surrendered.

"A house divided against itself cannot stand", Lincoln told the delegates, and continued: "I believe this government cannot endure permanently half slave and half free". Two years later, Lincoln was elected President of the United States. Five months after that, the war to preserve the Union and free the slaves began. In the next four years, the greatly increased variety and power of arms and armaments killed nearly 625,000 men on both sides. Those weapons included new revolvers such as the Colt Army Model of 1860, the Remington of 1858, and the Smith and Wesson Model No. 1. Among several rifles, the Springfield Model of 1861 became the most commonly used shoulder-arm of the war.

In addition, disease, an age-old scourge of war, caused the death of another 415,000 men. Almost 282,000 Union soldiers were wounded. President Lincoln himself was among the dead, assassinated on April 14 1865 by John Wilkes Booth, an actor and Southern sympathizer. Ten weeks later, on June 23, General Stand Watie was the last Confederate general to capitulate. But several more months passed before the final Confederate ship, the *CSS Shenandoah*, surrendered, on November 6 at Liverpool in England.

The first shots of the American Civil War were fired against Fort Sumter in Charleston Harbor, South Carolina on April 12,1861. Although the fort was within Confederate territory — South Carolina had been the first state to secede from the Union the previous December 24 — there had been a long-running dispute about its ownership. Four months after secession, the Confederates determined to retrieve the fort and sent Brigadier General Pierre Beauregard to demand that the Union garrison evacuate it.

On April 11, Beauregard sent a request to that effect, couched in impeccably polite terms, only to receive an equally polite refusal from Major Robert Anderson, of the 1st Artillery, in command at Fort Sumter. There was bravado in Anderson's refusal, as the garrison had no effective artillery to reply to a bombardment. The Confederates opened fire on Fort Sumter the next day and pounded it for the next 34 hours until it was virtually a ruin. As Anderson put it in his report, "the quarters were entirely burned, the main gates destroyed by fire, the gorge walls seriously injured, the magazine surrounded by flames ... four barrels and three cartridges of powder only being available". On the afternoon of April 14, Anderson was obliged to evacuate the fort. He marched his men out "with colors flying and drums beating."

The Confederates were lucky that at Fort Sumter circumstances had favored them, for they were the "poor relations" of the Civil War, less well equipped than the Union forces. For example, the Union army were better prepared for sieges, in which rifled

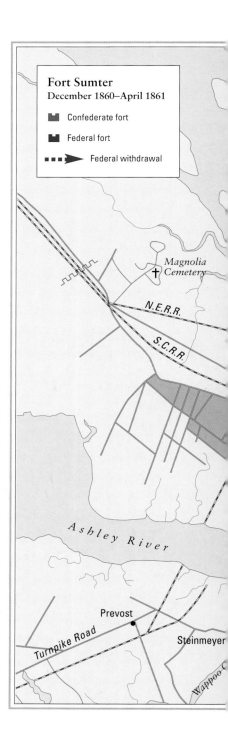

Fort Sumter
December 1860–April 1861
▪ Confederate fort
▪ Federal fort
▪▪▪▪➤ Federal withdrawal

artillery was used for the first time and was very successful against masonry fortifications. The Confederates, by contrast, possessed no effective siege train, and instead had to use a mixture of weapons captured from Federal arsenals and fortifications.

The action at Fort Sumter was not taken as a proper conflict by the Americans, who had a romantic view of the Civil War as an adventure that would soon be over. They were forced into a more realistic frame of mind when the Union army and Confederate forces met on July 21 1861 at the first Battle of Manassas, known in the North as Bull Run.

After skirmishing in which the Confederates threatened Washington with gun batteries on the River Potomac's approaches, the opposing armies converged on Manassas Junction, Virginia for a

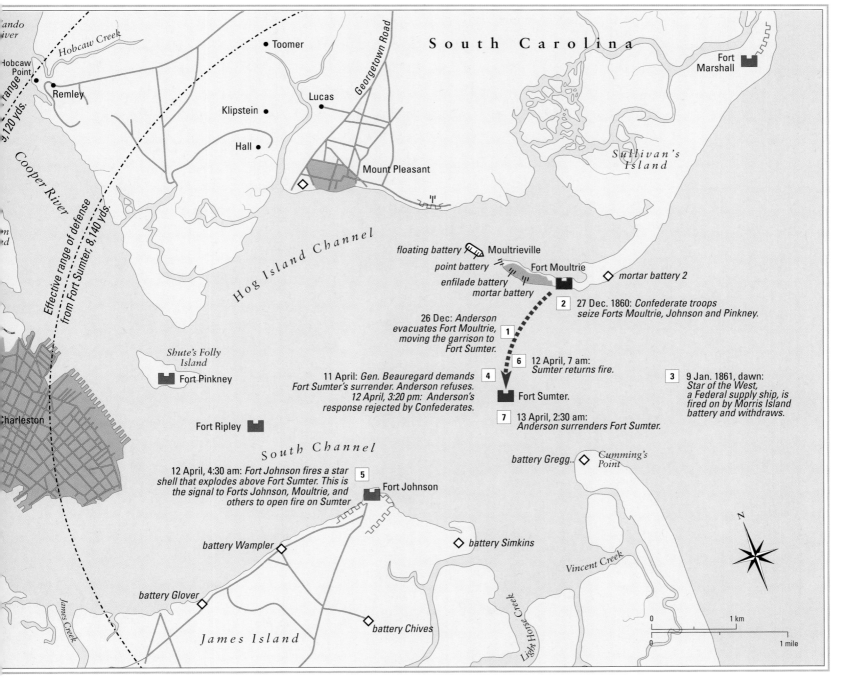

Opposite page: At Bull Run (Manassas) on July 21 1861, Union troops moved to encircle the Confederates, only to find their progress checked by Thomas J. "Stonewall" Jackson's Virginia Brigade. Next, the arrival of Confederate reinforcements by railroad sent Union troops fleeing in panic.

Below: The Battle of Manassas (1861) also called the First Battle of Bull Run, featured the stand made by Brigadier General Thomas J. Jackson and his Virginia Brigade, which halted the Union army advance. This action earned Jackson his famous nickname "Stonewall".

more serious showdown. During the battle, both sides used muzzle-loading single-shot muskets of .54, .58, and .69 caliber; officers carried swords and .36- or .44-caliber revolvers. The Union army attempted to launch a surprise attack on the Confederates' left flank but were checked by the stubborn stand of Brigadier-General Thomas J. Jackson's Virginia brigade. Jackson earned the nickname "Stonewall". His five regiments had 13 smoothbore artillery pieces. The Union forces had 11 more up-to-date rifled guns, which, ironically, turned out to be a liability. In the artillery duel, the Union gunners found that the 300 yd (274 m) that separated them from their opponents was too close: the rifled artillery kept overshooting while the Confederates' smoothbores were within comfortable range.

Unknown to the Union army, the Confederate army had been reinforced, and afterward an extra Confederate brigade had arrived by railroad. As a result, rather than enveloping the Confederates as they planned, the Union army found themselves enveloped by the Confederate forces. They fled the field in a panic, the Confederates followed snapping at their heels.

The Union defeat at Manassas shocked President Lincoln and his advisers into the sober realization that the Civil War was not going to be a short run but a long and painful haul. Meanwhile, the war was being fiercely fought in the west of the United States, where the Union army

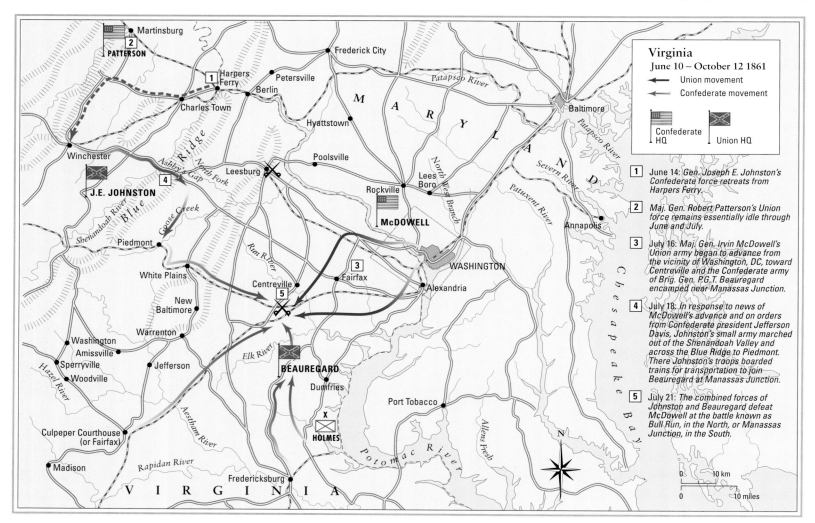

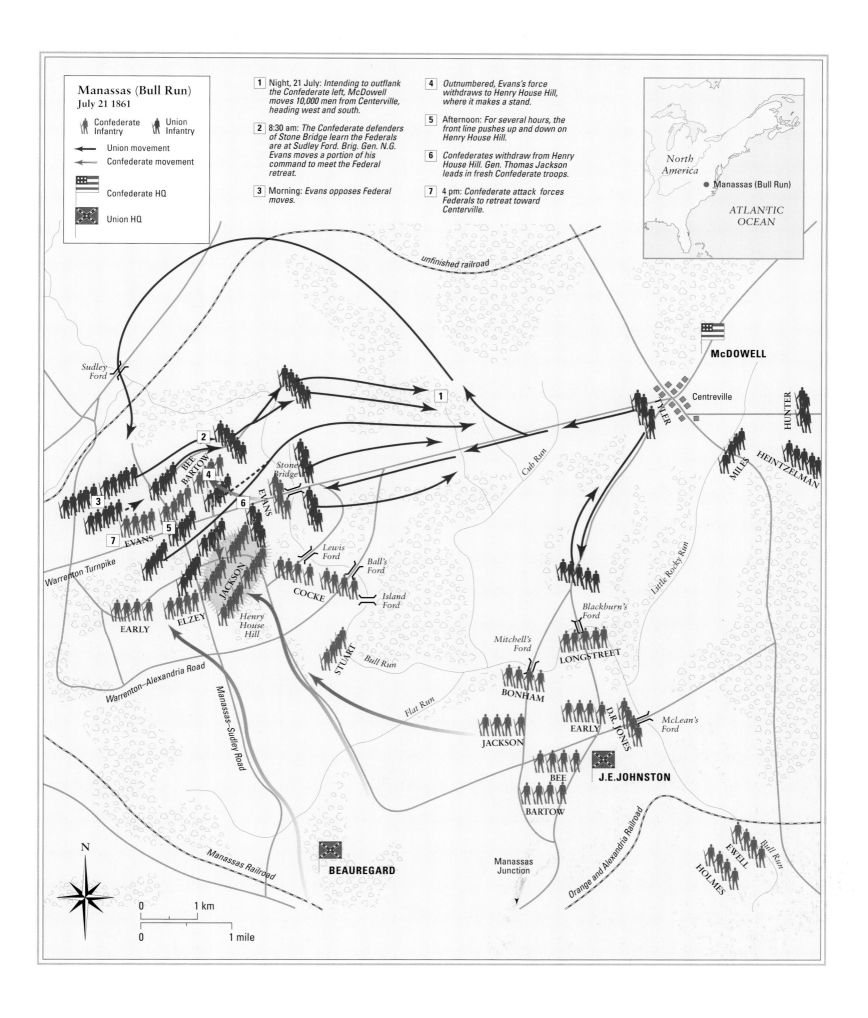

Manassas (Bull Run)
July 21 1861

👫 Confederate Infantry   👫 Union Infantry

← Union movement

← Confederate movement

Confederate HQ

Union HQ

1 Night, 21 July: Intending to outflank the Confederate left, McDowell moves 10,000 men from Centerville, heading west and south.

2 8:30 am: The Confederate defenders of Stone Bridge learn the Federals are at Sudley Ford. Brig. Gen. N.G. Evans moves a portion of his command to meet the Federal retreat.

3 Morning: Evans opposes Federal moves.

4 Outnumbered, Evans's force withdraws to Henry House Hill, where it makes a stand.

5 Afternoon: For several hours, the front line pushes up and down on Henry House Hill.

6 Confederates withdraw from Henry House Hill. Gen. Thomas Jackson leads in fresh Confederate troops.

7 4 pm: Confederate attack forces Federals to retreat toward Centerville.

North America

ATLANTIC OCEAN

Manassas (Bull Run)

unfinished railroad

Sudley Ford

McDOWELL

Centreville

TYLER

HUNTER

MILES

HEINTZELMAN

BEE BARTOW

Stone Bridge

EVANS

Cub Run

EVANS

Warrenton Turnpike

JACKSON

Lewis Ford

Ball's Ford

COCKE

Island Ford

EARLY   ELZEY

Henry House Hill

STUART

Bull Run

Little Rocky Run

Blackburn's Ford

Mitchell's Ford

LONGSTREET

Warrenton–Alexandria Road

Manassas–Sudley Road

Flat Run

BONHAM

JACKSON

Early

D.R. JONES

McLean's Ford

BEE

J.E. JOHNSTON

N

BARTOW

Manassas Railroad

BEAUREGARD

Manassas Junction

Orange and Alexandria Railroad

EWELL

HOLMES

Bull Run

0   1 km

0   1 mile

Opposite page: The ironclad Monitor (Union) and its opponent *Merrimack* (Confederate) in the Hampton Roads battle on March 8, 1862 were both revolutionary vessels. The *Monitor* was 172 feet (52 m) long, the *Merrimack*, 275feet (84m). Both carried Dahlgren smoothbores among their armaments.

were slowly gaining the upper hand. In May 1861, the nascent but fast-growing U.S. navy sealed off the Confederates with a blockade that stretched from the River Potomac to the Gulf of Mexico.

On March 8, 1862, the first battle of the Civil War at sea took place at Hampton Roads in south-eastern Virginia when the Confederate ironclad *CSS Merrimack* attacked a blockading squadron of wooden vessels. The *Merrimack*, formerly the *USS Virginia*, had been seized by the Confederates in a raid on the Norfolk Navy Yard in Virginia on April 20 1861. It was a formidable vessel, covered in a heavy oak and iron carapace with a crew of 282 men and carrying 10 large guns, of 7-and 9-inch calibers. The ironclad rammed and sank the *Cumberland* and badly damaged the *Congress*, which was forced to surrender. For all her virtually impenetrable surface, the *Merrimack* too had suffered damage: its smokestack had been riddled with cannon ball fire from the *Cumberland* and *Congress* and by fire from Union forces ashore. Two of its guns had been silenced; and in sinking, the *Cumberland* had severed her ram.

That night, while the *Merrimack* returned to the Norfolk Navy Yard for repairs, the Union armored warship *Monitor* arrived at Hampton Roads from New York. On the next day, March 9, the two ironclads went into battle. *Monitor*, the smaller of the two and lower in the water, carried two 11-inch guns mounted on a heavily armored revolving turret. *Monitor* and *Merrimack* spent four hours pounding away at each other, but the result was inconclusive. Hampton Roads was the first battle fought by either of the ironclads. It was also the last. In September 1862, the Confederate General Robert E. Lee moved north toward Maryland and established lines of communication through the Shenandoah Valley of

CSS Merrimack, the Conferderate vessel responsible for sinking the *Cumberland* and damaging the *Congress* on March 8, 1862.,

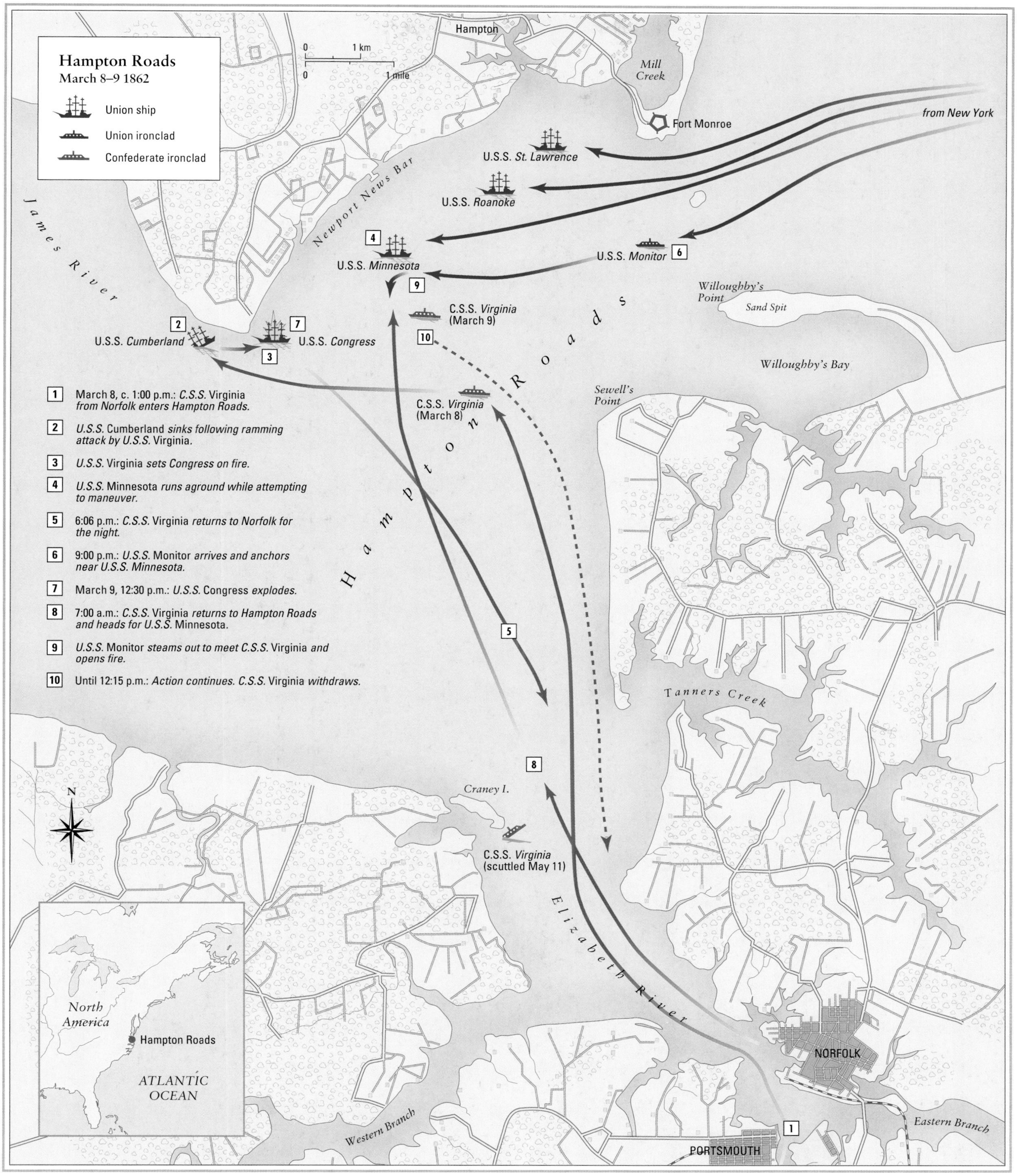

Hampton Roads
March 8–9 1862

Union ship

Union ironclad

Confederate ironclad

Hampton

Mill Creek

Fort Monroe

from New York

U.S.S. *St. Lawrence*

U.S.S. *Roanoke*

Newport News Bar

4 U.S.S. *Minnesota*

U.S.S. Monitor 6

9

Willoughby's Point

Sand Spit

C.S.S. *Virginia* (March 9)

10

2 U.S.S. Cumberland

7

3 U.S.S. *Congress*

Willoughby's Bay

James River

C.S.S. *Virginia* (March 8)

Sewell's Point

1 March 8, c. 1:00 p.m.: *C.S.S. Virginia* from Norfolk enters Hampton Roads.

2 *U.S.S. Cumberland sinks* following ramming attack by *U.S.S.* Virginia.

3 *U.S.S. Virginia* sets Congress on fire.

4 *U.S.S. Minnesota runs aground* while attempting to maneuver.

5 6:06 p.m.: *C.S.S. Virginia returns* to Norfolk for the night.

6 9:00 p.m.: *U.S.S. Monitor arrives* and anchors near *U.S.S. Minnesota.*

7 March 9, 12:30 p.m.: *U.S.S. Congress explodes.*

8 7:00 a.m.: *C.S.S. Virginia returns* to Hampton Roads and heads for *U.S.S.* Minnesota.

9 *U.S.S. Monitor steams* out to meet *C.S.S. Virginia* and opens fire.

10 Until 12:15 p.m.: *Action continues. C.S.S. Virginia withdraws.*

Hampton Roads

5

8

Tanners Creek

N

Craney I.

C.S.S. *Virginia* (scuttled May 11)

North America

Hampton Roads

ATLANTIC OCEAN

Elizabeth River

NORFOLK

Western Branch

Eastern Branch

1

PORTSMOUTH

Virginia and West Virginia. General George B. McClellan and his 97,000-strong Union army of the Potomac departed Washington and set off in pursuit. But catching up with the Confederates proved to be difficult. Two chances against Lee— at the battles of South Mountain on September 14 and Harper's Ferry on September 14-15 — failed to halt his advance. As a result, the Confederates were able to dig into good defensive positions along Antietam Creek in Maryland, where the Potomac River was behind them.

The Battle of Antietam began at dawn on September 17, 1862 when I Corps led by Major-General Joseph Hooker attacked the left flank of Lee's army. The fighting was ferocious from the start, with all-out attacks engulfing Miller's cornfield and the Dunker Church, only to be quickly answered by equally violent counterattacks.

Antietam, in which the Union army suffered 12,401 casualties killed, wounded, and captured or missing and the Confederates 10,316, was afterward termed the bloodiest one-day battle of the Civil War. The opposing armies were equipped with a wide range of mainly up-to-date weapons. Among them were the .69-caliber smoothbore Springfield 1842 musket, the Enfield, Richmond, and Sharps rifles and the Springfield rifle-musket. Several of the ruthlessly efficient Parrott guns featured in the artillery, such as 69 10-pound cannons and, on the Union side, 22 20-pound cannons. There were 3 12-pound Union howitzers and 58 in the Confederate batteries, as well as 4 24-pound howitzers. But the Union army outnumbered the Confederates in 3-inch ordnance rifles: 87 to the Confederates 48. Also, the Union army used 58 6-pound guns at Antietam. The Confederates had none. Burnside, Enfield Saddle Ring, and Sharps carbines were also used at Antietam, as was the Colt army revolver and the cavalry saber, one of which was carried by Major-General McClellan himself.

McClellan was well known for his insubordination, his tardiness in battle and his excessive caution when it came to exploiting an advantage. His diffident conduct at Antietam was no exception, and led to his subsequent dismissal by President Lincoln. He preferred the more enterprising Major-General Ambrose Burnside, commander

The Battle of Antietam Creek (Sharpsburg) on September 18 ,1862 was the most bloody battle of the entire Civil War, costing 23,000 casualties. The first substantial battle of the war, it was also the first to take place in Union territory.

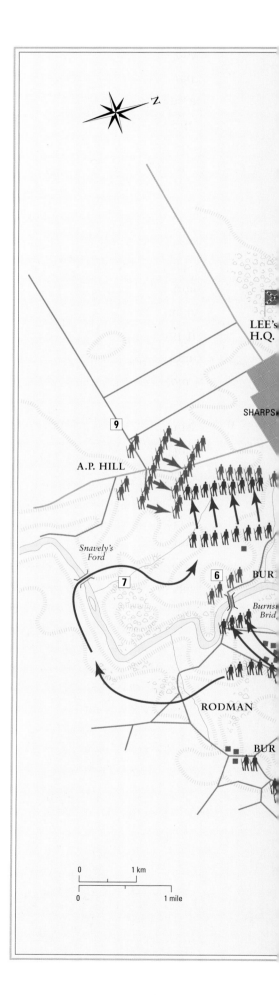

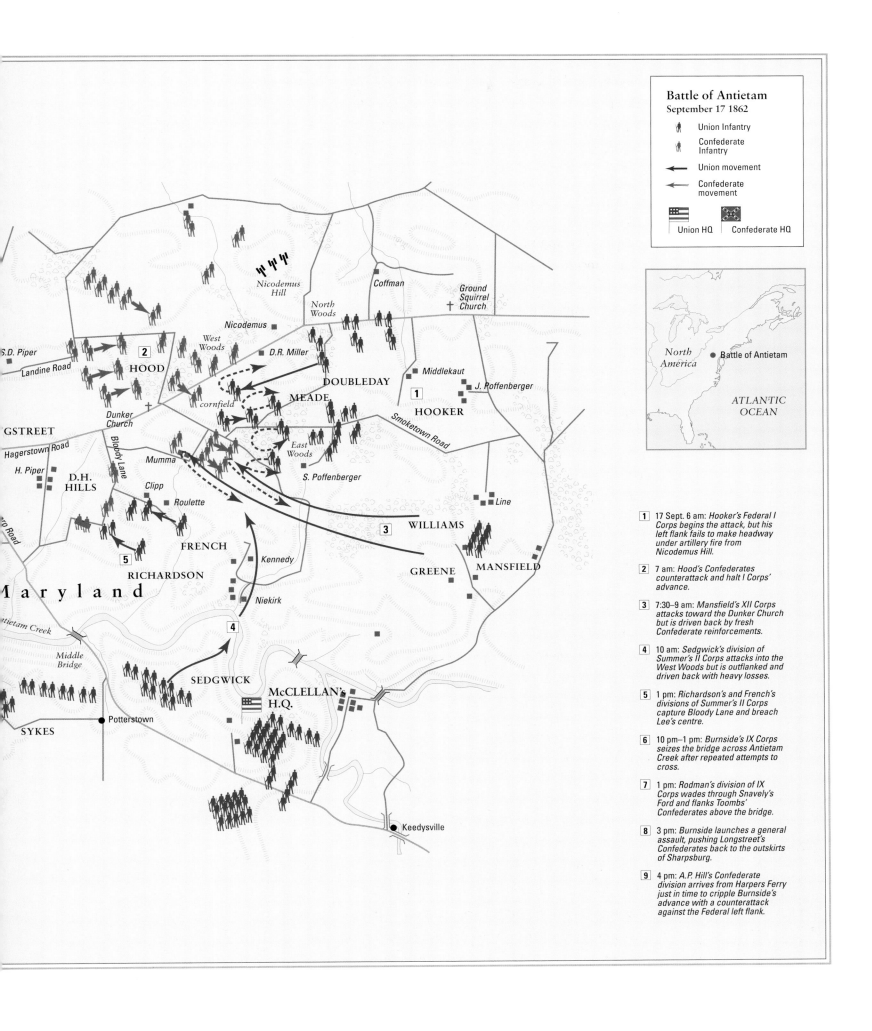

Battle of Antietam
September 17 1862

🏃 Union Infantry

👥 Confederate Infantry

← Union movement

← Confederate movement

🏴 Union HQ   🏴 Confederate HQ

North America • Battle of Antietam

ATLANTIC OCEAN

1 17 Sept. 6 am: *Hooker's Federal I Corps begins the attack, but his left flank fails to make headway under artillery fire from Nicodemus Hill.*

2 7 am: *Hood's Confederates counterattack and halt I Corps' advance.*

3 7:30–9 am: *Mansfield's XII Corps attacks toward the Dunker Church but is driven back by fresh Confederate reinforcements.*

4 10 am: *Sedgwick's division of Summer's II Corps attacks into the West Woods but is outflanked and driven back with heavy losses.*

5 1 pm: *Richardson's and French's divisions of Summer's II Corps capture Bloody Lane and breach Lee's centre.*

6 10 pm–1 pm: *Burnside's IX Corps seizes the bridge across Antietam Creek after repeated attempts to cross.*

7 1 pm: *Rodman's division of IX Corps wades through Snavely's Ford and flanks Toombs' Confederates above the bridge.*

8 3 pm: *Burnside launches a general assault, pushing Longstreet's Confederates back to the outskirts of Sharpsburg.*

9 4 pm: *A.P. Hill's Confederate division arrives from Harpers Ferry just in time to cripple Burnside's advance with a counterattack against the Federal left flank.*

of IX Corps at Antietam, to lead the Army of the Potomac. At Antietam, the Union army outnumbered the Confederates two to one, yet McClellan somehow allowed General Lee to fight his Union opponents to a dead stop. The Confederates suffered crippling casualties; but all the same, Lee continued to skirmish with the Union army throughout September 18 while withdrawing his much-depleted forces south of the Potomac River. With his vast reserves of men, McClellan should have been able to destroy the Confederates, but he failed to do so. He was fortunate that Lee's Maryland campaign, and in particular the battle of Antietam, had decimated and exhausted the Confederate forces, so that Lee's only real choice was to withdraw his men back to Virginia where his campaign in the North had begun. Tactically, Antietam was a Confederate victory but strategically, the winners were McClellan and the Army of the Potomac. At any rate, General Lee's invasion of the North was prevented, and that was enough for President Lincoln to head off the apparent intentions of Britain and France to recognize the Confederacy. On September 23, Lincoln was able to announce his Preliminary Emancipation Proclamation, granting freedom to the black slaves in the South.

The Siege of Vicksburg was the final stage in the Union army drive down the Mississippi River, which had begun in February 1862. Fifteen months later, Vicksburg, sited near the confluence of the Mississippi with the Yazoo river, was the last unconquered Confederate fortress, and it was still holding out after two attacks, on 19 May and 22 May. Those attacks had caused very heavy casualties and brought to an end a run of 19 days in which the Union General Ulysses Grant had severely disadvantaged his Confederate enemies.

During that time, Grant had marched his army over a distance of 200 miles (322 km) and crossed the Mississippi River unopposed on April 30. Subsequently, despite being outnumbered by the Confederates, Grant defeated them in five consecutive engagements and several skirmishes. The Union losses were considerable — 4,400 men in all — but the Confederates' were almost double, some 8,000. As a result of Grant's success, some 30,000 Confederates were isolated inside Vicksburg by May 16. They were, however, very well armed for the bitter fight that ensued. There were some 50,000 shoulder arms in Vicksburg, the majority of them British-made Enfield rifle-muskets of .577 caliber. In addition, the defenders at Vicksburg had at their disposal Springfield, Richmond, Mississippi, and Fayetteville models of the 0.58 caliber Minié rifles, .577 and .58 caliber French and Austrian rifle-muskets, and various other rifled muskets, rifles and British .75 caliber smoothbore muskets. The Confederates were also amply supplied with ammunition, to judge by the 600,000 rounds and 350,000 percussion caps that were surrendered to the Union forces when, finally, the Siege of Vicksburg was over on July 4.

The siege, which began on May 25, was the only feasible recourse for General Grant after the failure, of the two previous assaults. An important factor in Grant's decision to besiege Vicksburg was the advantage he knew he had due to the superiority his forces enjoyed in firepower. The Union forces came to the siege with some 180 cannons, later increased to around 47 artillery batteries comprising 13 heavy guns and 234 field pieces. Of the Union batteries, 29 had six guns each and 18 had four guns each. The U.S. Navy contributed even more firepower, with its 12-pounder howitzers and 11-inch Dahlgren smoothbores. But not all of them were fired from the decks of ships; some went ashore to serve as siege artillery.

By contrast, the Confederates inside Vicksburg had only 172 cannons, 103 of them fieldpieces, and 69 siege guns. Some 37 of the siege guns were sited overlooking the Mississippi River, together with 13

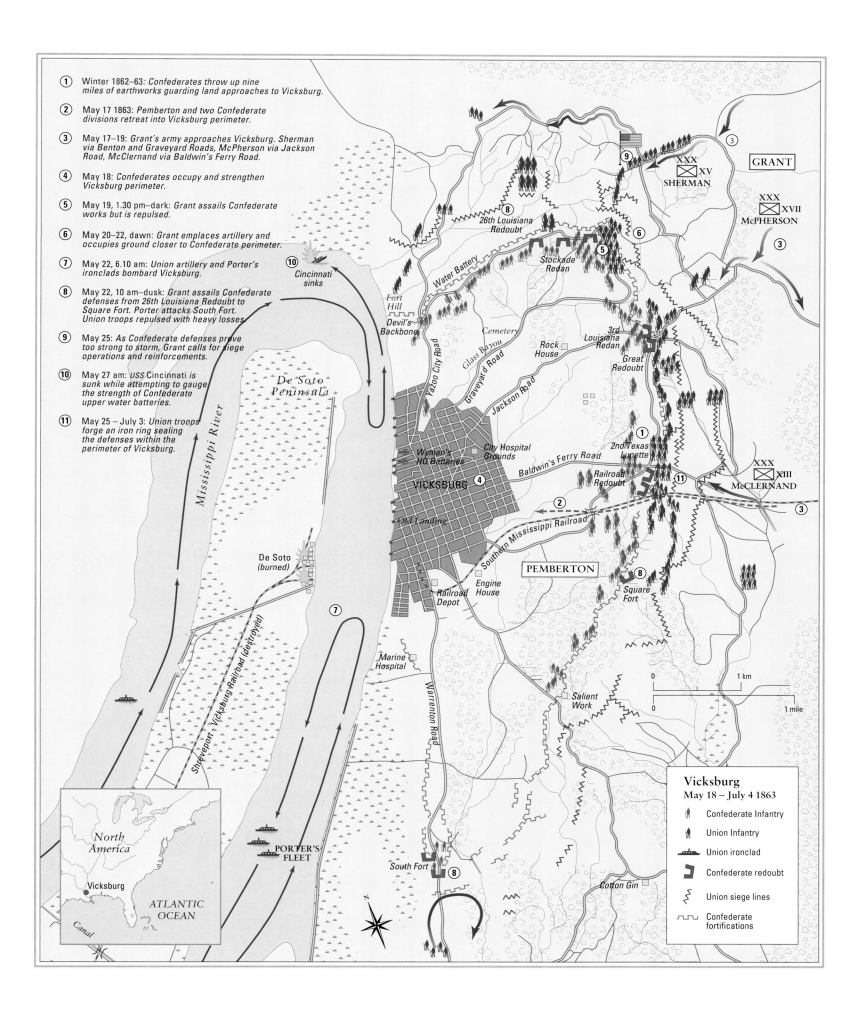

① Winter 1862–63: Confederates throw up nine miles of earthworks guarding land approaches to Vicksburg.

② May 17 1863: Pemberton and two Confederate divisions retreat into Vicksburg perimeter.

③ May 17–19: Grant's army approaches Vicksburg. Sherman via Benton and Graveyard Roads, McPherson via Jackson Road, McClernand via Baldwin's Ferry Road.

④ May 18: Confederates occupy and strengthen Vicksburg perimeter.

⑤ May 19, 1.30 pm–dark: Grant assails Confederate works but is repulsed.

⑥ May 20–22, dawn: Grant emplaces artillery and occupies ground closer to Confederate perimeter.

⑦ May 22, 6.10 am: Union artillery and Porter's ironclads bombard Vicksburg.

⑧ May 22, 10 am–dusk: Grant assails Confederate defenses from 26th Louisiana Redoubt to Square Fort. Porter attacks South Fort. Union troops repulsed with heavy losses.

⑨ May 25: As Confederate defenses prove too strong to storm, Grant calls for siege operations and reinforcements.

⑩ May 27 am: USS Cincinnati is sunk while attempting to gauge the strength of Confederate upper water batteries.

⑪ May 25 – July 3: Union troops forge an iron ring sealing the defenses within the perimeter of Vicksburg.

GRANT

XXX XV SHERMAN

XXX XVII McPHERSON

XXX XIII McCLERNAND

26th Louisiana Redoubt

Water Battery

Stockade Redan

Fort Hill

Devil's Backbone

Cemetery

Glass Bayou

Rock House

3rd Louisiana Redan

Great Redoubt

Yazoo City Road

Graveyard Road

Jackson Road

2nd Texas Lunette

Railroad Redoubt

Wyman's HQ Batteries

City Hospital Grounds

VICKSBURG

Old Landing

Baldwin's Ferry Road

Southern Mississippi Railroad

PEMBERTON

Square Fort

Railroad Depot

Engine House

Mississippi River

De Soto Peninsula

Cincinnati sinks

De Soto (burned)

Shreveport Vicksburg Railroad (destroyed)

PORTER'S FLEET

Marine Hospital

Warrenton Road

Salient Work

Cotton Gin

South Fort

North America

Vicksburg

ATLANTIC OCEAN

Canal

Vicksburg
May 18 – July 4 1863

Confederate Infantry
Union Infantry
Union ironclad
Confederate redoubt
Union siege lines
Confederate fortifications

0   1 km
0   1 mile

Reenactment of the American Civil War: Confederate soldiers overrun the Union Army's tents and cannons a soldier holding the Confederate Battle Flag ahead of other soldiers wearing Confderate uniforms and holding rifle muskets.

fieldpieces placed there to meet any amphibious invasion the Union army might attempt. But the Confederates failed to mass their guns, unlike their opponents, who concentrated theirs and were able to plaster Confederate targets with heavy amounts of shot. The Confederates, nevertheless, held out at Vicksburg for nearly six weeks as the Union artillery blazed away at their positions, not only from gunsites on land but also from the river, where the U.S. Navy kept up a continual bombardment from their ironclads.

Inside Vicksburg, the Confederate forces and the civilian population took to sheltering in caves, but their resistance — as much admired in the North as it was in the South — was basically hopeless, for food stocks ran low and starvation threatened. On July 4, General Grant prepared an assault on the fortress, but on learning of it, General John C. Pemberton, in command at Vicksburg, decided to surrender. Five days later, the Confederate garrison at Port Hudson also surrendered, giving command of the Mississippi to the Union. The Confederate surrender at Vicksburg gave the Union forces control of the Mississippi River for the rest of the war and split the Confederate forces in two. Along with defeat of the Confederate General Robert E. Lee at Gettysburg on July 3 1863 after a fierce two-day battle, Vicksburg is frequently considered the turning point of the war. In this context, Pickett's Charge, an infantry advance by the Confederate forces on the last day of Gettysburg, played its own part in the sense that the Confederate South was going to lose the war.

The Charge was named after Major General George Pickett, one of the Confederate generals at Gettysburg. On July 2, the Confederates failed in both the attacks they mounted on the Union flanks. Hoping for better luck with an assault on the Union center, General Lee decided to carry this out on the third day of the battle. Three divisions of nine brigades and 12,500 men were detailed to take part in a charge led by Major General Pickett, Brigadier-General Johnston Pettigrew, and Major General Isaac Trimble. The plan was to assault the center of the Union II Corps.

Opposite page: Pickett's Charge, named after one of the Confederate generals at the battle of Gettysburg, took place on July 3 1863. It was intended to smash the Union center but failed due to flawed equipment and ended with 6,555 Confederate casualties.

Unfortunately for Lee, his plans went awry from the start. The charge started late, after the morning July 3 was occupied with organizing the attack force. The artillery bombardment that preceded charge did not begin until 1 in the afternoon and was, in any case, ineffective owing to faulty leadership and flawed equipment. The guns in action included Napoleon, Parrott, and breech-loading Whitworth cannons and howitzers — all of them artillery of proven worth and strength — but the Confederate guns, numbering up to 170, were not accurately concentrated on the main target. The artillery exchanges lasted for nearly two hours. Confederate General Evander Law described it thus: "The cannonade in the center ... presented one of the most magnificent battle scenes witnessed during the War. Looking up the valley toward Gettysburg, the hills on either side were capped with crowns of flame and smoke as 300 guns, about equally divided between the two ridges, spewed out their iron hail upon each other".

However "magnificent" the bombardment may have seemed, it was ineffectual, with the Confederates frequently overshooting, a fact concealed by the smoke that covered large areas of the

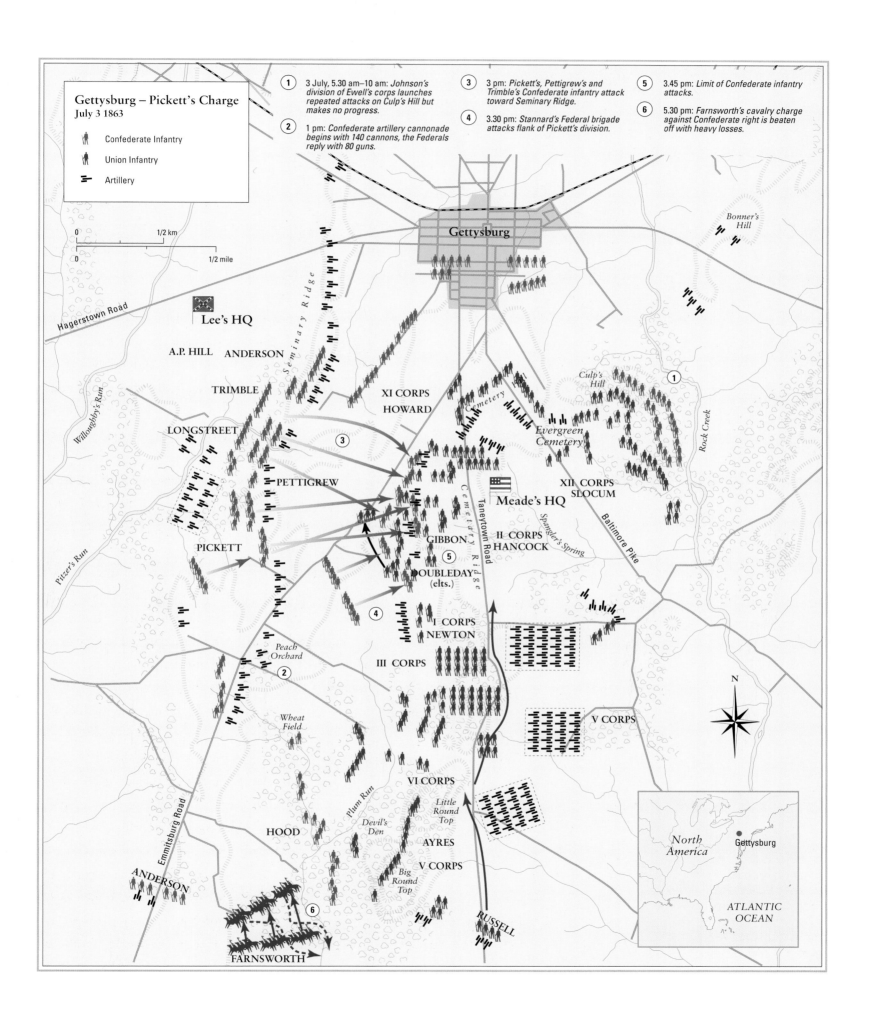

Gettysburg – Pickett's Charge
July 3 1863

- 🪖 Confederate Infantry
- 🪖 Union Infantry
- ⚏ Artillery

0 ———— 1/2 km
0 ———— 1/2 mile

① 3 July, 5.30 am–10 am: *Johnson's division of Ewell's corps launches repeated attacks on Culp's Hill but makes no progress.*

② 1 pm: *Confederate artillery cannonade begins with 140 cannons, the Federals reply with 80 guns.*

③ 3 pm: *Pickett's, Pettigrew's and Trimble's Confederate infantry attack toward Seminary Ridge.*

④ 3.30 pm: *Stannard's Federal brigade attacks flank of Pickett's division.*

⑤ 3.45 pm: *Limit of Confederate infantry attacks.*

⑥ 5.30 pm: *Farnsworth's cavalry charge against Confederate right is beaten off with heavy losses.*

Hagerstown Road

Lee's HQ

A.P. HILL   ANDERSON

TRIMBLE

Willoughby's Run

LONGSTREET

Seminary Ridge

Pitzer's Run

PETTIGREW

PICKETT

Peach Orchard

Emmitsburg Road

Wheat Field

HOOD

ANDERSON

FARNSWORTH

Gettysburg

Bonner's Hill

XI CORPS
HOWARD

Cemetery

Culp's Hill

Rock Creek

Evergreen Cemetery

XII CORPS
SLOCUM

Meade's HQ

GIBBON

Cemetery Ridge

Taneytown Road

II CORPS
HANCOCK

Spangler's Spring

Baltimore Pike

DOUBLEDAY
(elts.)

I CORPS
NEWTON

III CORPS

V CORPS

N

Plum Run

VI CORPS

Little Round Top

Devil's Den

AYRES
V CORPS

Big Round Top

RUSSELL

North America

Gettysburg

ATLANTIC OCEAN

battlefield. The Union artillery also overshot, causing havoc among the Confederate infantry lined up in the Seminary Ridge woods waiting to take part in the action. They suffered large casualties even before Pickett's Charge began.

Lieutenant General James Longstreet, who was in command of the charge, knew instinctively that the advance was going to fail, and fail disastrously. Nevertheless, he obeyed orders, as he was bound to do, and told Pickett, Pettigrew, and Trimble to lead the charge across ¾ mile (1.2 km) of open fields while Union artillery and rifles directed a storm of shot at them. Although some of the Confederate cavalry managed to break through the low stone wall that sheltered the Union soldiers, this was a brief success in what was otherwise a disasterous confrontation between Confederate and Union forces: the Confederates were thrown back with over 50 percent casualties. Overall, 6,555 Confederate soldiers were lost and some 3,750 were captured. The Union army lost some 1,500 killed and wounded. The disaster of Pickett's Charge served to underline the total failure of General Lee's campaign in Pennsylvania. Moreover, George Pickett never forgave him for ordering the charge that bore his name.

Cavalry played a prominent role in the fighting that took place in June 1864 around Cold Harbor, an important crossroads some 9 miles (14.5 km) from the Confederate capital Richmond, Virginia. The Union cavalry under the command of General Philip Sheridan seized the crossroads on May 31 1864. On the next day, modern repeater carbines were used to force back an attack by the Confederate infantry. These cavalry carbines had a shorter barrel than the rifle; and although they were less accurate, they were easier to handle on horseback. Most were of .52 or .56 caliber and were single-shot breech-loading weapons. The Confederate cavalry, by contrast, eschewed the saber favored by the Union forces and armed itself with six-shot revolvers of .36 or .44 caliber.

The offensive action by the Union cavalry at Cold Harbor exemplified one of five tasks routinely assigned to cavalry in the Civil War. The others were reconnaissance, screening, defensive delaying tactics, and raids on an opponent's lines of communication, railroads, or supply depots. On June 1 both sides were reinforced at Cold Harbor, the Confederates by extra troops sent from Richmond, the Union by the VI and XVIII corps. On June 3, the II and XVIII Corps, later augmented by the IX Corps, attacked along a 6⁴/₅ mile (11 km) front. They met disaster. Some 13,000 Union soldiers were slaughtered as they made a frontal assault on the Confederate defenses. Their opponents lost 2,500 men. The Confederate General Robert E. Lee was appalled by the scale of the casualties, afterward writing in his memoirs: "I have always regretted that the last assault at Cold Harbor was ever made." Although Cold Harbor was a Confederate victory, Lee went on: "No advantage whatever was gained to compensate for the heavy loss we sustained." In 1864, the Union forces set out to capture the important Confederate railroad and supply center, Atlanta. The Confederates had a terrible foretaste of what was to come when they suffered 13,300 casualties in two attacks on the Union forces on July 20 and 22. After these attacks, the Confederates had only 45,000 soldiers left. Falling back behind their defences inside Atlanta, they waited for the Union army. When the Northern forces arrived, they besieged the city and pounded it with heavy artillery for a month, leaving Atlanta in ruins. The Confederates burned whatever was left and on September 2 evacuated the city.

After his victory at Atlanta in September 1864, the Union General William Tecumseh Sherman set out to apply the most merciless form of warfare — total war — to break the Confederates both materially

Opposite page: During the 10-day Battle of Cold Harbor in June 1864, all Union assaults were repulsed, so violently that they lost 7,000 men in less than one hour. The Union losses had almost doubled by the time the operation was called off.

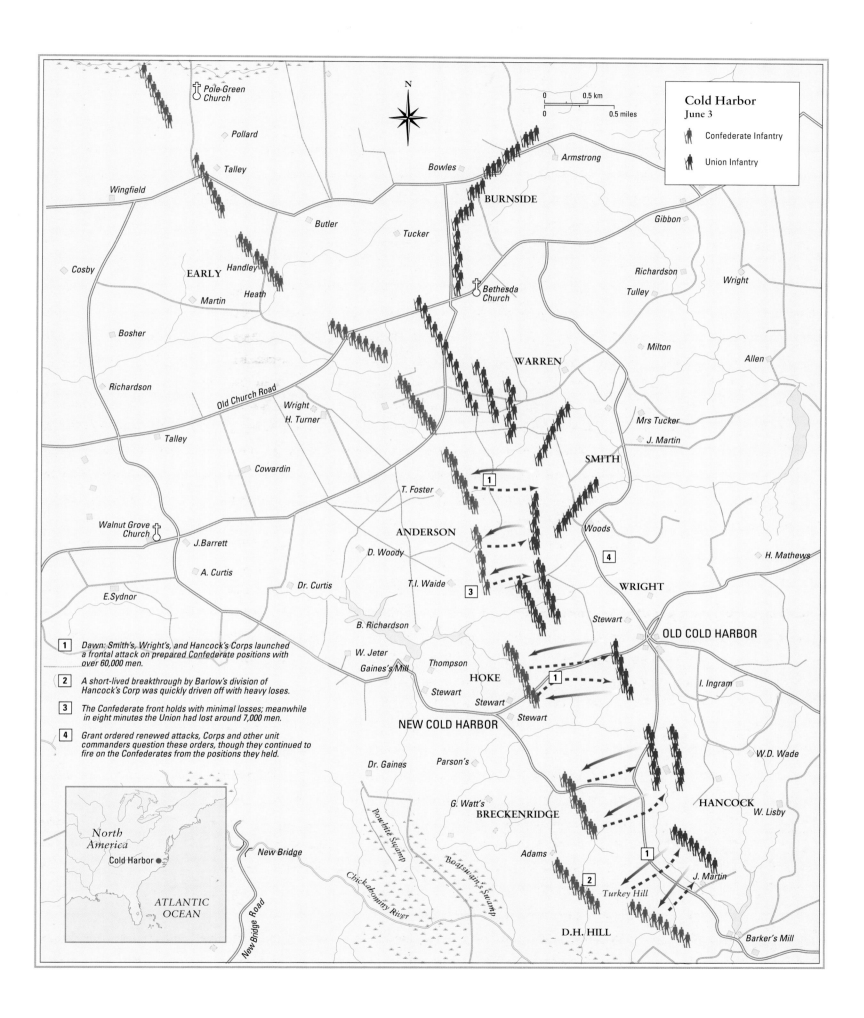

Pole-Green Church
Pollard
Talley
Wingfield
Butler
Tucker
Bowles
Armstrong
BURNSIDE
Gibbon
EARLY
Handley
Heath
Cosby
Martin
Richardson
Tulley
Wright
Bethesda Church
Bosher
Milton
Allen
WARREN
Richardson
Old Church Road
Wright
H. Turner
Talley
Mrs Tucker
J. Martin
Cowardin
SMITH
T. Foster
ANDERSON
Woods
D. Woody
Walnut Grove Church
J. Barrett
T.I. Waide
A. Curtis
Dr. Curtis
WRIGHT
H. Mathews
E. Sydnor
Stewart
B. Richardson
OLD COLD HARBOR
W. Jeter
Gaines's Mill
Thompson
HOKE
I. Ingram
Stewart
Stewart
Stewart
NEW COLD HARBOR
W.D. Wade
Dr. Gaines
Parson's
HANCOCK
G. Watt's
BRECKENRIDGE
W. Lisby
Adams
J. Martin
Turkey Hill
D.H. HILL
Barker's Mill

North America
Cold Harbor
ATLANTIC OCEAN
New Bridge
New Bridge Road
Chickahominy River
Powhite Swamp
Boatswain's Swamp

N

0   0.5 km
0   0.5 miles

Cold Harbor
June 3

Confederate Infantry

Union Infantry

1 Dawn: Smith's, Wright's, and Hancock's Corps launched a frontal attack on prepared Confederate positions with over 60,000 men.

2 A short-lived breakthrough by Barlow's division of Hancock's Corp was quickly driven off with heavy loses.

3 The Confederate front holds with minimal losses; meanwhile in eight minutes the Union had lost around 7,000 men.

4 Grant ordered renewed attacks, Corps and other unit commanders question these orders, though they continued to fire on the Confederates from the positions they held.

Opposite page: Union cavalry raids on Confederate-held Atlanta in July and August 1864 failed to cut the local railroad. On 27 August General Sherman led his three armies in a direct assault that forced the Confederates out of the town.

and psychologically. The stage Sherman chose for this exercise, which he viewed as the Confederates' punishment for starting the Civil War, was the state of Georgia, which he vowed would "howl" over his depredations.

On November 15 1864, Sherman marched out of Atlanta with 55,000 infantry, 5,000 cavalry, and 2,000 gunners with 64 pieces of artillery, together with 2,500 wagons and 600 ambulances carrying supplies, mostly ammunition. Heading for the Atlantic coast, Sherman proceeded to destroy everything that could be of use to the Confederates: plantations, shops, barns, crops, houses, and even complete towns. Sherman's army cut a swathe of destruction across Georgia that was 60 miles (97 km) wide and 300 miles (483 km) long, leaving behind it the wreckage of property and industry and ruined lives as civilians suffered immense personal loss. The damage cost around $100 million. About 300 miles (483 km) of Georgia's railroads were devastated and 22,000 farm and other animals were seized along with 9½ milllion lb (4.3 million kg) of corn and 10½ million lb (4.75 million kg) of fodder.

The Confederate forces that sought to stop Sherman failed to hold back his inexorable advance. General John Hood tried to distract the Union forces with an invasion of Tennessee while General Pierre Beauregard organized the defense of Savannah and Charleston, but all to no avail. Despite their efforts, Sherman's army invaded Savannah; and when he threatened to cut Confederate communications, Major General William Hardee, in command of the city, ordered an evacuation. Sherman moved in on December 21 and telegraphed President Lincoln, presenting Savannah to him as "a Christmas gift", complete with 150 guns and "plenty of ammunition".

After the march to Savannah, Ulysses Grant, General-in-Chief of the Union army, found another task for General Sherman. Across the Savannah River lay South Carolina, a state regarded in the North as the instigator of the Civil War and therefore due to pay a penalty for its turpitude. Another "march," through South Carolina and, beyond it, North Carolina, would be fit punishment; and in the early months of 1865, the time was ripe for Union revenge. By

Next page: After the fall of Atlanta, General Sherman led his forces on a march through Georgia, perpetrating a swathe of devastation aimed at destroying the state's economy. Sherman described his action as a way of "making Georgia howl".

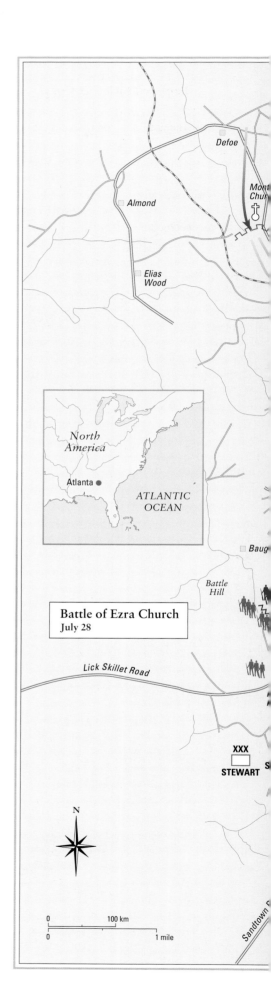

North America

Atlanta

ATLANTIC OCEAN

Battle of Ezra Church
July 28

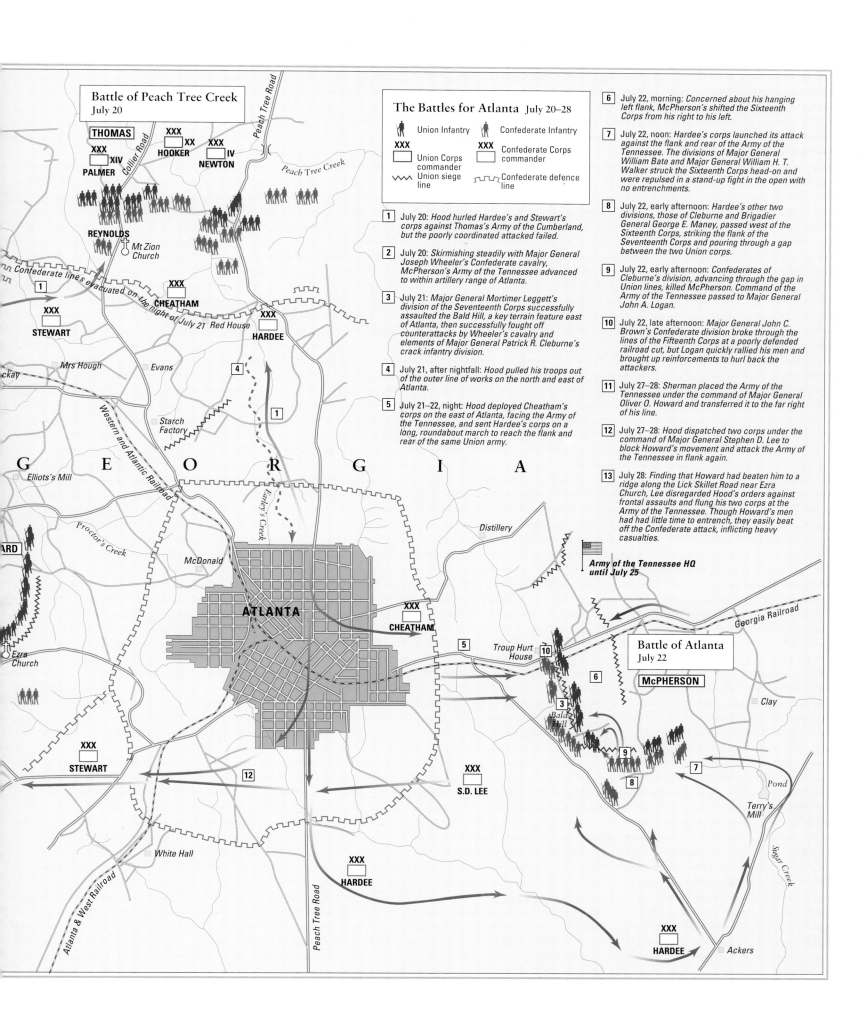

Battle of Peach Tree Creek
July 20

THOMAS

XXX PALMER
XIV

XXX XX
HOOKER

XXX IV
NEWTON

REYNOLDS

✝ Mt Zion Church

Peach Tree Road

Peach Tree Creek

Confederate lines evacuated on the night of July 21

1

XXX STEWART

Collier Road

XXX CHEATHAM

XXX HARDEE

Red House

4

1

Mrs Hough

Evans

Starch Factory

Western and Atlantic Railroad

Elliots's Mill

Proctor's Creek

Earley's Creek

G E O R G I A

McDonald

ATLANTA

XXX CHEATHAM

5

Troup Hurt House

Distillery

10

3

Bald Hill

9

8

7

Pond

Terry's Mill

Clay

Georgia Railroad

Sugar Creek

Army of the Tennessee HQ until July 25

Battle of Atlanta
July 22

McPHERSON

6

Ezra Church

XXX STEWART

12

XXX S.D. LEE

White Hall

Atlanta & West Railroad

XXX HARDEE

Peach Tree Road

XXX HARDEE

Ackers

The Battles for Atlanta July 20–28

👤 Union Infantry   👤 Confederate Infantry

XXX ☐ Union Corps commander

XXX ☐ Confederate Corps commander

〰 Union siege line

⌐⌐ Confederate defence line

1 July 20: Hood hurled Hardee's and Stewart's corps against Thomas's Army of the Cumberland, but the poorly coordinated attacked failed.

2 July 20: Skirmishing steadily with Major General Joseph Wheeler's Confederate cavalry, McPherson's Army of the Tennessee advanced to within artillery range of Atlanta.

3 July 21: Major General Mortimer Leggett's division of the Seventeenth Corps successfully assaulted the Bald Hill, a key terrain feature east of Atlanta, then successfully fought off counterattacks by Wheeler's cavalry and elements of Major General Patrick R. Cleburne's crack infantry division.

4 July 21, after nightfall: Hood pulled his troops out of the outer line of works on the north and east of Atlanta.

5 July 21–22, night: Hood deployed Cheatham's corps on the east of Atlanta, facing the Army of the Tennessee, and sent Hardee's corps on a long, roundabout march to reach the flank and rear of the same Union army.

6 July 22, morning: Concerned about his hanging left flank, McPherson's shifted the Sixteenth Corps from his right to his left.

7 July 22, noon: Hardee's corps launched its attack against the flank and rear of the Army of the Tennessee. The divisions of Major General William Bate and Major General William H. T. Walker struck the Sixteenth Corps head-on and were repulsed in a stand-up fight in the open with no entrenchments.

8 July 22, early afternoon: Hardee's other two divisions, those of Cleburne and Brigadier General George E. Maney, passed west of the Sixteenth Corps, striking the flank of the Seventeenth Corps and pouring through a gap between the two Union corps.

9 July 22, early afternoon: Confederates of Cleburne's division, advancing through the gap in Union lines, killed McPherson. Command of the Army of the Tennessee passed to Major General John A. Logan.

10 July 22, late afternoon: Major General John C. Brown's Confederate division broke through the lines of the Fifteenth Corps at a poorly defended railroad cut, but Logan quickly rallied his men and brought up reinforcements to hurl back the attackers.

11 July 27–28: Sherman placed the Army of the Tennessee under the command of Major General Oliver O. Howard and transferred it to the far right of his line.

12 July 27–28: Hood dispatched two corps under the command of Major General Stephen D. Lee to block Howard's movement and attack the Army of the Tennessee in flank again.

13 July 28: Finding that Howard had beaten him to a ridge along the Lick Skillet Road near Ezra Church, Lee disregarded Hood's orders against frontal assaults and flung his two corps at the Army of the Tennessee. Though Howard's men had little time to entrench, they easily beat off the Confederate attack, inflicting heavy casualties.

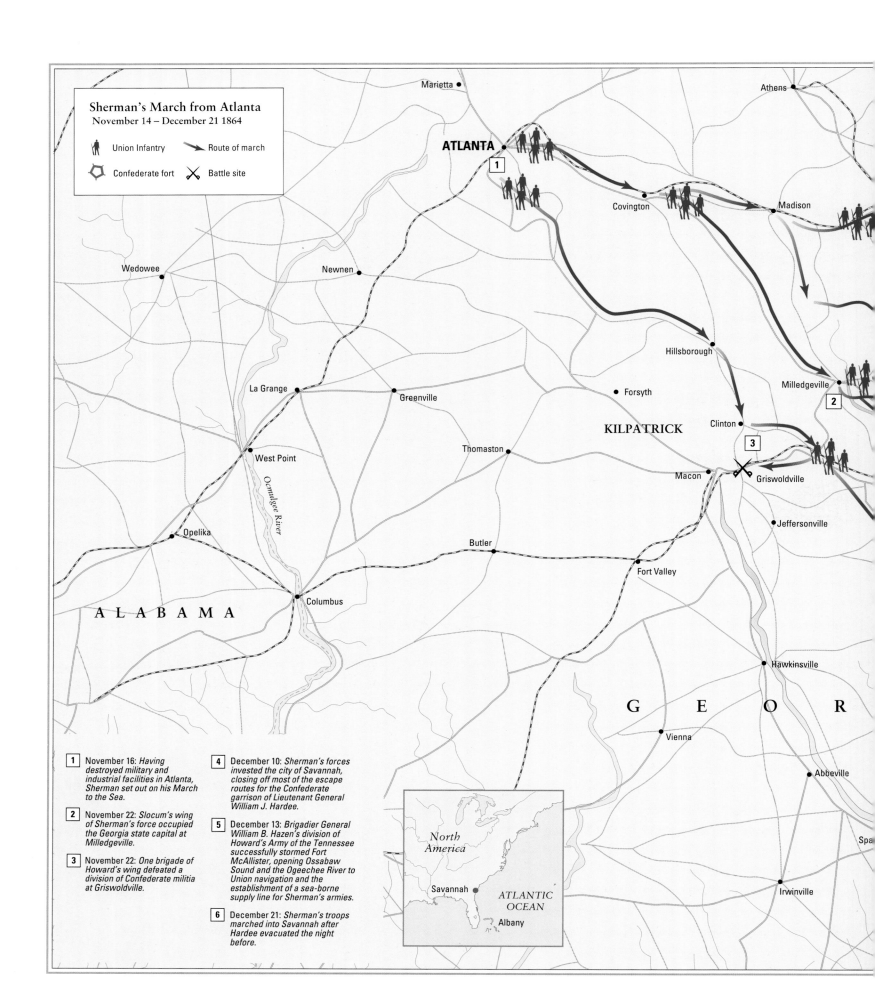

Sherman's March from Atlanta
November 14 – December 21 1864

🚶 Union Infantry   ➤ Route of march

⬡ Confederate fort   ✗ Battle site

Marietta

Athens

ATLANTA

1

Covington

Madison

Wedowee

Newnen

Hillsborough

Milledgeville

La Grange

Greenville

Forsyth

2

KILPATRICK

Clinton

Thomaston

3

Ocmulgee River

West Point

Macon

Griswoldville

Jeffersonville

Opelika

Butler

Fort Valley

A L A B A M A

Columbus

Hawkinsville

G E O R

Vienna

Abbeville

Spa

1 November 16: *Having destroyed military and industrial facilities in Atlanta, Sherman set out on his March to the Sea.*

2 November 22: *Slocum's wing of Sherman's force occupied the Georgia state capital at Milledgeville.*

3 November 22: *One brigade of Howard's wing defeated a division of Confederate militia at Griswoldville.*

4 December 10: *Sherman's forces invested the city of Savannah, closing off most of the escape routes for the Confederate garrison of Lieutenant General William J. Hardee.*

5 December 13: *Brigadier General William B. Hazen's division of Howard's Army of the Tennessee successfully stormed Fort McAllister, opening Ossabaw Sound and the Ogeechee River to Union navigation and the establishment of a sea-borne supply line for Sherman's armies.*

6 December 21: *Sherman's troops marched into Savannah after Hardee evacuated the night before.*

North America

Savannah

ATLANTIC OCEAN

Albany

Irwinville

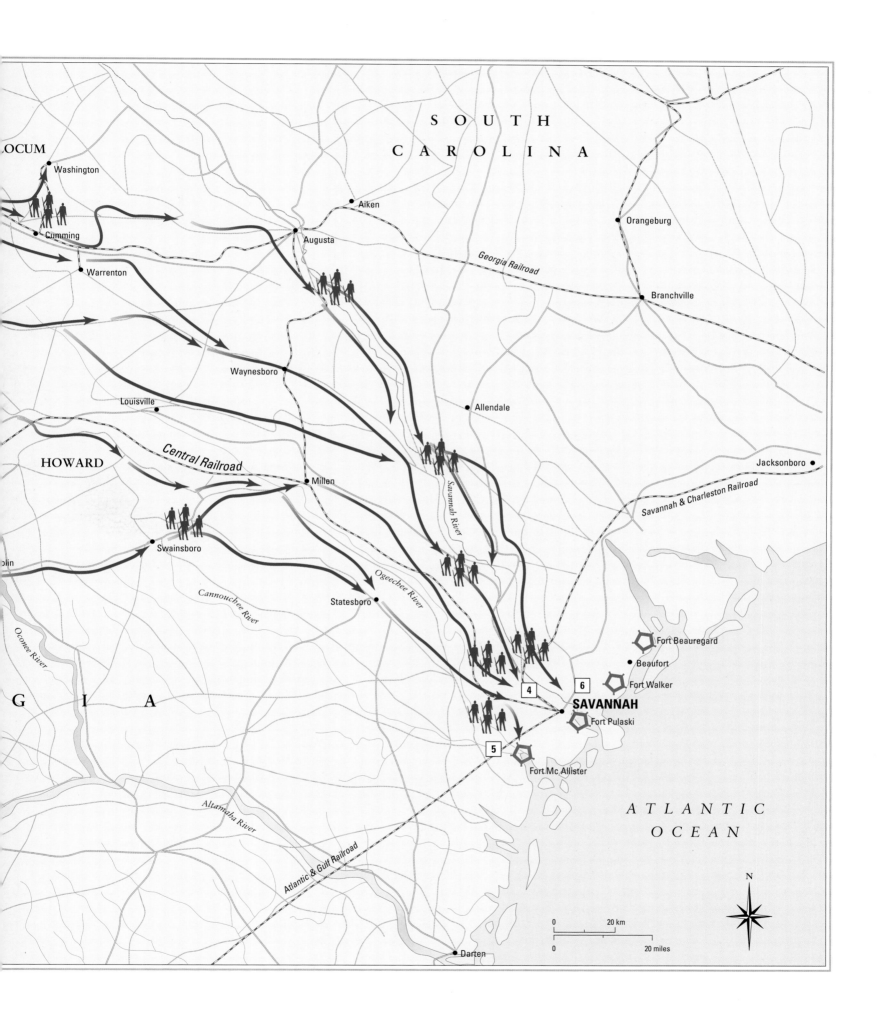

SOUTH
CAROLINA

LOCUM

Washington

Cumming

Warrenton

Aiken

Augusta

Orangeburg

Georgia Railroad

Branchville

Waynesboro

Louisville

Allendale

HOWARD

Central Railroad

Millen

Jacksonboro

Savannah & Charleston Railroad

Savannah River

Swainsboro

olin

Cannouchee River

Statesboro

Ogeechee River

Oconee River

Fort Beauregard

Beaufort

4

6

Fort Walker

G I A

SAVANNAH

Fort Pulaski

5

Fort Mc Allister

Altamaha River

ATLANTIC
OCEAN

Atlantic & Gulf Railroad

Darien

N

0   20 km

0   20 miles

Opposite page: General Sherman continued his march through North and South Carolina and on into Virginia, inflicting several defeats on the Confederate forces. Finally, the Confederates surrendered at Appomatox on April 4, 1865. Effectively, the American Civil War was over.

then, the Confederate forces were under intense pressure in northern Virginia, where Petersburg, 23 miles (37 km) south of Richmond, was under siege. A march through the Carolinas would intensify that pressure and enclose the Confederacy in a trap from which there was little, if any, chance of escape.

General Sherman and his 60,000-strong army moved into South Carolina on February 1 1865, foraging for supplies as it went. In the event, Sherman's forces met minimal opposition, and despite vile winter weather quickly advanced northward. The Confederates presumed that Sherman was heading either north-west, toward the munitions dump at Augusta, or north-east, to attack Charleston. He did neither, and instead attacked Columbia, the capital of South Carolina, which he captured on February 17. However, by midnight separate fires had merged into one great conflagration in the city that consumed an area nine blocks long and four blocks wide. Who started the fire, whether it was just an accident and whether the victorious Union army helped or hindered attempts to douse the flames have been a matter of controversy ever since.

Moving into North Carolina on March 15, Sherman was soon threatening Goldsboro on the Neuse River, where Confederate forces were preparing to resist. Sherman aimed either to meet up with another Union army which was also advancing on Goldsboro or to advance on Raleigh, the state capital of North Carolina, where he could threaten the Confederates' last supply line. On March 16, the Confederates attacked Sherman's left wing at Averasboro. Heavy fighting followed, with the Union army finally pushing their opponents back. Three days later, General Joseph Johnston launched an assault on Sherman's army at Bentonville with 27,000 troops, but had to withdraw on March 20 after the Union concentrated their forces. Sherman followed him, aiming, it seemed, to get into a position where he could strike a decisive blow against Johnston. But, at the last moment, the Union forces held back and allowed the Confederates to escape. Sherman appeared to have Johnston's force at his mercy, but it has been suggested that did not attack to save lives on both sides, as, by now, the Civil War was moving toward its close.

Sherman's men destroying railroad tracks in Atlanta, Georgia, 1864.

Instead, Sherman marched on to Goldsboro, which he reached on 23 March. By then, the Union army had covered 425 miles (684 km) since departing Savannah seven weeks earlier and on March 25 General Grant ordered Sherman to ensure that Johnston's forces did not escape a second time. But on April 9, at Appomattox, Virginia, a Confederate army, ordered by General Lee to attack the Union cavalry, was unexpectedly faced with a mass of Union infantry which had marched overnight to Sherman's aid. As the infantry deployed for battle, General Lee realized that his position was hopeless and asked General Grant for a ceasefire. The Confederate Army of North Virginia, comprising 28,356 men, surrendered at 3:45 in the morning. Effectively, the Civil War was over, and officially ended on May 29, when President Andrew Johnson, the murdered Lincoln's successor, proclaimed an amnesty.

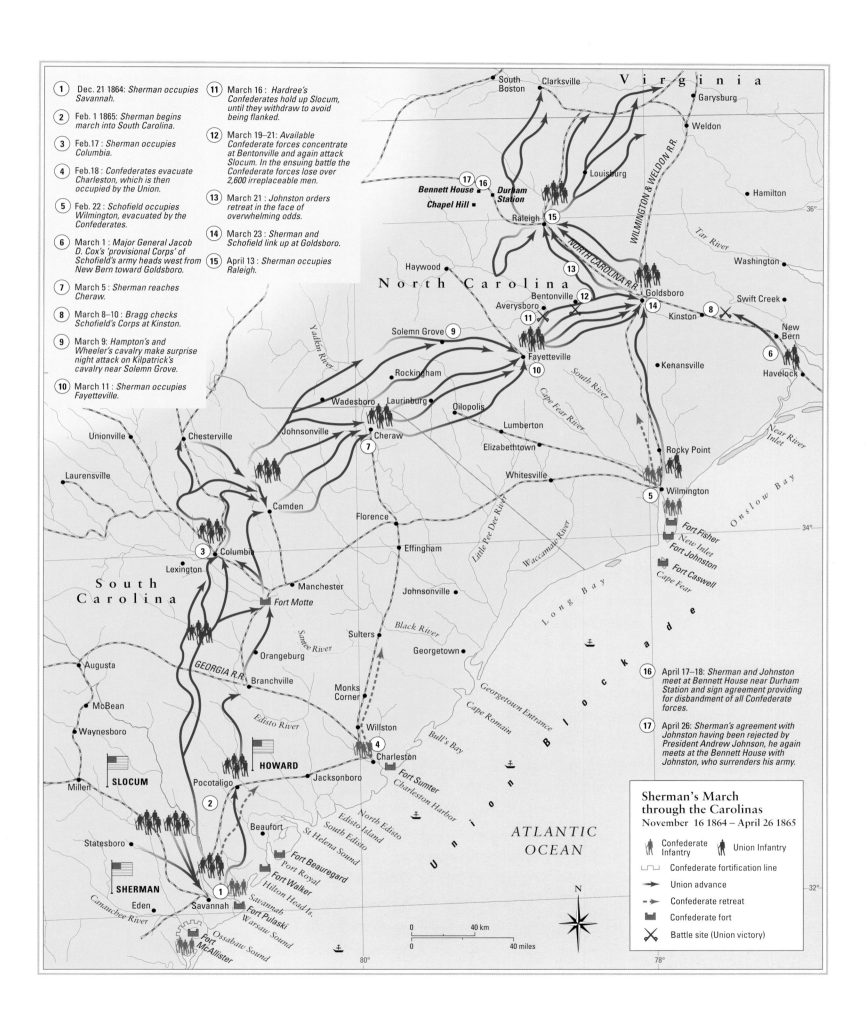

1. Dec. 21 1864: Sherman occupies Savannah.

2. Feb. 1 1865: Sherman begins march into South Carolina.

3. Feb.17: Sherman occupies Columbia.

4. Feb.18: Confederates evacuate Charleston, which is then occupied by the Union.

5. Feb. 22: Schofield occupies Wilmington, evacuated by the Confederates.

6. March 1: Major General Jacob D. Cox's 'provisional Corps' of Schofield's army heads west from New Bern toward Goldsboro.

7. March 5: Sherman reaches Cheraw.

8. March 8–10: Bragg checks Schofield's Corps at Kinston.

9. March 9: Hampton's and Wheeler's cavalry make surprise night attack on Kilpatrick's cavalry near Solemn Grove.

10. March 11: Sherman occupies Fayetteville.

11. March 16: Hardree's Confederates hold up Slocum, until they withdraw to avoid being flanked.

12. March 19–21: Available Confederate forces concentrate at Bentonville and again attack Slocum. In the ensuing battle the Confederate forces lose over 2,600 irreplaceable men.

13. March 21: Johnston orders retreat in the face of overwhelming odds.

14. March 23: Sherman and Schofield link up at Goldsboro.

15. April 13: Sherman occupies Raleigh.

16. April 17–18: Sherman and Johnston meet at Bennett House near Durham Station and sign agreement providing for disbandment of all Confederate forces.

17. April 26: Sherman's agreement with Johnston having been rejected by President Andrew Johnson, he again meets at the Bennett House with Johnston, who surrenders his army.

Sherman's March through the Carolinas
November 16 1864 – April 26 1865

- Confederate Infantry
- Union Infantry
- Confederate fortification line
- Union advance
- Confederate retreat
- Confederate fort
- Battle site (Union victory)

Virginia

North Carolina

South Carolina

ATLANTIC OCEAN

0   40 km
0   40 miles

N

THE FRANCO-PRUSSIAN WAR

THE WAR THAT PITTED FRANCE AGAINST PRUSSIA AND ITS GERMAN ALLIES REVEALED DRAMATIC CHANGES IN BOTH SMALL ARMS AND HEAVY ARTILLERY. THE LESSONS OF THE CONFLICT WOULD BE TAKEN UP BY MOST MODERN ARMIES, BUT WOULD ALSO BE FATALLY MISUNDERSTOOD BY NEARLY ALL OF THEM.

In July 1870, the Prussian chief minister Bismarck took advantage of an unofficial meeting between his own monarch, King Wilhelm, and the French ambassador to issue an insulting communiqué to the French press. Tensions were already high between Prussia and France, and the resulting furore in the French press and in parliament persuaded Napoleon III to declare war.

The reason why Bismarck and Wilhelm were confident of victory in a war against France was that they had won easy victories over Denmark in 1864 and Austria in 1866.

The Prussian infantry had in both wars achieved startling successes owing to the firepower of their needle gun — officially the *Dreyse Zündnadelgewehr*. This weapon had been developed in the 1840s and been upgraded regularly since then. It was the first rifle in the world to combine a bolt-action breech-loading mechanism with a pre-packed cartridge that included bullet, charge, and percussion cap in one packet, which was far more manageable. The name came from the needle used to ignite the percussion cap when struck by the hammer.

The needle gun displayed clear advantages over muzzle-loading rifles. It could be fired 10 times per minute, as opposed to the more usual two or three times. More important on the battlefield was the fact that the needle gun could be reloaded while the soldier was lying on the ground. A Prussian infantryman therefore presented a much smaller target than did his enemy.

Although Bismarck was relying on his needle-gun-armed infantry to win the war, he was unaware that the French army had recently re-equipped itself with a rifle superior to the Prussian weapon. The French *chassepot* rifle was built to a pattern similar to the needle gun, but with important advances. The seal when the breech was closed was a tough rubber ring and it was sealed to the bolt so that no gases

Opposite page: By the time the brief Franco-Prussian War ended in 1871, there was a new, mighty power in Europe: the German Empire, which united the multifarious German states under the leadership of Prussia.

Europe in 1871

0   200 km
0   200 miles

Arctic Circle

64°

ICELAND
Danish

Norwegian
Sea

60°

Faeroe
Islands
Danish

N

Finland

Bergen

Åbo   • St. Petersburg
Helsingfors

Christiana

Stockholm

S W E D E N

N O R W A Y

56°

SCOTLAND

North
Sea

Göthenburg

Baltic Sea

Glasgow • • Edinburgh

DENMARK
Copenhagen

R U S S I A N

52°

UNITED KINGDOM

Dublin
IRELAND

Liverpool •

Königsberg •

E M P I R E

Cork •

WALES

Birmingham •

Amsterdam •

• Hamburg

Warsaw •

Bristol •

NETHERLANDS

• Berlin

P o l a n d

London •

GERMAN EMPIRE

Calais •

Brussels

Rhine

BELGIUM

L.

• Frankfurt

• Prague

Lemberg •

Cracow •

ATLANTIC
OCEAN

• Paris

• Orléans

Vienna •

48°

Nantes •

AUSTRO-HUNGARIAN EMPIRE

Budapest •

F R A N C E

Bern
SWITZERLAND

ROMANIA

44°

Lyons •

• Milan

• Trieste

Bucharest •

Bordeaux •

Venice

Danube

Black Sea

Belgrade
SERBIA

BULGARIA

Marseille •

• Nice

Genoa •

I T A L Y

Adriatic Sea

ANDORRA

O T T O M A N   E M P I R E

MONTE-
NEGRO

Sofia •

• Constantinople

Corsica

• Barcelona

Rome •

Aegean
Sea

PORTUGAL

• Madrid

40°

Lisbon •

SPAIN

Balearic Is.

Sardinia

Naples •

Smyrna •

• Cagliari

Athens •

GREECE

• Cartagena

Cádiz •

Mediterranean

• Messina

Sicily

36°

Gibraltar
Tangier • *to Great Britain*

Crete

MOROCCO

A l g e r i a
to France

TUNIS
Ottoman

MALTA
to Great Britain

Sea

escape. This gave the *chassepot* a range of just over ¾ mile (1.4 km), compared to ⅓ mile (547 m) for the needle gun, and also prevented the user from being burned by escaping gases when he cradled the gun to his cheek. This meant that the French rifle could be fired much more accurately as well as over a greater range. The French army, realizing the advantage the *chassepot* rifle would hand them, had 1.2 million in use by the time war broke out.

Although the Prussians were going to war at a disadvantage in small arms, they had a very definite advantage in artillery. The famous steel-maker Alfred Krupp of Essen (see pages 168–170) had in the late 1850s developed a method allowing him to cast flawless steel shapes of up to two tonnes. He very quickly used this to produce steel tubes suitable for use as the barrels of large, breech-loading artillery. At the time, conventional military thinking held that large-caliber breech-loaders were unreliable in operational conditions. All armies were using muzzle-loading bronze guns. But King Wilhelm of Prussia was intrigued by Krupp's design, and ordered his army to undertake tests of the gun. These proved that Krupp's gun was not only reliable but that it would also outperform the muzzle-loader in range, accuracy, and rate of fire. Prussia placed a huge order with Krupp for both stationary harbor guns and for field artillery.

The Franco-Prussian War opened with a series of engagements at Wisembourg, Spicheren, Worth, and Mars-la-Tour. These were characterized by poor scouting by the French, rapid marches by the Prussians, and heavy casualties. They also saw the last large-scale cavalry actions in Europe. The famous "Death Ride" by General von Bredow's 12th Cavalry Brigade smashed a French attack and overwhelmed a battery of guns. The action cost von Bredow half his men.

The main French army of 113,000 men and 520 guns under Marshal Bazaine sought to halt the Prussian advance at Gravelotte on August 18, 1870. Having suffered the effects of the Krupp field artillery, Bazaine had his men dig into trenches and foxholes on the high ground above the Moselle. He placed his guns in concealed positions with orders not to open fire, and so reveal their position, until they had good targets at which to fire.

Marshal von Moltke, Chief of Staff of the Prussian Army, arrived at Gravelotte with 188,000 men and 732 guns. He began by bombarding the French positions with his artillery, and then sent forward his infantry while holding back his cavalry for the pursuit. The Krupp guns inflicted heavy losses, but the French lines were still intact when the German infantry advanced. The long-range accuracy of the *chassepot* rifle came as a nasty shock to the Germans. By 4 p.m. the attacks in the south had come to a halt. Von Moltke then attacked in the north, but this move had failed by 6 p.m. An attack in the center preceded by an even greater artillery bombardment fared a little better, but was likewise halted by the time night fell, around 10 p.m.

The day's fighting had seen 20,000 Germans and around 10,000 French soldiers killed or wounded. The vast majority of Germans fell to *chassepot* bullets while the French casualties were caused almost exclusively by artillery.

The next day Bazaine retreated, falling back eventually on strong static defenses at Metz, where he was laid under siege by the Prussians. Von Moltke marched his men quickly to Sedan, where Napoleon III was mustering the French reserves. He quickly defeated the French and captured Napoleon III himself. The war dragged on for another five months as a series of sieges,

but the result was not in doubt. France eventually surrendered and Prussia was able to build its Germany-wide empire, or Reich.

The lessons that the world's military men took from the war would influence the weaponry and tactics used for generations. It was recognized that breech-loading artillery was superior and that a preliminary artillery bombardment was necessary if enemy forces were dug in. Similarly, the long-range accuracy of the *chassepot* was seen to be lethally effective on open ground, although it would prove to be less effective in woodland, urban areas, or, eventually, in trench warfare. The success of the German cavalry at Mars-la-Tour caused many to believe that horsemen still had a role to play on the modern battlefield. The later failures by the cavalry when facing unbroken infantry were overlooked.

Franco-Prussian War
1870–1871

→ German attacks
→ Imperial French attacks
→ French Republic attacks

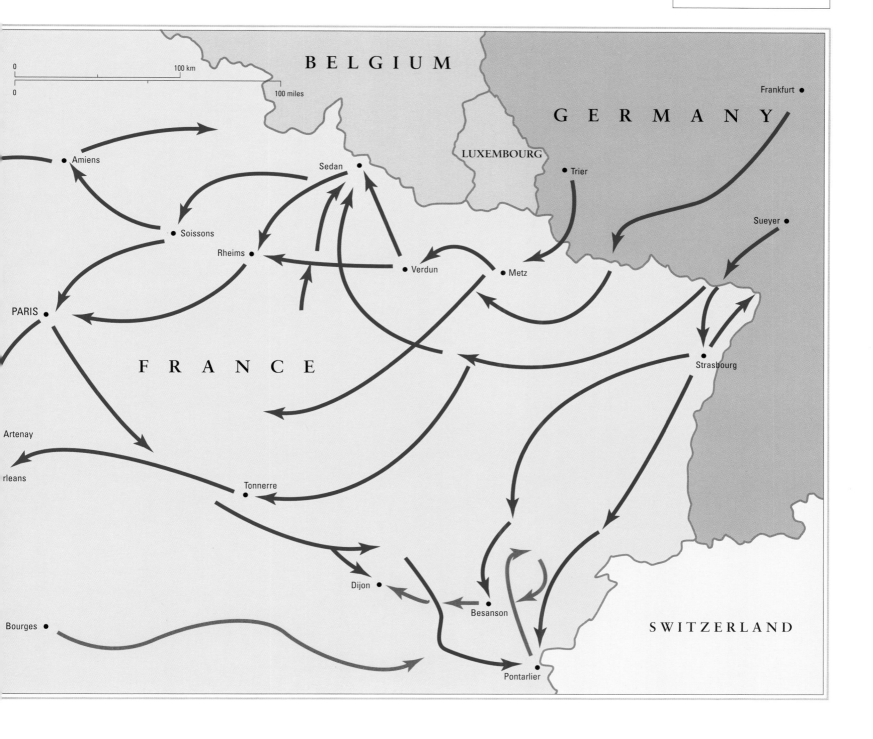

On August 18 1870, the French put up a vigorous defense at the battle of Gravelotte. Their armament — for instance, the *chassepot* bolt-action rifle — was superior but ultimately, the Prussians battered their way to victory.

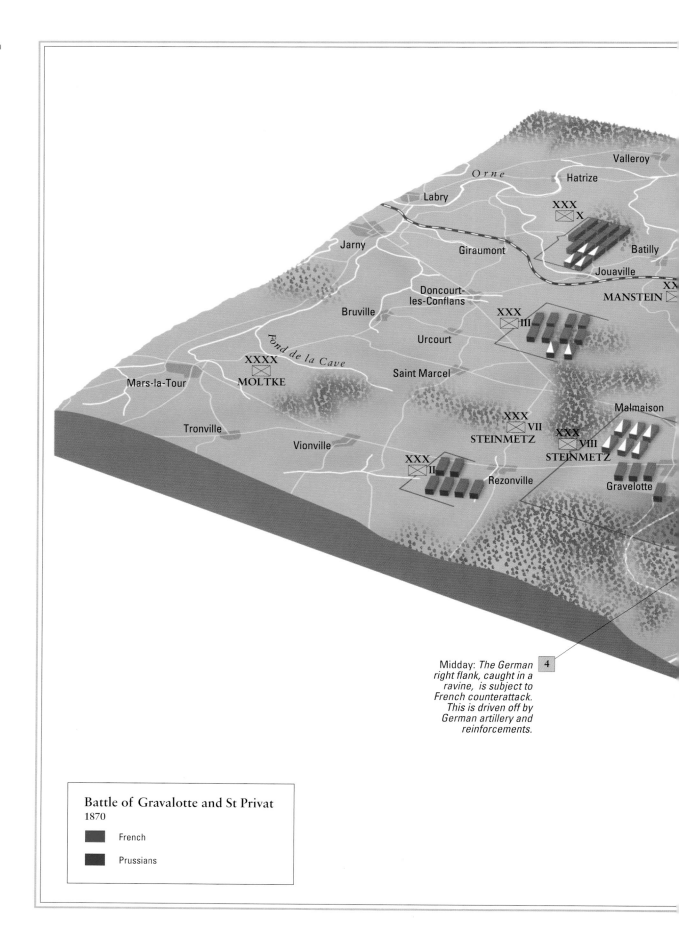

Midday: *The German right flank, caught in a ravine, is subject to French counterattack. This is driven off by German artillery and reinforcements.* 4

Battle of Gravalotte and St Privat
1870

French

Prussians

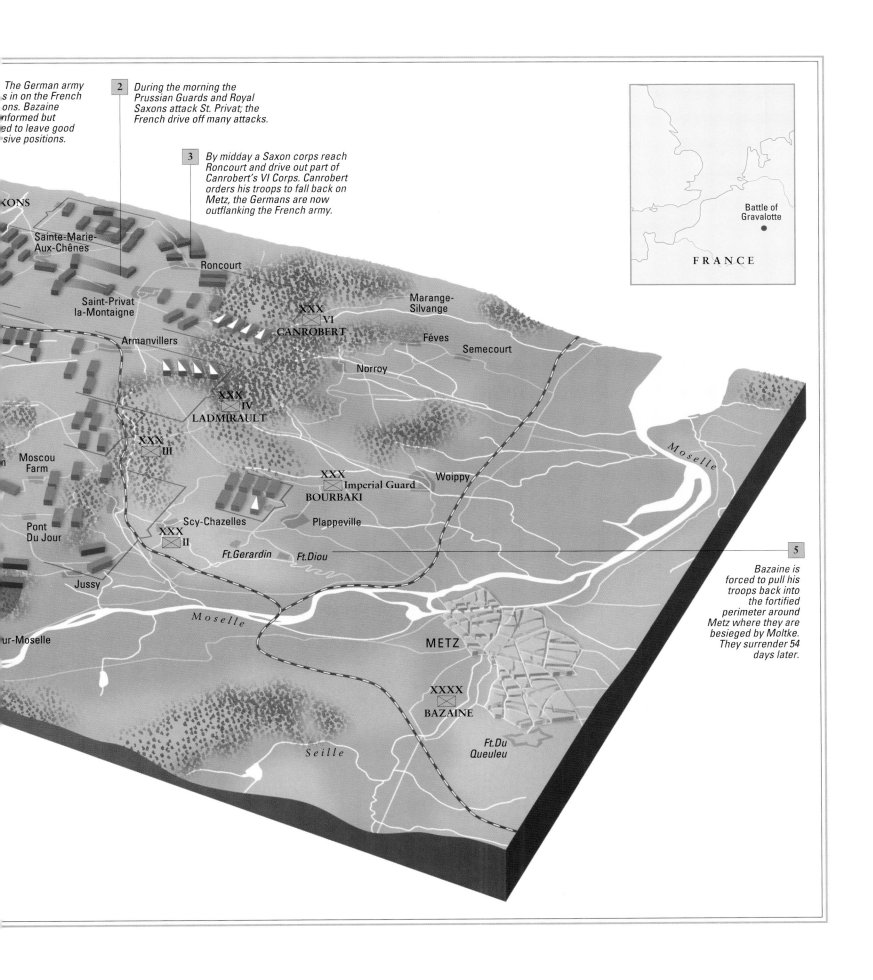

The German army
s in on the French
ons. Bazaine
nformed but
ed to leave good
sive positions.

2 During the morning the
Prussian Guards and Royal
Saxons attack St. Privat; the
French drive off many attacks.

3 By midday a Saxon corps reach
Roncourt and drive out part of
Canrobert's VI Corps. Canrobert
orders his troops to fall back on
Metz, the Germans are now
outflanking the French army.

Battle of
Gravalotte

FRANCE

KONS

Sainte-Marie-
Aux-Chênes

Roncourt

Marange-
Silvange

Saint-Privat
la-Montaigne

XXX
VI
CANROBERT

Féves

Semecourt

Armanvillers

Norroy

XXX
IV
LADMIRAULT

Moscou
Farm

XXX
III

XXX
Imperial Guard
BOURBAKI

Woippy

Plappeville

Pont
Du Jour

Scy-Chazelles

XXX
II

Ft.Gerardin

Ft.Diou

5

Jussy

Bazaine is
forced to pull his
troops back into
the fortified
perimeter around
Metz where they are
besieged by Moltke.
They surrender 54
days later.

Moselle

Moselle

ur-Moselle

METZ

XXXX
BAZAINE

Seille

Ft.Du
Queuleu

THE CLASH OF IRONCLADS

TECHNOLOGICAL IMPROVEMENTS IN STEEL SHIP-BUILDING COMBINED WITH INNOVATIVE GUN MANUFACTURING TECHNIQUES WOULD REVOLUTIONIZE NAVAL WARFARE BETWEEN 1870 AND 1890, BUT THE TRUE IMPORTANCE OF THE CHANGES IN WEAPONRY WAS NOT CLEAR UNTIL THE GREAT WAR OF 1914–1918.

Warships had been carrying iron armor since the 1850s, and the first all-iron warship was the British *HMS Warrior* of 1860. These early ironclads, as they were known, carried a similar armament to warships of three centuries earlier: muzzle-loading guns arranged to fire outward from the sides of the ship. It quickly became apparent that the old-style weaponry was useless against the new-style armor. At the same time, coal-fired steam engines were replacing sails as the main means of propulsion for warships. Compared to a sailing ship, a steam ship needed no masts and much fewer men, but it did need large below-deck space for the engines and the coal needed for long voyages. These factors resulted in a series of sometimes bizarre experimental designs.

One idea was to abandon guns when fighting a rival ironclad and ram the enemy instead. The U.S. Civil War saw some early experiments in ramming, but it was the Austrians who first used the weapon with real success. At the Battle of Lissa on July 20, 1866, Admiral Tegetthoff, with a fleet of seven ironclads and assorted wooden support vessels, attacked an Italian fleet under Admiral di Persano, of 12 ironclads and several wooden warships. Tegetthoff ordered his ironclads to fire only at the wooden enemy vessels and to engage the rival ironclads by ramming. Within an hour the Italian flagship and another ironclad were sent to the bottom of the Adriatic. The Austrians lost no ships, but one was damaged and a few men were killed.

The world's navies hurriedly began building ironclads with vicious-looking metal rams attached to greatly strengthened bows. The fashion for rams lasted for about 20 years, before admirals realized that the maneuvers to get a ram into action were unlikely to produce results in a battle in which the enemy was aware of the danger, unlike Persano in 1866.

Meanwhile the idea of mounting guns in armored and revolving turrets had been developing. Ships with such features were often termed monitors, after the *USS Monitor* of 1862. Ships with flat decks, low freeboards, and revolving turrets proved to be effective as coastal harbor guards, but could not survive

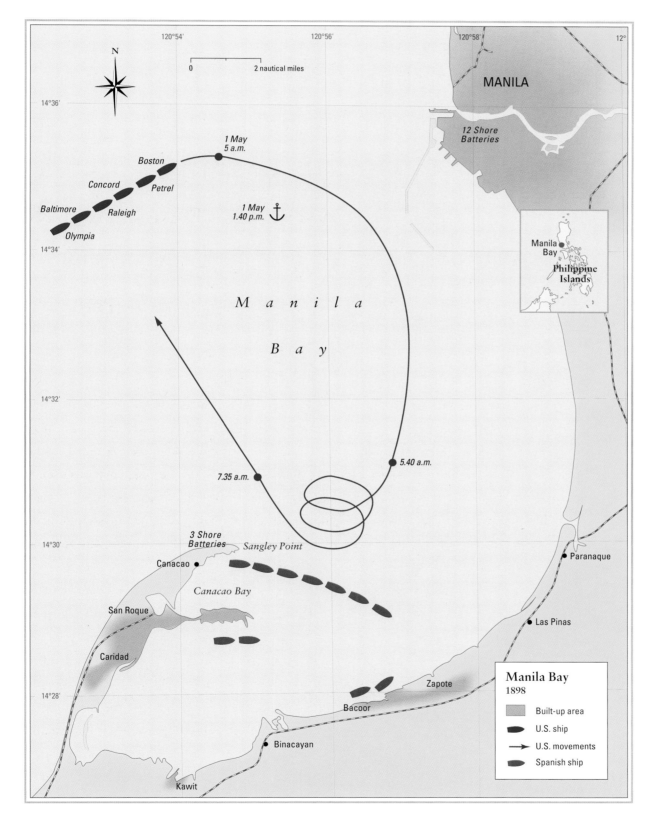

During the Spanish-American War of 1898, a Spanish squadron anchored at the Cavite naval yard in Manila Bay in the Philippine Islands was totally destroyed by American gunpowder and the nearby shore batteries were pounded into submission.

the heavy seas of the open ocean. A key drawback to this design was that the muzzle-loading guns then in use had to be withdrawn into the turret for reloading. This necessitated very large turrets that were cumbersome (several monitors capsized in only moderate seas) and also offered tempting targets to an enemy ship. Attempts to blend turrets with ocean-going hulls produced freaks such as the *HMS Agamemnon*, which had a turret midway along each side of the funnel and superstructure.

The answer to this design problem came in the shape of the *Esmeralda* and the *Blanco Escalade*, two cruisers built in the early 1880s for the Chilean Navy by the Armstrong shipyards at Keswick near Newcastle-upon-Tyne, England. The cruiser was a type of warship designed to cruise for long distances (hence its name) in search of enemy merchant ships or weakly defended ports. It would use its guns to sink or damage the targets. Some navies were also using cruisers to escort merchant convoys, raising the possibility of cruiser-versus-cruiser sea battles. The Keswick cruisers, as this design of ship became known as, were designed for such a role.

Like other cruisers of the time, the Keswick cruisers had capacious coal bunkers and food storage facilities so that the ship could remain at sea for weeks at a time. The revolutionary aspects were their armor and gun deployment. The ships were given a flat deck, with a drastically reduced superstructure of cabins, bridge, and lifeboats crammed into a small central area. The flat deck was made of steel armor able to withstand a plunging shell from an enemy cruiser. The engines, ammunition stores, and other key features were all below the armored deck.

The guns were breech-loaders, as was becoming the norm in warships. This allowed the guns to be mounted in small turrets that could therefore revolve in a relatively small area. One turret holding a 10 in (25.4 cm) gun was mounted near the bow, where the lack of superstructure allowed it to traverse and fire through the unprecedented arc of 180 degrees. A second 10 in (25.5 cm) turret was mounted at the stern with a similarly wide arc of fire. Both turrets were made of a solid carapace of armored steel in order to protect their crews from incoming fire.

The ships also had some distinctly old-fashioned features. These included a number of smaller guns mounted amidships. These were not in turrets and were protected only by steel shields. There were even machine guns mounted in crow's nests on the masts. The masts carried no sails; they were there for the hoisting of signal flags by day and lamps by night.

The combination of an armored deck and breech-loading guns in armored turrets with wide arcs of fire was recognized almost at once as being a battle-winning combination. The navies of the world began ordering such ships and converting older vessels to the new design. As well as cruisers, heavier battleships and smaller cruisers, usually termed second-class cruisers at this time, were ordered in the new configuration.

One of these new cruisers caused the Spanish-American War of 1898. The *USS Maine* was in Santiago, Cuba to protect American interests during a local rebellion against Spanish rule. The Spanish had protested against the ship's presence, fearing that the U.S. was about to intervene on the side of the rebels. On February 15 1898 the *Maine* suddenly exploded, killing 260 men. The American public and press at once concluded that a mine planted by the Spanish had sunk the ship. Congress passed a resolution demanding that Spain grant independence to Cuba and authorizing President McKinley to send soldiers to Cuba to enforce the decision. Spain responded by declaring war on the U.S. on April 25.

The massive explosion that destroyed the battleship *USS. Maine* (pictured) in Havana harbor, Cuba on February15 1898, led to the Spanish-American War that began on April 25 the same year. The dead numbered 252. The American press accused Spanish saboteurs of detonating a bomb from the shore.

Opposite page: In the war of 1904–1905, the Japanese scored an amazing victory over the Russians despite the fact that less than 40 years had passed since the previously "medieval" Japan was modernized and acquired an up-to-date navy.

Although Cuba was the cause of war, the first naval battle took place on the far side of the Pacific, in the Philippines. Admiral George Dewey was in Nagasaki Harbor with the U.S. Pacific fleet of four armored cruisers and two light gunboats. He hurriedly steamed south to Manila, where Admiral Don Patricio Montego was anchored with the Spanish Pacific fleet. Montego had eight battleships, most of them obsolete and a few equipped with armored rotating turrets. He was hampered further because the corrupt Spanish governor had sold the stocks of explosives intended for mines to local companies for quarrying operations.

Dewey arrived at dawn on May 1 1898. He steamed straight for the harbor, turning aside at the last minute to steam past the entrance while opening fire at close range. His order to his flagship captain, "You may fire when ready, Gridley", became famous in the U.S. Navy. By 11 a.m. every ship in the Spanish fleet had been sunk or battered beyond use. Dewey landed his marines to capture Manila.

In the Caribbean a fleet of six Spanish battleships and cruisers was in Santiago. As U.S. troops closed in on the port from land, the Spanish Admiral Pasqual Cervera decided to put to sea and head for Spain. An American fleet under Admiral Sampson was waiting. Once again the modern U.S. ships built along Keswick lines massacred the older Spanish vessels. Two of the Spanish ships had to be abandoned when their obsolete wooden decks caught fire.

The war ended soon after and Cuba became independent. The Philippines, Puerto Rico, and Guam were granted self-government, but under U.S. control. Such far-flung new responsibilities would mean that the U.S. had to acquire a much larger navy.

Also in 1898, Russia had coerced the Chinese government into leasing to them Port Arthur, giving them a naval port in the Pacific that did not freeze in winter. The move angered the Japanese, who had been expanding their influence and control in north-western China. Tensions rose and Japan decided on war.

Prefiguring events at Pearl Harbor in 1941, the Japanese fleet steamed to Port Arthur on February 9, 1904; and three hours before war was declared, it opened fire. The Russian Pacific fleet was taken entirely by surprise and lost two battleships and a cruiser before it could open fire. It never recovered from the blow, and in January 1905 Port Arthur surrendered to the Japanese.

The Russians had already begun preparing a fleet in the Baltic to steam to the Pacific and restore the situation. Under Admiral Rojdestvensky the fleet of four battleships, three cruisers, a dozen smaller warships, and a host of supply ships and colliers set off in October 1904. At Madagascar Rojdestvensky halted, to allow a number of obsolete warships from the Russian Black Sea fleet to catch up with him.

It was not until May 1905 that the mixed fleet arrived in Chinese waters. On May 27, Rojdestvensky was steaming past the island of Tsushima in two columns. A number of Japanese cruisers were shadowing him and had reported his position to Admiral Heihachiro Togo, who was approaching with the main Japanese fleet. The Japanese ships were faster than the Russians and came into sight just after noon.

Togo used his speed to get in front of the Russian fleet, steaming across the head of the enemy columns with his own ships in line ahead. This maneuver was known as "crossing the T", and allowed Togo to get all his guns to bear while only those guns on the bow of the Russian ships could be used. Despite this the Russians gave as good as they got in the opening salvos. Then Rojdestvensky was wounded and his flagship drifted, badly damaged, out of the fight. Almost at once the formation of the Russian fleet fell

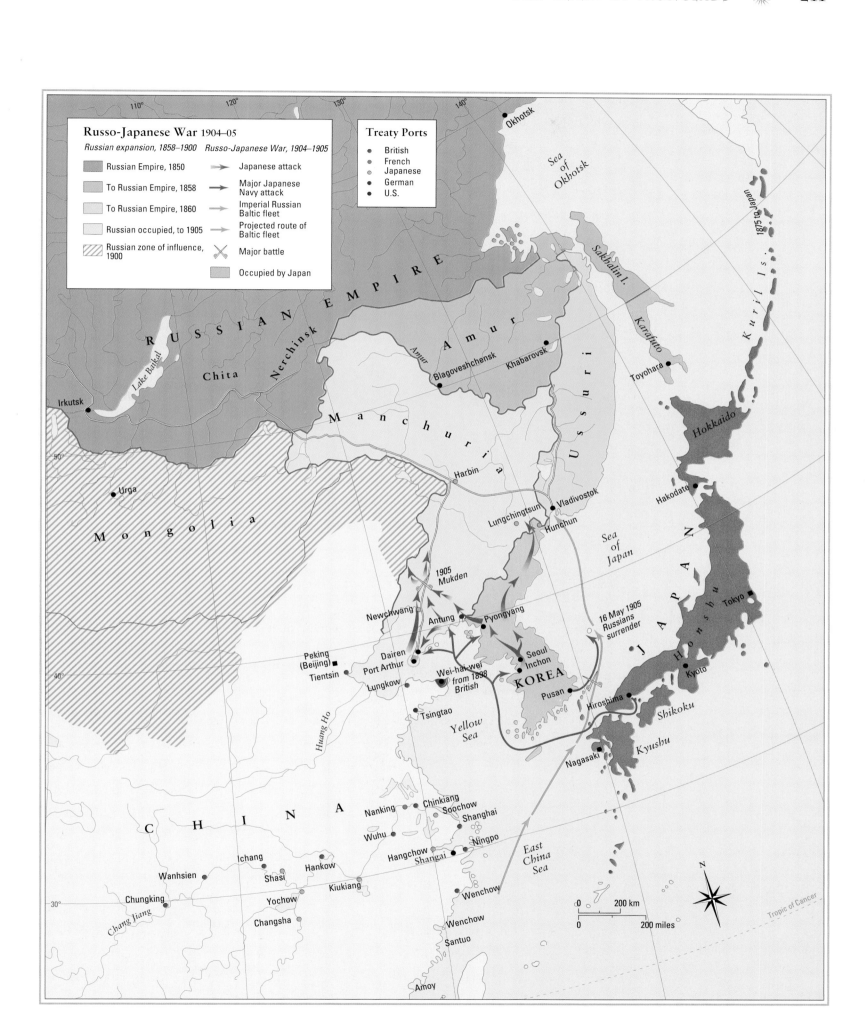

Russo-Japanese War 1904–05

Russian expansion, 1858–1900   *Russo-Japanese War, 1904–1905*

- Russian Empire, 1850
- To Russian Empire, 1858
- To Russian Empire, 1860
- Russian occupied, to 1905
- Russian zone of influence, 1900

- → Japanese attack
- → Major Japanese Navy attack
- → Imperial Russian Baltic fleet
- → Projected route of Baltic fleet
- ✕ Major battle
- Occupied by Japan

Treaty Ports
- British
- French
- Japanese
- German
- U.S.

Opposite page: As a result of their victory in the war against Russia, the Japanese replaced the Russians as the prevailing influence over the southern half of Inner Manchuria. The Japanese also acquired part of the Chinese Eastern Railway and Port Arthur.

apart, allowing the Japanese to concentrate their guns on one ship at time, sinking one before moving on to the next. Only three Russian ships survived the massacre — two destroyers and a light cruiser.

The immediate consequences of the Battle of Tsushima were catastrophic for Russia. Tsar Nicholas II hurriedly agreed to a peace deal that gave Port Arthur to Japan and recognized that Manchuria and Korea were in the Japanese sphere of influence for commercial expansion. Russian companies were forbidden to trade there.

For the world's naval powers, the clash of ironclads at Tsushima gave some important lessons. The first was that effective co-operation between the ships of a fleet was vital. Improved methods of communication were given priority so that an admiral could keep his ships in tight formation and maneuver them quickly even in the heat of battle. Secondly, the big guns of both fleets had proved to be effective at ranges of over $3^2/5$ miles (5.5 km). Previously it had been thought that accuracy at such a range was virtually impossible, and combat had been expected to take place at 1¾ miles (2.7 km) or closer. New guns with longer ranges were ordered and new tactics to use them were devised. This meant that the smaller guns usually mounted on battleships would be useless, lacking the range of the bigger guns. Third, speed in battle was seen to be vital.

The British were the first to put these lessons into practice when they produced *HMS Dreadnought* in 1906. New steam turbine engines that could push her through the water at an astonishing 21 knots powered the 18,000-ton ship. Her armament consisted of ten 12 inch guns mounted in armored turrets. Having only these big guns meant that she could carry more ammunition for them than older ships could carry for a mixed battery. *HMS Dreadnought* made every other battleship in the world obsolete. There began a frenzied race among naval powers to build their own "dreadnoughts", as the fast, all-big-gun battleship became known.

Two years later, the British produced an equally revolutionary type of cruiser. These ships displaced a massive 30,000 tons, mounted eight 12 in (19.4 cm) guns, had 6-in (15 cm) armor plating, and could steam at 27 knots. They were designed to be used as fast, hard-hitting raiders sent out to attack enemy convoys and ports and operate at a long range independent of the main fleet. It was said that they could sink anything they could catch and outrun anything they could not sink.

However, by the time the First World War broke out in 1914, the naval superiority the British had hoped to acquire was looking decidedly thin. In the shipbuilding "race" that followed the introduction of the Royal Navy's *HMS Dreadnought* in 1906, other nations had rushed to create their own ironclad battleships: they included Germany, France, Italy, the Austro-Hungarian Empire, Russia, Spain, the Ottoman Turkish Empire, and even minor powers such as Brazil, the Netherlands, and Greece. Britain's Super-Dreadnoughts had also been copied, first of all by the U.S. Navy.

In addition, hostilities at sea after 1914 revealed that the battleships were susceptible to new dangers. This peril to the supposedly unassailable dreadnoughts was posed by cheaper, smaller weapons. Arguably the most insidious was the submarine, which was considered so important by the Germans that they shrank from allowing their High Seas Fleet to engage the Royal Navy unless it was accompanied by a complement of U-boats. Sea-mines were another danger to battleships, and two Austro-Hungarian dreadnoughts suffered the embarrassment of being destroyed by torpedo boats and a team of frogmen.

The 1911 Revolt

Under Japanese influence from 1905

Chinese province in revolt

November 4 1911 Date of province's independence

S i b e r i a

Manchuria (Manzhouguo)

Fengtien

1912 independent

Chahar

Jehol
November 16 1911

November 10 1911

Peking (Beijing)
February 12 1912
emperor abdicates

Lushun
to Japan

Sea of Japan

K o r e a
1905 to Japan

Ningsia

Suiyan

Hopeh
November 7 1911

Shantung
November 3 1911

Yellow Sea

Nagasaki

K a n s u

Shansi
October 29 1911

Tsinghai

11 March 1912

Shensi
October 22 1911

Honan
December 1911 22

Kiangsu
November 5 1911

Anhwei
November 8 1911

Nanking
from January 1 1912
Sun Yat-sen provisional president

Hupeh
October 10 1911

Sikiang

Szechwan
November 22 1911

Wu-ch'ang
October 10 1911
revolution begins

Chekiang
October 23 1911

Hunan
November 4 1911

Kiangsi
October 22 1911

Kiangsi
October 31 1911

Fukien
November 8 1911

Formosa (Taiwan)

Kweichow

Yunnan
October 30 1911

Kwangsi
November 6 1911

November 9 1911

Kwangtung

Hong Kong
1841 to Britain

Macao
to Portugal

Kwangchonwan

South China Sea

Philippine Is.
from 1898 to U.S.

Burma
1886 to Britain

Indo-China
(1887–98
united by and to France

Hainau

SIAM

Tropic of Cancer

0   300 km

0   300 miles

N

THE SOUTH AFRICAN WARS, 1899–1902

THE ABILITY OF THE TINY BOER REPUBLICS IN SOUTHERN AFRICA TO HOLD OUT AGAINST THE GREAT MIGHT OF THE BRITISH EMPIRE FOR THREE YEARS AND INFLICT SEVERAL SERIOUS DEFEATS ON THE SUPPOSEDLY SUPERIOR BRITISH ARMY SHOCKED THE WORLD.

In the 1880s vast gold deposits were found in the Transvaal, an independent republic in southern Africa populated by European settlers of Dutch descent, the Boers. The Boer farmers had neither the skills nor the capital to exploit the finds, so foreign mining companies and engineers were brought in. By 1895 the number of foreigners, termed outlanders, had grown and become more than the Boers. Yet the Boer government refused to give any civil rights to the outlanders, and imposed heavy taxes on them from which Boer farmers were exempt. As most outlanders were British, they looked to Britain for protection. Britain suggested various reforms, but the Boers refused and war broke out on October 11 1899. The Transvaal was joined by the second Boer republic, the Orange Free State.

The only professional Boer armed forces were a few batteries of artillery, equipped with the latest guns from Krupp in Germany (see pages 168–170). The rest of the Boer army was composed of farmers and others who rode to war with their own guns, horses, and equipment. The Boers had large numbers of Mauser $^1/_3$ in (7.65 mm) rifles that were astonishingly accurate over long ranges, had a magazine of five bullets for rapid fire, and could be quickly reloaded from a pre-packed clip of ammunition.

Each district had its own unit, called a commando, which elected its officers for a campaign when mustered. The Boers called out their commandos and launched them on a rapid invasion of the two British colonies: Natal and Cape Colony. Within a week of war breaking out, the Boer commandos had about 30,000 men under arms. By mid-October 1899 the towns of Ladysmith, Mafeking, and Kimberley were under siege. The Krupp artillery was brought up and put into action. The style of the sieges soon developed into long-range sniping combat as the Boers waited for starvation to take a grip. Attempts by the British commander in southern Africa, General Redvers Buller, to relieve the towns led to the Battle of Colenso on December 15. The advancing British found themselves exposed in open country while the defending Boers were dug into trenches and foxholes. The long range of the Mausers took the British by surprise. One artillery battery was almost wiped out, thinking that they were out of rifle range of the Boers, and an infantry brigade suffered 500 casualties while unable to shoot back. In all the British lost 1,100 men killed, wounded or captured. The Boers lost fewer than 50. Several days later a second battle, at Spion Kop, led to 1,300 British and 300 Boer casualties.

After these defeats Buller was replaced by the popular Anglo-Indian Field Marshal Lord Roberts, known as "Bobs" to the army. Roberts abandoned Buller's frontal assaults and relied instead on movement. He was aided by the fact that the British Army had a better supply system than that resulting from the haphazard methods of the Boer farmers. Roberts sent cavalry columns on wide rides to cut behind the Boer armies and used his infantry to outflank defensive positions rather than attack them.

The two South African Wars of 1880-1881 and 1899-1902 arose from the refusal of the Dutch Boers in the independent Orange Free State and South African Republic to be ruled by the British, the colonial power of the time.

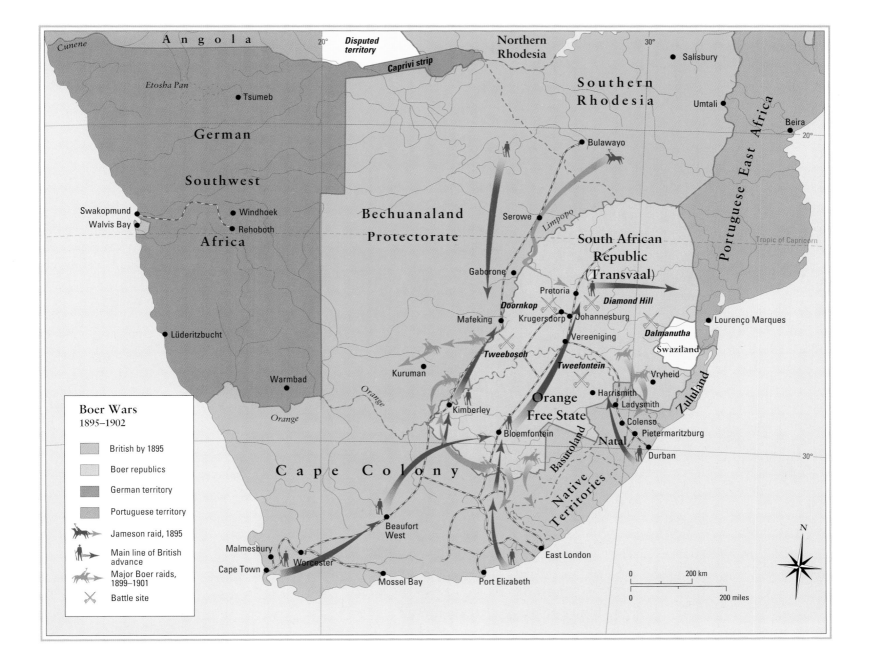

Boer Wars
1895–1902

- British by 1895
- Boer republics
- German territory
- Portuguese territory
- Jameson raid, 1895
- Main line of British advance
- Major Boer raids, 1899–1901
- Battle site

Boer commandos in the field during the Anglo-Boer war, 1900.

Opposite page: On December 15 1899, during the second South African War, the British force on its way to relieve the siege of Ladysmith ran into fierce Boer resistance at Colenso. Driven back with heavy losses, the British were forced to give up.

Using the new methods, Roberts soon relieved Ladysmith and Kimberley before overrunning the Orange Free State, announcing it occupied by the end of March 1900. Finally, on May 18, British troops relieved Mafeking and its garrison commanded by Robert Baden-Powell. By mid-June Roberts had captured the Boer capital Pretoria and occupied most of the Transvaal.

At this point Roberts considered the war to be over. He left for home and handed the task of pacifying the area to his second-in-command, Herbert Kitchener. In fact, the Boers simply abandoned formal battles for a campaign of guerrilla raids. The success of these raids forced Kitchener to change tactics. He built a network of 7,000 blockhouses at key points, each garrisoned by eight men and in sight of at least one other. Railroad lines were patrolled with armored trains from which men inspected the ground for signs of a passing commando. Cavalry patrols went out to find tracks of the commando horses. When a commando was located, cavalry units were sent to bring them to battle. The commandos were slowly eliminated and the areas where the Boers could operate safely became confined. Kitchener realized that the Boers had the full support of the Boer civilians and set about stopping the flow of supplies. Boer farms suspected of supplying the commandos were burned to the ground.and women and children from the farms were marched off to prison camps, termed concentration camps.

As a soldier, Kitchener concentrated on fighting the war. His concern for the Boers in the concentration camps was minimal, the camps were chronically short of supplies and plagued by poor hygiene. Disease broke out and claimed the lives of thousands. When news of the dreadful conditions in the camps reached Britain, a commission was sent out to investigate. Slowly conditions improved.

By late 1901 the Boer commandos were no longer effective offensive units and they were concentrating instead on keeping free of the increasingly effective British troops. The last of the commandos surrendered in May 1902 and the Treaty of Vereeniging was signed between Britain and the Boer leaders.

The lessons learned from the second Boer War were varied. Some recognized the importance of efficient scouting and intelligence. Baden-Powell, who had defended Mafeking, was the most vociferous of these and his later founding of the Boy Scout movement should be viewed as a sideshow to his military activities in the Boer War. The effectiveness of the mounted commandos and Kitchener's flying columns convinced many that cavalry in the form of self-contained units launched on raids was vital to modern warfare. The point was valid, but many military men overlooked the fact that the Boer War was fought over a vast, sparsely populated area, leading them to believe that cavalry still had a role on a more crowded battlefield than the action the Boer War had seen.

The main lesson to come out of the war, however, was that infantry fighting from trenches and armed with long-range rifles could inflict massive casualties on attacking infantry, but were themselves also vulnerable to heavy artillery fire. Roberts had been able to outflank the Boer trench lines, but again this was a result of the vast spaces involved. The debate over whether a future war would be dominated by trenches and rifles or by fast-moving columns and flanking attacks raged on.

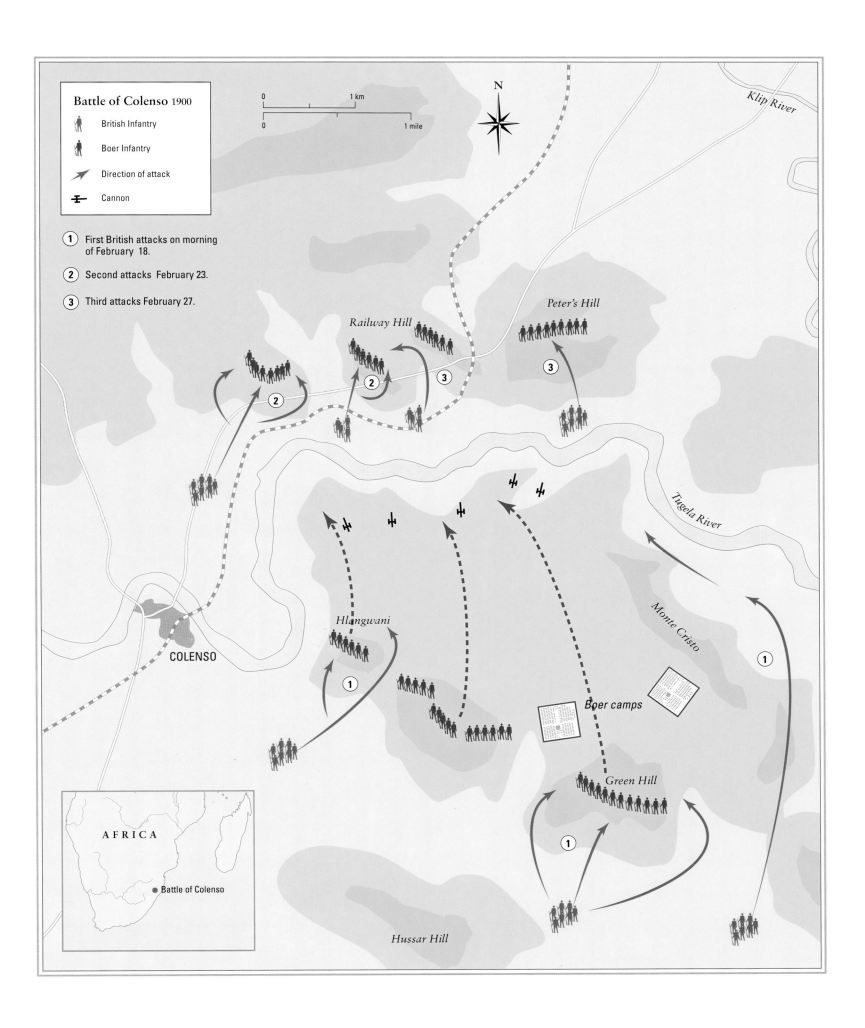

Battle of Colenso 1900

🚶 British Infantry

🚶 Boer Infantry

↗ Direction of attack

╪ Cannon

① First British attacks on morning of February 18.

② Second attacks February 23.

③ Third attacks February 27.

N

0   1 km

0   1 mile

Klip River

Peter's Hill

Railway Hill

Tugela River

Monte Cristo

Hlangwani

Boer camps

COLENSO

Green Hill

AFRICA

● Battle of Colenso

Hussar Hill

THE BALKAN WARS

AT THE TIME, THE BALKAN WARS WERE SEEN AS JUST ANOTHER STAGE IN THE GRADUAL DECLINE OF THE OTTOMAN EMPIRE, ALTHOUGH SOME SAW THE RISE OF SMALL BALKAN STATES AS A THREAT TO THE FUTURE. IN HINDSIGHT THE BALKAN WARS ANTICIPATED MUCH THAT WOULD BECOME WIDESPREAD IN WORLD WAR ONE.

The underlying cause of the two Balkan Wars of 1912 and 1913 was the decline of the Ottoman Empire. That decline was as much a product of corruption and incompetence among the Ottoman government officials as it was of long-term economic malaise. However, this was not the main cause of the Balkan Wars, which was a desire among Turkey's neighbors to grab provinces and lucrative trade routes, and the provinces themselves pushing for independence from each other.

In 1911 Italy had found a pretext to occupy the province of Libya and had defeated Turkey in the short war that followed. Libya passed from Ottoman to Italian control and this encouraged the small Balkan states to believe that they too could defeat Turkey. Montenegro struck first, on October 8 1912, quickly followed by Greece, Bulgaria, and Serbia, all of whom attacked Turkey. The Turks were swiftly beaten in the field, and they agreed to a peace that saw most of the remaining Ottoman lands in the Balkans handed over to the victors. However, the victorious allies promptly fell out among themselves over the ownership of the newly won lands. Bulgaria attacked Greece, only to find itself faced by Serbia and Montenegro as well. The Turks then joined in to grab land back from Bulgaria, followed by the Romanians who coveted some border territory. Bulgaria surrendered and the borders were redrawn by the new alliance of victors.

None of the combatants in the Balkan Wars was a leading power and their forces were equipped with weaponry considered obsolete by richer nations. They had used tactics that were thoroughly outdated, although, can also be seen in some instances as well suited to the rugged terrain. However, the rest of the world took note of several incidents that had taken place. The first of these came on November 16 1912, when the retreating Turkish army took up positions in the fortified lines of Catalpa. This series of

Opposite page: In the First Balkan War of 1912/1913, Bulgaria, Greece, Montenegro, and Serbia succeeded in breaking away from the Ottoman Turkish Empire. In the Second War, Bulgaria attacked Serbia and Greece, but lost most of the territory gained in the First.

The Balkans,
Crete and Cyprus
1912–1913

Ottoman territory in 1913

1913 Date of independence

20°

Tisza

KINGDOM

OF

HUNGARY

BOSNIA

• Mitrovica

• Belgrade

Drina

Morava

KINGDOM
OF
SERBIA • Nish

K. OF
MONTE-
NEGRO

1913 to
Montenegro

Cattaro •

Gusinje •

Scutari • Djakova
(Shkadra)

Durazzo •

Drin

PR. OF
ALBANIA

1913

EPIRUS

Corfu

MACEDONIA

1913 to Serbia

• Kumanovo

Üsküb (Skopje)

Vardar

Struma

1913
to Bulgaria

1913 to Greece

Janina •

THESSALY

KINGDOM

LIVADIA

OF

GREECE

PELOPONNESE

• Tripolis

• Navarino

*Ionian
Sea*

Ionian Islands

*Cerigo
(Kythira)*

Dniestr

Bug

RUSSIAN
EMPIRE

until 1917

MOLDAVIA

BESSARABIA

Siret

Prut

Ottul

KINGDOM OF ROMANIA

Galati • Izmail

• Bucharest

• Craiova

Danube

DOBRUJA

1913
to Romania

• Plevna

• Varna

KINGDOM OF

BULGARIA

Maritsa

• Sofia • Yamboli • Burgas

1913 to Bulgaria

• Adrianople
1915 to Bulgaria

THRACE
1913 to Bulgaria

• Dedeagach

Thasos

• Salonica

Lemnos

Aegean

Sea

*Mitilini
(Lesbos)*

Larisa •

Euboea

Corinth • Athens

Chios

Samos

Constantinople •

Sea of
Marmara

Gallipoli •

• Mudania

OTTOMAN

EMPIRE

• Smyrna

Dodecanese

Rhodes

1912
Italian occupied

Cyclades

Crete

Black Sea

40

Annexed in 1914
Cyprus

Mediterranean Sea

N

0   200 km

0   200 miles

concrete bunkers, gun emplacements, and a maze of trenches was built on the top of a ridge that rose steeply over 300 yd (274 m) from the plain in front of it. Much of that plain was covered by Lake Dermas and by the vast swamps that then surrounded it. The Bulgarians had shown themselves adept at moving their field artillery with speed and achieving heavy concentrations of fire in a short time. They moved up their guns and began to batter the fortifications. But no matter how hard they tried, the Bulgarians could not break through. Strong natural defences combined with a high standard of military engineering was shown to be proof against field artillery.

At sea the only ally with a navy was Greece. The naval war became a contest between the Turkish Navy, which was trying to stop merchant ships bringing supplies to the allies across the Mediterranean, and the Greek Navy, which sought to protect those ships. On December 16 1912 the two main fleets met at the Battle of Elli. They were equally matched, with three battleships apiece and a number of smaller craft. Almost all of these were of obsolete design, having been constructed in the 1880s and 1890s. The sole exception was the Greek flagship *Averof*, one of the new style of very big, very fast cruisers armed with 12 heavy guns and moderate armor.

Within minutes of sighting the Turkish fleet, the Greek admiral, Palos Kountouriotis ordered his ships to fight independently. He then pushed the *Averof* to top speed, quickly outstripping his older battleships and engaging the Turks alone. Kountouriotis threw his big ship into a series of high-speed turns and weaves in order to evade the large number of Turkish shells coming his way while opening fire with his own big guns. The result was a swift victory for the Greek fleet. The Turkish ships were badly damaged and hurriedly retreated to the safety of the Dardenelles, where they were protected by shore batteries.

The victory by the *Averof* convinced many admirals that the big-gun cruisers were highly effective battle weapons, not just powerful raiders. As a result, many navies began calling these ships "battle cruisers". The battle cruisers were removed from their previous fast strike role, for which they had been designed, and put in the main battle fleet. They thus ignored the fact that *Averof*'s success had been due to fast maneuvers in independent action. In a tightly controlled fleet action, such speedy turns would not be possible and the lightly armored cruisers would be easy targets for the enemy's big guns.

The final action of note came in June 1913, during the second Balkan War. A Greek Army launched an attack against an entrenched Bulgarian Army at Kilkis. The assault was preceded by an artillery bombardment and so the army pushed through at speed. The Greeks pushed the Bulgarians out of the trenches and began an advance that led to ultimate victory as the cohesion of the Bulgarians collapsed. This was thought to have shown that although well prepared, solidly built defenses such as those at Catalpa were almost impregnable, hastily constructed field trenches were vulnerable to a co-ordinated artillery and infantry assault. It was with this impression of the fighting during the Balkan Wars that the world went to war in 1914.

It did not, however, take long for the combatants to realize the truth about trench defenses. By September 1914, only a month after hostilities began, it was evident that the trenches on the Western Front in France were a recipe for stalemate. For once ensconsed, troops were largely impervious to small arms fire and artillery. Consequently, the front line barely moved until near the end of the fighting in 1918.

Opposite page: By 1914, many of the countries in Europe had already set themselves up for a future war, with a series of alliances that bound them to come to the aid of their allies if the latter were threatened or attacked.

Europe in 1914

Faeroe Islands
to Denmark

*Norwegian
Sea*

Arctic Circle

Finland

*North
Sea*

Christiana

Stockholm

Helsingfors

St. Petersburg

Baltic Sea

RUSSIAN

EMPIRE

Glasgow   Edinburgh

UNITED

KINGDOM

Liverpool   Hull

Birmingham

Bristol

London

Calais

DENMARK

Copenhagen

Hamburg

Amsterdam

NETHERLANDS

Brussels

BELGIUM

L.

GERMAN

Berlin

EMPIRE

Poland

Frankfurt

Prague

Cracow

Lemberg

Paris

Orléans

FRANCE

Bern

SWITZ

Vienna

Budapest

AUSTRO-HUNGARIAN

EMPIRE

ROMANIA

Bucharest

Black Sea

Lyon

Milan

Trieste

Bordeaux

Genoa

Venice

Belgrade

SERBIA

BULGARIA

Sofia

Marseille

ITALY

Adriatic Sea

MONTE-
NEGRO

ALBANIA

Constantinople

ANDORRA

Corsica

Rome

SPAIN

Barcelona

Madrid

Naples

Sardinia

*Aegean
Sea*

Balearic Is.

GREECE

Smyrna

Alicante

Athens

0   100 km

0   100 miles

Sicily

WORLD WAR ONE — AN OVERVIEW

IMAGES OF TRENCHES, BARBED WIRE, MACHINE GUNS AND ARTILLERY ARE USED TO DEPICT AND DEFINE WORLD WAR ONE, YET THERE IS ALSO MUCH MORE TO THE CONFLICT.

T he key feature of World War One that is often forgotten is that it was in fact, as well as name, a world war. Although trench warfare dominated the Western Front, the conditions that made it possible were not repeated in other theaters of war.

On the Western Front the combatants were able to field armies of millions of men that produced man-to-front ratios of dozens to the yard. Britain, France, and Germany could also afford the cost of concrete bunkers and other heavy engineering works that made the lines so difficult to break. Moreover, both sides kept their armies supplied through complex railroad systems that could move men, supplies, and weapons to wherever they were needed at high speed.

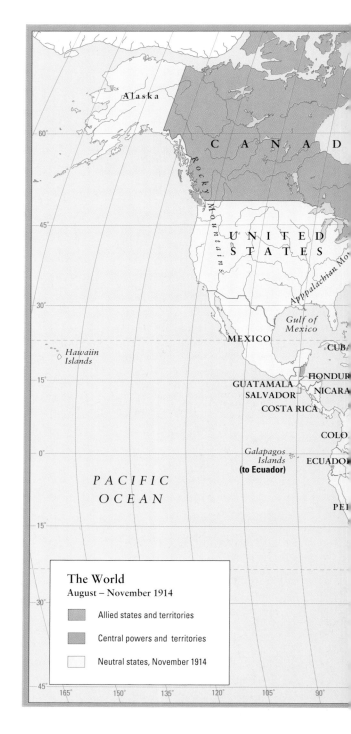

The World
August – November 1914

- Allied states and territories
- Central powers and territories
- Neutral states, November 1914

The closest theater to the Western Front in terms of fighting conditions was the Italian Front. There the Italians faced the Austrians, but in time both sides would call up reinforcements from their allies. The two armies were not as well equipped with heavy artillery, telephones, and other modern equipment as were the combatants on the Western Front, but they did have modern machine guns, barbed wire, and rifles. The commanders on both sides were well versed in the latest ideas about warfare, and these tended to produce tactics and defensive positions similar to those on the Western Front. Also, the Italian Front included mountains, gullies, deep rivers, and yawning chasms that dominated the terrain. Northern Italy was almost ready-made for defense, in a way that the plains and rolling hills and the general terrain of northern France was not.

World War One involved most of the world's great powers, assembled in two opposing alliances: the Allies (centered around the Triple Entente) against the Central Powers. Several alliances formed over the decades were involved, so within weeks the major powers were at war; with all having colonies, the conflict soon spread around the world.

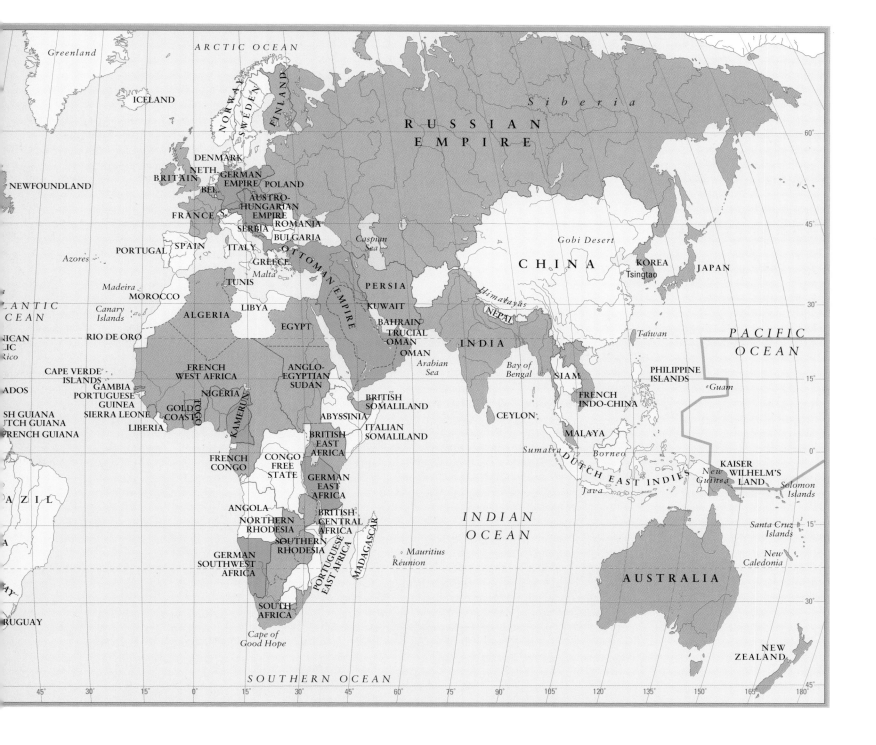

The Eastern Front offered quite different conditions owing to the geography and the combatants. The wide-open spaces of eastern Europe offered plenty of space for maneuver, flank attacks, and determined drives. It was here that cavalry were to be used in large numbers and to good effect. The barbed wire and machine guns that were so fatal to horses in the west were more thinly spread in the east, allowing the cavalry to fulfill its traditional role of scouting, raiding, and reconnaissance. The main combatants on the Eastern Front were Russia and Austria. Both sides could field large armies composed mostly of poorly equipped conscript forces raised from ill-educated peasant farmers who often did not have the ability to use modern equipment. In the case of the Russian Army, there was often a lack of equipment of all kinds. Some regiments were sent to the front without enough rifles for all. The unarmed men were expected to obtain weapons from colleagues who were taken sick, wounded, or killed as the campaign progressed.

When the Romanians joined on the Allied side, their army proved to be little better than those already engaged on the Eastern Front. Only the Germans fought with modern weapons and well-trained men, but they viewed the Eastern Front as a secondary priority and interfered only when they had to bolster the Austrians. Even more different were the colonial theaters of war. German south-east Africa (now Tanzania) offered around 360,405 miles² (580,000 km²) of bush without roads or railroads. Here the German commander Paul von Lettow-Vorbeck led a skillful guerrilla campaign that tied down large numbers of British troops and ships. At the outset Lettow-Vorbeck had about 3,000 German troops and 12,000 locally raised soldiers. With this small force he tied up over 40,000 British and imperial troops and also several warships, which patrolled off the coast. He and his men were still fighting in November 1918, and indeed Lettow-Vorbeck was about to attack the town of Katanga when he heard of the armistice. The German garrisons elsewhere did not fare so well. In south-west Africa (now Namibia), the German commander Victor Franke began the war with a strike into Portuguese territory to disrupt the Allied effort. With only 3,000 men, Franke was not in a position to withstand the tens of thousands of troops who poured over the border. He made a retreat, but cut off from supplies in the Kalahari Desert, he surrendered in July 1915.

The various theaters of war offered a wide variety of conditions, and the advance of technology created many more. World War One saw the advent of several types of weapon that would dominate warfare throughout the 20th century: in particular, tanks, armed aircraft, and torpedo-armed submarines. Other weapons, machine guns, heavy artillery, and mines had all been used in previous wars, but would be used in much greater numbers and to more deadly effect than ever before.

Every bit as startling as the technological advances were the changes in tactics. In 1914 all senior commanders believed that cavalry was essential to contemporary warfare. Detailed tactical doctrines had been developed for the use of the mounted soldier. By 1918 those tactics had mostly been discarded: cavalry was now thought of as fit only for specialized use in very particular circumstances.

Infantry tactics changed too. In place of the massed assaults with fixed bayonets seen in 1914, the various armies had developed novel methods of attack. The German stormtroopers had specialized methods of working through enemy trenches to the open land beyond. The British infantry developed different but equally effective trench-busting tactics, notably by tanks.

World War One was a very varied war that presented many problems to the men fighting it. The struggle placed great demands on the men and the generals, and the weapons with which it was fought.

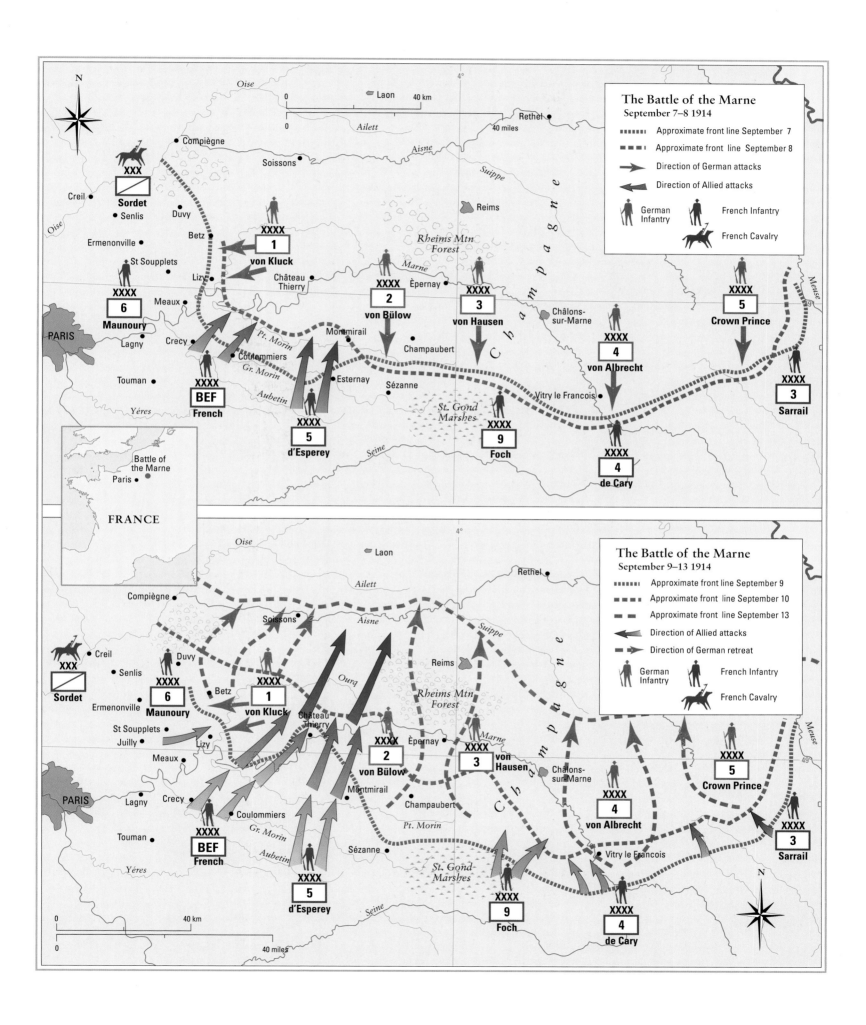

The Battle of the Marne
September 7–8 1914

- ▪▪▪▪ Approximate front line September 7
- ▪▪▪▪ Approximate front line September 8
- ⟵ Direction of German attacks
- ⟵ Direction of Allied attacks
- 🧍 German Infantry
- 🧍 French Infantry
- 🐎 French Cavalry

XXX Sordet

XXXX 1 von Kluck
XXXX 6 Maunoury
XXXX BEF French
XXXX 5 d'Esperey
XXXX 2 von Bülow
XXXX 3 von Hausen
XXXX 9 Foch
XXXX 4 von Albrecht
XXXX 4 de Cary
XXXX 5 Crown Prince
XXXX 3 Sarrail

PARIS

Compiègne
Soissons
Laon
Rethel
Reims
Creil
Senlis
Duvy
Betz
Ermenonville
St Soupplets
Lizy
Meaux
Château Thierry
Èpernay
Châlons-sur-Marne
Lagny
Crecy
Coulommiers
Montmirail
Champaubert
Vitry le Francois
Touman
Esternay
Sézanne
St. Gond Marshes
Rheims Mtn Forest
Champagne
Oise
Aisne
Ailett
Suippe
Marne
Pt. Morin
Gr. Morin
Aubetin
Yéres
Seine
Meuse

Battle of the Marne
Paris
FRANCE

The Battle of the Marne
September 9–13 1914

- ▪▪▪▪ Approximate front line September 9
- ▪▪▪▪ Approximate front line September 10
- ▪▪▪▪ Approximate front line September 13
- ⟵ Direction of Allied attacks
- ⟵ Direction of German retreat
- 🧍 German Infantry
- 🧍 French Infantry
- 🐎 French Cavalry

XXX Sordet

XXXX 6 Maunoury
XXXX 1 von Kluck
XXXX BEF French
XXXX 5 d'Esperey
XXXX 2 von Bülow
XXXX 3 von Hausen
XXXX 9 Foch
XXXX 4 von Albrecht
XXXX 4 de Cary
XXXX 5 Crown Prince
XXXX 3 Sarrail

PARIS

Compiègne
Soissons
Laon
Rethel
Reims
Creil
Senlis
Duvy
Betz
Ermenonville
St Soupplets
Juilly
Lizy
Meaux
Château Thierry
Èpernay
Châlons-sur-Marne
Lagny
Crecy
Coulommiers
Montmirail
Champaubert
Vitry le Francois
Touman
Sézanne
St. Gond Marshes
Rheims Mtn Forest
Champagne
Oise
Aisne
Ailett
Suippe
Marne
Ourq
Pt. Morin
Gr. Morin
Aubetin
Yéres
Seine
Meuse

STALEMATE ON THE WESTERN FRONT, FALL 1914

THE COMBATANT NATIONS ENTERED INTO WAR IN AUGUST 1914 CONFIDENTLY EXPECTING THAT THE WAR WOULD "BE OVER BY CHRISTMAS". EVENTS WERE TO PROVE THEM TERRIBLY MISTAKEN, AND PREPARED THE GROUND FOR FOUR YEARS OF SLAUGHTER.

The previous large-scale war fought between modern armies had been the Franco-Prussian War of 1870—1871. That had demonstrated that permanent, well prepared, and adequately manned defenses were almost invulnerable. But field defenses, such as trenches and rifle pits, had been vulnerable to well aimed artillery bombardments followed up by swift infantry attacks. Cavalry had been invaluable for scouting ahead of the armies and for exploiting breakthroughs when they had been made. It had also launched battlefield charges, though with mixed results.

Most of the senior commanders in 1914 assumed that they would be fighting a war broadly similar to that of 1870—1871. The battles of the Balkan Wars had done nothing to show otherwise. They drew up their plans accordingly.

The French generals were told by their political masters that in the event of war with Germany the prime goal was to recapture the provinces of Alsace and Lorraine that had been lost in 1871. Their Plan 17 called for a swift assault to capture Alsace and Lorraine while most of the French army stood on the defensive. There was a real worry that the Germans might invade by way of Belgium, but the French did not want to commit themselves to facing that threat if the main German thrust came directly across the border instead. Massive forts were built around Verdun which, it was hoped, would hold up the Germans, whichever way they came, long enough for the French army to get into position.

The Germans had devised the Schlieffen Plan, named for the staff officer who produced the original framework. This envisaged a holding action on the Franco-German border to halt the expected French

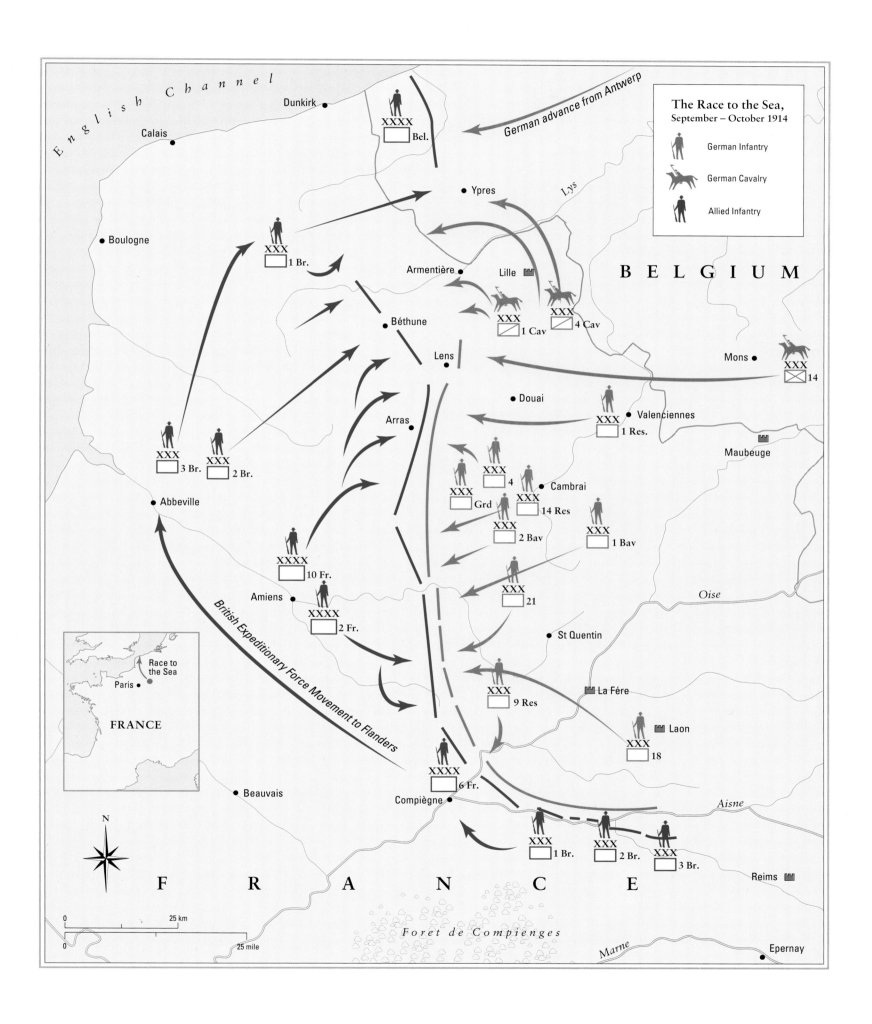

German advance from Antwerp

The Race to the Sea,
September – October 1914

German Infantry

German Cavalry

Allied Infantry

English Channel

Dunkirk

Calais

BELGIUM

XXXX Bel.

Ypres

Lys

Boulogne

XXX 1 Br.

Armentière

Lille

XXX 1 Cav

XXX 4 Cav

Béthune

Mons

XXX 14

Lens

XXX 3 Br.

XXX 2 Br.

Douai

XXX 1 Res.

Valenciennes

Maubeuge

Arras

XXX 4

Abbeville

XXX Grd

XXX 14 Res

Cambrai

XXX 2 Bav

XXX 1 Bav

XXXX 10 Fr.

Oise

Amiens

XXXX 2 Fr.

XXX 21

Race to
the Sea

Paris

St Quentin

FRANCE

La Fére

British Expeditionary Force Movement to Flanders

XXX 9 Res

Laon

XXX 18

XXXX 6 Fr.

Beauvais

Compiègne

Aisne

N

XXX 1 Br.

XXX 2 Br.

XXX 3 Br.

Reims

F   R   A   N   C   E

0   25 km

0   25 mile

Foret de Compienges

Marne

Epernay

attack into Alsace and Lorraine. Meanwhile the great bulk of the German army would march through Belgium and invade France from the north-west. The army would cross the Somme before turning south to surround Paris, cut off the French armies in Alsace and Lorraine from their bases, and thus win the entire war in one campaign.

At the tactical level, the French relied upon artillery to soften up the enemy and long-range rifle fire to decimate its ranks. A bayonet charge was the recommended way of taking enemy-held ground. The Germans had a more flexible method of attack: artillery moving swiftly alongside infantry to pound any resistance that the infantry could not dislodge.

The British Army was shaped by its experiences in the Boer War. It placed greater emphasis on accurate, long-range rifle fire than did either the French or the Germans. The British were also more inclined to move their men around the battlefield, seeking whatever advantages the ground might offer to either attack or defense.

The war began according to the German plan. The French attacked into Alsace-Lorraine but were halted within a few days with heavy losses. Meanwhile the German armies were marching rapidly through Belgium. The hastily mobilized Belgian army fought well but was pushed aside to the north while the main German columns surged on. At Mons the Germans unexpectedly ran into the British army, which had been hurriedly ferried across the Channel to help Belgium. The British were pushed back, but they did cause the German advance to slow down. More crucially, the extreme right wing of the German advance turned south earlier than planned, so that it was moving toward the eastern suburbs of Paris instead of hooking wide to the west to surround the city.

The prepared forts of Verdun held, providing a hinge on which the French line could swing back. The German advance was halted just south of the River Marne on September 5. The Germans then fell back to the River Aisne and dug in. A few attacks by the French and British failed to make headway, so they dug in as well.

Both armies had open flanks on the north-eastern edge of the fighting. There followed a series of attempts to outflank each other. Units were moved progressively north and east in an effort to work around the end of the opposing line. This had the effect of extending the defensive lines as each outflanking move ended in failure and troops digging in. By late September the lines had reached the sea. No more outflanking attempts could be made.

The defensive works of September 1914 were considered by both sides to be a temporary expedient. The generals knew the lesson of previous conflicts was that field defenses could be broken by a carefully coordinated assault by artillery and infantry, after which the cavalry could burst through to harry the retreating enemy. But winter was closing in and the generals recognized that their own forces had suffered heavy losses and had exhausted their stocks of ammunition. The attacks that were expected to break through the enemy trenches were planned for the spring of 1915.

Nobody expected the lines of trenches to be permanent. What the generals did not take into account was the impact on warfare at the tactical level of new weapons and improvements to existing weapons. Each on its own may have had a relatively modest impact, but taken together they made the field defenses of the trench lines invulnerable to the offensive weapons to hand in 1914. The stalemate on the Western Front was there to stay.

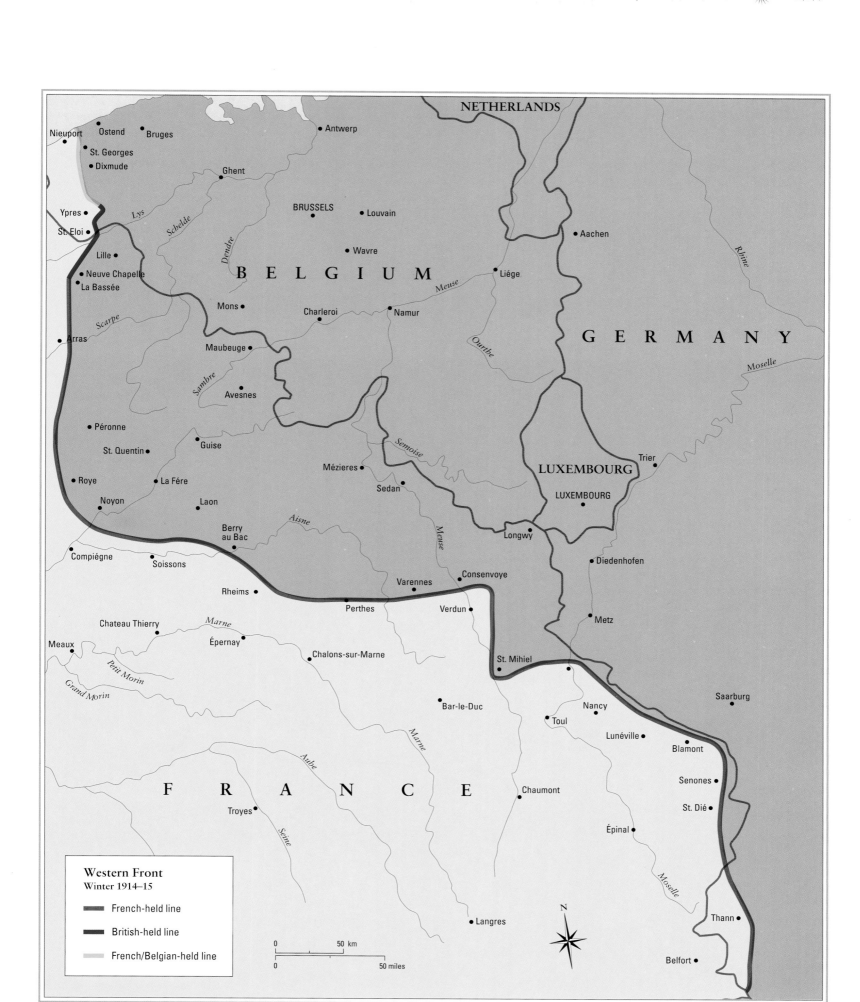

NETHERLANDS

Nieuport • Ostend • Bruges • Antwerp
St. Georges
• Dixmude
Ghent

BELGIUM

Ypres
St. Eloi
Lille
• Neuve Chapelle
La Bassée
Arras
Scarpe

BRUSSELS • Louvain
• Aachen
• Wavre
Liége
Mons • Charleroi • Namur
Maubeuge
Sambre
Avesnes
Péronne
St. Quentin • Guise
Roye • La Fére
Noyon Laon
Compiégne Soissons
Rheims
Chateau Thierry
Meaux Épernay
Chalons-sur-Marne
Petit Morin
Grand Morin

GERMANY

Rhine
Moselle

Meuse
Ourthe
Semoise
Mézieres
Sedan
Aisne
Berry au Bac
Varennes
Perthes Verdun
Marne
Bar-le-Duc
Marne

LUXEMBOURG

Trier
LUXEMBOURG
Longwy
Consenvoye
• Diedenhofen
St. Mihiel
Metz
Saarburg
Nancy
Toul Lunéville
Blamont
Senones
Chaumont St. Dié
Épinal
Moselle
Thann
Belfort

FRANCE

Troyes
Seine
Aube
Langres

Western Front
Winter 1914–15

—— French-held line
—— British-held line
—— French/Belgian-held line

0   50 km
0   50 miles

N

ARTILLERY

WHEN HOSTILITIES OPENED IN 1914, ARTILLERY WAS CONSIDERED TO BE AN ESSENTIAL PART OF ANY ARMED FORCE. ITS USE IN ATTACK WAS PARAMOUNT AND ALSO HAD A ROLE IN DEFENSE. THE IMPORTANCE OF THE GUNS INCREASED DRAMATICALLY AS THE WAR PROGRESSED AND EXPERIENCE TAUGHT HARSH LESSONS.

Opposite page: A regular feature of World War One was the massive, long-lasting artillery bombardments that preceded most of the major battles. These bombardments utterly devastated the locations on which they were fought and the blasted areas took years to recover.

The Franco-Prussian War of 1870 had ended with a clear lesson for artillery officers. The old-style muzzle-loaders used by the French were inferior in nearly every respect to the new breech-loading Krupp guns of the Prussians. Moreover, the German guns had been essential when the German infantry attacked field defenses held by the French infantry.

A fundamental problem with artillery at this time was how to move it about. Traditionally guns were mounted on two wheels with a trail acting as a third leg when in action. To move the gun, the trail was lifted onto a hook on the rear of a two- or four-wheeled vehicle called the limber. If the limber also carried the gun's ammunition, it was termed a caisson. The limber was then attached to a pole and traces to which were hitched six, sometimes four, horses. These horses were able to pull a standard field-artillery piece as far in a day as a man could comfortably march and so were considered adequate transportation for artillery. The gun crews marched alongside the guns. These field guns usually fired 8-pound (3.6 kg) balls or grapeshot and other ammunition designed for an 8-pound (3.6 kg) caliber.

During the latter 18th century a new form of artillery was introduced; light 2-pounder (0.9 kg) guns that were similarly hitched to caissons pulled by six horses, but the horses could now haul the guns as far as a cavalryman could ride in a day. On the field of battle the horses could pull the lighter guns at a trot for sustained periods, and at gallop in emergencies. The gun crews rode horses to keep up. This horse artillery was usually sent to accompany cavalry units on campaign. A third type of artillery was the big, heavy siege gun — too big to be easily pulled about the countryside by horses. It was usually dismantled for transportation and put back together again when it reached the city or fortress under siege.

Opposite page: The Battle of the Somme (July to 1 November 1916) was meant to break the stalemate of trench warfare. Instead, the Somme became a byword for mass slaughter as soldiers were mown down in rows by machine gun fire.

Siege guns were often of distinctive types called mortars or howitzers. Both forms of gun had a short barrel of very large diameter that could fire a heavy projectile over a short distance. Both weapons usually fired at a high angle, so that the shells fell onto the enemy defenses from above. This allowed the shells to land behind walls, destroy buildings, and kill personnel inside the fortress walls. It had the added advantage that plunging shot would often penetrate the soil before exploding; buildings' foundations would be shaken and they would tumble down. The key difference between the two was that the range of a mortar shot was determined by altering the amount of powder used when firing the gun. A howitzer altered its range by changing the angle of the barrel.

When World War One broke out in 1914, this basic division into field, horse, and siege artillery still existed. With a very few exceptions where motor trucks were used, most guns were pulled by horses. There had been advances in artillery but they had failed to make any significant impact on the way the guns were used according to the basic tactical doctrines of the day.

One critical advance had been made by the French in 1898, when they produced the 75 mm field gun that they called the *"Canon de 75"*. Soldiers from other nations called it the *"French 75"*, and marvelled at it. By 1914 the French army had 4,000 of these guns, organized into 1,000 batteries of four guns each. Although the gun was displayed in parades from 1899, the French were highly secretive about the true abilities of this weapon and even more so about how the design of the weapon achieved its astonishing accuracy and rate of fire.

The gun had been developed under conditions of absolute secrecy by the French state weapons factory, the *Atelier de Construction de Puteaux*. Work on the gun had begun in 1892, when the works commander, General Deloye, ordered his men to bring together a number of recent inventions in a new type of field gun.

The first of these inventions was a form of smokeless gunpowder developed in 1884. The great clouds of smoke produced by traditional gunpowder not only revealed the position of a gun to the enemy but also wreathed the gunners in smoke and prevented them from seeing their target.

The second advance was self-contained ammunition. Artillerymen had traditionally put the shell and propellant charge in separately. In self-contained ammunition the propellant powder was enclosed in a brass case. The shell was inserted into the top of the brass case, which was then crimped to hold the shell firmly in place. At the base of the case was the priming cap to set off the charge. This ammunition was more expensive but it was much easier to handle in action and safer for gunners to use.

The third advance was a form of rotating screw breech, which worked much more quickly than the conventional breech used by Krupp guns and most other artillery weapons by the 1890s.

The most important advance was the secret recoil system. When a gun is fired, the recoil tends to push it backward. In all artillery pieces up to the development of the French 75, this recoil had pushed the gun back several feet. The crew then manhandled it forward to its original position, ready to be reloaded. The French 75 did not recoil backward when fired.

This recoil-less action was achieved by a complex hydro-pneumatic system. When the gun was fired, the barrel slid back on rollers. As it slid back, the barrel moved a piston inside an oil-filled cylinder located under the barrel. The oil was forced through a small orifice into a second cylinder, which in turn had a piston that separated the incoming oil from a mass of compressed air at the far end of the cylinder.

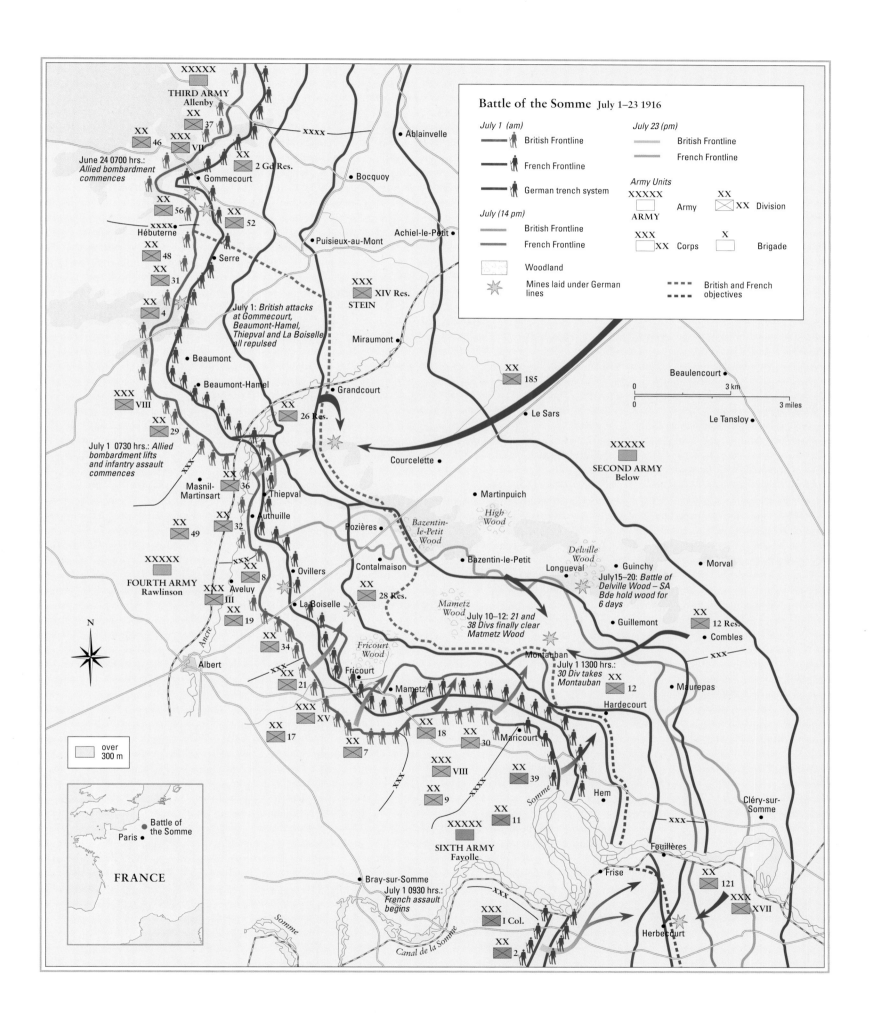

Battle of the Somme July 1–23 1916

July 1 (am)

British Frontline
French Frontline
German trench system

July (14 pm)

British Frontline
French Frontline

July 23 (pm)

British Frontline
French Frontline

Army Units

XXXXX / ARMY — Army
XXXX / XX — Division
XXX / XX — Corps
X — Brigade

Woodland
Mines laid under German lines
British and French objectives

XXXXX
THIRD ARMY
Allenby

XX 37
XX 46 XXX VII
XX 2 Gd Res.
• Ablainvelle
• Bocquoy

June 24 0700 hrs.: Allied bombardment commences

• Gommecourt

XX 56
XXXXX
Hébuterne
XX 52
• Puisieux-au-Mont
Achiel-le-Petit •

XX 48
• Serre
XX 31
XXX XIV Res.
STEIN
• Miraumont

XX 4

July 1: British attacks at Gommecourt, Beaumont-Hamel, Thiepval and La Boiselle all repulsed

• Beaumont
• Beaumont-Hamel
• Grandcourt
XX 185
• Beaulencourt •
• Le Sars
Le Tansloy •

XXX VIII
XX 29
XX 26 Res.

July 1 0730 hrs.: Allied bombardment lifts and infantry assault commences

• Courcelette
XXXXX
SECOND ARMY
Below

Masnil-Martinsart
XX 36
Thiepval
• Martinpuich
High Wood

XX 49
XX 32
• Authuille
Pozières •
Bazentin-le-Petit Wood

XXXXX
FOURTH ARMY
Rawlinson
XXX XX 8
• Ovillers
Contalmaison •
• Bazentin-le-Petit
Delville Wood
Longueval
• Guinchy
• Morval

XXX III
Aveluy
XX 19
• La Boiselle
XX 28 Res.
Mametz Wood
July 10–12: 21 and 38 Divs finally clear Matmetz Wood
July 15–20: Battle of Delville Wood – SA Bde hold wood for 6 days
XX 12 Res.

N

XX 34
Fricourt Wood
• Guillemont
• Combles
XXX

• Albert
XXX XX 21
Fricourt
• Mametz
Montauban
July 1 1300 hrs.: 30 Div takes Montauban
XX 12
Hardecourt
• Maurepas

XXX XV
XX 17
XX 7
XX 18
XX 30
Maricourt
Hem

XXX VIII
XX 9
XX 39

over 300 m

XX 11
XXXXX
SIXTH ARMY
Fayolle
• Cléry-sur-Somme
Feuillères
XX 121

• Bray-sur-Somme
July 1 0930 hrs.: French assault begins
• Frise
XXX XVII

Somme
XXX
XX I Col.
• Herbecourt

FRANCE
Paris •
• Battle of the Somme

Somme
Canal de la Somme
XX 2

Opposite page: On March 23 1918, Paris was unexpectedly bombarded by three huge German artillery pieces, named the Paris Guns, which were sited 70 miles (113 km) away. Built at Krupps Works, the Paris Gun was a 15-inch (38 cm) naval cannon normally used on battleships. Dashed line marks railway lines in and around Paris.

The oil flow compressed the air even further, forcing it to act as an enormously powerful spring that absorbed the force of the recoil. As the recoil force fell off, the air expanded again, pushing the oil out of the second cylinder back into the first and thus moving the piston arm to return the gun barrel to its original position. The whole process took about two seconds.

Allowing time for the gun to be reloaded after the barrel had returned to rest, the French 75 could fire 10 shots per minute — an unheard-of rapidity for the time. And because the gun did not move as it was fired, the wheels were locked into position — it did not need to be reaimed for each shot. Thus the second shot was as accurate as the first.

By 1914 other countries were experimenting with similar recoil-less systems for artillery pieces. Krupp had actually begun work on a similar mechanical layout in the 1880s, but had abandoned the idea because they had been unable to get it to work reliably in battlefield conditions. The French 75 was thus unique when the war began.

Another advance in artillery in the years before 1914 was the ability to fire indirectly, accurately. Gunners had usually fired at things they could see, but in 1882 the Russian artillery officer Colonel G.K. Guk published a book outlining his methods for shooting accurately at things he could not see. This gave the gunners the advantage of being able to open fire while hidden in gullies or behind buildings and thus being relatively safe from return fire. Guk's techniques depended on being able to measure very accurately both the elevation of the barrel, which determined range, and its azimuth, which determined direction. Guk's methods were sound, but his instruments were not.

In 1906 a German engineer named Goertz produced accurate methods for determining both azimuth and elevation. Guns could now be made to hit any spot with a relatively small error of margin anywhere in their field of fire without the gunner needing to see the target. Typically a spotter was placed under cover in a place from which he could see the target. He sent instructions to the gunners by telephone. Usually after the first shot, the spotter would instruct the gunner to adjust his aim accordingly.

This technique of indirect fire would be crucial in the trench warfare that was to dominate the battles to come, but it was not considered essential to the tactics and operations of open warfare expected in 1914.

When the campaigning season of 1915 opened, the Western Allies, Britain, France, and Belgium, expected to launch assaults that would break through the German trench lines. There would then follow a fluid war of movement in which infantry, artillery, and cavalry would co-operate in traditional fashion as the Germans were thrown back, surrounded, and crushed.

Attacks would begin with a heavy artillery bombardment of the German trenches by field artillery and siege guns. Then the infantry would go forward with bayonets fixed with the idea of clearing the trenches and opening the way

Boulogne

for cavalry, which would gallop forward and disrupt enemy rear areas and reinforcements. Finally the massed infantry columns would surge through.

The first assault took place in March at Neuve Chapelle, when the British General Douglas Haig deployed 60 batteries of field artillery to bombard the German lines. 48 battalions of infantry were massed for the assault, with significant numbers of cavalry standing ready behind them to exploit the

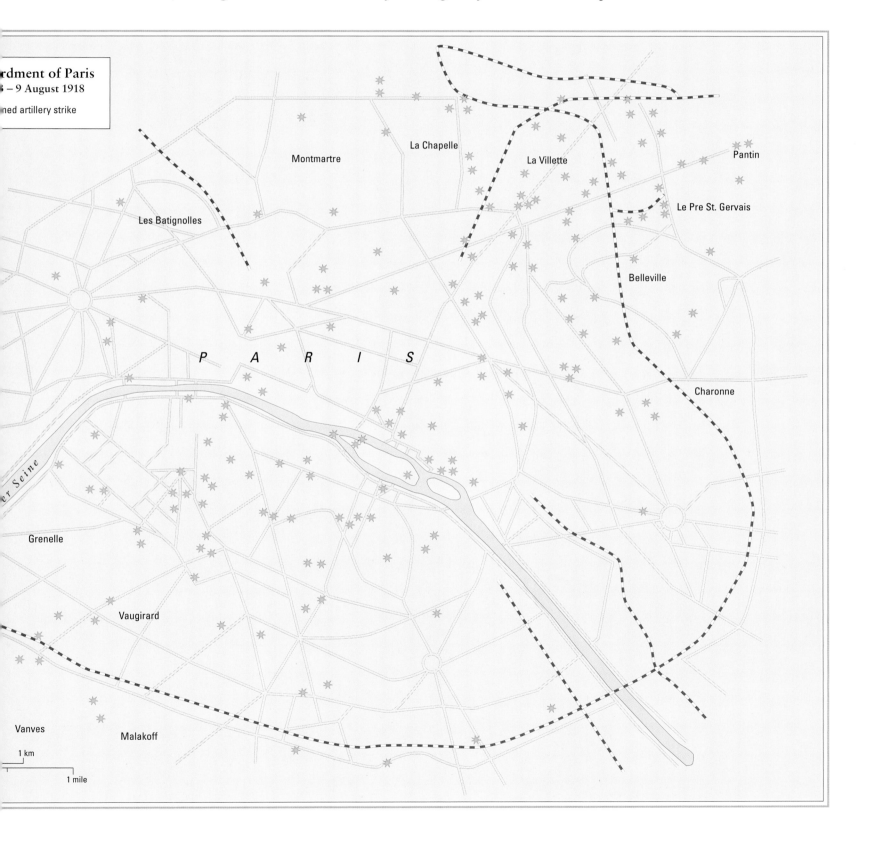

...rdment of Paris
... – 9 August 1918
...ned artillery strike

La Chapelle

Montmartre

La Villette

Pantin

Les Batignolles

Le Pre St. Gervais

Belleville

P A R I S

Charonne

er Seine

Grenelle

Vaugirard

Vanves

Malakoff

1 km

1 mile

Opposite page: The Franco-American forces in the Meuse-Argonne offensive of 1918 were on the brink of capturing the railroad hub at Sedan, which supplied the German army, when the armistice was declared on November 11, ending World War One.

expected breakthrough. The attack went ahead on March 10 and achieved breathtaking results. The artillery battered the German front-line trenches to pieces and the attacking infantry faced only lightly held fragmentary trenches. In several places the infantry fought their way through the German lines, and by late afternoon they had broken right through the German defenses into the open countryside beyond. Runners were sent back to call up the cavalry. And that was where it all began to go wrong.

The runners took longer than expected to find their way back over the shattered landscape to their base headquarters. Then the cavalry commanders waited until they received confirmed orders from army headquarters before advancing. That delay gave the Germans long enough to rush up a few reinforcements. By dawn, when the cavalry were picking their way forward over the shell-torn battlefield, the Germans were in place and hurriedly digging new trenches. The cavalry called for the field artillery to open fire on the new positions, but the guns had no ammunition left. The attack stalled, then failed. Haig tried again, at Aubers in May. This time the attacking infantry did not get through the German trench system and the cavalry did not move up. A third attack, at Loos in September, achieved nothing but heavy casualties among the attacking infantry.

Nevertheless the near-victory at Neuve Chapelle convinced Haig and most British generals that the basic plan of artillery bombardment followed by infantry assault was sound. What was needed, they thought, was more and heavier artillery firing more and heavier shells before the attack went in. This would lead to a massive increase in the number of guns on the Western Front.

It was soon realized that horse artillery was useless against trenches and that field guns were little better. The huge number of field guns in existence meant that they had to be used, but increasingly they were given the task of firing shrapnel to clear away barbed wire and men. The task of smashing trench networks was given to siege howitzers, now being produced in ever greater volume.

The climax of the traditional assault method of artillery bombardment followed by infantry attack would come at the Battle of the Somme in 1916. Once again the method failed and the infantry suffered appalling losses. Thereafter the generals looked for other methods of breaking through the front-line trenches and pursuing a war of movement, which they saw as the only means to achieve victory.

Meanwhile, the Germans had accepted that no breakthrough could be achieved. They perceived the Western Front as a grinding war of attrition where only futile bloodshed could be achieved by the expenditure of money on ammunition and fortifications. They kept their artillery for bombarding targets behind the Allied front lines and for inflicting heavy casualties on attacking infantry.

They also developed a number of specialist weapons. The first of these was Krupp's "Big Bertha", of which 12 were made. Big Bertha was a massive howitzer with a (16½ in) 42 cm barrel that fired an 1,830 lb (830 kg) shell. The gun weighed a mighty 48¼ ton (43.7 tonnes) and had to be mounted on special steel matting when fired in order to keep it from sinking into the ground. It was towed by a tractor produced by Daimler. More famous was the Paris Gun, officially the "Kaiser Wilhelm Geschütz", of which only one was completed by Krupp. This weapon was designed with the specific purpose of firing shells into Paris from behind the German front lines. It had a barrel 92 ft (28 m) long and 8¼ in (210 mm) in diameter that could throw a 207 lb (94 kg) shell more than 70 miles (113 km). The gun, including its special railway carriage, weighed 287 ton (260 tonnes). It fired for the first time on March 21 1918. About 350 shells were fired over the following five months, killing 250 Parisians and wounding 620 more.

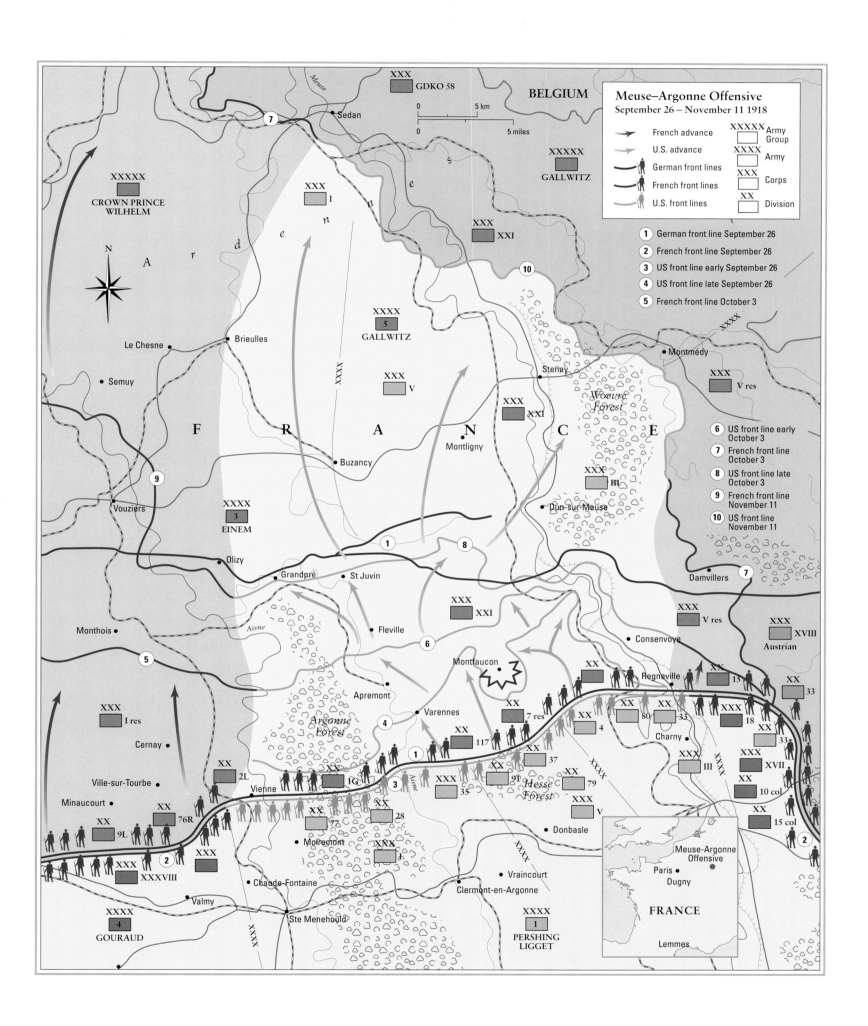

Meuse–Argonne Offensive
September 26 – November 11 1918

0   5 km
0   5 miles

→	French advance
→	U.S. advance
⚑	German front lines
⚑	French front lines
⚑	U.S. front lines

XXXXX	Army Group
XXXX	Army
XXX	Corps
XX	Division

1 German front line September 26
2 French front line September 26
3 US front line early September 26
4 US front line late September 26
5 French front line October 3

6 US front line early October 3
7 French front line October 3
8 US front line late October 3
9 French front line November 11
10 US front line November 11

BELGIUM

GDKO 58

Sedan

CROWN PRINCE WILHELM

GALLWITZ

I

XXI

A r d e n n e s

Le Chesne

Brieulles

Semuy

Montmédy

GALLWITZ 5

V

Stenay

Woëvre Forest

V res

F   R   A   N   C   E

Montligny

XXI

Buzancy

III

Vouziers

EINEM 3

Dun-sur-Meuse

Olizy

Grandpré   St Juvin

Damvillers

Aisne

Monthois

Fleville

XXI

V res

XVIII Austrian

Montfaucon

Consenvoye

Regneville

15

33

Argonne Forest

Apremont

Varennes

7 res

80   33

18

I res

Cernay

117

4

Charny

III

17

Ville-sur-Tourbe

2L

1G

37

91

Hesse Forest

79

10 col

Minaucourt

9L

76R

77

28

35

V

15 col

Moiremont

Donbasle

XXXVIII

Chaude-Fontaine

Vraincourt

Clermont-en-Argonne

GOURAUD 4

Valmy

Ste Menehould

PERSHING LIGGET 1

FRANCE

Meuse-Argonne Offensive

Paris

Dugny

Lemmes

FIREPOWER: MACHINE GUNS

THE MACHINE GUN DOMINATED THE BATTLEFIELDS OF WORLD WAR ONE. ITS ABILITY TO SPIT DEATH AT AN UNPRECEDENTED RATE MADE IT THE KEY DEFENSE WEAPON FOR ALL ARMIES.

T he dominance of the machine gun by 1915 makes it easy to forget that in 1914 it was a relatively new, untried weapon that in many ways was not thought suitable for modern warfare. Certainly most commanders considered it secondary to the infantry rifle.

The generals of 1914 expected to fight a war of open maneuver and swift movement. Experience in the Franco-Prussian, Boer, and Balkan Wars had shown that for this type of action, the long-range, magazine-fed rifle was ideal. The British Lee Enfield .303 MkIII, for instance, could reliably hit a target 1 in² (2.5 cm²) at ranges up to 500 yd (457 m), and an experienced rifleman could hit a man standing 1 mile (1.6 km) away. The German Mauser GEW98 and the French Label Model 98 were comparable.

These weapons generally weighed under 10 lb (4.5 kg) and had up to six bullets in the magazine. This enabled them to be fired rapidly if enemy soldiers got to close range, a situation in which rapidity of fire was more important than absolute accuracy. They could be fitted with bayonets for hand-to-hand action. By comparison, the machine guns of 1914 were cumbersome, awkward, and inaccurate. The standard British machine gun, for instance, was the Vickers. This weapon weighed over 50 lb (22.7 kg), more with the boxes of ammunition. It had an effective range of only 810 yd (741 m). Machine guns used by other combatant nations were comparable.

For infantrymen marching on foot over the long distances that tactical handbooks envisaged, the machine gun would be an encumbrance. And when soldiers entered action, it would easily be outranged by enemy rifles. The machine gun was thought to be useful for defending field fortifications against infantry attacks, but not for much else. Thus most armies equipped most infantry battalions with two or three machine guns in case they might be useful at some point. Machine-gunners tended to be pitied by the other men because they had to carry heavy loads and rarely fired their weapons.

Once trench systems began to develop, the relative usefulness of rifles and machine guns reversed. Action was now taking place at distances of generally less than 500 yd (457 m). Here the rate of fire of

Opposite page: In 1917, during the Battle of Arras, the Canadian Corps was tasked with capturing Vimy Ridge in the Pas-de-Calais region of France. It took three days of heavy fighting to achieve their objective, at the cost of 10,000 casualties.

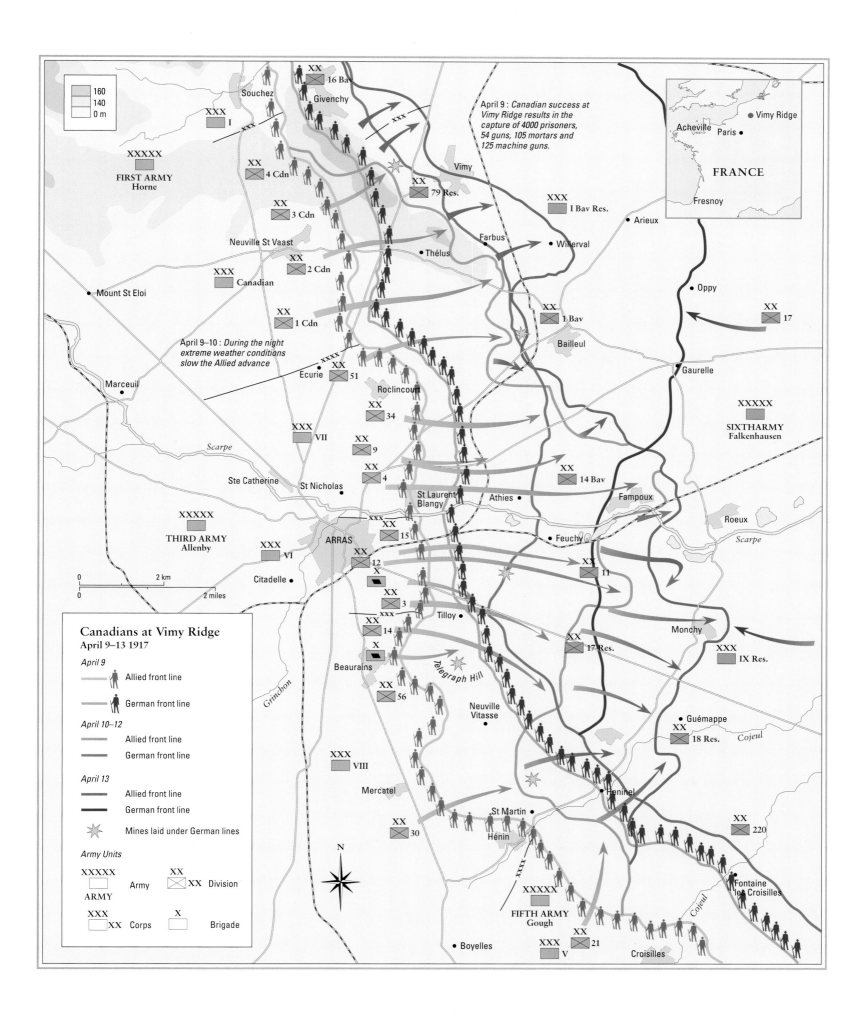

160	
140	
0 m	

Souchez

16 Ba

Givenchy

XXX I

XXXXX
FIRST ARMY
Horne

XX 4 Cdn

XX 79 Res.

Vimy

April 9 : Canadian success at
Vimy Ridge results in the
capture of 4000 prisoners,
54 guns, 105 mortars and
125 machine guns.

XXX I Bav Res.

• Arieux

XX 3 Cdn

Neuville St Vaast

Farbus

• Willerval

• Thélus

• Oppy

XX 2 Cdn

XXX Canadian

• Mount St Eloi

XX 1 Cdn

XX 1 Bav

Bailleul

XX 17

April 9–10 : During the night
extreme weather conditions
slow the Allied advance

• Marceuil

XXXX
Ecurie XX 51

Roclincourt

Gaurelle

XXXXX
SIXTH ARMY
Falkenhausen

XX 34

Scarpe

XXX VII

XX 9

Ste Catherine

St Nicholas •

XX 4

St Laurent
Blangy

XX 14 Bav

Athies •

Fampoux

Roeux

Scarpe

XXXXX
THIRD ARMY
Allenby

XXX XX 15

Feuchy

XXX VI

ARRAS

XX 12
X

XX 11

Citadelle •

XX 3

XXX

Tilloy •

Monchy

XX 14
X

XX 17 Res.

XXX IX Res.

Canadians at Vimy Ridge
April 9–13 1917

Beaurains

Telegraph Hill

April 9

👤 Allied front line

👤 German front line

XX 56

Neuville
Vitasse

• Guémappe

XX 18 Res.

Cojeul

April 10–12

Allied front line

German front line

XXX VIII

Mercatel

April 13

Allied front line

German front line

✳ Mines laid under German lines

Héninel •

XX 30

St Martin •

XX 220

Hénin •

Army Units

XXXXX
ARMY ☐ Army

XX ☒ XX Division

XXX
☐ XX Corps

X ☐ Brigade

N

XXXXX
FIFTH ARMY
Gough

XXX
V XX 21

• Boyelles

Croisilles

Fontaine
les Croisilles

Acheville *Paris •*

• Vimy Ridge

FRANCE

Fresnoy

0 — 2 km
0 — 2 miles

Grinchon

Cojeul

the machine gun was massively useful, and the long-range accuracy of the rifle was not. At first the number of machine guns per battalion was not increased, even though they were placed in camouflaged positions sited so that they could sweep the land between the trenches.

Later, the number of machine guns per battalion was increased, and from 1916 specialized machine gun units were developed by most armies. This new unit had the advantage that machine guns could now be moved from one part of the trench system to another, independent of where the infantry battalions were stationed. It gave the armies greater flexibility, especially in defense.

The machine gun was most effective when used in conjunction with a second military invention new to the armies of 1914: barbed wire. The entanglements that the armies put up in front of trenches and other defenses were designed both to slow down advancing infantry and to channel them into narrow openings in the wire where they could be mown down by pre-sighted machine guns. These entanglements were not simple wire fences but complex affairs up to 10 ft (3 m) high and 30 ft (9 m deep). They were often festooned with small bells so that any attempt to cut the wire at night in preparation for an attack at dawn could be heard and gunfire directed at the noise.

The combination of barbed wire and machine guns made the field defenses of the trench network effectively invulnerable to a conventional attack by mid-1915. The search was soon on for new weapons that would be more effective in the context of trench warfare than the rifle and bayonet.

Some of these were weapons improvised by the men in the trenches themselves. British officers from rural areas, for instance, got into the habit of bringing their sporting shotguns out from home. Once in France they sawed off at least half the barrel. This had the effect of dramatically widening the spray pattern of the pellets as they left the barrel. In the confined space of a trench this could be devastating. The sawn-off shotgun later became illegal in many countries.

Other weapons were developments of existing military equipment. The hand grenade is known to have been in use in China as early as 1044, but problems with finding a reliable fuse and keeping the gunpowder inside them dry meant that they were rarely used except in sieges. As the trenches of World War One were a siege on a vast scale, the hand grenade came back into fashion.

The British used the Mills Bomb No. 5. This weighed 30 oz (850 g) and could be thrown about 100 ft (30 m) by the average infantryman. When it went off, the grenade spewed lethal metal fragments to a distance of some 120 ft (36.5 m). Clearly, the thrower had to take cover. Typically he would toss the grenade into an enemy trench or roll it around a corner and then duck.

The Germans opted for the stick grenade, or *Stielhandgranate*, which had a wooden handle attached to the grenade itself. This made the weapon much easier to throw, with an average range of 170 ft (52 km). The explosive head did not have the metal fragments of the British weapon but it did have a much larger explosive charge. This produced a greatly increased blast effect, especially in confined spaces. It tended to stun its victims as often as kill them, the fatal blow being delivered by the infantryman following up the grenade blast with his rifle and bayonet.

The stick grenade was a key weapon in 1917 in the German stormtrooper tactics for negating the defensive power of the machine gun. Small groups of men would storm forward, often at night, taking advantage of ground cover whenever possible. Using grenades and light machine guns the men would overwhelm sections of enemy trenches, push on to the rear areas and attack machine gun positions from behind. Other stormtrooper units would push on to attack the enemy's headquarters and communication posts. With the machine guns neutralized and the enemy disorganized, the main infantry attack would be made. The British and French soon adopted similar tactics, and by the end of 1917 the machine gun was no longer as dominant on the battlefield as it had been in 1915.

During World War One, the machine gun had a fundamental influence on the way hostilities were conducted, for it proved to be a deadly mass killer. The value of a weapon that could produce such a result was not lost on military planners, who concentrated on developing the machine gun for use by the infantry during the years between World Wars One and Two.

By 1939, there were two basic types, the light and the heavy machine gun. Light machine guns were mobile and easy to carry from place to place. The heavy variety were also mobile, but were usually dug in along lines of defense. Of the two, the heavy machine gun had the greater firing rate. Whereas the light machine gun was magazine-fed, the heavy gun was fed with ammunition from a belt. It also had superior gun sights to enable it to maintain substantial and more accurate fire on the enemy.

All the major combatants in World War Two, which began in Europe in 1939 employed heavy machine guns, although the .311 in MG-34 used by the forces of Nazi Germany combined features of the light gun as well. The MG-34 could be used with a bipod or a tripod, weighing 26 lb (12 kg). with the former accessory or 43 lb (19 kg) with the latter, and had a firing rate of between 13 and 15 rounds per second.

The Russians, who were forced into World War Two on June 22, 1941 when the Germans invaded, opted for a weightier 12.7 mm heavy machine gun that remained in use throughout the hostilities. The Russian gun, which was cooled by air and operated by gas, measured more than 5 ft (1.5 m) in length, but had a lesser rate of fire than the German MG-34–between 9 and 10 rounds per second.

The British chose a gun, the 7.7 mm Vickers heavy machine gun, which had already proven its worth during World War One. One of these weapons had been fired on test for a week, and kept on firing throughout, pausing only to be reloaded. Weighing in at 40 lbs (18 kg), the 7.7 mm was cooled by water, with a steam-condensing radiator and measured 43 inches (1.1m) in length. Its rate of fire was rather less than the Russian 12.7 mm machine gun, at between 7.5 and 9 rounds per second.

In the Pacific war, the United States and Japanese forces faced each other with widely varying machine guns. The Americans chose the daunting Browning 12.7 mm in model, which in addition to infantry usage also served as an anti-aircraft weapon. This machine gun weighed 82 lb (37 kg)., measured 5½ ft (1.7 m) in length and fired at a rate of 7.5 rounds per second. The 7.7 mm type 99-1 machine gun, based on the French Hotchiss design, became the standard Japanese heavy machine gun. Weighing 70 lb (30 kg). with tripod, the 99-1 measured around 42 (1.1 m) in length and had a firing rate of 9 rounds per second.

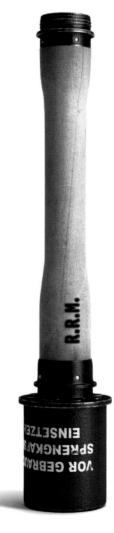

The stick grenade was introduced by the Germans in 1915 and lasted in use until 1945. The grenade had a cord at the base: when the cord was pulled, a five-second fuse began to burn.

ARMORED WARFARE: TANKS

AS TRADITIONAL ARTILLERY AND INFANTRY COULD NOT SMASH THROUGH TRENCH SYSTEMS, THE WORLD'S ARMIES BEGAN TO SEARCH FOR A NEW METHOD OF TRENCH-BUSTING. FOR THE BRITISH THE ANSWER WAS THE TANK.

The basic components of the tank were developed independently during the 1890s and 1900s. They only came together after the massive casualties of trench warfare forced military planners to look for new tactics and new weapons for breaking the trench stalemate.

In 1904 Hornsby & Sons of Grantham, England developed a new tractor. This featured continuous metal tracks that ran around the wheels. These tracks effectively formed a temporary road on which the wheels could run, spreading the weight of the tractor widely and stopping it from sinking into soft mud. The tractor was suggested to the army as a method for hauling artillery or supplies across muddy ground and would have armor plating to protect the driver, but was turned down owing to its low speed and heavy fuel consumption. Throughout the 19th century, there had been attempts to mount guns on wagons, but the heavy recoil of the gun always made this impractical. When the French produced the recoil-less French 75, this problem was solved.

It was Major Ernest Swanton of the British Royal Engineers who finally had the idea of mounting a recoil-less cannon on a tracked tractor and protecting it with plating. He suggested the idea to the army in the fall of 1914, but at this time the senior officers were still expecting to fight a war of open maneuver; they saw no point in Swanton's lumbering monster. But Winston Churchill, a politician who had fought in the Boer War, spotted the advantages of Swanton's idea. Churchill set up a committee of engineers to see if it would be possible to produce a machine able to break through enemy trenches. After consulting with army officers who had served in the trenches, it was decided that the machine had to fulfill three conditions. First, it had to be encased in armor able to stop a rifle or machine-gun bullet even at point-blank range. Second, it had to be able to cross a trench 8 ft (2.45 m) wide and climb a bank 5 ft (1.5 m) high. Third, it had to be armed with two machine guns and one light artillery gun able to fire through the armor without the gunners being exposed to enemy fire. It was a tall order.

A tank in action, plowing across a battlefield trench while keeping its crew safe from attack. When the Germans first saw tanks lumbering toward them, they were apparently so frightened that they leaped out of their trenches and ran away.

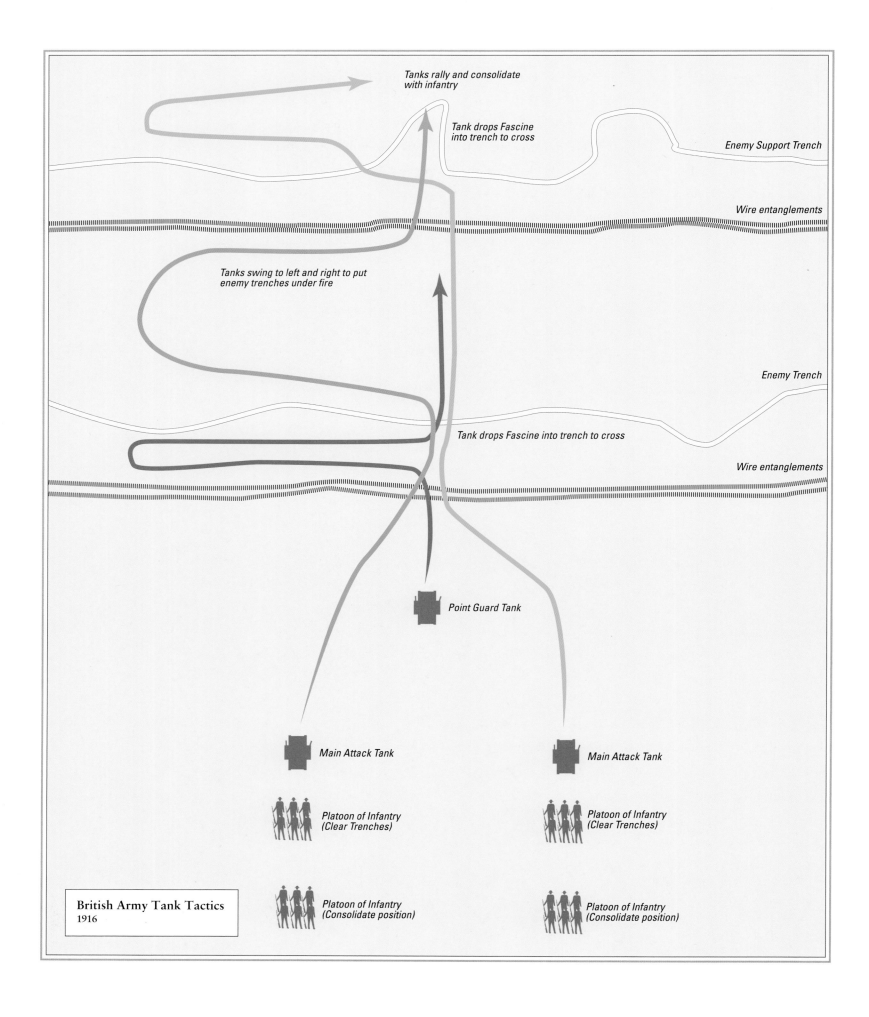

Tanks rally and consolidate
with infantry

Tank drops Fascine
into trench to cross

Enemy Support Trench

Wire entanglements

Tanks swing to left and right to put
enemy trenches under fire

Enemy Trench

Tank drops Fascine into trench to cross

Wire entanglements

Point Guard Tank

Main Attack Tank

Main Attack Tank

Platoon of Infantry
(Clear Trenches)

Platoon of Infantry
(Clear Trenches)

Platoon of Infantry
(Consolidate position)

Platoon of Infantry
(Consolidate position)

British Army Tank Tactics
1916

In January 1916 the first experimental models were put through their paces. The new weapons could move at only four miles (16 km) per hour, but this was fast enough to keep up with marching infantry and was considered adequate. The vehicles were fitted with naval 6-pound (2.7 kg) guns and machine guns, and the armor was proof against anything except a direct hit by an artillery shell. The only real problem was ventilation. The interiors of the vehicles were prone to fill with exhaust fumes from the engines, and the fumes expelled from the guns built up rapidly when they were used. Some crews actually passed out and had to be rescued. The army high command was impressed enough to order 150 of the new weapon. The vehicle now needed a name that was unique to it but would not give away its design or function to enemy spies. Because the men building the prototypes had been told that they were building self-propelled water tanks for use in desert areas, the name "tank" was agreed upon.

Tanks entered combat on September, 15 1916, when 32 were sent lumbering forward to accompany an infantry attack on the Somme with limited objectives. In the event, 23 of the tanks broke down or got stuck in mud before they reached the enemy trenches. The nine that did get into action were enormously effective. The British commander, Field Marshal Haig, was so impressed that he at once insisted that the army order 1,000 tanks and that special tank units be established. At the Battle of Cambrai in November 1917, new models of tank were sent forward in large numbers. In all 381 tanks were used in conjunction with infantry trained to co-operate with them and supported by artillery. The tanks overran the German trench system with ease, allowing the infantry to move forward. Unfortunately spies had alerted the Germans to the build-up of tanks in the sector and a reserve line had hurriedly been put together. The artillery put a number of tanks out of action and the attack eventually stalled. Nevertheless, a large amount of high ground had been captured for relatively little loss.

The French had been given the details of tank design by the British. Renault was asked to produce a tank, and in the summer of 1917 produced the FT17. At 7 ton (6.4 tonnes), it was much smaller than the 32½ ton (29.5 tonne) British tanks, but it had the same ability to cross trenches. The FT17 had only one gun, either a 7.92 mm machine gun or a 37 mm cannon and thus was much less well armed than the British tanks. But the gun was mounted in a revolutionary turret that could turn through 360 degrees, enabling the gunner to shoot at anything in sight. The FT17 used existing parts and could be put into mass production with ease. When the U.S. entered World War One, it chose to buy FT17 tanks for their tank units. They developed sophisticated tank tactics that relied on the tanks in a unit supporting each other with interlocking fire as they advanced. The Germans generally preferred to use the specialized infantry stormtrooper tactics to break through trench lines, and achieved much success with them. All the same, the German army was sufficiently impressed by British tanks to order their own to be developed. The result was the A7V, which entered service in March 1918.

On April 24, 1918, the world's first tank-against-tank battle took place when three A7V tanks were leading an infantry attack at Villers-Bretonneaux and were met by three British MkIV tanks. One British tank was damaged and withdrew; one German tank was knocked out. The German attack failed. By the end of the war, the tank was accepted by most military thinkers as the answer to the stalemate of the trenches. Even so, its slow speed and mechanical problems in battlefield conditions convinced many that it did not have a significant role in battles demanding speed of movement.

Opposite page: The tank, first used by the British at the Battle of the Somme in 1918, navigated barbed wire and other obstacles while protecting its crew from machine gun fire and outflanking enemy lines. This eventually broke the deadlock of trench warfare.

AIRCRAFT AT WAR

WHEN WORLD WAR ONE BEGAN, AIRCRAFT WERE REGARDED AS FIT ONLY FOR RECONNAISSANCE. THEY WERE LIGHTWEIGHT, PRONE TO MECHANICAL FAILURE, AND UNARMED. THE FOUR YEARS OF WAR WOULD SEE AIRCRAFT TRANSFORMED INTO A BATTLE-WINNING WEAPON OF POTENTIALLY AWESOME POWER.

World War One broke out only 11 years after the Wright brothers had first got a heavier-than-air machine off the ground. Since then, aircraft had been used mostly as toys for rich men, with races and other sporting events being organized for the amusement of the public. Those military men who did think about aircraft viewed them as useful only for long-range reconnaissance, a role traditionally taken by light cavalry.

The U.S. was the first nation to form a military air unit, the Air Division of the Signals Corps in 1907 but there were only two aircraft, used for scouting missions, as late as 1911. The British formed the Air Battalion of the Royal Engineers in 1911, which became the Royal Flying Corps in 1912. The French followed suit, but did not get very far owing to the views of Commander-in-Chief Marshal Foch, who declared in 1911 that "aviation is useless for the army". The Germans had a number of scouting aircraft, but generally preferred Zeppelin airships with their much greater range and flying height.

Of more interest were the activities of the Italian Air Corps. This force had only 39 men and nine aircraft, but it led the way. During the Italian-Turkish war of 1911—1912, the Italians regularly took cameras into the air so that they could photograph enemy camps and troop formations. They also dropped propaganda leaflets on towns and villages. On November 1 1911, Lieutenant Giulio Gavotte took four grenades into the air with him and dropped them on a Turkish encampment at Ain Zahra. Thus the Italians were the first to use aircraft for photo-reconnaissance, propaganda, and bombing. During the Balkan Wars only the Bulgarians had aircraft, which they used for reconnaissance.

By the time World War One began, most pilots and observers were in the habit of taking pistols or rifles into the air with them. The first air combat took place on August 15 1914 when a French pilot shot

Opposite page, top: After centuries of experiment, people were at last able to fly after the Wright Brothers built this heavier-than-air machine carrying a suitably light but powerful engine. The Wright Flyer first took to the air on December 17 1903.

at a German aircraft with a pistol. No damage was done. The first combat with a result occurred on October 5 when the French observer Joseph Quenault produced a machine gun from his cockpit and riddled a German scout aircraft with holes, causing it to crash.

The British had been developing special explosive devices to drop from aircraft. Unlike Gavotti's grenades, they had fins to stabilize them as they fell and were fitted with contact fuses so that they exploded when they hit the ground, not five seconds after being dropped. The first effective use of these bombs, as they were called, came on October 8 1914. Flight Lieutenant R. Matrix dropped four bombs onto a Zeppelin storage shed at Dusseldorf, setting it on fire and destroying a Zeppelin airship inside. Later that day Squadron Commander Spenser Grey bombed the railroad station at Cologne.

The German *Taube*, used by the Germans, Austrians, and Italians in 1914, was built by the Rumple company and was typical of pre-war design. It was lightweight and powered by a 99-horsepower Mercedes engine. It could reach 60 mph (96.6 kph) and altitudes of 10,000 ft (3,048 m) with a range of 80 miles (130 km). Like many early aircraft it had complex wire-operated wings to enable it tp change direction.

As the war progressed, aircraft manufacturers rapidly began producing models specialized for the different roles in which aircraft were being employed. As trench

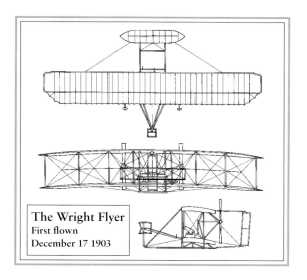

The Wright Flyer
First flown
December 17 1903

Below: French aviator and inventor Louis Blériot became the first pilot to make an international flight when he flew his Blériot XI monoplane, an aircraft of his own design, across the English Channel from Calais to Dover on July 25 1909.

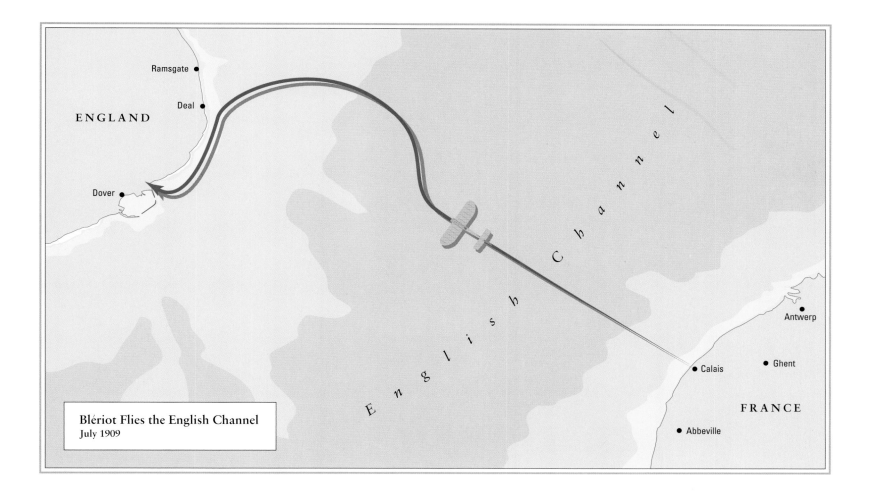

Blériot Flies the English Channel
July 1909

warfare stagnated, scouting behind enemy lines became the preserve of two-seater aircraft. The pilot flew the machine while the observer studied the ground below. Some aircraft were fitted with a radio. This enabled the observer to send back messages instantaneously. The radio was widely used for artillery spotting: the observer watched where artillery shells were landing and sent back corrections in order to ensure accuracy.

For defense these two-seater aircraft soon gained a machine gun. The gun was fitted onto a metal ring so that it could slide from side to side and be brought to bear on an enemy. An aircraft might have the propeller at the front, in which case the observer and his gun were in the rear cockpit. Alternatively the propeller might be at the rear of the fuselage in what were called "pusher aircraf", which allowed the observer to sit in the front. Here he had a much better view of the ground, and a wider arc of fire for his gun.

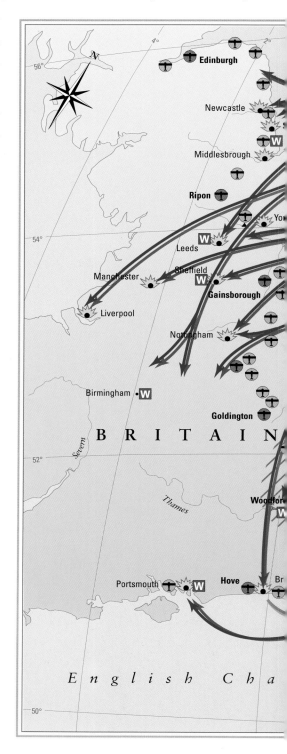

An early two-seater was the Albatros BII, a German biplane. Its performance was only marginally better than the *Taube*, but it had a much-increased range. Better was the French pusher, the Farman F40. This biplane had a top speed of 83.8 mph (135 kph), could reach 13000 ft (3,962 m), and was able to stay in the air for well over two hours. The observer had a 7.7 mm machine gun mounted in his cockpit on a swivel mounting and had the option of carrying up to 10 light bombs in racks under the fuselage. It entered service in 1915 and remained in service until 1917, by which time several hundred had been built.

The two-seater reconnaissance aircraft continued to develop through the war. The most advanced was probably the Albatros CXV, which entered service with the Germans in 1918. It was a biplane able to reach 110 mph (177 kph) and 17,000 ft (5,182 m), and designed to stay airborne for more than three hours. The observer in the rear cockpit had a 7.92 mm machine gun; the pilot had a second machine gun that fired forward.

Aircraft specialized for bombing were also being produced. Bombers needed to be able to lift the heavy weight of bombs and to have the endurance to fly them the often long distance to their target.

One of the first aircraft to be designed specifically for bombing was the British single-engine RE8. This aircraft entered service in mid-1916 and remained in service to the end of the war, even though by late 1917 it had become in effect obsolete. More than 4,000 were built. It was a biplane able to reach 102 mph (164 kph) and 13,500 ft (4,115 m) while carrying up to 225 lb (102 kg) of bombs. For defense the observer had twin .303 machine guns; the pilot had a forward-firing machine gun. The RE8 was nicknamed the Harry Tate, after a popular music-hall singer, and proved itself to be an effective bomber. However, it was vulnerable to fighters, which led to disaster in an engagement on April 13 1917 when a flight of RE8 bombers was attacked by a squadron of German aircraft. Every RE8 was shot down in less than five minutes.

Designers soon began using more than one engine in bombers, as this provided more power to lift the heavy aircraft into the air. The Russians actually had one such bomber in service when the war began:

Civilians experienced the terror of air raids in war when German Zeppelin airships first flew across the North Sea to bomb British cities, starting with the Zeppelin LZ38, which dropped its incendiaries on London on June 1 1915.

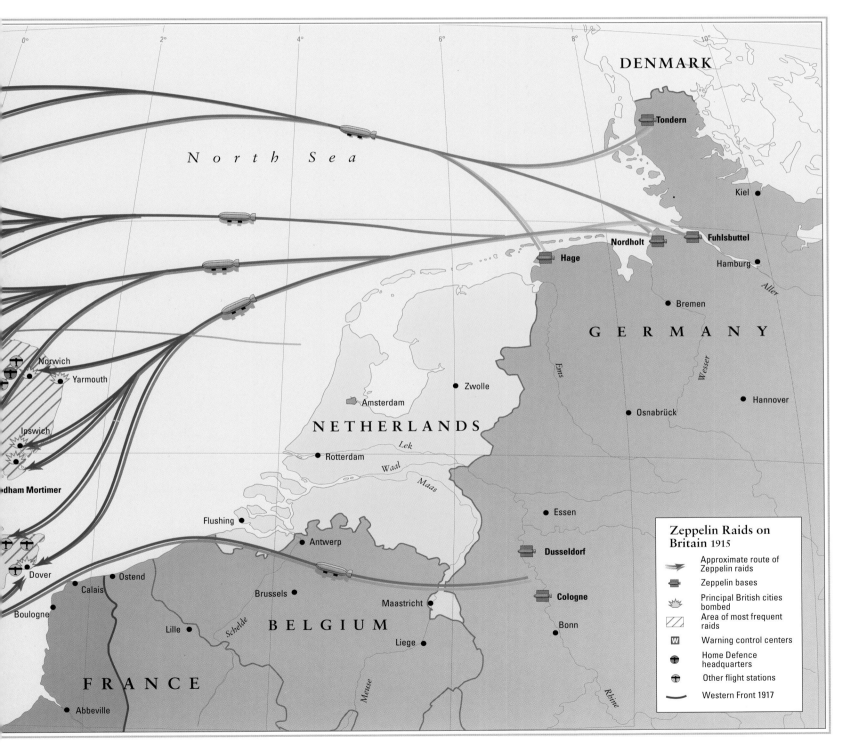

Zeppelin Raids on Britain 1915

- ➤ Approximate route of Zeppelin raids
- Zeppelin bases
- ✸ Principal British cities bombed
- ▨ Area of most frequent raids
- Ⓦ Warning control centers
- Home Defence headquarters
- Other flight stations
- Western Front 1917

the Ilea Marmosets. With a wingspan of 100 ft (30 m), this was a much larger aircraft than any other in 1914. It could lift 108 lb (49 kg) of bombs and stay airborne for up to 10 hours as it flew at a speed of 6 mph (9.6 kph) to find its target. Short on precision engineering capability and with limited use for such a weapon, the Russians built only 73 of these aircraft.

Almost as large was the Italian Capron Ca.3 of 1916. This aircraft had a 75 ft (23 m) wingspan and could lift over 3750 lb (1,700 kg) of bombs and carry them for 360 mph (579 km) at a speed of 80 mph (129 kph). It proved to be a very reliable and successful bomber despite having a defensive armament of only two machine guns. Capron later produced the monstrous Ca.4, a triplane with a wingspan of 108 (33 m). It entered service in the summer of 1918 and played little part in the war, although it seems to have been a successful bomber and a popular aircraft with its crews.

The most impressive bombing raids of the war were carried out by German Gotha bombers. With a range of over 500 miles (805 km), the Gotha G.V. was able to fly from German-occupied Belgium across the North Sea and reach London. The first raid on London was on June 13 1917. The city was unprepared for attack, so the bombers had an easy task in picking out their targets. A total of 162 people were killed and 432 were injured. Ten raids followed, but by October British defenses had improved to the extent that losses mounted and the raids were called off. A raid in May 1918 resulted in heavy losses for the Gothas, and London was not attacked again.

French built Nieuport 11, also known as "Bebe". The Nieuport 11 was also used by the British and was integral in the fight against the might of the German Fokker warplanes.

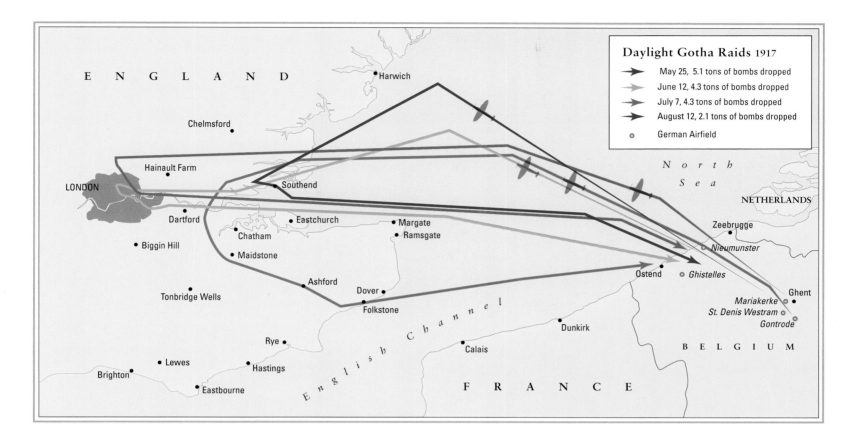

Daylight Gotha Raids 1917

→ May 25, 5.1 tons of bombs dropped
→ June 12, 4.3 tons of bombs dropped
→ July 7, 4.3 tons of bombs dropped
→ August 12, 2.1 tons of bombs dropped
◦ German Airfield

Reconnaissance aircraft and bombers had a profound effect on the war on the ground, but it was the fighters that captured the imagination of the people. The first truly effective fighter was the Fokker E1. This was an unimpressive pre-war design, but what made it special was the interrupter gear. This device was perfected by the Dutch aircraft designer Anthony Fokker, who was working for the Germans. It consisted of a rod linking the propeller hub to the machine gun in such a way that whenever a propeller blade was in front of the gun, the latter stopped firing. This enabled pilots to shoot directly forward through the propeller for the first time. Now the pilot could aim the gun simply by pointing their aircraft at the enemy.

So devastating was the new weapon that within a matter of weeks the Germans achieved total air superiority. The "Fokker Scourge", as the period became known to the Allies, saw high casualties among Allied airmen. It was not until the French Nieuport 11 entered service in January 1916 that the Allies ended the Fokker Scourge. As the rival air forces produced ever-faster and more maneuverable fighters, the men who flew them gained glamor. None was better known than Baron Manfred von Richthofen, the famous Red Baron. Richthofen gained his nickname by painting his aircraft red and insisting that all aircraft in his squadron had red on them somewhere. He shot down 80 Allied aircraft before he himself was shot down on April 1918 21.

The Red Baron was most closely associated with the Fokker Dr.1, a nimble little triplane with a top speed of 115 mph (185 kph) and a ceiling of around 20,000 ft (6,096 m). But most of the Red Baron's victories were gained in the Albatros D.III, a biplane that entered service in January 1917. There followed the notorious "Bloody April", when the Germans displayed their superiority in the air. During that month, the Allies lost 245 of their aircraft compared with a German loss of only 66. "Bloody April" was

The German Gotha heavy bomber first struck Britain with a raid on Folkestone, Kent, on May 25 1917, which killed 95 people. This and later raids made the Gotha the principal anti-civilian terror weapon in World War One.

brought to an end by the arrival of the British Sopwith Camel, with its top speed of 115 mph (185 kph) and an astonishing ability to snap around in a turn far faster than other aircraft.

Famous as the Red Baron was, most flyers recognized that Oswald Boelke was the better combat pilot. It was Boelke who developed the famous Dicta, a list of key instructions given to all new pilots. These included:

- Try to attack with the sun behind you.
- Only open fire if the enemy is in your sights.
- Always continue with an attack once you have begun.
- If you are attacked, turn to meet the enemy.
- Try to attack from behind.

Like Richthofen, Boelke did not survive the war. He died when he accidentally collided with a comrade in October 1916.

Also killed in 1916 was the first pilot to gain fame, Max Immelmann. He began the war as a reconnaissance pilot but soon transferred to fighters. In late 1915 he became known as the "Eagle of Lille" because of his string of victories above that city. Immelmann is known to have shot down 15 aircraft and may have had other victories. He is best known for developing a number of aerobatic maneuvers for use in air combat. The best known of these was the Immelmann Turn, in which he soared up steeply until his aircraft almost stalled, then flicked it over on full rudder to enter a steep dive.

Other fighter pilots too managed to gain a large number of victories. Although the system was never official, the press and public came to term any pilot who had shot down more than five enemy aircraft as

A Zeppelin airship photographed as a sinister silhouette hanging in the sky. The bombing of residential districts had a traumatic effect during the two years the air raids lasted, for it had long been supposed that home was the safest place.

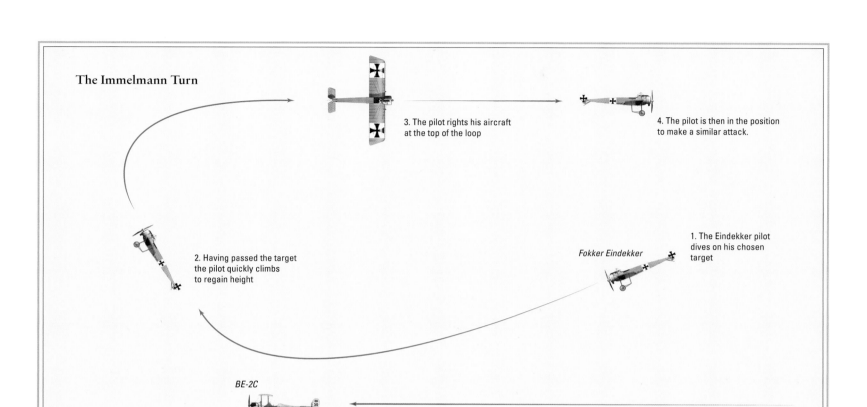

The Immelmann Turn

1. The Eindekker pilot dives on his chosen target

2. Having passed the target the pilot quickly climbs to regain height

3. The pilot rights his aircraft at the top of the loop

4. The pilot is then in the position to make a similar attack.

Fokker Eindekker

BE-2C

an "ace". Britain's Edward Mannock shot down over 70 aircraft, although exactly how many is not known. The Canadian Billy Bishop certainly shot down 72. He survived the war, returning to duty in 1939 as an air marshal of the Royal Canadian Air Force.

As well as heavier-than-air flying crafts, World War One saw the use of airships, most notably the German Zeppelins. Named for Count Zeppelin, who was largely responsible for their development, the Zeppelins were designed primarily for maritime reconnaissance. Over 1,200 scouting missions were flown over the North Sea during the war and there were many successes when the Zeppelins led German surface ships to intercept Allied convoys. In January 1915 there was a change of tactic when the Zeppelins were used to bomb British ports. The first raid, on January 19, was the bombing of Great Yarmouth and King's Lynn. The London docks were hit for the first time in March 1915. The success of these raids led to a program of numerous raids on Britain by these great airships.

The hydrogen-filled Zeppelins were vulnerable to enemy attack, as they were at risk of bursting into flames from the smallest spark. However, the great height at which they operated continued to keep them safe, that is until a raid on September 2, 1916 when a Zeppelin was shot down. Lieutenant William Robinson, flying a BE2c fighter, managed to get alongside Zeppelin SL11 over Hertfordshire and opened fire. The airship burst into flames immediately and crashed, killing all on board. Robinson was awarded the Victoria Cross for bravery and eagerly passed on to other pilots the method of attack he had used extinguish the airship.

By the spring of 1917 it was recognized that Zeppelins had become too vulnerable to attack from enemy aircraft to continue to be used for bombing raids. They were returned to their naval duties, where they could operate reconnaissance missions out of range of British land-based aircraft.

The Immelman Turn was a dogfighting tactic in aerial warfare devised by Max Immelman, a German air ace of World War One. The Turn enabled a pilot to escape an enemy aircraft following him and reverse their relative positions.

POISON GAS

THE HAGUE TREATY OF 1899 SPECIFICALLY BANNED THE USE OF POISON GAS IN WARFARE. DESPITE THIS THE WEAPON WOULD BE USED BY BOTH SIDES DURING WORLD WAR ONE, USUALLY WITH HORRIFIC RESULTS FOR THOSE AFFECTED.

Signed in 1899 by most European nations, the Hague Convention laid down many rules for the conduct of war, the treatment of prisoners and other matters. At the time it was widely believed that poison gas of all types had been banned. However, the actual wording of the relevant clause stated: 'The Contracting Powers agree to abstain from the use of projectiles the object of which is the diffusion of asphyxiating or deleterious gases.' That wording would be important as soon as World War One broke out.

It was the French who first used gas. In fighting in Alsace in August 1914, the French preceded their attacks on prepared German defences with hand grenades containing an ethyl-based tear gas. The grenades were so ineffective that the Germans did not even notice them. Tear gas was used again in November, with only slightly better results. The Germans retaliated in October against British positions near Ypres, but there too the gas had little effect.

The Germans believed that the tear gas had not worked because it had been used in small quantities. On January 31 1915 a total of 18,000 shells containing tear gas were fired at Russian lines near Warsaw. This huge concentration failed to have any effect: the weather was so cold that the gas froze solid in puddles on the ground.

All the while, the Germans had been stockpiling deadly chlorine gas. On April 22 1915 a total of 152 tonnes of chlorine gas in 5,700 cylinders was distributed to German units along the trenches at Ypres. Starting at 5 p.m. the Germans opened the valves of the cylinders and pushed them over the top of their trenches into no man's land. The gray-green gas spurted out, formed a large cloud and was carried toward the Allied lines by a gentle easterly breeze.

First to be struck by the gas was a division of French Algerian troops. As men began to fall down dead and others began clawing at their throats in agony, the rest turned and fled. They were swiftly

Opposite page: The French were the first to use gas as a weapon in World War One, in August 1914. The gas used by the French, containing xylyl bromide, was not fatal, unlike the poison chlorine gas used by the Germans at Ypres eight months later.

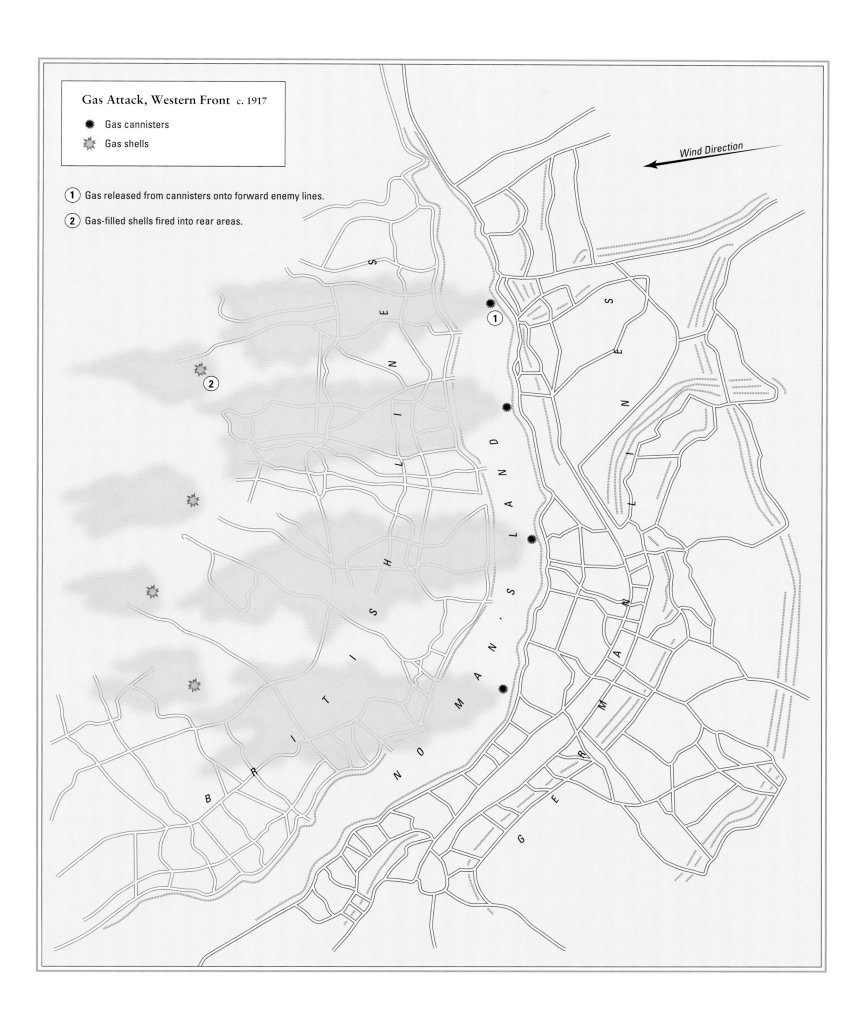

Gas Attack, Western Front c. 1917

✳ Gas cannisters
✴ Gas shells

① Gas released from cannisters onto forward enemy lines.

② Gas-filled shells fired into rear areas.

Wind Direction

followed by a Senegalese unit and regular French regiments. A stretch of trenches of approximately 23,000 ft (7,315 m) wide was simply abandoned as the men fled the gas. To the north a Canadian division was struck by the edges of the deadly cloud. Some men fled; others ran only as far as nearby trenches where the gas did not reach. Confusion spread. At 5:50, the fleeing men reached the town of Ypres; 10 minutes later the gas followed them. By now the gas was dissipating, but it could still be fatal. An officer in the Durham Light Infantry who had been a chemist before the war recognized the smell and ordered his men to urinate into handkerchiefs and wrap them around their faces — the ammonia in the urine blocked the chlorine. He led his men forward into the gas, to find the trenches empty.

On the German side, the infantry were refusing to advance until the foul, deadly gas had dissipated. Chlorine gas is heavier than air, so it lurked in the abandoned French trenches long after it was blown away on the surface. The Canadians were meanwhile hurrying south to take over machine guns abandoned by the French and to jump into the trenches that were clear of gas. By the time a German attack was sent in, it was too late.

Within days British and French troops were issued with rudimentary face pads made of folded cloth impregnated with chemicals that would filter out the gas. The British also protested that the gas attack had breached the Hague Convention. The Germans responded that they had not used shells to deliver the gas and so had not broken the letter of the rules.

The British tried using gas at the Battle of Loos in September 1915, but the wind changed and blew it back to the British lines. The French had developed phosgene, which had the advantage of being colorless and almost odorless and thus difficult to detect, but it was slower-acting than chlorine. The two gases were usually used together in a mixture called "white star gas" by the Allies, owing to the labels attached to the cylinders. The Germans quickly copied the mixture, using it for the first time in December 1915.

In July 1917 the Germans unleashed a new gas that was soon dubbed "mustard gas" by the British. The gas was less deadly than phosgene but it disabled men much more quickly. Mustard gas had the effect of inflaming all mucus membranes, especially those of the throat and eyes, resulting in choking and blindness. In severe cases the skin would erupt in yellowish blisters and vomiting would occur. In such cases death was invariable after an agonizing illness that could last weeks. Mustard gas was for this reason greatly feared even though it was usually less fatal than the other gases. Mustard gas was more long-lived in the environment than the earlier forms of poison. It could seep into the soil and afflict those who turned the soil over even several days later. On occasion the Germans fired shells containing mustard gas into areas that were on the flanks of the section of line they were about to attack. It was intended that the gas would make the areas impossible to use, thus guarding the flanks of the advancing troops.

In all about 100,000 men are believed to have died as a result of poison gas during World War One. In terms of the total death toll, this was a relatively small figure. However, the injuries inflicted by gas were often horrible, and the gas had a profound psychological effect on many who encountered it. Certainly the need for men to wear gas masks, hoods, and overalls whenever a gas attack was suspected contributed greatly to the miseries of trench warfare. In 1925 the Geneva Protocol was signed, banning all uses of poison gas. In World War Two, all combatant nations had sizeable stockpiles of poison gas. However, none of them used the gas in battle, because of fear that enemy sides would use it in retaliationor might have developed more deadly forms since the previous war.

This French soldier and his dog are shown wearing crude gas masks as a defense against gas attacks during World War One. Gas was forbidden under the Hague Convention of 1899, but that did not stop it being used.

SUBMARINE WARFARE

THE GERMAN U-BOAT CAME CLOSE TO WINNING WORLD WAR ONE.
BUT DECISIVE ACTION BY THE ROYAL NAVY CURBED THE THREAT, AND
THE MAIN EFFECT OF THE U-BOAT CAMPAIGN WAS TO BRING THE
U.S. INTO THE WAR – WITH DISASTROUS RESULTS FOR GERMANY.

The submarines of 1914 had one great advantage in warfare but several serious drawbacks. Their main advantage was that they could submerge beneath the waves, where they would be invisible to lookouts on ships and, in view of the restricted technology of the time, beyond the reach of any weapons. The drawbacks to the submarine included its slow speed — 12 knots on the surface and 8 knots when submerged — and the facts that it could stay submerged for only a few hours and had a limited range: it could not venture more than a few hundred miles from base. Furthermore, submarines could carry only three or four torpedoes, which were generally reserved for use against warships. Their main weapon against merchant ships was the gun, and that involved surfacing.

In the opening months of the war, the German Navy under Admiral von Tirpitz aimed to destroy the British Grand Fleet and gain control of the seas. Submarines, or U-boats (*Unterseeboot*), were put to work to help achieve this aim. Given their slow speed, U-boats could neither keep up with German warships nor chase British ones. Instead their captains sought to position their U-boats in places where they guessed British ships would be encountered.

On September 22 1914 the tactic was used with great success when U-9 sank three British cruisers in an action lasting less than an hour. Another cruiser was sunk in October, and in December the battleship *Formidable* was sunk by U-24. Early in 1915 the British realized that a U-boat commander needed time to aim his torpedoes, taking into account the speed and heading of the target ship. By altering speed regularly and following a zigzag course warships would be safe from attack. No more warships were to be sunk by U-boats.

The Germans had by this time changed strategy. Britain would now be starved into surrender by blockade. But international agreements to which Germany was a party forbade sinking a merchant

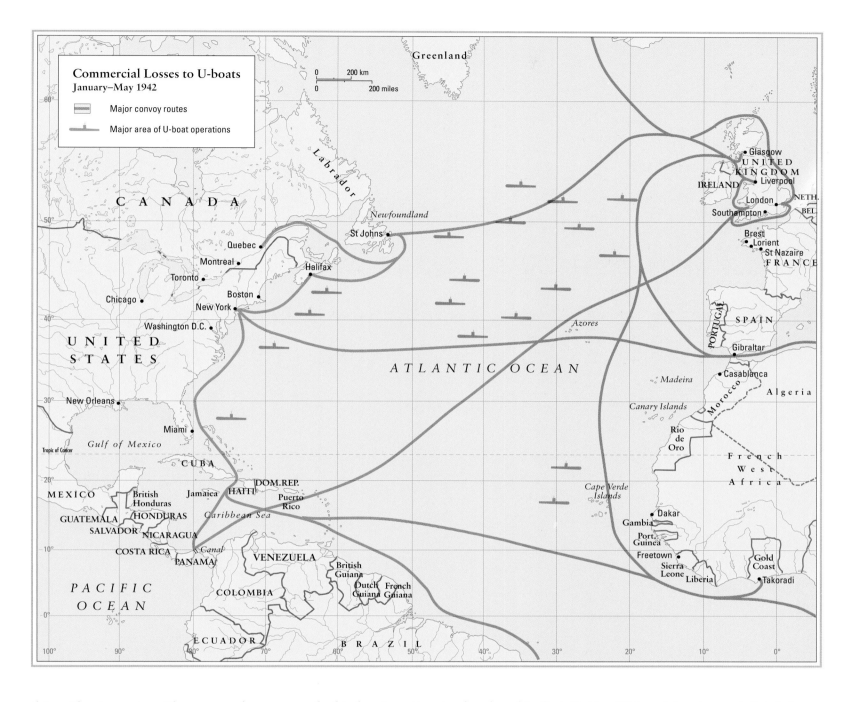

Commercial Losses to U-boats
January–May 1942

— Major convoy routes

— Major area of U-boat operations

ship without warning. The crew and passengers had to be given time to abandon ship first. But by 1915 most merchant ships had radios and could send out distress signals. Given the U-boat's slow speed, it was unlikely that a U-boat could evade the fast destroyers that would race to the merchant ship's aid. The Germans therefore decided to declare unrestricted naval warfare within an area covering the sea approaches to Britain. Within this area, all ships would be sunk on sight.

Neutral governments were appalled. They protested that their ships heading for other neutral states such as Norway or the Netherlands frequently used these areas. The Germans promised to try to avoid such attacks, advising neutral ships to fly prominent flags. Inevitably mistakes occurred. The most famous incident was when U-20 sank the liner *Lusitania* on May 7 1915 off Ireland. A total of 1,198 people died, 128 of them U.S. citizens. The American public was outraged, and President Woodrow Wilson protested in such strong terms that the Germans modified their campaign and then called it off altogether.

Submarines made their first impact in action during World War One, as a means of preventing military and other supplies reaching Europe from the Americas. Unrestricted submarine warfare was announced by the Germans on January 9, 1917.

Opposite page: During World War One the production of German submarines and the number of Allied ships they sank peaked in 1917. The Germans produced specialized submarines, some of which could carry 48 mines as well as torpedoes. Others carried deck guns.

Thereafter U-boats operated farther afield, where targets were harder to come by but British naval ships were less likely to intervene. U-boat attacks were made on the surface using guns, in response, the British began using Q-ships, merchant ships with concealed weapons and naval crews. If a U-boat surfaced to attack, the naval flag was raised and the guns were revealed and brought into action. At the same time, normal merchant ships were given guns with naval crews. Those without guns were advised to try to ram any U-boat that surfaced. Although the merchant ships claimed relatively few U-boats, the new, aggressive tactics caused U-boat captains to surface and begin their attack at a great range, which enabled the faster merchant ships to get away. The British realized that the U-boats were reaching the open ocean by traveling through the heavily patrolled English Channel when submerged. A massive steel net was, therefore, strung across it from England to France. Dubbed the "Dover Barrage", the net was festooned with mines. The barrage had to have safe channels for the passage of Allied ships and thus was not a complete block on U-boat activity. Nevertheless it did restrict their movements.

The Germans had by this time developed a mechanism by which mines could be laid by a submerged U-boat. These were first used to lay mines off British ports in the summer of 1915. Once the British realized what was happening, there were few losses of ships to mines; but the approaches to ports had to be swept routinely by minesweepers, which took much time and effort.

In 1916 the British introduced the depth charge, an explosive device set to go off at a predetermined depth. Finally they had a weapon that could reach the U-boat when it was submerged. The U-boat still had to be found, of course, and that was usually possible only if the warship saw it submerge and got to the spot quickly enough to be reasonably certain that the U-boat was in the immediate area. Throughout this time of changing tactics the U-boat had a profound impact on the surface fleets. After the successes of 1914, British admirals had a perpetual fear that they might steam into a U-boat ambush. On several occasions British warships failed to follow up an advantage in battle when their German protagonists turned away suddenly. Worried that they were about to be led into a U-boat ambush, the British declined to follow, allowing the German ships to escape.

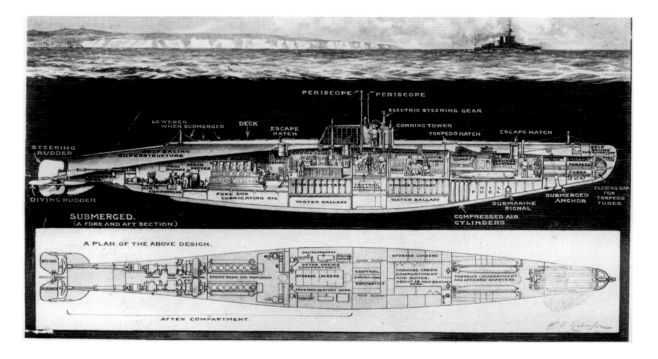

A Bristish magazine drawing showing a German U-boat on patrol in the English Channel. Including the U-boat in cutaway and as a plan of the internal layout of the submarine.

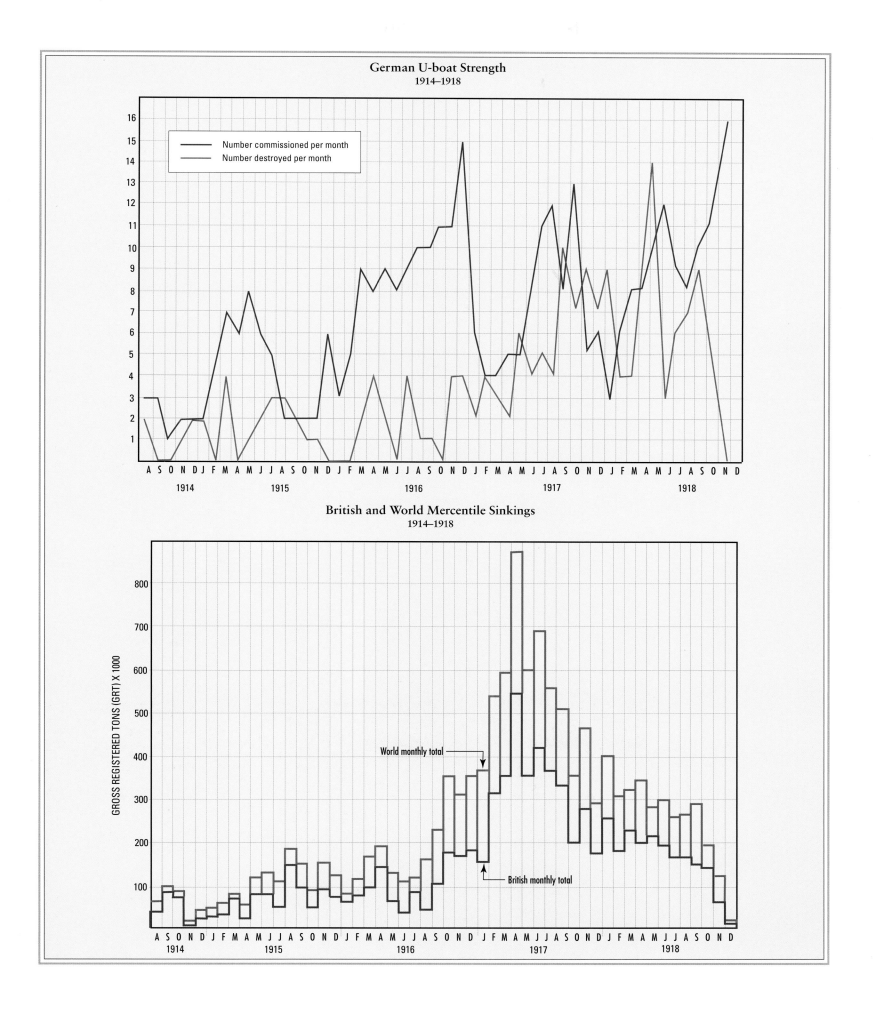

German U-boat Strength
1914–1918

Number commissioned per month
Number destroyed per month

16
15
14
13
12
11
10
9
8
7
6
5
4
3
2
1

A S O N D J F M A M J J A S O N D J F M A M J J A S O N D J F M A M J J A S O N D J F M A M J J A S O N D
1914   1915   1916   1917   1918

British and World Mercentile Sinkings
1914–1918

GROSS REGISTERED TONS (GRT) X 1000

800
700
600
500
400
300
200
100

World monthly total

British monthly total

A S O N D J F M A M J J A S O N D J F M A M J J A S O N D J F M A M J J A S O N D J F M A M J J A S O N D
1914   1915   1916   1917   1918

Opposite page: Merchant shipping sailed in convoy for safety in both world wars. After the Germans' successes in World War One, the Treaty of Versailles (1919) banned them from building submarines. They were constructed nevertheless and posed deadly danger to Allied shipping in World War Two.

By late 1916 Germany's prospects were deteriorating. The naval chiefs asked the Kaiser to approve a resumption of unrestricted U-boat warfare and the campaign began in February 1917. British merchant losses soared. In January only 83,775 tons (76,204 tonnes) of shipping had been lost. In February that leapt to 559,974 tons (508,023 tonnes) and to 962,318 tons (873,800 tonnes) in April. By May, Britain had food stocks left for only six weeks. However, the resumption of unrestricted U-boat warfare caused the U.S. to cut off all diplomatic ties with Germany immediately and issue an ultimatum. When Germany persisted with her actions, the U.S. declared war on April 6 1917. The U.S supplied large numbers of destroyers and other ships to escort convoys across the Atlantic. Monthly merchant shipping losses fell to 392,000 tons (355,616 tonnes). This was still serious, but ship-building industries could replace these losses and crucially Britain began to receive more food than it was consuming. The crisis was over.

Late in 1917 the new, Type-151 U-boats entered service. These were much larger than earlier models, carrying 18 torpedoes and dozens of mines. They had a range of 25,000 miles (40,234 km). In the spring of 1918 they were sent to the eastern seaboard of the U.S., an area previously free of U-boat activity. In their first foray 23 ships were sunk without loss. A later voyage was less successful, with one U-boat lost and fewer merchant ships sunk. The U-boat campaign continued until the end of the war. In October 1918 a total of 120,402 tonnes of merchant shipping was sunk by U-boats. As the Germans never had more than 133 U-boats, half of which always were under repair or maintenance, being resupplied, or in harbor for other reasons, the U-boat fleet did remarkably well. They almost brought Britain to the brink of starvation. It was a lesson that one German U-boat officer, Karl Donitz, would learn and remember.

This graph from World War Two shows monthly losses of Allied and Neutral ships at sea from German U-boat and other raider activity. The graph also reveals that losses reduced after improved defense against attacks was introduced in 1943.

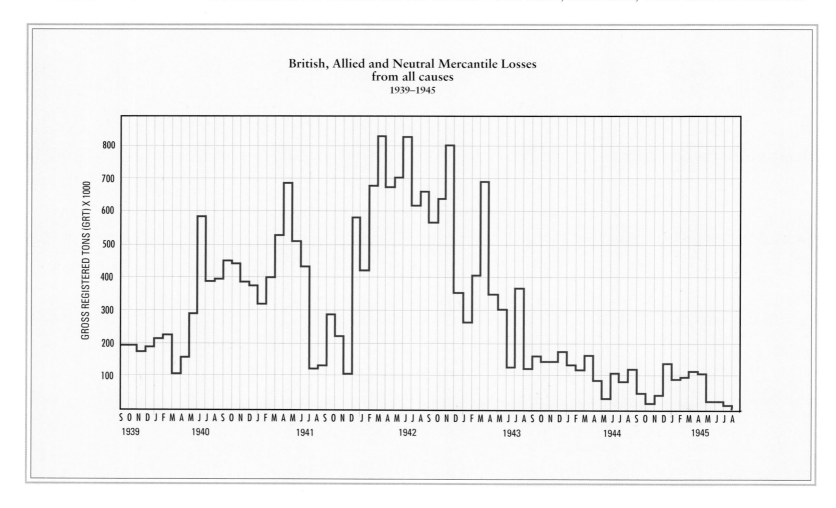

British, Allied and Neutral Mercantile Losses
from all causes
1939–1945

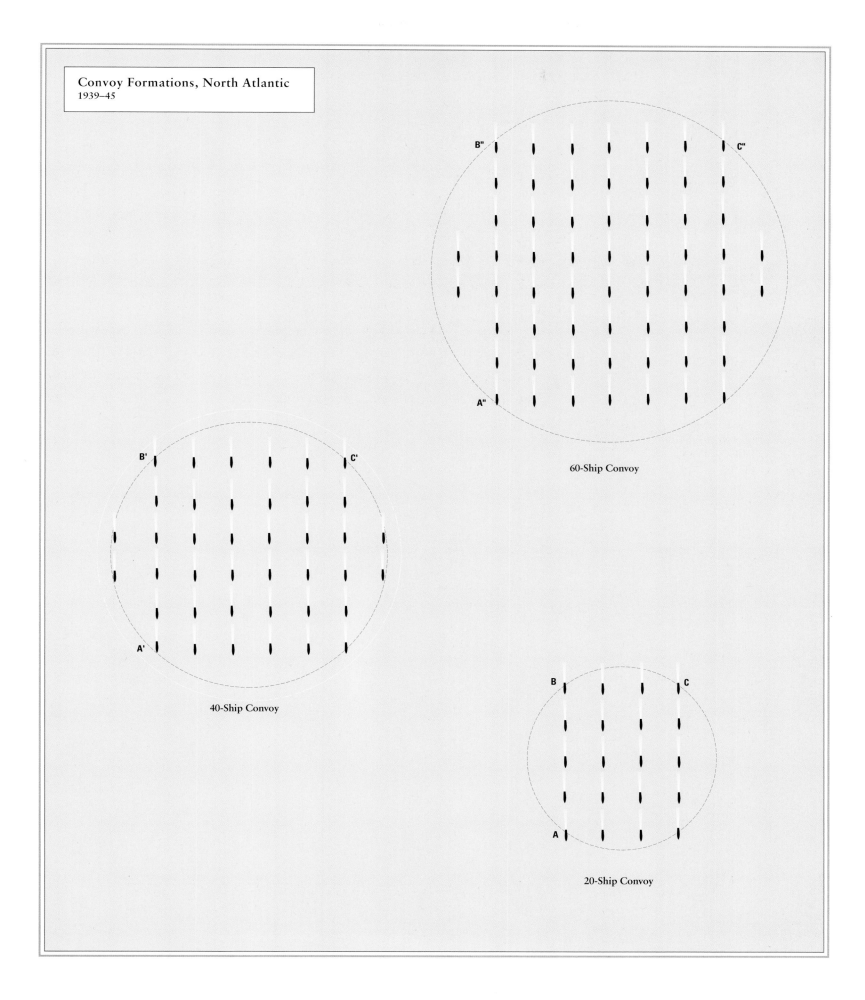

Convoy Formations, North Atlantic
1939–45

60-Ship Convoy

40-Ship Convoy

20-Ship Convoy

DREADNOUGHT BATTLESHIPS

THE DREADNOUGHT BATTLESHIPS WERE THE MOST POWERFUL WEAPONS AFLOAT IN 1914. NAVAL COMMANDERS EXPECTED THE NAVAL WAR TO BE DECIDED BY A CATACLYSMIC CLASH OF THESE POWERFUL WARSHIPS, BUT THIS NEVER HAPPENED.

Opposite page: The Royal Navy suffered a severe defeat at the Battle of Coronel on November 1, 1914, but wreaked their revenge on December 8 when they located and vanquished the German cruiser squadron responsible at the Battle of the Falkland Islands.

There was a grim joke in Britain during World War One that Admiral Sir John Jellicoe, commander of the Grand Fleet, was the only man who could lose the war in an afternoon. There was much truth in this. Jellicoe commanded the main battle fleet of the Royal Navy. If it were sunk or crippled, the German Navy would control the seas, cut Britain off from overseas supplies, and starve it into submission.

The destructive power of the big guns of large naval ships was immense. Merchant ships could be sunk with ease at ranges counted in miles. Coastal towns could be reduced to rubble in minutes. Port facilities could be destroyed with ease. Once a fleet had undisputed control of the seas, the damage it could inflict on an enemy was great. But to achieve that the rival fleet first had to be found and destroyed.

Most navies had several classes of warship, as well as submarines, coastal patrol craft, minesweepers, and other specialist crafts. The smallest of these were destroyers, used to hunt for submarines and torpedo boats. Then there were cruisers, designed as long-distance raiders and armed with guns up to 8 inches in caliber and with a large hold to store coal for long voyages. Larger than cruisers were the heavy cruisers, also termed battlecruisers. These great ships had guns of up to 13 inches in caliber and were extremely fast, but achieved their speed by forgoing heavy armor. They had been designed as raiders, like cruisers, but their huge guns tempted many admirals to use them in warship battles. Most powerful of all were the battleships, armed with 12-inch, 14-inch, or even 15-inch guns and protected by thick armor plating. As their name suggests, battleships were intended to fight battles against other warships.

When the war began, the German admiral Graf von Spee was at German-ruled islands in the Pacific with two heavy cruisers and three light cruisers. Other German cruisers were in the Pacific and Indian

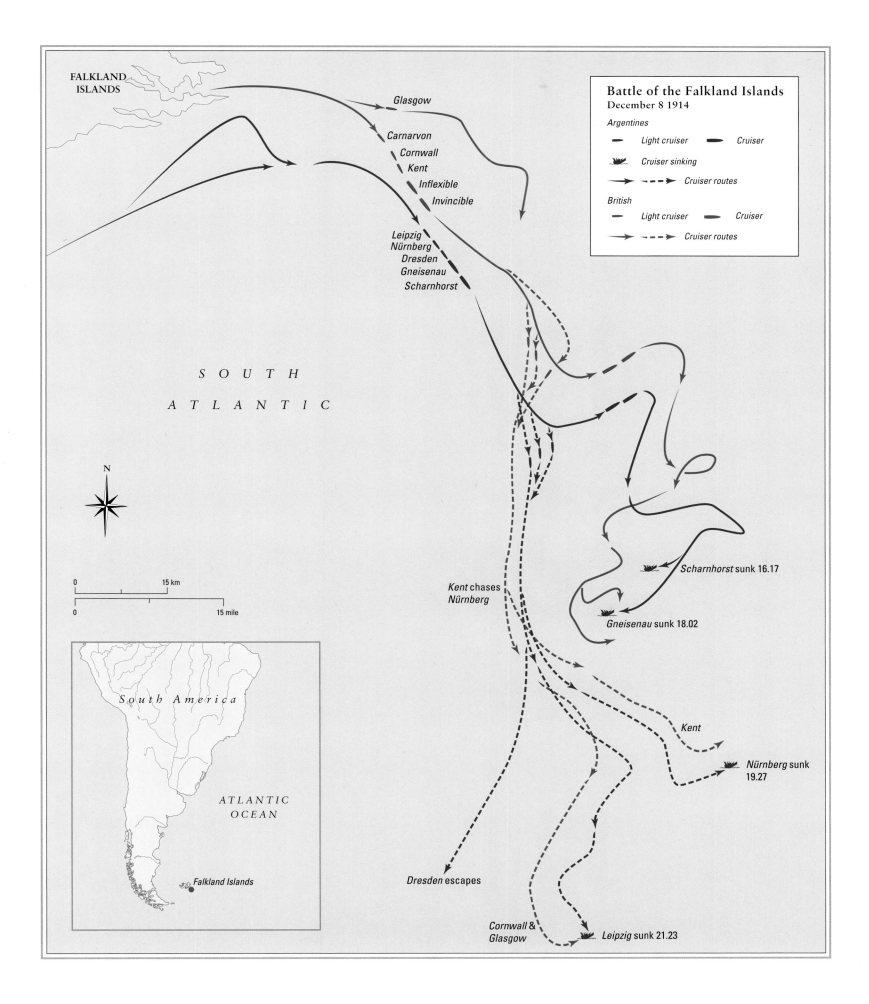

FALKLAND
ISLANDS

Glasgow

Carnarvon

Cornwall

Kent

Inflexible

Invincible

Leipzig
Nürnberg
Dresden
Gneisenau
Scharnhorst

Battle of the Falkland Islands
December 8 1914

Argentines

Light cruiser   Cruiser

Cruiser sinking

Cruiser routes

British

Light cruiser   Cruiser

Cruiser routes

S O U T H

A T L A N T I C

N

0   15 km

0   15 mile

Kent chases
Nürnberg

Scharnhorst sunk 16.17

Gneisenau sunk 18.02

Kent

Nürnberg sunk
19.27

South America

ATLANTIC
OCEAN

Falkland Islands

Dresden escapes

Cornwall &
Glasgow

Leipzig sunk 21.23

F. M. Panzerkreuzer „Seydlitz".

HMS Seydlitz, launched in 1913, was a cruiser of the Imperial German Navy in World War One. *Seydlitz* saw action in the North and Baltic Seas but was scuttled in 1919 along with the rest of the German fleet.

Oceans. Between them they sank dozens of merchant ships, bombarded Madras, and sank a Russian cruiser. In October, von Spee steamed to the west coast of South America to prey on British ships in that area. He was met off Coronel on November 1 by the British Admiral Sir Christopher Craddock, who had two cruisers and two light cruisers. The Germans opened fire at a range of 36,000 ft (10,973 m). Both British cruisers were quickly sunk and Craddock was killed, but the light cruisers were able to use their speed to escape.

Von Spee then received orders from Germany to return home. He abandoned his attacks on merchant ships, steamed around Cape Horn, and was heading north when he encountered a second force of British cruisers off the Falkland Islands. Admiral Sir Doveton Sturdee had three cruisers and two of the most modern battlecruisers mounting 12 in (30 cm guns). After a battle lasting over four hours, four of the five German ships were sunk. The *Dresden* got away.

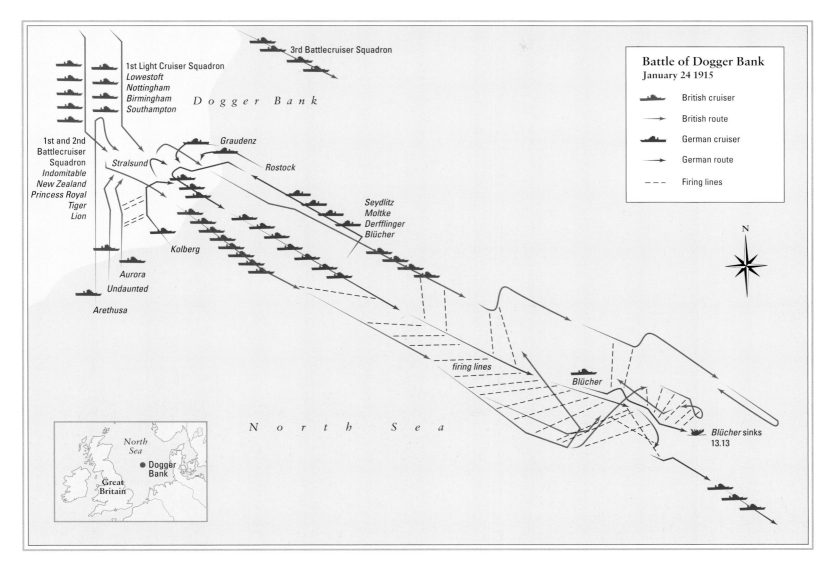

Battle of Dogger Bank
January 24 1915

3rd Battlecruiser Squadron

1st Light Cruiser Squadron
Lowestoft
Nottingham
Birmingham
Southampton

D o g g e r   B a n k

British cruiser

British route

German cruiser

German route

Firing lines

1st and 2nd
Battlecruiser
Squadron
Indomitable
New Zealand
Princess Royal
Tiger
Lion

Stralsund

Graudenz

Rostock

Seydlitz
Moltke
Derfflinger
Blücher

Kolberg

N

Aurora

Undaunted

Arethusa

firing lines

Blücher

N o r t h   S e a

Blücher sinks
13.13

*North
Sea*

● *Dogger
Bank*

*Great
Britain*

Isolated German cruisers would continue to plague merchant ships in distant waters until the last of them, the *Konigsberg*, was sunk in July 1915. By that time, the main naval focus of the war had shifted to the North Sea. As soon as war was declared, the British Navy announced a blockade of Germany. Warships patrolled the English Channel and the northern entrance to the North Sea. All German merchant ships were captured and all neutral ships were searched. Ships heading for Germany were allowed to take only goods of no possible use to the war effort. Anything the British considered would be of use to the Germans was removed and compensation was paid. The policy did no immediate harm to Germany, but as the war dragged on the blockade took effect.

On November 3 1914 German battle cruisers raced across the North Sea, bombarded Great Yarmouth, and returned home safely. On December 16 Hartlepool, Scarborough, and Whitby were shelled by German ships, which again got home without incident. On January 13, 1915, the German battlecruisers came out again, to attack the British Dogger Bank fishing fleet. But this time five British battlecruisers were in the area under Admiral David Beatty. In the battle of Dogger Bank, one German battle cruiser was sunk and one was damaged; Britain had one battle cruiser badly damaged.

The next months saw several raids and counter-raids. The Germans generally had the upper hand in these small encounters. For example, a flotilla of British minesweepers was wiped out in February

On January 24 1915, at the Dogger Bank (North Sea), the Royal Navy intercepted cruisers of the German Grand Fleet on their way to raiding the English coast. The Navy sank a heavy cruiser, but tho other German ships got away.

Opposite page: The Battle of Jutland, 3 May 1916, between the Royal Navy and the German High Seas Fleet was the greatest naval battle of World War One. The outcome was a draw, but the German fleet never challenged the Royal Navy again.

by German light cruisers. In April Lowestoft was shelled heavily and the attackers escaped home. Most operations, however, ended in fruitless maneuvering, with few if any shells fired in anger.

Then, on May 31 1916, Admiral Reinhard Scheer ordered the German battlecruisers under Admiral von Hipper to steam up the Norwegian coast and attack British shipping. Von Hipper followed with the main High Seas Fleet of battleships in case British battleships appeared. In fact, the British had intercepted some careless radio signals and knew that Hipper was at sea. British battlecruisers under Beatty set out to intercept. Jellicoe followed with the Grand Fleet of battleships in case Beatty needed support. Both fleets had cruisers and destroyers out acting as scouts.

Early in the afternoon a British cruiser and a German cruiser sighted each other. Both sent signals alerting their battlecruiser squadrons. Beatty and Hipper raced to the scene and opened fire on each other at 3:45 p.m. Two British ships were quickly sunk and a third was crippled. "There seems to be something wrong with our bloody ships today", remarked Beatty.

Von Hipper then turned south, as if heading for home, but in reality he was luring Beatty towards Scheer and the German battleships. At 4:58 p.m. Scheer opened fire, and Beatty turned his battle cruisers around. Now he was luring Scheer toward Jellicoe, and the great conflict between battleships seemed set to happen. At 6:17 p.m. the main battle fleets came in sight of each other and opened fire. But mist came down and gave Scheer the opportunity to turn away with his outnumbered battleships. At 7:10 p.m. the battleships again sighted each other and opened fire, but again Scheer slipped away into mist. At dusk the battlecruisers sighted each other and opened fire, but then night fell. More sporadic fighting took place in the night between individual ships. By dawn, Scheer was safely back at base.

The Battle of Jutland had cost the British three battlecruisers, three cruisers, and eight destroyers. The Germans lost one battleship, one battlecruiser, four cruisers, and five destroyers. In terms of numbers it had been a draw, but in the long term it was clear that the British had won a major victory. Scheer had been deeply shaken by the battle. Never again did he sanction a major sortie that risked his whole fleet. The High Seas Fleet spent the rest of the war lying idle in harbor.

Jellicoe's great warships were far from idle. They continued to enforce the blockade, and by the end of 1917 a lack of raw materials was affecting German war industries. Also, big-gun ships were sent to shell German trenches, barracks, and ammunition dumps close to the Belgian coast.

On April 22 1918 the Grand Fleet launched the Zeebrugge Raid. The Belgian port was being used as a base by German U-boats, and the aim of the raid was to close the narrow harbor entrance. The attack began just before midnight with an intensive bombardment by big-gun ships while lighter craft dashed in at high speed to lay down a smokescreen. Three ships filled with concrete were steamed into the harbour entrance and sunk while a third, packed with explosives, was tied to the harbor wall and detonated. At the same time, parties of marines and engineers had stormed ashore to blow up the harbor facilities. The plan worked well, even though the German defenses were stronger than expected. Owing to their ingenuity and engineering skills, the Germans had the port back in partial operation by May 14.

On October 29, 1918 the German High Seas Fleet erupted in mutiny. It was the first of a series of disaffections that spread throughout all the German armed forces. On November 11 the Germans agreed an armistice. The war was over.

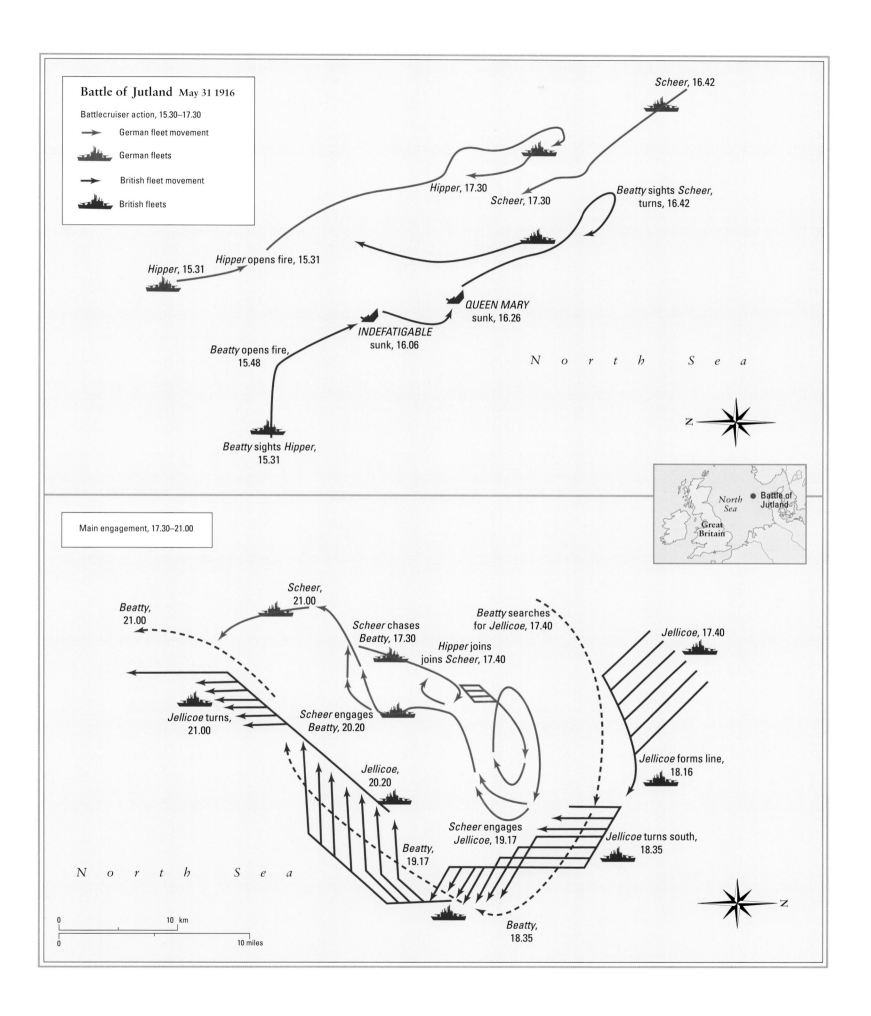

Battle of Jutland May 31 1916

Battlecruiser action, 15.30–17.30

→ German fleet movement

German fleets

→ British fleet movement

British fleets

Scheer, 16.42

Hipper, 17.30

Scheer, 17.30

Beatty sights *Scheer*, turns, 16.42

Hipper opens fire, 15.31

Hipper, 15.31

QUEEN MARY sunk, 16.26

Beatty opens fire, 15.48

INDEFATIGABLE sunk, 16.06

N o r t h   S e a

Beatty sights *Hipper*, 15.31

North Sea *Great Britain* *Battle of Jutland*

Main engagement, 17.30–21.00

Beatty, 21.00

Scheer, 21.00

Scheer chases *Beatty*, 17.30

Beatty searches for *Jellicoe*, 17.40

Jellicoe, 17.40

Hipper joins *Scheer*, 17.40

Jellicoe turns, 21.00

Scheer engages *Beatty*, 20.20

Jellicoe, 20.20

Jellicoe forms line, 18.16

Beatty, 19.17

Scheer engages *Jellicoe*, 19.17

Jellicoe turns south, 18.35

N o r t h   S e a

Beatty, 18.35

0   10 km

0   10 miles

BETWEEN THE WARS

THE PERIOD BETWEEN THE TWO GREAT WARS OF THE 20TH CENTURY LASTED JUST 20 YEARS. IN MILITARY TERMS THERE WERE SIGNIFICANT ADVANCES IN BOTH TECHNOLOGY AND TACTICS DURING THAT PERIOD, BUT THESE CHANGES WERE NOT RECOGNIZED BY ALL. MANY SENIOR COMMANDERS, POLITICIANS AND ALSO RANK-AND-FILE MEN EXPECTED THE WAR THAT BROKE OUT IN 1939 TO BE FOUGHT ALONG LINES BROADLY SIMILAR TO THAT OF 1914–1918. THEY COULD NOT HAVE BEEN MORE WRONG.

The years immediately after the coming of peace in 1918 were ones of disarmament and massive cuts in spending on the military. This was understandable. The combatant nations could now devote their wealth to more peaceful pursuits. There was also a deeply held feeling that the Great War, as it was then called, had been a "war to end all wars". So great had been the carnage, so heavy the death toll, and so costly the expense of the war that many thought it proved war was not worth the cost.

The founding of the League of Nations as an international organization through which the states of the world could discuss their disagreements and reach a peaceful resolution gave hope to many that the era of armed conflict was truly over. Never again, it was thought, would the world's civilized nations go to war for selfish ends.

At first it seemed as though those hopes would be fulfilled. Both Poland and Germany claimed the mineral-rich area known as Upper Silesia. In 1921 a plebiscite was held in the area and the population voted to join Poland. Germany respected the decision. In 1923 a group of Italian diplomats in Albania was ambushed and killed near the Greek border. The Italians claimed the Greeks were to blame and sent warships to the Greek coast. The dispute was settled by the League of Nations, which decided that

Opposite page: European territories after World War One. Compare this map with the one on page 221. Poland, Czechoslovakia, and Yugoslavia gained their independence and a "corridor" had been created out of German territory to allow Poland access to the Baltic Sea.

Europe in 1919–1920

Greece had to pay compensation even though the killers were never identified. Both Greece and Italy accepted the decision.

But even as peace seemed possible on the world stage, everyone accepted that there would be a role for the armed forces. Britain, France, and other colonial powers faced routine and numerous border clashes with tribes and peoples who were not part of the League of Nations. British India, for instance, fought a war against Afghanistan in 1919, and tribal wars in the area were endemic.

The response of most countries was to maintain their armed forces at a level commensurate with the threat. The British and the French maintained their land armies with infantry and artillery, and with a reduced cavalry force, to patrol their empires. Both put many warships into storage, scrapped older ships and did not order new ones. Their air forces also saw little in the way of new hardware. Large numbers of aircraft of old design were used to patrol the borders of the colonies while a handful of new aircraft impressed crowds at air displays.

The first signs of rearmament came in an unexpected area, the Pacific. During World War One, Japan had seized the German colonies in the Pacific and on the Asian mainland. It kept them after 1918 and soon began developing them into the basis of a maritime empire and sought to formalize long-standing Japanese influence in Korea and Manchuria. This led to the Washington Naval Treaty of 1922, signed by Britain, Japan, France, Italy, and the United States.

The treaty sought to avoid a naval arms race and to preserve a balance of power in the western Pacific that would ensure no country had such a preponderance of naval power that it might be tempted to go to war seeking easy victory. The treaty regulated the size of battleships, the size of the guns they could carry, and how many ships each country could have. It also laid down rules about the new-fangled aircraft carriers then under construction. It reflected the naval thinking that had emerged from World War One. This saw the battleship as the most important ship in the navy, it was expected to win battles and thereby wars. The few battles fought between the navies of Britain and Germany had been decided by gunfire. Generally the bigger ships with the bigger guns had won. All other kinds of ship were seen as auxiliary to the big-gun battleships. Torpedo-armed submarines had scored some successes over big ships early on

in the war, but improved tactics had ended that threat. German U-boats had come close to imposing an economic stranglehold on Britain, but again it was thought that this threat had been contained by the use of escorted convoys and improved tactics. Cruisers of various sizes had been useful for raiding but had proved to be vulnerable in pitched battles.

Messerschmitt Bf-109 (Gustav) in flight.

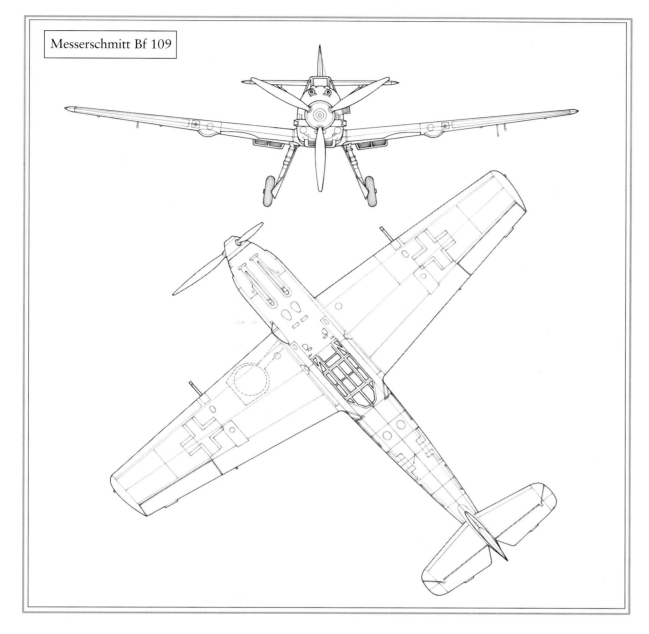

Messerschmitt Bf 109

The Messerschmitt Bf 109 fighter was to feature in World War Two as one of the German Luftwaffe's best aircraft. However, when it was developed in the mid-1930s Germany was forbidden to have an air force.

In the latter 1920s, the Japanese began to push at the limitations of the Washington Naval Treaty by constructing a new class of destroyer, the *Fubuki* class. At over 2240 tons (2,032 tonnes), it was bigger than contemporary destroyers and was armed with six 127 mm guns, nine torpedo tubes, and numerous depth charges and anti-aircraft machine guns. The ships incorporated a number of technological advances, such as fully enclosed gun turrets for the lighter guns and armored torpedo tubes. The *Furutaka* class of heavy cruiser mounted a main armament of six 8-inch guns, but like destroyers it also had torpedoes, anti-aircraft guns, and depth charges. They were also very fast, being able to achieve 35 knots.

The large number of anti-aircraft guns on the new Japanese ships was due to a series of experiments carried out in 1921 by the American air service officer General Billy Mitchell. Mitchell believed that the bomber aircraft could revolutionize war, and set out to prove his theories by attacking the old German battleship Ostfriesland with bombs. The tests included light bombs and heavy bombs. As Mitchell expected, the light bombs inflicted only superficial damage. The three heavy 2,000 lb (907 kg) bombs sent the battleship to the bottom.

The creation of the Luftwaffe, the air force of Nazi Germany, took place in secret, which was kept until 1935 when the Führer (leader) Adolf Hitler shocked the world by announcing that Germany had been re-arming since 1933.

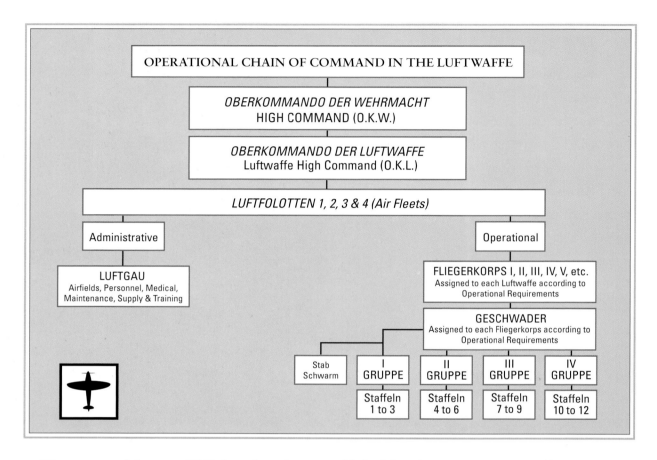

OPERATIONAL CHAIN OF COMMAND IN THE LUFTWAFFE

OBERKOMMANDO DER WEHRMACHT
HIGH COMMAND (O.K.W.)

OBERKOMMANDO DER LUFTWAFFE
Luftwaffe High Command (O.K.L.)

LUFTFOLOTTEN 1, 2, 3 & 4 (Air Fleets)

Administrative

Operational

LUFTGAU
Airfields, Personnel, Medical, Maintenance, Supply & Training

FLIEGERKORPS I, II, III, IV, V, etc.
Assigned to each Luftwaffe according to Operational Requirements

GESCHWADER
Assigned to each Fliegerkorps according to Operational Requirements

Stab Schwarm

I GRUPPE

II GRUPPE

III GRUPPE

IV GRUPPE

Staffeln 1 to 3

Staffeln 4 to 6

Staffeln 7 to 9

Staffeln 10 to 12

The success of the tests did little to dent the general belief that the awesome power of big naval guns remained paramount, but it did persuade all navies that they had to fit more and better anti-aircraft guns to their ships.

One naval weapon that saw significant advances between the wars was the torpedo. The weapons of 1918 tended to be driven by compressed air at speeds of around 35 knots and to carry warheads of about 300 lbs (136 kg) of TNT. Ranges of around 900 ft (2,747 m) were usual. Most navies went into World War Two with comparable weapons, but ranges had extended to around 4,500 ft (1,372 m). The Japanese had developed the Type 93 "long-lance" torpedo. This weapon could deliver a 1,000 lb (454 kg) warhead to distances of over 120,000 ft (36,576 m) at speeds of 38 knots. The crucial advance that made this possible was the development of a compressed-oxygen power plant.

The Japanese were not content to develop a new torpedo; they also developed a new delivery system. The Japanese produced the "Betty", officially the Mitsubishi G4M. This twin-engined aircraft was designed to be based on Pacific islands and to deliver the "long-lance" torpedo over the ocean's enormous distances. It had a range of 1,900 miles (3,058 km) and a speed of 260 mph (418 kph). A defensive armament of five machine guns and a 20 mm cannon was considered to be adequate against any aircraft-carrier-based fighters it was likely to meet. The Betty had the advantage over other torpedo bombers that it could drop the robust "long-lance" from a height of 500 ft (152 m), avoiding the need to come down to the suicidally low heights demanded by the more easily damaged torpedoes of other nations.

The Betty was but one of the many new forms of advanced aircraft that entered service in the 1930s. The vast majority of air forces were constrained by a lack of investment and most technological advances were made by civilian aircraft manufacture and only then applied to military aircraft.

The Bristol Aircraft Company, for instance, produced the Type 143 passenger aircraft in 1936. Britain's military chiefs were embarrassed to realize that at 250 mph (402 kph) this aircraft was faster than any fighter then in service with the RAF. The aircraft were the first in Britain to have advanced features such as a stressed skin, a retractable undercarriage, and flaps. The RAF hurriedly ordered a military version of the Type 143, which became the Blenheim light bomber.

Among the improvements that aircraft designers introduced in the interwar years were much more powerful and reliable engines. The famous Sopwith Camel of World War One had entered combat with a 130 horsepower engine. By 1939 fighters had engines with 1,400 horsepower. Increased power meant greater speed — from about 110 mph - 350 mph (177 kph -

The captured German battleship Ostfriesland being bombed by U.S. Army Air Corps aircraft, during tests on the effects of aerial bombing on warships, June 21, 1921.

563 kph) for fighters. This in turn led to much greater attention to aerodynamics, robust construction, and more precise controls. The results of this process were to produce aircraft that were made predominantly of metal, in place of wood and canvas, and that were sleek, streamlined monoplanes in place of the ungainly biplanes of the earlier war.

Under World War One fighter ace Hermann Goering, the German Luftwaffe was one of the first air forces in the world to equip itself exclusively with modern types of aircraft. The showpiece fighter was the Messerschmitt Bf109, which was being produced as the Bf109E variant by the time war broke out. This fighter had a top speed of 340 mph (547 kph), a range of 1,000 miles (1,609 km), and a ceiling of 34,450 ft (10,500 m). This gave it a performance better than almost any other fighter in the world, and the Bf109E packed a real punch. World War One fighters had been armed with one or at most two machine guns, but the Bf109E had two machine guns in the engine cowling and two 20 mm cannons in the wings. Later versions had a third 20 mm cannon firing through the propeller hub.

Goering and his staff had thought hard about what aircraft they would need. The Bf109 was designed to gain control of the air, but its limited range and high cost made it of limited use in other roles. They therefore commissioned the Messerschmitt Bf110, which was nicknamed the "*Zerstorer*" (Destroyer). This twin-engined fighter had a range of 600 miles (966 km) and had more armament than the Bf109. Its main task was to patrol the skies, seeking out and destroying enemy bombers. A key weapon for this task was the heavy machine gun in the rear cockpit operated by the observer. The Bf110 would fly below or alongside bombers, maneuvering to get into a blind spot, and then open fire with deadly effect.

First Troop Movement by Air
Spanish Civil War, September 1936

Troop-carrying aircraft
Air defense fighter
Republican fighter

Air defense drives off Republican attempts to disrupt airlift.

Ju52s airlift 12,000 men of the Nationalist "Army of Africa" in 677 flights during August and September 1936.

Republican warship patrols

The use of aircraft in war developed quickly after 1918. During the Spanish Civil War of 1936–1939, in which Nazi Germany provided support to the Nationalist side, troops were airlifted and fighters were used in a defense role.

Opposite page: In the Spanish Civil War, the Condor Legion sent from Nazi Germany to support General Francisco Franco, the Nationalist leader, was able to rehearse new methods of aerial warfare, such as dive-bombing, which later featured in World War Two.

To strike at the enemy, the Luftwaffe had the Heinkel He111, which was being manufactured in the P variant in 1939. This bomber had a range of 1,300 miles (2,092 km) and a top speed of 200 mph (322 kph) and could carry up to 4,500 lb (2,041 kg) of bombs. This bomber was intended to fly far over enemy territory and hit military and industrial targets. The Dornier Do17 had a broadly similar performance and was intended for a similar role. The Junkers Ju88 was of a similar type, but it was faster and had a greater range. It would be used to give close support to the army, bombing enemy strongpoints in advance of a ground assault. Another Junkers bomber that was designed from the very start to co-operate with the army was the famous Junkers Ju87 Stuka. The Stuka was a light, single-engined bomber both slow and limited in range. It was able, however, to deliver its 4,000 lb (1,814 kg) bomb load with pinpoint accuracy. As a dive-bomber, it could drop from the sky at great speed, allowing the pilot to drop his bomb from low level while keeping the target in view. To increase its power and to shatter enemy morale, it was fitted with a siren that produced an ear-splitting howl as the dived. The Focke-Wulf company produced the Fw200 Condor long-range bomber. Able to fly over 2,700 miles (4,345 km) at 150 mph (241 kph) and carry 3,300 lb (1,497 kg) of bombs, the Condor was given the task of maritime patrol. As a scout for the German Navy, it was unequaled. The Luftwaffe led the way in both design and numbers, but other air forces were not far behind. The British had Spitfire and Hurricane fighters. The Spitfire was of comparable performance to the Messerschmitt Bf109E, but was available in smaller numbers in 1939. The Hurricane was more robust and less sophisticated, but it was cheaper and easier to maintain. Both were armed with eight .303 machine guns. The French Dewoitine D520 had a similar performance to the Hurricane but heavier armament. The Italian Reggiane Re2000 had a performance not far short of the Bf109 and the Spitfire, but with only two machine guns it lacked the firepower to bring down modern bombers. Poland's PZL P11 had only two machine guns.

Other nations kept their expansionist ambitions and aircraft under wraps. Japan had the high-speed, and heavily armed Mitsubishi A6M2 Zero fighter in 1939. It was a nasty shock when it appeared over Pearl Harbor in 1941.

Spanish Civil War 1936–1939

- Extent of Nationalist control, 1938
- Nationalist offensives
- Republican counter-offensives
- ○ Airfields

ATLANTIC OCEAN

FRANCE

SPAIN

PORTUGAL

Santander
Bilbao • Guernica
León
Burgos
Huesca
Girona
Soria
Salamanca
Segovia
Barcelona
Tarragona
Madrid
Toledo
Valencia
Lisbon
Badajoz
Albacete
Alicante
Cordoba
Cartegena
Saville
Malaga

Mediterranean Sea

Spanish Morocco

ALGERIA

MOROCCO

N

0   100 km
0   100 miles

Opposite page: In 1905, the Japanese started to create an empire, first by annexing Korea after their victory in the Russo-Japanese War. Intrusions into China began in 1931, when the Japanese seized Manchuria where they set up the puppet state of Manchukuo.

The use to which these aircraft would be put was the subject of much debate between the wars. Most countries, notably Britain, France, and the United States, saw their air forces principally in terms of bombers. They expected to fight wars in which there would be extensive land conflict and airfields would be fairly close to the front lines. Some bombers were earmarked for ground attack roles in support of the army — the British Fairey Battle was a single-engined light bomber designed for this role. Other bombers were intended to penetrate deeper into enemy territory and bomb armaments factories, naval dockyards, power plants and other targets of military value if not always of direct military ownership.

Events would prove that bombers were exceedingly vulnerable to modern fighters in daylight. Longer-range raids were moved to nighttime; but navigating at night is a difficult art, and precision bombing in darkness is next to impossible. Most air forces undertook few joint exercises with their armies, so although they had light bombers designed for co-operation, the crews were poorly trained for the task. This was especially the case in that most military men expected a static, trench-based war as in World War One.

The exception was Germany. The German military placed great emphasis on tight and swift co-operation between the air force and the army, and they trained for this relentlessly. This cooperation was part of a new style of warfare that the Germans dubbed *blitzkrieg*, or lightning war. It would dominate not only World War Two but also military thinking into the 21st century.

The basic principle of *blitzkrieg* was to identify the key, strategic point in the enemy's defenses and attack that point with overwhelming force. Once through the enemy defenses, the attacking units would race on at speed to capture transportation links, headquarters, communications, and other necessary features of a military command structure. With the enemy commanders disorganized, the attacking force could then mop up the scattered and bewildered enemy armies with ease. Speed, decisive force, and aggression were the essential features. The Luftwaffe, in the shape of the Stuka and the Ju88, was expected to come up at very short notice and hammer any enemy units that seemed likely to offer resistance. To achieve this the Germans made use of a civilian invention: radio. By the latter 1930s radio sets were small enough to be fitted to aircraft and ground vehicles, and could even be carried about by infantrymen. The Germans were lavish in their supply of radio sets so all units could keep in touch with each other.

The Messerschmitt BF110 long-range fighter was a highly effective night-fighter and ground-attack aircraft and was used extensively in the Greman *blitzkrieg* campaign.

For *blitzkrieg* to work properly, the spearhead of the attacking force had to be able to move quickly and deploy great firepower. An early decision was taken by the Germans to make the main attack using tanks, or *panzers* in German, accompanied by infantry riding in trucks, and artillery pulled by trucks. These motorized units would be used to race to the enemy's rear, thereby spreading confusion and terror, while the foot-slogging infantry and horse-drawn artillery came on behind to mop up.

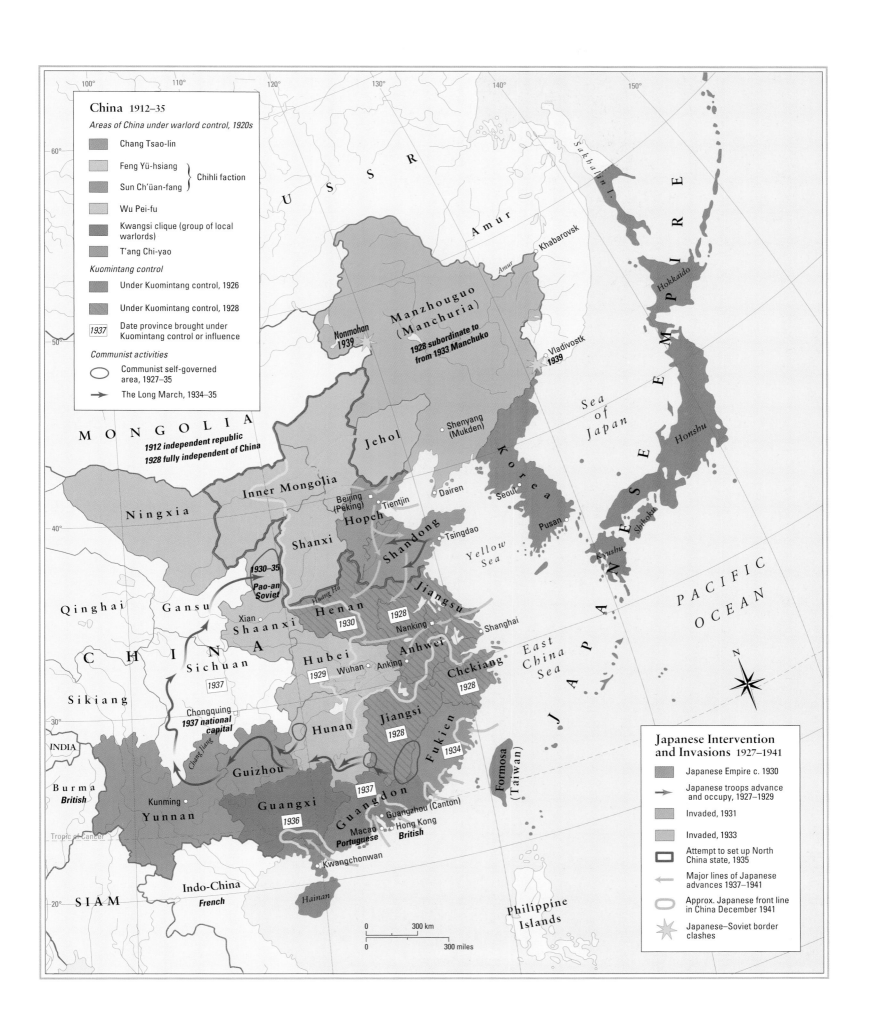

China 1912–35

Areas of China under warlord control, 1920s

Chang Tsao-lin

Feng Yü-hsiang } Chihli faction
Sun Ch'üan-fang }

Wu Pei-fu

Kwangsi clique (group of local warlords)

T'ang Chi-yao

Kuomintang control

Under Kuomintang control, 1926

Under Kuomintang control, 1928

1937 Date province brought under Kuomintang control or influence

Communist activities

Communist self-governed area, 1927–35

The Long March, 1934–35

Japanese Intervention and Invasions 1927–1941

Japanese Empire c. 1930

Japanese troops advance and occupy, 1927–1929

Invaded, 1931

Invaded, 1933

Attempt to set up North China state, 1935

Major lines of Japanese advances 1937–1941

Approx. Japanese front line in China December 1941

Japanese–Soviet border clashes

U S S R

Amur

Khabarovsk

Sakhalin I.

J A P A N E S E   E M P I R E

Hokkaido

Amur

Manzhouguo (Manchuria)
1928 subordinate to from 1933 Manchuko

Nonmohan 1939

Vladivostk 1939

Jehol

Shenyang (Mukden)

Sea of Japan

Honshu

M O N G O L I A
**1912 independent republic
1928 fully independent of China**

Inner Mongolia

Korea

Seoul

Dairen

Beijing (Peking)   Tientjin

Pusan

Shikoku

Kyushu

Ningxia

Shanxi

Hopeh

Shandong

Tsingdao

Yellow Sea

PACIFIC OCEAN

Qinghai

Gansu

1930–35 Pao-an Soviet

Huang Ho

Henan 1930

Jiangsu 1928

Nanking

Shanghai

East China Sea

N

C   H   I   N   A

Xian

Shaanxi

Sichuan

1937

Hubei

Wuhan Anking 1929

Anhwei

Chekiang 1928

Qinghai

Sikiang

Chongquing **1937 national capital**

Chang Jiang

Hunan

Jiangsi 1928

Fukien 1934

East China Sea

J   A   P   A   N

INDIA

Guizhou

Burma **British**

Kunming

Yunnan

Guangxi 1936

1937

Guangdon

Guangzhou (Canton)

Macao **Portuguese**   Hong Kong **British**

Formosa (Taiwan)

Tropic of Cancer

Kwangchonwan

Indo-China **French**

SIAM

Hainan

Philippine Islands

0   300 km

0   300 miles

July 1941: Panzer units of the German Army pass through a blazing Russian village on their one-way journey to the battlefront.

The expansion of Nazi Germany began in 1936 with the occupation of the demilitarized Rhineland and continued in 1938 with the *Anchluss*, the union of Germany and Austria. In 1939 the Nazis annexed Czechoslovakia and on 1 September, they invaded Poland.

Like most armies, the infantry and artillery were equipped with updated, but not noticeably different, versions of the weapons they had used in World War One.

German Panzers in 1939 consisted principally of the Panzer II, Panzer III, and Panzer IV, each of which had its role on the battlefield. The Panzer IV was the main breakthrough tank, intended to deal with serious opposition in the initial phases of fighting through enemy defenses. It was armed with a 75 mm gun firing both high-explosive and armor-piercing shells and with a machine gun. It could manage 25 mph (40 kph) on roads and had a range of 125 miles (201 km) before it would need to be refuelled. The Panzer III was slightly faster and more armored than the Panzer IV, and had a gun and ammunition specialized for piercing armor. It was intended to be the main tank-destroying tank: it would be brought up to deal with any enemy armored units that appeared. The Panzer II was lighter, smaller and faster than the other two. It was armed with a 20 mm cannon able to fire over 200 rounds per minute and with two machine guns.

The main role of the Panzer II was to attack soft targets such as infantry, transports, depots, and other strategic targets once the breakthrough had been made. The tanks that the Panzers came up against in the early years of World War Two were not markedly inferior. The British Matilda tank, for instance, had a two-pounder gun, the equivalent of the Panzer III's weapon, and somewhat heavier armor. The tanks used by the French, the Char D2 had a 47 mm gun and two machine guns and was similarly well armored. The American M2 tank had a 37 mm gun but it was more lightly armored than the other tanks. The key advantage that the German Panzers had over their rivals was not so much in the technology or

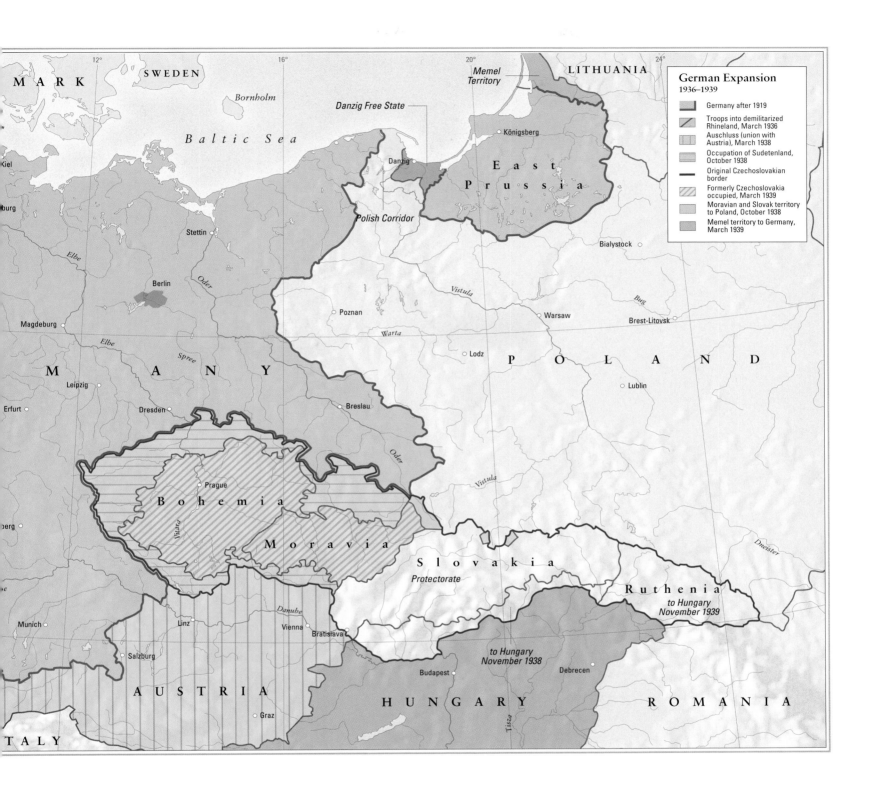

German Expansion
1936–1939

- Germany after 1919
- Troops into demilitarized Rhineland, March 1936
- Auschluss (union with Austria), March 1938
- Occupation of Sudetenland, October 1938
- Original Czechoslovakian border
- Formerly Czechoslovakia occupied, March 1939
- Moravian and Slovak territory to Poland, October 1938
- Memel territory to Germany, March 1939

the design of the tanks, but in the way they were used. Nearly every country's tactical doctrine required tanks to disperse along the entire front line and act as infantry-support weapons. However, the Germans massed their Panzers together in specialized Panzer divisions and threw them forward in large numbers to overwhelm and break through enemy defenses. Backed up by motorized infantry and artillery, and supported from the air by Stukas, the Panzer attack proved to be irresistible when it was unleashed against the Allied forces in World War Two.

WORLD WAR TWO — AXIS EXPANSION

WORLD WAR TWO OPENED WITH A SPECTACULAR SERIES OF SUCCESSES FOR THE AXIS POWERS, THE RESULT OF A REVOLUTION IN WEAPONS AND TACTICS THAT GAVE THE GERMANS AND JAPANESE BATTLEFIELD SUPREMACY. BY THE SUMMER OF 1942 IT LOOKED AS IF NOTHING COULD STOP THEIR RAPID VICTORY.

Opposite page: During September 1939, the forces of Nazi Germany swept through Poland, throwing aside all resistance with their *Blitzkrieg* (lightning war) method of fast-moving armored warfare. This was accompanied by punishing air raids, notably featuring the Luftwaffe's terrifying Stuka-JU87 dive bombers.

The armed forces that went to war in 1939 were deceptively similar to those that had ended the last great war in 1918. In many respects weaponry and supply systems had not changed very much. A majority of the senior commanders had held command at divisional level in the earlier conflict, and their views on tactical and strategic questions had been conditioned by their experiences 20 years earlier.

This continuity was more pronounced among the states that had won World War One. They had ended the war with vast amounts of military equipment of all kinds and, with peacetime defense budgets cut to a minimum, there had been little opportunity or enthusiasm to replace it. Moreover, the victors were inclined to think that they had the key to victory. Those countries that had been defeated were less affected. They were building up their armed forces from scratch with the most modern equipment. Moreover, their commanders were more inclined to be open to new ideas and concepts, as the methods they had used in World War One had failed.

At sea the big-gun battleship was still considered to be the key weapon in achieving and maintaining control of the shipping lanes. Submarines, cruisers, destroyers, and other craft were considered useful for attacking merchant ships, undertaking small actions, and other secondary roles, but the battleship was seen as the final arbiter of naval power.

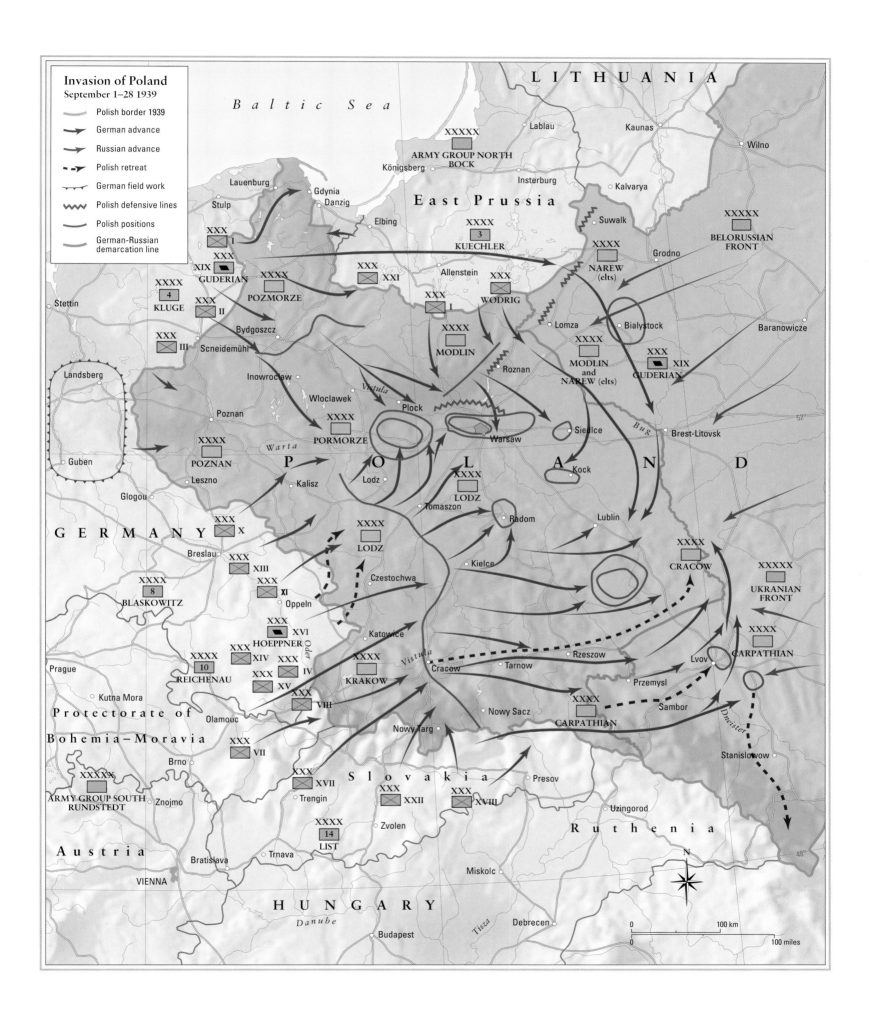

Invasion of Poland
September 1–28 1939

- Polish border 1939
- German advance
- Russian advance
- Polish retreat
- German field work
- Polish defensive lines
- Polish positions
- German-Russian demarcation line

L I T H U A N I A

Baltic Sea

Lablau

Kaunas

Wilno

XXXXX
ARMY GROUP NORTH
BOCK

Königsberg

Insterburg

Kalvarya

East Prussia

Elbing

Suwalk

XXXXX
BELORUSSIAN
FRONT

Lauenburg

Gdynia
Danzig

XXXX
3
KUECHLER

XXXX
NAREW
(elts)

Grodno

Stulp

XXX
I

XXX
XXI

Allenstein

XXX
WODRIG

Baranowicze

Stettin

XIX
GUDERIAN

XXXX
4
KLUGE

XXXX
POZMORZE

XXX
I

XXX
MODLIN

Roznan

Lomza

Bialystock

XXXX
MODLIN
and
NAREW (elts)

XXX
XIX
GUDERIAN

XXX
II

Bydgoszcz

Landsberg

XXX
III

Scneidemühl

Bug

52°

Inowroclaw

Wloclawek

Vistula

Plock

Warsaw

Siedlce

Brest-Litovsk

Guben

Poznan

XXXX
POZNAN

Warta

XXXX
PORMORZE

Lodz

Kock

P O L A N D

Leszno

Kalisz

Glogou

XXXX
LODZ

Tomaszon

Radom

Lublin

G E R M A N Y

XXX
X

Breslau

XXXX
LODZ

Kielce

XXXX
CRACOW

XXXXX
UKRANIAN
FRONT

XXX
XIII

Czestochwa

XXX
XI

Oppeln

XXX
XVI
HOEPPNER

Katowice

Oder

XXXX
8
BLASKOWITZ

Prague

XXXX
10
REICHENAU

XXX
XIV

XXX
IV

XXX
XV

XXXX
KRAKOW

Vistula

Cracow

Tarnow

Rzeszow

Lvov

XXXX
CARPATHIAN

Kutna Mora

XXX
VIII

Przemysl

Sambor

Dneister

Protectorate of
Bohemia–Moravia

Olamouc

Nowy Sacz

XXXX
CARPATHIAN

XXX
VII

Brno

Nowy Targ

Stanislowow

Znojmo

XXX
XVII

Trengin

S l o v a k i a

XXX
XXII

XXX
XVIII

Presov

Uzingorod

XXXXX
ARMY GROUP SOUTH
RUNDSTEDT

Zvolen

XXXX
14
LIST

R u t h e n i a

A u s t r i a

Bratislava

Trnava

Miskolc

48°

VIENNA

N

H U N G A R Y

Danube

Budapest

Tisza

Debrecen

0   100 km
0   100 miles

Opposite page: On May 10 1940, Nazi Germany invaded Belgium, the Netherlands, Luxembourg, and France. The first three surrendered quickly, although France held out for six weeks before capitulating on June. 22 Afterward, Vichy, a French collaborationist state, was established in the south.

On land the combination of artillery and infantry that had dominated the earlier conflict was still relied upon by most armies. The majority of senior commanders envisaged warfare similar to that of 1914–1918: static defenses would dominate and only limited assaults led by tanks and supported by heavy artillery were possible.

A typical infantry support tank was the French Char B1 bis. This weighed 35 tons (32 tonnes) and had armor up to 2.4 in (60 mm) thick. It was designed to clamber over all manner of field obstructions and defensive works. It had a 47 mm gun mounted in a turret and a huge 75 mm howitzer firing directly forward from the hull. Because it was intended to aid infantry attacking fixed defenses, it was slow and had a limited range. The smaller tanks designed to race through gaps in enemy lines were typified by Italy's Fiat Ansaldo. This tank weighed only 3.58 tons (3.25 tonnes) and had armor 2/3 in (15 mm thick), which was adequate for stopping bullets but not much else. The two-man crew consisted of a driver and a gunner — the latter had a pair of machine guns, a 20 mm anti-tank gun, or a flamethrower. With a top speed of 28 mph (45 kph) and a range of 78 miles (126 km), the Ansaldo was expected to create mayhem behind enemy lines.

In the air, most air forces envisaged undertaking missions similar to those of 1918. Bombing raids would be undertaken in daylight against specific military targets, but more daring advocates of long-range bombing suggested attacking weapons factories in enemy towns that lay within range. Because the emphasis was on precision bombing of small targets, the actual weight of bombs to be carried was generally quite low. The Soviet Ilyushin DB3 was a typical bomber. It had twin engines of 960 horsepower each, giving it a top speed of 267 mph (430 kph), a range of 1,600 miles (2,575 km), and a ceiling of 33,000 ft (10,058 m). It could carry 2,200 lb (998 kg) of bombs and was protected by three 13 mm machine guns. Italy's G50 Freccia fighter entered service in 1938 as a low-wing monoplane powered by an 840 horsepower Fiat A74 engine. This gave the machine a top speed of 293 mph (472 kph), a ceiling of 33,000 ft (10,058 m), and a range of 620 miles (998 km). Nimble and quick, the Freccia was much admired at home and abroad. It was armed with twin 12.7 mm machine guns.

Hitler, it was said, had "missed the bus" by attacking Poland on September 1 1939. It was confidently predicted that the Poles would be able to delay the German advance in a series of defensive battles until the winter came. By spring 1940 the British and French would be fully mobilized and would launch an assault into Germany in the west. Faced by a war on two fronts, Germany would collapse, just as it had done 20 years earlier. That this did not happen was due to the concept of *blitzkrieg*, developed and perfected in the 1930s by a small group of younger German officers. Hitler recognized the advantages of the idea and used his power as dictator to impose the doctrine on his older and more senior commanders, who recognized only the risks of the new concept.

The principal tank in the new battle plan was the Panzer IV, manufactured by Krupp. This weapon entered service in 1936 and remained in production to the closing days of the war, with almost 9,000 produced. There would be much variation between the different models of the Panzer IV in guns, levels of armor, and assorted secondary armament. The models with which Germany went to war were models A to D. These generally had 1 1/5 inch (30 mm) armor and were armed with a 75 mm general cannons and a 7.92 mm machine gun. The tank could manage 20 mph (32 kph) on roads, less cross-country; it had a range of 206 miles (332 km).

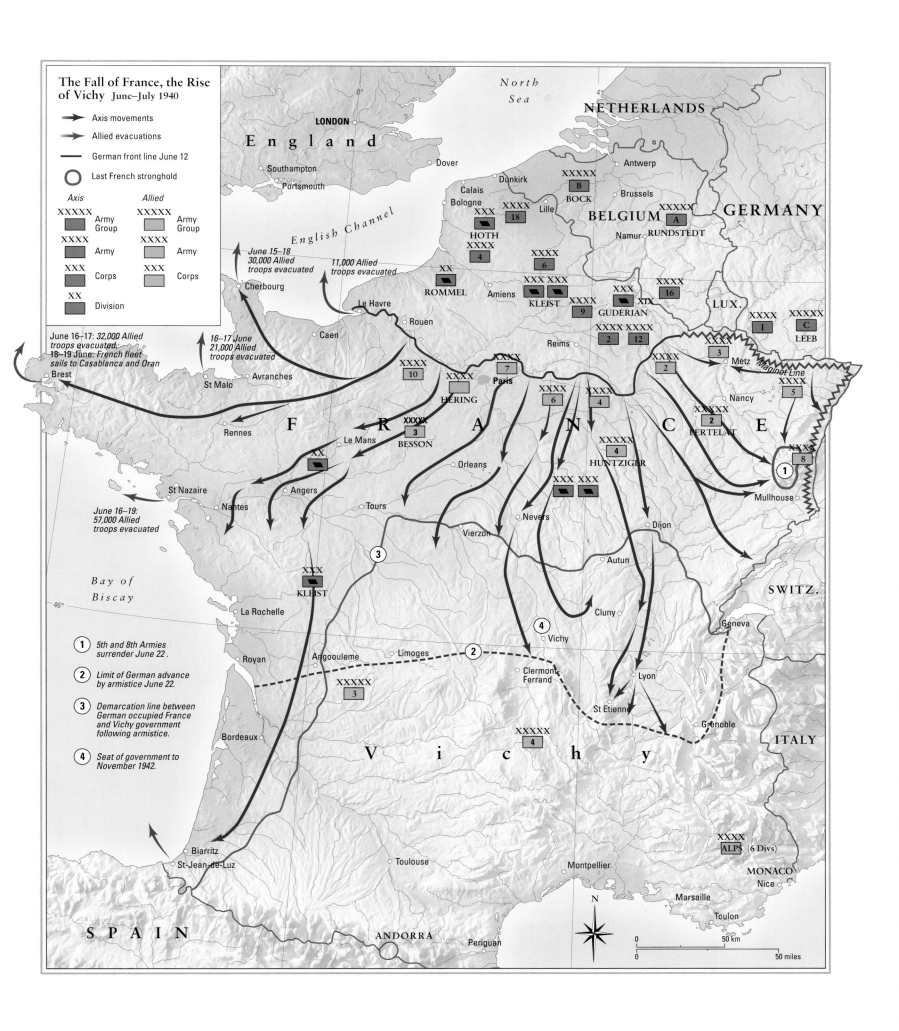

The lighter and faster Panzer III made by Daimler-Benz was produced in larger numbers. It was equipped with a lighter gun and armourpiercing ammunition. The Panzer III was to attack enemy tanks, artillery, and bunkers while the Panzer IV got on with the main fighting.

Perhaps the key features of these tanks have been often overlooked. They were equipped with a two-way radio and were large enough to carry a tank commander whose sole job was to use the radio and command the other crew members. In nearly all other tanks the commander also had to man the gun, drive, or carry out other tasks. He was thus not distracted by other tasks in battle and could fight his tank more effectively. The provision of radios allowed the tanks to keep in touch with each other and with other units — crucially with the Luftwaffe.

The new German way of fighting war was unleashed on Poland on September 1 1939. Five armies organized into two army groups marched into Poland. Prepared for a conventional war, the Poles were caught entirely by surprise by the *Blitzkrieg* tactics. The Poles saw the Panzer columns break through on a narrow front and then tried to close their front lines behind them. They expected to be able to isolate and defeat the few tanks that their tactical doctrines said would have broken through. But they were entirely unprepared for large, self-contained motorized units of armor, artillery, and infantry roaming in the strategic heartland of Poland.

As early as September 9, the first German tanks were on the outskirts of Warsaw, the Polish capital. Although they failed to penetrate its defenses, their mere presence caused the Poles to order a general retreat the next day. It was too late. The Panzers had already overrun key transport links and had destroyed the headquarters units of many divisions. The Poles fought gallantly but without any clear strategy and often without orders about what to do. They surrendered on September 27 after the Russians had invaded eastern Poland.

The German invasions of Denmark and Norway in April 1940 were amphibious operations carried out mainly along conventional lines. This caused the Allied commanders to imagine that they would face a similarly conventional German attack into France when it came. As a consequence, the Germans were able to repeat their *Blitzkrieg* success in the west against largely unprepared British, French, Dutch, and Belgian armies.

The assault began on May 10 1940. Not only did the Germans use *Blitzkrieg* tactics, they also opted for strategic surprise by launching the main armored thrust through the Ardennes hills. The French thought that the narrow, twisting roads of the area were too restricted to allow for the advance and supply of a major force. The Germans thought differently, and were proven correct.

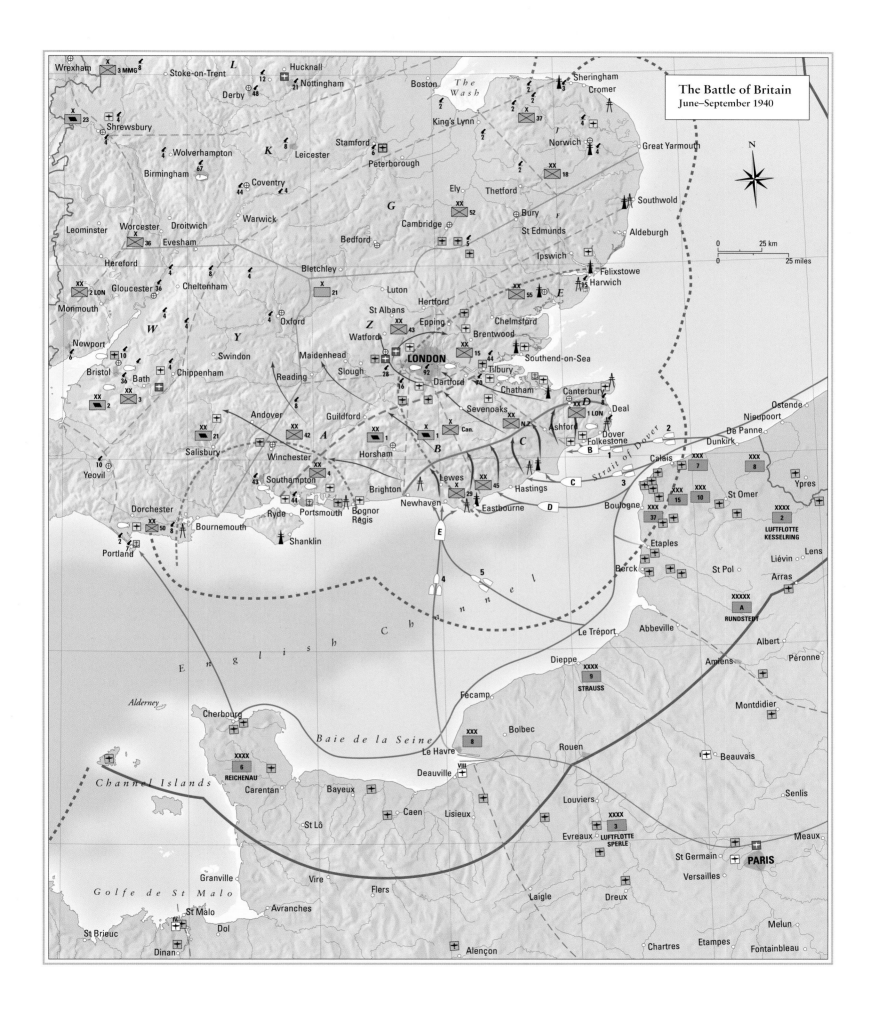

The Battle of Britain
June–September 1940

The crucial role was assigned to General Heinz Guderian, one of the younger generals who had developed the *Blitzkrieg* concept in the 1930s. His XIX Panzer Corps was to advance through the Ardennes and race ahead to secure river crossings over the Meuse River at Sedan, which would then be used by the rest of von Kleist's Panzer group, which would come up as quickly as it could.

At noon on May 12 Guderian reached Sedan. He studied the enemy artillery and infantry positions on the far bank of the river and radioed his Luftwaffe support. At 2 p.m., 12 squadrons of Stukas arrived, protected by a fighter escort, and began the systematic destruction of the French positions. The Stukas came back time and again. Under cover of their attacks, at 4 p.m. the motorized infantry climbed down from their trucks, inflated some rubber dinghies brought along for the task, and paddled over the river. By 5 p.m. the infantry had secured a bridgehead and begun bringing over artillery and armored cars on boats. By nightfall the Germans had established a pocket 10 miles (16 km) wide and 5 miles (8 km) deep. Under cover of dark, Guderian got a few tanks across. On the next day he captured a bridge and all three of his Panzer divisions poured over the river. On May 14 his forces attacked and broke through the thin line of French troops facing his men, they had come into countryside without any enemy troops. He deployed his tanks and motorized support.

There then occurred an astonishing argument in the German high command. Guderian and other younger officers wanted the Panzer units to race ahead, spreading destruction and confusion far and wide. The older generals worried that the Panzers would be cut off and forced to surrender for lack of supplies. Hitler imposed a compromise. The Panzers would halt for two days on the river Oise, to allow the foot-slogging infantry to come up and establish a firm defensive line facing north against an Allied counterattack. Once the infantry had come up, Guderian was unleashed again. This time he did not stop until he had reached the coast, cutting off the main French and British armies in Belgium and north-eastern France. There then followed the magnificent evacuation of almost the entire British army, together with many French and Belgian units, from Dunkirk. In part, the evacuation was successful because the Germans pulled many Panzer units out of the front line in order to repair damage, service the tanks and rest the men before the renewed assault south toward Paris. When that attack came, it was as successful as the first. On June 16 the French prime minister, Petain, surrendered.

Stunning as the victories achieved by *Blitzkrieg* had been, the limitations of the concept became obvious. Everything about *Blitzkrieg* had been designed for land warfare. But Britain was on the other side of the sea. The German military commanders had no doubt that they could defeat the British army within a few weeks, but only if they could get over the English Channel.

German battleship Bismark, as seen from an allied war ship. At 41,000 tonnes and packed with anti-aircraft weapons and mounted with guns it was one of the largest German battleships of World War Two.

III
Luftlandsturmregiment

III
Fallschirmjägerregiment 3

Kissamos

Kasteli Selianou

17,000 t
Royal

Hitler had hoped that once all its allies were defeated, Britain would be willing to make peace. He offered what he considered to be reasonable, almost generous terms, but Britain's new prime minister, Winston Churchill, refused even to listen. Hitler then turned to his navy. Admiral Erich Raeder was a talented but fairly conventional naval commander.

Germany had been constrained in the 1920s and early 1930s by international treaties that banned it from having any warships of over 11,200 tons (10,160 tonnes) — well below the minimum size for a battleship. So German ship designers produced the "pocket battleship". This was effectively a heavy cruiser but with larger guns and thicker armor. A 15 percent saving in weight was made by using expensive welding throughout rather than the cheaper riveting used by other nations. With six 11-inch guns, eight 5.9 inch guns, and numerous anti-aircraft weapons, each of these pocket battleships was a powerful ship. Once Hitler was in power, he told Raeder to ignore treaties, and order four new battleships. The *Scharnhorst* and *Gneisenau* were of 34,720 tons (31,497 tonnes) and armed with nine 11-inch guns, 12 5.9-inch guns, and batteries of anti-aircraft weapons. *Tirpitz* and *Bismarck* were even larger, at 45.195 tons (41,000 tonnes), and mounted eight 15-inch guns, 12 5.9-inch guns, and anti-aircraft weapons.

Neither of the two very large battleships was ready in 1940, and without them Raeder did not fancy risking a major battle against the Royal Navy: it could put 15 mainly elderly battleships into the fray. He

The German invasion of Crete, May 20 1941 followed their success in capturing Greece and involved the most extensive airborne attack ever attempted. British and other Allied defenders had to be rescued by the Royal Navy as Crete was evacuated.

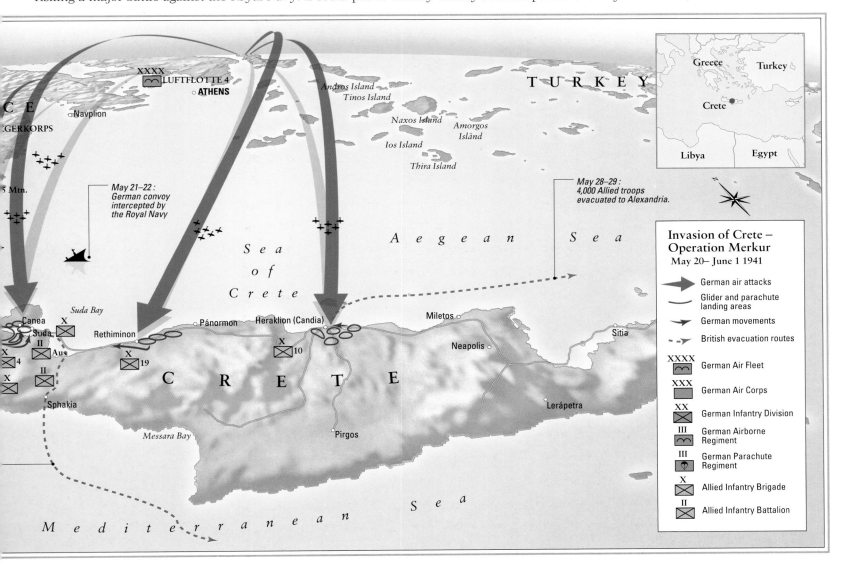

had already lost one pocket battleship, *Graf Spee*, to the British in 1939 and had suffered further naval losses during the Norwegian campaign. After studying the needs of the army for the protection of an invasion fleet, Raeder reported that he could guarantee that the main invasion fleet would get across but could not guarantee to stop the British Home Fleet once it steamed down from Scotland to intervene. Also, German troops in Britain would be cut off from supplies and reinforcements. Only if the Luftwaffe could guarantee to support his ships with continual air cover and frequent bombing attacks on the British fleet, could he hope to keep control of the Channel and carry supplies across it. That meant that the Luftwaffe had to gain and keep total control of the air over the English Channel. The Royal Air Force (RAF) had to be defeated.

The air campaign that was to become known as the Battle of Britain began in late July 1940, but the major German raids opened on August 13. They were codenamed Eagle Day by the Luftwaffe's commander Hermann Goering. Germany's tactics varied considerably during the battle. In the early stages it sent over fairly large formations of bombers, escorted by fighters, to attack and destroy RAF airfields, aircraft factories, and other targets. After August 20 the emphasis shifted to ambushing RAF aircraft in the air. Small bomber formations would come over the coast accompanied by fighters, but with a much larger fighter formation lurking nearby. A British squadron of fighters moving in on the German bombers would be attacked by overwhelming numbers of German fighters. Between August 24 and September, 6 the RAF lost 269 fighters, 171 were badly damaged; the Germans lost only 180 fighters.

By September 7, Goering was convinced, from faulty intelligence reports, that the RAF's fighter strength had been almost eliminated. He ordered a change of tactics: to soften up Britain's defenses for the invasion, expected to take place on September 12. The Luftwaffe switched its attacks to London and other cities in an effort to spread despair among the civilian population and to bring chaos to road and rail transportation links. In the event the change hardened British civilian determination and gave

During World War Two, German submarines prowled the Atlantic Ocean to prevent American supplies from reaching Britain. Until 1943, when the British developed effective techniques of detecting and sinking the submarines, the losses suffered by supply convoys were considerable.

Submarine Warfare in the Atlantic
June 1940 – March 1941

— Pan-American Neutrality Zone
▬ Extent of air escort cover
- - Extent of surface escort cover
▤ Major convoy routes
• Allied merchant ships sunk by U-boats
⚓ U-boats sunk
▨ Territory under Allied control
▨ Territory under Axis control
▨ Territory under Vichy government (unoccupied France)
▫ Neutral territory

the RAF breathing space to repair battered air bases and bring in new aircraft and pilots. The road and rail network did suffer but not as bad as the Luftwaffe thought.

On 9 September Hitler studied the reports and postponed the invasion to September 24. On September 17, forecasts of awful weather

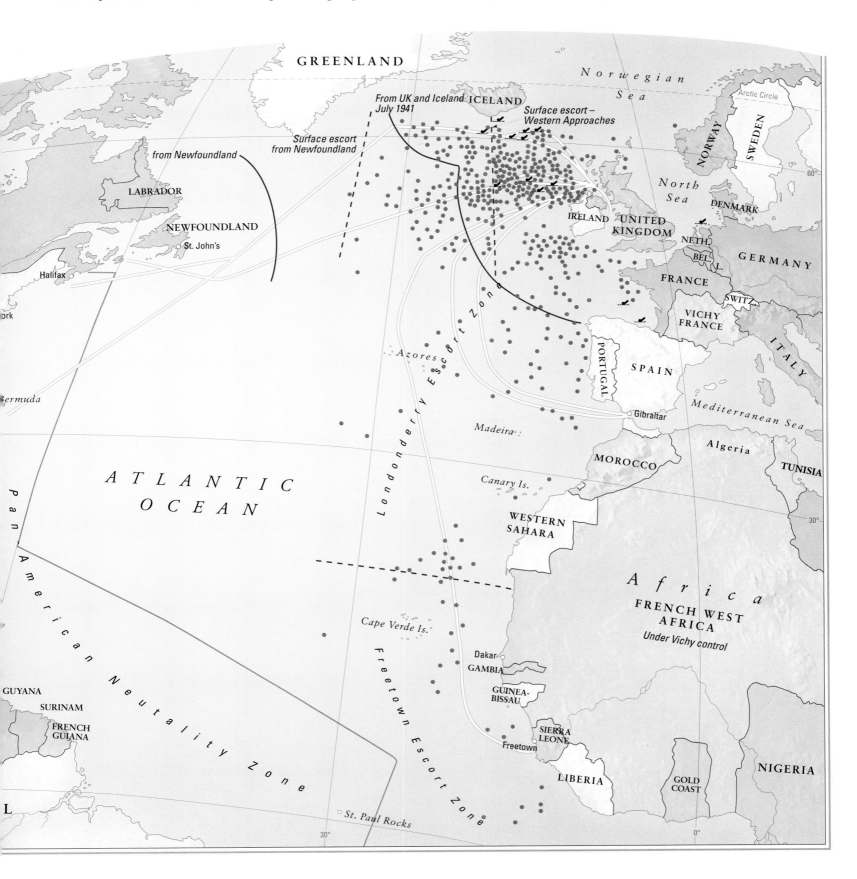

Opposite page: The Japanese attack on Pearl Harbor, December 7 1941—"A Day that will live in infamy"— was designed to cripple the U.S. Fleet and so allow Japan to spread its power over the Pacific Ocean.

1 Tender *Whitney* and destroyers *Tucker, Conyngham, Reid, Case,* and *Selfridge,*
2 Destroyer *Blue*
3 Light cruiser *Phoenix*
4 Destroyers *Aylwin, Farragut, Dale,* and *Monaghan*
5 Destroyers *Patterson, Ralph, Talbot,* and *Henley*
6 Tender *Dobbin* and destroyers *Worden, Hull, Dewey, Phelps,* and *Macdough*
7 Hospital Ship *Solace*
8 Destroyer *Allen*
9 Destroyer *Chew*
10 Destroyer-minesweepers *Gamble,* and *Montgomery,* and light-minelayer *Ramsey*
11 Destroyer-minesweepers *Trever, Breese, Zane, Perry,* and *Wasmuth*
12 Repair vessel *Medusa*
13 Seaplane tender *Curtiss*
14 Light cruiser *Detroit*
15 Light cruiser *Raleigh*
16 Target battleship *Utah*
17 Seaplane tender *Tangier*
18 Battleship *Nevada*
19 Battleship *Arizona*
20 Repair vessel *Vestal*
21 Battleship *Tennessee*
22 Battleship *West Virginia*
23 Battleship *Maryland*
24 Battleship *Oklahoma*
25 Oiler *Neosho*
26 Battleship *California*
27 Seaplane tender *Avocet*
28 Destroyer *Shaw*
29 Destroyer *Downes*
30 Destroyer *Cassin*
31 Battleship *Pennsylvania*
32 Submarine *Cachalot*
33 Minelayer *Oglala*
34 Light cruiser *Helena*
35 Auxiliary vessel *Argonne*
36 Gunboat *Sacramento*
37 Destroyer *Jarvis*
38 Destroyer *Mugford*
39 Seaplane tender *Swan*
40 Repair vessel *Rigel*
41 Oiler *Ramapo*
42 Heavy cruiser *New Orleans*
43 Destroyer *Cummings* and light-minelayers *Preble* and *Tracy*
44 Heavy cruiser *San Francisco*
45 Destroyer-minesweeper *Grebe,* destroyer *Schley* and light-minelayers *Pruitt* and *Sicard*
46 Light cruiser *Honolulu*
47 Light cruiser *St. Louis*
48 Destroyer *Bagley*
49 Submarines *Narwhal, Dolphin* and *Tautog* and tenders *Thornton* and *Hulbert*
50 Submarine tender *Pelias*
51 Auxiliary vessel *Sumner*
52 Auxiliary vessel *Castor*

caused him to postpone the invasion again. It never happened. Hitler's mind was gradually turning back to what had been his original objective: a redrawing of the maps of eastern Europe in Germany's favor. Poland had already been divided between Germany and Russia. Czechoslovakia, Romania, Hungary, Bulgaria, and Yugoslavia had all been so overawed by German military might that they had become more or less willing allies. What could not be ignored was the Soviet Union. The Russian dictator Stalin had not only taken eastern Poland in fall 1939 but also had annexed Latvia, Lithuania, and Estonia. If Hitler were to dominate eastern Europe, he would have to defeat Russia first.

The Soviet army was in a terrible condition. More than 75 percent of all senior officers had been removed from their command, and many had been shot without trial, during the horrific purges that Stalin ordered in the late 1930s. Morale was low and expertise in the higher ranks was almost non-existent. Nor was Soviet weaponry in much better condition. The Red Army had around 20,000 tanks, but its tactical doctrine insisted that the armored vehicles should be scattered among the infantry units in order to provide close support. They should not act independently, like the Germans used them.

The Soviet T27 was a two-man tank armed with a machine gun and ¼ in (9 mm) armor. Many of them were adapted to be used as battlefield tractors for pulling artillery or supply wagons. Slightly larger was the T26. It had a turret carrying a 37 mm gun or flamethrower and was protected by $2/3$ in (15 mm) armor. These and similar models were designed to push through any opening in an enemy line and disrupt rear areas at speed. To batter a gap in enemy defenses in the first place was the task of heavy tanks such as the colossal T35, which weighed 50 tons (45.7 tonnes). It mounted a 76 mm howitzer in the main turret and had four smaller turrets that had two mounted 45 mm guns and two machine guns. This monster was being replaced from 1940 by the KV2, which was almost as big but had only a single turret mounting a variety of weaponry up to its heaviest armament, the 152 mm howitzer. Like the T35, it was agonizingly slow and cumbersome. Only tanks holding the unit commander had radios. The other tank commanders had to watch the lead tank and follow its movements in action.

But before Hitler could attack Russia, his armed forces had to deal with two distracting side campaigns. Mussolini had declared war on Britain and France as soon it was obvious that France would be defeated. The refusal of Britain to surrender meant that the Italian Army faced the British Army in the North African desert on the border of Italian Libya and British Egypt. The Italians did not do well, so Hitler sent them two divisions of Germans, one of them Panzers under the command of the capable Erwin Rommel. Rommel won a series of spectacular victories and stabilized the situation.

More serious was the Italian war against Greece that had begun in October 1940. Again Italy failed to deliver a knockout blow, but Hitler hoped to ignore the stalemate. Then, in March 1941, the Yugoslavs threw off the enforced German alliance and turned openly hostile to both Germany and Italy. Hitler could not afford to have a hostile Yugoslavia on his southern flank during an invasion of Russia. He sent the German army to crush Yugoslavia and Greece, which they did with brutal efficiency in less than two weeks. The Italians insisted that the island of Crete had to be captured. It was in a strategic location and its use as a base for the British Navy would be a serious drawback for the Italian Navy. The island was held by a mixed force of Greeks, British soldiers, and New Zealanders, but many had been evacuated from Greece and were disorganized and ill equipped. The Germans opted for an aerial assault using paratroops to secure key targets followed by light infantry coming in by glider and aircraft. The most

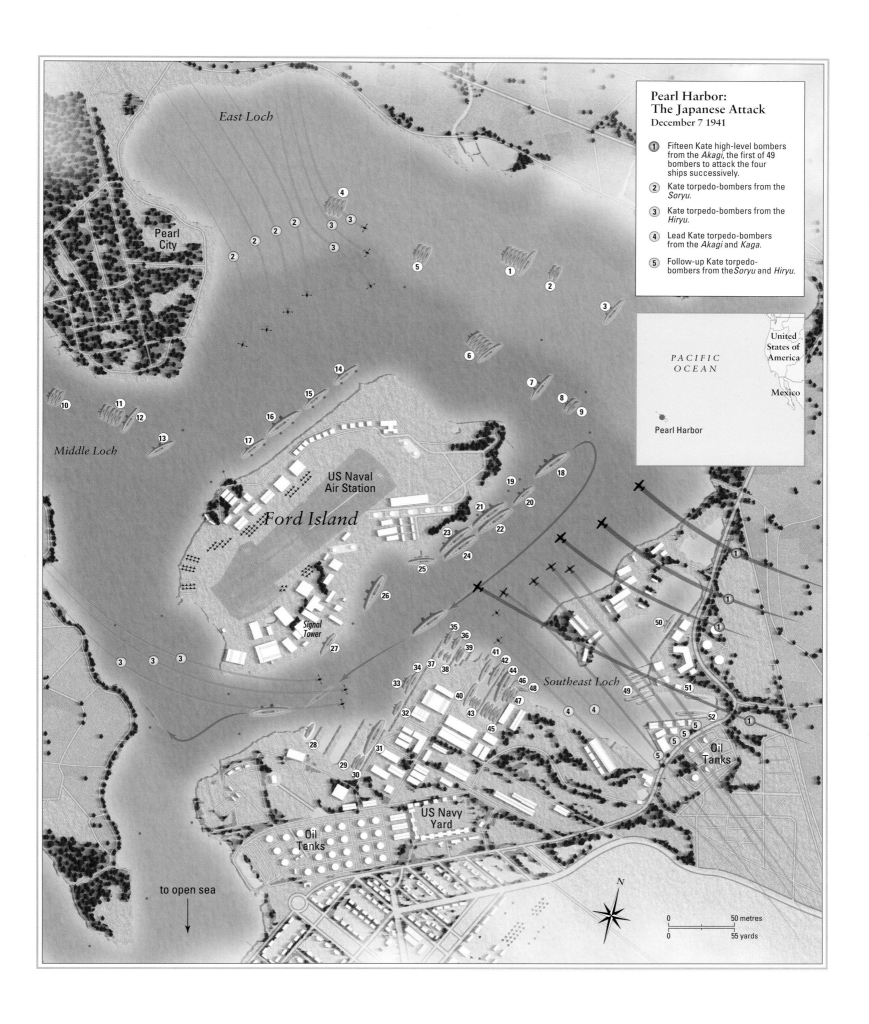

**Pearl Harbor:
The Japanese Attack**
December 7 1941

① Fifteen Kate high-level bombers from the *Akagi*, the first of 49 bombers to attack the four ships successively.

② Kate torpedo-bombers from the *Soryu*.

③ Kate torpedo-bombers from the *Hiryu*.

④ Lead Kate torpedo-bombers from the *Akagi* and *Kaga*.

⑤ Follow-up Kate torpedo-bombers from the *Soryu* and *Hiryu*.

East Loch

Pearl City

Middle Loch

US Naval Air Station

Ford Island

Signal Tower

Southeast Loch

Oil Tanks

US Navy Yard

Oil Tanks

to open sea

PACIFIC OCEAN

United States of America

Mexico

Pearl Harbor

N

| 0 | | 50 metres |
| 0 | | 55 yards |

important effect of this small operation was that it delayed the German invasion of Russia by a month. It finally began on June 22 with Operation Barbarossa. German Panzers rampaged across Russia using *Blitzkrieg* tactics. But the Soviet Union was much larger than either Poland or France and sheer distances involved meant that the Germans and their allies were never able to utterly destroy the Soviet armed forces. In Asia, a new theater of war was about to open up. The Japanese invasion of China had been progressing in brutal but desultory fashion since 1933. The U.S. and other countries had protested and imposed increasingly severe trade sanctions on Japan, including an oil embargo. By the summer of 1941 the situation was critical. Vast oil resources were located in the Dutch East Indies (now Indonesia); and having been defeated by Germany, the Dutch were in no position to stop the Japanese from invading and taking the oil. The U.S, however, was bound to intervene so Japan decided to attack it first.

WEAPONS PRODUCTION OF THE MAJOR POWERS 1939-1945

AIRCRAFT

	1939	1940	1941	1942	1943	1944	1945
U.S.A	5,856	12,804	26,277	47,826	85,998	96,318	46,761
U.K.	7,940	15,049	20,094	23,672	26,263	26,461	12,070
U.S.S.R.	10,382	10,565	15,735	25,436	34,900	40,300	20,900
Germany	8,295	10,247	11,776	15,409	24,807	39,807	7,540
Japan	4,467	4,768	5,088	8,861	16,693	28,180	11,066

MAJOR WARSHIPS

	1939	1940	1941	1942	1943	1944	1945
U.S.A	-	-	544	1,854	2,654	2,247	1,513
U.K.	57	148	236	239	224	188	64
U.S.S.R.	-	33	62	19	13	23	11
Germany (U-boats)	15	40	196	244	270	189	-
Japan	21	30	49	68	122	248	51

TANKS

	1939	1940	1941	1942	1943	1944	1945
U.S.A	-	c.400	4,052	24,977	19,497	17,565	11,968
U.K.	989	1,399	4,841	8,611	7,476	5,000	2,100
U.S.S.R.	2,950	2,794	6,590	24,446	24,089	28,963	15,400
Germany	c.1,300	2,200	5,200	9,200	17,300	22,100	4,400
Japan	c.200	1,023	1,024	1,191	790	401	142

The attack on the base of the U.S. Pacific Fleet at Pearl Harbor took place without warning on December 7 1941. Believing that battleships would decide a naval war, the Japanese concentrated their attacks on the U.S. battleships, sinking five and badly damaging six more. Dozens of other ships and aircraft were also destroyed, along with 2,403 people killed. The attack had been delivered by dive bombers and torpedo bombers equipped with the new and top-secret Japanese "long-lance" torpedo.

With the U.S. Navy effectively knocked out for months, the Japanese launched sea-borne invasions of the East Indies, Malaya, and Burma. All were overrun within a few months. The overwhelming Japanese victories had been achieved not so much by innovative weaponry, although some of their aircraft were superb, as by surprise, skill and suicidal bravery. The Japanese hoped that their sudden spectacular victories would induce the U.S. to make a form of peace that would secure Japan's oil supplies and allow it to continue the war in China. But the Americans refused and began preparing for a counterattack.

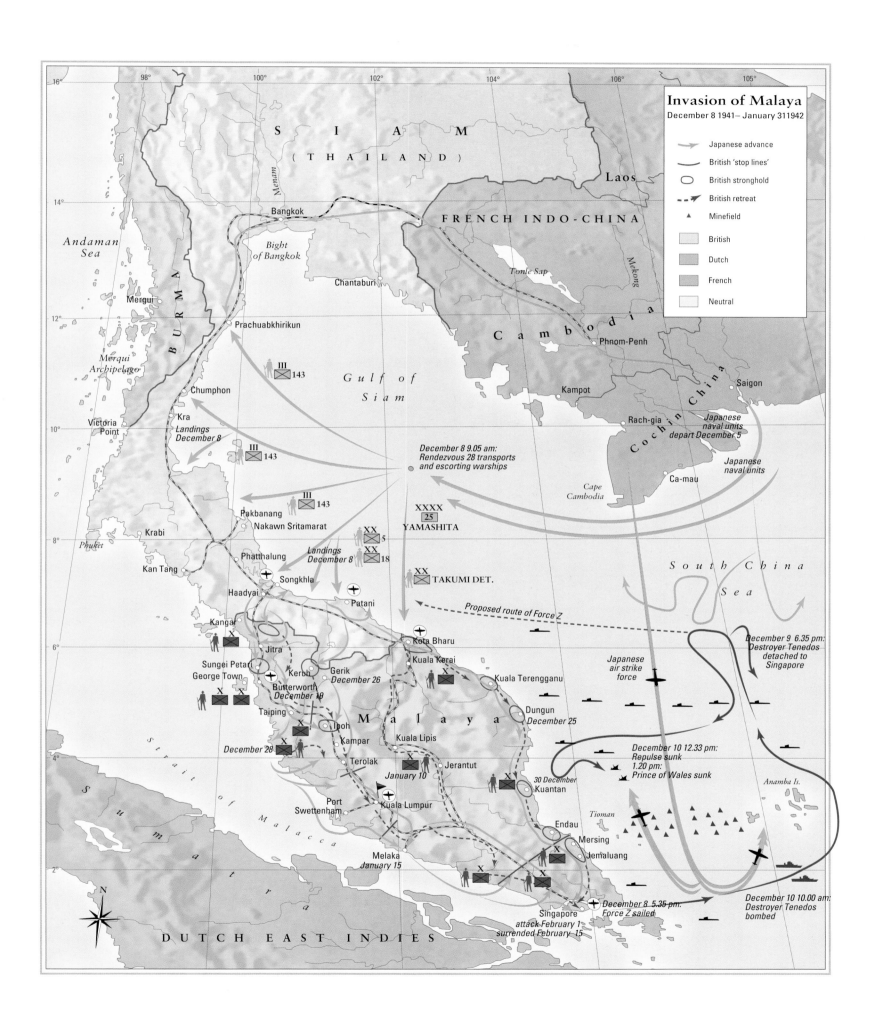

Invasion of Malaya
December 8 1941– January 311942

- Japanese advance
- British 'stop lines'
- British stronghold
- British retreat
- Minefield
- British
- Dutch
- French
- Neutral

Andaman Sea

S I A M
(T H A I L A N D)

Laos

Bangkok

Bight of Bangkok

FRENCH INDO-CHINA

Chantaburi

Tonle Sap

Mekong

B U R M A

Mergui

Prachuabkhirikun

III 143

Gulf of Siam

Phnom-Penh

C a m b o d i a

Kampot

Merqui Archipelago

Chumphon

Kra
Landings December 8

III 143

Rach-gia

Japanese naval units depart December 5

Cochin China

Saigon

Victoria Point

Pakbanang
Nakawn Sritamarat

III 143

Cape Cambodia

Ca-mau

Japanese naval units

Krabi

Krabi

Phuket

XXXX
25
YAMASHITA

XX 5

December 8 9.05 am:
Rendezvous 28 transports
and escorting warships

Kan Tang

Phatthalung

Landings December 8

XX 18

S o u t h   C h i n a   S e a

Haadyai

Songkhla

Patani

XX TAKUMI DET.

Proposed route of Force Z

Kangar

Jitra

Kota Bharu

Japanese air strike force

December 9 6.35 pm:
Destroyer Tenedos
detached to
Singapore

Sungei Petani
George Town

Kersh

Kuala Kerai

Gerik
December 26

Kuala Terengganu

Butterworth
December 19

Taiping

Ipoh

M a l a y a

Kampar

Kuala Lipis

Dungun
December 25

December 28

Terolak

Kuala Lipis

Jerantut

30 December
Kuantan

December 10 12.33 pm:
Repulse sunk
1.20 pm:
Prince of Wales sunk

Anamba Is.

Port Swettenham

January 10

Kuala Lumpur

Tioman

S
u
m
a
t
r
a

Endau

Mersing

Jemaluang

Melaka
January 15

Singapore
*attack February 1
surrended February 15*

December 8 5.35 pm:
Force Z sailed

December 10 10.00 am:
Destroyer Tenedos
bombed

D U T C H   E A S T   I N D I E S

Strait of Malacca

N

WORLD WAR TWO — AXIS DOMINATION

BY MAY 1942 THE AXIS POWERS OF GERMANY, JAPAN, ITALY, AND THEIR ALLIES WERE AT THE HEIGHT OF THEIR POWER AND MANY NEUTRAL OBSERVERS BELIEVED THAT AN AXIS VICTORY WAS INEVITABLE. MINDS BEGAN TO TURN TO WHAT SUCH A VICTORY WOULD MEAN.

The armed forces of the Axis powers had been the instruments of victory, but the politicians behind them had grand plans for how to use the conquests.

Mussolini had probably the least ambitious plans of the three main Axis partners. He intended to incorporate Albania and parts of Yugoslavia into Italy. Greece would become an Italian possession. French and British possessions in North Africa and the Middle East would become Italian colonies, creating a 20th century version of the Roman Empire around the Mediterranean Sea.

Hitler was not convinced by Italian ambitions, and planned to turn Greece and a partitioned

Yugoslavia into German puppets. Germany's allies, such as Finland, Bulgaria, Romania, and Hungary, would be enlarged at the expense of their mutual enemies but would remain quite secondary to Germany in the "New Order" of Europe.

The Soviet Union would be reduced to the status of a slave state, entirely at the disposal of Germany. Nazi racial theories held that the Slavs were inferior to the Germans and so could be used as the Nazis wished. The Soviet Union would be carved up into five main regions. The Slavs would be herded into cities to work as slave labor. All land would be taken over by the government and parcelled out on leases to farmers from Germany or allied countries. Each farm would be given a number of enslaved workers whose condition would be similar to that of the medieval serfdom from which the Russian peasants had emerged a century or so earlier.

Japan's war aims centered on what it called the Greater East Asia Co-Prosperity Sphere. This was promoted as a friendly economic community of Asian countries free of European imperialism and economic domination. The Japanese envisaged that it would cover all of mainland Asia apart from the Soviet Union. In practice the Japanese wanted to free these regions of European occupation in order to subjugate them to Japanese economic power. The newly independent states of Asia were expected to supply raw materials to Japanese industry and to follow the lead of their Japanese "liberator."

The Axis invasions in the early years of World War Two changed the world map to show large swathes of newly-occupied territory and almost the whole of Western Europe was now under the rule of Nazi Germany.

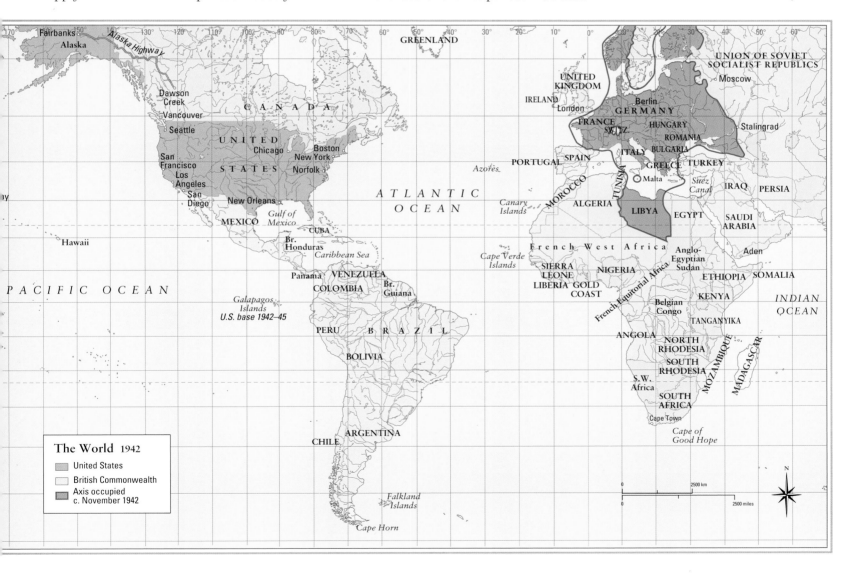

The World 1942

- United States
- British Commonwealth
- Axis occupied c. November 1942

WORLD WAR TWO — ALLIED COUNTERATTACK

THE OPENING MONTHS OF WORLD WAR TWO WERE DOMINATED BY VICTORIES FOR THE AXIS POWERS, BUT THEY WOULD ALL FACE DEFEAT EVENTUALLY AND BE FORCED TO ACCEPT UNCONDITIONAL SURRENDER.

The first of the Allies to produce weapons that could face those of the Axis on equal terms was Britain. The Spitfires and Hurricanes of the RAF Fighter Command had kept control of the skies over the English Channel and southern Britain during the crucial weeks of the Battle of Britain. But this was a defensive battle and the fighters were defensive weapons. If the Allies were going to win the war, they would have to go on the offensive.

It was in the Pacific theater of war that the Allies first managed to score a significant offensive success against the enemy. The main weapon in this victory had been developed during the interwar years without attracting much attention: the aircraft carrier.

During the 1920s the Washington Naval Treaty restricted the size and number of large warships that a country could have. Because most naval experts believed the big-gun battleship was the key weapon at sea, the aircraft carrier was neglected. It was not until the Washington Naval Treaty expired that navies began to build aircraft carriers. The U.S. and Japan began by converting two battle cruisers each to the new role. Their guns were removed, insides stripped out, and hulls decked over with a flush deck that acted as a landing field. The results were the *Lexington* and the *Saratoga* for the U.S. and the *Akagi* and the *Kaga* for Japan. The British and French followed suit. In 1937 Britain began construction of *HMS Illustrious*, the first large purpose-built aircraft carrier to enter service. It had the unique feature of an armored deck and armored sides to the hangars as protection primarily against gunfire and secondarily against bombs. No other navy regarded armor as necessary for the carriers they were building.

The carriers needed specialized aircraft. These had to be able to land and take off in very short spaces, be robust enough to cope with touching down on a pitching deck, and small enough to be taken down below on the elevators common to all aircraft carriers. Most carrier aircraft would be designed with folding wings, to aid storage and movement around the ship. These constraints generally made naval aircraft inferior in fighting ability to their land-based counterparts. They tended to be slower, more lightly armed, and less agile. That was good enough when facing other carrier-based aircraft but not when going after land targets.

A startling exception was the Mitsubishi A6M2, better known by the name given it by pilots: the Reisen or Zero. The Japanese had kept this fighter a strict secret during development in the latter 1930s. Even after it entered service, it was used only when the chances of one being shot down over enemy territory were negligible. In September 1940, 13 Zeros attacked 27 Chinese fighters and shot them all down without loss. Rumors of a high-performance Japanese fighter inevitably leaked out of China, but earlier Japanese fighters had been so inadequate that nobody took the stories seriously. The first the U.S. knew of the Zero's abilities was when swarms of them appeared over Pearl Harbor.

The Zero had a top speed of 282 mph (454 kph) and a ceiling of 32,848 ft (10,012 m). Its phenomenal range of 1,926 miles (3,100 km) was achieved with external fuel tanks that could be jettisoned when empty. It was armed with two 7.7 mm machine guns and two 20 mm cannons and could be adapted to carry a pair of 140 lb (64 kg) bombs, but this reduced its performance. The Zero would undergo five major variations by 1945 and a total of 10,964 would enter combat.

Complementing the Zero was the Nakajima B5N Kate carrier bomber. This versatile three-man bomber was able to carry either 1,764 lb (800 kg) of bombs or a torpedo. It was this aircraft that sank so many U.S. ships at Pearl Harbor and in the Coral Sea. Unlike the Zero, the Kate was replaced as the war progressed by faster carrier bombers, such as the Tenzan.

An early success for aircraft in a sea battle came on December 10 1941. Most naval officers believed that ships maneuvering at speed and protected by anti-aircraft guns would in most circumstances be able to fight off air attack. When Japanese bombers and torpedo bombers attacked the battleship *HMS Prince of Wales* and the battlecruiser *HMS Repulse* off the Malayan coast near Kuantan, this idea was disproved. In less than an hour the Japanese scored eight hits with 49 torpedoes and sent both capital ships to the bottom. Their sinking was even more shocking as the two big ships were accompanied by four destroyers with specially upgraded anti-aircraft weaponry.

The two Japanese victories at Pearl Harbor and Kuantan convinced some, but not all, naval officers that it was the aircraft carrier and not the battleship that would now decide fleet actions. That point was proved beyond doubt at the Battle of Midway in June 1942. Signal intercept intelligence showed that the Japanese were about to launch an attack on Midway Island, the site of a large U.S. Marine base. Admiral Spruance was sent with three aircraft carriers, the *Enterprise*, *Yorktown*, and *Hornet* and six cruisers and a number of destroyers to ambush the attackers. When the attack came, it was led by the top Japanese admiral, Yamamoto, with four aircraft carriers and support from four battleships, six cruisers, and a number of destroyers.

The battle began when the Japanese aircraft carriers launched an attack on Midway Island early on June 4. The battle was confused by dense cloud causing the rival fleets to lose touch with each other from

Opposite page: The Battle of Midway June 3 –6, 1942, was the first naval battle fought solely between the naval air forces of the two sides. Half the Japanese aircraft carrier force was lost, a crucial blow to their war effort.

time to time. It ended with all four Japanese carriers and the *Yorktown* sunk by air attack alone. Spruance moved west the next day to attack the remaining Japanese ships, but turned back when he became worried about what the big guns of the enemy battleships could do to his aircraft carriers. Nevertheless, Japanese naval power had been broken and the supremacy of the aircraft carrier over the battleship had been clearly demonstrated.

Naval warfare was having an equally clear effect in the Mediterranean, although in a very different way. On March 28 1941 off Cape Matapan in southern Greece, the British and Italian navies had fought a relatively old-fashioned gun battle when an Italian fleet of one battleship, four cruisers, and 14 destroyers met a British fleet of three battleships, four cruisers, and 18 destroyers. The battle was a significant British victory and, combined with other actions, gave the British Navy effective control of the eastern Mediterranean, even though Italian ships, submarines, and torpedo boats continued to operate

As a result, convoys of supply ships heading from Italy to North Africa became smaller, less frequent and more liable to suffer losses. This, in turn, meant that German and Italian land forces under General Erwin Rommel in the North African desert came to be short of supplies, reinforcements and — perhaps most importantly — Panzers and trucks. This culminated in the failure of Rommel to extend his headlong advance of 1942 from Libya all the way to the Suez Canal. Instead he came to a halt at Ruweistat Ridge on June 30.

One of the new weapons that gave Rommel and other German commanders an advantage was the assault gun. This was an artillery piece mounted onto a tank chassis. The gun was not mounted in a turret and the vehicle lacked other key features, but it did have excellent cross-country performance, provided the gunners with some armored protection, and delivered impressive firepower. In the view of the German high command, they had the advantage of being cheaper to produce than tanks.

The most numerous of these assault guns was the StuG III, 10,600 of which saw action. It was a 75 mm cannon mounted onto a Panzer III chassis. Despite their name, the assault guns were highly effective in defense; and as the Germans found themselves increasingly under pressure, the number of these guns increased. The StuG IV was a similar gun mounted on a Panzer IV chassis. The Elefant was an 88 mm gun mounted on a Tiger chassis. There were numerous variants on the concept of the assault gun, and later other armies copied the idea.

On October 23 1942 the British commander General Bernard Montgomery launched his counterattack in the desert near the tiny settlement of El-Alamein. The battle raged until November 4, by which time Rommel had only 30 tanks fit for action and was almost out of fuel. Even then, he managed to extricate most of his men by a combination of skillful rearguard actions and taking advantage of bad weather. The escape was only temporary, and by February 1943 the German and Italian forces in North Africa were trapped in a pocket around Tunis. They surrendered on May 13 1943, by which time Rommel was in Germany, a sick man, and increasingly convinced that his country could not win the war.

The battles of Midway and El-Alamein had been won by superior Allied numbers and better intelligence reports, not by superior weaponry. It was on the Eastern Front that the Germans first came across an Allied weapon greatly superior to their own, and it came as a nasty shock.

Russian tank designers, led by M. Koshkin, had begun to think along the lines of German designers in 1939. They began to favor a medium tank that was heavy enough to batter through defenses and

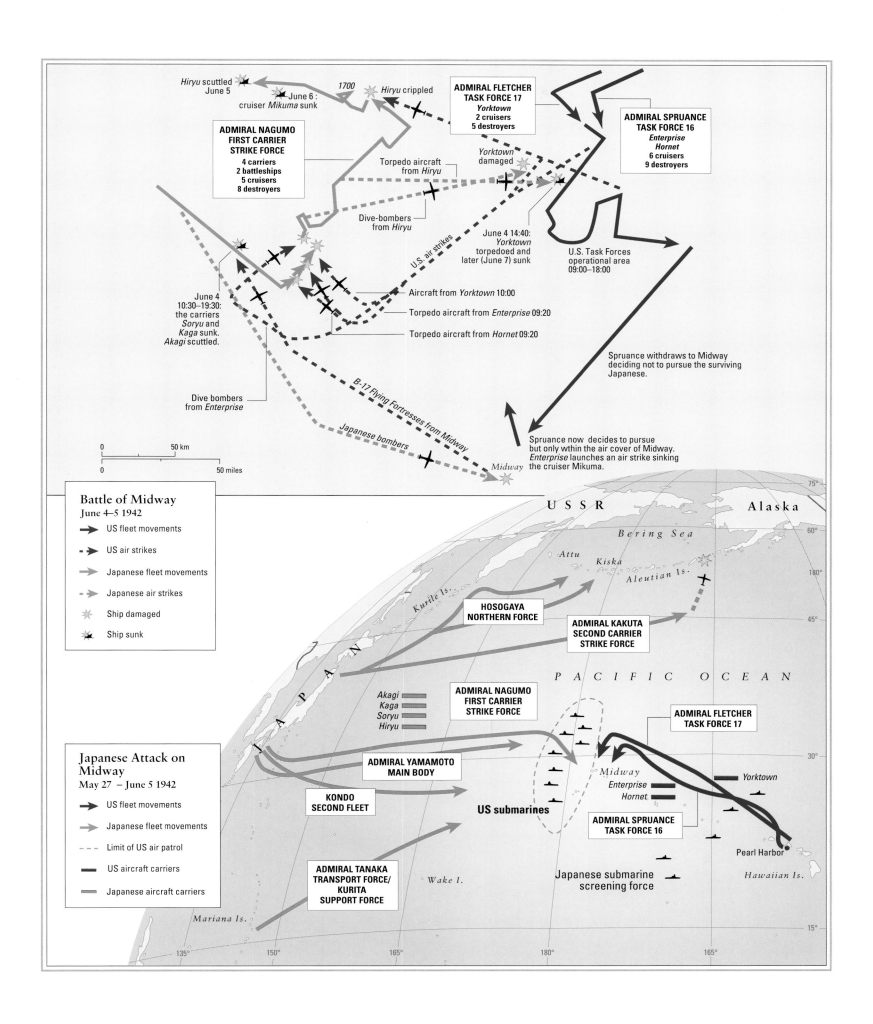

Hiryu scuttled
June 5

June 6 :
cruiser *Mikuma* sunk

1700

Hiryu crippled

**ADMIRAL FLETCHER
TASK FORCE 17**
Yorktown
2 cruisers
5 destroyers

**ADMIRAL SPRUANCE
TASK FORCE 16**
Enterprise
Hornet
6 cruisers
9 destroyers

**ADMIRAL NAGUMO
FIRST CARRIER
STRIKE FORCE**
4 carriers
2 battleships
5 cruisers
8 destroyers

Torpedo aircraft
from *Hiryu*

Yorktown
damaged

Dive-bombers
from *Hiryu*

June 4 14:40:
Yorktown
torpedoed and
later (June 7) sunk

U.S. air strikes

U.S. Task Forces
operational area
09:00–18:00

June 4
10:30–19:30:
the carriers
Soryu and
Kaga sunk.
Akagi scuttled.

Aircraft from *Yorktown* 10:00

Torpedo aircraft from *Enterprise* 09:20

Torpedo aircraft from *Hornet* 09:20

Spruance withdraws to Midway
deciding not to pursue the surviving
Japanese.

Dive bombers
from *Enterprise*

B-17 Flying Fortresses from Midway

Japanese bombers

Midway

Spruance now decides to pursue
but only wthin the air cover of Midway.
Enterprise launches an air strike sinking
the cruiser Mikuma.

0   50 km

0   50 miles

Battle of Midway
June 4–5 1942

➤ US fleet movements

▪▪➤ US air strikes

➤ Japanese fleet movements

▪▪➤ Japanese air strikes

✴ Ship damaged

✴ Ship sunk

U S S R

Alaska

Bering Sea

Attu

Kiska

Aleutian Is.

**HOSOGAYA
NORTHERN FORCE**

**ADMIRAL KAKUTA
SECOND CARRIER
STRIKE FORCE**

Kurile Is.

P A C I F I C   O C E A N

J A P A N

Akagi
Kaga
Soryu
Hiryu

**ADMIRAL NAGUMO
FIRST CARRIER
STRIKE FORCE**

**ADMIRAL FLETCHER
TASK FORCE 17**

**ADMIRAL YAMAMOTO
MAIN BODY**

Midway
Enterprise
Hornet

Yorktown

**Japanese Attack on
Midway**
May 27 – June 5 1942

➤ US fleet movements

➤ Japanese fleet movements

▪▪▪ Limit of US air patrol

▬ US aircraft carriers

▬ Japanese aircraft carriers

**KONDO
SECOND FLEET**

US submarines

**ADMIRAL SPRUANCE
TASK FORCE 16**

Pearl Harbor

**ADMIRAL TANAKA
TRANSPORT FORCE/
KURITA
SUPPORT FORCE**

Wake I.

Japanese submarine
screening force

Hawaiian Is.

Mariana Is.

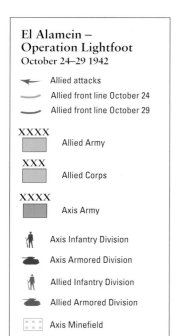

El Alamein – Operation Lightfoot
October 24–29 1942

— Allied attacks

— Allied front line October 24

— Allied front line October 29

XXXX Allied Army

XXX Allied Corps

XXXX Axis Army

Axis Infantry Division

Axis Armored Division

Allied Infantry Division

Allied Armored Division

Axis Minefield

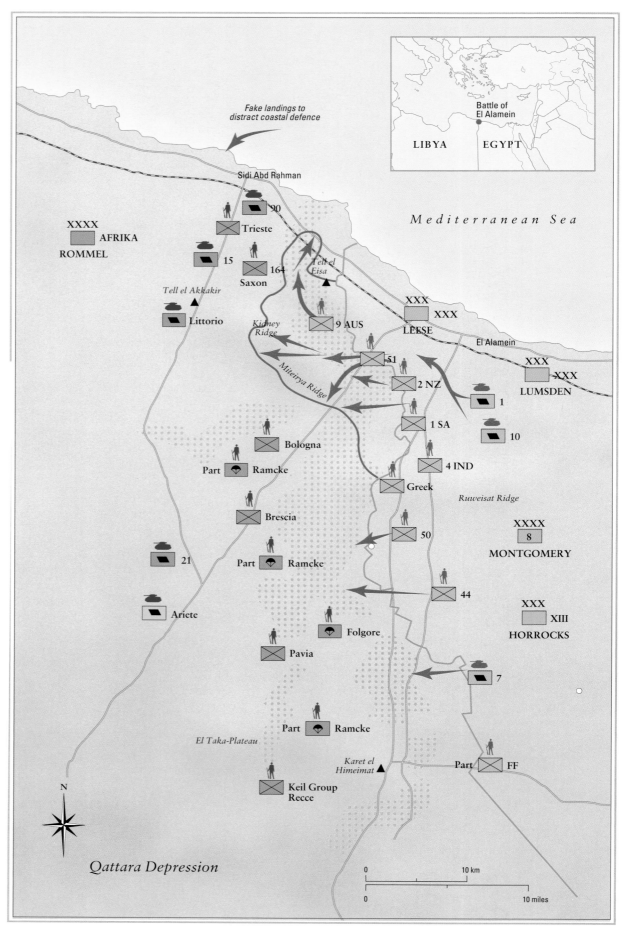

Fake landings to distract coastal defence

Mediterranean Sea

Battle of El Alamein

LIBYA   EGYPT

Sidi Abd Rahman

90

Trieste

XXXX AFRIKA

ROMMEL

15

164

Saxon

Tell el Eisa

Tell el Akkakir

Littorio

Kidney Ridge

9 AUS

XXX LEESE **XXX**

El Alamein

Miteirya Ridge

51

2 NZ

XXX LUMSDEN **XXX**

1

1 SA

10

Bologna

Part Ramcke

4 IND

Greek

Ruweisat Ridge

Brescia

50

XXXX 8

MONTGOMERY

21

Part Ramcke

44

Ariete

XXX XIII

HORROCKS

Folgore

Pavia

7

Part Ramcke

El Taka-Plateau

Karet el Himeimat

Part FF

N

Keil Group Recce

Qattara Depression

0   10 km

0   10 miles

Operation Lightfoot was the codename for the second Battle of El Alamein, 24 October 1942, between the British Eighth Army and the German Afrika Korps. El Alamein signalled the start of the ultimate German defeat in North Africa eight months later.

light enough to race ahead at speed and exploit a breakthrough. The result was the T34, the most revolutionary tank of the war and a weapon that made all other tanks obsolete.

The T34 was a medium tank armed with a 76.2 mm gun and protected by armor up to 2 in (52 mm) thick. It had an operational range of 250 miles (402 km) and a top speed on roads of 33 mph (53 kph). This alone made it superior to the 1939 models of the Panzer IV and Panzer III, but the tank included several revolutionary design features. The turret was cast in one piece, giving it added strength, and the hull was designed in a series of sloping facets so that incoming shells would often glance off without exploding. Its cross-country performance was boosted by having five large road wheels and wide tracks to spread the tank's 29 ton (26.4 tonne) weight more evenly across the ground. Of crucial importance for fighting in Russia, all the controls and instruments were designed so that they could be used easily by men wearing gloves.

The T34 did have some drawbacks compared to German machines. The turret could accommodate only two men, so the tank commander had to double as either gunner or loader. The early models lacked a radio, which hindered co-operation on the battlefield, but this was corrected in later models. So successful was the T34 that it remained in production into the 1970s for export markets, and some armies still had T34 tanks in their arsenal in 2010. The high point of the T34's success came in the Stalingrad campaign of 1942–1943. In the summer of 1942 the Germans abandoned their main aim of 1941, capturing Moscow. Instead they thrust south to capture the Caucasus oilfields, secure the grain fields of the Black Sea and Caspian Sea areas, and thus position themselves for a northward sweep over the Don and Volga Rivers to the great city of Stalingrad on the Volga. It was not really necessary for the success of the campaign to capture Stalingrad — laying siege to it would have sufficed, but Hitler committed his first major blunder of the war when he insisted that the city had to be captured. This move sucked in most of the German reserves, to be lost in bitter street fighting, where the superior equipment that gave the Germans their advantage in open battle was lost.

On November 19 1942 massed attacks led by T34 tanks burst through the German lines north and south of the city. Using *Blitzkrieg* tactics, the Russian columns raced on to surround and isolate the huge German forces in and around Stalingrad. The pocket was then squeezed mercilessly until a lack of supplies and mounting casualties caused Field Marshal von Paulus to surrender the remnants of his 6th Army. The campaign had cost the Germans 250,000 men, and by February 1943 they were back where they had started. The appearance of the T34 prompted an arms race in tank design. The Germans copied many of the new features of the T34 in their Panzer V Panther. This superlative tank was arguably the best armoured vehicle produced by any nation during World War Two. Armed with a 75 mm cannons and two 7.92 mm machine guns, the Panther could travel faster than the T34 and could cope with rugged terrain just as well. With armor up to 3 in (80 mm) thick, it was better protected than the T34. In a straight battle the Panther had the edge. Even more formidable was the Panzer VI, better known as the Tiger Tank. This awesome tank weighed 56 tons (50 tonnes) and had armor up to 4¾ in (120 mm) thick in places. It was armed with the famous 88 mm gun and also two machine guns. A speed of 24 mph (39 kph) was impressive for a vehicle of this weight, as was its range of 120 miles (193 km). Properly handled the Tiger was supreme on the battlefield. It was vulnerable only to a hit at point-blank range or from behind.

At Villers Bocage in Normandy a few days after D-Day, a single Tiger held up an entire Allied armored division, destroying 24 vehicles. One Tiger commander, Kurt Knispel, destroyed 168 Russian tanks in 18 months without suffering any serious damage to his   own vehicle. Impressive as the Tiger was, and the improved Tiger II was even better, they were faced by large and growing numbers of enemy tanks and artillery. The war on the Eastern Front, and to a lesser extent on other fronts, was becoming one of German quality against Allied numbers. The German war industries were remarkable for continuing to produce new and improved weapons in the face of great difficulties. And few of those difficulties were greater than the Allied strategic bombing campaign.

The idea of strategic bombing had been born in the final days of World War One. Enthusiastic military aviators had noted the successes gained by bombers attacking military targets and predicted that the time would come when similarly spectacular results could be gained against war industries. As soon as there were aircraft with the range to carry bombs to enemy cities, they said, weapons factories, oil plants, and transportation networks would be laid waste. So effective would such bombing become, they said, that all the armies would need to do would be to march in and occupy the enemy territory. Nobody took such ideas seriously until the Spanish town of Guernica was destroyed in 1937 in the Spanish Civil War. In Britain and America the idea of strategic bombing was taken up and orders were placed with manufacturers for heavy, four-engined bombers able to carry heavy bombloads over long distances. The early years of the war seemed to undermine the concept, when bombers of all types were too vulnerable to fighters to make long-range raids feasible.

However, by 1940 neither the British Navy nor their army could get at the enemy. Only bombers could hit the Germans and Italians in any effective way. Because daylight raids were suicidal, the RAF opted for night raids. This made precision bombing of individual factories impossible. Instead the RAF adopted the tactic of area bombing. This involved identifying an area of a city where armaments factories, rail junctions, canal locks, or other prime targets were concentrated in a small area. That area would be saturated with bombs to destroy everything that stood above ground. Inevitably homes, churches, and other civilian buildings were destroyed as well as the intended targets, but nobody in the RAF lost much sleep over that after the German bombing of London, Coventry, Plymouth, and other British cities.

In time, the concept of area bombing would be extended until it resulted in the virtual destruction of entire towns and cities. Some German cities saw the destruction of over 80 percent of their buildings.

The principal weapons used to wage this war of attrition were the three "big brothers": the Stirling, the Halifax and the Lancaster. The Stirling entered service in 1941. It was able to carry up to 14,000 lb (6,350 kg) of bombs over a range of almost 2,000 miles (3,219 km). This far outclassed any other bomber then in active service, but its relatively slow speed of 260 mph (418 kph) and low ceiling of 17,000 ft (5,182 m) made it vulnerable to German fighters. Next into action, also in 1941, was the Halifax. Although its performance was only marginally better than the Stirling's, it was a robust and dependable aircraft that was popular with crews. Outclassing both these was the Lancaster, which entered service in 1942. The Lancaster had a top speed of 290 mph (467 kph) and could reach 25,000 ft (7,620 m) while achieving a range of 2,700 miles (4,345 km). The Lancaster could carry 14,000 lb (6,350 kg) of bombs, and the bomb bay could be easily converted to carry a range of specialist weapons, making it the ideal aircraft for special raids. It had eight .303 inch machine guns in three turrets: two in the front, two in the dorsal turret, and four in the rear. This was inadequate for daylight raids but it was useful at night, when enemy fighters would appear for only fleeting seconds of action. The aircraft was, in addition, relatively roomy and comfortable for the crew and its construction was robust, able to absorb a surprising amount of damage and still get home. It became the main heavy bomber of the RAF, with 7,377 built.

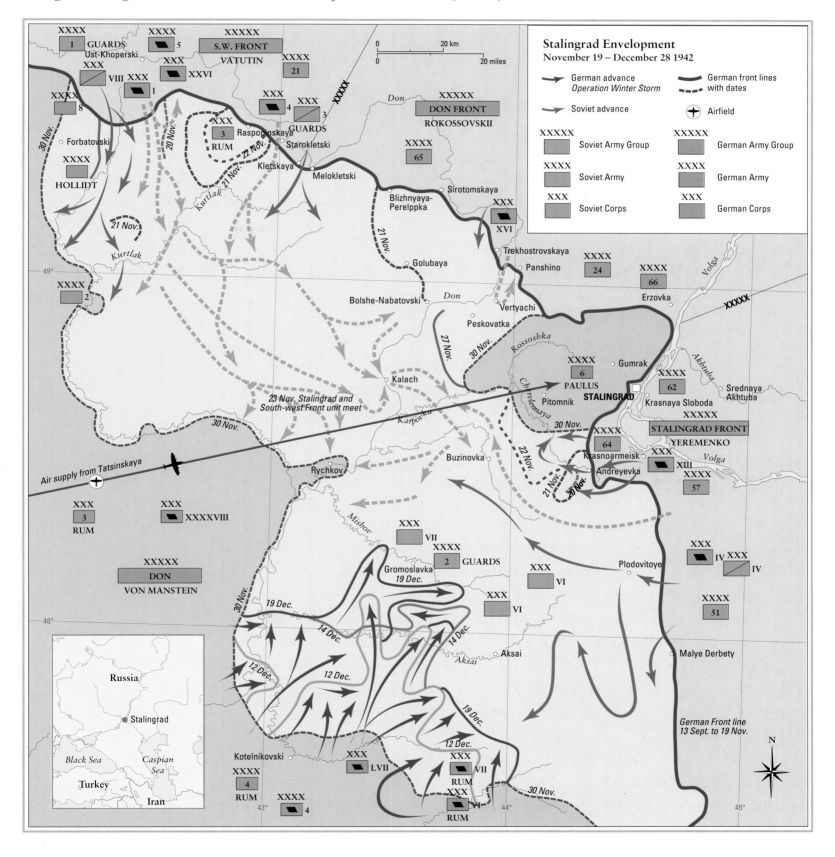

Stalingrad Envelopment
November 19 – December 28 1942

Opposite page: During Operation
Bagration, June 22 – August
19 1944, the Soviet Red Army
cleared the Germans out of
Belorussia and so handed them
the "most calamitous defeat of
all the German armed forces in
World War Two."

The most famous raid carried out by the Lancaster was the Dambuster Raid, undertaken on the night of May 16, 1943. It was aimed at destroying three major dams in the hills east of the Ruhr industrial region. If the dams were smashed, the steel industries of the Ruhr would be deprived of the water they needed to operate. The lakes behind the dams also served as the header tanks for the German canal system, on which were transported most heavy loads such as iron, steel, coal, and completed weaponry.

The main problem was that dams were very strong structures and presented only a narrow profile to bombs dropped from the air. They had been ruled out as practical targets. But the inventor Barnes Wallis devised a way to make a large bomb skip over the water surface like a pebble and then sink to the base of the dam and explode, causing maximum damage.

The raid successfully destroyed two of the target dams and damaged the third. Eight of the Lancasters were lost on the raid, of 19 that took part — making this one of the costliest raids in terms of the proportion of crews killed that the RAF undertook. The immediate results were impressive, but the Germans repaired the damage faster than expected.

While the heavy four-engined bombers were slowly but methodically destroying the industrial cities of Germany, a quite different type of bomber was proving itself to be equally effective. In 1938 the De Havilland company, based in Wales, had proposed to the RAF a small, very lightweight bomber aircraft that was stripped of gun turrets and all other extraneous weight in order to achieve high speed and high altitude. De Havilland believed that such an aircraft could race to its target, bomb successfully, and return to base before enemy fighter aircraft had time to react. The RAF discarded the idea and commissioned the big bombers. De Havilland persisted in their plans and in November 1940 flew the prototype of what they dubbed the Mosquito.

Made primarily of balsa wood and equipped with twin engines, the Mosquito proved to be an instant hit and was soon nicknamed the Mozzie by its crews. This aircraft could reach 341 mph (549 kph) and 28,000 ft (8,534 m) while operating over a range of 2040 miles (3,283 km) with a bomb load of 4,480 lb (2,032 kg). So agile was the bomber that the RAF soon ordered fighter versions for nightfighter duties and photo-reconnaissance versions for undertaking long-range reconnaissance flights over the Reich. The Mosquito was so effective that it had the lowest loss rate of any of the aircraft in the war despite undertaking a variety of hazardous missions, such as bombing Cologne in broad daylight in May 1942.

The Mosquito was the favored aircraft for specialist crews flying on RAF raids. These included crews manning the Master Bomber, whose task was to circle the target throughout the raid, issuing instructions to the other bombers by radio, checking that the bombs were falling on target, and monitoring enemy fighter actions. Other Mosquitoes would meanwhile be dropping flares to show bombardiers where to drop their loads, patrolling the area around the target in search of nightfighters and swooping down low to attack searchlights and anti-aircraft batteries.

While the RAF was concentrating on the bombing of German cities at night, the U.S. Army Air Forces (USAAF) flew daytime sorties. Their missions were generally against targets in occupied countries where precision was essential in order to minimize civilian casualties, and during these sorties the bombers would be in hostile airspace for only a limited time. When the Americans did penetrate deeply into the Reich and its occupied territories, they suffered heavy casualties. The worst single raid was on the Schweinfurt ball-bearing factory on October 14 1943. Of the 291 bombers that took part, 60 were shot

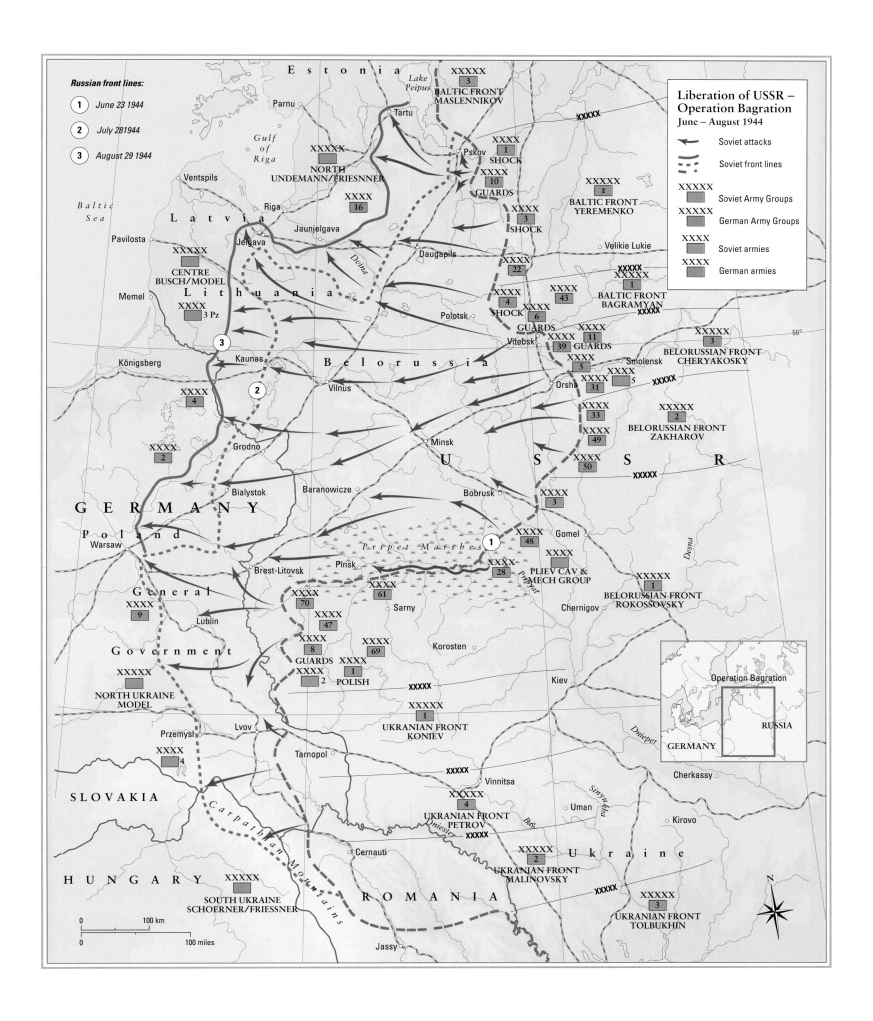

Russian front lines:

(1) *June 23 1944*

(2) *July 28 1944*

(3) *August 29 1944*

**Liberation of USSR –
Operation Bagration**
June – August 1944

Soviet attacks

Soviet front lines

XXXXX — Soviet Army Groups

XXXXX — German Army Groups

XXXX — Soviet armies

XXXX — German armies

E s t o n i a

Lake Peipus

Parnu

Gulf of Riga

Ventspils

Baltic Sea

Pavilosta

Riga

Jaunjelgava

L a t v i a

Jelgava

Memel

Dvina

Daugapils

Königsberg

Kaunas

L i t h u a n i a

Vilnus

B e l o r u s s i a

Polotsk

Vitebsk

Orsha

Smolensk

Velikie Luike

G E R M A N Y

P o l a n d

Grodno

Bialystok

Baranowicze

Minsk

U S S R

Bobrusk

Gomel

Warsaw

Pripet Marshes

Pinsk

Brest-Litovsk

Pripyat

G e n e r a l

Lublin

Sarny

Korosten

Chernigov

Desna

G o v e r n m e n t

Kiev

Cherkassy

NORTH UKRAINE
MODEL

Przemysl

Lvov

Tarnopol

Dnieper

S L O V A K I A

Vinnitsa

Uman

Kirovo

Carpathian Mountains

Cernauti

U k r a i n e

Bug

Dniester

Sinyukha

H U N G A R Y

SOUTH UKRAINE
SCHOERNER/FRIESSNER

R O M A N I A

Jassy

BALTIC FRONT
MASLENNIKOV

Pskov

XXXX 1 SHOCK

XXXX 10 GUARDS

BALTIC FRONT
YEREMENKO

XXXX 3 SHOCK

NORTH
UNDEMANN/FRIESNNER

XXXX 16

XXXXX
CENTRE
BUSCH/MODEL

XXXX 3 Pz

XXXX 22

XXXX 4 SHOCK

XXXX 6 GUARDS

BALTIC FRONT
BAGRAMYAN

XXXX 43

XXXX 39 GUARDS

XXXX 11 GUARDS

XXXX 5

XXXX 31

XXXX 5

BELORUSSIAN FRONT
CHERYAKOSKY

XXXX 33

XXXX 49

BELORUSSIAN FRONT
ZAKHAROV

XXXX 4

XXXX 2

XXXX 50

XXXX 3

XXXX 48

XXXX 28

PLIEV CAV &
MECH GROUP

BELORUSSIAN FRONT
ROKOSSOVSKY

XXXX 9

XXXX 70

XXXX 61

XXXX 47

XXXX 8 GUARDS

XXXX 69

XXXX 1 POLISH

XXXX 2

XXXX 1

UKRANIAN FRONT
KONIEV

XXXX 4

XXXX 4

UKRANIAN FRONT
PETROV

UKRANIAN FRONT
MALINOVSKY

XXXX 3

UKRANIAN FRONT
TOLBUKHIN

56°

Operation Bagration

RUSSIA

GERMANY

0   100 km

0   100 miles

N

The doctrine of strategic bombing was total war transferred from ground to air action. As applied over German-occupied Western Europe during World WarTwo, the aim was the destruction of the enemy's economic capacity to continue hostilities.

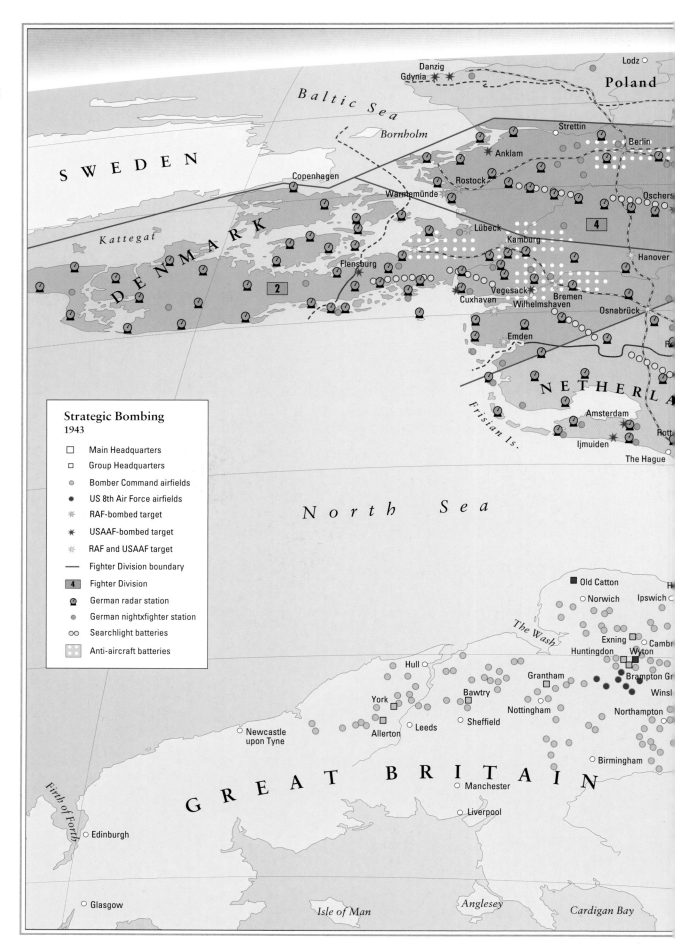

Strategic Bombing
1943

◻ Main Headquarters
◻ Group Headquarters
● Bomber Command airfields
● US 8th Air Force airfields
❋ RAF-bombed target
✳ USAAF-bombed target
❋ RAF and USAAF target
— Fighter Division boundary
4 Fighter Division
☗ German radar station
● German nightxfighter station
∞ Searchlight batteries
⠿ Anti-aircraft batteries

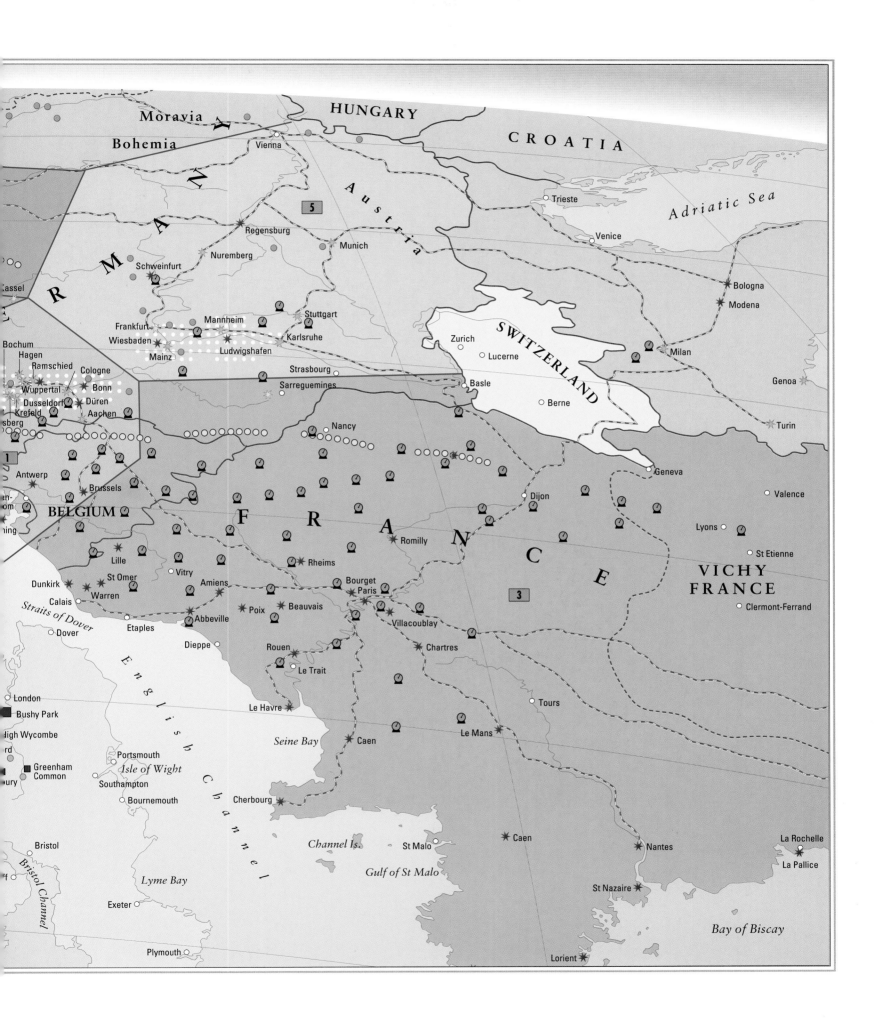

Moravia

HUNGARY

Bohemia

CROATIA

Adriatic Sea

Vienna

5

Austria

Trieste

Regensburg

Venice

Munich

Nuremberg

Schweinfurt

Bologna

Kassel

Modena

Mannheim

Stuttgart

Frankfurt

SWITZERLAND

Wiesbaden

Karlsruhe

Zurich

Milan

Bochum

Ludwigshafen

Lucerne

Hagen

Mainz

Ramsched

Strasbourg

Basle

Genoa

Cologne

Bonn

Berne

Wuppertal

Düren

Turin

Dusseldorf

Aachen

Krefeld

...sberg

Nancy

1

Geneva

Valence

Antwerp

Dijon

Brussels

Lyons

...m

BELGIUM

FRANCE

Romilly

...ning

St Etienne

Lille

Rheims

VICHY
FRANCE

Dunkirk

St Omer

Vitry

Amiens

Bourget

3

Clermont-Ferrand

Calais

Warren

Poix

Beauvais

Paris

Straits of Dover

Abbeville

Villacoublay

Dover

Etaples

Dieppe

Chartres

Rouen

Le Trait

Le Havre

Tours

English Channel

London

Le Mans

Bushy Park

igh Wycombe

Caen

...rd

Seine Bay

Portsmouth

Greenham
Common

Isle of Wight

...ury

Southampton

Bournemouth

Cherbourg

Bristol

Channel Is.

St Malo

Caen

La Rochelle

Nantes

La Pallice

Lyme Bay

Gulf of St Malo

Exeter

St Nazaire

Bristol Channel

Bay of Biscay

Plymouth

Lorient

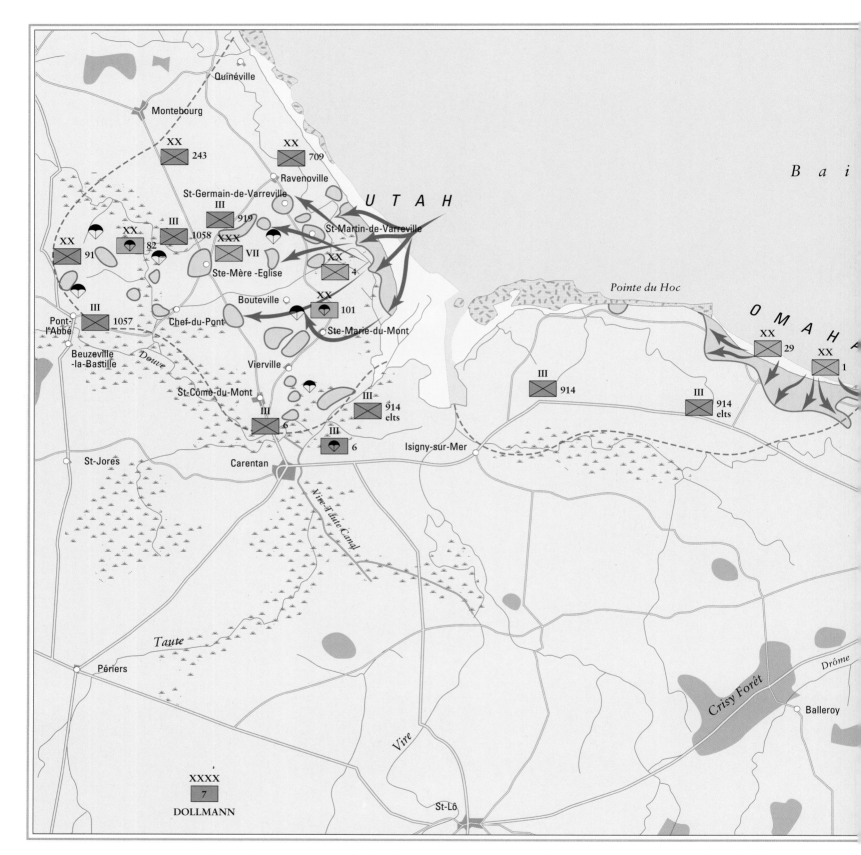

down, 17 more were so badly damaged that they were deemed to be beyond repair, and 122 needed substantial repair.

The bombers taking part in these raids over Europe were Boeing B17 Flying Fortresses. This large bomber had entered service in 1940, though it was not until 1942 that the definitive B17G model was

e la Seine

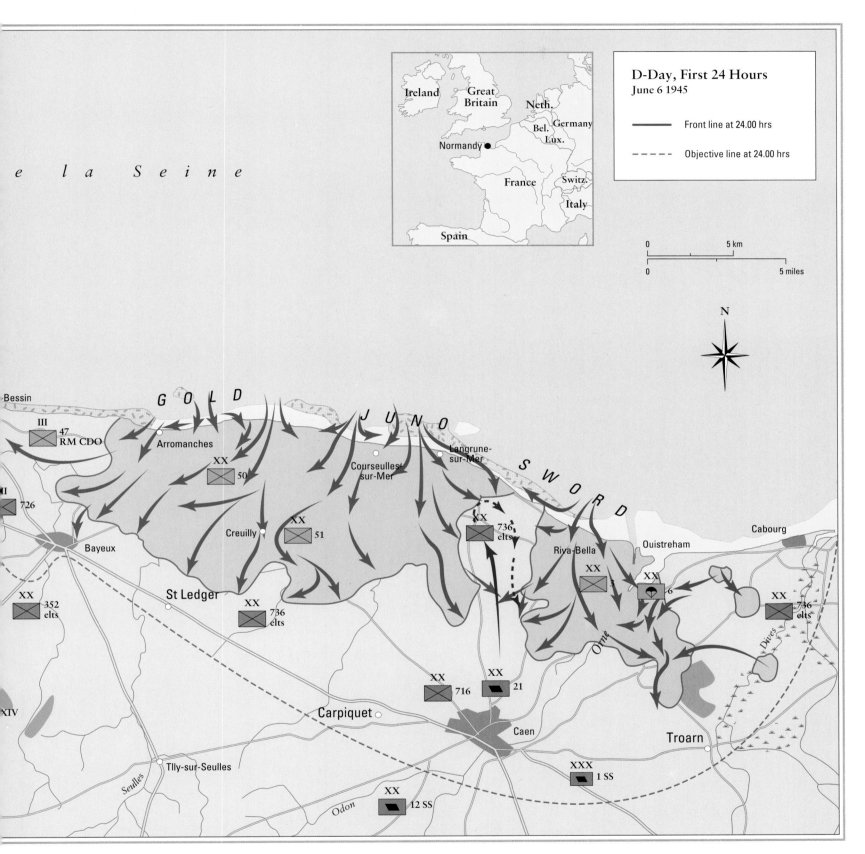

D-Day, First 24 Hours
June 6 1945

——— Front line at 24.00 hrs

- - - - - Objective line at 24.00 hrs

Ireland
Great Britain
Neth.
Bel.
Germany
Lux.
Normandy ●
France
Switz.
Italy
Spain

0   5 km
0   5 miles

N

-Bessin
GOLD
JUNO
SWORD

III
47
RM CDO

Arromanches

XX
50

Courseulles-
sur-Mer

Langrune-
sur-Mer

Cabourg

726

Creuilly

XX
51

XX
736
elts

Riva-Bella

Ouistreham

Bayeux

XX
3

XX
6

XX
736
elts

St Ledger

XX
352
elts

XX
736
elts

Orne

Dives

XIV

XX
716

XX
21

Carpiquet

Caen

Troarn

Tilly-sur-Seulles

XXX
1 SS

Seulles

XX
12 SS

Odon

produced. This superb aircraft had a bomb load of 4,000 lb (1,814 kg), but could carry 9,600 lb (4,354 kg) on short missions. Its top speed was 290 miles (467 kph), its ceiling was 35,600 ft (10,850 m), and range almost 2,000 miles (3,219 km). The nickname Flying Fortress came from its defensive armament of 13 .5-inch machine guns mounted in five positions, including a belly ball turret to guard the underside.

The D-Day invasion of Normandy on June 6 1944. 175,000 troops landed on day one, with varying successes, except at Omaha Beach where German resistance was at its fiercest.

The U.S.A.A.F 8th Air Force's losses of bombers in daylight over Europe remained heavy until the introduction of the long-range P51 Mustang fighter in early 1944. The Mustang was a good fighter in action, but its great advantage was its enormous range. With large fuel tanks, good economy, and extra drop tanks the Mustang had a range of 1,600 miles (2,575 km). This meant that it could escort the USAAF's daylight bombers as far as Berlin. Once a substantial number of Mustangs were in operation by the end of 1944, American bomber losses fell dramatically, allowing larger raids to more distant targets to be undertaken with great precision.

The combination of heavy bombing disrupting weapons production and the appearance on the battlefield of high-quality ground weapons in large numbers sealed the fate of the European Axis powers. Italy surrendered first, in September 1943. Allied troops rushed to occupy the country, but the Germans got there first. The Allies faced a long, arduous campaign fighting their way north through Italy in 1944 and into 1945.

Allied planners had been looking at ways to get a large army onto the European continent since the British were driven out in 1940. The British Prime Minister Winston Churchill favored a route through Greece, pointing out that the British bases in Egypt and Malta would provide the springboard and supply centers. He was deeply worried about Stalin's plans for post-war eastern Europe and wanted to get there first. Once the Americans joined the war, however, it became clear that an invasion through France was more favoured. Planning began for an invasion, code-named Operation Overlord but now better known as D-Day. The invasion took place on June 6 1944; and very soon it was obvious that owing to Allied numbers, supply systems, and air superiority, it was only a matter of time before the Germans were defeated. The American M4 Sherman tank was the most numerous tank used by the invaders, seeing service in British and Canadian armies as well as the U.S. Army. This tank weighed 88 lb (39.9 kg) and had armor up to 2½ in (63 mm) thick. It could reach 25 mph (40 kph) on roads and had a range of 120 miles (193 km). The main weapon was a 75 mm cannon; three machine guns were the secondary armament. Later models had a specialist anti-tank gun, and there were a variety of special models such as the M4 (105) with a 105 mm howitzer.

The Sherman was no match for the Tiger and was outclassed by the Panther, but it was equal to the Panzer IV; and sheer weight of numbers enabled it to overwhelm the better German tanks. By the winter of 1944, the western Allies were on the Rhine and were clearly poised for an invasion of Germany early in 1945.

On the Eastern Front, the steady Soviet advances of 1943 culminated in the massive Operation Bagration of summer 1944. The attack began on June 22 near Vitebsk. Despite tenacious resistance by the outnumbered German units, the Russians broke through after five days. The Soviet assault then spread outward to embrace the entire central area of the Eastern Front. Using *Blitzkrieg* tactics on a grand scale, the Soviets drove the overstretched German forces back.

The confusion of the German retreat was shown by the fact that nine generals were killed and 22 were captured. In all the Germans lost about 25 percent of their manpower on the Eastern Front in the battle and an even higher percentage of tanks, heavy artillery, and aircraft. By the end of August the Soviet advance had liberated nearly all the Soviet Union: the Germans were pushed back to where they had started from in June 1941. More serious for the Germans, it was clear that they could not withstand another

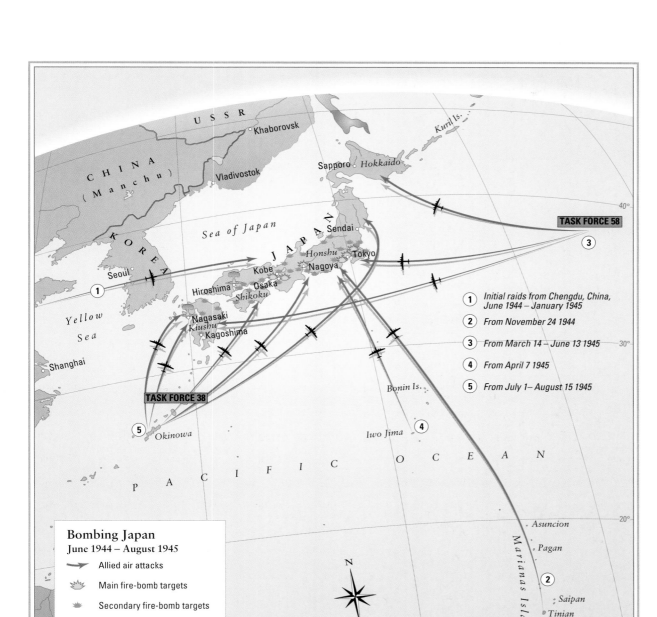

Bombing Japan was not feasible until the American air forces had captured island bases close enough to the Japanese home islands. Not until early 1945 were they able to bomb Japanese cities from bases in the Mariana Islands or Okinawa.

Bombing Japan
June 1944 – August 1945

→ Allied air attacks

🌸 Main fire-bomb targets

🌸 Secondary fire-bomb targets

💣 Atomic bomb targets

1. Initial raids from Chengdu, China, June 1944 – January 1945
2. From November 24 1944
3. From March 14 – June 13 1945
4. From April 7 1945
5. From July 1– August 15 1945

attack. It would take time for the Soviets to replace their losses and to rebuild their always ramshackle supply system. But when that had been achieved, they would advance again and the Germans could do nothing to stop them. Many German generals recognized the inevitability of defeat and expected Hitler to seek some sort of peace deal, as the Kaiser had done in 1918. Hitler refused to contemplate surrender and insisted that his men had to fight to the end, promising them secret weapons of awesome power to keep morale high. Hitler may well have known that the atrocities perpetrated on Russian civilians and the mass murder of Jews, gypsies, and others meant he faced certain execution after an Allied victory. The puzzled German commanders knew something of the atrocities, but very few knew the full extent of the Nazi horrors. Caught in a system in which the Gestapo secret police would murder the families of any commander who surrendered without good cause, the German army fought on.

The end came in spring 1945. In March the western Allies crossed the Rhine and marched into the heart of Germany. A simultaneous attack by the Soviets smashed through the German defenses and

Opposite page: American forces closed in on the Japanese home islands with an island-hopping campaign that began in the Solomon Islands in 1943, and by 1945 took them to Okinawa in the Ryukyu Islands 330 miles (530 km) from the home island of Kyushu.

surrounded Berlin. Hitler killed himself on April 30, with other senior Nazis joining him in death. The Berlin garrison surrendered on 2 May. Germany itself surrendered on May 8.

In the Far East the war against the Japanese was less dominated by military weapons technology than by the open spaces of the Pacific and the dense jungles of South-east Asia. The fighting involved heavy casualties on both sides, with the Japanese fighting to the death and often launching suicide attacks. Given the terrain over which this fighting took place, most of it involved infantry armed with rifles and sub-machine guns. The use of tanks was rare and aircraft acted more as mobile artillery than as bombers. Incurring high casualties on each Pacific island that they captured, the Americans adopted an "island-hopping" strategy. This meant that they attacked and occupied only those islands that were needed for use as naval and air bases for future operations. Islands without good harbors and airfields, or which were off the main route of advance, were simply left alone. The bombing campaign against Japan was very effective. In February 1945 the USAAF switched tactics to fire-bombing. Civilian casualties were very heavy and those who survived were homeless. Weapons production declined to a near halt. However, Japanese resistance remained fanatical. Allied military planners anticipated that the Japanese military would defend the home islands to the last man and that Allied casualties would be enormous. This consideration prompted President Harry Truman to order the dropping of atomic bombs on Hiroshima and Nagasaki in August 1945.

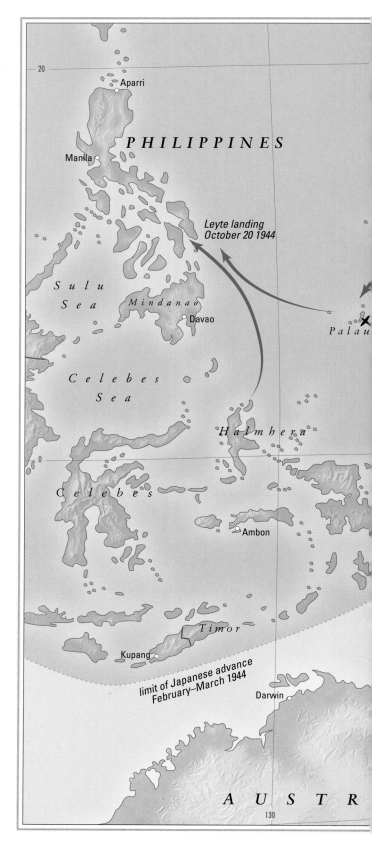

The horrific casualties and fear of more finally induced the Japanese to surrender. The war was over.

On September 2, 1945, the Japanese signed their formal surrender on board the United States battleship USS *Missouri* which was anchored in Tokyo Bay, together with other ships of the U.S. Navy

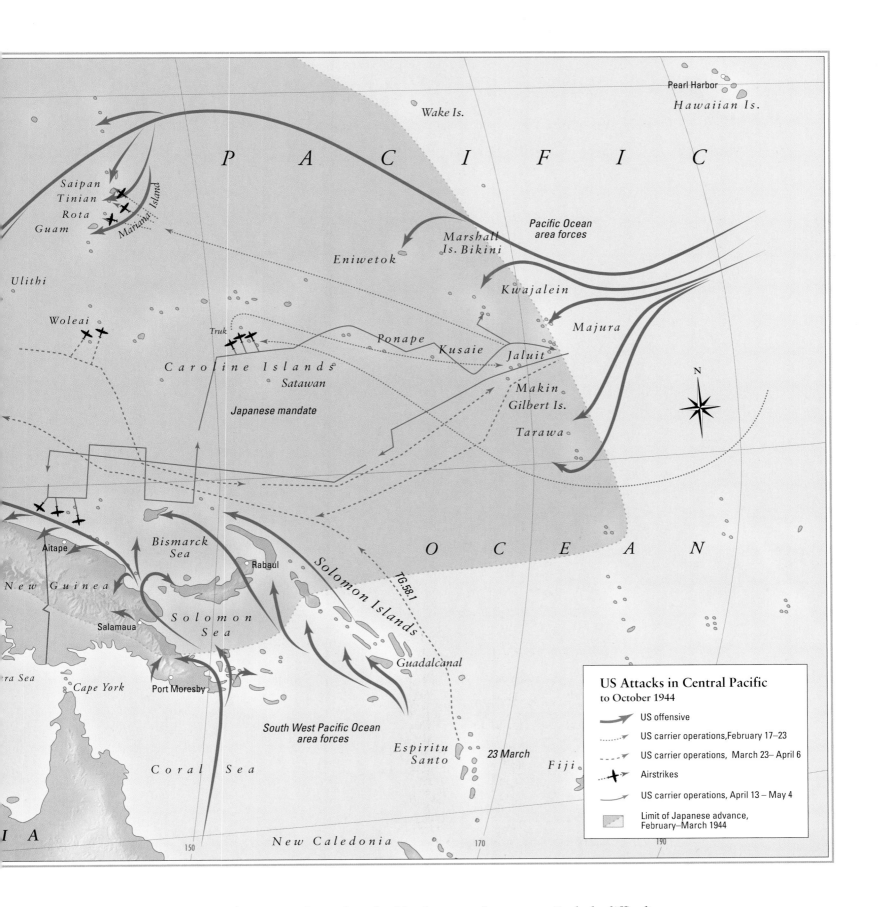

Pearl Harbor

Hawaiian Is.

Wake Is.

P A C I F I C

Saipan
Tinian
Rota
Guam

Mariana Island

*Pacific Ocean
area forces*

Eniwetok

Marshall
Is. *Bikini*

Kwajalein

Ulithi

Woleai

Truk

Ponape

Kusaie

Majura

C a r o l i n e   I s l a n d s

Satawan

Jaluit

Makin
Gilbert Is.

Japanese mandate

Tarawa

N

Aitape

*Bismarck
Sea*

Rabaul

O   C   E   A   N

New Guinea

Solomon Islands

Salamaua

S o l o m o n
S e a

TG.58.1

ra Sea

Cape York

Port Moresby

Guadalcanal

**South West Pacific Ocean
area forces**

*Espiritu
Santo*

23 March

Fiji

I A

C o r a l   S e a

New Caledonia

150   170   190

US Attacks in Central Pacific
to October 1944

—→ US offensive

·····▾ US carrier operations, February 17–23

– – –▾ US carrier operations, March 23– April 6

✈ Airstrikes

—→ US carrier operations, April 13 – May 4

▨ Limit of Japanese advance,
February–March 1944

and vessels of the Royal Navy. The ceremonies took under 30 minutes and were a particularly difficult

experience for the Japanese, who were culturally programmed to consider surrender a shameful act.

WORLD WAR TWO — ROCKET WARFARE

WORLD WAR TWO WAS FOUGHT WITH UPGRADED AND GREATLY IMPROVED VERSIONS OF WEAPONS THAT HAD BEEN ON THE BATTLEFIELD DURING WORLD WAR ONE. SUBMARINES, TORPEDOES, AIRCRAFT, BOMBS, TANKS, AND ARTILLERY HAD ALL BEEN IN ACTION IN 1918. HOWEVER, ONE ENTIRELY NEW WEAPON SAW EXTENSIVE SERVICE IN 1944 AND 1945: THE UNMANNED MISSILE.

Opposite page: The Germans built sites for launching their VI pilotless rocket bombs in occupied Belgium and northern France. Around 8,000 VIs ("V" stood for "vengeance") were launched against England, though less than one-fifth of them reached their targets.

Missiles of a sort had been used in combat for centuries before World War Two. The Chinese and, later, soldiers in India had long been using gunpowder-fuelled rockets to launch explosive charges. The development of these weapons reached its most sophisticated form in the early 19th century when the British engineer William Congreve produced a number of rockets designed to supplant conventional artillery. Congreve's rockets had a range of up to 2 miles (3.2 km) and could deliver an explosive charge of 24 lb (10.9 kg) that sprayed an area with shrapnel when it went off. But all these weapons were for tactical use and were erratic and inaccurate.

It was a shock to the British population when missiles carrying warheads of nearly a ton (0.9 tonnes) of high explosives began falling from the sky in 1944. The weapon was officially the *Vergeltungswaffe* (vengeance-weapon) 1, but was more widely known as the V1. It was also dubbed the "doodlebug" or "*buzzbomb*" because of its characteristic noise.

The British government had known for some time that a number of top-secret weapons were under construction. Although they had little idea of what the weapons were, they knew that they were being developed at a top-secret base on the Baltic island of Peenemunde.

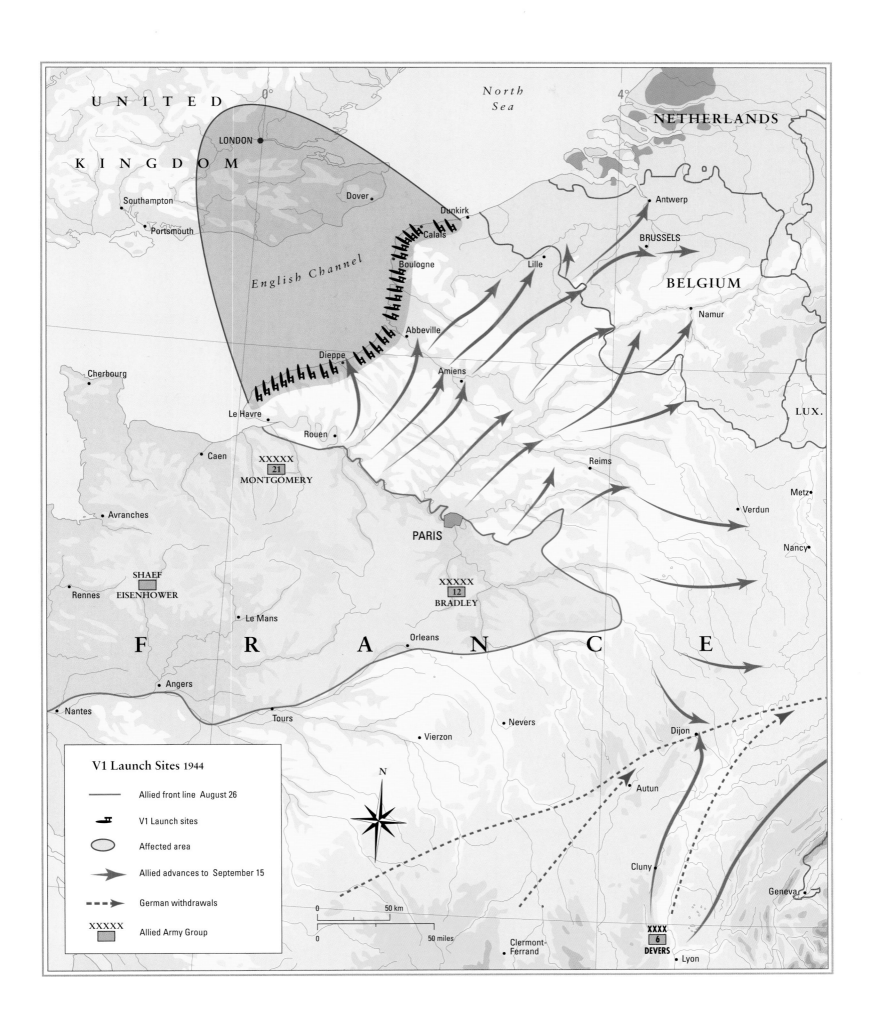

UNITED

KINGDOM

0°

North
Sea

4°

NETHERLANDS

LONDON

Southampton

Dover

Portsmouth

Dunkirk

Calais

English Channel

Boulogne

Abbeville

Dieppe

Le Havre

Cherbourg

Rouen

Caen

XXXXX
21
MONTGOMERY

Avranches

Lille

Antwerp

BRUSSELS

BELGIUM

Amiens

Namur

LUX.

Reims

Metz

Verdun

Nancy

PARIS

SHAEF
EISENHOWER

Rennes

Le Mans

XXXXX
12
BRADLEY

Orleans

FRANCE

Angers

Nantes

Tours

Vierzon

Nevers

Dijon

Autun

Cluny

Geneva

Clermont-
Ferrand

Lyon

XXXX
6
DEVERS

N

V1 Launch Sites 1944

— Allied front line August 26

⎯ V1 Launch sites

⬭ Affected area

→ Allied advances to September 15

--➤ German withdrawals

XXXXX ▢ Allied Army Group

0   50 km

0   50 miles

On August 17 1943 a bomber raid had been sent to Peenmunde in an effort to halt the work. The raid did do extensive damage to the development and construction site. But the Germans responded by moving the main factories producing the weapons to other sites.

The V1 was in reality a pilotless aircraft rather than a rocket. It had wings to provide lift and a conventional tail to control it in flight. Power came from a simple ram-jet, or pulse-jet, which powered it at up to 400 mph (644 kph). A complex arrangement of gyroscopes, pendulums, and a compass acted as a simple autopilot to keep it flying in a straight line at a set altitude. Its range was governed by the amount of fuel on board. The weapon was pointed in the right direction and fell to earth when the fuel ran out. As this was inaccurate, the V1 was usually sent against large cities — mostly London. When the V1 entered service in the summer of 1944, it was initially very successful. Its high speed and small size made it very difficult to shoot down. However, within a few months the installation of a line of barrage balloons along the English coast, each of them trailing stout wires, served to snare many V1s or at least to divert them off course. Soon after this, a small number of anti-aircraft crews were trained in destroying V1s, and came to achieve a high hit rate. RAF fighter pilots also became adept at shooting them down.

Just as the Allies believed they had overcome the V1, the V2 arrived on the scene. Against this weapon there was no defense. It consisted of a true rocket that followed a ballistic route to its target, reaching as high as 50 miles (80 km) above the Earth's surface before falling back to the ground on a course carefully controlled by its internal guidance system. The rocket was powered by an alcohol mixture that burned with liquid oxygen under pressure. It was guided by a sophisticated gyroscopic device, which made it marginally more accurate than the V1.

The first V2 fell on London on September 8 1944, and over the next months more than 1,300 rained down on the city. An estimated 2,754 civilians were killed; another 6,523 were injured. London was not the only target. Norwich, Ipswich, Lille, Paris and Cambrai all suffered attack, but only a few dozen rockets hit any of them. Later, the main weight of the V2 offensive fell on Antwerp, as the Allies began using the docks in the city to supply their forces in Europe. The hugely impressive V2 had an important impact on morale in Germany. The launch of the weapons and the all-too-obvious concern of the Western Allies allowed Hitler and the Nazis to spread rumors and reports about even more revolutionary secret weapons, which were promised for the summer of 1945.

German V1 doodlebug flying bomb, view from underneath.

After the war, the Allied countries raced to grab as much information about the revolutionary V2. The Americans captured the main designer who had worked on the V2, Werner von Braun, and also 126 of his top associates. They also captured 300 railway wagons full of V2 parts and complete rockets. The Soviets managed to capture a few intact rockets and a handful of scientists while the British and Canadians captured a few key personnel, but agreed to pool their resources with the Americans in return for gaining access to whatever secrets were revealed. Both the Soviets and the Americans used the V2 design as the basis for their ICBMs and space rockets.

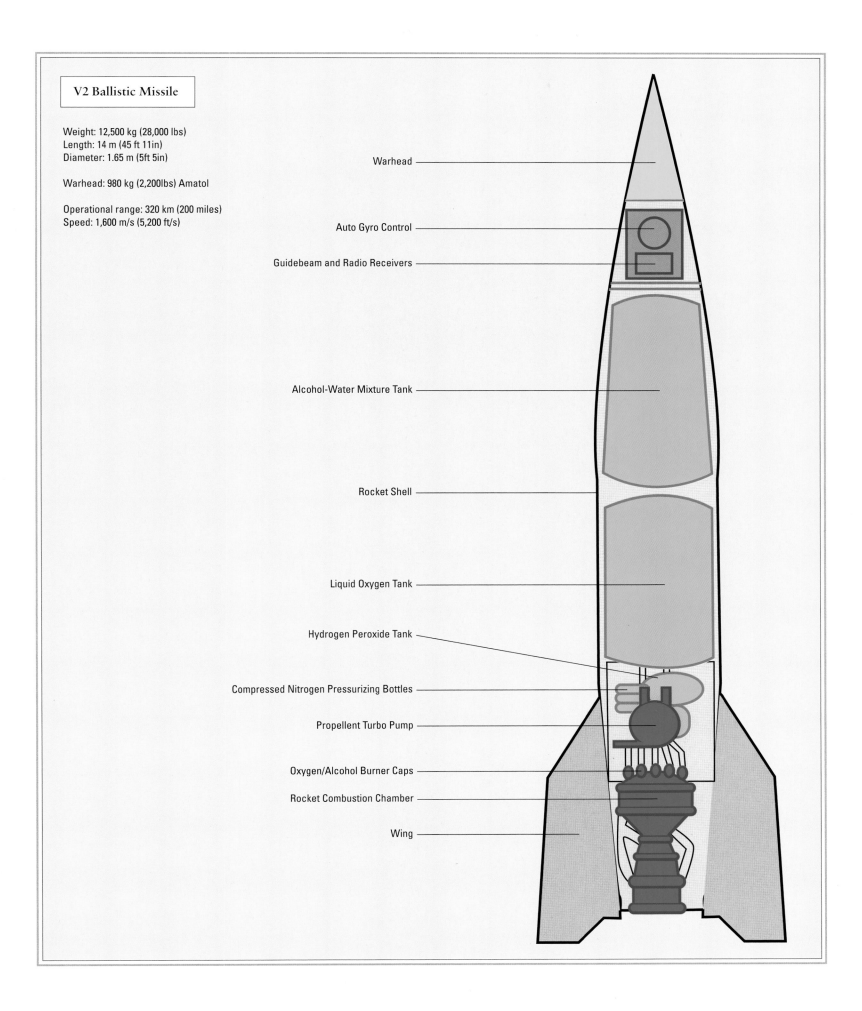

V2 Ballistic Missile

Weight: 12,500 kg (28,000 lbs)
Length: 14 m (45 ft 11in)
Diameter: 1.65 m (5ft 5in)

Warhead: 980 kg (2,200lbs) Amatol

Operational range: 320 km (200 miles)
Speed: 1,600 m/s (5,200 ft/s)

Warhead

Auto Gyro Control

Guidebeam and Radio Receivers

Alcohol-Water Mixture Tank

Rocket Shell

Liquid Oxygen Tank

Hydrogen Peroxide Tank

Compressed Nitrogen Pressurizing Bottles

Propellent Turbo Pump

Oxygen/Alcohol Burner Caps

Rocket Combustion Chamber

Wing

WORLD WAR TWO — ATOMIC WARFARE

THE ATOMIC BOMB BLASTS AT NAGASAKI AND HIROSHIMA AT THE END OF WORLD WAR TWO SHOCKED THE WORLD. THE IDEA OF A NUCLEAR BOMB WAS NOT NEW IN 1945, BUT THE U.S. WAS THE FIRST TO PRODUCE A WORKING WEAPON. OTHER COUNTRIES ALSO BEGAN TO DEVELOP ATOMIC WEAPONS.

The discovery of radiation in 1898 by Pierre and Marie Curie had started the study of sub-atomic physics, which would eventually lead to both atomic power plants and the atomic bomb. In 1934 the study of atomic reactions had progressed to the point at which the Hungarian physicist Leo Szilard postulated circumstances under which a chain reaction could be set off. He patented an idea for a bomb based on a nuclear chain reaction but had no idea of how to construct such a device. He took his work to the British government. In 1938 two German scientists, Otto Hahn and Fritz Strassmann, successfully produced nuclear fission in uranium. The tests were replicated at Columbia University in the U.S. by Enrico Fermi, Herbert Anderson, and others.

Working under conditions of utmost secrecy, the Germans had been continuing their work, funded by the German Army's weapons research department. Working under Kurt Diebner and Erich Schumann, a team of scientists tried to solve the practical problems of producing the type of atomic bomb that had been proved possible in theory. In the spring of 1942 the team reported that they could make an atomic bomb, but estimated that it would take them at least four years, possibly longer, to complete their work. At this point in the war the Germans were at the zenith of their power. It seemed to Adolf Hitler and to many of his senior military staff that the war in Russia would be won by late 1942 or the summer of 1943. For this reason, the enormously costly atomic research project could be sidelined until after victory had been won by conventional means. Funding for the project was cut, never to be restored.

The Japanese too were working on an atomic bomb project, codenamed Ni-Go. The details of this project are sketchy as all the records, equipment, and personnel were located in Korea and were captured by the U.S.S.R in 1945. It is thought that the project had solved all the theoretical and technical problems involved and would have produced a working weapon by about 1948.

The Americans, although suffering a series of catastrophic military defeats and setbacks, had virtually unlimited resources for scientific experiment and investigation. Therefore, they made the decision to throw huge amounts of money and scientific brainpower at the development of an atomic weapon. The British scientists who had been working on Szilard's ideas were brought into the growing project, as was Szilard himself. The project was led by J. Robert Oppenheimer and was codenamed the Manhattan Project: the initial team of scientists had met in Manhattan.

President Roosevelt and Britain's Prime Minister Winston Churchill decided not to tell their ally Soviet Russia, led by Josef Stalin, of the project; they were worried about his post-war ambitions for Soviet power. But Stalin had a number of spies active in the U.S. and Britain. Almost all of them were scientists, artists, and others who had left-wing views and who were sympathetic to the plight of the U.S.S.R as it took the brunt of the land war against Germany. The Soviet spymasters persuaded, bribed or blackmailed them into passing secrets to the U.S.S.R. By 1942 the Soviets were aware of the atomic bomb project and were given regular updates on how work was progressing.

Below: The Manhattan Project was the code-name for the building of the atom bomb from 1942–1945. The bomb was constructed on the mistaken assumption that Nazi Germany was doing the same. The Nazis were, in fact, more interested in rocketry.

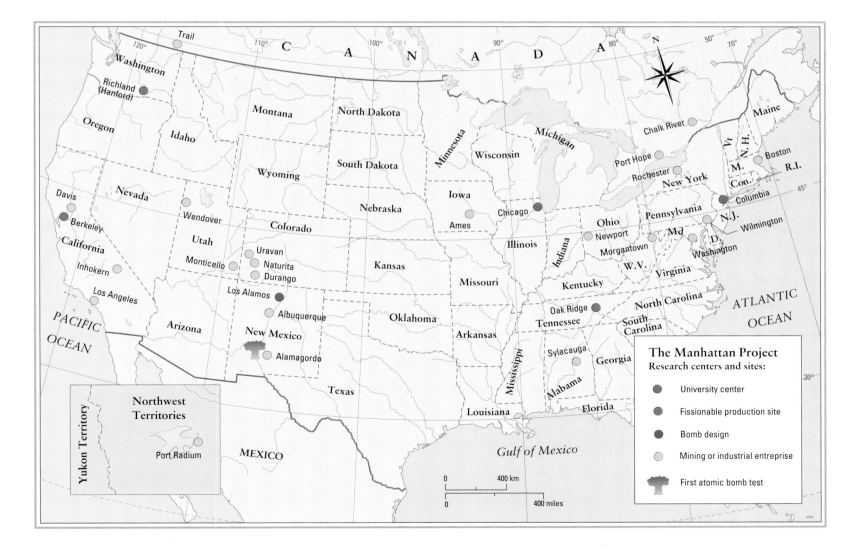

The Manhattan Project
Research centers and sites:

● University center

● Fissionable production site

● Bomb design

● Mining or industrial entreprise

First atomic bomb test

Opposite page: After the first atom bomb, dropped on Hiroshima on August 6 1945, failed to secure the surrender of Japan, a second was dropped on Nagasaki on August 9. Almost a week went by before the surrender was announced on August 15.

The Manhattan Project grew rapidly as vast resources were thrown into it. Over 30 sites across the United States were involved in producing components, carrying out tests, and refining uranium. As the work progressed, it was realized that there were two major problems. The first was how to extract the uranium isotope uranium-235 from uranium ore. The ore contained 99.3 percent other isotopes and only 0.7 percent of uranium-235, but for a bomb to work the uranium core needed to be more than 80 percent uranium-235. The second problem was how to set in motion a chain reaction powerful enough to result in a titanic atomic blast rather than a more muted cascade of reactions.

The issue of producing enough uranium-235 was solved in part when it was realized that plutonium-239 could also, under certain circumstances, be induced to produce a chain reaction. Plutonium-239 could be manufactured from stable isotopes of uranium; and although the process was long and costly, it was at least reliable.

The triggering mechanism proved more difficult to devise. Uranium could be set off by slamming together two lumps of uranium with sufficient force to generate an initial reaction. If the piece of uranium was of sufficient size — 1,400 lb (635 kg) was finally decided upon — there would be enough to cause a violent chain reaction resulting in an instantaneous blast. This could be achieved by placing the two pieces of uranium at opposite ends of a metal tube and sending one racing down the tube with an explosive blast — rather like firing a bullet down a gun barrel. This "gun-type" method of setting off the bomb was considered to be reliable, but the supply of adequate amounts of uranium-235 was still in doubt. The weapon was codenamed "Little Boy".

To set off a plutonium bomb a much more complex system was needed. A hollow sphere of plutonium had to be produced and then mounted within an outer sphere of steel lined with explosives. When the explosives were set off, the plutonium sphere would be crushed together and heated in order to set off the atomic blast. If there were even the slightest variation in the explosive, the weapon would not go off. Less reliable, but using the more plentiful plutonium, this "implosion-type" weapon was codenamed "Fat Man".

On July 16 1945 the first successful test, codenamed "Trinity", of an implosion-type bomb was conducted. President Truman then had to decide whether or not to use the weapon on Japan. The clinching argument was almost certainly the very high number of casualties expected among American and British troops if a land invasion of Japan were needed. Truman ordered that two atomic bombs should be dropped on Japanese cities, after which a threat to use dozens more would be made, although at this time there were no others in existence.

Consequently a gun-type bomb was dropped on Hiroshima on August 6 and an implosion-type was dropped on Nagasaki on August 9. The targets were chosen because they were industrial cities that were producing weapons and other war equipment; they were also relatively free of historic buildings and cultural heritage sites. The two bombs killed about 100,000 people instantly, and many tens of thousands more died of after-effects in the following months and years.

Japan surrendered on August 15, but it would be several weeks before all units of the Japanese armed forces accepted the decision and surrendered in turn.

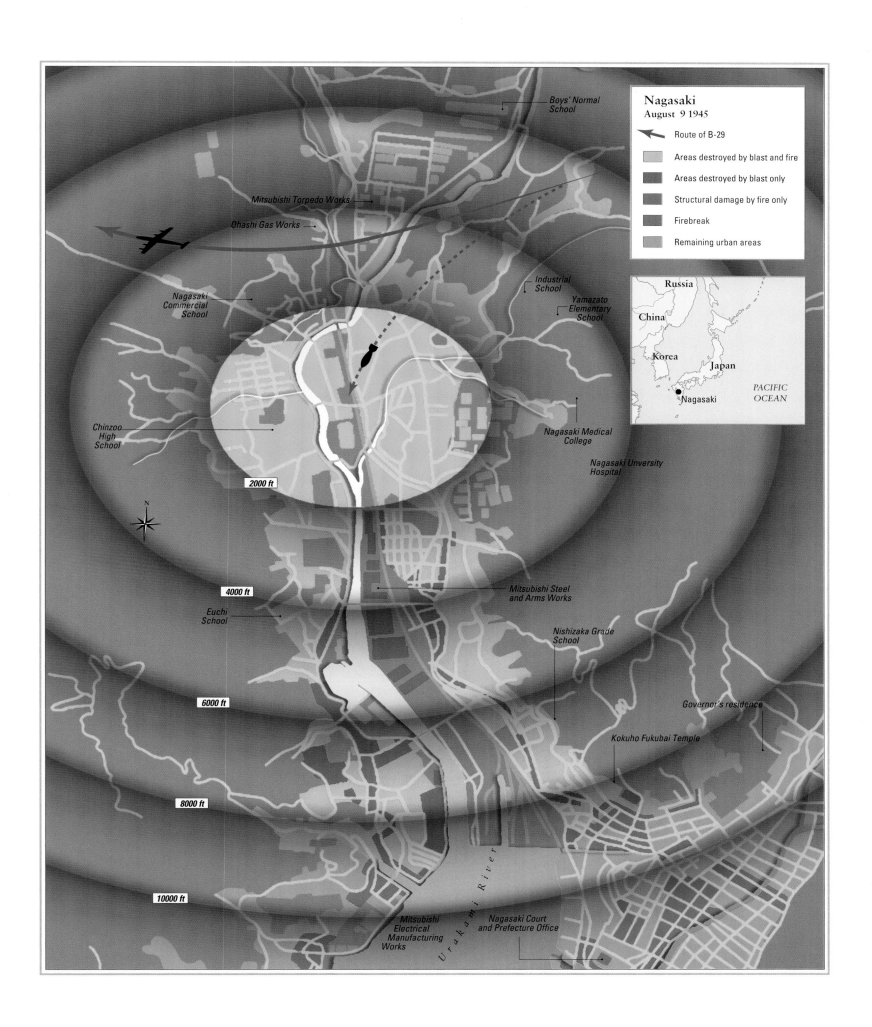

Boys' Normal School

Nagasaki
August 9 1945

⬅ Route of B-29

Areas destroyed by blast and fire

Areas destroyed by blast only

Structural damage by fire only

Firebreak

Remaining urban areas

Russia
China
Korea
Japan
Nagasaki
PACIFIC OCEAN

Mitsubishi Torpedo Works

Ohashi Gas Works

Nagasaki Commercial School

Industrial School

Yamazato Elementary School

Chinzoo High School

2000 ft

Nagasaki Medical College

Nagasaki Unversity Hospital

4000 ft

Mitsubishi Steel and Arms Works

Euchi School

Nishizaka Grade School

6000 ft

Governor's residence

Kokuho Fukubai Temple

8000 ft

Urakami River

10000 ft

Mitsubishi Electrical Manufacturing Works

Nagasaki Court and Prefecture Office

WORLD WAR TWO - INDUSTRY AT WAR

DURING A WAR, THE INDUSTRIAL RESOURCES OF A STATE TEND TO BE DIVERTED FROM THE PROFITABLE BUSINESS OF INTERNATIONAL TRADE AND CONCENTRATED ON WEAPONS PRODUCTION. THIS INVOLVES NOT ONLY A CHANGE IN PRODUCT FOR FACTORIES BUT ALSO A SHIFT IN THE CONSUMPTION OF RAW MATERIALS.

T he problems of keeping war industries supplied surfaced early in the history of warfare. The trees of Ancient Greece did not produce enough of the strong, straight poles over 2 yd (1.8 m) long that were needed for spear shafts. Wood had to be imported from farther north, and blocking supplies of it was an early aim of Persia's war effort in 480BC.

The nations engaged in World War Two faced different problems in organizing and supplying their war industries. And the ways in which these problems were solved varied greatly.

In Germany the most pressing initial problem was to secure supplies of iron ore from Sweden, which were transported to Germany across the Baltic in summer and by way of Norway in winter when the Baltic froze. This was solved by invading Norway in 1940 and by sinking much of the Soviet Baltic fleet. Germany was later to conquer much of mainland Europe, which ensured a steady supply of most raw materials used in weaponry, but rubber and copper would be in short supply throughout the war. The increasing demands of the German Army for men drew workers from the factories. They were replaced by laborers brought from the occupied countries.

Britain suffered most acutely from a lack of raw materials. These materials, along with much food, had to be brought in by sea on ships that were constantly threatened by German U-boats and, intermittently, by powerful surface warships. The loss of merchant ships to the Germans was at times high, and in 1942

Opposite page: The Japanese, who lacked their own natural resources, relied heavily on merchant shipping to bring supplies to Japan. This was why they wanted to set up a "Co-Prosperity Sphere" to provide them with access to resources elsewhere in south-east Asia.

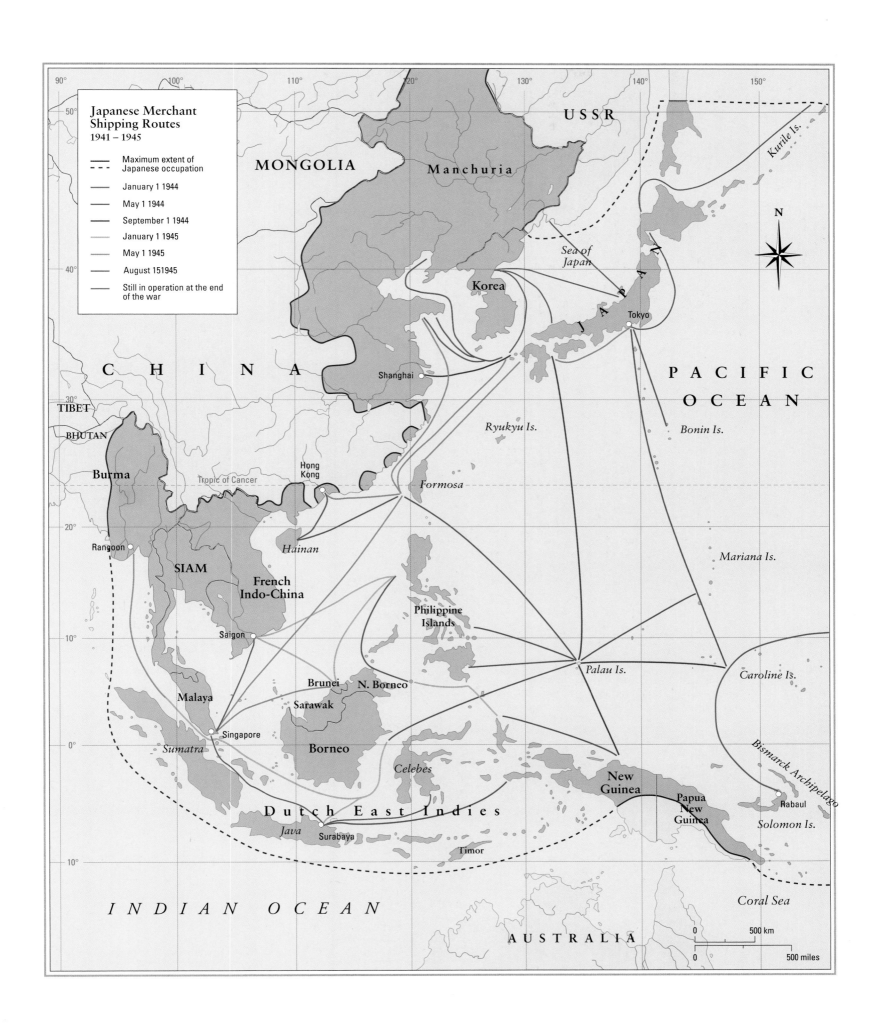

Japanese Merchant
Shipping Routes
1941 – 1945

Maximum extent of
Japanese occupation

January 1 1944

May 1 1944

September 1 1944

January 1 1945

May 1 1945

August 151945

Still in operation at the end
of the war

USSR

MONGOLIA

Manchuria

Kurile Is.

N

Sea of
Japan

Korea

J A P A N

Tokyo

PACIFIC
OCEAN

C H I N A

Shanghai

Ryukyu Is.

Bonin Is.

TIBET

BHUTAN

Burma

Tropic of Cancer

Hong
Kong

Formosa

Mariana Is.

Rangoon

Hainan

SIAM

French
Indo-China

Philippine
Islands

Palau Is.

Caroline Is.

Saigon

Malaya

Brunei
Sarawak

N. Borneo

Singapore

Sumatra

Borneo

Celebes

Bismarck Archipelago

New
Guinea

Rabaul

Papua
New
Guinea

Solomon Is.

Dutch East Indies

Java   Surabaya

Timor

Coral Sea

INDIAN OCEAN

AUSTRALIA

0   500 km

0   500 miles

After March 1941, before entering the war, the U.S. furnished vast quantities of military material, under Lend-Lease arrangements, to Britain, the U.S.S.R, China, France and other Allied countries crisscrossing the Atlantic and Pacific Ocean with their supply routes.

it threatened to starve British factories of the materials necessary to produce weapons. Japan suffered similar problems, but in this case it was U.S. submarines and fighting ships that were taking a toll on merchant ships. Unlike the British Navy, which was strong and adaptable enough to defeat the U-boat menace by late 1943, the Japanese Navy was severely overstretched by demands to support the army on distant Pacific islands and could not counter the American submarines.

Britain, Japan, and Germany all suffered at various times from heavy bombing of their factories and industrial towns. Britain and Germany countered this by a policy of dispersal: the various stages in the manufacture of weapons were spread between different workshops, often located in small towns and

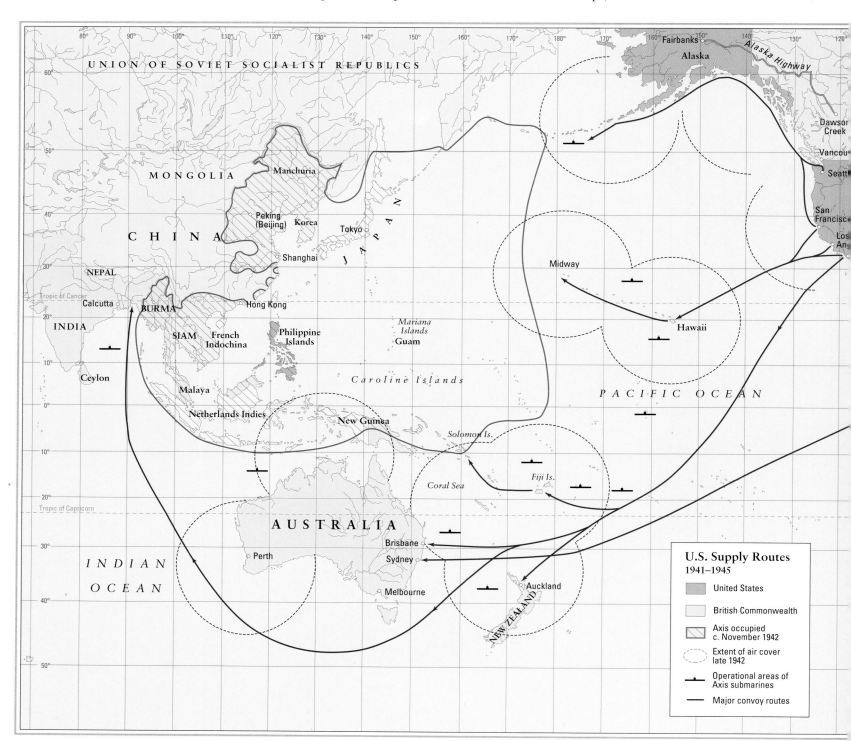

U.S. Supply Routes
1941–1945

United States

British Commonwealth

Axis occupied
c. November 1942

Extent of air cover
late 1942

Operational areas of
Axis submarines

Major convoy routes

Anti-communist posters were widely displayed in Malaya during its 12 year struggle against a communist takeover in the then British colony after World War Two. One poster calls them "terrorists" who "chose to live by violence, extortion, murder..."

Because communists led the anti-French forces, they attracted the support of the new Chinese Communist government of Mao Zedong. This support soon took the practical form of rifles, machine guns, and other light weapons along with large quantities of ammunition sent from the surplus stores left over from the war against Japan. The U.S.S.R later joined the cause, sending food, trucks, and ammunition to the communist forces.

Neither China nor the U.S.S.R wanted to spend much money on Vietnam, and China in particular did not want to create an independent state on its southern border. Therefore, they sent only light weapons that were so old as to be of little use. This resulted in a war fought chiefly by ambush, raid, and guerrilla operations. The sort of conventional warfare in which French heavy weaponry would have a clear advantage did not take place.

Other wars of independence followed a similar pattern. In 1948 the Malayan Communist Party began an armed uprising along the lines launched by their counterparts in Vietnam. Again the rebels gained support from China and again they concentrated on guerrilla activities. Unlike the French, however, the British responded with guerrilla tactics of their own, along with a consistent campaign to win the support

Eurasia and Africa
1946–55

Former colonial possession

Colonial possession with date of independence

- British
- French
- Dutch
- Portuguese
- Spanish
- USA
- Italy
- New Zealand
- Belgium
- Australia

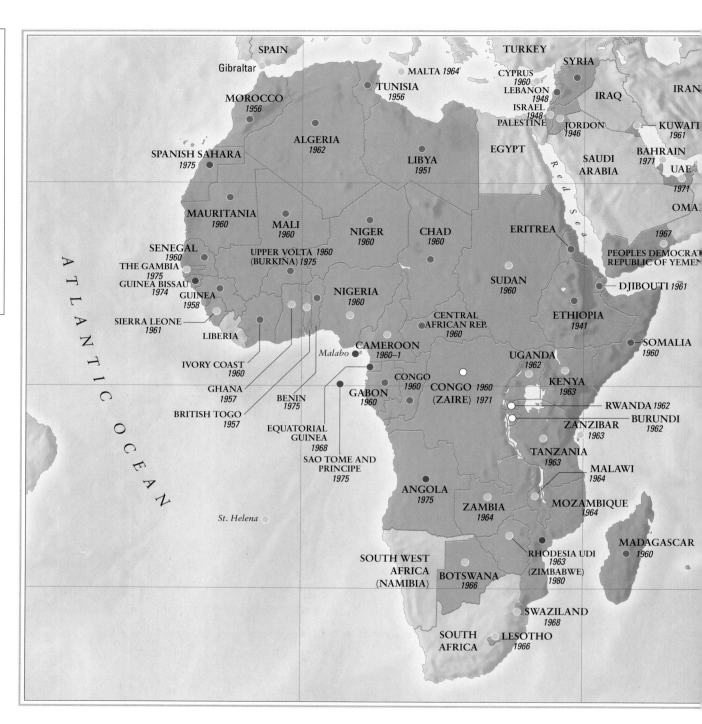

of the Malay population with propaganda and civil engineering projects that improved living conditions in rural areas. By 1955 the serious fighting was over, but it was not until 1960 that the Malay communists gave up and sought sanctuary in China.

Rather different was the Mau Mau uprising in Kenya. This was a complex movement that had its roots in African secret religious societies and drew upon the unrest within the Kikuyu tribe. The Mau Mau was a secret society that sought to kill white settlers, restore Kikuyu power, implement land ownership reforms, and assert labor union powers. Independence from Britain was adopted later, when the Mau Mau leadership realized that their aims could not be achieved under British rule.

Separated by thousands of miles from the nearest communist country, the Mau Mau were unable to gain access to large quantities of small arms and remained short of weapons throughout the conflict. The

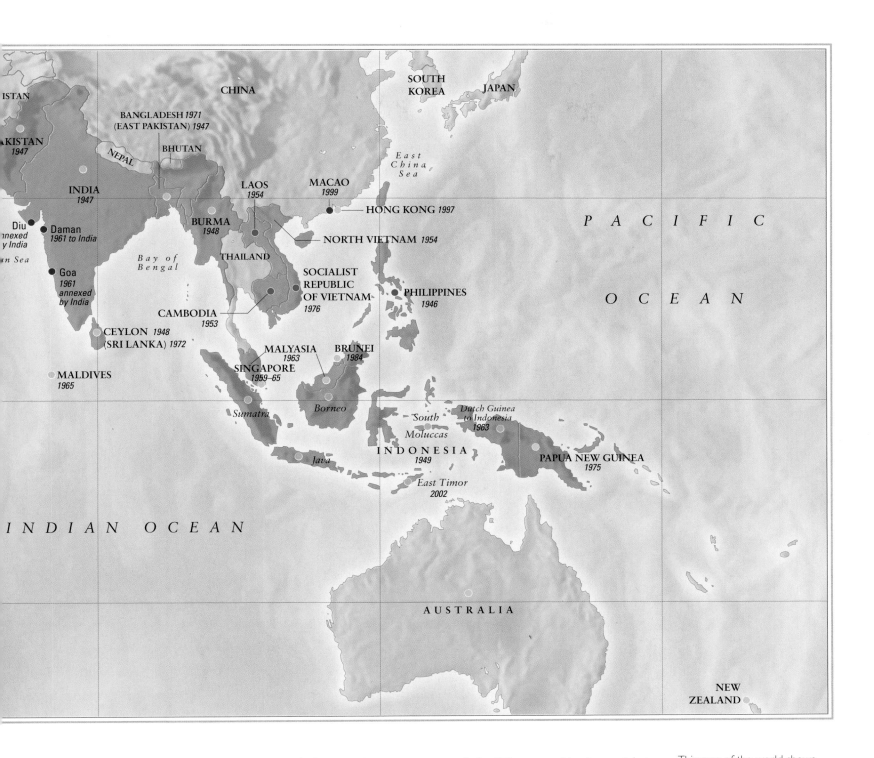

This map of the world shows countries (colored green) that gained independence after World War Two. The first of them were India and Pakistan, in 1947, when the former British colony of India was partitioned between Hindus and Muslims, respectively.

British were aided by the fact that many tribal groups in Kenya opposed the Kikuyu and had no wish to live in an independent state dominated by militant Kikuyu. The uprising began in October 1952. By 1957 it had been put down, but some isolated Mau Mau groups remained in action until 1963.

Other post-war struggles for independence broke out in widely separated areas of the globe. Algeria and Morocco erupted against French rule in 1952; the Sudan rose against British rule in 1955; and Indonesia began to contest Dutch rule in 1947. Elsewhere unrest took the form of disorganized rioting and bloodshed or of peaceful political protest and organization. All these contributed to the increasing cost of maintaining colonies. By the 1960s the economic benefits of overseas colonies had, in most cases, disappeared. European powers began a process of granting independence to their colonies, a process generally complete by the late 1970s.

THE NUCLEAR THREAT

THE USE OF NUCLEAR WEAPONS AGAINST JAPAN BY THE U.S. IN 1945 SHOCKED THE WORLD BY THE DEVASTATION THAT COULD BE CAUSED BY A SINGLE BOMB. DEVASTATION ON THIS SCALE HAD BEEN PERPETRATED BEFORE, BUT ONLY BY PROLONGED ASSAULTS. THE APPARENT EASE AND SPEED OF THE MASS CARNAGE THAT COULD BE INFLICTED WAS SOMETHING NEW.

In 1945 only the United States had atomic weapons. These worked by a process of nuclear fission, that is, by breaking atoms apart. They were dropped from a high-altitude B-29 Superfortress bomber. The B-29 was ideal for this task, as it had the range necessary to reach distant targets and could fly high enough to be out of range of the blast of the weapon by the time it had detonated. The main drawback to the B-29 as a delivery system for an atomic bomb was that it could be shot down on its way to the target. Despite this limitation, the fact that only the U.S. had atomic weapons, and had shown itself prepared to use them, made it supremely powerful.

On August 29 1949 the U.S.S.R exploded an atomic bomb at a test site in the deserts of Kazakhstan. The Soviet bomb was almost identical in design and power to the American weapon, for the simple reason that it had been built largely using designs and techniques acquired by Soviet spies in the U.S. This test ended its monopoly of nuclear weaponry and initiated a costly and dangerous arms race.

In November 1952 the U.S. tested its first fusion bomb, usually termed an H-bomb, as it uses isotopes of hydrogen. Fusion bombs are many times more powerful than fission weapons. Indeed they use a fission bomb as the trigger to set off the fusion blast. This first test weapon had a blast yield of 10.4 megatonnes, about 450 times greater than the fission bomb dropped on Nagasaki. The U.S.S.R then hurried up its development program and was able to stage its first test of an H-bomb in August 1953.

Other countries quickly recognized that possession of nuclear weapons gave the U.S. and the U.S.S.R a huge military advantage that could be translated into diplomatic muscle. Britain acquired an atomic weapon in October 1952, France in 1960, and China in 1966. In 1998 both India and Pakistan tested nuclear weapons. Israel is thought to have the capacity to produce nuclear weapons, and may actually have done so, but this has never been officially confirmed by any organization. Iran and North Korea currently have programmes of nuclear development that may lead to the production of weapons. At various times Sweden, Brazil and Argentina have begun nuclear weapons programmes, but they have abandoned them without producing an operational weapon.

This huge ballistic missile is seen on a traveling carriage for transportation to and from missile sites. For security, the missiles were moved at a very slow pace and were accompanied all the way by guards riding alongside on motor bicycles.

Opposite page: In February 1946, George F. Kennan's "Long Telegram" from Moscow helped to articulate the U.S. government's increasingly hard line against the Soviets, and became the basis for US strategy toward theU.S.S.R for the duration of the Cold War. The U.S. and the U.S.S.R. pursued nuclear rearmament and developed long-range weapons with which they could strike the territory of the other.

The growth of the "nuclear club", as the group of countries possessing atomic weapons is called, made it necessary for them to develop a nuclear strategy. In the 1950s the U.S. adopted a policy of massive retaliation. This stated that any large-scale attack on it or any of its allies would be met by a large number of counterattacks using atomic weapons. An initial attack did not need to be nuclear in order to trigger a nuclear response but only large in scale. This was quite clearly aimed at any attack by the U.S.S.Rand its allies on Western Europe using conventional weapons. Although not stated so clearly, it was generally assumed that the targets of the nuclear attacks would be large cities.

The preeminent problem of the doctrine of massive retaliation was that it assumed the U.S. nuclear weapons would be intact and able to respond to an attack. If the U.S.S.R preceded an invasion of Western Europe by atomic attacks on the U.S., this might not be the case. The policy of massive retaliation remained officially in force in the 1960s, but in fact had been replaced by a policy of mutually assured destruction. This relied on the U.S. having a second-strike capability, an ability to hit back with nuclear weapons no matter how destructive a Soviet first strike might have been. This relied on American nuclear weapons being kept hidden from view or out of range of Soviet attack. At first, this involved having bombers armed with primed nuclear weapons sitting on runways ready to take off at a moment's notice, but later it relied on missiles that could be launched from submarines.

The scale of devastation that would be unleashed by a war of mutually assured destruction between the United States and the U.S.S.R was immense. Various studies indicated that the amount of radiation and radioactive fallout generated by such a war would lead to the slow but certain annihilation of life on Earth— but only if nuclear weapons were used on a massive scale. Other studies concentrated on the concept of a "nuclear winter". This outcome was said to be possible if the smoke and dust created by nuclear explosions was thrown up into the stratosphere. There it would spread around the globe and persist for years before falling back to earth. Global temperatures might fall to such an extent that there would be no summer weather for crops to grow in and global famine would result. Neither scenario was proven, but they did become widely accepted.

All along, the world's military were developing other forms of nuclear weaponry. The U.S. developed the neutron bomb in the 1970s. This was a form of fusion weapon, which resulted in a small explosion but a huge outburst of neutron radiation. In practical terms this means that a neutron bomb would leave buildings standing but kill the humans in them. Its prime tactical military use would be as an anti-tank weapon because it would kill the crews of tanks over a wide area and halt a large armored offensive.

Another form of nuclear weapon is the salted bomb. This is a fission bomb that has been wrapped in a thick layer of metal, such as zinc or cobalt. The metal jacket would be pulverized to dust by the blast and would absorb the radiation from the blast. The heaviness of the metal would ensure that the fine dust fell in a relatively restricted area around the blast, where its radioactivity would remain for months or years. In effect, it would render an area of land uninhabitable for a long time.

A variation on this weapon is to wrap radioactive material around a conventional bomb that then sprays the radioactive material around. This is known as a dirty bomb. It would have a much less widespread and less deadly impact than a salted bomb, but could quite easily render several blocks of a city uninhabitable unless costly and complicated cleanup operations were carried out promptly.

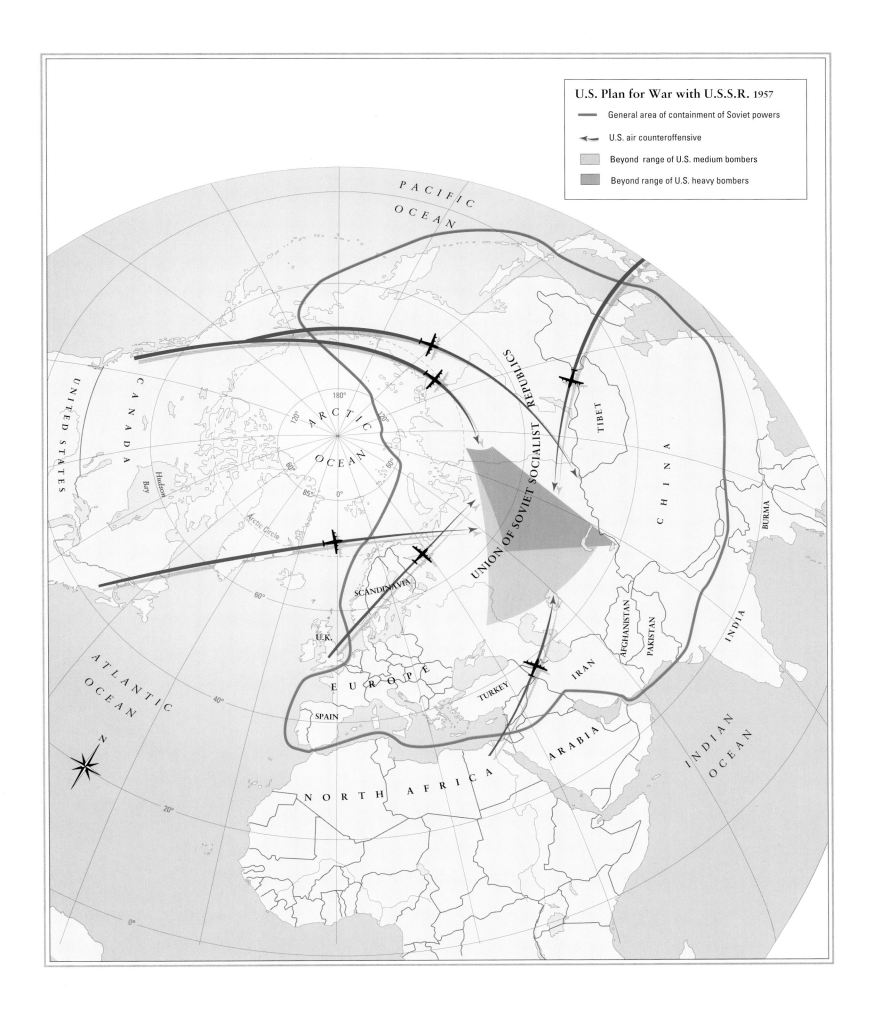

U.S. Plan for War with U.S.S.R. 1957

⎯ General area of containment of Soviet powers

← U.S. air counteroffensive

▢ Beyond range of U.S. medium bombers

▢ Beyond range of U.S. heavy bombers

MISSILE WARFARE

THE SELF-PROPELLED MISSILE WAS THE MOST SIGNIFICANT DEVELOPMENT IN BATTLEFIELD WEAPONRY IN THE LATE 20TH CENTURY AND IS CONTINUING TO DOMINATE NEW RESEARCH AND DEVELOPMENT IN THE 21ST CENTURY.

The German V weapons of 1944–1945 introduced the world to what could be achieved by missile weapons on the strategic level. Although these weapons were relatively inaccurate, they had a profound effect on military planners, as they showed what might be achieved by missiles that were more accurate and used in greater numbers.

For a missile to be effective it must have four features: a warhead, an engine, a flight system, and a guidance system. To this should be added a fifth essential component, which is not a part of the missile itself: the operator needs to know where the missile's target is. Without this knowledge, the missile is essentially useless. Locating a target may be the task of reconnaissance aircraft, scouts working on the ground, or the intelligence services. However the target is identified, the location and nature of the target must be passed on to the missile crew.

The warhead of a missile is the key component, as it inflicts the damage on the target. The most common form of warhead has always been a high explosive. This material produces a powerful blast when detonated, causing damage to anything in the vicinity. Explosive warheads are sometimes surrounded by a material that will form shrapnel on detonation. Shrapnel consists of sharp pieces of material, usually metal, that are thrown out by the blast to inflict injury and damage.

A variation on the explosive warhead is the shaped charge. This is made of an explosive charge packed around a metal cone, which has its open end toward the target and is encased within a tough cylinder. When the charge detonates, the explosive force is concentrated on the metal liner. The metal is liquefied by the heat and accelerated forward at hypersonic speed — typically around 6 miles (9.7 km) per second. Denser metals, such as lead, magnesium, or uranium, make the most effective liners, but alloys and other metals are used for specialist purposes.

The main task of a shaped charge is to smash a hole through a hard, solid object such as the armor on a tank or other armored vehicles. The stream of molten metal traveling at high speed will drill through

Opposite page; Between 1960 and 1985, mutually assured destruction (MAD) was touted as a method of preserving world peace by the two superpowers, the U.S. and the U.S.S.R. Both possessed nuclear weapons that could destroy the world.

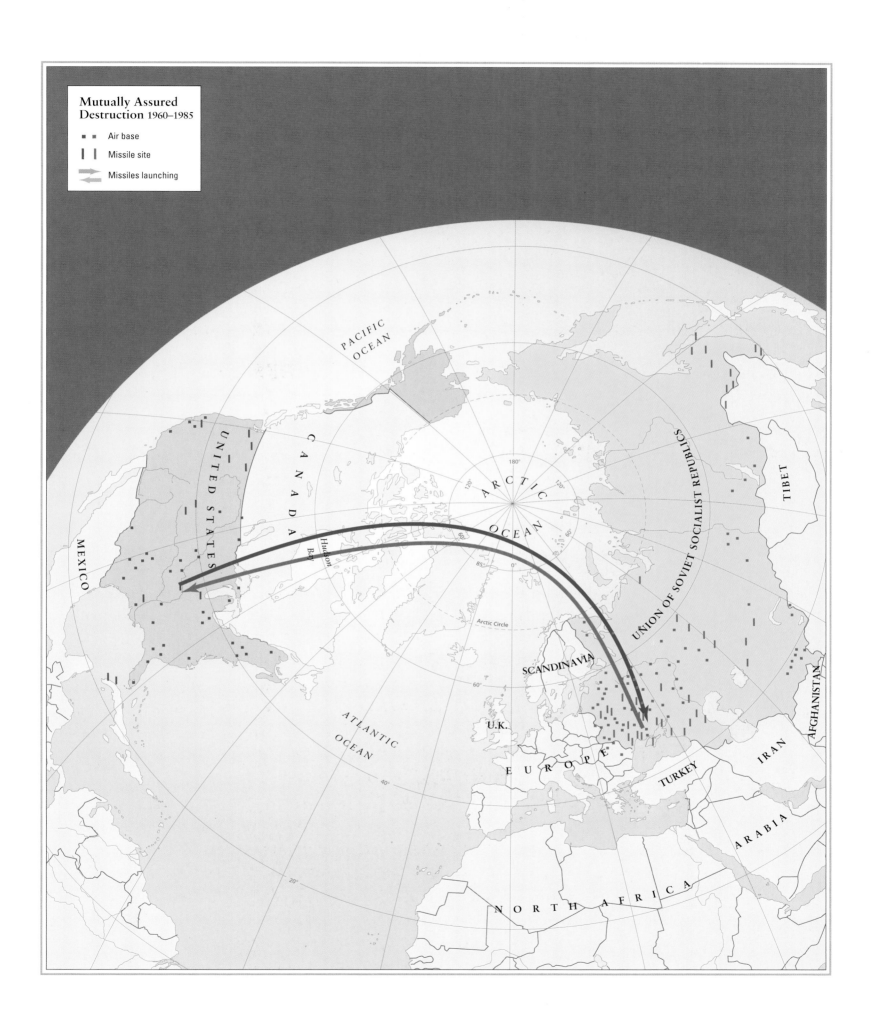

Mutually Assured Destruction 1960–1985

■ ■ Air base

❘ ❘ Missile site

➤ Missiles launching

Packages to Cuba 1962

⟵ Supply route from Soviet ports

U.S. and NATO allies

U.S.S.R. and Warsaw Pact allies

Neutral

GREENLAND ICELAND

NORWAY SWEDEN FINLAND

DEN. USSR

UK

IRELAND NETH. POLAND

BEL. E.G.

W.G. CZ.

FRANCE AUS. HUN.

ROM.

USA

Montreal S. YUG. B.

Toronto PORTUGAL SPAIN ITALY

Chicago GREECE

New York

Cincinnati Washington TUNISIA

Memphis MOROCCO

Atlanta

Dallas ALGERIA LYBIA

New Orleans

Houston Spanish

Gulf of Mexico Miami Sahara ATLANTIC

OCEAN MAURITANIA MALI NIGER

MEXICO CUBA

JAMAICA HAITI DOMINICAN SENEGAL

Br. Honduras REPUBLIC Gambia VOLTA

Guatamala Haiti Port. Guinea GUINEA NIGERIA

El Salvador NICARAGUA S. LEONE IVORY CEN. AFRICA

Costa Rica LIBERIA COAST

Panama VENEZUELA TOGO CAMEROON

MRBM Range British Guiana DAHOMEY

COLOMBIA Dutch Guiana GABON CONGO

French Guiana CONGO

ECUADOR

IRBM Range B R A Z I L ANGOLA

PERU

BOLIVIA

In 1961, U.S. spy plane surveillance discovered that the U.S.S.R was supplying missiles to Cuba, which was situated only 90 miles (150 km) from U.S. territory. The US responded with the threat to intercept future shipments to Cuba. This period bcame known as the Cuban Missile Crisis and is generally regarded as the moment in which the Cold War came closest to a nuclear war.

the armor and spray around the crew cabin and kill the crew. Other forms of shaped charge are designed to crack open concrete bunkers, bomb shelters, or gun emplacements.

Another warhead often fitted to missiles is the cluster bomb. This bomb scatters, across a wide area, a number of much smaller explosive devices or "bomblets" that then explode on impact. This saturates an area in lethal blasts and shrapnel. There is a growing consensus against the use of cluster bombs because they tend to leave behind a number of unexploded devices that are difficult to detect but may cause death or injury to civilians long after a conflict has ended.

Other warheads that have been fitted to missiles include incendiaries, smoke dischargers, poison gas, biological weapons, and chemical weapons. Many of these are now illegal under various international treaties and agreements.

The motive power for a missile is either a jet engine or a rocket engine. Rockets are the more common option as they are tough and reliable, need little in the way of maintenance, and can be deployed rapidly and effectively. The typical solid-fuel rocket is a more sophisticated form of the firework rocket used at

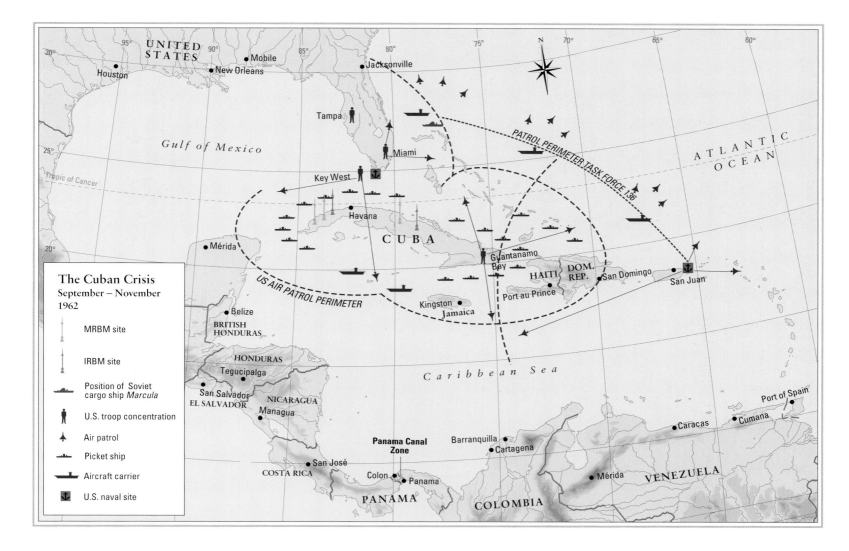

The Cuban Crisis
September – November 1962

⬆ MRBM site

⬆ IRBM site

⚓ Position of Soviet cargo ship *Marcula*

🧍 U.S. troop concentration

✈ Air patrol

⚓ Picket ship

⚓ Aircraft carrier

⚓ U.S. naval site

parties, carnivals, and other celebrations. A tube is packed with a combustible material that will create large quantities of hot gas when burned. The fuel is ignited and the gas is allowed to escape through a narrow nozzle at the rear, producing the force that drives the rocket forward. The rocket engine burns for as long as the fuel lasts and then stops. Solid-fuel rockets tend to be used for short-range missiles.

The more elaborate liquid-fuel rocket contains two tanks in which are stored a fuel and an oxidizer, often liquid oxygen. Pumps push carefully controlled amounts of each into a combustion chamber where they are ignited. The hot gases created are then pushed out through a nozzle as in a solid-fuel rocket. The liquid-fuel rocket has the advantage that varying the amount of fuel put through the pump can control the amount of thrust. This also allows for a longer burn time to be produced more reliably. For this reason, it tends to be used for longer-range missiles.

Longer-range missiles intended to fly close to the ground are often powered by a jet engine. Most often, this is a turbojet mounted inside the missile itself, but occasionally it may be fitted on the outside of the missile.

The flight system is the means by which the missile is kept in the air and steered toward its target. For rockets it is the engine that keeps the weapon in the air. Most rockets accelerate continuously for as long as the engine is burning. The energy produced by the engine provides the lift. The fins fitted to the missile, usually at its tail, are there only for steering. Often the fins are angled so that they spin the

More missiles were already heading for Cuba, but to universal relief, the ships carrying them turned back and the missiles already installed were removed. In 1964, Soviet premier Nikita Krushchev, who was responsible for the episode, was ousted for "hare-brained scheming".

Opposite page: Deterrent patrols by U.S. nuclear-powered ballistic missile submarines began on November 15 1960 at the height of the Cold War, and have continued ever since. In 2008, for instance, 31 deterrent patrols were carried out.

rocket as it surges forward. This serves to keep it on a stable trajectory as it flies. Only tweaks are needed to alter the direction of the rocket in flight. Sometimes the trajectory of the rocket is determined before it is set off.

Jet missiles operate on a system more like that of conventional aircraft. They are often fitted with wings that generate lift and with tail assemblies that control pitch and direction.

Guidance systems for missiles vary depending on what the target is, but generally they conform to one of two types. The first is usually termed "fire-and-forget"; the second is called a guided missile.

The fire-and-forget systems are internal to the missile itself and require no input once it has been launched. If operated on a satellite global positioning system (GPS) , the missile will be programmed with the co-ordinates of the target. An on-board computer then monitors the flightpath of the missile towardsthe target, making steering corrections and engine changes as necessary to ensure that the missile hits its target. Those missiles powered by a jet engine and guided by a GPS computer are usually termed cruise missiles.

Rather more basic and less accurate is a missile in which the on-board computer is programmed with the range and distance to be flown but does not monitor progress by way of using GPS. Other missiles may have heat-seeking devices, so that they steer themselves to the jet engines of hostile aircraft, or they may have a radar detector so that they head toward any object that is sending out a radar signal.

Guided missiles operate in a variety of methods. The earliest examples used in World War Two trailed behind them a pair of long, thin wires that were connected to a joystick with which the operator could steer the missile. In a more modern variation, a missile will steer toward a specific laser light wavelength. The guider has a laser, which he shines on the target, so that the missile heads for the reflected light scatter. Other guided missiles have a small TV camera fitted so that the operator can see where the missile is going and direct it accordingly.

This American soldier is about to fire a 54-inch (137 cm) long M1 bazooka, a recoil-less rocket anti-tank weapon first used in 1942, during World War Two. The bazooka went on to serve in the Korean War of 1950-1954.

The majority of military missiles are categorized not so much by their design as by their purpose. Exceptions are ICBMs. As their name suggests, these missiles travel from one continent to another along a ballistic path that takes them up to the margins of space before they fall back to Earth. Almost invariably these carry nuclear warheads.

Cruise missiles are used to attack small, static targets such as individual buildings, bridges, or other structures. Their usefulness in a campaign is usually restricted to the opening phases, when enemy headquarters, TV stations, government buildings, transportation links, and other static targets can be hit.

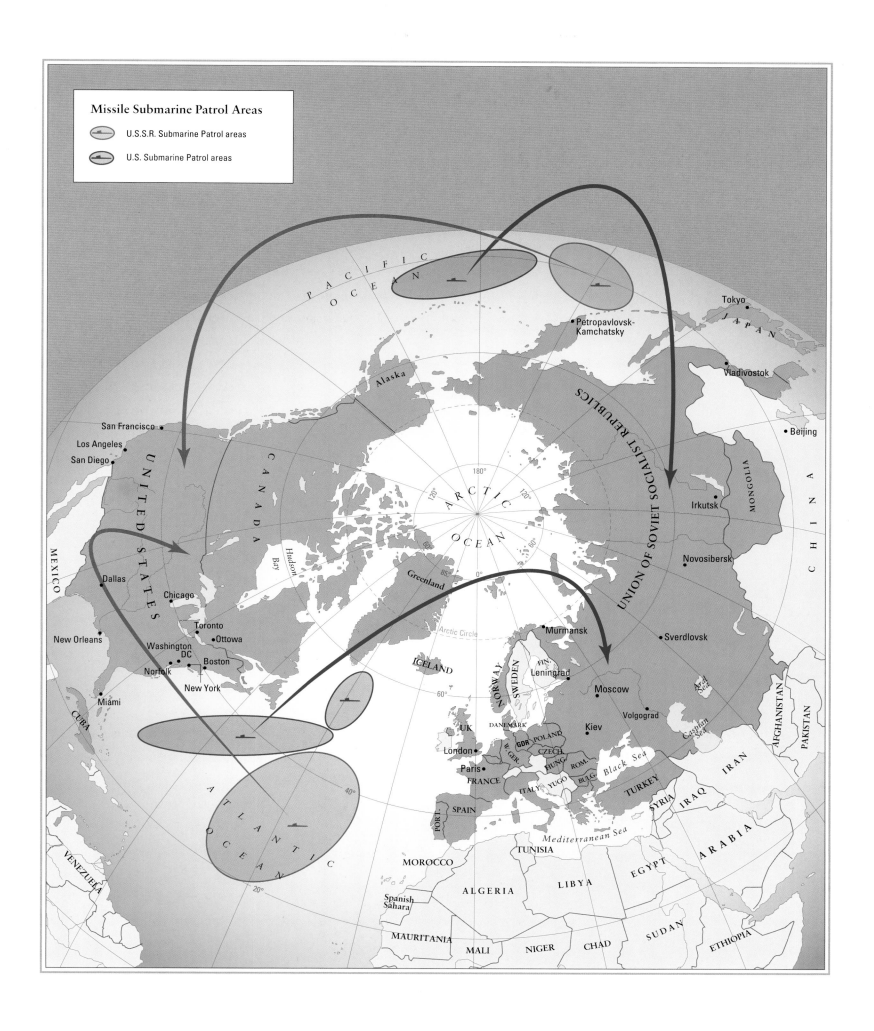

Missile Submarine Patrol Areas

U.S.S.R. Submarine Patrol areas

U.S. Submarine Patrol areas

PACIFIC OCEAN

Tokyo

JAPAN

Petropavlovsk-Kamchatsky

Vladivostok

Alaska

Beijing

UNION OF SOVIET SOCIALIST REPUBLICS

San Francisco

Los Angeles

San Diego

UNITED STATES

CANADA

Irkutsk

MONGOLIA

CHINA

ARCTIC OCEAN

Novosibersk

MEXICO

Dallas

Chicago

Hudson Bay

Greenland

Sverdlovsk

Murmansk

Toronto

Ottowa

New Orleans

Washington DC

Boston

Norfolk

New York

Miami

CUBA

ICELAND

NORWAY

SWEDEN

FIN.

Leningrad

Aral Sea

Moscow

Volgograd

Kiev

Caspian Sea

AFGHANISTAN

PAKISTAN

UK

DANEMARK

London

Paris

FRANCE

W. GER.

GDR

POLAND

CZECH

HUNG.

ITALY

YUGO

ROM.

BULG

Black Sea

TURKEY

IRAN

SYRIA

IRAQ

PORT.

SPAIN

Mediterranean Sea

ARABIA

ATLANTIC OCEAN

VENEZUELA

TUNISIA

MOROCCO

Spanish Sahara

ALGERIA

LIBYA

EGYPT

MAURITANIA

MALI

NIGER

CHAD

SUDAN

ETHIOPIA

Arctic Circle

Opposite page: The SDI Missile Defence System known as "Star Wars" was proposed in 1983 to protect against attack by nuclear ballistic missiles. However, in 1987, it was decided that presentday technology was insufficiently advanced to build this ground- and space-based system.

Perhaps the best-known cruise missile is the Tomahawk, which was developed by the U.S. General Dynamics Company in the 1970s and remains in production. The missile has gone through a number of variations and upgrades in its long history. The 109E model is the current basic version. This missile weighs about 1½ tons (1.4 tonnes) and is 19.7 ft (6 m) long with a diameter of about 20 in (50 cm). It can carry a warhead of up to 1½ tons (1.4 tonnes) and can carry many types of warhead in its domed nose. It is powered by an internal turbofan jet that can propel it at up to 600 mph (966 kph) over a range of 1,500 miles (2,414 km). Although it is usually launched from vertical tubes, one version has been produced that can be launched underwater from a submarine's torpedo tubes.

The Tomahawk was used extensively during the 1991 Gulf War: U.S. forces launched 288 at targets in Kuwait and Iraq. In 1999 the British used Tomahawks in Kosovo, launching an estimated 20 missiles. In these operations it was estimated that the Tomahawk missiles hit their target about 85 percent of the time and achieved a near miss about 10 percent of the time. The remaining 5 percent of the missiles were lost for one reason or another.

The various types of anti-ship missile use radar to locate their targets. They may be launched from other ships or from aircraft and are pre-programmed to travel to a certain area before the internal radar is switched on. This radar then scans the area around the missile for any large, metallic object. As they operate exclusively at sea, the only objects likely to be detected are ships. The missile's on-board computer then directs it to strike the ship.

The best-known anti-ship missile is the Exocet, made by the French MBDA company. The Exocet has been in service since 1979, undergoing frequent modernization. The 40MM3 is the latest model. The missile weighs 1,500 lb (680 kg) and has a length of 15 ft (4.6 m) and a diameter of 14 in (35.6 cm). It is powered by a solid-fuel rocket to achieve speeds of up to 720 mph (1,159 kph) over distances of up to 90 miles (145 km). The 350 lb (159 kg) warhead is usually high-explosive.

Anti-tank missiles first saw use in World War Two in the form of the bazooka and the Panzerfaust (tank fist). These were short-range weapons, with an effective range of only 300 ft (91 m) or so. By the 1960s longer-range infantry-operated weapons were available to most armies. The Soviet 9K11 Malyutka was typical. It entered service in 1961, was manufactured in huge numbers, and was widely distributed to foreign armies and insurgency groups supported by the U.S.S.R. It had a range of about 1.2 miles (1.9 km) and delivered a 6 lb (2.7 kg) warhead. The operator steered the missile with a joystick, connected to the missile by wires. It could penetrate conventional armor of up to 8 in (200 mm) in thickness but had a hit rate of only about 25 percent. Its variations are still in service in some countries.

Anti-aircraft missiles can be fired from the ground, from ships, or from aircraft. They tend to be small, light weapons with an explosive warhead powered by solid-fuel rockets. The earliest versions in the 1940s were unguided, but in the 1950s guided missiles able to home in on hot engines or directed by radar were entering service.

A typical anti-aircraft missile is the AIM-9 Sidewinder, made by the U.S. and operated by over 40 air forces. This air-launched rocket weighs 200 lb (91 kg) and is more than 9 ft (2.7 m) long. It carries a 6 lb (3 kg) warhead consisting of an explosive charge and a fragmenting case. It has a range of 11 miles (17.7 km) and operates at speeds of up to almost 2,000 mph (3,219 kph), homing in on its target by means of an infrared detector, which picks up the heat signature of a jet engine.

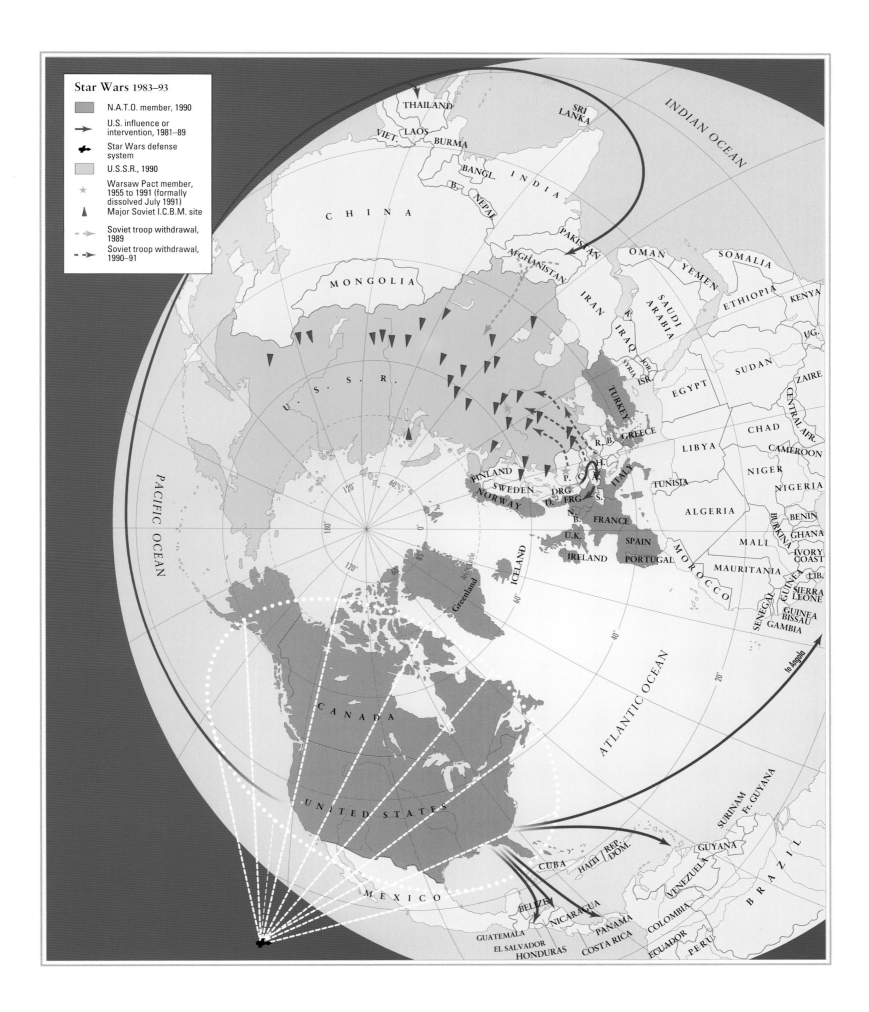

Star Wars 1983–93

N.A.T.O. member, 1990

U.S. influence or intervention, 1981–89

Star Wars defense system

U.S.S.R., 1990

Warsaw Pact member, 1955 to 1991 (formally dissolved July 1991)

Major Soviet I.C.B.M. site

Soviet troop withdrawal, 1989

Soviet troop withdrawal, 1990–91

INDIAN OCEAN

THAILAND

SRI LANKA

VIET. LAOS

BURMA

BANGL.

B. NEPAL

INDIA

CHINA

PAKISTAN

OMAN YEMEN SOMALIA

AFGHANISTAN

IRAN

K.

SAUDI ARABIA

ETHIOPIA

KENYA

MONGOLIA

IRAQ

JOR.

SYRIA ISR.

SUDAN

UG.

U. S. S. R.

TURKEY

EGYPT

ZAIRE

CENTRAL AFR.

LIBYA

CHAD

CAMEROON

R. B. GREECE

NIGER

NIGERIA

FINLAND

SWEDEN

NORWAY

DRG

D. FRG

N. S.

B. FRANCE

ITALY

P. C. A.

H.

TUNISIA

ALGERIA

MALI

BENIN

GHANA

IVORY COAST

U.K.

IRELAND

SPAIN

PORTUGAL

MOROCCO

MAURITANIA

BURKINA

SENEGAL

GUINEA

LIB.

SIERRA LEONE

GUINEA BISSAU

GAMBIA

PACIFIC OCEAN

120

60

180

0

120

60

ICELAND

Arctic Circle

Greenland

60

85

ATLANTIC OCEAN

to Angola

40

20

C A N A D A

U N I T E D   S T A T E S

M E X I C O

CUBA

HAITI

REP. DOM.

SURINAM

Fr. GUYANA

GUYANA

VENEZUELA

COLOMBIA

B R A Z I L

BELIZE

GUATEMALA

EL SALVADOR

HONDURAS

NICARAGUA

COSTA RICA

PANAMA

ECUADOR

PERU

THE JET AGE

THE CONCEPT OF THE JET ENGINE WAS PATENTED IN 1932 BY THE BRITISH ENGINEER FRANK WHITTLE. THE OUTBREAK OF WORLD WAR TWO PROVED THE NEED FOR AN ENGINE THAT COULD POWER AIRCRAFT AT HIGH SPEED. THE JET ENGINE WAS FINALLY PERFECTED AND IT REVOLUTIONIZED AIR WARFARE.

It was the Germans who won the race to be first to get a jet aircraft into action. The Messerschmitt Me262 outclassed every other fighter in the world when it entered combat in June 1944. It had a top speed of 450 mph (724 kph), a ceiling of 37,500 ft (11,430 m), and a range of 650 miles (1,046 km). It packed a real punch, with four 30-mm cannons mounted in the nose, and was deadly to Allied aircraft. However, the Me262 entered service in relatively small numbers: only 1,433 aircraft were built, compared to over 20,000 Spitfires and 15,000 Mustangs. Despite its fame, the Me262 was not the only German jet aircraft of the war. The Arado Ar234 Blitz was the world's first jet bomber, entering service in November 1944 and playing a lead role in German air operations during the Battle of the Bulge the following month. The Blitz could reach 460 mph (740 kph), faster than most fighters, and had a ceiling of 32,800 ft (10,000 m) and a range of up to 1,000 miles (1,609 km). It could carry 660 lb (299 kg) of bombs and had a primitive form of on-board computer to aid aiming bombs at high speeds. As it could outrun almost any fighter in existence, its defensive armament consisted of only two 20 mm cannons firing directly backward. Only 210 of these aircraft entered service.

The Allies were not far behind the Germans in developing jet aircraft. The Gloster Meteor fighter went operational in July 1944, although it was produced in even smaller numbers than the Me262, with only 210 seeing active service before the end of World War Two. After the war more than 3,500 Meteors were produced, and it offically became the standard RAF fighter in 1947. The Meteor had a top speed of 415 mph (668 kph), a ceiling of 44,000 ft (13,411 m), and a range of 1,340 miles (2,156 kph). It was

also armed with four 20 mm cannons in the nose. As with all very early jets, engine reliability and maintenance were real problems.

The first jet aircraft to see combat after World War Two, entering service with the U.S.A.A.F., was the F-80 Shooting Star. This fighter was produced by the Skunk Works, a top-secret department within the Lockheed manufacturing company charged with designing advanced military aircraft. The fighter had a top speed of 600 mph (966 kph), a ceiling of 46,000 ft (14,021 m), and a range of 1,200 miles (1,931 km). Its standard armament was six 12.7 mm machine guns, but variants carried eight unguided rockets or two 1,000 lb (454 kg) bombs. It entered service in July 1945 but only saw active service in the Korean War. The F-80 made history on November 8 1950, when one flown by Lt. Russell Brown encountered a Soviet MiG-15, flown by a Chinese pilot, near the Yalu River in North Korea in an area dubbed "MiG Alley". In a short dogfight Brown shot down his opponent, scoring the first known jet-versus-jet kill in history.

Despite Brown's success, the MiG-15 soon proved itself to be superior in nearly every way to the Shooting Star. It had a top speed of 670 mph (1,078 kph), a ceiling of 50,000 ft (15,240 m), and a range of 750 miles (1,207 km). It was armed with three cannons. The main advantage of this aircraft in combat was its nimble handling. The steeply swept-back wings and tail planes greatly improved handling at high speed, but it had a tendency to roll at lower speeds and handled erratically when diving. Despite

US B-29 Superfortress in flight. The B-29 was a four-engine propeller-driven heavy bomber used by the U.S. military in World War Two and the Korean War, however, the B-29 was soon made obsolete by the development of the jet engined fighter plane. The B-29 was reclassified as a medium bomber. The B-29 suffered from engine overheating issues and engine failures throughout its service (1944–1960).

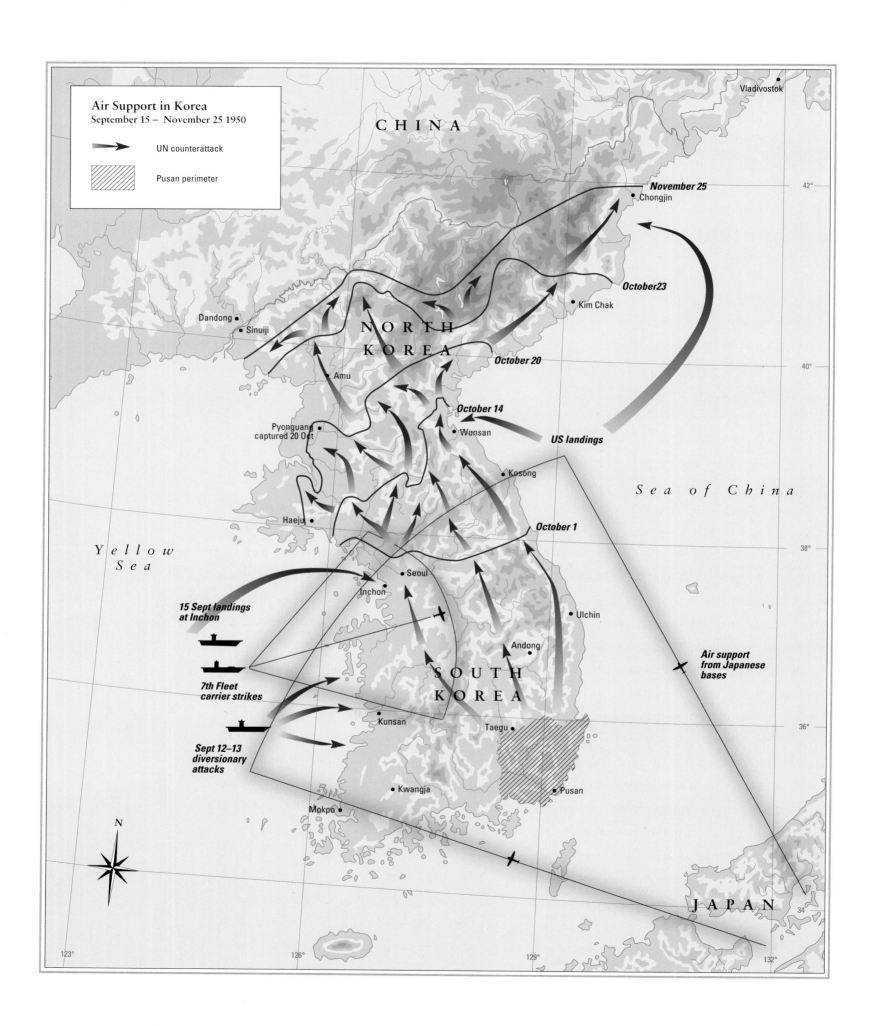

Air Support in Korea
September 15 – November 25 1950

→ UN counterattack

▨ Pusan perimeter

CHINA

Vladivostok

November 25
Chongjin

Dandong
Sinuiji

NORTH KOREA

Kim Chak

October 23

October 20

Amu

October 14

Pyonguang
captured 20 Oct

Wonsan

US landings

Kosong

Sea of China

Haeju

October 1

Yellow Sea

Seoul

Inchon

15 Sept landings
at Inchon

Ulchin

Andong

7th Fleet
carrier strikes

SOUTH KOREA

Air support
from Japanese
bases

Kunsan

Taegu

Sept 12–13
diversionary
attacks

Kwangja

Pusan

Mokpo

N

JAPAN

its successes in dogfights, the MiG-15 was deployed primarily to counter the high-flying American B29 bombers. This task it performed well, as a result of which the Americans switched to night bombing.

In all, 12,000 MiG-15 aircraft were built. Although it was outclassed by newer models by the late1950s, it remained in service with the Soviet Air Force as a trainer until the 1970s and with foreign air forces as a combat aircraft for almost as long.

By the late 1950s all jet aircraft were following the swept-wing layout of the MiG-15. Britain's Lightning, America's F86 Saber, and the French Mirage were typical. However, a debate then began among designers of jet fighters as to the best concept to follow. Emphasis was increasingly put on a combination of high-speed and high-technology weapons. Essentially the fighter was being seen as a delivery vehicle for weapon systems.

The McDonnell Douglas F-4 Phantom was a typical product of this train of thought. For a fighter the aircraft was heavy, at 41,000 lb (18,597 kg), but it was fast, with a top speed of more than 1,700 mph (2,736 kph). It had a range of 1,615 miles (2,599 km), but its combat radius was reckoned to be about 422 miles (679 km), with a ceiling of 60,000 ft (18,288 m).

It was the weapon systems that the Phantom could carry that made it a successful combat aircraft. There were nine "hardpoints" to which weapons could be fixed, and they could carry up to 4 lb (1.8 kg) of weapons. They included Sidewinder air-to-air missiles, a Vulcan 20 mm cannon, Sparrow air-to-air missiles, Slammer air-to-air missiles, Maverick air-to-ground missiles, Walleye bombs, and a variety of other weapons. This impressive range was beyond the ability of a single pilot to operate properly, so the Phantom had a two-man crew: a pilot to fly the aircraft and a technician to operate the weapons. It entered service in 1960 and remained in production until 1979, by which time 5,195 had been built. It served with the U.S. Air Force, the U.S. Navy and the U.S. Marine Corps and also with 11 allied nations.

In the 1960s the British had been experimenting with a novel concept: the jump jet. This resulted in 1969 in the Hawker Harrier, which was able to take off and land vertically. The Harrier was conceived as a strike/defense fighter able to operate without the need for a conventional airfield. In combat situations the Harrier could operate from forest clearings, fields, or urban spaces. All it needed was a support unit of technicians, maintenance crews, and supply systems mounted in trucks. Although it could operate vertically, the aircraft could carry a heavier load of weapons and fuel if it took off conventionally. The shortest of runways, and short stretches of straight road, were adequate. The naval version of the Harrier was launched from aircraft carriers equipped with a "ski-jump", an angled section of deck that allowed the aircraft to gain upward motion as it accelerated forward off the deck.

The Harrier's great advantage has always been its ability to take off from sites not available to other jet aircraft. Its performance in the air has been adequate and it has a top speed of 662 mph (1,065 kph) and a combat radius of around 300 miles (482 km).

Meanwhile, theories of fighter requirements were changing. U.S. Air Force Colonel John Boyd had for some years been promoting his idea that maneuverability, not speed, should be the key feature of fighter performance. He and his supporters pushed for a smaller aircraft with a larger wing; one that was slower but nimbler. The result was the Lockheed Martin F-16 Falcon fighter. Although it was controversial when it first appeared, the Falcon has become one of the most successful combat aircraft ever. Over 4,400 have been built and it is still in service with 25 air forces.

The Korean War of 1950–1953, in which a United Nations force led by the U.S. fought to prevent communist North Korea taking over South Korea, was the first in which jet aircraft and helicopters were widely used.

Opposite page: The Six Day War of 1967 between Israel and some of her Arab neighbors was the third in a series of short, but fierce, conflicts whose origin derives from the creation of the Jewish State of Israel in 1948.

The Falcon has a top speed of over 1,500 mph (2,414 kph), a ceiling of 60,000 ft (18,288 m), and a combat range of 340 miles (547 km) further if drop tanks are fitted. It has an internal 20 mm cannon and a total of 11 hardpoints to which can be fitted up to 17,000 lb (7,711 kg) of weaponry. The various models of the Falcon have been successfully fitted with air-to-air missiles, air-to-ground missiles, anti-ship missiles, conventional bombs, laser-guided bombs, cluster bombs, nuclear bombs, mines, and a range of other systems.

The Falcon first entered combat with the Israeli Air Force in April 1981, when it went up against Syrian aircraft in the Bekaa Valley. Its first victim was a helicopter, but it soon accounted for a Syrian MiG-21 fighter with a Sidewinder missile. Later that year Israeli F-16 aircraft were used in a ground-attack role for the first time when they attacked the Osirak nuclear reactor outside Baghdad. This action was credited with halting Iraq's nuclear weapon research program. In 1986 the Falcon again saw action, this time with the Pakistani Air Force. The aircraft were patrolling the border with Afghanistan when Afghan aircraft strayed over the border. Four Su22 bombers were brought down, and other successes followed.

The first large-scale deployment of Falcons in combat came in the 1991 war in the Gulf when U.S. and allied forces in Operation Desert Storm liberated Kuwait from Iraqi occupation. A total of 249 Falcons were deployed, carrying out 13,340 sorties in both fighter and ground-attack roles. Three of these aircraft were shot down. The F-16 has continued to see action with the U.S. Air Force over Iraq and in other theatres. On February 25, 2009, a USAF F16 shot down an Iranian Ababil 3 reconnaissance aircraft that had strayed into Iraqi airspace.

The success of the maneuverable Falcon led fighter designers to emphasize agility over speed while utilizing the increasingly sophisticated electronics of modern weapons systems. The latest fighter to enter service is the Lockheed Martin/Boeing F-22 Raptor. Among its advanced features are combined radar and infrared devices that track and identify all aircraft in the vicinity. These project data to the pilot's helmet visor, overlaying identification data into the pilot's view so that he does not need to guess when he glances but can take instant decisions on how to react. The aircraft also features integrated electronic warfare systems technology, to link on-board systems to those of the command HQ and allow seamless information sharing and communications. The Raptor also features stealth technology. This reduces its radar signature so that defending fighters and anti-aircraft weaponry are less able to counter intruding Raptors. High technology comes at a price, and each Raptor is thought to cost about $140 million.

Meanwhile the heavy two-seat fighter had led to the two-seat ground-attack jet, of which the Anglo-French Jaguar was a prime example. Entering service in 1973, the Jaguar is still in operation in some air forces. The Jaguar has a maximum speed of more than 1,200 mph (1,931 kph) and a combat range of 335 miles (539 km). It is armed with two 30 mm cannons, two Sidewinder air-to-air missiles, and 18 air-to-ground Matra rockets and is able to carry up to 10,000 lb (4,536 kg) of bombs or other external weaponry.

The Jaguar is now being phased out by front-rank air forces. Its place is being taken in part by the Typhoon, also known as the Eurofighter. This multi-role aircraft was long dogged by political and technical problems, but it finally entered service in 2003 and now equips six air forces. The project began in 1979 as a joint British-German concept for a European combat fighter. The French joined in 1980 but they insisted on leading the project, thus causing the others to pull out.

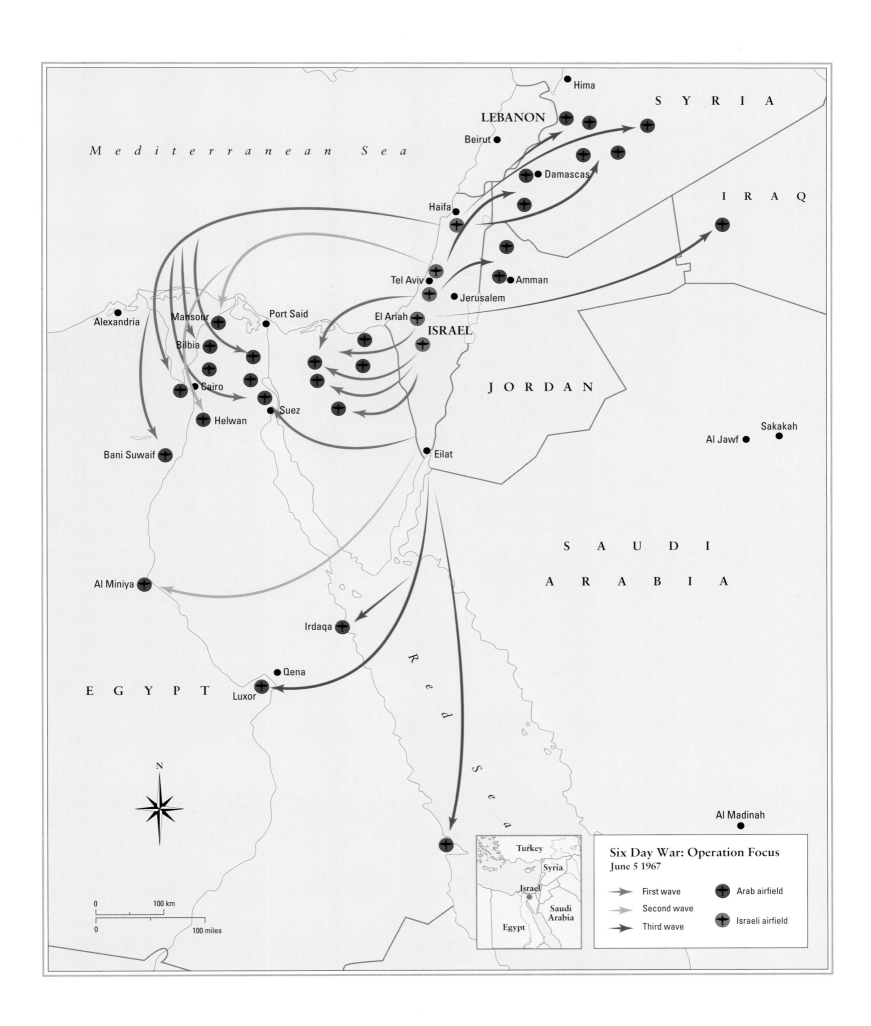

Hima

LEBANON

S Y R I A

M e d i t e r r a n e a n   S e a

Beirut

Damascas

Haifa

I R A Q

Tel Aviv

Amman

Jerusalem

Alexandria

Mansour

Port Said

El Ariah

ISRAEL

Bilbia

Cairo

J O R D A N

Helwan

Suez

Bani Suwaif

Eilat

Al Jawf

Sakakah

S A U D I

A R A B I A

Al Miniya

R e d

Irdaqa

Qena

S e a

E G Y P T

Luxor

Al Madinah

N

Turkey

Syria

Israel

Egypt

Saudi
Arabia

Six Day War: Operation Focus
June 5 1967

0   100 km

0   100 miles

→ First wave   ✛ Arab airfield

→ Second wave   ✛ Israeli airfield

→ Third wave

This was followed by a British-German-Italian project, the Future European Fighter. Political considerations led to the French being included and again they laid down strict conditions causing others to pull out of the project. Finally, in 1986, the Eurofighter Consortium was founded in Germay with British, German, and Italian ownership. Spain joined later, to form the company as it remains today.

The prototype Eurofighter was flown in 1994. The consortium opted for the name Typhoon in 1998, choosing a name that was pronounced and spelled similarly in most major languages. There was a delay when German government officials recalled that the Hawker Typhoon had been a ground attack aircraft in World War Two, but they eventually gave way.

The Typhoon is a lightweight, twin-engine aircraft with a delta-wing canard layout: the "tail" fins are located in front of the main wing. The design is inherently unstable, and the aircraft relies on a complex arrangement of control surfaces operated by the on-board computer to remain in the air. The instability is of great use when dogfighting, as it allows the Typhoon to twist and turn with great agility. It has a range of defensive measures, including a general radar, a missile-specific radar, and a laser-warning receiver. It can launch chaff or flares to divert incoming missiles. The 13 hardpoints are designed so that they can carry a wide range of weaponry for both air-to-air combat and air-to-ground attacks. There is also an internal 27 mm cannon. The Typhoon's first operational mission came on August 17, 2007 when one was sent up to intercept a long-range Russian bomber that was heading toward British airspace, no doubt to test the response of the RAF. The aircraft has a maximum speed of 1,500 mph (2,414 kph), a ceiling of 65,000ft (19,812 m), and a combat radius of 800 miles (1,287 km).

The introduction of the jet engine had a similar impact on the design and operation of bomber aircraft, although neither as immediate nor as far-reaching as for fighters. The first development came in the latter 1940s: bombers were produced that could fly higher than contemporary fighters and thus evade interception.

The British Canberra, which entered service in 1949, was typical of such aircraft. It was powered by jets but was of a fairly conventional design, and even included several wooden and plywood components. It had a top speed of 580 mph (933 kph), a ceiling of 48,000 ft (14,630 m), and a range of around 2,000 miles (3,219 km). It had four 20 mm cannons for defensive purposes and could carry up to 8,000 lb (3,630 kg) of bombs, rockets, or missiles.

The Canberra fought in many operations, including the 1956 Suez crisis, the Malayan Emergency, and the Vietnam War. It remained a front-line bomber with the RAF until the early 1970s and with other air forces until the 1990s. A special high-altitude, long-range reconnaissance version remained in active service with the RAF until 2006, and played a leading role in contemporary operations in Afghanistan.

In addition to the requirement for a tactical bomber such as the Canberra, there was a need to produce a bomber that could carry an atom bomb over intercontinental distances — long-range missiles had not been perfected in the 1950s. This led to the American Boeing B-52.

The B-52 entered service in 1955 and remains the only long-range heavy bomber active with the U.S. Air Force. The aircraft has a wingspan of 184 ft (56 m), making it almost as large as a 747 jumbo jet airliner. It has a maximum speed of 650 mph (1,046 kph), a ceiling of 50,000 ft (15,240 m), and a combat radius of 4,500 miles (7,242 km). Depending on the configuration of the bomb bay, the B-52 can carry up to 70,000 lb (31,751 kg) of bombs, missiles, mines, or a combination of all three.

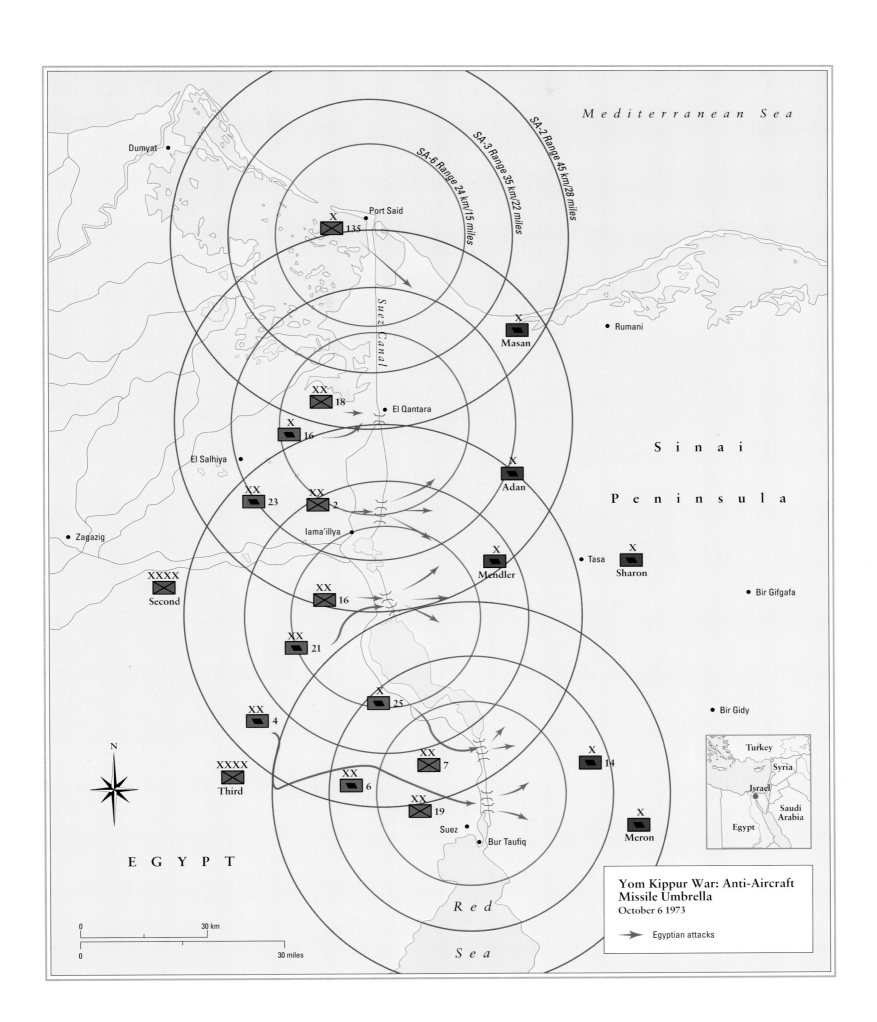

Mediterranean Sea

Dumyat

SA-2 Range 45 km/28 miles
SA-3 Range 35 km/22 miles
SA-6 Range 24 km/15 miles

Port Said

X 135

Rumani

X
Masan

Suez Canal

XX 18

El Qantara

X 16

El Salhiya

S i n a i

X
Adan

P e n i n s u l a

XX 23

XX 2

Iama'illya

Zagazig

Tasa

X
Sharon

X
Mendler

Bir Gifgafa

XXXX
Second

XX 16

XX 21

X 25

Bir Gidy

XX 4

XX 7

X 14

XXXX
Third

XX 6

XX 19

Suez

Meron
X

Bur Taufiq

E G Y P T

Turkey
Syria
Israel
Egypt
Saudi Arabia

R e d

Yom Kippur War: Anti-Aircraft Missile Umbrella
October 6 1973

→ Egyptian attacks

S e a

N

0   30 km
0   30 miles

The McDonnell-Douglas F-4J Phantom II was a supersonic, all-weather interceptor with full ground attack capability. Between 1955 and 1979, 5,057 of them were built. They served with U.S. forces as well as the militaries of seven other countries.

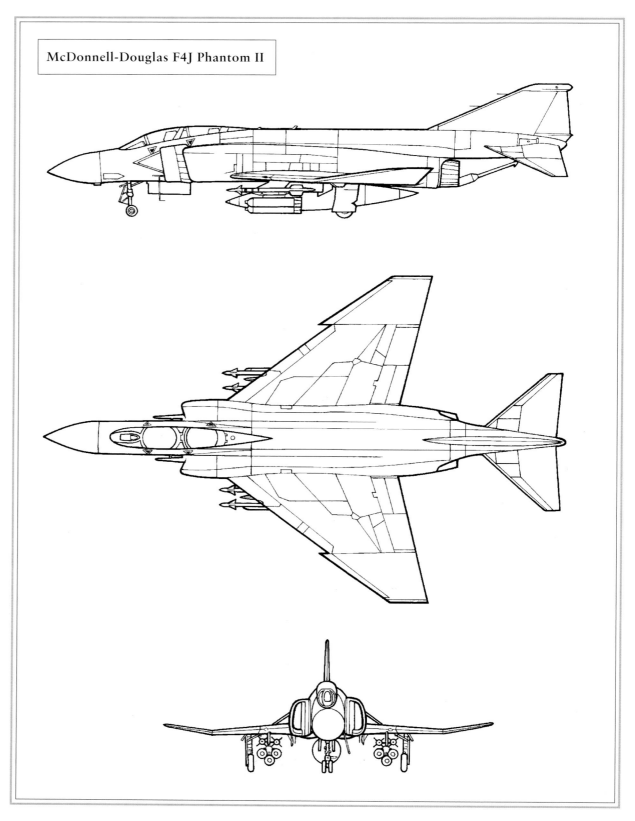

McDonnell-Douglas F4J Phantom II

Although it was conceived of as a nuclear bomber and carried out many tests with nuclear weapons, the B-52 has seen action as a conventional bomber in several theaters. It entered combat for the first time in 1964 when 28 of them were sent to Vietnam. The B-52 was used for carpet-bombing missions. These involved dropping a large number of smaller bombs in a set pattern so as to achieve total destruction of an area. It proved especially useful when attacking guerrilla camps and supply lines that were hidden

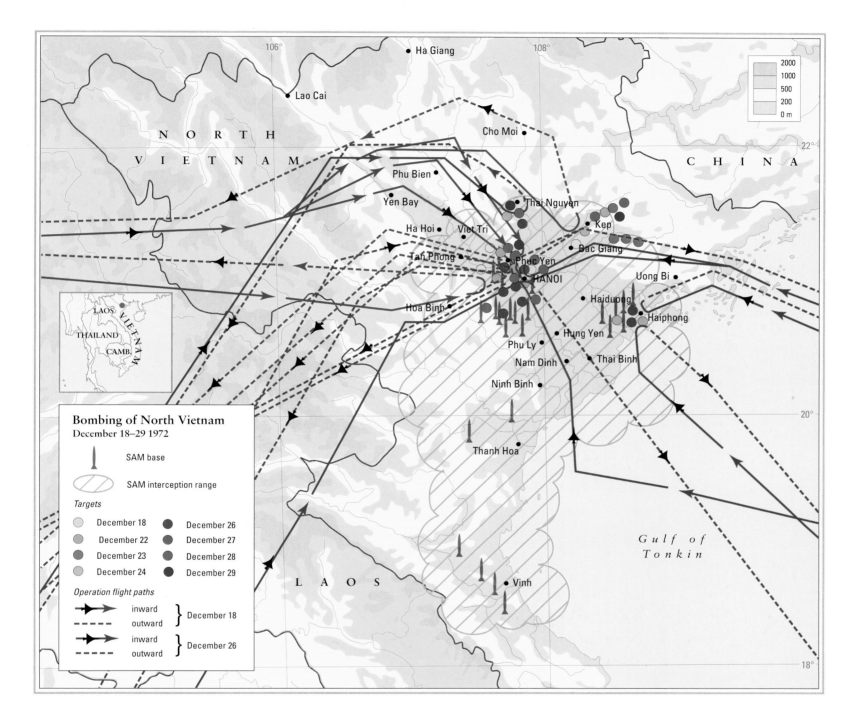

Bombing of North Vietnam
December 18–29 1972

SAM base

SAM interception range

Targets

December 18
December 22
December 23
December 24
December 26
December 27
December 28
December 29

Operation flight paths

inward
outward
} December 18

inward
outward
} December 26

beneath the jungle canopy of trees. Smaller, precision bombers would have been unable to locate the target, but beacause of its size the B-52s could carpet the whole area with bombs.

This tactic was costly in cash terms but it did produce results. The most intensive bombing of the Vietnam War came with Operation Linebacker II, when waves of B-52s flew a total of 729 sorties in 12 days and dropped 17,060 ton (15,481 tonnes) of bombs. The aircraft also operated over Cambodia, hitting communist supply lines such as the Ho Chi Minh Trail.

The Soviet answer to the B-52 came in the form of the Tupolev Tu-95, known to Western air forces as the Bear. The owered by four turboprop engines, the Bear can achieve up to 575 mph (925 kph); it has a ceiling height of 45,000 ft (13,716 m), and a combat range of 9,000 miles (14,484 km). It has a pair of 23 mm cannons for defense and can carry up to 33,000 lb (14,969 kg) of bombs, missiles or mines.

In April 1972, U.S. B-52 bombers attacked Vinh in North Vietnam. The priority targets were the SMA-2 missile sites, which the Americans considered to be "the most sophisticated air defenses in the history of air warfare".

Bombing Baghdad, Primary Targets January 17 – February 28 1991

(1) Directorate of Military Intelligence
(2) Telephone switching station
(3) Ministry of Defense National Computer Complex
(4) Electrical transfer station
(5) Telephone switching station
(6) Ministry of Defense HQ
(7) Ashudad highway bridge
(8) Telephone switching station
(9) Railroad yard
(10) Muthena airfield
(11) New Iraq Air Force HQ
(12) Iraqi Intelligence Service HQ
(13) Telephone switching station
(14) Secret Police complex
(15) Army storage depot
(16) Republican Guard HQ
(17) New Presidential Palace
(18) Electrical power plant
(19) SRBM assembly factory
(20) Baath Party HQ
(21) Government conference center
(22) Ministry of Industry and Military Production

(23) Ministry of Propaganda
(24) TV transmitter
(25) Communication relay station
(26) Jumhurlya highway bridge
(27) Government control center South
(28) Karada highway bridge
(29) Presidential Palace Command Center
(30) Presidential Palace Command Bunker
(31) Communication relay center
(32) Secret police HQ
(33) Iraqi Intelligence Service Regional HQ
(34) Telephone switching station
(35) National Air Defense Operations Center
(36) Al Dawrah oil refinery
(37) Electrical power plant
(38) Rasheed electrical power plant
(39) Rasheed barracks and airfield
(40) Baghdad ammunition depot
(41) Saddam International Airport
(42) Amiriyah shelter
(43) Baghdad International Radio reception
(44) Baby milk factory

The Gulf War of 1991 followed the refusal of Saddam Hussein of Iraq to co-operate with United Nations weapons inspectors.

As far as is known, the Bear has not been used in combat. However it was one of the most active and operationally important Russian aircraft during the Cold War. It was used to test the air defenses of Western nations on a regular basis, making almost weekly flights toward NATO air space at a variety of heights and locations. Presumably the Soviets were probing to see how quickly NATO air forces responded and in what fashion. A naval variant of the Bear was fitted with a powerful air-to-sea radar that could detect warships at a range of 200 miles (322 km). NATO carrier-based aircarft were kept busy intercepting Bears that sought to shadow ships on maneuver.

The Bear continues its probing missions to this day. On September 10 2009 a pair of Bears left northern Russia and headed over the North Pole toward Canada. They were intercepted by a pair of U.S. Air Force F-15 fighters, after which the Bears turned aside and patrolled the frozen wastes for 10 hours before returning home. The missions are not as frequent as they were in the Cold War era, but the aircraft remain a potent threat to the ships, land forces, and infrastructure of other nations.

The British produced the Vulcan in 1956 as its own nuclear bomber. Constructed on a delta-wing design, Vulcans were loved by their crews as comfortable aircraft that were easy to fly. They were adapted for use as maritime patrol aircraft and conventional bombers. Although they remained in service for over 30 years, the aircraft saw combat only once. In 1982 Vulcans were used to bomb Argentinian positions on the Falkland Islands as part of preparations to oust the Argentinian invaders.

The Vulcan could carry up to 21,000 lb (9,525 kg) of bombs over a range of 2,600 miles (4,184 km). Its top speed was 627 mph (1,009 kph) and its ceiling was 56,000 ft (17,000 m). In all, 136 of these fine

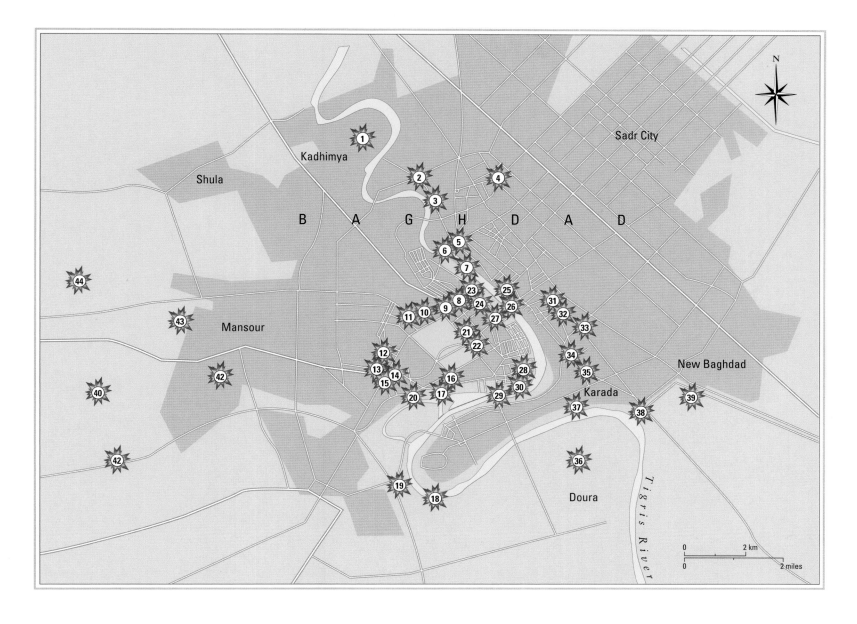

The center of Baghdad, the Iraqi capital, was extensively bombed in the 1991 war. Strategic targets included airfields, bridges, and government departments.

aircraft were built. Several of them survive as static displays at museums and one has been restored to flying condition for use at air shows.

As these large bombers became operational in the 1950s, the need for heavy bombers began to be questioned. The primary role of heavy bombers was the strategic bombing of enemy cities, factories, and other distant high-value sites. Once intercontinental missiles were developed that could carry nuclear weapons from one side of the Earth to the other, the primary role of the big bomber was taken away. Although several nations began planning for more advanced heavy bombers that would enter service in the 1970s, none of them were built. Instead, air forces concentrated on the cheaper option of upgrading their existing designs. The carpet-bombing of enemy positions, as carried out by B-52 bombers in the Vietnam War, has become outmoded by advances in technology. As detection equipment became more sophisticated and accurate, it became possible to find enemy positions even when they were camouflaged or hidden. Low-flying strike aircraft able to deliver precision weapons became a more reliable and cost-effective option than carpet-bombing. Thus designers and the military placed greater emphasis on aircraft such as the Jaguar, Eurofighter, MiG27, and A-10 Thunderbolt.

HELICOPTER WARFARE

THE HELICOPTER HAS PROVED TO BE A HIGHLY ADAPTABLE WAR MACHINE. IT HAS BEEN USED IN A VARIETY OF ROLES AND HAS BEEN LIKENED TO THE LIGHT CAVALRY OF PREVIOUS GENERATIONS. IN THE MODERN BATTLEFIELD NO ADVANCED ARMY CAN AFFORD TO BE WITHOUT HELICOPTERS.

The Germans were the first to put the helicopter on the battlefield, and they anticipated most of the roles that it would perform. The Focke Achgelis Fa223 Drache entered service in 1941. The Drache (Dragon) had been designed as a pre-war passenger and transportation aircraft for use in remote areas without a proper airfield and runway. It had a speed of 108 mph (175 kph), a ceiling of 8,163 ft (2,488 m), and a range of 435 miles (700 km). The Flettner Fl282, similar in performance, was significantly smaller. Fewer than 50 of these helicopters entered service, but they were used for a wide variety of tasks. These included ferrying senior officers, transporting equipment between ships, reconnaissance, artillery-spotting, and mountain transportation. The Luftwaffe was so impressed that it placed orders for hundreds of helicopters, intending them to be used to drop mines at sea, to evacuate the wounded from battlefields, and to engage in ground attack, in addition to the tasks they were already performing. However, technical problems and the bombing of the production factories by the RAF and the USAAF meant that the various models never came into production.

In the United States too, the potential uses of the helicopter had been identified, and the Sikorsky R-4 Hoverfly entered service in small numbers in 1944. It was used primarily for evacuating wounded men or for transportation in areas where runways were impossible to construct, such as Burma and the Aleutian Islands. Like the Flettner helicopter, the Hoverfly was small and able to lift only two passengers or an equivalent weight of equipment in addition to the pilot.

After World War Two, the military temporarily lost interest in helicopters for any purpose other than transportation in difficult terrain. It was the French fighting a guerrilla war in Algeria who led the way in bringing the helicopter back to the battlefield with the Bell 47. This small, fairly slow helicopter had been acquired for evacuating wounded soldiers on stretchers mounted on the skids. However, commanders soon began removing the stretchers and putting two men armed with machine guns into the helicopter instead. The craft were then used to attack positions in rocky mountains and hills. The first known instance of this came in 1955. It was so successful that within a year the French military began modifying the larger Sikorsky H-34 helicopter by adding a 20 mm cannons and rocket-firing racks.

By 1958 the French were developing air-assault tactics that would later be copied by every other army with access to helicopters. H-34 helicopters would attack a target first with rockets and cannons.

The Battle of Ap Bac in Vietnam, January 2 1963, was significant as the first important victory scored by the Viet Cong over American and South Vietnamese forces, who were well equipped with armored vehicles and support helicopters.

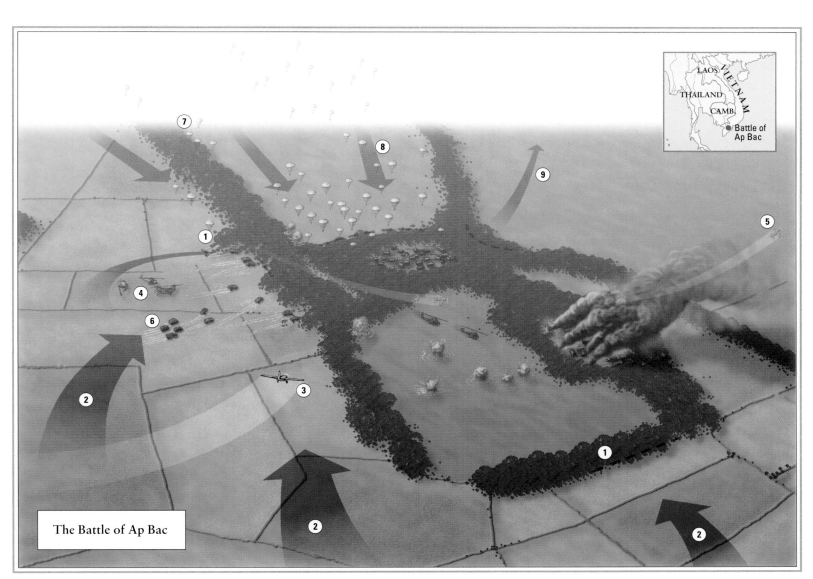

The Battle of Ap Bac

1. Original Viet Cong positions.

2. 1st Battalion of civil guard arrives. Concealed Viet Cong open fire. Civil guard falls back in disorder, their commanding officer among the killed.

3. U.S. advisor flying overhead in spotter plane orders helicopter- borne infantry reinforcements.

4. These reinforcements land too close to the Viet Cong positions. Many are wounded and survivors withdraw.

5. Sky raider fighter-bombers launch napalm attack but hit villages and miss Viet Cong positions.

6. In an attempt to rescue the downed helicopter crews, armored personnel carriers are ordered forward. Thought invulnerable to small arms fire, the carriers approach the eastern tree line. At point-blank range the Viet Cong open fire, killing the machine gunners riding on top of the vehicles. The Viet Cong then rush forward throwing grenades and the carriers withdraw.

7. The senior American advisor still flying overhead persuades the South Vietnamese Commander to order a parachute drop to seal in the Viet Cong. The drop is badly handled and the troops land in front of the Viet Cong positions and come under heavy fire. They are therefore unable to launch an attack.

8. 7th South Vietnamese infantry division approaching from the north are unable to co-operate with dispersed and pinned down airborne troops.

9. During the night the Viet Cong withdraw, having tied down a force many times their size and vastly better equipped. In the process only 18 of their own men were killed.

Then Sikorsky CH-34 helicopters would land and disgorge infantry who would attack and occupy the enemy positions. Once the enemy had been defeated, the French troops would be airlifted out again by the CH-34 helicopters while the H-34 craft laid down covering fire.

The French lost the Algerian War, but the success of their helicopter assault tactics was noticed. During the 1960s the U.S. Army began arming its UH-1B Huey helicopters with rockets and machine guns while the CH-47 Chinook was given improvised bomb racks for dropping bombs on bunkers. The Soviet Union adapted its MiG Mi8 in a similar way, and the British Royal Navy began using helicopters equipped with magnetic detectors in order to find submerged submarines. The British Royal Navy soon fitted them with depth charges for dropping on any target located.

It was the Americans who took the next step in helicopter warfare, by producing the first purpose-built air attack helicopter. This was the Bell AH-1 Cobra, which entered service in 1967. The Cobra had a two-man crew, one to pilot the craft and one to operate the weapons. It had a top speed of 219 mph (352 kph), a ceiling of 11,400 ft (3,474 m), and a range of 450 miles (563 km). Its armory consisted of twin 7.62 mm machine guns, or twin 40 mm grenade-launchers, in a turret under the chin of the craft. There was also provision for up to 19 70 mm rockets, a 20 mm cannon, or a 7.62 mm minigun. The craft remains in service today, but has undergone numerous modifications

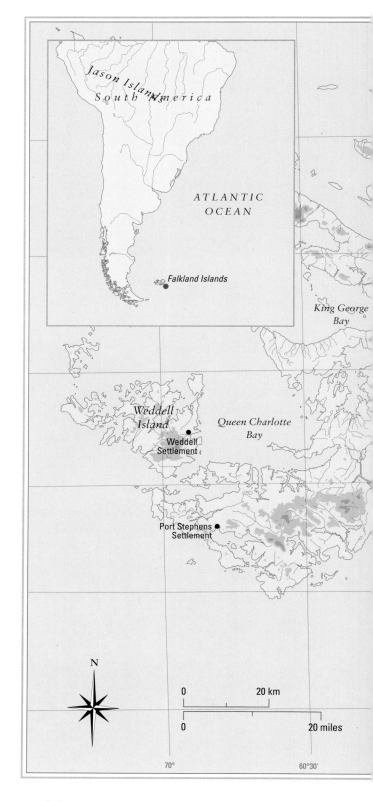

so as to improve its performance or to allow it to carry different weapons. Most recently it was adapted to carry a 20 mm Gatling cannons and eight anti-tank missiles. In Vietnam, Cobras flew over a million operational hours. Their primary role was to attack enemy ground positions in support of ground forces, but they also flew as armed escort to unarmed transport helicopters. This latter role led to the "hunt-kill patrols" in which a pair of Cobras flew behind and above an unarmed reconnaissance helicopter. If enemy troops opened fire on the scout helicopter, they would be detected and destroyed by the Cobras.

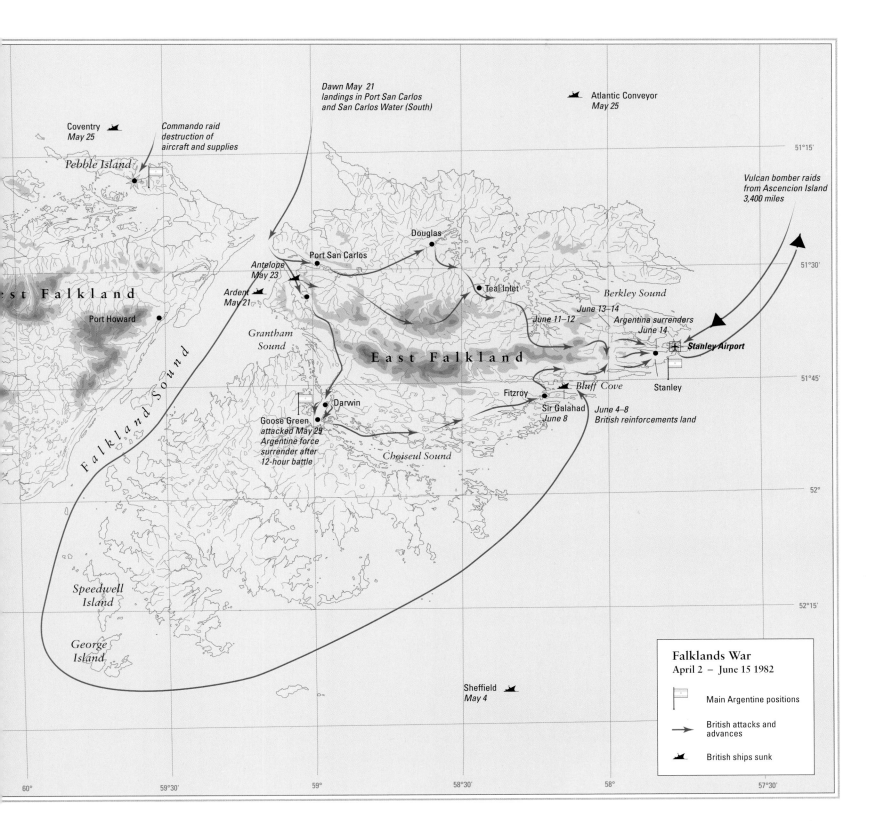

Dawn May 21
landings in Port San Carlos
and San Carlos Water (South)

Atlantic Conveyor
May 25

Coventry
May 25

Commando raid
destruction of
aircraft and supplies

Pebble Island

Vulcan bomber raids
from Ascencion Island
3,400 miles

51°15'

Douglas

Port San Carlos

Antelope
May 23

East Falkland

Teal Inlet

Berkley Sound

June 13–14

June 11–12

Argentina surrenders
June 14

51°30'

Ardent
May 21

Port Howard

Grantham
Sound

East Falkland

Stanley Airport

Stanley

51°45'

Falkland Sound

Darwin

Goose Green
attacked May 29
Argentine force
surrender after
12-hour battle

Fitzroy

Sir Galahad
June 8

Bluff Cove

June 4–8
British reinforcements land

Choiseul Sound

52°

Speedwell
Island

52°15'

George
Island

Sheffield
May 4

Falklands War
April 2 – June 15 1982

Main Argentine positions

British attacks and
advances

British ships sunk

60°   59°30'   59°   58°30'   58°   57°30'

The Cobras were moved to a secondary role by the latter 1980s, attacking secondary targets only when air superiority had been gained by more advanced aircraft. They remain in use with U.S. forces and with other nations such as Pakistan, Israel, Thailand, and Turkey.

The attack helicopter that replaced the Cobra was the McDonnell Douglas AH-64 Apache, which entered service in 1984 and remains the main U.S. attack helicopter. The two-man crew sits in tandem in the narrow fuselage, with the twin turboshaft engines and four-bladed rotors positioned behind them.

The Falklands War began after Argentine forces invaded the Falkland Islands on April 2 1982. The Falklands, a British territory, were claimed by the Argentines who called them Las Malvinas. The British prevailed after some 10 weeks of unequal fighting.

American Apaches have been used since 1989 in Panama, the Gulf War, Bosnia, Kosovo, and in the Iraq war. During the Iraq invasion of 2003 more than 200 American Apaches were used.

Opposite page: Apache AH-1s support UK and Coalition forces in the south of Afghanistan, during the current conflict between Coalition forces and the Taliban. The Apaches use Longbow Fire Control Radar; coalition forces say that it improves situational awareness and avoidance of other aircraft during tactical maneuvers.

The Apache's top speed is 227 mph (365 kph); it has a ceiling of 21,000 ft (6,400 m) and a combat radius of 300 miles (482 km). It is armed with a 30 mm cannon and 70 mm air-to-ground rockets. It also has hardpoints on which can be mounted a variety of missiles for use against ground targets, aircraft, or ships. The weapons master has a range of highly sophisticated radar and infrared devices that allow him to operate by day or night and in fog, rain, and other adverse weather conditions.

The Apache entered service in 1984 and first saw combat in the 1989 invasion of Panama. In 1991, Apaches undertook the first mission of Operation Desert Storm when they flew in low to attack Iraqi radar bases on the night of January 17 1991. The destruction of these targets allowed bomber and ground-attack aircraft to invade Iraqi air space undetected. The Apache then switched to a specialized anti-tank role, destroying an estimated 600 tanks and other armored vehicles and several hundred trucks and transport vehicles. During operations in the Balkans in the latter 1990s, there were problems with the night-vision equipment, but this was rectified by the time the helicopter returned to Iraq for the invasion of 2003.

The Iraqi military had learned important lessons and on March 24 2003, the Apache suffered a rare defeat. A force of 33 helicopters was sent to attack a brigade of tanks that had halted in open country. It was a trap, as a massive ring of anti-aircraft weapons surrounded the tanks. As the Apache helicopters

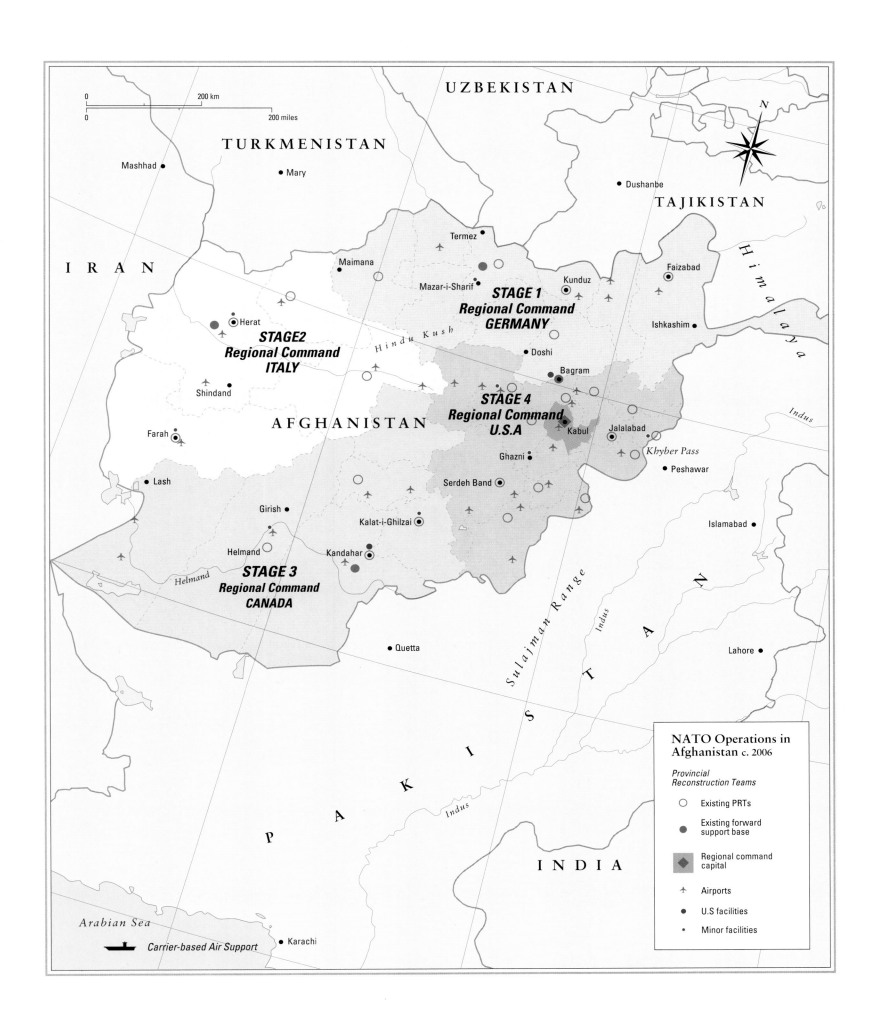

UZBEKISTAN

TURKMENISTAN

TAJIKISTAN

IRAN

AFGHANISTAN

PAKISTAN

INDIA

Mashhad

Mary

Dushanbe

Termez

Maimana

Faizabad

Mazar-i-Sharif

Kunduz

STAGE 1
Regional Command
GERMANY

Ishkashim

Herat

STAGE2
Regional Command
ITALY

Hindu Kush

Doshi

Bagram

STAGE 4
Regional Command
U.S.A

Kabul

Jalalabad

Khyber Pass

Shindand

Ghazni

Peshawar

Farah

Serdeh Band

Lash

Islamabad

Girish

Kalat-i-Ghilzai

Helmand

Kandahar

Helmand

STAGE 3
Regional Command
CANADA

Quetta

Lahore

Sulaiman Range

Indus

Indus

Indus

Himalaya

Arabian Sea

Karachi

Carrier-based Air Support

0   200 km
0   200 miles

N

NATO Operations in Afghanistan c. 2006

Provincial Reconstruction Teams

○ Existing PRTs

● Existing forward support base

◆ Regional command capital

✈ Airports

● U.S facilities

· Minor facilities

Opposite page: The second war against Iraq, which began on 17 March 2003 was much more extensive than had been attempted in 1991. Invasions took place in the north of Iraq and also in the south, where Allied forces converged on Baghdad.

attacked, they came under heavy fire. One was shot down and 30 were damaged, several of them beyond repair. The attack was called off.

Other countries have developed their own attack helicopters. The Franco-German Tiger entered service in 1991. This helicopter is very lightweight and agile. The hull is made of 80 percent carbon fiber, 11 per cent aluminum, and 6 per cent titanium; the rotors are made of plastic. It is one of the very few helicopters able to perform a loop. As in the Apache, the crew are equipped with sophisticated equipment for finding targets and evading gunfire.

The Tiger has a top speed of 196 mph (315 kph), a ceiling of 13,000 ft (3,962 m), and a range of 500 miles (805 km). It is armed with a 30 mm cannon in the chin turret and has four hardpoints that can mount a variety of cannons, machine guns, rockets, and missiles. In July 2009 the Tiger entered service in Afghanistan with the French army, its first combat deployment.

The Russian Kamov Ka-50 is known to Russian troops as the Black Shark and is similar to the Apache in its performance and roles. It entered service in 1995 and saw action in the Chechnya War, in which it successfully attacked a number of ground targets.

By the early 21st century, the tactical use of helicopters had moved on from its inception by the French. Combat helicopters have been used mainly against guerrilla forces. These forces typically operate on foot or on trucks and have low-technology weaponry, but they do have a measure of support from the local civilian population. Helicopters are used to transport patrols to and from their area of operation so that they are not ambushed on access roads. They are also used to rush reinforcements up to any patrol that comes under attack while attack helicopters move in to destroy the enemy force. Helicopters are also useful in carrying supplies to an isolated garrison if ground routes prove too dangerous for trucks. Essentially the helicopter can be used to gain an element of surprise for conventional forces dealing with a guerrilla opponent.

Most armies recognize that they may be called upon to face a powerful, high-tech enemy at some point and have developed helicopter tactics for such a war. Combat helicopters are envisaged to have two prime roles. The first is to act as a highly mobile anti-tank force. A screen of light scout helicopters would fan out to locate enemy armor. A smaller force of attack helicopters equipped with anti-tank missiles would then dash forward at very low height and destroy the enemy armor.

The second role is to attack and destroy or occupy enemy positions. This role would be especially important in an offensive in which bridges and other transport bottlenecks had to be secured for use by advancing troops. Helicopter gunships would open the attack, hitting enemy positions and troops. Transport helicopters would then land infantry units that would launch an assault. If a position had to be occupied, the attack helicopters would return and provide support fire in the event of an enemy counterattack. If possible, larger transport helicopters would be flown in to land light artillery and light tanks for supporting the infantry.

In addition to these combat roles, helicopters are used by many modern armies for transportation and for evacuating the wounded. Some commanders believe that the presence of helicopter ambulances able to move a wounded man quickly from the front line to a hospital is essential to morale.

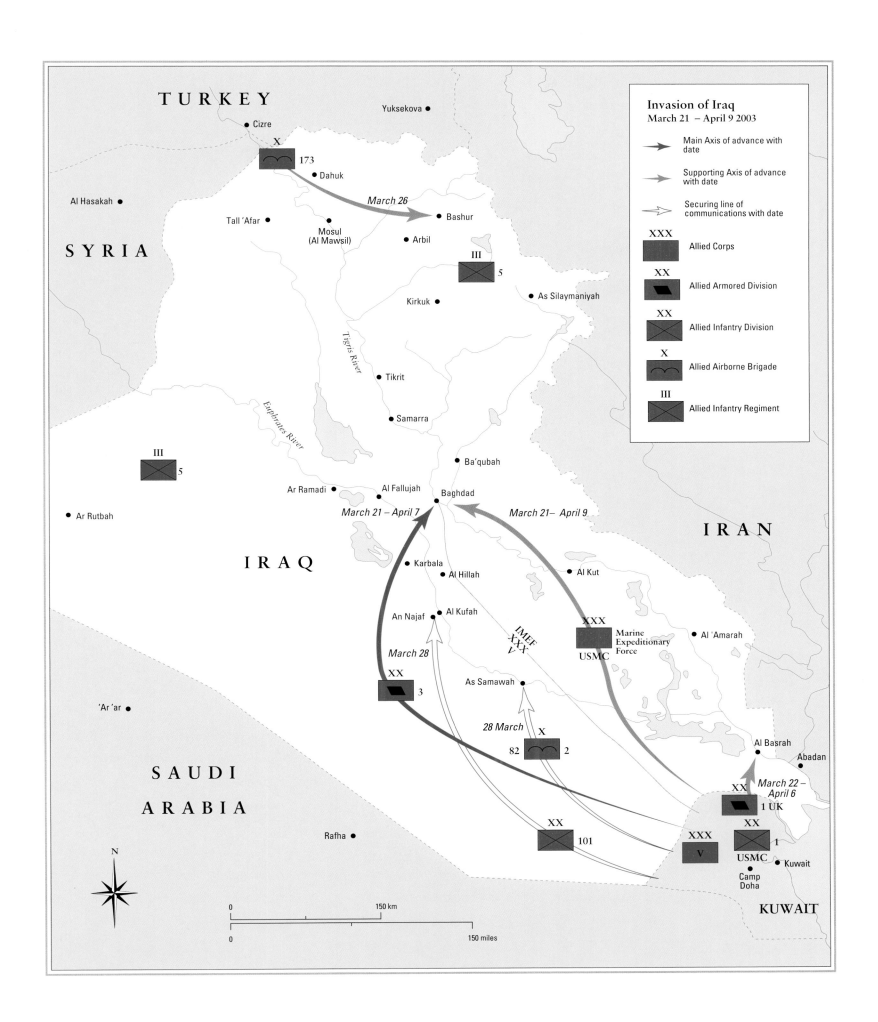

TURKEY

Yuksekova •

• Cizre

X
173

• Dahuk

March 26

• Bashur

Al Hasakah •

Tall 'Afar •

Mosul
(Al Mawsil) •

• Arbil

SYRIA

III
5

Kirkuk •

• As Silaymaniyah

Tigris River

• Tikrit

• Samarra

III
5

• Ba'qubah

Euphrates River

Ar Ramadi •

Al Fallujah •

Baghdad •

March 21 – April 7

March 21– April 9

• Ar Rutbah

IRAQ

IRAN

Karbala •

• Al Kut

Al Hillah •

An Najaf •

Al Kufah •

March 28

IMEF
XXX
V

XXX
USMC

Marine
Expeditionary
Force

• Al 'Amarah

XX
3

As Samawah •

28 March

X
82   2

'Ar 'ar •

XX
1 UK

March 22 –
April 6

SAUDI

ARABIA

Rafha •

XX
101

XXX
V
USMC

XX
1

• Kuwait

Camp
Doha

Al Basrah •

• Abadan

N

KUWAIT

Invasion of Iraq
March 21 – April 9 2003

→ Main Axis of advance with
date

→ Supporting Axis of advance
with date

⇒ Securing line of
communications with date

XXX
■   Allied Corps

XX
◪   Allied Armored Division

XX
☒   Allied Infantry Division

X
◠◠   Allied Airborne Brigade

III
☒   Allied Infantry Regiment

0   150 km

0   150 miles

THE SUPERCARRIER

"SUPERCARRIER" IS NOT A TERM OFFICIALLY RECOGNIZED BY ANY NAVY BUT IT IS WIDELY USED TO MEAN AN AIRCRAFT CARRIER LARGE ENOUGH TO CARRY A COMPLETE AIR GROUP. SUCH SHIPS ACT AS THE CENTRAL CRAFT IN A NAVAL TASK FORCE WITHOUT THE NEED FOR ANCILLARY AIRCRAFT-CARRYING VESSELS.

The Americans developed the concept of a supercarrier as a result of their experiences in the Pacific during World War Two. An arduous series of campaigns had demonstrated that air cover was essential to naval and amphibious operations. The critical naval battles of the Pacific War — Pearl Harbor, Midway, Leyte Gulf and the Philippine Sea — had all been dominated by aircraft launched from aircraft carriers.

American naval planners decided that any naval operations in the foreseeable future would need air cover. As it was not possible to guarantee that land airfields would be available within range, the navy would need to have aircraft carriers. The increasing sophistication of air warfare showed that no single aircraft carrier of the size used by the U.S. in World War Two could provide all the types of aircraft needed for a future campaign. The U.S. Navy had a choice: to provide two or more carriers equipped with different but complementary aircraft types or to build a new class of aircraft carrier able to hold everything that would be needed. It opted for the latter, and created the supercarrier.

The first supercarriers to be launched were the *USS Forrestal* and three sister ships. The *Forrestal* entered service in 1955 and remained active until 1993. It was the first aircraft carrier built for the use of jet aircraft. It was also the first one built with an angled flight deck, a steam catapult, and landing lights —other carriers had been fitted with those features, but only after entering service.

The *Forrestal* was enormous. It measured over 1,000 ft (305 m) long, had a beam of 131 ft (40 m) at the waterline, and a draft of 35 ft (10.7 m). It displaced 67,199 tons (60,962) tonnes and had 4,378 crew members, and its powerful steam turbine engines could push it through the water at 34 knots at top speed. For close defense she had eight 5 inch anti-aircraft guns, later modified to 84 anti-aircraft missiles. All this was intended to ensure that the ship carried everything needed to keep 100 aircraft of various types in action as well as if they were on a large land airfield.

The ships of the *Forrestal* class saw action in Vietnam, launching their aircraft to hit land targets and to patrol the coastline and inshore seas. In 1986 the *Saratoga* saw action in the Mediterranean after Libya's Colonel Gaddafi had claimed the Gulf of Sirte as part of Libyan national waters. The *Saratoga* led a U.S. naval task force into the Gulf, defying Gaddafi and engaging a number of Libyan aircraft and ships. It took part in the 1991 Gulf War, launching air attacks against Iraq and Kuwait. All the aircraft carriers of this class were decommissioned during the 1990s.

The place of the *Forrestal*-class supercarriers was taken by the 10 ships of the *Nimitz* class. These began entering service in 1975, when the *USS Nimitz* itself was commissioned. The most recent to enter service, in January 2009, was the *USS George H.W. Bush*. These ships are even larger than the *Forrestal* class. They displace about 113,119 tons (102,620) tonnes, are 253 ft (77 m) long and 108 ft (33m) wide, and draw 36 ft (11 m). Their nuclear engines provide unlimited endurance, although the ships need to restock with food and other supplies from time to time, and can achieve speeds in excess of 30 knots. For defensive purposes they have up to 40 anti-aircraft missiles.

Each ship of the *Nimitz* class can accommodate up to 90 fixed-wing aircraft or helicopters or a combination of the two. Among the fixed-wing aircraft flown from the ships are the FA-18 Super Hornet multi-role fighter and the EA-6B Prowler electronic weapons aircraft. Each carrier forms the heart of an aircraft-carrier strike force. This consists of a number of warships, including cruisers and destroyers. They provide anti-aircraft protection in depth, act as launch pads for cruise missiles, and are able to lay

"Supercarrier" is an unofficial term for the largest aircraft carriers, that is those which displace over 77,161 tons (70,000 tonnes). The present Supercarrier standard was set in 1954 with the launch of the *USS Forrestal*, which displaced 85,950 tons (78,000 tonnes) when fully loaded.

down gunfire in support of amphibious landings. Two cruisers and five destroyers, for example, escort the *USS Nimitz*.

The U.S. navy is now planning the next generation of supercarriers, dubbed the *Ford* class after President Gerald Ford. These ships, of which three have been ordered for 2020, will use the basic hull shape of the *Nimitz* class but will contain a large amount of improved equipment, such as better radar, catapults, and arresting gear, improved engines, and an entirely redesigned island structure.

The United States is currently the only country operating supercarriers, but two other navies have similar ships on order. The British Royal Navy has ordered two supercarriers, to be named *Queen Elizabeth* and *Prince of Wales*. Each of these ships will displace 72,798 tons (66,042 tonnes), will be 918 ft (280 m) long and will be 128 feet (39m) in the beam. They will be capable of 25 knots and will be able to travel about 9,975 miles (16,053 km) without refuelling.

The aircraft carried by the two British supercarriers will be 36 Lockheed F-35 Lightning II multi-role fighters and four airborne early-warning radar aircraft. The Lightning was designed for use on carriers and is a versatile aircraft able to carry out bombing, dogfighting, and ground-attack missions. In theory each carrier could carry an additional 10 aircraft, but it is expected that these will be helicopters rather than fixed-wing aircraft.

The arrival of the two aircraft carriers will solve a long-standing problem experienced by the Royal Navy. Its existing aircraft carriers are a trio of 22,000-ton vessels that were built in the 1970s specifically to provide anti-submarine patrols across the North Atlantic. In the 1982 Falklands War, however, *HMS Invincible* was hurriedly converted to a more conventional aircraft carrier role. This convinced the Royal Navy to convert all three to a multi-task role, for which they had not been built. The new ships will be the first British aircraft carriers designed for wide-ranging duties since the 1950s.

The French announced in 2008 that they would be ordering a supercarrier similar to the British ships

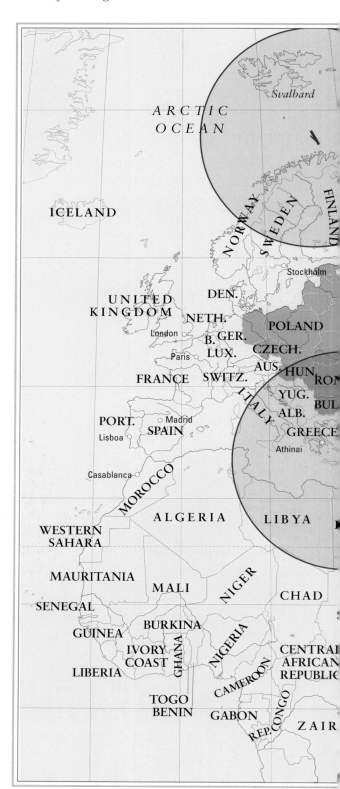

and built by the same consortium. The ship, provisionally named *Richelieu*, would be slightly larger than the British ships and contain some distinctively French features, such as two command islands. It is expected to carry 32 Rafaele fighters, three early warning aircraft and a number of helicopters. However, in 2009 the French government announced a delay to the project owing to the economic crisis and so the projected completion date of 2017 is now in doubt.

U.S supercarrier deployment, heavily focused around the Middle East region.

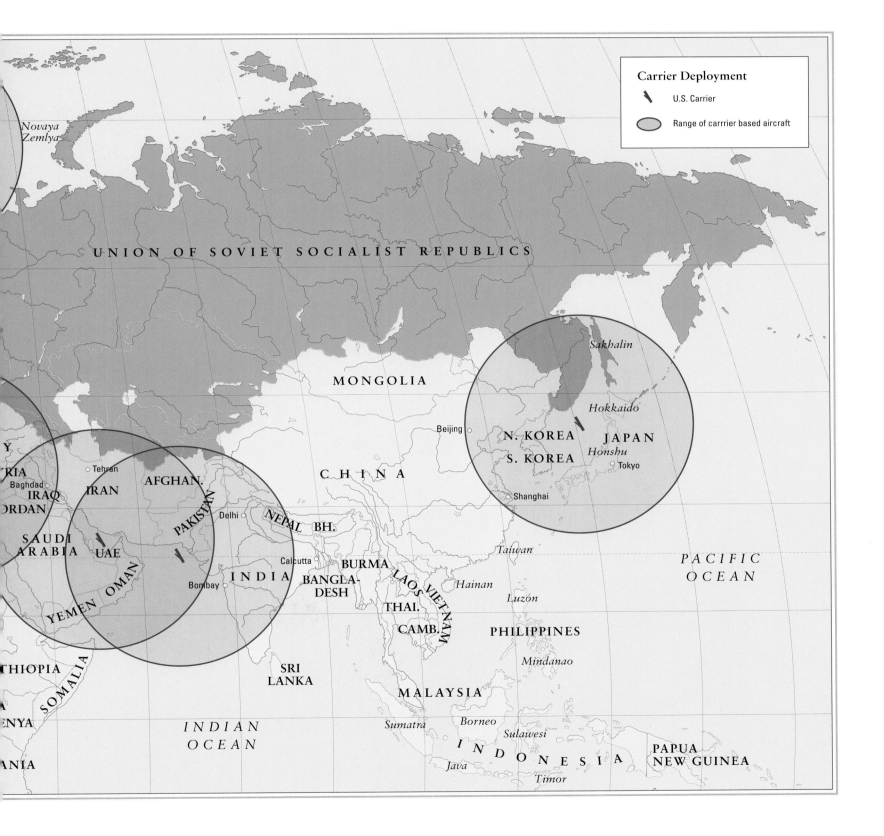

GUERRILLA WARFARE

THE ADVENT OF INCREASINGLY EFFECTIVE WEAPONRY HAS MADE CONVENTIONAL WARS COSTLY TO WAGE AND POTENTIALLY SUICIDAL TO INITIATE. AS A CONSEQUENCE, MANY NATIONAL, RELIGIOUS, AND POLITICAL GROUPS NOT ABLE TO ACHIEVE THEIR AIMS THROUGH PEACEFUL MEANS HAVE TURNED TO GUERRILLA WARFARE.

Opposite page: FARC-EP, a Marxist-Leninist revolutionary guerrilla organization based in Colombia, has fought in the ongoing Colombian Civil War for more than 40 years. During the mid-1990s, drug war analysts have stated that the FARC-EP have become increasingly involved in the drug trade, controlling farming, production, and exportation of cocaine in those areas of the country under their influence. This claim has been also been made by U.S. and Colombian authorities.

There is nothing new about guerrilla warfare. The name was coined to describe the irregular units in Spain that were fighting against the French occupation of that country between 1807 and 1814. The word literally means "little war", which first applied to the style of fighting but later to the nature of the combatants engaged in the war as well.

A typical guerrilla army is composed of irregular units. Some of the personnel may be fully trained soldiers, but the units are composed of whoever is willing to join them on an *ad hoc* basis rather than officially recruited and trained military units. The fighters are usually only lightly equipped, often having only personal weapons such as rifles, pistols, or grenades. Almost invariably, a guerrilla army lacks artillery, tanks, ships, aircraft, and other heavy weapons. This imposes on the guerrilla a style of fighting that makes the best use of his light weaponry. Ambushes and raids have long been typical guerrilla tactics, as have assassination and propaganda campaigns.

For a guerrilla army to be successful, it needs to be able to escape the superior weapons and technology of the enemy. There are two basic methods of doing this. The first is to operate from a base in inhospitable terrain such as mountains, swamps, or forests. The second is to hide among the local civilian population. Guerrillas are often part-time soldiers who work as farmers or factory hands by day but take up arms at night.

The aim of a guerrilla campaign is not to defeat the enemy in conventional terms but to ensure that the effort required to obtain victory is out of proportion to the benefits to be gained. The campaign seeks to defeat the enemy by convincing him that the struggle is not worth his time and effort.

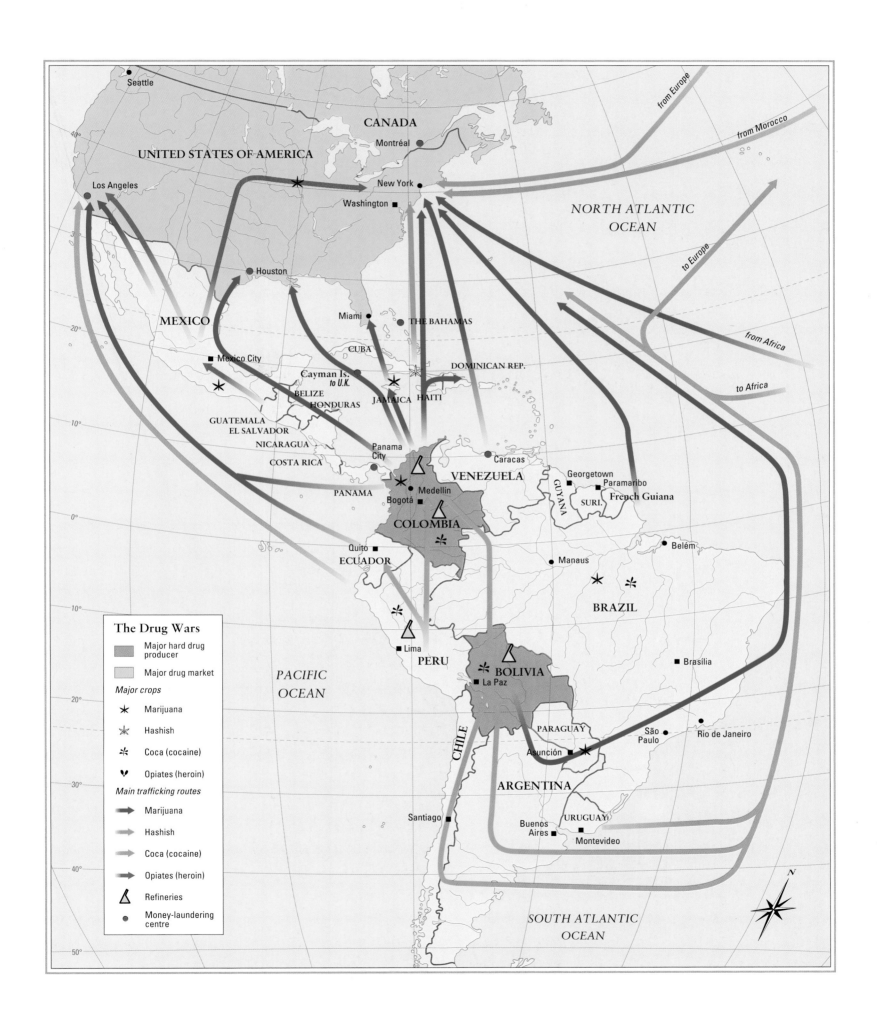

Seattle

CANADA

UNITED STATES OF AMERICA

Montréal

Los Angeles

New York

Washington

NORTH ATLANTIC
OCEAN

from Europe

from Morocco

Houston

to Europe

MEXICO

Miami

THE BAHAMAS

from Africa

Mexico City

CUBA

to Africa

Cayman Is.
to U.K.

BELIZE

DOMINICAN REP.

HONDURAS

JAMAICA

HAITI

GUATEMALA
EL SALVADOR

NICARAGUA

COSTA RICA

Panama
City

Caracas

Georgetown

Paramaribo

PANAMA

Medellín

VENEZUELA

GUYANA

French Guiana

Bogotá

SURI.

COLOMBIA

Belém

Quito

ECUADOR

Manaus

PACIFIC
OCEAN

BRAZIL

Lima

PERU

The Drug Wars

Major hard drug
producer

Major drug market

Major crops

✳ Marijuana

✳ Hashish

✳ Coca (cocaine)

v Opiates (heroin)

Main trafficking routes

➤ Marijuana

➤ Hashish

➤ Coca (cocaine)

➤ Opiates (heroin)

△ Refineries

• Money-laundering
centre

BOLIVIA

La Paz

Brasília

PARAGUAY

São
Paulo

Rio de Janeiro

Asunción

ARGENTINA

Santiago

CHILE

Buenos
Aires

URUGUAY

Montevideo

SOUTH ATLANTIC
OCEAN

N

A Pakistani soldier walks past seized ammunitions and weapons recovered during military operations against Taliban militants. As of 2010, a strong insurgency in the form of a Taliban guerrilla war continues in Afghanistan.

There are two methods of responding to a guerrilla campaign. The first is to seek a military decision by launching search-and-destroy patrols, large-scale sweep campaigns, and other operations designed to find and eradicate the guerrilla units. The second is to adopt what has become known as a "hearts and minds" approach. This seeks to undermine the guerrilla force's support among the local population by putting forward an alternative vision of the future and supporting it with constructive actions and programs, constantly seeking to keep the local population friendly, and to avoid giving offense. Both approaches have achieved successes and failures, but the most successful counter-guerrilla operations have combined the two approaches. The two most high-profile guerrilla wars of the early 21st century are in the Middle East. The campaign against the Taliban in Afghanistan began in 2001 after the Taliban government was overthrown by local and Western forces, but it grew rapidly in size and scope in 2006. It has been estimated that as of 2010 the Taliban consisted of about 2,000 full-time guerrillas and another 8,000 part-time fighters with varying degrees of commitment to the cause.

Although the Taliban publicly claims to be a fundamentalist Islamic movement, the situation is greatly complicated by Afghan tribal loyalties and feuds. It can be difficult for outsiders to be certain if any particular unit is based on religious belief or tribal identity. In general, the Taliban have followed a conventional guerrilla strategy of seeking to prolong the campaign and to increase its cost to the Western military based in Afghanistan while attempting to gain control of rural areas, from which they can draw supplies, funding, and recruits.

In Iraq the insurgency campaign is being waged by the Iraqi government, backed by U.S. and Allied military forces, against a loose coalition of local militias and sectarian units. An underlying problem in Iraq is that the state is not based on any natural ethnic or religious boundaries, so the the north is populated by Kurds, the south-east by Shia Muslims, who are backed by Iran, and the center by Sunni Muslims. Each of these groups has its own political agenda and for the most part its own irregular armed forces willing to take up arms to achieve it. In both these conflicts the guerrillas have largely failed in their stated aims. However, the government and the Western forces have likewise failed either to defeat the guerrillas militarily or to win over the local population. The conflicts seem likely to drag on for some time to come. There are several other guerrilla campaigns active in 2010 including an Islamist uprising in the Philippines, a separatist campaign waged in the ethnically Malay areas of southern Thailand, a religious rebellion in northern Uganda led by the Lord's Resistance Army, the Shining Path communist movement in Peru, and the drugs money-funded political violence in Colombia.

Opposite page: In the late 19th and early 20th centuries, Africa was extensively colonized by European powers. The first colony to achieve independence, in this case from Italian rule, was Libya in 1951. As the map shows, the rest followed.

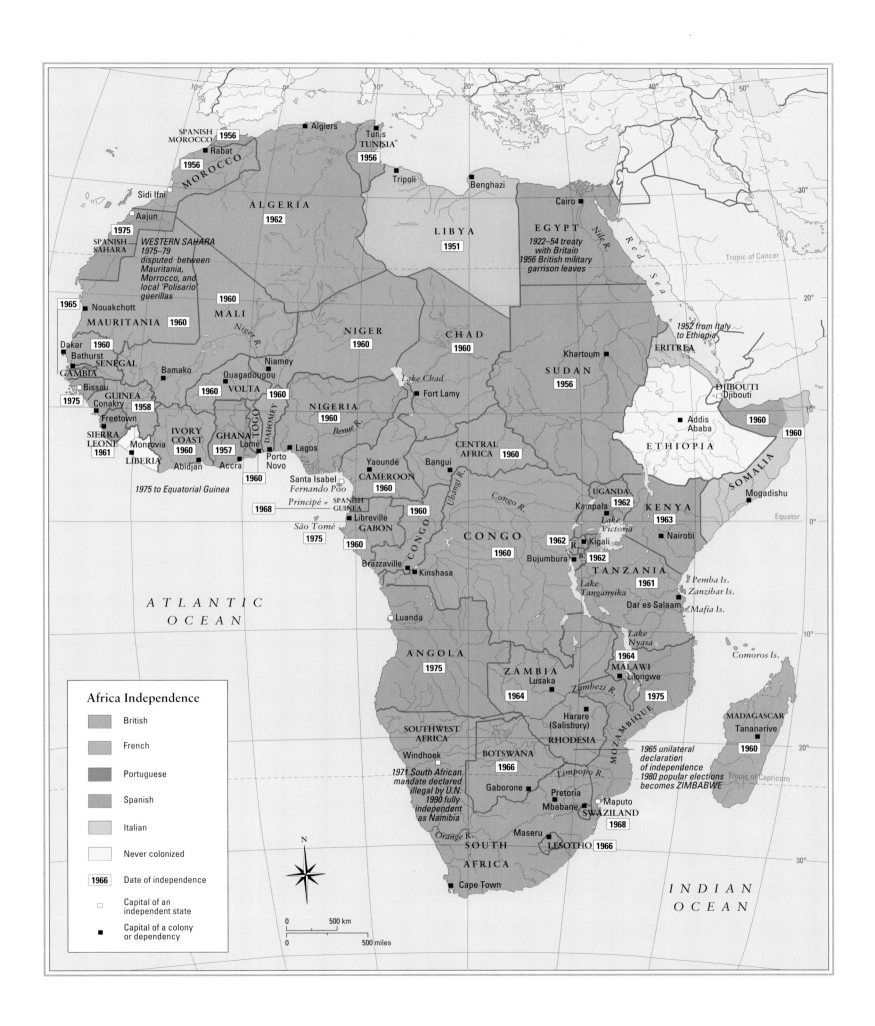

SPANISH MOROCCO **1956**
1956 Rabat
MOROCCO
Sidi Ifni
Aajun
1975
SPANISH SAHARA
1965
Nouakchott
MAURITANIA **1960**
WESTERN SAHARA
1975–79 disputed between Mauritania, Morrocco, and local 'Polisario' guerillas
Algiers
ALGERIA **1962**
Tunis
TUNISIA **1956**
Tripoli
LIBYA **1951**
Benghazi
Cairo
EGYPT
1922–54 treaty with Britain 1956 British military garrison leaves
Nile R.
Red Sea
Tropic of Cancer
MALI **1960**
Niger R.
Dakar **1960**
Bathurst
SENEGAL
GAMBIA
1965
Bissau
GUINEA **1958**
1975
Conakry
Freetown
SIERRA LEONE **1961**
Monrovia
LIBERIA
Bamako
Ouagadougou
VOLTA **1960**
NIGER **1960**
CHAD **1960**
Lake Chad
Fort Lamy
Khartoum
SUDAN **1956**
ERITREA *1952 from Italy to Ethiopia*
DJIBOUTI
Djibouti
Addis Ababa
ETHIOPIA **1960**
1960
SOMALIA
Niamey
GHANA **1957**
Lomé
TOGO **1960**
DAHOMEY
Accra
Porto Novo
1960
IVORY COAST **1960**
Abidjan
Lagos
NIGERIA **1960**
Benue R.
1975 to Equatorial Guinea
Santa Isabel
Fernando Póo
Principé **1975**
São Tomé **1975**
SPANISH GUINEA **1968**
CENTRAL AFRICA **1960**
Yaoundé
Bangui
CAMEROON **1960**
Libreville
GABON **1960**
Ubangi R.
Congo R.
CONGO **1960**
Brazzaville
Kinshasa
Mogadishu
UGANDA **1962**
Kampala
Lake Victoria
KENYA **1963**
Nairobi
1962
R.
Kigali
B.
1962
Bujumbura
1962
TANZANIA **1961**
Pemba Is.
Zanzibar Is.
Dar es Salaam
Mafia Is.
Lake Tanganyika
Equator
ATLANTIC OCEAN
Luanda
ANGOLA **1975**
Lake Nyasa
Comoros Is.
1964
MALAWI **1975**
Lilongwe
ZAMBIA **1964**
Lusaka
Zambezi R.
MOZAMBIQUE
MADAGASCAR
Tananarive
1960
SOUTHWEST AFRICA
Windhoek
1971 South African mandate declared illegal by U.N. 1990 fully independent as Namibia
BOTSWANA **1966**
Gaborone
Harare (Salisbury)
RHODESIA
Limpopo R.
Pretoria
Maputo
Mbabane
SWAZILAND **1968**
1965 unilateral declaration of independence 1980 popular elections becomes ZIMBABWE
Tropic of Capricorn
Orange R.
SOUTH AFRICA
Maseru
LESOTHO **1966**
Cape Town
INDIAN OCEAN

Africa Independence

	British
	French
	Portuguese
	Spanish
	Italian
	Never colonized
1966	Date of independence
☐	Capital of an independent state
■	Capital of a colony or dependency

N

0   500 km
0   500 miles

THE AGE OF TERROR

THE USE OF TERROR AS A WEAPON HAS A LONG HISTORY. THE TERM "TERRORISTS" TODAY REFERS TO SMALL GROUPS OF EXTREMISTS WHO SEEK TO IMPOSE THEIR WILL ON SOCIETY THROUGH ACTS OF VIOLENCE AND FORCING GOVERNMENTS TO MAKE CONCESSIONS.

The basic difference between a guerrilla campaign and a terrorist campaign is that in the former the guerrillas focus their attacks on military targets; terrorists often attack civilian targets. There is overlap in a number of conflicts, which has allowed terrorist groups to claim that they are guerrillas, but governments have routinely denounced guerrillas as terrorists.

A good example of an organization that blurred the distinctions was the Irish Republican Army (IRA) during its campaigns from 1916 to 1923. The IRA aimed to win Irish independence from Britain and then to impose its own vision of republicanism on the newly independent state. At this time, it engaged in both guerrilla warfare against British Army units and in terrorist activities against Irish and British civilians.

The Irgun group of Jews aiming in the 1940s to establish a Jewish state in Palestine adopted the terrorist tactics of the IRA, as they lacked the numbers and resources to wage a guerrilla campaign. Irgun blew up railroads and government buildings, murdered politicians and government officials, and launched attacks on civilian targets. The group later abandoned violence for a political agenda.

In Algeria the FLN (National Liberation Front), founded in 1954, aimed at achieving independence from France. The FLN operated on political, economic, and military levels, but it also had a terrorist arm that pioneered the tactic of coercive terrorism. This involved armed FLN men moving into a rural village and forcing the village elders, at gunpoint, to recognize the FLN as the legitimate government. The village would then be forced to pay taxes to the FLN and to accept the FLN rule and judicial rulings. Dissenters against the newly imposed FLN rule were shot. Having achieved rule over one village, the group would move on to the next, returning only if resistance surfaced. In this way the FLN gradually gained control of the countryside, restricted the French to the towns, and eventually gained independence for Algeria.

ETA (Basque Homeland and freedeom) have run a terrorist campaign aimed at gaining Basque independence from Spain since 1959. Attacks have concentrated mostly on the murder of those deemed to be co-operating with the Spanish "occupation"; police officers, local government officials, and journalists have all been killed but ETA has still not achieved its aims.

In 1965 the Palestinian Liberation Organization (PLO) began an armed struggle against Israel that from the start had a strong terrorist element. The PLO was never a single group, more an umbrella organization for various political, paramilitary and terrorist groups that all shared the aim of eliminating Israel as a state. In 1972 a PLO group known as Black September took 11 Israeli athletes hostage at the Munich Olympics. The raid ended in a gun battle with German police in which all the athletes and five of the eight terrorists were killed. The PLO made a specialty of hijacking civilian aircraft and holding the passengers and crew hostage until various demands were met.

Olympic Committeeman (R) knocks on door where Arab guerrillas hold Israeli athletes hostage, January 1972.

In 1969 a splinter group of the IRA, termed the Provisional IRA or Provos, resumed the armed campaign for a united and independent Ireland. This renewed campaign concentrated almost exclusively on terrorist attacks: bombs were planted in pubs, bars, streets, and civilian buildings. Intercommunal violence between Protestants and Catholics in Northern Ireland became endemic as tit-for-tat killings and bombings became normal.

In Sri Lanka in the 1970s, the minority Tamil ethnic group began to agitate for greater local autonomy from the central government. The campaign began as a political one, but extremists took up arms in the 1980s, to begin a struggle that used both guerrilla and terrorist tactics. Calling themselves the Tamil Tigers, armed fighters sought to emulate FLN tactics and impose their rule on Tamil areas of Sri Lanka. In 2009 the Sri Lankan Army recaptured all such areas, killing nearly the entire Tamil Tiger leadership.

Although these and other terrorist groups had claimed thousands of lives during the 20th century, many people consider the Age of Terror to have started on September 11 2001. On that day 19 terrorists affiliated to the Islamic terror group Al Qaeda hijacked four jet airliners over the U.S. Two of them were flown into the World Trade Center in New York and a third was flown into the Pentagon in Washington, DC. The fourth was apparently heading for the U.S. Capitol in Washington D.C., when passengers on board fought back and overpowered the terrorists, at which point the terrorists flying the aircraft crashed it into the ground. In all, 2,976 people were killed in addition to the terrorists. One particularly shocking element of the 9/11 attacks was that the terrorists had deliberately killed themselves in order to inflict the greatest possible damage on their targets. More usually terrorists make a point of escaping the scene of an attack so that they can launch further attacks. Indeed, the choice of targets is often motivated by the desire to get away safely, a fact that has caused many such attacks to be described as cowardly.

However, the use of human beings in suicide attacks was not as novel as many people thought in 2001. In the closing stages of World War Two, the Japanese launched a number of suicide attacks. These mostly took the form of pilots crashing aircraft filled with explosives into Allied warships in attacks known as *kamikaze*. Some 3,900 *kamikaze* aircraft were launched, of which about 15 percent hit their target. The Allies suffered 81 ships sunk and 368 damaged; there were 4,900 deaths and 5,000 wounded.

Islam also has a tradition of suicide attacks. In medieval times the minority Ismaili sect led by Hassan I Sabah used assassination as a political and military weapon. The assassins very often attacked their targets knowing that they could not escape alive. In 1897 an uprising among the tribes on India's Northwest Frontier — in what is now Pakistan and Afghanistan — was fomented by a religious preacher who recruited young men prepared to launch a series of suicidal attacks on British military personnel. One such assault, on Malakand, was made by 40 men posing as firewood sellers. As soon as they saw an officer's uniform, they attacked with knives. They were all killed in the attack, but they slew one British officer, one sergeant, and 21 other ranks, and wounded five officers and 32 other ranks. Most other attacks were on a smaller scale, but the results could be every bit as shocking.

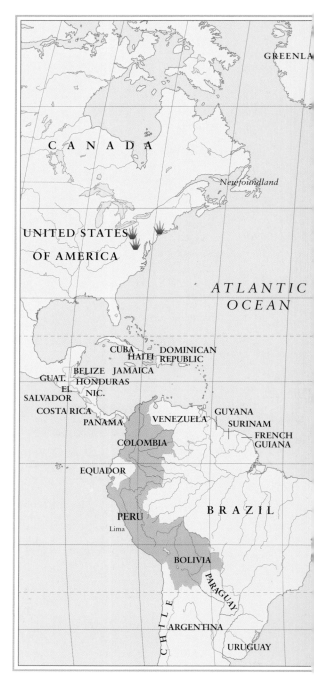

It was on these traditions that Al Qaeda and related groups of Islamic militants drew for the attacks of 2001 and other incidents. Al Qaeda was founded in the latter 1980s by the wealthy Saudi Arabian businessman Osama bin Laden to fight against the Soviet occupation of Afghanistan. When the Soviets withdrew, bin Laden transformed Al Qaeda into an organization dedicated to fighting holy war, or *jihad*, against non-Muslims. He targeted particularly the United States, as he perceived American foreign policy as a barrier to his ultimate aim of uniting all Muslims into a political state founded on fundamentalist Islamic teachings. In 1996 bin Laden issued a *fatwa*, or religious ruling, calling on all Muslims to attack and expel non-Muslim soldiers from Islamic countries as a religious duty.

In 1998 Al Qaeda organized bomb attacks on U.S. embassies in Tanzania and Kenya that left over 300 dead, most of them local workers. In October 2000 the organization mounted a suicide attack when a small boat loaded with explosives was steered against the destroyer *USS Cole* in Aden Harbor. The two bombers and 17 U.S. sailors were killed in the attack, but the ship was saved. A similar attack on the *USS The Sullivans* was made but failed when the attacking boat foundered in the swell.

After the attacks of 9/11, there followed a string of other suicide attacks and attempted attacks. The precise role of Al Qaeda in these attacks has never been clear. Some of the terrorists had been trained at Al Qaeda camps, but whether the attacks were part of a wider Al Qaeda campaign was less certain. A few of the attacks were intended to create mass casualties; others were more minor in scope. A series of bombs detonated in the tourist district of Bali on October 12 2002 claimed 202 lives.

Similarly operating at arm's reach from Al Qaeda were the suicide bombers who struck in London on the morning of July 7 2005. Three subway trains and a bus were blown apart by four suicide bombers working together, causing 56 deaths and 700 injuries. The bombers were killed along with their victims. They were all British Muslims who had links to Al Qaeda training camps but seem to have acted alone in the attack.

Although Al Qaeda has been substantially broken up after the 2001 attacks, the confederation of extremist Islamists that it inspired seems set to continue to use suicide bombings to inflict casualties.

Suicide attacks across the globe have become a familiar feature of modern warfare. Islamic militants and Al Qaeda are among those linked to recent suicide attacks. Map data as of 2009.

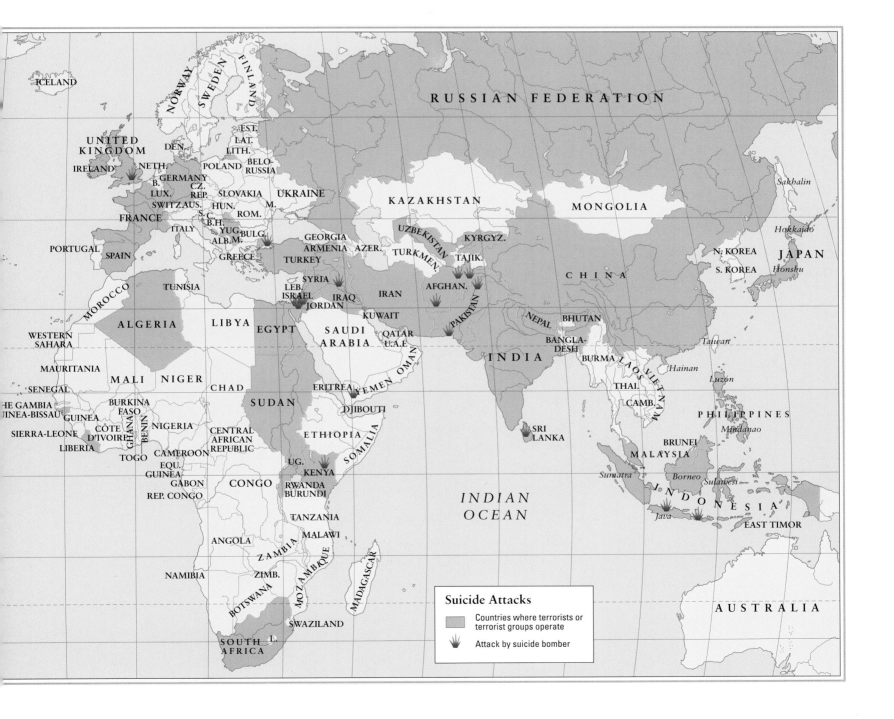

Suicide Attacks

Countries where terrorists or terrorist groups operate

Attack by suicide bomber

HIGH-TECH WAR

THE USE OF ADVANCED TECHNOLOGY ON THE BATTLEFIELD HAS BECOME A HALLMARK OF MODERN WARFARE. AS TECHNOLOGICAL PROGRESS ACCELERATES, NEW INVENTIONS AND DEVELOPMENTS APPEAR IN WARFARE WITH BEWILDERING SPEED.

Many advances in weapons technology are still highly classified. Some military hardware has been seen in action, so that its abilities can be evaluated without the ways in which they were achieved becoming known. Other military weapons remain top secret, and their existence is unknown outside the military units in which they are deployed.

The development of the stealth aircraft for the U.S. Air Force shows how military technology can advance in secret, revolutionizing the battlefield without the outside world being aware of the fact. It was in 1975 that engineers at Lockheed's top-secret Skunk Works research department realized that new composite materials produced a much lower radar signature than did conventional aircraft construction materials. Combined with on-board computers able to control aerodynamically unstable aircraft, these materials offered the promise of producing a combat aircraft almost invisible to radar.

Development work progressed, and tests and trials were undertaken in secret. Early test flights of stealth aircraft produced sightings of black aircraft of strange shapes that did not show up on radar, which at the time were classified as UFO sightings. The program produced the B-2 Spirit heavy bomber and the F-117 Nighthawk, which, despite being popularly dubbed the Stealth Fighter, was in fact a light bomber. The Nighthawk entered service first, seeing combat for the first time over Panama in 1989. The Gulf War of 1991 saw the Nighthawk fly about 1,300 sorties. The B-2 entered combat in 1999 over Kosovo, later operating over Afghanistan and Iraq.

A growing trend among weapons manufacturers is to produce fighting vehicles that have no human crew, thus saving casualties should they be destroyed. Cruise missiles were an early example of this tendency. They could be steered and controlled remotely by an operator hundreds of miles away and still deliver a warhead with the precision of a manned bomber — but at a much higher financial cost.

Cruise missiles are among the most expensive of single-use weapons, and this has led to questions over their efficiency. However, supporters of cruise missiles argue that they are cheaper than human pilots when total training and infrastructure costs are looked at and in terms of loss of life.

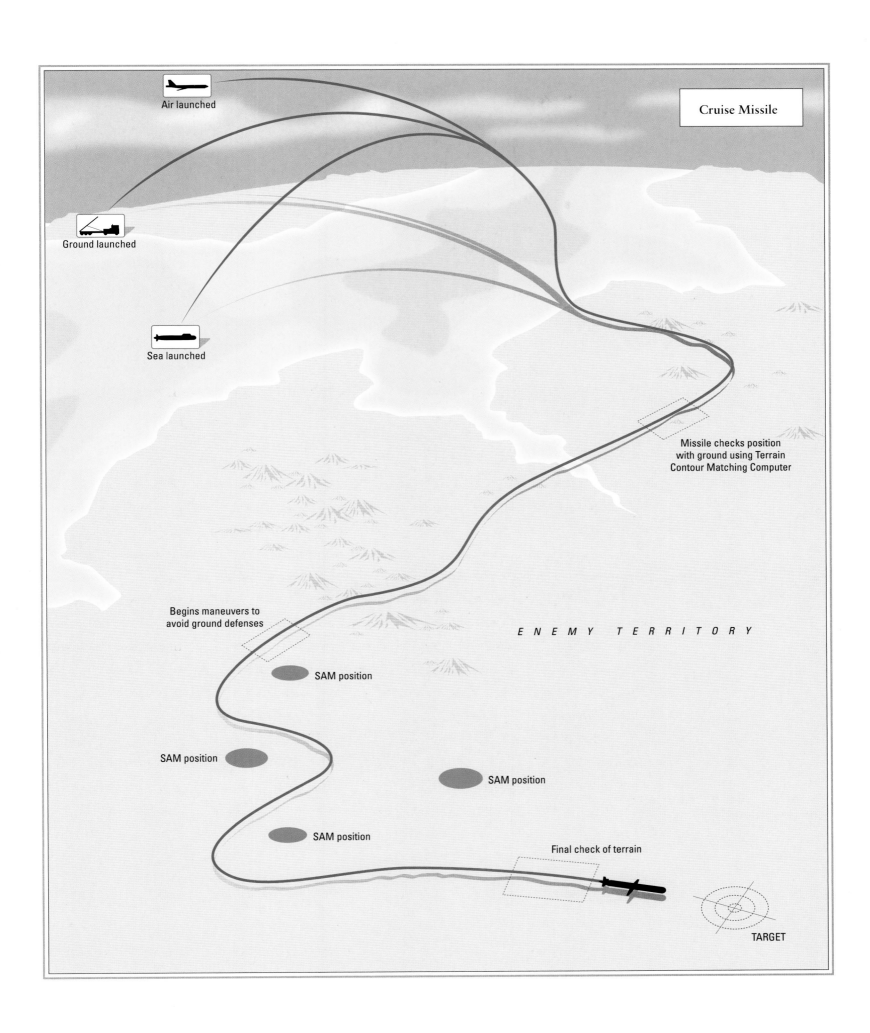

Cruise Missile

Air launched

Ground launched

Sea launched

Missile checks position with ground using Terrain Contour Matching Computer

Begins maneuvers to avoid ground defenses

ENEMY TERRITORY

SAM position

SAM position

SAM position

SAM position

Final check of terrain

TARGET

Opposite page: The intensively high-tech style of 21st century warfare illustrated here includes using laser munitions and designator pods and missiles. In future conflicts, these could be some of the precursors to a new type of warfare, launched and guided from afar.

The U.S. Air Force is said to be considering a project known unofficially as the 2037 Bomber. It aims to introduce a high-tech heavy bomber in the year 2037 ready to replace the B-52, which will reach the end of its operational life in 2040. Details are of course top secret, but it would seem that the aircraft is planned to be supersonic and stealthy and able to carry a heavy payload over a long distance. It is also said to be unmanned. An intermediate design for a stealthy, subsonic medium-range manned bomber is expected to enter service in 2018.

Already some unmanned vehicles are in operation using GPS technology to ensure accuracy. Unmanned Aerial Vehicles (UAVs) are already widely used by several countries for reconnaissance and scouting. But the U.S., and possibly other countries, is using them for more aggressive purposes. The MQ1 Predator, for example, entered service in 1995, and about 180 are in operation. This UAV has a top speed of 135 mph (217 kph), a ceiling of 25,000 ft (7,620 m), and a range of about 2,000 miles (3,219 km). It can carry a wide range of surveillance equipment, or weaponry. It can carry two missiles, usually either AGM114 Hellfire air-to-ground missiles or AIM92 Stinger air-to-air missiles. It is thought that the armed version first entered combat in 2002, but details are still classified. The Predator is vulnerable to anti-aircraft fire, owing to its slow speed. More advanced armed UAVs are planned.

Unmanned ground vehicles are in operation with a few units. The U.S. marines, for instance, use the Gladiator, a miniature tank-like vehicle. The version made public mounts a 7.92 mm machine gun, but it is understood that other weaponry can be mounted. The smaller Talon, used by the U.S. Army, can carry a grenade-launcher and an incendiary device as well as a machine gun.

Much smaller scout vehicles are proposed for ground-troop support. Termed micro air vehicles, these crafts are currently larger than a football. They can be sent up to scout ahead of a ground unit by flying a mile or so over enemy territory to look for concealed tanks, artillery, and other hazards. It is envisaged that by about 2025, these vehicles may have been reduced to the size of a dragonfly.

Ground forces serving in advanced militaries are also benefiting from a range of high-tech devices that in the U.S go by the name of Future Combat Systems. It is foreseen that a self-contained brigade will consist of tanks, artillery, motorized infantry, unmanned aerial vehicles, unmanned ground vehicles, and micro air vehicles. All the vehicles and personnel will be linked to a central computer, which will manage incoming data to produce a virtual representation of the battlefield on which are marked all friendly and hostile troops, vehicles, and weaponry. Using head-up display visors, any soldier on the battlefield will have access to this virtual view as well as the scene he can see with his own eyes.

The high-tech combat zone of the future will be a very different place from the battlefield of today.

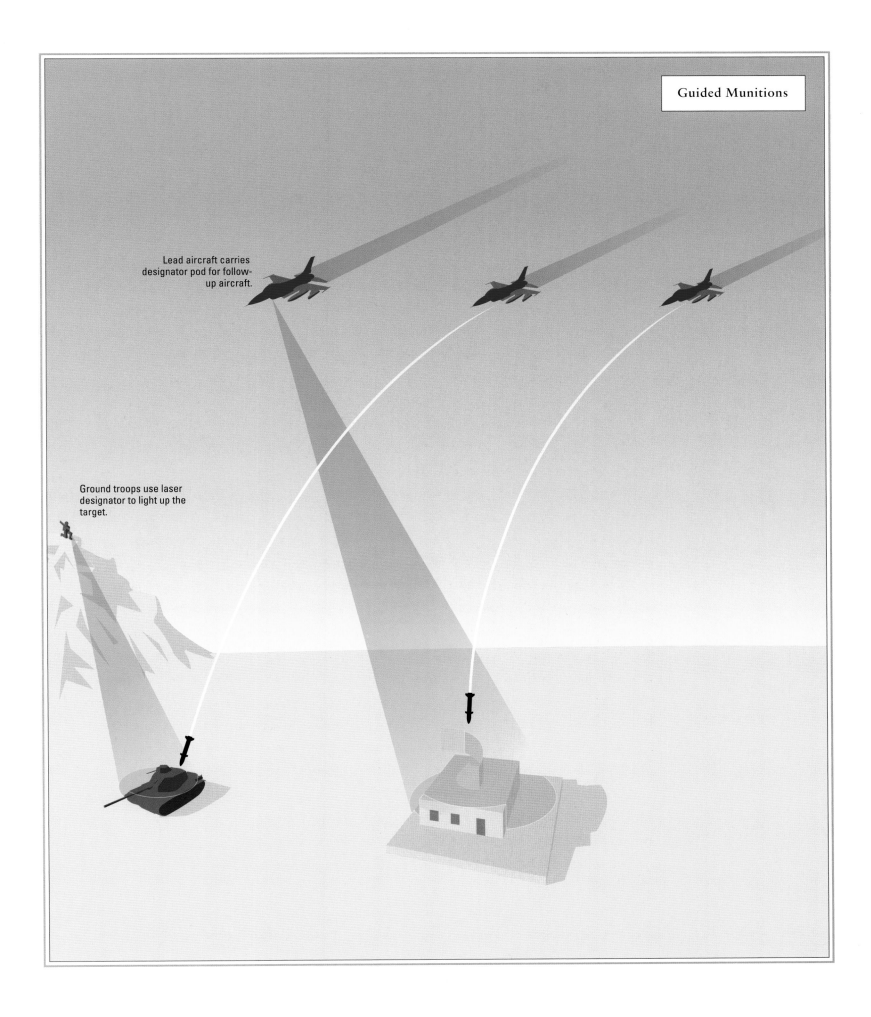

Guided Munitions

Lead aircraft carries designator pod for follow-up aircraft.

Ground troops use laser designator to light up the target.

CYBER ATTACK

INCREASING DEPENDENCE ON COMPUTERS BY THE DEVELOPED WORLD HAS INCREASED PROSPERITY AND IMPROVED COMMUNICATIONS SYSTEMS. IT HAS ALSO OPENED UP A NEW AREA FOR WARFARE: THE VIRTUAL WORLD OF THE INTERNET, GOVERNMENT COMPUTERS, COMPUTERIZED INDUSTRIAL AND ELECTRONIC SYSTEMS.

The purpose of war is not simply to destroy the enemy's military forces; that is only a means to an end. The aims of war usually include the conquest of a state, the annexation of disputed territory, or the imposition of a political or religious ideology on an unwilling population. All these may be achieved by destroying the ability of the target to resist. Destroying the military forces of the target state or population is but one method of attack.

Cyber warfare is waged principally over the Internet. Its aims are to disrupt the enemy state in any way possible. The battlefield is a virtual one ranging over web servers, enterprise information systems, client server systems, communications links, network equipment, and the desktops and laptops in businesses and homes. The battlefield also encompasses information systems such as electrical grids, telecommunications systems, and various corporate and military robotics systems.

There have been a number of cyber attacks detected over the past 20 years or so. Among the most common is cyber espionage. This involves a person gaining unauthorized access to a computer network in order to access and download information. Not all cyber espionage is military in nature, as private corporations have been known to hack illegally into the computers of their rivals in order to steal industrial secrets.

The Titan Rain cyber espionage attack of 2003 targeted companies manufacturing weapons for the U.S. military. It is known that the computers of Lockheed Martin and NASA were penetrated and that highly classified information was downloaded from them, but the true scope of the attack and its success remains classified. The attack originated in China but opinion differs as to whether it was launched by the Chinese government or by Chinese companies.

A denial of service (DoS) attack is designed to render the target computer system unable to operate fully for a time. A relatively simple method for achieving this is to deluge it with automatically generated incoming messages or data so that its processing power is fully consumed. Alternatively the system may be hacked into so that the attacker can plant malware into software and make the system fully or partially inoperable. A variation is the distributed denial of service (DDoS) attack. This involves distributing a form of malware, termed a worm, to as many other computers as possible. The worm infects a computer but takes no action until a specified date or set of circumstances, when it is activated. The infected computer will then seek to access a targeted computer with a DoS attack.

The most famous example of a DDoS attack was the MyDoom worm of 2004. This worm appeared in January, spreading rapidly to thousands of computers linked to the Internet. On February 1, it was activated and launched a DDoS attack on the computers of the SCO software company. SCO offered a reward of $250,000 for the identification of the originator of the attack, but nobody was caught.

Of particular concern to the military are equipment disruption (ED) attacks. These are highly sophisticated attacks that require not only the ability to hack into a system but also the knowledge required to alter the internal software. The aim of an ED attack is to ensure that the attacked system does not work properly. In the context of modern, computerized weapons systems, the attacker would aim to render weapons inoperable or faulty. Cruise missiles, for instance, would not hit their target but would be deflected to hit another area. Aircraft operating on-board computers might suddenly drop out of the sky. Tanks would be unable to fire their guns. Although an ED attack is difficult to carry out and relatively easy to detect, its potential gains are enormous.

A nation's infrastructure may also be vulnerable to cyber warfare. Banking systems, stock markets, and other crucial economic systems are all computerized. An effective cyber attack could cause financial meltdown and paralyze a nation's ability to pay its way. If such an attack were launched at the outset of a conventional war, it might render the targeted country unable to wage war. Other infrastructure systems that could be paralyzed by a cyber attack in support of a conventional war would be telephone and other communications systems, power supplies, water supplies, traffic lights, and broadcasting networks, and almost anything else that relies on computerization — in a developed country, this is almost everything.

In the spring of 2007 Estonia came under an intense and prolonged cyber attack that is widely believed to have been the most serious to date. At the time the Estonian government was in dispute with the Russian government over the treatment of war memorials dating from the Soviet era. Estonia had been occupied by the Soviet Union, which had used severely repressive measures against the Estonians, including mass murder, mass deportations, and arbitrary imprisonment of political dissidents. The Soviets had erected a number of monuments celebrating the Soviet "liberation" of Estonia from German occupation in 1944. As the newly independent Estonian government viewed the Soviet regime to have conducted an occupation every bit as illegal and brutal as that of the Germans, it did not appreciate the monuments and wanted them moved. On April 27 2007 in the midst of this dispute, the cyber attacks began. The website of the Estonian Parliament was swamped by a mass of incoming emails and data

The spread of computer usage across the world has been an on-going theme of the late 20th and early 21st centuries. Nevertheless, as the map shows, the advantage, as in so much else, lies with the richer, more developed countries

requests so that it crashed and became inoperable. Estonian newspapers, radio stations, and television stations were likewise attacked by massive internet traffic and crashed. Political parties then found their computer systems subjected to defacement attacks. Estonian government ministries then suffered a range of attacks that varied from attempts to access classified information to defacement and DDoS attacks. Banks also suffered cyber attacks, causing them to shut down their systems while they were cleansed of malware. The Estonian banking system was closed for several days: no payments could be made, money withdrawn, or cash paid in.

Experts from the UN were called in to investigate and very quickly concluded that the scale and range of the cyber attacks on Estonia had been beyond the ability of a single person or a small group to orchestrate. Clearly a large number of very talented and well trained computer experts had been at work.

When the scale of the operation became clear, the Estonian government blamed the Russian government for the attacks. However, the attackers covered their tracks well, and to date no clear evidence has been found that the Russian state was involved. On the other hand, the Russian government has refused to co-operate with the investigation and has refused Estonian police access to Russia or to Russian data logs. In 2008 Dmitri Galushkevich, a Russian student living in Estonia, was convicted of carrying out one of the defacement attacks. It is thought that he made this attack as a solo effort once the news of the more general attack became known.

One direct result of the attacks on Estonia was a June 2007 meeting of the defense ministers of NATO countries. Details of what was discussed are classified but are understood to have included the start of a major and ongoing review of cyber security among NATO defense computers.

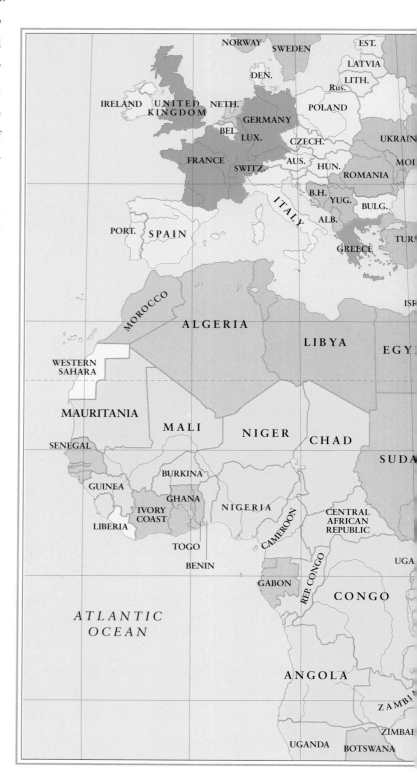

In 2008 the Georgian invasion of South Ossetia was preceded by a wave of cyber attacks on Ossetian websites and computer systems. Every media organization in Ossetia was temporarily shut down and other systems suffered DoS and defacement attacks. A few days later the Georgian Parliament website went down while several government ministries suffered attacks, followed by Georgian media networks and banking systems. Responsibility for the attacks has never been proven, but it was widely alleged that the Georgian military had launched the initial cyber attacks on Ossetia and that Russian organizations had launched the counter attacks.

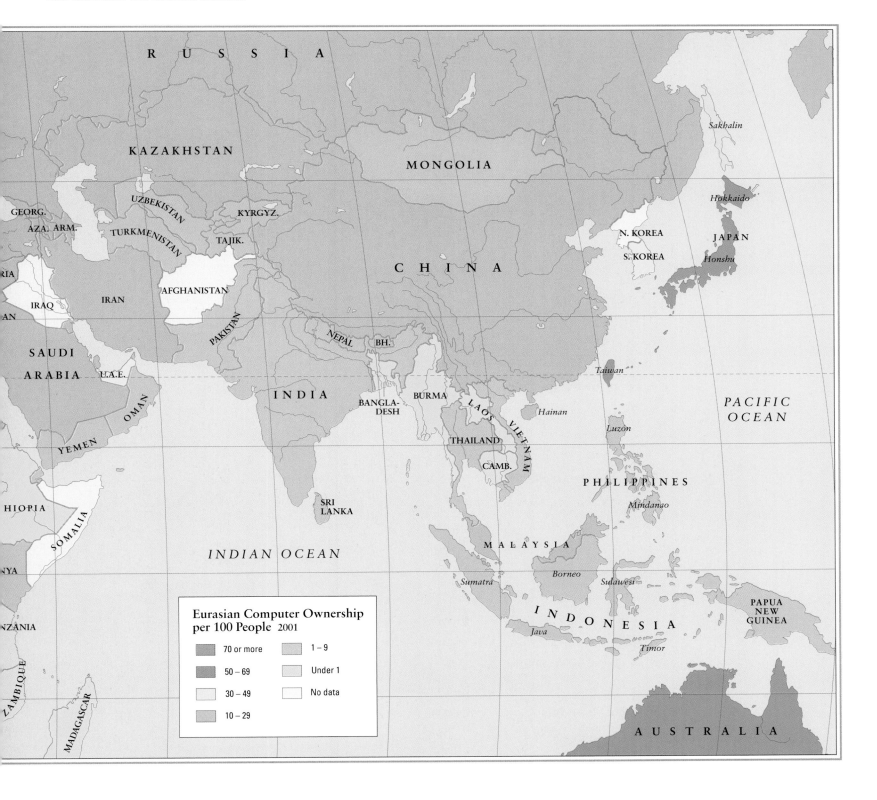

Eurasian Computer Ownership per 100 People 2001

- 70 or more
- 50 – 69
- 30 – 49
- 10 – 29
- 1 – 9
- Under 1
- No data

WORLD DEFENSE INDUSTRIES

THE MANUFACTURE OF WEAPONS AND MILITARY HARDWARE IS COMPLEX AND VARIABLE. IN AFGHANISTAN SMALL CRAFT WORKSHOPS TURN OUT AMMUNITION BY HAND. IN THE UNITED STATES FACTORIES USE MODERN TECHNOLOGY TO MASS-PRODUCE WEAPONRY.

The manufacture of arms occurs in almost all countries. Some governments prefer to manufacture their own weapons in secret — weapons that will give them an advantage over others in war. Employing defense industries can also be seen as a way to provide jobs for the population, especially if export sales can be achieved.

Governments have been the most important customers for weapons manufacturers for the past 500 years, and there has always been a close relationship between arms companies and the governments they serve. In some countries there are clear guidelines about the nature of a relationship between weapons manufacturers and governments to avoid claims of bribery or corruption.

Typically, a government will issue a requirement specification for a new weapon, setting out its desired capabilities. This specification is based on the calculation of the expected needs of the country's military and an appreciation of the possibilities of current and future technology. The specification will be tendered out to a number of weapons manufacturers and one or more companies will then produce designs and plans to meet the requirement. The government will assess the plans in terms of how closely they meet the specified requirements and also on grounds of cost. A prototype may then be ordered from one or more companies, from which the best design will be selected and the contract awarded.

The escalating cost of high-tech weapons in the 20th and 21st centuries has put the production of frontline weaponry beyond the means of many countries. Only countries with large economies such as the United States, Russia, and China can bear the costs of research and development involved in producing modern ships, UAVs, and tanks. Even wealthy countries such as Germany, Britain and Italy will often collaborate on weapons projects in order to spread the costs of development, for example in 1985 Italy, West Germany, Spain, and the UK agreed to go ahead with production of the Eurofighter. The profits from this joint venture were then spread among the partners by dividing up the production in order to ensure jobs in each country. Production of the Eurofighter was apportioned so that the Italians manufactured the left wing and rear fuselage, the British made the front fuselage and tail, the Germans the central fuselage, and the Spanish the right wing. By 1986, the cost of the program had reached $290 million.

European Defense officials, from Germany, Spain, Italy, and Britain in front of the Eurofighter jet during a presentation ceremony in Manching, June 30 2003. The Eurofighter aircraft, a four-nation collaboration designed to boost European military capabilities, was officially licensed June 30, almost half a century after the ambitious project began.

The concentration of the manufacture of high-tech weapons in a small number of countries and companies has led to a growing trade in weapons. Countries unable to bear the costs of developing high-tech weaponry are eager to purchase weapons. Governments of countries where those weapons are made are understandably reluctant to see them sold to potential or actual enemies. Most countries, therefore, operate an export license system under which companies seeking to sell weapons abroad must first gain authority from their government. Generally a government will grant an export license only if the weapons are to be sold to an ally or to a friendly country.

Arms licenses may be granted as part of a wider trade deal, in effect becoming bargaining chips in a complex discussion about trade barriers, production quotas, and tariffs. Some governments use the promise of an arms deal as a way to encourage another government to adopt certain policies either internally or in relation to a third country. Those wishing to buy arms may pursue a particular foreign policy in the hope of persuading an arms-exporting country that they are friendly and thus deserve an export license.

The international arms trade is conducted largely in secret, and it is almost impossible to get accurate figures for what is taking place. It is generally recognized, however, that the world's leading arms exporter is the U.S., with an estimated export market of around $7.5 billion in 2008. Russia came second with $4.6 billion, Germany third with $3.4 billion, and France fourth with $2.7 billion.

Figures for arms imports are not available, but the total expenditure on the military is disclosed by most governments. The U.S. spends the most on its military, with an annual budget of $528 billion, or 3.9 percent of gross domestic product (GDP) in 2008. Britain came second, spending $59 billion (2.5 percent of GDP). France was third, with a budget of $53 billion (2.4 percent of GDP), and China was fourth, spending $50 billion (1.8 percent of GDP).

Total world spending on the military is estimated at about $1,158 billion; but this is only a rough guess, as many governments hide spending on the military under other departmental headings. It has been estimated that there are some 1,138 companies in 98 countries manufacturing weapons of various types. Although stocks of heavy weapons such as tanks, ships, and aircraft are usually carefully controlled, lighter weapons are more difficult to keep track of. One estimate puts the number of rifles, assault rifles,and sub-machine guns in circulation around the world at about 639 million.

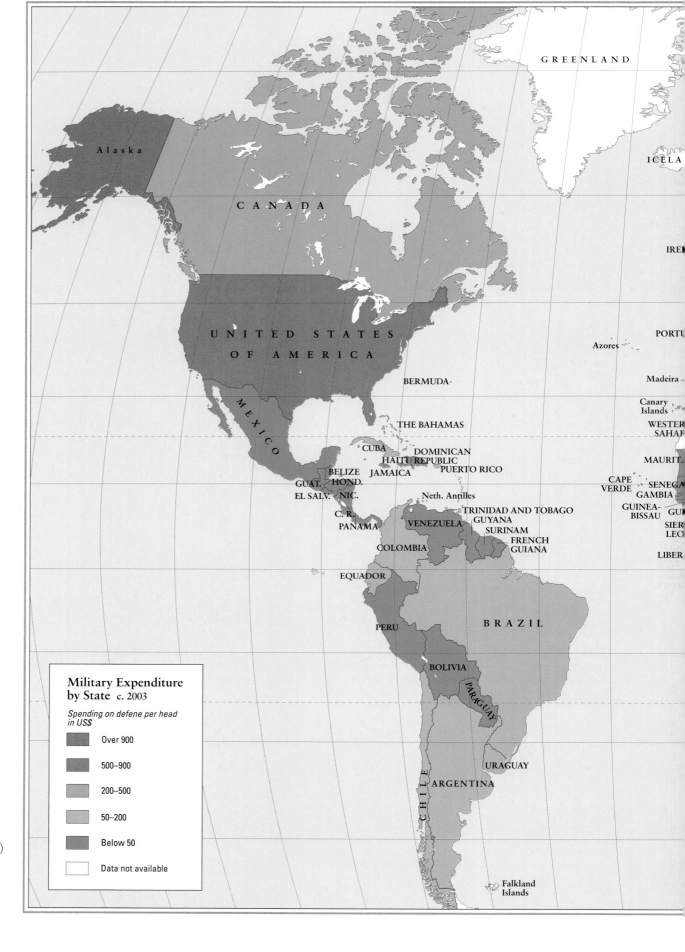

Military expenditure in 2003. The map reflects the rising cost of high-tech weapons in modern times. Only the fastest growing countries (U.S., Russia, and China) can afford to develop new weapons; other countires share the cost burden by collaborating on weapons projects.

Military Expenditure by State c. 2003

Spending on defene per head in US$

- Over 900
- 500–900
- 200–500
- 50–200
- Below 50
- Data not available

ARMED CAMPS

MILITARY ALLIANCES BETWEEN COUNTRIES HAVE EXISTED FOR CENTURIES. MOST ALLIANCES HAVE BEEN, OR HAVE CLAIMED TO BE, DEFENSIVE, WHEN TWO OR MORE SMALL COUNTRIES ALLY THEMSELVES AGAINST A LARGER COUNTRY. A FEW HAVE BEEN OFFENSIVE, WHEN A NUMBER OF COUNTRIES JOIN TOGETHER SPECIFICALLY TO ATTACK ANOTHER COUNTRY.

For most of the latter 20th century the world was dominated by two huge military alliances: the communist Warsaw Pact and the capitalist NATO. Each of these power blocs possessed enough nuclear weaponry to destroy not only the other but also much of the world. Many people believed that there was a real possibility that humanity might annihilate itself in a global nuclear war.

In 1991 the Warsaw Pact was dissolved by its member states after the collapse of the communist regimes in those countries. NATO was left as the pre-eminent military alliance in the world. Inevitably the nature of NATO changed after its main rival ceased to exist. Instead of concentrating on the prospect of a major nuclear or conventional war against an alliance of comparable power, NATO found itself managing peace-keeping operations and lending military forces to help with humanitarian missions. The size of NATO also expanded, as Estonia, Latvia, Lithuania, Slovenia, Slovakia, Bulgaria, and Romania all joined. Meanwhile other military alliances formed as the countries of the world adapted to the new, post-Cold War era.

In 1992 the Collective Security Treaty Organization (CSTO) was formed by seven former states of the U.S.S.R.: Russia, Belarus, Armenia, Kazakhstan, Kyrgyzstan, Tajikistan, and Uzbekistan. The CSTO alliance is a defensive pact: its terms come into operation only if a member state is attacked, not if it is the aggressor.

The CSTO holds large-scale annual maneuvers in order to ensure that the militaries of its member states are able to co-operate easily. In 2009 the CSTO set itself the aim of maintaining on standby a force that would be equal to that kept on standby by NATO. This seemed to indicate CSTO accepted that NATO would have larger forces available when mobilization was complete.

In 1994 the Council for Peace and Security in Central Africa (COPAX) was formed by Cameroon, the Central African Republic, the Republic of Congo, Gabon, Equatorial Guinea, and Sao Tome and Principe. COPAX is a non-aggression pact: its members have undertaken not to attack each other. COPAX keeps a brigade-sized force on standby for instant deployment on missions agreed by its members. These are stated to be peace keeping and humanitarian missions, but defensive military operations have not been ruled out.

Russia, China, Kazakhstan, Kyrgyzstan, Tajikistan, and Uzbekistan founded the Shanghai Cooperation Organization (SCO) in 2001. India, Iran, Mongolia, Pakistan, Sri Lanka, Afghanistan, and Belarus are observers at meetings but not members. The organization is intended to deal with security issues of mutual concern in Central Asia. This is usually taken to mean Islamist terrorism and separatist movements, although the organization's charter does not state this.

The South American Defense Council (SADC) was formed in 2008 by all the independent states of South America. The organization is a loose defensive alliance, which is still in the process of formation. It is envisaged that the military forces of all the member states will undertake joint maneuvers on a regular basis and that their police forces and intelligence services will co-operate against terrorists and drugs cartels.

Next page: Global Defense Organization membership offers states a buffer against aggression.

The world's "hotspots" reflect problems that prevent a a peaceful situation. For example, Colombia has severe and longstanding drug problems and Afghanistan, Iraq, Sudan, and Somalia suffer ongoing wars.

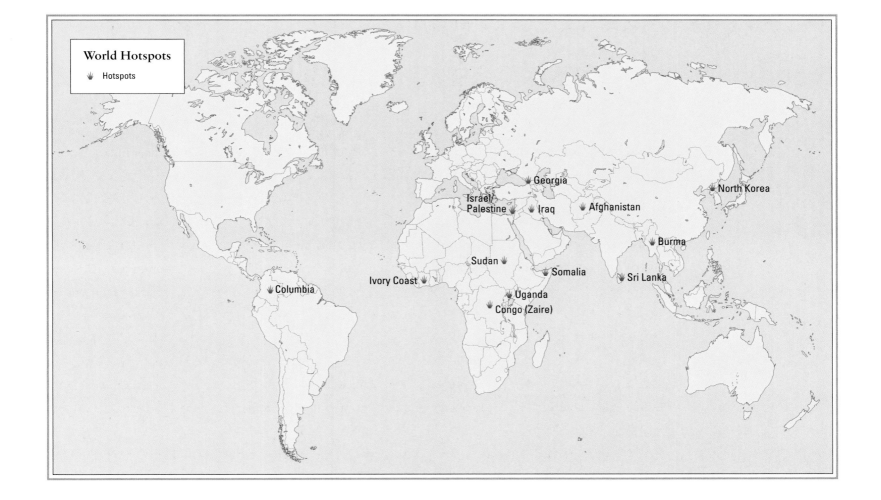

World Hotspots
꙰ Hotspots

Georgia · Israel/Palestine · Iraq · Afghanistan · North Korea · Burma · Sudan · Somalia · Sri Lanka · Ivory Coast · Columbia · Uganda · Congo (Zaire)

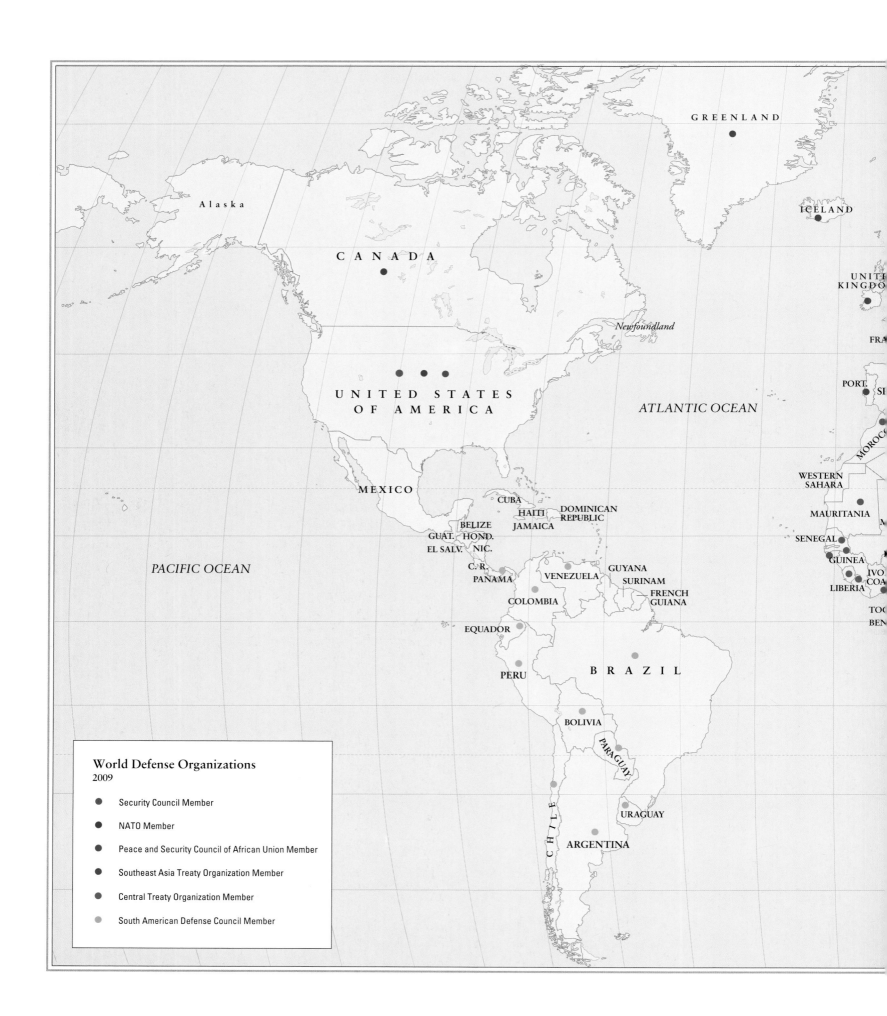

GREENLAND

Alaska

ICELAND

UNITE
KINGDO

CANADA

Newfoundland

FRA

PORT.   SI

UNITED STATES
OF AMERICA

ATLANTIC OCEAN

MOROC

WESTERN
SAHARA

MEXICO

CUBA
HAITI   DOMINICAN
JAMAICA REPUBLIC

MAURITANIA

BELIZE
GUAT. HOND.
EL SALV. NIC.

SENEGAL

PACIFIC OCEAN

GUINEA
C. R.
PANAMA   VENEZUELA   GUYANA
                     SURINAM
                     FRENCH
COLOMBIA   GUIANA

IVO
COA
LIBERIA

TO(
BEN

EQUADOR

BRAZIL

PERU

BOLIVIA

PARAGUAY

CHILE   URAGUAY

ARGENTINA

World Defense Organizations
2009

● Security Council Member

● NATO Member

● Peace and Security Council of African Union Member

● Southeast Asia Treaty Organization Member

● Central Treaty Organization Member

● South American Defense Council Member

Svalbard

Novaya
Zemlya

NORWAY
SWEDEN
FINLAND

N.
EST.
LAT.
LITH.
POLAND
RMANY
UX.
CZECH.
VITZ.
AUS.
HUN.
ROM.
ITALY
CR.
SEB.
MAC.
BULG.
ALB.
GREECE
TURKEY

UNION OF SOVIET SOCIALIST REPUBLICS

MONGOLIA

Sakhalin

Hokkaido

N. KOREA
S. KOREA
JAPAN
Honshu

CHINA

Taiwan

SYRIA
LEB.
ISRAEL
JORDAN
IRAQ
IRAN
AFGHAN.

PAKISTAN

NEPAL
BH.

BURMA
BANGLA-
DESH

LAOS
VIETNAM
Hainan

Luzón

PACIFIC OCEAN

LIBYA
EGYPT
SAUDI
ARABIA
UAE
OMAN

INDIA

THAI.
CAMB.

PHILIPPINES

Mindanao

NIGER
CHAD
YEMEN

SRI
LANKA

MALAYSIA

ERIA
SUDAN

CAMEROON
CENTRAL
AFRICAN
REPUBLIC

ETHIOPIA

SOMALIA

Sumatra
Borneo
Sulawesi

PAPUA
NEW GUINEA

BON
REP. CONGO
ZAIRE
UGANDA
KENYA

INDONESIA

Java
Timor

ANGOLA
ZAMBIA
TANZANIA

INDIAN OCEAN

ZIMBABWE
MOZAMBIQUE
MADAGASCAR

NAMIBIA
BOTSWANA

AUSTRALIA

SOUTH
AFRICA

NEW
ZEALAND

BIBLIOGRAPHY

Volkman, Ernest: *Science Goes to War* (Wiley Books, 2009)

Fowler, Will: *Modern Weapons and Warfare; The Technology of War from 1700 to the Present Day* (Lorenz Books, 2000)

Tzu, Sun : *On the Art of War* (Create Space, 2009)

Weapon: A Visual History of Arms and Armor (DK Publishing, 2006)

Fowler, Will: *Ancient Weapons - History Detectives* (Southwater Publishing, 2002)

Adcock, Frank E.: *Greek and Macedonian Art of War* (University of California Press, 1962)

Williams, Brenda: *Ancient Egyptian War and Weapons* (Heinemann Library, 2002)

Gabriel, Richard A and Metz, Karen S: *From Sumer to Rome: The Military Capabilities of Ancient Armies* (Greenwood Press, 1991)

Williams, Brian: *Ancient Roman War and Weapons* (Heinemann Library, 2002)

Soar, Hugh H. D.: *The Crooked Stick: A History of the Longbow* (Westholme Publishing, 2004)

Nossov, Konstantin: *Ancient and Medieval Siege Weapons* (Lyons Press, 2005)

Smith, Robert D and DeVries, Kelly: *Medieval Weapons: An Illustrated History of Their Impact* (ABC-CLIO, 2007)

Nicolle, David and Thompson, Sam: *Medieval Siege Weapons: Byzantium, the Islamic World and India AD 476-1526* (New Vanguard 2003)

Fraoli, Deborah A: *Joan of Arc and the Hundred Years' War* 2005

Bennet, Marrew; Bradbury, Jim; DeVries, Kelly and Thompson, Sam: *Fighting Techniques of the Medieval World: Equipment, Combat Skills and Tactics* (Greenwood Press, 2005)

Gravett, Christopher and Turner, Graham: *Medieval Siege Weapons (1): Western Europe AD 585-1385* (Osprey Publishing, 2002)

Bradbury, Jim: *The Medieval Archer* (Boydell Press, 2008)

Allmand, Christopher: *The Hundred Years' War: England and France at War c1300-c1450* (Cambridge University Press, 1988)

Dougherty, Martin J: *Weapons and Fighting Techniques of the Medieval Warrior 1000-1500* (Blue Jacket Books, 2008)

Kelly, Jack: *Gunpowder: Alchemy, Bombards and Pyrotechnics: The History of The Explosive that Changed the World* (Basic Books, 2004)

Norris, John: *Gunpowder Artillery 1600-1700* (Crowood Press, 2005)

Chartrand, René and Hutchins, Ray: *Napoleon's Guns 1792-1815 1) Field Artillery* (Osprey Publishing 2003)

Smith, Anthony: *Machine Gun: The Story of the Men and the Weapons that Changed the Face of War* (St. Martin's Press, 2003)

Persico, Joseph: *Eleventh Month, Eleventh Day, Eleventh Hour: Armistice Day 1918* (Random House, 2004)

Miller, David: *Fighting Men of World War II: Volume 2: Axis Forces - Uniforms, Equipment and Weapons* (Stackpole Books, 2007)

Scoffern, John: *Projectile Weapons of War and Explosive Compounds* (Bibliolife, 2009)

Yenne, Bill: *Secret Weapons of the Cold War: From the H-Bomb to SDI* (Berkley Books, 2005)

Blackman, Haden: *The New Essential Guide to Weapons and Technology* (Del Rey, 2004)

Townshend, Charles: *The Oxford History of Modern War (Oxford University Press*, 2005)

Bishop, Chris: *The Encyclopedia of Weapons: From World War II to the Present Day* (Thunder Bay Press, 2006)

INDEX

Acknowledgments

For Cartographica Press
Maps: Jeanne Radford, Alexander Swanston, Malcolm Swanston, and Jonathan Young

The publishers would like to thank the following picture libraries for their kind permission to use their pictures and illustrations:

Alamy: 32, 134, 168, 180, 216, 278, 288, 318

Getty: 45, 56, 79, 148, 173, 175, 190, 198, 231,242, 250, 275, 280, 373, 385

Istock: 8, 9,11, 12, 13, 22, 26, 27, 29, 30, 38, 39, 40, 44, 51, 54, 60, 71, 74, 76, 80, 88, 93, 105, 112, 114, 157, 241, 252, 333

Photolibrary: 22, 33, 164, 252

Robert Hunt Library: 329

Library of Congress: 169, 244, 257, 260, 340

Naval Historical Foundation: 184, 209, 266

Shutterstock: 147, 272

United States Air Force Museum: 318

U.S. Air Force: 345

U.S. Department of Defense: 360

U.S. Navy: 364 - 365

Wikimedia.org: 143

Every effort has been made to contact the copyright holders for images reproduced in this book. The Publisher would welcome any errors or omissions being brought to their attention and apologizes in advance for any unintentional omissions or errors. The Publisher will be pleased to insert the appropriate acknowledgement to any companies or individuals in any subsequent eddition of the work.